Donald Trump's no outlier, but epitomizes the malignant heart and soul of American evangelicalism; they are a *match made in heaven.*

Both a timid, ignorant liberal media establishment *and* a cloistered, largely indifferent class of American academic drones—dwelling in what Mary Douglas might call the hallowed groves of Pentecostalism—have completely whiffed on the social, political, cultural, and theological origins of the revolution of disenchantment that carried an evangelical-inspired-and-infested Trump administration to power.

In *Paradise Joe's*, a rogue cultural sociologist demonstrates how evangelicalism came to occupy the ideological heart of American society and politics. He transforms what might have been a conventional academic case study into an entertaining, jargon-free tale of one small Christian college community, an account filled with memorable local and national characters, all the while gleaning from it the larger meaning and significance of evangelicalism in American life.

Why has evangelicalism made a progressive, European-style social democracy—and universal healthcare—a virtual impossibility? Why the corrosive distrust of government and science? Why the malingering legacy of slavery and Jim Crow, of legal and economic inequality? Why the persistent urban/rural antagonisms? In sum, why are we so different from our closest European ancestors and kin?

Paradise Joe's takes these and other daunting questions head on.

In a second extended bonus appendix for academicians, the author tacks his 95 theses of *Paradise Joe's* onto the Wittenberg door of a deeply compromised American sociology of religion.

Observe here the crazy old aunt of evangelicalism getting dragged down from the attic and cast out into the open, exposed to the light of day for the first time.

D1523040

Paradise Joe's

A Cultural Sociology of a Christian College Community

An Exploration into the Meaning and Significance of American Evangelicalism

Michael F. Sparks

Jacket and hardcover design by José Manuel García
cuestiondegustos.com

First Edition

Published by BookBaby
www.bookbaby.com

For Carol Rae, Maya Cathleen, Kiri Roselee
&
Our very own ancient one, my dear mother,
Patricia Handlin Sparks

Contents

Acknowledgments

Typically, the authors of academically-oriented books fill this space with some rather predictable content.

First, they unburden themselves of a seemingly overwhelming weight of debts or obligations that have been incurred and accumulated. A multitude of colleagues, research assistants, departmental secretaries, librarians and libraries, grant-dispensing foundations, editors, and the like are thanked, no doubt deservedly so. For without these invariably wonderful, considerate, and generous people the book could not have been written.

Second, they issue a blanket pardon. Colleagues unfortunate enough to have been roped into reviewing the manuscript are thereby absolved of responsibility for any mistakes or errors of judgment that remain. Time and again this rendering of absolution occurs. Which possibly gives others no less skeptical than myself pause to wonder: so if the book still contains a residue of mistakenness, are *others* ultimately to blame for failing to sift the chaff from the wheat, for not taking the author to task for it? No wonder, again, that some might prefer the cloak of anonymity.

Unfortunately, the author of this book has arrived here on this platform largely debt free, although not entirely unscathed. He has received next to no help or support whatsoever, from anyone. And so accordingly, obviously, he alone is to blame for what follows. Sometimes he wishes it were otherwise—although not that often, and only sort of. Indeed, there is something to be said for being given free reign over a project, and now a book, like this one. Indeed I rejected one questionable publisher because he demanded nothing less than total surrender—of the title, dust cover, price, marketing strategies, my soul, and conscience. I refused to part with any of them. If you'll pardon a tenuous analogy drawn from a fellow northwesterner, the late Kurt Cobain, but appropriate for the times: the assumption that complete control over things ought be relinquished smells not like teen spirit, but rotting white privilege. In time, I hope the reader will come to appreciate the results of that unbridling, and yet also the authorial self-discipline it inevitably demands in its stead.

And yet again, on the other hand, not so fast. As it turns out, no author is an island entirely unto himself, no matter how inadvertently self-marooned. It did not take too long for this one to discover that although I had gone over the manuscript with a fine-tooth comb for what seemed like a million times, errors kept popping up like pimples on adolescent skin. Without the close editing of my partner in life, Carol Flotlin (whose critical eye was sharpened to a razor's edge by Catholic school nuns, she claims), I would have been thrown to the wolves, literally, and with some justification. What is more, long ago I recall that at least one administrator at Seattle Pacific University, who upon receiving official notification that I was in fact a doctoral candidate from the University of Chicago—although I had been lurking about in the shadows for some time unbeknownst—approved the distribution of a very large questionnaire to a random sample of students through the campus post office. Certainly, that was generous, and of course thanks are in order, even at this late juncture. Of course, again, it didn't undermine my case at all that I took along my first daughter in toddling clothes to crawl around on the gentleman's office carpet while we negotiated, delighting us both. And finally, more recently, thanks are due my Spanish son-in-law, José Manuel García, for his riotous jacket cover graphics. Burdens were indeed either shouldered by or shifted onto others.

At one particularly daunting low point in my quest for a distinguished university press publisher one—and only one—editor actually responded to my inquiries with anything other than the usual canned rejection notice. Seemingly out of the blue, this editor from a major university press located somewhere within the core of the Big Apple, after having brushed me off once or twice before—suggesting that I go compile a resume of bylines in journals or magazines and come back with it in hand—took the time to actually read a short chapter, the introduction to *Paradise Joe's*, that I had attached to an e-mail. Doubtless she was the first—and most likely only—editor to have ever done so. And so I was somewhat unprepared for her almost gushing response: "What an inviting introduction!" Over the course of the next month or so we exchanged a flurry of e-mails. She peppered her communications with topical questions and also explained the system—the restraints mainly—under which she worked. It all boiled down to the fact that I had no credentials whatsoever to present to court, that which her fellow editors would require at mashup roundtable time. And so, seemingly inevitably, the bloom began to fade from the rose of an initially promising association.

But understandably so, as I had labored on with no successful journalistic publishing breakthroughs to report. No matter what I sent out—even pieces that academicians who I admired, with whom I was not even acquainted or "networked," called "fascinating" or "intriguing"—my entreaties went unrequited. In due course it became increasingly apparent that editors of newspapers, periodicals, and journals could not make head or tail of what I was trying to explain to them about Donald Trump, evangelical religion, and

American life and politics. Perhaps I had too strange or unconventional a story to tell.

Editors at other equally prestigious university presses echoed the message. This is no *talent alone matters* blind audition before a selection committee of a symphony orchestra. Don't kid yourself. No matter the quality of your tome, it will not see the light of day. A prominent editor at Oxford University Press explained that she had given up forwarding submissions from authors with no academic curriculum vitae glitter to the Oxford faculty for initial clearance. Invariably, they came back unexamined, and almost immediately. Now she no longer even bothers.

And so my situation and this occasion of acknowledgement differ markedly from those of most academically-ensconced authors. As will become all too apparent, I have feathered my own nest and proudly present this one big egg and now fledgling of a book that has emerged from it—at least the only one *so far*—all by my lonesome. To extend the barnyard metaphor, I am left feeling much like Wilbur the pig and Charlotte the spider as they gazed up at the unique web that would ultimately save his life. I too occupy a niche largely of my own making, but happily cite and celebrate (with apologies for any erroneous spellings from memory) the following posse of acquaintances and accomplices who may have contributed in some way or other to the feathering of that eventual launching pad, a few of whom, sad to say, are most likely no longer with us.

Many thanks then to Sandra Sharpe, Lois Hudson, Markham Harris, Lynne Iglitzen, Barbara Melber, Guenther Roth, Harvey & Blix Bresler, Andy Miller, and Wendy Bebié—students, teachers, and fellow travelers whom I encountered at the University of Washington.

And also to Wendy Guentner, Mohammed Bashir, Yvonne McDonald, Edward Shils, Stephen Toulmin, Jim & Ruth Block, Jimmy & Dorothy Fuerst, and Jerry & Julie Dorfman—students, teachers, and friends met, or re-united with, while in Chicago and at the University of Chicago; elsewhere, to Jim Fielder (whom I failed miserably as a friend—RIP), Susan Lemagie, and another noble ancient one, Fran Ennis.

I may have occasionally annoyed the hell out of altogether too many of you, but you have more than occasionally rattled and warmed the cockles of my heart.

Caveat Emptor

Given the potential jeopardy into which certain members of this community may have fallen by becoming my informants or helping out in other respects, I have changed some names, dates, and other details—the time period of my fieldwork on campus, for example—in order to shield the innocent from possible recrimination. All students, of course, were assigned pseudonyms.

A few not so innocent figures—particularly those too obvious or nationally prominent to disguise—are left to fend for themselves.

But, alas, the social critique of all ideas, which Louis Dupré in an exemplary essay on culture sees as one of the main tasks of twentieth-century sociology, has been applied only spottily to the effects of modernization on religion. . . . It is tempting to interpret the myopia in sociological studies as a failure of modernization that could have been avoided if certain anthropological methods of inquiry had been adopted.

Three assumptions that dominate contemporary religious studies, and that seem most questionable to me, tend to protect the subject from the probing of sociological criticism and from uncomfortable comparisons. The most fundamental of these assumptions writes into the definition of the subject the notion that religion is good for the human psyche. To assume that religion has integrative functions or is otherwise conducive to the good life makes immediate sense to those who start from the same assumption. However, the usefulness of a definition depends on the use to which it is to be put. Clearly this definition leaves out a lot of religious behavior that is widely regarded as emotionally restrictive, bigoted, fanatical, or psychotic. Thus the first question is why the subject should be so selectively defined. . . .

Not being committed to supposing that people are always better off with religion, anthropology has a wider perspective. Anthropology was founded in a mood of rationalism in which scholars rejoiced in intellectual liberty and freedom from arbitrary ceremonial and moral constraints. Religion as such was not thought necessarily to be good for people, and supernatural was no more a good word than was taboo. If they were not rationalists, likely as not anthropologists had been bred in a Christian missionary tradition that deplored heathen darkness. Consequently, with no other axe to grind but the need to establish a comparative field, anthropologists tried to start with as unloaded a definition of religion as possible. I am not especially fond of the one based on belief in spiritual beings, but at least it defines a field without begging any questions about the integrative power—moral, intellectual, or social— of religion. Nor does it teach that modern times show a decline from ancient standards of piety. Indeed, reflection shows that the evidence for old-time sanctity comes from suspect sources such as hagiography, panegyrics, and sermons. If we were to read even that biased evidence more critically, we would notice the professionals upbraiding the mass of ordinary people for lack of faith, as if the gift of which, we are told, modernity has deprived us was always rather the exception. Just as fundamental, there can be no evidence that there is more unhappiness and mental disturbance now than in those famous ages of faith.

How can anyone possibly say? The evidence is weak, the arguments weaker. In many of the writings of religious sociology we cannot but recognize the sermons of our childhood. The idea that humans are beings who need religion belongs to creation mythology. To say that only religion heals the sick soul is traditional evangelism. The idea that modernization is bad for religion echoes preaching that directly opposes worldliness to salvation. To insist that culture is autonomous is saying that the spirit moveth where it listeth. To have no interest in the social mechanisms by which faith is roused and sustained is to be faithful to the model of pentecostal inspiration. It is proper to use empirical evidence only as illustrative material when the object of the discourse is spiritual counseling. None of this helps to understand better the relation of beliefs to society, yet this is the very problem at issue for understanding religious change.

Mary Douglas, 1982

PART ONE

INTRODUCTION

CHAPTER 1

CONTEXTS: PERSONAL & ETHNOGRAPHIC

G rowing up in a small logging town along the western slopes of the state of Washington, one experienced Christianity in all sorts of ways, almost unavoidably. And yet, strangely enough, as far as its physical presence, only a couple of actual buildings—one Catholic, one Protestant—stand out, having left any sort of impression at all, but perhaps there were others. Diversity came from a best friend, Dave Fitzgerald, who was a Mormon, but never let on about it, not even to try to explain away the large stash of canned goods lining the shelves of his family's tiny, one-bathroom rambler of a house that I would often visit.

Like most American parents, mine felt an overwhelming obligation—and only rarely an urge—to expose their offspring to religion. No matter how lukewarm their own prior encounters with it, good parenting demanded periodic appearances at the local downtown First Baptist Church; for appearances—those either effecting or affecting the normal—were, and still remain, among the highest aspirations of small-town American life. I recall the rather strange affinity my father had for a man named George Valley, who owned an appliance store right next to the only music store in town, Johnny's Music Box, half a block over from the only movie house, the Blue Ox theatre. We seemed destined to follow this man everywhere—to his church, to basketball nights out for wheezing old men, to some sort of all male breakfast club convened at the Timberline Lodge, the only motel in town. Like many American youths, I grew up in a small town where there was only one of anything seemingly essential—or frivolous.

And yet oddly enough again, I don't recall any serious repercussions for failing to embrace the religious norm; disbelief simply went unchallenged, unacknowledged, although it certainly was never brazenly practiced or broadcast. Perhaps it was more a feeling of being left out of the proper mix. Either way, no one seemed to mind all that much. No one really felt threatened by much of anything—religious or otherwise. Not even the Harlem Globetrotters coming to town, although they couldn't get a meal after the game, ending up twenty miles away in Olympia, the state capitol, still driving around in their bus, looking for a restaurant that would serve them. The phony white all-stars who played against them so ineptly night after night had no problem. No wonder the trotters seemed so lean and hungry. Unlike these days?

From a very early age on, I harbored a quite different cache of aspirations from most of my mates—becoming a college basketball player, for one, a necessary intermediate step up that challenging set of rungs on Jacob's ladder to the earthly paradise of Bill Russell's Boston Celtics. Although again, seemingly unavoidably, religion got drawn into the mix also. Somehow or other, to no one's surprise, the only high school basketball coach in town ended up teaching my fifth-grade Sunday school class—teaching perhaps proving too generous a term. Calm and controlled on the outside, this Paul Daugherty guy's eyes flashed like crystalline daggers. We worms squirmed through bone-rattling accounts of the fires of hell awaiting unrepentant sinners. Deeply stirred, I became determined to eliminate any stray, undisciplined thoughts and feelings. With the benefit of hindsight—as most have now been made aware, of course—such attempts tended to lead seemingly, ineluctably, to the exact opposite. Or worse.

One very long week at our church's Black Lake summer Bible camp provided the occasion for setting the first phase of my spiritual growth in motion. There I inadvertently confessed to our barrack's counselor, a man named Fred Archer who was the father of our high school's star quarterback (of course), that I had answered the call to come forward issued by a guest speaker missionary from Formosa—now Taiwan—earlier that evening. No doubt I mistakenly thought that by lying through my teeth he might then go away and leave me alone. Instead, he hovered beside my top bunk bed for what seemed like hours, initiating me into the full range of the wonders and responsibilities of my decision, suffocating the life out of me with the worst human dog breath I had ever encountered. Would he never stop talking, emoting, and exhaling all over me?

That summer I sat under a tree during morning silent Bible reading hour and gave my life to Jesus. Indeed, that a fellow camper could run screaming out of the barracks, having had a finger nearly sliced off by the scissor-like metal frame of a collapsing bunk bed, blood spurting all over his body and us, sealed the deal. Obviously, there was much more to this religion business than just roasted marshmallows and flush-faced homilies. No doubt this unfortunate character had been caught red-handed, alone in his bunk, engaged in some sort of foul deed, and all hell had broken loose. Perhaps the Old Testament God hovering over us all had let him have it directly, mercilessly. An eye for an eye, a tooth for a tooth, a finger for a . . . hand.

Back home I immediately set up shop along tar-graveled Harvard Avenue, way atop so-called "snob hill," where a good many of the fathers with advanced degrees in science (although mine claimed only a lowly BS) who worked for the ITT Rayonier Olympic Research Division had settled their families. Having felt the hand of God upon me, I could be seen waving an abridged paperback edition of the New Testament above my head, calling for sinners to repent. Upon hearing such exhortations, my younger brother had run home, out of breath, gasping to our mother about the "good news" of getting "born again . . . Is it true?"—this all potentially good news to a pudge who had been dealt a particularly bad hand in life so far. The looks I subsequently received were those from a respectable parent who had unexpectedly created a monster that she would now be hard-pressed to rein in and control, the best of intentions having gone awry.

Luckily (not *verily*), the town's only pharmacy, located along main street Railroad Avenue, openly displayed a rack of *New York Times* bestsellers; this, besides radio and television, was our only contact with the outside world. There I discovered an array of Jewish authors, whose *Herzog, The Chosen, The Natural, Portnoy's Complaint*, et al., soon filled my horizons with other possibilities, *and neuroses*. And yet it was only an additional summer's very different kind of encounter, following a year or two on a pagan university campus, with Bertrand's Russell's *Why I'm Not A Christian*, that finally broke the spell. The habit of nightly prayers from summers past *absconded* first, no doubt offset by the arrival of a new technical term into my vocabulary along with other less orthodox items. Perhaps for quite a few other American youths these pivotal moments eventually arrived also, along with some variation upon the realization that *I've been had (not bad), and boy do I feel borderline stupid about it.*

Then again, and much more likely for an even greater number of adolescents, the impact of such early training and routines lingered on, many remaining in force throughout a lifetime. I recall Gordon Tang, the notorious slum landlord owner of a series of hacked-up "duplex" houses in the U-District of Seattle taking one look at my room—the bed in particular—and commenting: "We're you in the army?" Nope, just summer Bible camp.

In this respect, as Luigi Barzini once wrote of his fellow Italians, we Americans are indeed quite *alone in the world*. There is nothing quite like us, *anywhere*, as we will see in the explorations that follow.

Looking back, my near fatal brush with evangelical religion seems rather ordinary, perhaps even predictable, no different from that of millions of other American boys and girls. Indeed nothing has surprised me more than that I would return to the religion of my youth for the topic of a dissertation.

For when I went off originally to the University of Chicago for graduate school training in sociology I did so thinking my areas of concentration would be that of urban sociology and Weberian social theory, with nary a sideways glance at anything so remotely uninteresting as American religion. It was just one among many other memories I sought to expunge, drawn east to the Midwest mainly by the lodestars of Edward Shils (due to a Richard Hofstader footnote), Marshall Sahlins, Stephen Toulmin, and Saul Bellow, among others. They were the graying academic sugar plum fairies dancing in my dreams.

Then again, given such an imposing line-up of luminaries—and not all Jews, mind you—go figure how the topic of American Christianity seems to have largely escaped the attention of virtually all of them. Given the thrust of the book you hold in your hands, it may prove the ultimate irony of a splendid multi-disciplinary education that even though a leading scholar of Max Weber, Guenther Roth (my mentor at Washington), had offered and I had taken his class in the sociology of religion—and that I had then subsequently spent months, literally years, on-and-off with the other academicians mentioned above—I cannot recall a single mention or nod in the direction of religion in America, let alone *evangelical* religion. Not one. For it appears they all shared and reinforced my own malingering indifference, if not a finely-honed and burnished disgust, about such matters.

And yet, fortuitously also, the multi-disciplinary genius of the University of Chicago—the Committee on Social Thought, in particular—and the freedom the sociology department had given me to range far afield generated interests and options that no graduate school experience anywhere else could possibly have orchestrated. Just imagine, if you will, a class on *The Ancient City* of Fusel de Coulanges taught by Marshall Sahlins, an anthropologist, and James Redfield, a classicist,[1] among a good many others equally rich and challenging. But evangelical religion in America? Nary a whisper.

When I convened my dissertation committee of two sociologists and the above Marshall Sahlins to formally present a proposal, after having spent a season or two exploring an evangelical college community campus, my initial primary object of study, it seems as though the brief document I earlier forwarded to them had arrived like a bolt of lightning out of the blue, or a ton of bricks. As I sat among them I must confess luxuriating—if not thoroughly

---

[1] The latter the author of *Nature and Culture in the Iliad*, among others. The course boasted a reading list of Descartes, Vico, Hume, Rousseau, Michelet, Maine, Marx, Morgan, Engels, Durkheim, Lévi-Strauss, and Foucault.

basking—in their astonishment. Who'd have thunk up such a thing? And where on earth did I find this place?

Sahlins, who did well to mask and muffle his dismal opinion of sociology, giggled uncontrollably, mouthing the anthropological mantra, "exotic," aloud several times. Not unexpectedly, one of the sociologists—an overt Christian himself, I later learned, who to his credit made no mention of any personal connection or interest—mulled things over and then raised certain orthodox departmental social scientific expectations, laying down the gauntlet in a subsequent private conversation: "But can you prove it?" As the diligent reader will eventually discover, yes I can, *and have*, much to the ultimate delight and satisfaction—perhaps even surprise—of the sociologists.

And so given this quite deep, rich, and varied palette of a graduate school training, the first impression imparted here might be that of a doctoral candidate for whom the religion of his youth was the furthest thing from his mind as he returned home to Seattle in search of a dissertation topic. Fortunately, it was only a matter of time before past experience and the pressure to come up with something *defensible* began to generate some possibilities. I had originally gone to Chicago thinking "community case study" (as in Gerald Suttles's *The Social Order of the Slum*—the author of which, upon hearing about my project, later asked to join the committee and made some substantial contributions) and so as I continued the quest, casting about for leads, one in particular began to intrigue me, over time coming to demand the lion's share of my attention.

Preconceptions or biases—be they theoretical, methodological, religious, or experiential in origin—are not easily set aside or overcome. In my own case, I did not arrive upon the Seattle Pacific University campus in complete innocence, my vision unclouded by anticipations of any sort. In fact I chose this small community, out of several I might have otherwise, due to a rather unusual kind of familiarity. My first sustained experience[2] with Seattle Pacific College came seemingly ages ago in 1977 when stationed for a year on campus as a member of a CETA (President Carter's Comprehensive Employment and Training Act) crew. I worked as a jack-of-all-trades in the plant maintenance department, performing carpentry, masonry, building demolition and restoration, among other jobs. Our crew was a motley bunch of misfits: a couple of college graduates, an unemployed teamster, a drifter, a

---

[2] Actually it was my second, as I had been recruited by coach Les Habegger to play basketball, and paid a visit, but turned the offer down to become a Washington Husky (under Tex Winter) instead.

longshoreman from Queens, an aspiring rock-and-roll star, two or three black autoworkers from Detroit, a newly-minted history Ph.D., and several shell-shocked Vietnam veterans. One vet we called "Moses" for his streams of wild and long flowing red hair and occasional extemporaneous flights into preaching, gospel singing, and speaking in tongues (*glossolalia*); another we called "Crazy Eddie," for his, well, general craziness. Eddie wore a stocking-cap every day regardless of the weather and drove an old black hearse with the back cut open for collecting waste metals, one of his many supplemental sources of income. Puddles, his little poodle dog, sat all day long in the front seat of the hearse, eagerly awaiting Eddie's routine lunch time visits. During the demolition of the old biology building the crew discovered a vat of dead cats soaking in formaldehyde and Crazy Eddie just went, well again, kind of nuts. He pushed us all aside to get a look, eyes wide and gleaming, saying he'd back the hearse up to the building and load 'em aboard. Later, during a break, Eddie was resting, leaning his head and back against a wall, remarking casually aloud to no one in particular: "You know sometimes I just feel like climbing that clock tower over there [the administration building] with a hunting rifle and wasting anything that moves." Although this barely raised an eyebrow among the vets, needless to say, few of the other crew members turned their backs on Eddie for any extended period of time. Prone to flights of fancy and bouts of melancholy, Crazy Eddie, by the end of our stint, would become Eddie the Rat, turning into a stool pigeon informant for "Big Bad Bud," our boss, parlaying reports on internal "troop movements" (scuttle-butt, dissension, meetings with our City of Seattle adviser) of the crew into a hoped-for permanent position in the campus auto shop.

We weren't pretty, just a bunch of grunts, and after a while it seemed as though we had worn out our welcome, which I found puzzling, given that the members of the crew were some of the nicest guys I had ever worked with and we got along so well. Yet controversy and conflict swirled around us. Department head squared off against department head over our presence and treatment; rumors rippled through the staff about "conspiracies" and "ring leaders." There were confrontations and sweat-room interrogations. One of the "smart-ass" Detroit blacks—a young man named Don Vaughn, I recall—was sent in to demolish a wall in a building in which the electricity had been "inadvertently" left on. Whacking into a junction box with a crow-bar, he was leveled by 120 volts. Knocked breathless and unconscious, he nonetheless survived, waking up in a hospital bed with no feeling in his legs. The next day, our boss, Big Bad Bud, summoned us to his office to drive the point home, joking, "That'll knock some sense into him."

So went my introduction to Seattle Pacific. Welcome to the big leagues. These Nickerson Avenue dudes play hardball. Check your Bible—the beatitudes, in particular—at the door. Where were the meek and mild-mannered children, the soft and cuddly lambs of God, we—and I, especially— wondered? Bizarre, unpredictable, and yet strangely amusing, our stint there had the feel of some kind of weird divine comedy. Jeff, the student "work-study" coordinator of the CETA crew paid the author the highest of compliments: "You remind me of Hawkeye on *M.A.S.H.*" Sure, I was kind of a smart ass and we *were* conscripts, outsiders in a militarized, free-fire zone of sorts, and yet none of us could really understand why. To say the least, I left with the lingering impression that there was much more to these folks than that advertised in the mission statement of the promotional brochure. Much more indeed.

So that I appreciate, perhaps as well as anyone, the challenge of wiping away preconceptions. Due to these and other more conventional academic experiences, my mind was scarcely a blank slate when I returned to the campus a good many years later. Obviously I chose a small community case study for some reason. Laurence Wylie's marvelous *Village in the Vaucluse*[3] and other community studies come immediately to mind, having persuaded me of the value of the small-scale fieldwork approach. I was inspired and guided by the notion that each morsel of American society bore some sort of relationship to a larger cultural whole, and that one ought to be able to plunk down temporary roots in any such community and tease out the extended relationship. To me this seemed more a matter of common sense than anything else.

My background in general American and social history lay behind an almost congenital suspicion of the loose application of sociological constructs. However great my admiration for and benefit from the work of Max Weber in the sociology of religion, for example, I relied more on his *micro* vision and formulation of social behavior[4]—and his personal example—than his larger *macro* concepts, deriving as they did from European sociological and historiographical traditions. Accordingly, I assigned myself the daunting task of developing social, cultural, and historical concepts and categories more appropriate to the American terrain; I continually exhorted myself to ground my interpretations in concrete observations and experience, and to resist any initial falling back upon convenient disciplinary theoretical crutches. The reader will encounter a few generic terms, such as "social" and "cultural" defined and employed in a somewhat idiosyncratic manner, their

---

[3] Cambridge: Harvard University Press, 1974. And closer to home, Arthur Vidich and Joseph Bensman's classic *Small Town in Mass Society: Class, Power and Religion in a Rural Community* (Princeton University Press, 1968).

[4] As in a paper I wrote for Stephen Toulmin, "Ambiguity and Social Behavior in Max Weber: A Systemization."

meanings bent in conformity with my particular designs. In many respects I have been forced to develop a new descriptive and analytical language more amenable to my projected task. Some academicians may find this problematical or disconcerting.[5] So be it.

Now although I did not enter this community laden with some conception in the sociology of religion to test,[6] one preeminent guiding question dogged my deliberations, an early formulation of an eventual major theme: why is evangelical religion so oddly and noisily important in American society? Like some sort of squeaky wheel. For it seemed to me that all sorts of intriguing things were happening *out there*—or *in here*, rather—that virtually no one in academia was addressing. Such as, why is evangelical religion so seemingly inextinguishable a presence or force in our American culture, perhaps the most modern society in the "post-industrial," "post-modern" world? Why no such comparable presence in European societies, our closest cultural ancestors? For some of the reasons alluded to above, I hoped to explore quite

---

[5] To wit, if I had taken Christian Smith's sociological theory of religion and research suggestions to heart this book would never have even been conceived, let alone written. Much as I admire the ambition and comprehensiveness of *Religion: What It Is, How It Works, and Why It Matters* (2017), it scarcely could have guided or improved my project had it been available when I sat down to make sense of my findings. Indeed it could very well have stopped my effort dead in its tracks. Smith might find my reaction to his 2017 book rather unanticipated: it feels both glutted by details and yet spread too thin. What is more, although he is an avowed evangelical Christian who too easily dismisses critics of religion like Richard Dawkins as "sadly ignorant about their object of critique" (132) and is ensconced within a Catholic University (Notre Dame), he nonetheless succeeds rather well in practicing "methodological agnosticism" (13) throughout the work; unfortunately, the reader just might come away convinced that religion is indeed nothing more than superstition cloaked in mystery.
—The reader may compare the above dismissal of Richard Dawkin's ignorance with Smith's own reductionism in an ironic critique of "explanatory reductionism" as called out in Francis Crick's declaration that "You're [i.e., we all, humans] nothing but a pack of neurons."; as though there were nothing more to Crick's view of the matter; as though he too wouldn't marvel at what we've all done with our basic construction tool kits of neurons. (ibid., 60)

[6] Predictably enough, University of Chicago professor Wendy Griswold, a "sociologist of culture," upon perusal of an early chapter, wrote back that she couldn't make head or tail of it: "What concept in the sociology of religion are you trying to test?"
—And I was (quite happily) violating the rules of some doyens of the field: ". . . . Jane Harrison comments on the erroneous approach of those inquirers who start with a general term religion of which they had a preconceived idea, and then try to fit into it any facts that come to hand. Instead she proposes no initial definition, but remarks that 'we shall collect the facts that admittedly are religious and see from what human activities they appear to have sprung' (1912: 29). It is yet more tempting for the inquirer into societies farther removed from our own tradition than that of ancient Greece to adopt a similar approach, and quietly to overlook the definitional problems. The dangers, however, outweigh the advantages." (Jack Goody, "Religion and Ritual: The Definitional Problem," *The British Journal of Sociology*, Vol. 12, No. 2, June, 1961, 142.)

a few of these matters in this small community, but I had only vague, barely sketched out versions of them to guide me.

Now I must acknowledge also that however much I strove to sweep my mind clean of ingrained theory and methodology, there were social scientific materials that I later drew upon heavily in the evaluation of my field experience. A good many from anthropology and psychology proved instrumental, as will become readily apparent from here on out. Indeed although my project began as something else, it evolved over the course of time into an *ethnography* of sorts, as they call such things in anthropology, and no one was more surprised than I.[7]

And so upon my arrival on campus I sought to immerse myself in the unimpeded flow of the historical and contemporary details of the life of this academic community. I would encourage the full wash of culture to spill over me, flooding my senses with the unvarnished sights, sounds, thoughts, and behaviors of the community. Accordingly (and perhaps ironically), I labored for months in the archives, poring over old college newspapers, community documents, and collections of letters, compiling volumes of notes and transcriptions, selecting what seemed significant and yet not really knowing what might prove meaningful later on—continually collecting and collating, unsure where it all might lead. I squandered a small fortune on the Weter library's two antiquated copy machines; it seemed as though I was forever scaling those stairs from the archives to the machines. Several months of tedious labor persuaded me to go on: there may be something here. One day I wandered into an adjacent room during a break and discovered shelves lined with cassette recordings of the college's chapel services—several hundred, dating back nearly twenty years. I began listening to them, eventually reviewing three hundred or so, transcribing a few word for word, a chore requiring two or three hours, sometimes more, for each thirty-minute chapel session. The tapes contained both intriguing and redundant material, and much in between, but I wasn't sure precisely why; I was unsure what to save through transcription and which to pass over and so I devoted a few more months to the tapes alone. The next year I moved my study out of the library completely and began meeting more people and sticking my nose into everything, expanding this sort of documentary habit to my observations of live chapels and other campus events and encounters, taking copious, almost verbatim notes. Such was the extent of my commitment to an unguided immer-

---

[7] Again, when Marshall Sahlins christened an earlier version of this book "a marvelous ethnography" I did my best to effect *mais bien sûr*, as though it had all simply come together according to plan.

sion, an approach encouraging the community to speak for itself, telling me in its own voice just what it was or sought to be. I was loathe to arbitrarily narrow my focus too soon, but there did eventually come a time when the materials and experiences began to repeat themselves; then I sensed that enough was enough; I had absorbed and recorded the full range and texture of the community. Only then did I really turn my attention to what it all might mean.

The extent to which I succeeded in keeping preconceptions to a bare minimum receives some corroboration from my own belief, and now confession, that *virtually everything I observed or experienced on campus surprised me*. I was simply unprepared for what I found. And what I managed to make of it all later on surprised me even more. It never occurred to me, for example, that there was such a tangible, identifiable thing as "secular society"; that I, and others like me, were members of this malevolent behemoth and that we were in fact the sworn enemies of evangelical Christianity. It simply never occurred to me, at least not in so blisteringly blatant a form. The depth and intensity of their apprehensions was simply stunning. Persons who have lived around or had occasional dealings with this institution will find bewildering some of the emotions and thoughts the members of this community have been harboring and expressing among themselves over the years. *Exotic*, a favorite term of anthropologists, scarcely captures the full gist of it.[8]

In any event, I proceeded under the guiding assumption that when one's initial focus is upon community particulars (with general themes or conceptions temporarily put on the back burner) then observations and interpretations can flow more freely out of the nature and structure of the materials themselves. Later one even feels a little more confident when drawing upon or fashioning more general conclusions that the interpretation has been well-grounded in reasonably un-incriminating concrete details.

What sort of form will these interpretations and conclusions assume? Throughout this study I will dwell upon the kinds of social and cultural details and dynamics which distinguish communities and societies from one another. As intimated above, I aim to discover and explain what makes evangelicalism a prominent, uniquely American phenomenon. Time and again I will call attention to the ways in which large cultural idioms and historical dynamics translate into small behaviors, and conversely, how small be-

---

[8] Phil Zuckerman who also took an ethnographic, "qualitative" approach to his study of Denmark and Norway, was similarly dumfounded at times: "I ended up 'discovering' aspects of religion and irreligion in Scandinavia that I had never anticipated or expected. . . . so many interesting and compelling contours to their secularity that I had never even considered before, had never experienced . . . hadn't even really known were possible. . . ." (*Society Without God. . .* , 97.)

haviors and events invoke a much larger historical and cultural cosmos. I will seek a blend of the particular and the general, attempting to locate within the confines of this small academic community and along the larger contours of American history and culture developmentally unique elements which set the American society apart from its closest European ancestors. Although the reader will find themes and concepts drawn from many different academic disciplines, perhaps what ultimately lends coherence to this interdisciplinary mix is not so much a particular method or technique as an emerging vision of the way in which the smaller and larger pieces of American society may fit together into a whole. The entire fieldwork and scholarly experience has strengthened my conviction that there is a seminal quality to American evangelicalism and culture that defies generalization.[9] It must be explored and understood in its own terms and in its own way. There is simply no substitute for *getting out there and mixing it up*: seeing, feeling, and living among the object or objects of study.[10] In the larger methodological scheme of things this suggests a concentration more upon molding and shaping our techniques to reflect the phenomena we seek to understand than an all-too-common quite different approach, that of scouring the social landscape for phenomena conforming to and validating our research designs and data collection tools.[11] This kind of social scientific sensitivity and flexibility, this kind of out-in-the-bush *mentalité*, for lack of a better term, might be thought of

---

[9] The main comparison here is with modern industrialized Europe. There are, however, particular features or dynamics within American evangelicalism and fundamentalism that can be found in fundamentalist religions around the world, particularly those of the Islamic variety. Numerous parallels—those concerning assorted, often complicated, reactions to "modernism"—can be found in the mammoth six-volume series, *The Fundamentalism Project* (University of Chicago Press, 1991-1996), edited by Martin Marty and R. Scott Appleby.

[10] There is no better demonstration of this than Daniel Everett's monumental ethnography, *Don't Sleep, There Are Snakes: Life and Language in the Amazonian Jungle* (London: Profile Books, 2008). Should be required reading for every social science course in American higher education.

[11] In many respects my approach shares much with the anthropologist Saba Mahmood, with whose work I became acquainted (unfortunately) long after the final drafts of my book were largely completed. I too, ultimately, ". . . . had to transcend [my ethnographic site and experiences] in order to make sense of *what* I had encountered" in both theoretical and historical dimensions, as the reader will soon discover. For indeed it is a matter of taking apart compounding observations but also of dislodging "fragments of the past congealed into the present." (*Religious Differences in the Secular Age: A Minority Approach*, Princeton University Press, 2016, 23.)

modestly as a *cultural sociology*.[12] Then again, *rogue sociology* has a nice ring to it also.[13]

---

[12] One telling example of how an unmitigated "sociological" approach to matters religious can obscure social scientific insight—let alone comparative cultural understanding—comes from Christian Smith's monumental sociological theory of religion mentioned earlier, *Religion: What It Is*. . . . (2017). In an "Excursus: What People Seem to Pray About" in Chapter Four, "Why Are Humans Religious?" he explains that "one way to learn more about what religious people are looking for in their religious practices is to examine the things for which they pray." He lists two American studies (of Protestants and Catholics) and a rare Dutch study and concludes from them—See! They all largely pray about "worldly issues." Smith totally ignores, mentioning only in passing, one monumental statistical discrepancy: The Dutch pray *much less* frequently than Americans. His only concern: that they pray about the same things; his only observation that "Because the Netherlands is a relatively secularized society, the percentages shown here are lower than those found in more religious countries." Did it ever occur to him to ask: Why is that? What is the nature or the source of that statistical difference? And to actually fully explore his own title question: "Why it matters?" Why does *it* matter? Indeed not once in all the books Professor Smith has written that I have reviewed has it occurred to him to ask or address this question.

—One indication of how hopeless this project for a meaningful, significant *cultural sociology* may be is found in Penny Edgell's desultory review of the prospects in "A Cultural Sociology of Religion: New Directions," *Annual Review of Sociology*, 2012, Vol. 38. Her pathetic offhand reference to Marshall Sahlins's *Culture and Practical Reason* (let alone calling Mary Douglas a sociologist) mentioned as "Other work [that] concentrates on how religion becomes defined as something distinct from other institutions or realms of activity. . . ." (255) simply reveals how clueless she is as to the "structural" basis of culture; hence the analysis of *structure* that must inform any *cultural* sociology. *Paradise Joe's* would not exist without *Culture and Practical Reason*. A similar disappointment followed my review of Ruth Marshall's "Christianity, Anthropology, Politics," *Current Anthropology*, Vol. 55, Supplement 10, December 2014, but for altogether different reasons that I will expand upon elsewhere in due course.

—A 2012 compilation that attempted, aside from its title, to recount how religion has been addressed in the fields of sociology, anthropology, and history, observed that: ". . . . it is not hard to diagnose a certain balkanization of the study of religion that divides up the object of study in ways that reproduce the fault lines among the different fields themselves. . . . Meanwhile, interdisciplinary studies are often merely 'multidisciplinary' rather than truly syncretic and synthetic. . . . Yet it should also be said the 'interdisciplinary' often serves as an excuse for a lack of rigor." (Philip S. Gorski et al., 13-14.)

—Later, I was literally shocked to discover that my use of the term, *cultural sociology*, had been preempted by the afore-cited sociologist, in his quite valuable, "The Return of the Repressed . . . ," 165 and elsewhere. A rare *sociological* work of insight.

[13] But please note that none of this should be taken to mean that data-crunching ought play no role in a "cultural sociology." Indeed, see my own statistical tests (Appendix A) of the central *cultural* proposition informing this book. See also, for example, Lisa A. Keister's marvelous use of data to test a culturally-based proposition in her "Religion and Wealth: The Role of Religious Affiliation and Participation in Early Adult Asset Accumulation," *Social Forces*, Vol. 82, No, 1, September 2003. The same applies, once again, to Michael Hout et al.'s breathtakingly skilled "The Demographic Imperative in Religious Change in the United States," *American Journal of Sociology*, Vol. 107, No. 2, September 2001. I wish the same could be said of Greeley and Hout's atrocious later 2006 study, *The Truth About Conservative Christians*. . . .

Many years later, just a few days in fact before sending the manuscript off to the publisher, I came across a quite telling, almost prophetic, aphorism that both captures and affirms my initial intentions *and* anticipates the broadest, most general conclusions at whose sweeping doorstep I would ultimately arrive.

> Everything we think of as a cause of culture is really an effect of culture, including us.[14]

And finally, in a somewhat lighter vein, one last introductory word on a perennially controversial matter, this having to do with the expression and reception of religion in American public life. Sociologists refer to this as the private/public sphere question. Looking back, I recall that perhaps one of the most rigorous discussions of the issue during this earlier period followed the 1993 publication of Stephen Carter's *The Culture of Disbelief: How American Law and Politics Trivialize Religious Devotion*, a polemical work that became a much cited favorite of President Bill Clinton. The by-now-familiar argument runs that a state-enforced "public secularism" has managed to marginalize and "trivialize" piety in American life, quarantining it far from serious discussions of public policy; that the nation's liberal elites have "come to belittle religious devotion, to humiliate believers and, even if indirectly, to discourage religion as a serious activity."[15]

As the reader of this volume will soon come to appreciate, most secular academicians and journalists didn't have a clue where Carter "was coming from,"[16] and still don't. For a Yale professor, it was a surprisingly dire siren song. The words were vaguely familiar, but the tone-deaf "liberal establishment" couldn't hear or feel, let alone dance, to the music. *Their* incomprehension notwithstanding, the indictment rang dead true in other more pedestrian quarters elsewhere. Evangelicals could hum more than a few bars

---

[14] This actually only one sentence in Judith Shulevitz's review of Joseph Heinrich's *The WEIRDest People in the World: How the West Became Psychologically Peculiar and Particularly Prosperous*, in *The Atlantic*, October 2020, 95.

[15] New York: Basic Books, 1993.
—Wendy Kaminer begs to differ: ". . . . contemporary public policy discussions: left and right . . . are suffused with piety. The rise of virtue talk—which generally takes the form of communitarianism on the left and nostalgia for Victorianism on the right—has resulted in a striking remoralization of public policy debates. Today, it's rare to hear a non-normative analysis of social problems, one that doesn't focus on failings of individual character or collective virtue. . . ." ("The Last Taboo," 26.)

[16] But social internationalist critics within evangelicalism surely did. Prominent evangelical author Michael Horton, for example, begs to differ: "Rather, we are the rock of offense and we are not being insulted, persecuted, and falsely accused because of Christ, but because of our own follies and quests for political power." (*Beyond Culture Wars. . . ,* 35)

and knew the chorus by heart. Although my own reading of the liberal status quo's posture toward religion suggests more a callous indifference than calculation or conspiracy,[17] we need not belabor the point. Our greater interest here lies in this notion of "trivialization." Why and whence it comes? And who proves ultimately responsible? Bear with me, now, as I direct the reader's attention to the title of this volume.

Paradise Joe's[18] was an old hamburger joint that sat across the street, just east of the Seattle Pacific campus. Indeed the reader may have surmised something more from its appearance in the title of this work than mere light-hearted Miltonian word play. Its prominence serves to presage and illustrate a rather important dynamic within evangelicalism (whose more formal exposition will follow later). Over the course of my trips back and forth to campus, the *Paradise Joe's* sign always caught my eye and left an indelible impression. Although I know next to nothing of the place beyond the name and never really inquired further (a year or so later the building was converted into a laundromat, I believe, and is now a *Subway* franchise), in time the significance of the venue began to dawn on me. How oxymoronic this marriage of Milton's exotic, exalted lost Paradise with the mundane vending of burgers and fries! And yet *how typical of evangelicalism*: the prosaic and the sublime—side by side—mingling all in the same breath, part and parcel of the same sublunary institution.

Behold, if you will, patrons of God's chosen hamburger joint—God's MacDonald's?—bowing their heads and muttering grace before scarfing down burgers and fries. Would Christ take onions, pickles, and cheese—the works—on his burger? All sorts of irreverent imagery leap out at the innocent bystander: "Miracle Fries," "Communion Shakes," "Last Supper Whopper," and perhaps even a "Leper Corner" tucked away somewhere out of

---

[17] Aside from the occasional sarcasm, and in spite of all that has occurred over the last few decades, American academicians are still reluctant to acknowledge evangelicalism as a legitimate and serious force in American life. It is this kind of indifference—due partially to ignorance—and a refusal to engage the evangelical element in genuine debate, to take them seriously intellectually, that makes Stanley Fish and John Niehaus's exchange in *First Things* so unprecedented and noteworthy—and so out of character in academia. The results were well worth waiting for. See Stanley Fish, "Why We Can't All Just Get Along," Richard John Neuhaus, "Why We Can Get Along," and especially, "Stanley Fish replies to Richard John Neuhaus," in *First Things* 60, February 1996.
—You know that a dent, at least, in the façade of indifference has been made when a New York Jewish liberal icon like Norman Mailer writes a book *about Jesus*. (*The Gospel According to the Son*, New York: Random House, 1997.)
—In popular American culture, by marked contrast, Christian themes abound. The Hollywood science-fiction blockbuster, *Star Wars*, ought be seen as galactic-scale *Passion Play*.

[18] The original dissertation was titled, *Paradise Joe's: Seattle Pacific, Evangelical Religion, and American Culture.*

sight, the various patrons' "needs" attended to by a solicitous staff of student "apostles," the purveyors of an immediately forthcoming fast-food goodness.[19]

As the reader might imagine, this kind of religious imperialism can get out of hand. Get even more whimsical and ride this ideological vehicle to a ridiculously sublime conclusion. Take the notion of "Secret Rapture" in dispensational millenarian theology: the moment during the Second Coming—or *Parousia*—when believers are whisked away to meet and dwell with Jesus among the clouds, thereby spared the agony of the Tribulation and Apocalypse. Just think of the possibilities! Why not a Brothel? There are, after all, Biblical precedents: the prosperous, well-established Israeli institution of "sacred prostitution," for instance.[20] Imagine the marquee: *SECRET RAPTURE* in flashing red neon, a rumbling, trembling aquamarine canvass sky lashed to an aluminum scaffold, pasty cotton candy clouds, and pink-cheeked cherubs lounging about here and there. Nestled right smack dab in the middle of a "blinding white light district," on a "Miracle Row" of sorts, with competing institutions—the *Second Coming?*—rounding out the block. Inside the *Rapture*: screaming white zonkers, a stairway disappearing into a mist of cheap (or expensive—C. Klein's *Eternity*) perfume, and Led Zeppelin's *Stairway To Heaven* pulsing from enormous triaxal speakers. Clients choose from among several theme room offerings: "Samson and Delilah," "Adam, Eve, and the Serpent," "Sodom and Gomorrah," "Ahab and Jezebel," "Fallen Angel" (with wings), and the ever-popular "Mary Magdalen—The Wild Years." And nary a clumsy mixed metaphor intrudes.[21] Years later I discovered that Margaret Atwood had without the benefit of such an ethnographic experience imagined just such an institution, albeit a

---

[19] Much later I discovered that my imagination wasn't all that far off the mark. Daniel Radosh writes of the "Holy Land Experience" theme park that opened in 2001 in Orlando, Florida, wherein hungry visitors can frequent the Oasis Palms Café. On the menu: "Goliath Burgers," "Jaffa Hot Dogs," "Tabgha Tuna," "Bedouin Beef," and to top it all off, the "Holy Land Sampler." (*Rapture Ready! Adventures in the Parallel Universe of Christian Pop Culture*, Scribner 2008, 26.) Among Radosh's many examples of how these trivializations of the sacred can cover almost any angle is Stephen Baldwin, "one of the country's voices for Christian teen rebellion . . . the first Jesus psycho . . . whose skate and sermon video [is] called *Livin' it*." (138) Recall also that back in 1986, before the fall, Jim and Tammy Faye Bakker's Heritage Village Theme Park, "Heritage Village," was the *third largest* in the country, behind the two Disneys. (ibid.)

[20] Berger, *The Sacred Canopy* . . . , 115.

[21] Well, not so fast actually: here's Mars Hill pastor Mark Driscoll's take on "Porn-Again Christianity," wherein good Christian wives are charged ". . . . to fight for their husbands by providing an archive of *redeemed images*." (Jessica Johnson, *Biblical Porn: Affect, Labor, and Pastor Mark Driscoll's Evangelical Empire*, Duke University Press, 2018, 111.) {emphasis added}

somewhat more modest and secretive dive, the dystopian Gilead brothel *Jez-ebel*, in her brilliant 1985 work of secular prophecy, *The Handmaid's Tale*.

Theatrics aside, the more serious academic point here being that when an ever-expanding circle of formerly pedestrian phenomena are drawn into the sanctifying orbit of the sacred a seemingly inevitable trivialization and vulgarization occurs. More specifically, as we will readily see in the chapters ahead, cultural oxymorons tend to flow naturally from a wholesale extension of the evangelical logic of "wholeness" into every nook and cranny of a religious community. Perhaps most importantly, when practically every object or activity is made sacred or Christian (no matter how clear and sharp the original demarcations) *then virtually nothing remains truly sacred or set apart from the contamination of the profane.* This strikes me as a *deeper*, more genuine source of any perceived trivialization or vulgarization of religion in contemporary American life. When preachers such as Pat Robertson enter the formerly secular arena of politics they are invariably soiled by the indiscriminate filth of politics. When Creationists carry their beliefs into the arena of scientific discussion—all the while displaying an ignorance of the elementary facts and methods of science, as well as advancing *specific* claims un-related to any body of corroborating evidence—those claims and beliefs are eventually drawn under scientific scrutiny, which may bring criticism and even ridicule.

These are scarcely developments without precedent. The Australian tribe of Karadjeri, for instance, routinely reenacts a cosmogony of its founding heroes, two of whom were enshrined in myth engaging in an immortal (not *immoral*, mind you) act of urination, the particular style of which is still ritually performed today.[22] And, closer to home, we musn't overlook one of our own Puritan fathers, Cotton Mather, recorded in his autobiographical writings exhorting himself to "think noble thoughts" while similarly venting his bladder.[23] Are not vulgarity and ignobility the often unintended

---

[22] Mircea Eliade, *The Sacred and the Profane: The Nature of Religion*, New York: Harcourt Brace Janovich, 1959, 168.
—In this context, that Laura M. Hartman's, *The Christian Consumer: Living Faithfully in a Fragile World* (New York: Oxford University Press, 2011) could be published by a major university press speaks volumes as to the cluelessness of the academic publishing world about the evangelical ideological agenda.
—Evangelicals often use the expression, "walk with God," or "Christian walk." This is, however, a traditional sacralization: "Even the most habitual gesture can signify a spiritual act. The road and walking can be transfigured into religious values, for every road can symbolize the 'road of life,' and any walk a 'pilgrimage,' a peregrination to the Center of the World. . . . [pilgrims, ascetics] proclaim by their 'walking,' by their constant movement, their desire to leave the world, their refusal of any worldly situation." (ibid., 183) A huge bestseller among liberal evangelicals is a book by Scott Peck entitled, *The Road Less Traveled*.
[23] Philip Greven, *The Protestant Temperament: Patterns of Child-Rearing, Religious Experience, and the Self in Early America*, New York: A Meridian Book of The New American Library, 1979, 67.

outcomes of this quest for sacred unity? for a more "naked public square"? Our ancient Greek friend, Diogenes, would feel right at home among these noble, righteous savages.[24]

Although these observations can serve to impugn the claim of Stephen Carter and others, suggesting that the source of trivialization may lie more *within* evangelicalism than *without*, more importantly they return us to this business of secularization and all its attending complications. For if a believer performs an ostensibly profane behavior in a thoroughly pious manner—or the larger group or community routinely engages in such activities, for that matter—practices that some may deem a contamination of sorts, are these instances of "accommodation" and "secularization?"[25] Or might they represent something altogether different?[26]

Actually, I think there is much more to these questions than the either/or evaluations of conventional schemes. Foremost, we ought resist the temptation to characterize or dismiss these kinds of incidents or developments as part of a larger unilinear process of secularization; instead, we should take them very seriously, and better think of them as various kinds of sacralizations and sanctifications, links in a larger chain of casuistry[27]; for they are as

---

[24] See "Diogenes the Cynic," in M. I. Finley, *Aspects of Antiquity* (New York: The Viking Press, 1969). The larger Diogenesian *social* context is addressed later in my Chapter 8.
—One finds similar kinds of pressures in Jewish halakhic fundamentalism. As Avishai Margalit observes: "To follow Halakha strictly is to have religion intervene in every aspect of human life, including the most private and the most trivial." ("Israel: The Rise of the Ultra-Orthodox," *The New York Review of Books*, 9 November 1989, 38.)
—As does also Moshe Halbertal in his review of a massive study of the Hasidic movement in Judaism by David Biale et al., *Hasidism: A New History* (Princeton University Press, 2018): the second of four "fundamental element[s] of the emerging sensibility. . . was the call for worshipping in the material world. . . . to include mundane secular activities as well. . . . Since God's presence is all-encompassing, including in human desires and mental states, by delving into such alien thoughts the worshipper can 'uplift them' . . . . even such embarrassments of the flesh might be embraced as religiously meaningful." This, however, an element unlike the prominence of the "rebbe" that has "receded to the margins." ("The Dance Goes On," *The New York Review of Books*, 5/24/2018, 32.)

[25] Although Christian Smith rejects the traditional sociological/empirical secularization claim, he nonetheless still validates the concept itself: "Secularization denotes *some reduction in the performance of the culturally prescribed practices* that seek to access, communicate with, or align people with superhuman powers." No, as with Weber's wonderfully rich and nuanced notion of *casuistry*, it can be a good deal more complex than that, even though Smith continues on to elaborate the matter comparatively. (*Religion: What It Is. . . ,* 244.)

[26] R. Laurence Moore makes a compelling case in a similar vein that evangelicals have throughout their long American history served to promote the faith by employing commercial business techniques, hence not vulgarizing but strengthening it. See *Selling God. . . ,* 1994.

[27] *Casuistry* is, of course, a favorite concept of Weber, who surely would enjoy the implicit sacralization of our "Secret Rapture" brothel. As he wrote about "specifically extramarital sexual life, which has been removed from the everyday":

integral to the integrity, strength, and, yes *purity* of contemporary evangelicalism as any so-called traditional processes. I intend then to demonstrate that developments which strike some observers as anomalous to more ideal conceptions of Christianity may nonetheless prove integral to the continuing identity, prosperity, and longevity of American evangelicalism.[28] For indeed the Jimmy Swaggart dimension of the presidency of Donald Trump ultimately proves as emblematic, as *pure* an expression, of the evangelical ideological heart of American culture as Jonathan Edwards bitter farewell sermon, or the Salem witch trials, or a George Whitefield revival meeting.[29] For indeed vulgarism and meaning abounds, the one side by side with the other, part and parcel of an   inevitable collusion of the sacred and the

---

> Under these conditions, the erotic relation seems to offer the unsurpassable peak of the fulfillment of the request for love in the direct fusion of the souls of one to the other. The boundless giving of oneself is as radical as possible in its opposition to all functionality, rationality, and generality. . . . It is so overpowering that it is treated 'symbolically': as a *sacrament*. The lover realizes himself to be rooted in the kernal of the truly living, which is eternally inaccessible to any rational endeavor. ("Religious Rejections of the World and Their Directions," in *From Max Weber*. . . , 346-7.) {emphasis added}

[28] Another way to think of the evangelical's apprehension of modern skepticism is advanced by T. M. Luhrmann in her intense study of a small evangelical sect, the Vineyard: ". . . . they understand their God in a way that adapts to the skepticism. . . . takes shape out of an exquisite awareness of doubt. . . . This God is not, as some people have argued, a rejection of modernity—a refusal to embrace the modern or a denial of modern ways of thinking. This near-magical God is an expression of what it is to be modern." (*When God Talks Back*. . . , 301.)
—There are broader issues and dynamics at work here also, as Saba Mahmood demonstrates among the Coptic Christian and Bahai minorities of modern Egypt, where "religious difference has proliferated and metastasized. . . even as its raison d'etat secularized. I hope to show how the regulation of religion under secularism has not only tamed its power, but also transformed it, making it more, rather than less, important to the identity of the majority [Sunni] and minority populations." (*Religious Differences in the Secular Age: A Minority Approach*, Princeton University Press, 2016, 14.)

[29] Winiaerski, op. cit., 483.
—There are, of course, other ways to view these matters. Some dismiss these developments as a corruption or degradation: ". . . . many evangelicals have trivialized the Christian faith and turned it into a superficial commodity. . . . have instead created a counterfeit culture . . . . baptizing the products they desire to market. Evangelicals have been prone to give secular institutions and commodities a Christian makeover. . . . Evangelicals have not created a Christian America. Rather, they have developed an Americanized Christianity and *they cannot tell the difference between the two*." (Richard G. Kyle, *Popular Evangelicalism in America*, London: Routledge, 2018, 167, 2.) {emphasis added} Later, Professor Kyle proves as equally confused about their "market mentality,"(127) demonstrating almost no awareness of the "moral market" (from Garry Wills) spin of much of their *mentalités*. The reader will, later also, come to understand how they do indeed fully distinguish "between the two."
—Ross Douthat dismisses these sacralizations as simply corruptions of, or decline in, the former integrity of mainline American Christianity, manifestations of *Bad Religion*. . . . (2012).

profane, the one seemingly inevitably hemorrhaging and bleeding into the other.

In this little hamburger shack, *Paradise Joe's*, we encounter but one telling metaphor, one off-hand iteration and reminder of an elemental theme and feature of American evangelicalism; an abbreviated image of a complex, sprawling, expansive, but ultimately coherent evangelical vision of community and culture, to whose full exploration we now turn.[30]

---

[30] Originally, a second much longer introductory chapter followed chapter 1. As it was in many respects more technical and academic in nature, with hundreds of supporting footnotes, it was moved to the end of the book, to an Appendix B. Most influential in this decision was the example of Robert Wright's *The Evolution of God* (2009), wherein in my estimation the most compelling portion of the book was relegated to an appendix, "How Human Nature Gave Birth to Religion." May I suggest the same proves the case with my Appendix B. It represents the macro-level theoretical punch line that the much longer case study narrative sets up. It directly addresses the larger meaning and significance of the ethnographic details of this small evangelical community for American life and politics. Academicians may prefer to skip ahead to it now; general readers most likely will not. But later, having worked their way up to it, the latter should feel adequately prepared to take it on. In either sequence, please do not avoid it, for it contains—nay, even slams home—the essential meaning and significance of this book. *At the very least*, the reader should attempt to wade through pp. 383-400, paying particular attention to the concepts of "existential security"—and "economic" and "cultural insecurity."

PART TWO

HISTORY

CHAPTER 2

LOCAL HISTORY: FROM SEMINARY TO UNIVERSITY

Seattle Pacific College began in a garden plot of a neglected orchard at the foot of Queen Anne hill more than a century ago. The five acres of land, known as the "Victory Addition Reserve," represented but a small portion of an eighty-acre parcel first settled upon by a Norwegian immigrant named Nils Peterson, a fellow who due to premillenarian[31] apprehensions had come to regard the lay of the land as much too valuable for the mere idle cultivation of fruits and vegetables, offering the rights to the annual national Conference of the Free Methodist Church convened in Seattle in June of 1891. Build a school to train missionaries and other Christian workers, he urged the Conference, relating that these instructions had come directly from God.

The locals called the northern base of Queen Anne Hill, Ross, after John Ross, who along with Peterson was a major landowner and homesteader. Up the hill went a dirt road—several meandering trails actually that branched and then rejoined one another—that the residents in the early days of the settlement, before the arrival of the trolleys, climbed single file to attend church downtown, a couple of miles away to the south. In the other direction the land sloped down to a stream, a wandering snake of a brook that drained the unpredictable Lake Union, dispensing her steady runoff and occasional overflows into the contracted, kidney-shaped Salmon Bay, a body of water that with the inrush of the salty tide waters from its ultimate outlet and destination, Puget Sound, would occasionally back up into the canal, forming swimming holes in the summer. Paul Mason, then a young kid who had learned to swim in a mill race (a slick, sloped chute for sawmill logs) back in Pennsylvania, recalls the difficulties this early training later caused him out west:

---

[31] As opposed to postmillennialism, which seeks to establish the "Kingdom of God" on earth in the present time. In the words of Dwight Moody: "I look upon this world as a wrecked vessel," he said; "God has given me a life-boat and said to me, 'Moody, save all you can.' " (In William G. McLoughlin, *Revivals, Awakenings, and Reform: An Essay on Religion and Social Change in America, 1607-1977*, University of Chicago Press, 1968, 144.)

There was no water if the tide was out and when it was in the water was pretty stationary. We had a hard time swimming . . . never [understood] how a kid could learn to swim in still water.[32]

Above the brook Mason remembers a beautiful meadow, beds of watercress here and there, and an even smaller stream trickling down from Peterson's garden plot. A narrow bridge arched over the often waist-deep, crystal-clear main brook and during a salmon run the neighborhood folks stood on the bridge and the banks and lampooned Coho and Chinook with five-pronged spears; salmon "so thick you could walk on them." [33]

At Third West Etruria sat a two-room shack that because of a steep slope had one-half resting in the dirt and the other balanced upon stilts like an Asian hut. It was out of the ordinary, beamed the neighbors, because it had a coat of paint on it in a part of town where nothing else did. Paul Mason recalls that "a colored boy [sic] had rented it and was barbering. We would go down and get him to show us how to shoot. He would take an air gun and split bullets by shooting at a sword. We kids picked up the bullets."[34]

There wasn't even a grocery in Ross, the closest being a general store a half-mile away in Fremont run by "Brother" F.M. Bird, a proprietor who galloped around on a horse taking orders once a week and then delivered the goods the following day in a wagon. As late as 1903, Fremont was considered a "dry town," falling as it did within the "four-mile circle of sobriety then surrounding the University of Washington," its distant neighbor along the lake to the northeast.[35]

Such was the condition of Ross and the Fremont district in June of 1891 when Nils Peterson extended his offer to the Free Methodist conference. B.T. Roberts, the founder of Free Methodism, caught a trolley to Fremont, walked on over to Ross, and found the feral qualities of the site to his liking.[36] So began Seattle Seminary. Elected to the initial board of trustees, along with Peterson,[37] was a fellow named Hiram Pease.

---

[32] Anita Weier interview with Paul Mason, *Queen Anne News*, 27 January 1982.

[33] C. Dorr Demaray interview with Paul Mason, 2/21/80. {Archives}

[34] Weier, interview.

[35] Paul Dorpat, "Now and Then: Fremont," *Pacific Magazine, Seattle Times*, 11 August 1985.

[36] Adelaide Beers, *The Romance of the Consecrated Life: A Biography of Alexander Beers* (Winona Lake, Indiana: Free Methodist Publishing House, 1922), 95.

[37] The seven others were Isaac W. Zeek, Roger S. Greene, James C. Scott, John C. Norton, Henry M Frankland, William M. Copeland, William Campbell. (Victor W. Jones, compiler, "Some Antecedents and Descendents of Mr. and Mrs. Marion Phillips, Oregon Pioneers of 1845-46 with Collateral Ancestors and Descendents of Allied Families," unpublished manuscript, August 1954 / revised 1973.) {Archives}

Hiram Pease played a central, intriguing role in these beginnings. The son of a wealthy eastern beer magnate, he left Pennsylvania in 1873 at the age of fifty for health and moral reasons, perhaps seeking a kind of regeneration out West.[38] He began a second-hand junk business, nickeling-and-diming his way to financial health and investing the accruing marginal profits in downtown Seattle real estate.[39] More importantly for our purposes, Pease became in time a health and hygiene fanatic. So that although he was Free Methodist, pro-temperance, and all that went with them, he brought an additional agenda to the 1891 conference, seizing the moment to press for the institutionalization of his ideas. Pease rose before the Annual Conference with a strings-attached offer: "If they eliminate pork and its products, with tea and coffee, from the bill of fare, and recommend the use of grahm [*sic*] bread and make it, I will give $2,500 toward the enterprise."[40] Without hesitation, the conference accepted the offer and made Pease a Trustee. And B. T. Roberts recommended for headmaster a minister from Spottsylvania, New York, Alexander Beers.

Alexander and Adelaide Beers arrived in Seattle in March of 1893 to find a city awash in a spring downpour, a downtown in the final stages of recovery from the Great Fire of 1889,[41] and an elementary trolley system that took them only as far as Fremont, leaving a half-mile or so traverse with

---

Of these seven, Greene and Norton alone were non-Free Methodists. John C. Norton was a banker and a Baptist preacher who would later serve as principal for a term. Roger S. Greene, also a prominent Baptist, was Chief Justice of the Territorial Supreme Court (David M. Buerge, "Missions in the Wilderness: Seattle's early religious leaders imposed moral order on an unruly frontier town . . . ," *The Weekly*, 25-31 December 1985, 28), of whom C. Dorr Demaray (S.P.C. President, 1959-1968) remarked while conducting one of his oral history interviews (with Philip F. Ashton, 9/25/79), he "really wrote the [school] charter—and got it through the department or province, I guess it was a province in those days—he got it through and all that sort of thing."

I believe this is the same Judge Greene who figures so prominently (nearly heroically) in the notorious 1882 courthouse lynching incident in Murray Morgan's *Skid Road Seattle—Her First Hundred Years* (New York: Ballantine Books, 1971), 76-78.

[38] Jones, "Some Antecedents and Descendents . . . ," *Response*, September 1981.

[39] C.W. Shay, "Reminiscences of the Early Days of Seattle Seminary," unpublished, undated manuscript. {Archives}

[40] Richard Gladwin Hedges, "A Historical Study of Seattle Seminary and Seattle Pacific College, 1891-1926" (M. Ed. Thesis, University of Washington, 1962), 15; Charles Hoyt Watson ("The Christian Liberal Arts College: The Story of the First Seventy-Five Years of Seattle Pacific College in Christian Higher Education," unfinished manuscript, terminated August, 1969) quotes the *Seattle Post-Intelligencer*. Characteristically enough, Pease argued against the proposed Oregon site on the grounds that a large farm was simply *too filthy*. {Archives}

[41] 1890 Seattle population: 42,837. (Watson, "The Christian Liberal Arts College . . . .")

luggage over a muddy, split-log trail to the Seminary.[42] There they found an unfinished four-story brick building and a $15,000 mortgage.[43] Unprepared for quite this monumental a leap of faith, Beers begged to be relieved of his duties, offering to refund travel monies if he were allowed to cut his losses and move on. The Board of Trustees pleaded for a trial run; he relented and stayed—twenty years or more, as it turns out.[44]

The Seminary opened its doors on April 14, 1893 with an initial enrollment of twelve students,[45] offering grades one through twelve, elementary grammar through college preparatory courses, and a one-year Christian Worker's course.[46] Classical emphasis upon history, Latin, Greek, and the sciences made this no mere Bible or missionary training school.[47] Teachers and students lodged together in the single building. Socially, there were clear distinctions regarding gender. To reduce confusion, students ascended the appropriate male and female sides of a divided staircase to third floor dormitories. Outside, a central flagpole partitioned the campus grounds into re-

---

[42] "History of the School," 1933 *Cascade*. {Archives} (In 1910, the *Cascade* was a monthly publication, becoming a kind of yearbook around 1915 and the first formal yearbook in 1929.)

[43] Hedges, "A Historical Study . . . ," 19.

[44] Jones, "Some Antecedents and Descendents . . . ." Adelaide Beers claims the Lord intervened to change his mind, recalling the first Sunday meeting on the new school community: "No sooner had he begun to pray than the Heavens seemed to open above and the room was filled with the presence of Jehovah . . . . This wonderful outpouring of the spirit swept away all harassing doubts from Mr. Beers' mind. Great assurances were given, both that the two of us were in Divine order and that money would be given to lift the mortgage." (Quoted in Watson, "The Christian Liberal Arts College . . . ," 8.)

[45] Jones, "Some Antecedents and Descendents . . . ." Nils Peterson recalled the dedication ceremonies: "The Lord at different times has sent special Pentecostal showers upon this school; which evidences to us his good will and approbation. . . . the glory cloud rested down and filled the whole building . . . all . . . shouting and praising the Lord." (Watson, "The Christian Liberal Arts College . . . .")

[46] Hedges, "A Historical Study . . . ," 21.

[47] Although we find in the 1933 yearbook, the *Cascade* {Archives}, the passage "History of School. . . . On October 29 of the same year ground was broken for the construction of the first building of Seattle Seminary, a school for the training of missionaries and ministers," Dr. Joseph Davis, a long-time faculty member, contends the original intention may have been much broader: "As I read the story, the Oregon-Washington Conference people of the Free Methodist Church passionately wanted a Christian high school for their children and neighbors. They called the school Seattle Seminary, which meant high school. . . . Rather the program was solid liberal arts in scope and content." (Dr. Joseph Davis, "Seattle Pacific: As I Have Seen It," *Response*, October 1980.)
  Curriculum aside, the school did in fact produce many missionaries. From 1901-1911, twenty-two faculty, students, or alumni went abroad to Africa, Japan, China, India, and the Dominican Republic, and by 1954 the school had "provided 247 missionaries worldwide." (*Seattle Pacific College Bulletin*, March 1954.)

spective male and female sexual territories.[48] Sexual apartheid was severe and enforced: intermingling of the sexes was forbidden except in "general social interviews."[49]

Headmaster Beers presents a difficult emotional puzzle. He was many things to many different people. The contradictions abound: stern disciplinarian ("Legend has it that a Seminary ten-year old who had suffered the rod . . . at the hand of the principal nailed this belligerent thesis to the principal's door: 'Down with Beers and all other liquors.' ")[50] yet a patsy with children; gracious, yet often petty and vindictive; broadminded and thoughtful, yet prone to prolonged moments of anti-intellectualism and bathos; successful money raiser and financial agent,[51] yet a sloppy bookkeeper whose questionable habits eventually sunk the school deeply into arrears. A faculty member who alternated with him at the post of headmaster remarked that "his power was mysterious."[52] Cyril Hill recalls with great fondness: "Well, I practically worshipped him. . . . He was a self-made literary scholar . . . he would quote from the old Greek, he'd quote poetry—numerous things— word for word."[53] But he was also, in many respects, a very simple man. Consider Adelaide Beers's account of her husband's final seminary oral examination:

> The Examination took place in the woods with the participants seated on a moss-covered log. The reverend John La Due conducted the examination which concerned English, geography, and the "more elementary outlines of theology." Mr Beers was unable to answer the questions but each time a question was asked he would reply: "Brother La Due, I don't quite understand that particular question you are asking me, but one thing I am certain of, and that is, on the 18th day of November, 1881, the Lord wonderfully pardoned all my sins, and now I am conscious of the fact that I am his child."[54]

Over the course of the next twenty years, Beers (alternating as both principal and "business agent") and three or four others shared the principal's

---

[48] Hedges, "A Historical Study . . . ," 13; The *Falcon* (12 December 1939) school newspaper reported on "S.P.C Rules of Yesteryear"(1919) to the effect that: "The campus was divided into two sections, the division line between the flag pole, one side for the boys and the other for the girls."

[49] 1893-94 *College Catalog*, Rule 6. {Archives}

[50] Hilda Bryant, "A short Historie of ye olde college," (*SPC Alumni*, Autumn 1965).

[51] Jones, "Some Antecedents and Descendents . . . ."

[52] Watson, "The Christian Liberal Arts College . . . ."

[53] C. Dorr Demaray interview with Cyril Hill (10/18/79). {Archives}

[54] Quoted in Schoenhals,"Higher Education . . . ," 50.

chair. Together they added three more acres and several new buildings to campus. Student enrollment grew as did the size of the faculty. Beers proved an exceptional fund-raiser, year after year extracting generous contributions from wealthy Christian businessmen and church supporters. In 1915, when the Seminary officially became Seattle Pacific College and after twenty years of service, he was appointed president, a post he held for an additional year until he was driven from the community because of alleged malfeasance in office. Sloppy bookkeeping practices, scandalous personal behavior (cigar smoking and delivering flowers to another man's wife), $53,000 of institutional debt, and an accumulation of detractors eventually sank this unconventional, controversial man. Yet he was only the first to leave in such a humbled fashion. His successor would suffer a similar fate.

But, perhaps more importantly for our purposes, what was the ultimate *raison d'être* of this school? Premillenarian missionary (Peterson)? Asceticism (Pease)? Denominational expansionism (Free Methodist)? Surely, all these lent an impetus, yet some hint of a larger, more all-encompassing cultural intention can be discovered in "What Seattle Seminary Stands For," a short anthem reproduced in catalogs and yearbooks for nearly twenty years. Herein we discover themes that will recur again and again in both this particular institution and throughout American evangelicalism at large. And it is these larger connections that will ultimately justify our scrutiny of such an apparently diminutive institution.

The establishment of separate Free Methodist schools has become "imperative," Beers writes, because of "certain tendencies in the public schools." What tendencies? Those linked with a much larger and chronic deterioration and corruption of public society: "there has been a great departure from the principles laid down and regarded as fundamental by our forefathers, there can be no doubt. A cold commercialism is found everywhere and in many places is the very atmosphere of the home and office. The glitter of gold, the greed for wealth, the glare of fashion and show, have formed a circle around which all things political, business, and social revolve." The sins, sinners, and consequences of the Gilded Age were manifold: corrupt politicians, fraudulent bankers, rising divorce rates, broken homes, and a rapid decline in parental responsibility, to enumerate just a few. Characteristically, Seattle Seminary would swim against the swelling tide of modernity and decline, "these modern fads . . . this bosh of unbelief and skepticism." Within the walls of a Christian academy, the Christian student becomes "noble, broad, and unselfish"—and in marked contrast to the coruscating show of life "outside," the paralyzing, depreciating world of artifice—develops true "nobility of character," demonstrating upon graduation a superior personality, one exemplifying genuine "intrinsic value of character."[55]

On display here are some rather intriguing—and perhaps not unfamiliar—sentiments of *cultural* antagonism, insularity, and separation. They offer us a late nineteenth-century glimpse or introduction to what we will encounter later as a more general evangelical cultural logic of *invidious distinction*.[56] Observe here in somewhat crude form the outlines of a discriminating worldview, wherein an interior *Christian* world of true, concrete, and noble characters is set in direct opposition to a *secular* carnival of fleeting, superficial appearances and pretense, socially evanescent and unreal. Here was the first wedge in the door of cultural hermeticism, presaging future categorizations and elaborations of social worlds into the Christian and the secular, the fallen and the redeemed, the transcendent and the terrestrial. The Christian academy fashions a Christian personality in every way superior to its secular counterpart. Its graduates cannot be improved upon by any secular example or experience. The intended relationship is not one of exchange or interaction with the larger society or world; no, rather, the school fashions her students into perfectly polished projectiles to be launched at a defiled, decadent world. Indeed upon the platform of the second floor assembly room was etched a motto which succinctly captured this singular, unreflective purpose: "Not to be ministered unto but to minister."[57]

Let us explore the social and cultural origins of these sentiments. Whence do they come? Upon what are they based? Are they indigenous to this particular denomination? to the Pacific Northwest? to American evangelicalism in general? And, even more broadly, are they uniquely or distinctly American? Do they in some manner resonate deeply within our collective cultural memory? And what sort of relationship might they have with some rather more contemporary—and recurring—cultural phenomena? These are intriguing—and timely—questions. To approach them, oddly enough, a closer examination of the career and personality of Hiram Pease is in order.

The *quid pro quo* of Hiram Pease's gift to the Seminary is all too apparent in the 1893-94 Catalog: "The table will be filled with an abundance of wholesome food. The boarding department will be conducted on scientific and

---

[55] Alexander Beers, "What Seattle Seminary Stands For," *The Olympiad Yearbook 1909*. {Archives}

[56] Throughout this book I will be liberally borrowing or coining phrases drawn from or inspired by that master of critical cultural analysis and expression, Thorstein Veblen—*invidious distinction* and *conspicuous consumption*, in particular.

[57] Jones, "Some Antecedents and Descendents. . . ."

hygienic principles." Pease was a constant presence—perhaps even a nuisance—in the Seminary kitchen. He delivered deadly serious lectures to the student body[58] on matters of concern, promoting such activities as the daily immersion of the feet in a pan of ice-cold water—preferably at the crack of dawn—to enhance bodily vigor. He would stand before the assembled student body brandishing a terry-cloth towel like a matador's cape, pulling taut the ends and then allowing it to slacken, passing the institutional white towel in and out of human hills and valleys, abrading skin and bone with great force, firming the body's tissue and the spirit contained therein. Such was the proper use of a bath towel, he instructed.[59] The quest for moral and physical rigor knew no repose, no idle pause from regimen. Under such a program even the most mundane daily behaviors became invested with all manner of spiritual consequences. (Perhaps not an unwarranted concern given the incidence of disease in the community: small pox, whooping cough, typhoid fever, and, yes, parasites. As one resident wrote: ". . . . I had a spasm from stomach worms choking off my breath trying to come up my throat from the stomach. He and the folks thought for sure I was dying.").[60]

What are to make of this? Mere eccentricity? Faddism?

Consider that Pease had been troubled throughout his childhood with illness and had journeyed west not only to put some distance between himself and his father, who had grown rich through either the brewing or peddling of beer and other alcoholic beverages, but also to seek a more salubrious climate for his physical infirmities. Once established in his junk business, somehow or other he became acquainted with the program of the Battle Creek Sanitarium and went east to Michigan to matriculate in the college.[61] He studied diet, hygiene, physical exercise, and mental discipline, returning to Seattle a fervid apostle of John Harvey Kellogg. The budding Seminary became an all too convenient and appropriate outlet for his exuberance. Indeed he was there in the fields, working alongside the masons to erect the first building.[62] In the midst of one financial crisis he mortgaged his own home to raise an immediate loan for the school. When he died in 1919 it was

---

[58] Clark Shay's recollections, reported in Schoenhals, "Higher Education . . . ," 256.

[59] Hedges, "A Historical Study . . . ," 16.

[60] "Letters of Ella Colson . . . ."

[61] C. Dorr Demaray interview with Harold McNeese (10/9/81). {Archives} C.D.D.: ". . . . and while he [Pease] was here, he went to Battle Creek Sanitarium to see what they believed in diet and exercise—to their college—and he got the whole line—their diet and their exercise program—and he tried to bring it back here when the school was founded— the whole works."

[62] Hedges, "A Historical Study . . . ," 14.

disclosed that he had donated some $65,000 to the school—a near fortune. What to make of it? Is there some larger significance to his relationship to the Battle Creek Sanitarium than mere idiosyncrasy, some broader historical and cultural linkage? Let us dwell for a moment on the legacy of Battle Creek and John Harvey Kellogg.

We are of course familiar with the corn flakes and other cereal products, provender perhaps more American than apple pie. A good deal less familiar are his views on sanitation, health, and moral development, attitudes which dominated Battle Creek and environs as well as pervaded the more bourgeois regions of Victorian American society. Without doubt, Kellogg was an extremist residing on the fringe of Victorian moral culture, someone who allowed his own obsessive temperament to roam freely over the prim and proper moral landscape of the era, inflating to irrational proportions whatever caught his immediate fancy. Yet through him we can obtain a feel for the kind of cultural mood to which the impressionable Pease was so irresistibly drawn.

Mid-and-late nineteenth-century America, although it must seem true of nearly every period in American history, was undergoing an unusually brisk social and economic transformation. A rapidly expanding market economy brought increasing fragmentation of traditional work and family relationships and loyalties, the obsolescence of earlier forms of social control, and an apparent corresponding dilution and dispersion of moral authority. Traditional master/journeyman/apprenticeship work relationships, with their tightly integrated, live-in social relationships, arrangements that preserved a measure of stability and continuity, appeared threatened by the development of wage-labor-based industries. Eastern cities swelled with second-wave Catholic immigrants, inciting fears of their manipulation by corrupt political machines[63] and the usurpation of a Protestant moral and cultural hegemony that had been in force throughout the first full century of national existence.[64] As the American society continuously molted and transformed itself, shedding one obsolescent social skin after another, undermining older forms of social control based upon the physical proximity of bosses, workers, and their families and children, (relatively) common languages and cultural backgrounds, and the (again, relative) stability of populations in urban

---

[63] "A tide of immigration unfriendly to American institutions is pouring in upon us. The votes which are for sale are largely confined to the ignorant class of foreigners that is thronging to our shores." Excerpt from the graduation oration of the Seminary's first graduate, Winfred A. Grantham (*Seminary Echo*, May 1896). {Archives}

[64] Paul Boyer, *Urban Masses and Moral Order in America, 1820-1920*, Cambridge: Harvard University Press, 1978.

neighborhoods and rural towns and communities, some observers have argued that those seeking to re-assert Protestant cultural domination turned to more subtle, internalized forms of moral authority. Business and community leaders promoted Christian revivalism to distract and narcotize increasingly unruly industrial laborers, as they had done so successfully in other contexts prior to the Civil War.[65] Rapid movement through recently evolved but relatively stable social and economic levels[66] produced a mélange of ill-assorted-and-fitted social actors. Protestant ministers joined with physicians, educators, and social reformers in an attempt to re-assert a wavering cultural authority. Casting about for a response, Jackson Lears contends, their attention turned from older, fading, more external forms of authority to newly-conceived strategies emphasizing the internalization of moral codes.

> Oppression had to yield to repression. . . . By the 1880s, whether sanctioned by secular or religious authority, an internalized ethic of self-control had become the unquestioned norm for the middle and upper classes as well as for much of the rest of society.[67]

---

[65] Paul E. Johnson, *A Shopkeeper's Millennium: Society and Revivals in Rochester, New York, 1815-1837* (New York: Hill & Wang, 1978). Consider also:

> D. L. Moody's revival meetings, on the other hand, might be characterized as the result of superabundant confidence among evangelical businessmen in the 1870s. These captains of industry believed that an effective lay preacher (as Moody was), together with a sentimental "gospel singer" (like Sankey), given thousands of dollars to spend on highly organized six-to-eight week revival campaigns in the nation's largest cities, could reach the unemployed clerks, salesgirls, and working people with a Christian message that would calm their anxieties over unemployment and turn their attention to higher thoughts than labor agitation. . . . Friedrich Engels called "Moody and Sankey and the like" the tools of the capitalist class. . . .
> [And later, from 1905-1920:] . . . [Billy Sunday's] style was slangy and flamboyant; he leaped around his revival platform like an acrobat, shouting and telling funny stories and waving the American flag as he stood on the top of the pulpit. His theology was blatantly Fundamentalist [drawing 15,000-20,000 a meeting], and, at a time when many religious liberals were concerned about the exploitation of the working class by the "robber barons" of industry, Sunday's campaigns (like Moody's) were being financed by some of the leading industrial exploiters. (William G. McLoughlin, Revivals, Awakenings, and Reform: An Essay on Religion and Social Change in America, 1607-1977, University of Chicago Press, 1978, 142, 144, 147.)

[66] Michael B. Katz, *The People of Hamilton, Canada West: Family and Class in a Mid-Nineteenth-Century,* Cambridge: Harvard University Press, 1975; Stephen Thernstrom, *Poverty and Progress: Social Mobility in a 19th-Century City,* New York: Athenium, 1978.

[67] T. J. Jackson Lears, *No Place Of Grace: Anti-Modernism and the Transformation of American Culture, 1880-1920,* New York: Pantheon Books, 1981, 12-13. Much as I admire and have profited from this book, I find that Lears relies too heavily on the kind of historical evidence—essays, books, letters—that an educated, bourgeois elite tends the leave behind and has overlooked

In many respects late nineteenth-century Seattle represents a quintessential slice of America caught in the grips of this social transformation. And yet obviously no local variant anywhere in the country exactly mirrored these processes in the general forms and interpretations historians have employed to conceptualize and understand them. The Pacific Northwest was probably more radical politically than the rest of the country,[68] a traditional judgment handed down and embellished over the years, perhaps most deliciously in the anecdotal account of U.S. Postmaster General James A. Farley's visit to Seattle in the mid 1930s, during which he is held to have offered the toast, "To the forty-seven states and the soviet of Washington."[69] The salutation followed closely upon the heels of a few decades of conflict between workers and owners, whose more notable incidents and altercations became the stuff of labor legend, both locally and nationally (a brief account and exploration of which follows in the next chapter). Western Washington also was home to several utopian socialist communities: small, independent communitarian groups seeking radical departures from the kind of new industrial social and economic relationships they observed developing around them, the emerging order too vaguely reminiscent of what many had experienced in the factory towns and cities of the East. Perhaps these radical insurgents drew inspiration from the sheer unspoiled nature of the Pacific Northwest environment; perhaps they came west looking for social, political, and economic transcendence; perhaps also the sheer number of young, restless, unassimilated workers lent greater force to their social and political aspirations. For quite obviously the Pacific Northwest had not yet developed the kind of comfortable, respectable middle class that was so integral a feature of the established eastern urban order. In any event, the kinds of social, economic, and political tensions and conflicts, and the social experiments, that were occurring elsewhere can be found in abundance in the Northwest of this period— however more feral or picaresque they might appear to jaded Eastern eyes. Although the work and the industries were different—the extraction and harvesting of natural resources rather than more complex manufacturing—

---

or failed to search out evidence (if indeed such exists) of the common wo/man's response to social and cultural change. In this particular instance I find it difficult to believe that so precipitous and uniform a change from "external" to "internal" forms of social control occurred. And surely in any age families and communities exert a moral direction and authority that is much more subtle and complex than the term "oppression" can possibly capture.

[68] But Roger Sale argues that the "labor movement" developed later in the West than elsewhere. (*Seattle: Past to Present*, 38.)

[69] Charles Pierce LeWarne, *Utopias On Puget Sound, 1885-1915*, Seattle: University of Washington Press, 1975, 3.

just about everything that was happening in the towns and cities across the country was also happening here.

In the mid-1860s to the end of the century Seattle swelled to the brim with transient single men who worked in the local lumber mills or the logging operations in the surrounding region. Others mined copper, silver, and gold in the back hills of Monte Cristo and Mount Index in King and Snohomish counties[70] or coal to the southeast in Renton, Newcastle, and the Cedar River Valley.[71] In the 1880s and '90s even more arrived with the railroad construction gangs that laid the Northern Pacific Railroad line and then the Great Northern line farther to the north, gandy dancers who were sporadically hired, fired, and re-hired as the projects moved west in fits and starts, spewing a trail of often unemployed workers in their wakes. Later in 1897 with the Nome and Klondike gold rushes came the prospectors buying supplies or passing through on their way to the mineral fields to the north, or river pilots from the Yukon drawn south of the border for supplies and a little excitement.[72] Their presence brought along the inevitable supporting institutions of the saloon and brothel (often under the same roof), much to the chagrin of the religious leaders who had spearheaded the original settlement—the Dennys, Borens, Blaines, among others—civic-minded patricians who had assumed the guidance of some form of divine mandate.[73] In 1869, John Pennell opened the Illahee, "one of the largest brothels in the Northwest," in the "lava beds" of south Seattle amongst the distilleries, saloons, and the hotels and tenements housing itinerant laborers, procuring native Indian women from eastern Washington and a large number of white prostitutes from as far away as San Francisco. There ensued years of conflict between the propertied families and classes of the original missionary order and their middle-class supporters, and the entrepreneurs and patrons of the "squaw brothels" in the lava beds. In 1879, the Illahee burned to the ground and in 1881, following the shooting deaths of a businessman and a policeman, a mob ("Many of the actors were professed Christians," reported Judge Roger Sherman Greene, who attempted to stop the thing) broke into the city

---

[70] Don Duncan, "Dunc's People: Two spelunkers find adventure in long-forgotten Northwest mines," *Seattle Times*, 19 July 1987.

[71] Sale, *Seattle: Past to Present*, 33.

[72] Murray Morgan, *Skid Road* . . . , 125.

[73] "The Blaines' letters home are often rife with allusions to the survival of the fittest: how cheering it was to see the great trees of the forest fall to the advance of the ax and plow, the weaker yielding to the strong, or how inevitable and proper it was that the debased savages should die off or otherwise surrender their land to a superior people following a divine mandate to possess it and make it prosper." (Buerge, "Missions in the Wilderness . . . .")

courthouse and "dragged three prisoners out into the street and lynched them."[74] By 1884, several distinguished citizens (the "Apple Orchardists," after the "trees in the lot where they met") turned their supporters' attention to more effective political methods of reform, turning out a slate of candidates who won enough city and county seats to implement their prohibitionist program.

> Saloons were shut down, the sale of liquor was banned on Sunday, and gamblers and pimps were prosecuted. . . . But if the reformers were inspired, their reforms were simplistic and economically disastrous. Deprived of the pleasures of Seattle, the loggers, mill workers, and miners went elsewhere to spend their money. The economy, exacerbated by a national slump, took a nose dive, and by '85, the Apple Orchardists were voted out of office. Worse was the plight of women: Their votes [pressured by reformers, the Territorial Legislature in 1883 gave women the vote: "At a stroke, the voting power of the reformers increased enormously"] had so infuriated businessmen that in 1887 the franchise was revoked and not returned until 1910.[75]

Foremost among those putting the economic interest of the city before the pursuit of piety were the "New Seattle" businessmen, those who, although regular churchgoers and members, regarded the inevitable vices and excesses—drinking, gambling, and prostitution—of a vibrant and prosperous city a tolerable price to pay for continued prosperity. The opposition of this group of entrepreneurs to reform and the subsequent revocation of female suffrage served to dampen the enthusiasm of the reformers, and there]followed only episodic reminders of once virulent conflict.

The next fifteen years or so brought an infusion of Japanese, Chinese, and other ethnic and religious immigrants into the city, not all driven by high-minded purpose ("In the early 1900s it was estimated that there were nearly 200 Japanese prostitutes in Seattle"). Swamped by ethnic diversity, the established Protestant order was sent reeling, traditional assumptions of cultural hegemony now undermined by a challenge of an altogether different nature. Many churches worked to accommodate and absorb the new Asian immigrants, drawing them into the Christian community. The Reverend Mark Allison Matthews, dynamic, progressive leader of Seattle's First Presbyterian church, soon—with a congregation of 6,000—to become the largest of that denomination in the world, envisioned Seattle as "a righteous

---

[74] Judge Greene: "Those hangmen were in revolt against Magna Carta. In that respect the lynchers were co-criminal with the lynched. Many of the actors were professed Christians. Unwittingly they were illustrating the doctrine of original sin and total depravity, but without pity for their victims, who had been darkly illuminating the same dogma." (Quoted in Buerge, "Missions in the Wilderness . . . ," 28.)

[75] Ibid.

community that would be an important staging area from which missionaries could embark for Asia to complete the Christian conquest of the world and usher in its transformation." Matthews, a "fanatical prohibitionist," regarded the malodorous social condition of Seattle a serious impediment to its ascension as a genuine "holy city." Upon the election of Mayor Hiram Gill in the first decade of the new century (a candidate who foresaw a "wide-open town" and who promised his supporters "that he would protect saloons and gambling halls and permit prostitution in the skid road district. 'Hell!,' he once said to a friend, 'this is a seaport town, ain't it?' ") and then subsequent revelations of political arrogance and misfeasance ("He had promised to keep prostitution within the skid road area, but then it was made public that he had given some of his friends the contract to build what was described as 'the world's largest brothel' south of it in Georgetown."), new fire was kindled in the breasts of the reformers. The 1910 restoration of the female vote enabled Matthews to engineer the recall of Gill and close down the brothels. In 1917, he lead an initiative campaign culminating in state legislation prohibiting the manufacture, importation, and sale of liquor, a move portending the eventual ratification of the 18th Amendment to the Federal Constitution in 1919, which brought Prohibition nationwide.

An all too familiar pattern begins to emerge from these apparently sporadic surges and retreats of evangelical reform fervor. In each instance the vigorous promotion and implementation of a moral program occurs in a socially diverse city (or a nation, to extend the generalization), the denizens of which, although they may not all share the enthusiasm of the zealots, nonetheless admire the goals of the movement, since they seem founded upon beliefs they also embrace or recall from their adolescence or appear the possession of the more prominent and successful individuals and families. This, if only tacit, compliance ensures an electoral victory which ushers in an era of reform the social and economic consequences of which the average citizen could only vaguely anticipate. In time, the evidence of social conflict and economic dislocation persuades a majority of citizens (a judgment perhaps aided by a vocal opposition) that the costs of reform are greater than society can bear and the mandate of the zealots is withdrawn. The years pass; a new generation emerges. It encounters the same kinds of nagging, festering social ills that are all too easily attributed to a category of behavioral vice the evangelical moral elite abhors. An earlier generation's experiences of the social and economic consequences of the total application of piety has by now faded from immediate memory and the evangelical cultural core spearheads another rush to reform, implementing programs to re-invigorate the moribund social and body politic. And so on it goes, one generation after another, cycles of pietistic expansion and contraction that dot the landscape of American cultural history. These have become in the more familiar, formal academic treatments conceptualized as, and reduced to, three or four "Great Awakenings,"[76] the complex and varied contents of which this brief portrait can only begin to suggest. Yet not always, I should mention, do these cycles concern the application and subsequent relaxation of "temperance" of one kind or another, although the former was for many reformers in the early twentieth century the cynosure of all political effort.[77] They can also characterize the development of individual institutions or communities, or serve to explain particular periods in their histories. The waxing and waning of piety, the coming and going of "reform" or "revival" is a predictable, ineradicable feature of evangelicalism (and, by implication, of American cultural history), as will become apparent throughout the course of this study.

I mean to argue also that the strategies of the reformers to redeem the pagan elements of society and purify their towns and cities were a good deal more subtle and protean than is commonly thought. We sometimes dwell unduly upon the campaigns to keep the pagan man from his pleasures and overlook the diverse nature and motivations of the evangelical social and spiritual machine. Instead what one finds in any highly motivated evangeli-

---

[76] See, for example, "The Third Great Awakening, 1890-1920" in McLoughlin, *Revivals, Awakenings, and Reform*. . . . Although evangelicalism has undoubtedly contributed to many positive social reform movements, it is McLoughlin's particular bias to, for the most part, elevate evangelicalism (unjustifiably) to the leadership of some of our greatest reform movements and overlook detrimental aspects of its influence and history. I also have serious problems with his formulation and interpretation of the third (1890-1920) and fourth (1960-1990?) "Great Awakenings," especially the fourth where he lumps the new left and the counterculture together with "neo-evangelicalism," un-prophetically dismissing the latter as a largely escapist religious phenomenon: "Neo-evangelicalism offers a moratorium on politics—a rejection of the turbulent sixties." (213-14) It is the nature and structure of this "rejection" that he so thoroughly misunderstands. The rampant reductionism is most tellingly illustrated by this bibliography entry: "The shift from a postmillennial optimism to a premillennial pessimism, evident even among intellectual sophisticates in this awakening, is evident in: Robert L. Heilbroner, *An Inquiry Into The Human Prospect* (New York: Norton, 1971); Hal Lindsey and C. C. Carlson, *The Late Great Planet Earth* (Grand Rapids, Michigan: Zondervan, 1973). . . ." (227-28) The latter book is a popular evangelical account of the last days before the *Parousia*, or the second coming of Christ. The most the two have in common is that neither dwells exclusively upon history.
For a telling critique of this notion of uniform, identifiable "Awakening" periods, see Jon Butler, *Awash*. . . , esp. Chapter 6, "The Plural Origins of American Revivalism."

[77] Martin Marty detects elements of cultural backlash and resentment—with often disparate objects of aspersion—in the Prohibition movement: "The Wets were immigrant newcomers, supporters of the great city machines; they were infidels and heathens who violated Sabbath laws and they were snobbish eastern 'society people'—classes who were above the level of dry forces as others were below them." (*Pilgrims In Their Own Land: 500 Years of Religion in America*, New York: Penguin Books, 1985, 376.)

cal community of this period—or any other for that matter—is a multi-pronged and -textured approach to the education of its youth and to the proselytization of the unchurched. And so we shouldn't be surprised to learn that during a period characterized by great political victories, and equally great debacles, evangelical reformers were active in other, less obvious, arenas:

> Not only did they try to impose morality, they actively sought to attract the unchurched to their congregations. Revivals, camp meetings, and the Sunday School movement of the 80s were directed at those who had lapsed, but for the broad secular audience, the Chautauqua Literary and Scientific circles proved to be very popular. Rapidly separating itself from its Methodist Episcopal beginnings, in the latter decades of the 19th century the Chautauqua movement became virtually a national institution, and locally it promoted public education and provided support for the university. The YMCA and the YWCA were also developed during this time to broadcast a nominally Christian message to the public, and offered assistance in a club-like setting.
> More significant, however, were the health and welfare programs sponsored and maintained by the churches. The Catholic Sisters of Providence built the first major public hospital in the city and pioneered a popular form of health insurance. The Seattle Union of the Christian Temperance Union Women sponsored a day nursery to help a new phenomenon: the working mother. In 1885, the Ladies Relief Society, made up of women from several denominations, started the orphanage that was to become the Seattle Children's Home. And in a more compassionate response to prostitution, Harriet Parkhurst and her friends organized the Florence Crittenden Rescue Circle, a home for prostitutes which provided shelter, counseling, child care, and vocational education. The Sisters of the Good Shepard, a Catholic order, ran a home similar to the Crittenden home, and members went on forays to the skid road area to offer aid to the women.[78]

It is then in this larger local and national context of a dominant evangelical Protestant community and ethos coming to terms with a perplexing social and cultural transformation that we ought to view Hiram Pease's hejira to Battle Creek and the subsequent founding of Seattle Seminary. Given Judge Roger Greene's experiences downtown (during the lynching incident), no wonder he lent his good name to the enterprise (as a trustee). There was a war being waged for the souls of American youth; Hiram Pease went east looking for spiritual ammunition and discovered a Victorian powder keg in John Harvey Kellogg.

---

[78] Buerge, "Missions in the Wilderness . . . ." The influential Reverend Mark Allison Matthews, for example, mentioned earlier, "called for the development of city parks, art galleries, and libraries, and the development of a medical school at the University of Washington. He campaigned for the concepts of initiative, referendum, and recall, worked for the institution of the direct primary and supported labor-management negotiations and consumer protection." (ibid.)

The most concentrated dose of Kellogg can be found in his very popular, widely-read-and-consulted success manual for boys, *Man, the Masterpiece, or Plain Truths Plainly Told, About Boyhood, Youth and Manhood* (1886). Kellogg laid down the fundamentals of adolescent emotional and physical development in such chapters as "The Masterpiece" (the physical body), "Social Ethics," "Getting a Wife," "How to Make Life a Success," "Stomaches," "Biliousness," "The Rum Family," "Germs," "What to Wear for Health," "How to Bathe," "Sexual Sins and their Consequences," and "Diseases of the Sexual Organs," among others. Every ten pages or so yields an authoritative colored plate illustrating perfect and imperfect anatomy or posture, or a stony pink masterpiece of a model performing dumb-bell exercises. Foremost among Kellogg's concerns, however, was the orchestration of all personal and family energies for the prevention of the principal threat to character formation, "sensual self-indulgence." Caution need be exercised to guard against children routinely eating too much or sleeping too long, since any initial indulgence here in these relatively benign areas may render the child vulnerable at later stages to the most spiritually damaging of all practices, the "secret vice" of masturbation. Against this great usurpation, Kellogg devised a program of denial and discipline to enhance the exercise of the will, having for its ultimate goal the elimination not only of conscious, deliberate acts of masturbation but even any loitering hint of sensuality that may slip into the unguarded moments of dreams. He advised rigorous daily exercise in self-abnegation (and -abuse) in order that the finely-honed and-tested will might respond almost automatically to any subliminal temptation, "snapping the youth awake and out of his dream in time to prevent nocturnal emission." The regimen included:

> 1) Kneading and pounding on the abdomen each day to promote evacuation before sleep and thus avoid "irritating" congestions.
> 2) Drinking hot water, six to eight glasses a day (same end in view).
> 3) Urinating several times each night (same end in view).
> 4) Avoiding alcohol, tobacco, and tea because they stimulated lecherous thoughts.
> 5) Taking cold enemas and hot sitz baths each day.
> 6) Wearing a wet girdle to bed each night.[79]

These prophylactic measures proved far less discomfiting and mortifying than the potential horrors of indulgence and habituation they sought to forestall, of which Kellogg warned:

---

[79] Lears, *No Place Of Grace* . . . , 14. I could not find this exact formulation of the regimen in my copy of *Man, the Masterpiece* and must assume Lears rearranged the items somewhat for greater effect.

How many times has a poor victim of this vice said to us, with tears streaming from his eyes, and dark despair written upon every lineament of his face, "Oh, why was I not warned of the terrible suffering I must endure? Why was I not told of the horrible wickedness of this filthy vice?" No tongue can describe the mental anguish, the despair, the shame of one of these victims, who, after years of transgression, is suddenly awakened to a realization of his folly, when he discovers the ruin he has wrought. Never to have been born would be far better than this living death.[80]

However extremist, idiosyncratic, and yes, occasionally even pathological, the ministrations of Kellogg and his acolytes, they nonetheless represent an attempt by prominent late 19th-century Americans to re-invigorate an apparently waning cultural authority and discipline in a society undergoing rapid social transformation; an effort, paradoxically, that sought to introduce and apply many of *the very same techniques and routines so integral to the growing rationalization of the economic marketplace to the emotional life of individuals.* The logic and rigor of the marketplace would be harnessed to control its consequences.

Although I might take issue with Jackson Lears's claim that under the banner of these particular ideas—i.e., those supposedly arising out of cultural anxiety and *emanating from the educated bourgeoisie*—a national cultural consensus had emerged,[81] clearly the middle and upper-middle classes wrestled with

---

[80] Kellogg, *Man, the Masterpiece*, 395. We find here in this chapter, "Sexual Sins and Their Consequences," all the dietary restrictions and recommendations that Pease insisted be a part of the culinary curriculum, as well as the hygienic practices—even the use of a towel: "Immediately on rising in the morning, take a sponge or towel bath, occupying one or two minutes, and rub dry with a coarse towel. The vigorous glow of the skin which follows a cool bath taken in this way has a most happy effect upon the body and mind" (402). In extreme cases where "moral suasion" fails to eliminate onanism Kellogg recommends in "To Cure the Practice in Children":

> A method which is wholly successful, though productive of some pain, is the following:—Draw the prepuce down beyond the glans, passing a silver wire through the skin on either side, and twist the ends together in such a way as to draw the two sides of the prepuce so close together that it cannot be drawn back from the glans. This, in exceptional cases in which the prepuce is unusually long, will effectively prevent erection, and consequently interrupt the habit. This method, for which we are indebted to Dr. Archibald, Superintendent of the Iowa Asylum For Feeble Minded Children, we have employed in a number of cases with entire success. The pain produced by it is not great, and is in most cases an advantage rather than an objection, as it has a decided tendency to diminish the desire to continue the practice. (404)

[81] ". . . . the Victorian ethic of self-control was engrained widely and deeply enough to constitute the mainspring of the dominant culture . . . undergirded the values disseminated by the

the problem of the installation and preservation of moral character in American youth. In this respect the lessons of Battle Creek were not lost on Hiram Pease. Here was an impressive, coherent system of ideas and techniques whose implementation could enhance the evangelical moral development program. The more direct clinical references to sexuality would be tempered, lest they inadvertently stimulate impure thoughts, but the underlying essence and spirit of Kellogg survived intact. Seminary students and teachers may very well have turned aside to conceal their bemusement at the demonstrative antics of Hiram Pease, but the anxieties (and phobias) that so drove him were shared by many of his contemporaries. Pease amused nearly everyone, but the laughter came uneasily, for they had seldom encountered a man who took so seriously, literally, and so urgently acted upon—spelling out in so graphic and almost clinical a manner—what everyone else seemed to take for granted. Toilet functions were not your everyday boarding room banter, let alone nocturnal emissions. Yet whatever mishmash of Victorian pseudo-science Pease brought back from Battle Creek, everybody seemed to get the point. Surely downtown Seattle businessmen of faith got the point; so did orthodox Free Methodists and, above all, the students. For all the smirks and smothered laughter there was an underlying consensus in force here, however vague, of how all these ideas hung together. There was some sort of relationship between the particular manner in which one's bodily desires and appetites were controlled and the development of moral character; and there was an additional relationship between the acquisition of this character and society at large. The dark forces of both physical and moral nature had to be reined in and controlled.[82] Indeed however much Free Methodist

---

educated bourgeoisie . . . official standards of conduct [bringing] coherence to a potentially fragmented society." (Lears, *No Place Of Grace* . . . , 14-15.)

[82] Consider Joseph Kett's particular take upon these developments:

> The extraordinary emphasis on achievement, purity, and self-restraint in success tracts suffused both middle-class family values and the institutions created for middle-class young people in the 1880s and 1890s. . . . the impetus behind the creation of institutions for adolescents came from men and women whose values approximated those of the success writers. The values of success writers and those of the architects of new institutions for youth, such as the Boy Scouts and church youth societies, were complementary in many ways. Each group located the social evils of the day in big cities; each preferred the virtues of the country boy; each celebrated Puritan thrift and self-denial; each castigated political and economic corruption; and each, finally, saw value in prolonging the period of preparation.

The establishment of these institutions reflects both the larger developmental forces of the changing role of children in the economic household which produced the increasing cultural

businessmen countenanced these elemental forces (for surely a little greed[83] oils the wheels of the capitalist locomotive), they nonetheless understood that a stable, disciplined workplace and market depended upon the continued dispersion and implementation of ascetic ideals.[84] A sober, stable, morally-upright Christian society found them indispensable. Not a few Seattle businessmen concurred, parting with thousands of dollars so that a fledgling Seminary (and eventual college) could survive. And Pease gave the most because he believed the most, as he once explained: ". . . .my dollars must back my doctrines."[85]

---

segregation of youth from adults and the intentional prolongation of childhood, and the narrower aims of the reassertion of evangelical cultural hegemony:

> For all the talk about activity, however, the motive force behind Christian youth societies in the 1880s and 1890s was defensive, a desire to shield young people from contamination by the alien culture of big cities and immigrants. A set of values which can be located in medical and educational literature as early as the 1840s and 1850s had finally found embodiment in institutions. A common thread which ran through college "life," the high school curriculum, and Christian youth organizations was hostility to precocity, to adult behavior in youth. As it acquired institutional forms, the long-standing fear of precocity changed its shape. The avoidance of precocity no longer entailed merely the removal of intellectual pressures and social stimulants from youth, but the creation of a self-contained world in which prolonged immaturity could sustain itself.
> (Joseph F. Kett, Rites of Passage: Adolescence in America, 1790 to the Present, New York: Basic Books, 1977, 170, 210.)

[83] Pease himself was scarcely averse to easy money, going off to Nome, Alaska when news of the gold rush reached Seattle. Characteristically, he preached the gospel to fellow passengers on the boat up. (Response, September 1981; Watson, "The Christian Liberal Arts College. . . .")

[84] Especially in view of local labor unrest, as Seattle was the northwest headquarters for the I.W.W.—Industrial Workers of the World, the Wobblies—and served as the launching point in November of 1916 for the Verona, a steamer carrying a phalanx of Wobblies north to Everett to break a blockade forbidding labor radicals to set foot in the lumber mills and city, the ship and her activist passengers surprised on the docks by a hundred armed deputies who perpetrated what became known as the "Everett Massacre." (Norman H. Clark, Mill Town: A Social History of Everett, Washington, from Its Earliest Beginnings on the Shores of Puget Sound to the Tragic and Infamous Event Known as the Everett Massacre, Seattle: University of Washington Press, 1972, 168-214.)

And in local city politics, which often pitted urban populists against the "Interests"; and later, when indigenous labor disputes culminated in the second general strike the country had experienced, the Seattle General Strike of 1919. (Morgan, Skid Road . . . , 194-214; Sale, Seattle: Past To Present . . . , 71, 113-35.)

Although the Seattle General Strike is widely regarded as the country's first "General Strike," Nell Irvin Painter instead lays that honor upon the "St. Louis Commune" of 1877. (Standing at Armageddon: The United States, 1877-1919, New York: Norton 1987, 18.)

[85] Schoenhals, "Higher Education . . . ," 256.

So that, oddly enough, all the while wealthy benefactors gave the school monies, one of whose major intentions was to encourage the building of the sort of "character" needed to quell disorder and continually nourish and propel the industrial and managerial revolution, her very own faculty[86] and students harbored seemingly conflicting ideas and sentiments. Winfred A. Grantham, for example, the first graduate of Seattle Seminary, who marked his departure with these words:

> We live in a time when the race for wealth and self-advancement entirely engrosses the minds of most men. . . . The poor are wailing, from miserable hovels, for the necessities of life, while the rich revel in palaces of luxury. . . . Step into the road that leads to true and enduring honor. Build up character rather than wealth.[87]

What is meant here by "character"? Indeed, in these aspirations and pronouncements can be found the source of some confusion in everyday American moral thinking, past and present. Consider the mythologies (and realities) of the self-made man and other celebrated characters dotting the

---

[86] W.H. Boddy, "Seminary Training":

> By precept and by example they have disabused his mind of mercenary ideals of life and he [the student] has seen the transcendent beauty of a life of self-denial . . . the principles of self-abnegation and sacrifice are not merely characteristics of the visionary idealist, but in them are found the highest ends of human life. (*1909 Olympiad Yearbook*) {Archives}

[87] *Seminary Echo*, no. 7, May 1896; also, from the 1915-16 *Bulletin*:: "Seattle Pacific has no aristocracy save that of merit. The students who are dependent upon the work of their own hands have as much attention as would sons of millionaires. The institution believes in the dignity of labor and hence the opportunities afforded for a number of industrious students to pay their expenses in part by work. . . ." {Archives}

> Education, in the popular American sense, involves concepts of material success, professional accomplishment and civic service [read: secular] and makes use of these as incentives and objectives. The fundamental principle of the Christian religion is self-denial and altruism; faith in God and love to man. The fundamental principle of education [secular] is self-realization and complete living; faith in natural law and a cooperative spirit. . . . one's philosophy is altruistic [Christian] rather than egoistic [secular], man and God-centered [Christian] rather than self-centered [secular]. It means righteousness, purity, chastity, love, and service. And it gives pre-eminence to the great fundamental truths: that humanity needs a savior, that God is a personal, loving Father, that the Bible, as a revelation from God, is a more secure guide than the discoveries of humanity. (President C. Hoyt Watson, "Objective of a Conservative Christian College." 1926 inaugural address. Published in *School and Society*, no. 660, 20 August 1927.)

historical landscape.[88] Our entrepreneurial ancestors, we are often reminded, struggled and scrapped, marshalling the virtues of self-discipline and patience, postponing immediate consumption while reaping meager marginal profits which accumulated and were then re-invested in the service of anticipated future enterprises. Such trials and tribulations were the very stuff of character formation, as exemplified by the career of Hiram Pease.[89] Fortunes were amassed by individuals exhibiting such virtues: those who eschewed the indolence and indulgence of the more temporary pleasures of the moment; those who invested their wages and surpluses not in the booze and whores of the Lava Beds but rather in some higher, more distant entrepreneurial purpose.

Such is the quintessential *moral market* experience.[90] Perhaps more so than any other society, we Americans render all sorts of moral judgments

---

[88] I rely here upon James Oliver Robertson's *American Myth, American Reality* (New York: Hill & Wang, 1980).

[89] The reality, of course, may have been more complex. For example, how did Pease, at the age of fifty, amass enough money from a junk business to buy his own home, invest in Seattle real estate, afford to travel to Battle Creek to matriculate in the school, and, to top it all off, sail to Alaska in quest of gold? Perhaps he brought along some sort of endowment from his wealthy eastern family associations?

[90] It is this moral market social, cultural, and historical context that Jonathan Haidt overlooks when he frames five innate "taste receptors" of his "Moral Foundations Theory." Particularly problematical is #2, "The Fairness/Cheating Foundation," of which in a particular application to politics *in general* he writes: "Everyone cares about fairness, but there are two major kinds. On the left, fairness often implies equality, but on the right it means proportionality—people should be rewarded in proportion to that they contribute, even if it guarantees unequal outcomes." (*The Righteous Mind*, 161.) Presumably this foundation has little to do with any religious intonation, elsewhere formulated as the #5 "Sanctity/Degradation Foundation." But for American Puritanism/evangelicalism "proportionality" has much more to do with a larger moral market sensibility than with any mere behavioral violation of the Ten Commandments, or any other "secular" ethical standard as well. What matters here is *character* and *personality*, not so much cheating as an individual outcome of sin, or other cultural violations that "trigger" more general reactions of disgust. What is more, it is this larger, albeit culturally specific, moral market sense that lies behind the transformation of traditional Protestant notions of sin from an individual property or matter into a trans-personal, social and cultural phenomenon characteristic of groups—as we will see.

No wonder then that Haidt can lay claim to having found the same five foundation's pattern in "many countries besides the United States." (Although it's suggestive that in the footnote following the preceding quote he expands the claim to "The basic pattern I've reported here holds in all of these countries and regions." "Many" grows into just about everywhere.) But again, to *de-culturalize* such "trigger intuitions" into more general universally-applicable forms and questionnaire statements is to increase the likelihood of generating common patterns. "Proportionality" might be thought of in terms of a similar general trigger intuition item like "murder is wrong" ("Care/Harm Foundation"?) or "parents should be respected" ("Authority/Subversion Foundation"?) In which cultural context? Capital punishment in the United States? Female genital mutilation in Islam?

upon the apparent results of a kind of testing in the economic market arena. Our evaluations of the character and personality of individuals and even social groups are colored by the evidence of their participation (or, more importantly, their non-participation) in the marketplace, a kind of "moral market thinking" which to my mind represents one of the centerpieces of American society, politics, and culture.[91] (A peculiarly and intensely American outlook that I will contrast with more conventional European "Protestant Ethic" conceptions in the following chapter.)[92]

The more immediate point here is that the embrace and promotion of such assumptions and doctrines (in their political guises particularly) have created, and continue to create, considerable confusion in the minds of

---

One further indication of how Haidt misses the cultural interpretation boat comes in an acknowledgement that his original "Fairness/Cheating Foundation" formulation wasn't broad enough, as it was limited to notions of equality alone, failing to fully appreciate the conservative moral intuition "trigger" of proportionality. So expanded, it becomes: "It was the fairness of the Protestant work ethic and the Hindu law of karma: People should reap what they sow. People who work hard should get the fruits of their labor. People who are lazy and irresponsible should suffer the consequences." But *it* wasn't and isn't both of these things. Not only are the two mentioned items cultural apples and oranges that cannot be turned into indistinguishable moral intuition triggers, indeed within the more particular American cultural context the so-called Protestant work ethnic and moral market thinking are equally distinct cultural idioms that cannot be generalized into a common concept term, proportionality. (*The Righteous Mind*, 185, 408, 196.) What is more, cultural idioms cannot be reduced to mere generalized feelings, however partially referenced. Referring to an experimental research situation, Haidt observes: "Why did most players pay to punish? [cheaters in the game] In part, because it felt good to do so.[47] We hate to see people take without giving. We want to see cheaters and slackers 'get what is coming to them.' We want the law of karma to run its course, and we're willing to enforce it." (ibid., 209) But as we have seen, one culture's cheating (healthcare is a privilege—proportionality) is another culture's just deserts (healthcare is a basic human right—fairness). And there's a social calculus as well. For a wealthy Donald Trump, tax evasion is not cheating, it's just being "smart." Proportionality has all sorts of social and cultural layers.

[91] It is instructive that even the abolitionist movement of the American North in the midst of their efforts to end slavery were nonetheless guided by preemptive anticipatory moral market evaluations: "Not surprisingly, a sometimes overbearing tone of paternalism also pervaded the white abolitionists' efforts, in endless calls for blacks to prepare themselves for freedom by abandoning vice in favor of thrift and industry." (Sean Wilentz, "Abolition's First Wave," *The New York Review of Books*, 5/14/2020, 42.)

[92] An expression and account of which I first encountered in Garry Wills's monumental *Nixon Agonistes: The Crisis of the Self-Made Man* (1968).
—"This was evident in the frequent assertion that Christ's teaching about stewardship did not center on raising money for the church but rather upon developing Christian character. . . . as Julius Crawford wrote [in 1930] . . . . 'The entire end of Christian stewardship,' opined Methodist Luther Lovejoy [1924], was improving human character. Guy Morrill [1922] insisted that all forms of property—land, houses, businesses, and stocks—were 'God's appointed agency' for developing Christ-like character." (Gary Scott Smith, "Evangelicals Confront Corporate Capitalism," in Larry Eskridge & Mark A. Noll eds., *More Money, Money and Evangelicals in Recent North American History*, Grand Rapids: Eerdmans, 2000, 61.)

evangelicals and in their communities. By this I mean to suggest that in this ideological currency the practical economic *process* so central to the creation and development of an individual's habits, outlooks, and motivations—the formation of moral character, along with the epiphenomenal accumulation of individual fortunes and derivative expansion of general prosperity—often becomes, ironically, disassociated from the personal and social moral *results* of the process.[93] This is an early instance of what I will describe more extensively later on as the confusion of economic and moral market arenas. In our particular case, observe the founders of Seattle Seminary championing a moral regimen which, to say the very least, generates a system of motivation that when writ large into the enveloping society becomes the principal driving force behind (or, at the very least, merely accelerates) the accumulation of capital, the creation of wage labor, and the growth and organization of markets, only to spurn the inevitable outcomes of industrialization in the end—the abstract "evil" commercialization and wealth of the Gilded Age and all its sundry social and political ramifications. (Just as in the more contemporary social context most modern evangelicals would, if pressed, likely disassociate the American free enterprise system from its undeniable role in the usurpation of traditional values and institutions, apologists locating the sources of dislocation and upheaval elsewhere, as we will see.)[94]

---

[93] Lears, citing the work of Edmund S. Morgan, refers to this attitude as "American ambivalence" and dates it from the Puritans. (*No Place Of Grace* . . . , 26.) Joseph Kett writes of John Harvey Kellogg:

> Yet by the 1880s, ideas like Kellogg's were pushing towards center stage. *Man, the Masterpiece* was itself a success tract disguised as a treatise on health and physiology; a chapter on the workings of the stomach succeeded one on "how to make life a success." At times, moralism gave way to momentary lapses into religious terminology. Straining for the right metaphor to underscore the value of the daily cold water douche, Rev. C. Cuthbert Hall compared it to baptism! The mixture of Protestant moralism, religion, health, and success was incongruous, but behind it lay a distinctive paradox of late 19th century thought. *The same writers who exhorted youth to rise in the world were usually critical of business enterprise, associating the latter with luxury and corruption* [,] *and advocating extreme denial in youth.* Kellogg was no exception. He associated city life, frailty, and intellectuality with sexual indulgence, and rural life with sexual restraint. Kellogg generalized even beyond village life; all things natural and wild—Indians, savages, even apes—were chaste. It was if the road to the boardroom ran through the jungle. (Joseph F. Kett, *Rites of Passage: Adolescence in America, 1790 to the Present,* New York: Basic Books, 1977, 165.) {emphasis added} [See also McLoughlin, 161.]

[94] These observations are, of course, not original with me. Daniel Bell dwells upon similar matters in *The Cultural Contradictions of Capitalism* (New York: Basic Books, 1976). And even conservative pundits, such as George Will, acknowledge the often paradoxical consequences

In this instance the irony merely serves to illustrate an old and familiar theme of unintended social consequences: that in the campaign to re-assert control over an apparently deranged and self-indulgent society, prominent people, the founders and faculty of the Seminary among them, formulated theories and programs of moral development that had for a goal the enhanced rationalization of the inner life, the internal logic and consequences of which underpinned, buttressed, and perhaps even accelerated the social transformation they sought to reverse.[95] The irony will compound even further in the next chapter when we examine the social and political beliefs of the faculty and students in the first few decades of the twentieth century,

---

of an unbridled free market society. See "The Disease of Politics," *Newsweek*, 1 November 1976. What this volume will contribute is an understanding of the role the moral market ethos plays in evangelicalism and, furthermore, the unique role evangelicalism plays in the larger American cultural arena.

[95] Max Weber discerned the irony of such unintended consequences more generally: "In the great twist of *The Protestant Ethic*, Weber argued that all these antiworldly attitudes finally led to the development of an all-too-worldly spirit. . . . Quite unwittingly, Calvinist beliefs fostered the spirit of secular capitalism. A people worried about wealth and luxury created the ethic that would amass vast amounts of wealth. . . . the devout pursuit of Calvinist piety had brought about nothing less than the modern secular order." (Abram C. Van. Engen, *City on a Hill: A History of American Exceptionalism*, New Haven: Yale University Press, 2020, 212.)
—R. Laurence Moore documents a concurrent process with respect to the efforts of 19th-century Protestant leaders to inject moral content into popular, sensational literature. Drawn into the business of making religion "competitive with other cultural products," their efforts led to a growing commodification of religion through "moral sensationalism," in the form of books and magazines designed to both titillate and edify. Hence an unintended consequence of trying to control the market for sexually imaginative material was an "expansion of the cultural marketplace that fed on desire." The producing and selling of these quickly read materials "fed a habit of addictive buying. . . . Protestantism [its "extreme subjectivism" and imaginative "manipulations"] was excellent preparation for the pleasures of reading novels and more generally for modern consumer hedonism." So that not only were evangelical Protestant moral market schemes and regimens deployed to instill virtue and self-discipline, thereby spurring production, and then deployed again in the attempt to discourage—or in the mopping up after—the various pagan abuses and excesses of consumption, but their promoters and bearers were also deeply involved in the creation and expansion of these market demands as well. As Moore concludes, " . . . production and consumption chased each other and became mutually-dependent values in the Protestant world of antebellum America." (*Selling God: American Religion in the Marketplace of Culture*, New York: Oxford University Press, 1994, 38-39.)
—I do not mean to leave the impression that this moral agenda was formulated or arose overnight in reaction to a specific apparent cultural development. No social phenomena demonstrate such a clean one-to-one correspondence. Obviously, the evangelical communities were in the business of moral character enhancement long before the arrival of the Gilded Age. We should instead regard these efforts as amplifications or accelerations of inherited values and doctrines. There were of course other non-religious efforts to decelerate the trends towards greater routinization and rationalization that Jackson Lears discusses. These efforts were informed by a greater understanding of the origins of modern capitalism but proved no less futile.

opinions which will put them even further at odds with some of the intentions of the founders.

CHAPTER 3

DEEP (AND SHALLOW) HISTORY: THE LAYERS OF EVANGELICAL CULTURE

There is another dimension to the conventional narration of events in the early history of any community or society that must be explored if we are to fully grasp the contemporary meaning and significance of what has gone before. By this I mean to examine the various types or levels of cultural logics and dynamics characterizing this particular community and American evangelicalism in general. The concepts *meaning* and *significance* will play an important role here. In the Weberian sense of "complexes of meaning,"[96] meaning refers here mainly to how our interpretations and understandings of the world foster motivations that translate into behavior; significance concerns the inevitable assessment of the impact or consequences of such intended behaviors, both individual and collective. Significance signifies a reflection back upon meanings and motives and their relationships with actions; its use may imply or trigger an evaluation of sorts—as, for example, when intentions misfire and things go awry, significance becomes problematical or is denied. We might even link the two via a proposition: the greater the intensity of meaning and the motivations they generate the greater the likely significance or impact of the behaviors spawned by them. And, conversely, the greater the impact or significance of behavior in and upon the world the greater the verification of the intensification of original meaning. Such as, for instance, the *significance* of taking down the Twin Towers of the World Trade Center reflected back upon and confirmed the intensity of the *meaning* of *Jihad* and *Allah* within radical Islam. Just as, in a less violent context, successful completion of each stage in the ascent of the "project to become fully human"[97] validates and further enhances the significance of the meaning of Confucianism.

In this sense cultural logics are the structural vehicles that carry interpretations of the world, *meanings*, into *significance*. Through them patterns of ideas are organized and translated into motivations that generate or end up expressed as patterns of behavior. This may raise a host of questions. Do they have anything in common with what we conveniently—and

---

[96] Drawing upon an unpublished paper that I wrote for Stephen Toulmin, "Ambiguity and Social Behavior in Max Weber: A Systemization," 1993.

[97] Huston Smith, *The World's Great Religions: Our Great Wisdom Traditions*, HarperSanFrancisco, 1991, 86.

conventionally—think of as "worldviews?" What is their effective range and scope? Do they hold sway merely within the bounds of this particular community, within American evangelicalism and the larger American society in general—or, casting our gaze even farther afield, are they present in foreign nations and cultures, and perhaps even in earlier historical periods of the above-mentioned divergent communities and societies? Although I intend in the course of this study to identify, explain, and demonstrate the operation of culturally-transmitted ideas or logics in this community and thus will in large measure rely upon the unfolding of its contents to define and illuminate my use of these terms, let me begin here by introducing and making more explicit some of the general theoretical assumptions (particularly those of range and historical precedent) guiding my employment of these terms and categories. With respect then to the system of ideas or logics present in this community, I will employ terms and concepts occupying three different, but closely related, levels of generalization. And, as noted earlier, all three of these arose later, after the fact, at the tail end of both the community field-work and associated historical research. Above all, they represent subsequent assessments and interpretations, not preliminary guiding theoretical lode-stars.

The Sacred and the Profane

Perhaps the most universal logic or dynamic we will encounter is this propensity of dividing the world (i.e., one's community, city, region, society, nation, continent, etc., and the individuals and groups contained therein) into diametrically-opposed sacred and profane categories, a tendency common to most religious groups, although generally deemed characteristic of more traditional or "pre-literate" tribes and cultures. And this isn't always a benign or un-problematical process. Observe that the *greater* the apparent external threat or danger to a religious group or community—or, conversely (yet often concurrently), the *greater* the aggressive promotion and projection of an internal religious world view outward into a potentially hostile, unreceptive social environment—the *greater* the corresponding inclination to draw invidious lines of demarcation, particularly in the formulation of wholesale declensions of persons, objects, and relationships in sacred / profane (or Christian/secular) terms. The practice occurs most simply in those primordial tribes which employ binary symbols to render comprehensible and stable, if not innocuous, the environmental dangers buffeting them, and secondarily in conceptualizing the role and threat of different or competing tribes and groups.[98] Closer and more germane to the Judeo-Christian tradition, we discover in Max Weber's *Ancient Judaism* a "pariah community" whose inheritance and transmission of prophetic theological distinctions produced "ritualistic segregation" and the "dualism of in-group and out-group morality," demarcations that became honed and intensified through recurrent encounters with enemies and enslavers; a combination, all told, of theologically-inspired cultural hubris ("chosen"-ness) and labile social and political environments (among many other factors) which produced the extreme swings of the withdrawal and submission of the Babylonian and Egyptian exiles on the one hand and the belligerency of the warrior state in the ancient Israel confederacy on the other.[99]

Much later on there is evidence of similar pressures and dynamics in an entirely different context in the New Testament Christian communities, wherein the departure of Jesus leaves the members of a callow, fledgling charismatic sect alone to squabble among themselves, in time growing increasingly petty and litigious, prone to promulgate and distinguish orthodoxy from heresy, setting off appropriate Christian thought and behavior from

---

[98] "One of the outstanding characteristics of traditional societies is the opposition that they assume between their inhabited territory and the unknown and indeterminate space that surrounds it. The former is the world (more precisely, our world), the cosmos; everything outside it is no longer a cosmos but a sort of 'other world,' a foreign, chaotic space, peopled by ghosts, demons, 'foreigners'. . . ." (Mircea Eliade, *The Sacred and the Profane: The Nature of Religion*, New York: Harcourt Brace Jovanovich, 1959, 29.)

This is of course not the only role sacred/profane (and other logical) distinctions perform in traditional cultures. It simply appears that once the original antinomy is in place other demarcations flow epiphenomenally from this more fundamental *structural* one. Hence the sacred totem represents for Durkheim in *The Elementary Forms of the Religious Life* (New York: The Free Press, 1965) the self-conjured identity ("idealism") of the clan, the primary source of the system of classification generating the meanings and understandings upon which the social relationships of the group hinge. As Marshall Sahlins writes it is these almost unconscious idioms and mechanisms, this "structure [that] is the organization of conscious experience," that proves "Unfathomable and yet powerful enough to make the difference between the peoples, to makes us right and you wrong, something like that has indeed intimations of the sacred." And *vice-versa*, as we will see. ("Two or Three Things I Know About Culture," *The Journal of the Royal Anthropological Institute*, Vol. 5, No. 3, September 1999, 413-4.)

This is not, however, to argue that all cultural categorizations, dualisms, world views are necessarily ideological, in the sense of immediately reflecting changes in the perception, or reality of, external physical or social danger. There is, after all, such a thing as habitual social and cultural life betraying very little ideological animus; hence the emphasis upon ideology as an "*extraordinary* source of meaning and motivation" in my chapter one definition.

[99] Max Weber, *Ancient Judaism*, New York: The Free Press, 1952, 336-55, 356-82, 90-146. Extremes that persist in modern times: contrast the passivity of the Holocaust with the militarism of Zionist Israel. However, keep in mind that the mere existence of a threat is not in and of itself sufficient grounds to produce the kind ideological reaction that I describe in this study. There are a host of other pre-conditions—a victimization theology, for example—that must be present to generate sacred/profane distinctions.

untutored pagan equivalents—severe, often finicky measures and distinctions designed, in part, to establish and impart a singular identity, increase solidarity, and enhance prospects for survival. The epistles of Paul are riddled with references to partisan social and theological antagonisms. It is just these ideological currents and pressures that are so largely absent from the apostles' (and others) accounts of the teachings of Jesus, who so clearly (although scarcely uniformly) enunciated the principle of a fundamental terrestrial unity (spiritual equality) of all individuals and social groups.[100]

Throughout the history of Christianity one detects the waxing and waning of ideological pressures to formulate public signals and codes distinguishing the sacramental from the blasphemous, the saved from the damned. What then is an inherent tendency in all religious groups to demarcate sacred from profane objects and practices, insiders from outsiders, and, with routinization and codification, orthodoxy from heresy, in turn *assumes in and among particular historical and cultural contexts an intensity and expression appropriate to each*.[101] Above all, cultural (and environmental) variation ensures that different religious groups will be predictably more *or* less prone to adopt and employ these kinds of blanket invidious distinctions. On this basis alone one might predict, for instance, that reasonably isolated, homogeneous religious groups or societies of relative independence and prosperity will be less likely to develop elaborate insider/outsider distinctions than say more het-

---

[100] I should mention that Paul also had his moments of universalism, as when, for instance he wrote: "For all alike have sinned, and are deprived of the divine splendour . . . ." (Romans 3:23-24, *The New English Bible*, New York: Oxford University Press, 1971), although I should add that Paul sandwiches this observation between the more exclusive claims of the conditions of God's justice, resting upon "faith alone. . . . God's justice. . . . it is God's way of righting wrong, effective through faith in Christ *for all who have such faith—all, without distinction*. . . . all are justified by God's free grace." (3:21-24) {emphasis added}

[101] For example, Jerome Kagan recounts the struggle of European intellectuals against the authoritarian nature of knowledge under the church, sketching the historical context of "John Locke's metaphor of the *tabula rasa* and the desire of so many seventeenth-century intellectuals to make experience primary in the shaping of man's mind" (versus the "innate ideas" conceptions of Spinoza, Leibniz, and the continental rationalists), remarking that

> In addition to the desire to weaken the church's powerful hold on the citizenry, there was a deep belief in egalitarianism. The church held as a basic tenet that some were born *superior to others because they were born in wedlock to Christian parents*. Hence, from the beginning, their minds were stocked with superior ideas and sentiments, and nothing the non-Christian could do would make it possible for him to attain spiritual equality. To Locke and those like him who believed in political egalitarianism, the doctrine of innate ideas was an intellectual obstacle to the attainment of political equality. . . . (*The Growth of the Child: Reflections on Human Development*, New York: Norton, 1978, 75.) {emphasis added}

erogeneous groups and societies enmeshed in webs of habitual social, political, and economic antagonisms.[102] Yet we should keep in mind that however much allowance is made for the influence of these variable conditions at some remove from the religious ideology itself, they pale in importance to the nature and content of the logics underpinning a particular community or society.[103] Indeed how else does one explain the plethora of cultural ideologies that even one major religion, such as Islam or Christianity, has spawned in relatively similar social and economic milieus? Granted, with respect to this diversity it has proven fruitful to analyze the relationship between the social background of individuals and the characteristic patterns of their attraction to particular kinds of cults, sects, or denominations, and such

---

[102] Then again these kinds of distinctions may develop over time, as we saw in Moorish Spain: "At the same time, the fanaticism and intolerance of the Spaniards seems to have been *an acquired characteristic, a product of history*. At an earlier date they had been reproached by other Christians for their laxity, their resort to infidel doctors, their visits to Moorish courts, so long as the Muhammadans remained in the peninsula. The enduring conflict with the infidel, and the religious propaganda connected with it, helped to make Spain more firmly Catholic, more intolerantly orthodox, than any other country." ((Herbert Butterfield, "Christianity in History," in Philip P. Wiener, ed., *Dictionary of the History of Ideas, Vol. 1*, New York: Scribners, 1973, 393.)
—But as Marshall Sahlins suggests these sorts of cultural dynamics evince a more general geographic aspect as well:

> Consider again this surprising paradox of our time: that localization develops apace with globalization, differentiation with integration; that just when the forms of life around the world are becoming homogeneous, the peoples are asserting their cultural distinctiveness. 'An increasing homogenization of social and cultural forms,' as Marilyn Strathern says, 'seems to be accompanied by a proliferation of claims to specific authenticities and identities'. . . . many other students of globalization point out the linkage of these seemingly opposed processes, noting that the marking of cultural difference is responsive to the hegemonic threat of world capitalism. The short answer to the paradox is thus 'resistance.' Problem is, the people are not usually resisting the technologies and 'conveniences' of modernization, nor are they particularly shy of the capitalist relations needed to acquire them. Rather, what they are after is the indigenization of modernity, their own cultural space in the global scheme of things. ("Two or Three Things. . . ," 410.)

[103] Need I add here the obvious qualification that a host of social, geographic, historical, economic, and other elements interact with one another to produce a community, nation, or culture, and that the process of the formulation of a religious or cultural logic is never-ending? I don't mean to argue that a definable logic is ever *prior* to this ongoing process of cultural creation and change, is ever a big-bang *first cause* of things that follow. Rather I assume that once a particular course of cultural development has produced a discernible cultural entity that can be momentarily apprehended (and that continues to evolve as we scrutinize it) it becomes plausible to examine it for evidence of these kinds of logical, religious, sacred/profane declensions.

studies obviously have value in and of themselves; but what I mean to emphasize here is how in certain identifiable contexts *changes in the perception of impending cultural dangers or threats produce a corresponding acceleration or diminution in the intensity of religious ideology*, most noticeably as a systematic variation in this tendency to sunder the surrounding world into diametrically-opposed sacred and profane realms.[104]

This approach not only serves (perhaps too superficially) to distinguish the more contemplative insular religion of, say, Buddhism from the more aggressive warrior religions of Islam and Christianity, but may also prove useful in distinguishing divergent approaches within the religions themselves. Reflect for a moment upon the possible links or parallels between this kind of ideological dynamic and the different responses to cultural upheaval Clifford Geertz recounts in the respective legends of two Muslims—the Indonesian apostle, Sunan Kalidjaga, and the Moroccan Sufi scholar, Sidi Lahsen Lyusi: the former, deemed to have "introduced Islam into Java and, more or less single-handedly and without resort to force, converted its population to the new creed," living during a "time without order," experiencing the dissolution of the old Indic civilization (Hindu-Buddhist) and the triumph of the scriptural one of "Islamic times"; the latter living during the "sectarian anarchy of the Maraboutic Crisis," observing the eventual disintegration of 17th-century Morocco into aggressive, competing polities ruled by "holy men of one sort or another . . . [a political climate producing] aggressive utopian communities":

> Both men lived in times when their societies were moving, hesitantly, painfully, and, in the nature of the case, quite incompletely, toward form, after having been disrupted by fundamental religio-political upheaval. But where Kalidjaga attempted to direct that movement by representing it in his consciousness, creating in microcosm the harmony sought for in macrocosm, Lyusi attempted to direct it by struggling against it, by exposing in his teachings and his actions the internal contradictions it was desperately seeking to contain. The first approach is essentially aesthetic; it portrays its ideal. The second is essentially moral; it commands it.[105]

---

[104] Candida Moss has traced the history of this idea of persecution of Christians throughout history in her marvelous *The Myth of Persecution: How Early Christians Invented a Story of Persecution* (2003). Although she acknowledges that "there are places in the world where Christians face real violence. . . . [that] often goes unpublicized and unnoticed.", it is more often the case that such mythologies are ". . . . easily adapted by the powerful as a way of casting themselves as victims and justifying their polemical and vitriolic attacks on others." (9) As with the Bible, the accounts were ". . . . written long after the time in which these people supposedly lived, by authors who were preserving folklore, not facts." (18, 124.)
—E.g.: David Limbaugh [brother of Rush], *Persecution: How Liberals Are Waging A War Against Christianity*, Wash. D.C.: Regnery, 2003.

[105] Clifford Geertz, *Islam Observed: Religious Development in Morocco and Indonesia*, New Haven: Yale University Press, 1968, 30.

The internal contemplations of Kalidjaga represent then a humbling search for direction and answers, this well-born wanderer turned highwayman turned spiritual seeker waiting "by the side of the river for years," exhibiting an heroic patience, an affecting projection outward of an all-transforming inner grace. Lyusi, by contrast, sought the transformation of an insurgent culture by force of personality and behavior, drinking foul, infectious water rung from a diseased nightshirt in a virtuosic performance, bending the intentions of others to his will. The one became lost in thought; the other, lost in action.[106] These two legendary figures loom as mythological evocations of their cultures' respective apprehensions of an encroaching modern world; two different—but in a sense ultimately synchronized—responses to the perception of an external cultural malaise or danger:

> . . . the scripturalist response to the challenge posed by the secularization of thought have been differently represented in our two societies. Both are present in both. But Indonesia [Kalidjaga], with her ingrained inclination to try to absorb all styles of thought into one broad, syncretic stream, has been naturally more receptive to the argument that Islamic doctrine and scientific discovery are really not conflicting but complementary forms of belief; while Morocco [Lyusi], with her as deeply ingrained inclination toward religious perfectionism and moral rigor, has been more receptive to the attempt to isolate a purified Islamic faith from contamination with everyday life.[107]

The cultural chasm dividing these two worldviews is spanned by an ideological bridge or continuum running from the cooler contemplation of spiritual universalism on one side to the more incendiary eruptions of social separatism and Puritanism on the other. All manner of religious groups and cultures fall into the cracks and fissures lacing the expanse between these ideological extremes; all may be understood and analyzed in terms of the systematic relationship they assume with one another along this continuum of religious intensity.[108] We observe then a dynamism (with all its attendant

---

[106] This is similar in many respects to Weber's distinction between "exemplary" and "emissary" prophecy. ("The Social Psychology of the World Religions," in C. Wright Mills & H. H. Gerth eds., *From Max Weber: Essays in Sociology*, New York: Oxford University Press, 1946, 285.)

[107] Geertz, *Islam Observed* . . . , 106.

[108] Consider Peter Berger's characterization of Asian forms of religiosity:

> It's very syncretistic. People see no problem going to a Shinto shrine on certain seasons of the year, being married in a Christian-like ceremony, and being buried by a Buddhist monk. This eclecticism is not just apparent in Japan—it's in all of East Asia; China is similar in that respect. It's very

features) which although present and embodied to some degree in all religious practitioners and groupings assumes a form, expression, and intensity particular to each.

In one sense the recognition and appreciation of this generality or universalism is what I have in mind by a "deeper" level of cultural analysis (although the reader should not immediately infer an implicit evaluation of "better" or more "profound"). Both the historical *and* contemporary phenomena most central to the explanation of the thought and behavior of the Seattle Pacific community I studied and American evangelicalism at large fall along a continuum that bears a striking resemblance to these traditional kinds of dynamic relationships between the sacred and profane.[109] I will devote the bulk of this study to the description and elaboration of the systematic nature and content of this particular cultural idiom.

The Moral Market

At a second, lower, more national level of generalization, we encounter the cultural logic of "moral market"[110] thinking, a social sensibility which represents to my mind an uniquely American phenomenon. Although there are certainly European precedents—elements in Weber's *The Protestant Ethic and the Spirit of Capitalism* leap immediately to mind—there remains something so indigenously American in our propensity for making individual prowess in the economic marketplace (or conversely, the absence thereof) an ultimate litmus test or barometer in the personal evaluation of character to

---

different from Western notions, which probably come from monotheism. You either believe or you don't believe. There's a Japanese philosopher. . . Nakamura who wrote a book. I've forgotten everything about it except one sentence . . . in which he says that the West has been responsible for two basic mistakes. One is monotheism—there's only one God—and the other is Aristotle's principle of contradiction—something is either A or non-A. Well, those are *deep-seated cultural habits of mind*, and they make both religion and secularity where it exists take on a very different form. (As quoted in Charles T. Mathewes. . . , 154.) {emphasis added}

[109] This kind of cultural declensionism extends far beyond commonly understood sacred and profane distinctions. See Marshall Sahlins, *Culture and Practical Reason*. . . . and his Sandwich Islands history co-author, Patrick Vinton Kirch's, "When Hawaii Was Ruled by Shark-Like Gods," *The New York Review of Books*, 12/3/2015, wherein he writes that "The Hawaiian system of *kapu* had evolved beyond elsewhere in Polynesia, pervading all aspects of daily life. Pigs, certain kinds of red fish (red was the sacred color), and bananas were *kapu* to women; indeed, the food of men and women had to be cooked in separate houses. As Moore writes, 'time itself could be placed under a *kapu*,' with nine days out of each lunar month consecrated to particular deities."

[110] Again, the expression comes from Garry Wills, *Nixon Agonistes*. . . , 1969.

warrant the claim that it has become over the course of our brief two hundred year national existence a fundamentally distinct cultural trait.

Now while most evangelicals embrace the assumptions and anticipate the social and political consequences of this logic with an élan appreciably greater than that found among any other stratum in American society, by no means am I suggesting that moral market thinking evolved or emerged from within the mental precincts of American evangelicalism alone or that it harbors its only vigorous contemporary advocates. Rather, this conception reveals an exceedingly complex lineage that I am at present unable to fully unravel, one which blends European and American elements—from colonial Puritanism through Emersonian Transcendentalism to Carnegian/(Horatio) Algerian capitalism—into an exceedingly bracing concoction, full draughts of which only Americans seem able to down with much relish.[111] What evangelicalism has contributed (among other things) is a particular formulation of, or twist upon, this moral market ethos, accentuating the attendant anxieties and phobias of a social vision that most Americans have come to embrace, however subliminally. As we saw earlier, these anxieties surface most readily as a tension between the *process* of the production and accumulation of one major source of individual moral value (work in the marketplace) and the *results* of this work (affluence or wealth). Evangelicals have traditionally extolled the virtues of personal industry in the marketplace (and even more vehemently execrated its absence) and yet wrung their hands in despairing anticipation of its often lamentable spiritual consequences.[112]

---

[111] Like earlier occultisms drawn from Europe and Africa that the Puritans rooted out, as Jon Butler has documented, the emerging moral market ethos also sought to elbow traditional sensibilities aside:

> George Washington's successful eviction of squatters from his land west of the 'Apalacheon Mountains' between 1785 and 1795 was a struggle between two competing systems of land use. Washington treated land as an investment, while the 'common folk' saw the backwoods as commons. (Nancy Isenberg, "Left Behind," *The New York Review of Books*, 6/28/18, 18.)

[112] Recall the career of Henry Ward Beecher (1813-1887), "widely considered the best preacher of the age and was a front-runner for chief patriot":

> . . . .Beecher's message [in the midst of the "Gilded-Age"] was aimed at relieving the anxieties of his affluent Brooklyn suburbanite audience, who sensed a conflict between their new wealth and the stern Puritan morality in which they had been raised. Beecher, like all the popular preachers of the era, preached a gospel of virtuous wealth as a commendable moral example to the poor. (George M. Marsden, *Fundamentalism and American Culture: The Shaping of Twentieth-Century Evangelicalism, 1870-1925*, New York: Oxford University Press, 1980, 22-23.)

Phrased in this simple, preliminary manner, the above assertion invariably elicits the observation that these are scarcely original phenomena, that Weber dealt with similar issues in the aforementioned *Protestant Ethic,* that comparable anxieties vexed both old English and New England Puritans and theologians,[113] and that even Benjamin Franklin wrestled with the moral dilemma of the accumulation of wealth; in short, that the above represents nothing new under the sun, is but a mere gloss or variation upon some old and familiar themes. In anticipation of this understandable response, allow me to pause for a moment to defend my presumption of some sort of contemporary 19th- and 20th-century American difference.

---

[113] As Jackson Lears writes:

> American ambivalence toward material progress dated from the earliest Puritan times. Puritan divines urged diligence and frugality, then fretted over the prosperity resulting from those habits. Wealth was a sign of God's blessing but also an agent of corruption. Economic success contained the seeds of moral failure. As the historian Edmund Morgan has observed, "it was [the Puritans'] lot to be forever improving the world, in full knowledge that every improvement would in the end prove illusory."
> Morgan has shown the vitality of the Puritan ethic in the Revolutionary era, when republican ideologues had begun to enjoin diligence and frugality for political as well as religious reasons. English Whigs had taught their American counterparts that every republic had been destroyed by success. Whig historiography established a common pattern: the flourishing of trading centers inevitably bred an irresponsible leisure class and a vicious urban mob; the martial virtues declined among the elite, which soon established a hireling standing army; finally, demagogues led the populace on a chaotic crusade against their erstwhile leaders. (*No Place of Grace* . . . , 26-27.)

Unfortunately this look back proves to be the sole extent of Lears's recognition of the role evangelicalism has played in all these social and cultural developments. Even more recently he appears oblivious to the deeper cultural currents I have identified, returning again and again to the singular focus of "vitalism" in intellectual and leadership circles of the Progressive era as explanations of where we are now as a number-crunching, data-driven marketing society. Given all that we have experienced in the age of Trump, how odd—yet predictable—that his latest piece in *The Hedgehog Review* peters out thusly: " 'To understand God's thoughts,' she said, 'we must study statistics, for these are the measure of His purpose.' [Florence] Nightingale wrote at a time when Providence and Progress moved forward hand and glove; some people think they still do. But if we were to replace Nightingale's God with the money god of capital, *we would have a better sense of where we are today.*" [Summer, 2020] {emphasis added} As though religion and capitalism are not still familiar bed partners. To extend the metaphor, Lears, having made his thematic bed a certain way all these years, can't seem to become more than a one-trick bed-maker.
—"The social order, fixed by God, kept coming unfixed. Puritan piety exalted hard work; Puritan preaching excoriated the inevitable results—rising and falling saints." (Morone, *Hellfire Nation.* . . , 43.)

The Max Weber Calvinism thesis invoked success in a God-ordained "calling" and any resulting accumulation of wealth as a sign of redemption, the diligent Protestant seizing upon economic largesse as an indication of prior spiritual selection, he the unwitting beneficiary of any number of the gratuitous dispensations of God. Although in rigid Calvinistic terms there was nothing the ardent capitalist could do in the terrestrial arena to advance his own cause, he could nonetheless locate in the lucrative consequences of entrepreneurial endeavor some assurance of grace; similarly (and usually overlooked) for the lowly employee or factory worker, whose diligence, skills, and workmanship might prove equally demonstrative of spiritual selection and remuneration.[114] Hence to the more immediate material rewards encouraging daily toil, thrift, savings, and investment (and the probable enhancement of "social self-esteem," which paid both emotional and material dividends[115]) could be added the longer-term inducement of an eternity in

---

[114] "The power of religious asceticism provided him [the bourgeois businessman] in addition with sober, conscientious, and unusually industrious workmen, who clung to their work as to a life purpose willed by God. . . .

Now naturally the whole ascetic literature of almost all denominations *is saturated with the idea that faithful labour, even at low wages, on the part of those whom life offers no other opportunities, is highly pleasing to God.* . . . The treatment of labour as a calling became as characteristic of the modern worker as the corresponding attitude toward acquisition of the business man." (*The Protestant Ethic and the Spirit of Capitalism,* New York: Charles Scribner's Sons, 1958, 177-79.) {emphasis added}

[115] The notion of an individual interest in accruing "social self-esteem" as another motivation for entrepreneurial activity was appended to the original thesis in his "supplementary" essay, "The Protestant Sects and the Spirit of Capitalism" (Gerth & Mills eds., *From Max Weber . . . ,* 321):

> The Puritan sects put the most powerful individual interest of social self-esteem in the service of this breeding of traits. Hence *individual* motives and personal self-interests were also placed in the service of maintaining and propagating the "bourgeois" Puritan ethic. . . .
> To repeat, it is not the ethical *doctrine* of a religion but that form of ethical conduct upon which *premiums* are placed that matters. . . . a certain methodical, rational way of life. . . . The premiums were placed upon [1] "proving" oneself before God in the sense of attaining salvation—which is found in *all* Puritan denominations—and [2] "proving" oneself before men in the sense of socially holding one's own within the Puritan sects. Both aspects were mutually supplementary and operated in the same direction: they helped deliver the "spirit" of modern capitalism, its specific *ethos* . . . . {emphases in original}

Weber regarded the more individualistic American "self-made man" ethos the "old tradition," one rapidly disappearing, replaced by these more social, "Europeanized" (and I would add, Veblenesque) motivations for a vocational asceticism.

paradise. The entrepreneur, and to some extent even the plebian laborer, were thus doubly and trebly motivated to activity and prosperity.

Now, I will not dwell upon the inadequacies of the original Weber thesis, passing over the characterization of Calvinism and numerous other problems which others have examined at great lengths.[116] The evangelical moral market vision of work and wealth has evolved in an altogether different direction. Here in the American social arena the cultivation, demonstration, and assessment of *character*[117] and the promulgation of *invidious distinctions* supplant the Weberian quest for an assurance or "proof" of *redemption* and *grace* (although Weber's additional motivational element of an individual interest in enhanced "social self-esteem"—a truism of nearly any social grouping in any culture—is surely present in both.) For to cite the most obvious difference: virtually every evangelical assumes that redemption is available to anyone, at any time, simply for the asking. By contrast, the issues of character and anxieties about indolence and wealth (in the Weberian scheme) represented mere collateral concerns, secondary to the discernment or demonstration of a pre-determined salvation, if they were raised at all.[118]

---

[116] A concise, convincing early discussion of the question—consistent with the interaction model of social and cultural dynamics I employ throughout this study—can be found in Herbert Butterfield, "Christianity in History," in Philip P. Wiener, ed., *Dictionary of the History of Ideas, Vol. 1* (New York: Scribners, 1973), 396-97.
—Garry Wills illuminates the fundamental tension and complexity of the original concept that perplexed, if not tortured, antinomian believers from Anne Hutchinson on: "Since God's saving grace cannot be merited in Calvinist theology, all the soul can do is *prepare* itself for grace by lamenting its own insufficiency. . . . the only way to become a saint is to proclaim oneself a sinner. Thus, in an America that has retained its sense of being chosen and historically blessed, there has always been a tendency to stress each generation's personal unworthiness for the inscrutable blessings God has showered on the country." (*Under God. . .* , 69.) Hence how truly un-Calvinistic is the moral market conception.

[117] As William G. McLoughlin writes of the late nineteenth century version: "To evangelical believers in the Protestant ethic, the poor were poor because they had some flaw of character that conversion would quickly remove: 'It is a wonderful fact,' Moody preached, 'that men and women saved by the blood of Jesus rarely remain the subjects of charity, but rise at once to comfort and respectability.'. . . The way to end poverty and crime was to convert men to the principles of the Protestant ethic. . . ." (*Revivals, Awakenings, and Reform: An Essay on Religion and Social Change in America, 1607-1977*, University of Chicago Press, 1978, 144, 49.)
—To this complicating angst, Alexis de Tocqueville was largely oblivious, concluding more simply that "It is often difficult to ascertain from their [American preachers] discourse whether the principal object of religion is to procure eternal felicity in the other-world or prosperity in this." (Quoted in Mansfield, *Choosing Donald Trump. . .* , 80.)

[118] Jimmy Swaggart, for example, occasionally acknowledges (with characteristic paralipsis: "and there's no way I can say this without it appearing that I am boasting, and I assure you I am not") that although no one has brought more souls to Christ on the face of this earth than he, the sum total of his conversions—his work for God—confers not the slightest spiritual

As alluded to above, performance (and with especial virulence—non-performance) in the American marketplace becomes a premier litmus test of character. Now we must appreciate that while the majority of American evangelicals thoroughly embrace the ethos and structure underpinning this implicit testing, they tend to put a characteristic spin upon the resulting moral market evaluations.[119] Perhaps among the more affluent individuals and congregations there linger a few nagging anxieties over the New Testament passages upon wealth and poverty mentioned above—the parable of the rich man having to pass through the eye of a needle to enter heaven (Matthew 19: 21-26), in particular, might prove disconcerting to some. Increasingly these burdens are balanced and lightened by rather more comforting theological inventions, such as the relatively recent emergence of "prosperity theology." This new creed, grounded in a few isolated bits of scripture, assumes a celestial sanction for the accumulation of wealth, one issuing from a God who "wants you to prosper."[120]

On the surface at least, prosperity theology appears riddled with hypocrisy, serving as a hastily fabricated, retroactive theological rationalization for profligacy and greed; or, better yet, evidence of an encroaching "worldliness," as though if one were to scratch a "worldly" evangelical too forcefully the surface luster of holiness would come off to reveal a poseur with motivations and values no different from any materialistic non-Christian; only the hypocrisy is more pronounced. And so the television and print media seize

---

advantage in seeking redemption and grace. It is faith in the cleansing blood of Jesus alone—the singular petition for and acceptance of grace in a conversion experience—which ensures a sinner's salvation. (1986 television broadcast from the dais of his Family Worship Center church.)

[119] Variations upon this theme can be found operating more recently in what is known as "the house church movement" and/or "emerging evangelicalism," wherein social activism in small churches—and even large megachurches—has "emerged" (I guess) in response to the conservatism of the Religious Right. Yet in spite of more New Testament-flavored "social gospel"-like "outreach" moral market sensibilities still flourish. "Apostolic nostalgia" butts heads with "nationalistic nostalgia." The former invokes "rich social relations, such as those based on mutuality, which characterized the early Christian church"; the latter "sought accountability without the reciprocity of ongoing relationships, and when they didn't observe the accountability they expected, their commitment to engagement weakened. . . . based on an idealized American past characterized by independence, responsibility, and hard work." (Brian Steensland, op. cit., 387.) Now whereas Jonathan Haidt, op. cit., would characterize this ethos of "accountability" as a genetically passed-along moral "intuition," one among four others comprising his larger "Moral Foundations Theory," clearly this reluctance to excuse (let alone embrace) those down on their luck is grounded in a moral market cultural calculus or idiom, not any sort of inherited predisposition that enhances the survival prospects of the group.

[120] All told, it is my impression that *both* the imperative for hard work and the anxieties over its rewards have in more recent times diminished in intensity.

upon this discrepancy between the evangelical's public rejection of the world and his own private consumption of its pleasures and accumulation of its artifacts and, understandably, level the charge of "hypocrisy." Similarly in an academic context: American sociologists and scholars cite the more notorious abuses and scandals and other more general public opinion samples of the "liberalization" of attitudes among evangelicals as evidence of "accommodation."[121] *They* are becoming more like *us*. More egregiously: they appear to preach one thing and then do another. Following the delivery of impassioned pleas for the starving children of the world on the air, these American apostles slink away into chauffeured limousines or disappear into private leer jets, whisked home to mansions with innumerable bathrooms furnished with an array of gilded faucets and other garish baubles. The apparent discrepancy is explained as dishonesty or deceit of one form or another. Either they are lying to themselves or they are lying to us; or they simply are deluded beyond all measure of reason. Fair enough, but there is a coherent logic in operation here that has been largely overlooked. Consider just one example.

The occasion is a gathering (in 1983) of some of the most prominent charismatic and Pentecostal preachers and televangelists in the country. They convene in a large auditorium somewhere in Southern California, doing so under the auspices and sponsorship of TBN, the "Trinity Broadcasting Network," a local Christian television organization that under the direction of Paul Crouch has grown into the largest of its kind in the nation, if not the world. Nearly all the big names are here. On this particular evening, Jim Bakker is speaking to a packed auditorium. Viewers accustomed to the usually demure manner and charming banter of the *PTL (Praise The Lord) Club* television talk show host may be surprised by his aggressive verbal thrusts. He is clearly ticked off about something and is letting everyone know about it. Perhaps it was an article appearing a few weeks earlier in *Newsweek*, one revealing that at the very moment Jim and Tammy Bakker were airing a desperate, tear-jerking appeal for contributions to keep their *PTL Club* ministry on the air, the two claiming that they had given all that they owned for the show—"We've given near everything we have," Tammy wailed—the Bakkers were acquiring a $449,000 second home in Palm Springs for a "spiritual retreat."[122] And so at the present gathering Jim Bakker is feeling persecuted (and this was nearly a year before the Jessica Hahn sex revelations, which would eventually sink him), and although he makes no reference to the insinuations of impropriety that had surfaced in *Newsweek* and were first

---

[121] As cited in chapter one, see Hunter 1983, 1987; Wuthnow 1988; Bellah 1970.

[122] *Seattle Times*, 6 October 1984.

investigated by a local *Charlotte Observer* reporter, clearly these weigh heavily on his mind. He tells of his displeasure with a rampaging "judgmentalism," asking why we always have to be "against somebody or something?" Why can't we be "for something?" Surveying the national evangelical landscape, he discerns a petty litigiousness loose among the brethren; there are "spiritual groupies" out there along the spiritual highways and byways of America, women who migrate from preacher or televangelist to televangelist and who are never satisfied by what they find, always spreading gossip and rumors about the spiritual inadequacies of whomever they are shadowing at the moment. He is sick to death of it! Clearly, the flap over money and wealth in the ministries is eating away at him. Avoiding direct mention of his own problems, he launches into a defense of the apparent wealth and prosperity of the more successful televangelists, gesturing to Oral Roberts, who sits beside other evangelical notables on the stage, complaining of his treatment both within and without the evangelical community. He jabs the air with an index finger: "You think it's easy to create and run a successful ministry? You try it sometime! You try it and see if God blesses your ministry!"

In these few words Jim Bakker collapses the entire moral market universe of the prosperous modern evangelical onto the head of a pin. So *you* think just about anybody can be a televangelist, huh? That whoever rises to the top does so through naked ambition and greed, unrelated to virtue or the will of God? Perhaps we shouldn't be surprised to learn here that money, or the sum total of contributions attracted by a ministry, represents more than a mere material windfall; indeed, it becomes the measure of the evangelist's spiritual worth to God; it is the moral market barometer of his performance. Those who fail to raise the monies are judged unworthy or (un)"blessed" by God's favor and grace; they are clearly deficient in the qualities God seeks to promote and reward. For how can one criticize the continual accumulation of monies as unethical or un-Christian when such accumulation provides a clear demonstration of God's continuing favor? Indeed if God deemed the ministry at odds with His will and intention, if He disapproved of what Jim and Tammy did with the money, well then, quite simply, the moral market blessings spigot, controlled by God alone, would be turned off; the flow of money would reduce to a trickle and then dry up altogether. But does the money stop? My God, no! We're rolling in it. We still enjoy the blessing of God. Secular media accuse us of this and that indiscretion and yet the blessings of God continue flowing our way. Hence a *spiritual moral market evaluation* confirms the integrity and value of the Bakker ministry. Appreciate the logical force of the Bakker message: how dare the carping critics apply and judge us by the pedestrian morality of the pagan world when we submit ourselves daily to an even higher standard and measure of conduct. Such is the fusion of piety and wealth, the wedding of moral and spiritual market calculi.

These are precisely the standards the Oklahoman, Oral Roberts, invoked when he threatened that God just might "call me home" upon any failure to meet a certain fundraising goal and deadline. God was applying a spiritual market yardstick to his ministry. Raise the monies and affirm your value to the Lord, or leave the spiritual market arena to those more able and willing, to those more "blessed." However subterranean the motives, Roberts perhaps guilty here of extorting a spiritual market ransom in return for a postponed divine kidnapping, this particular melodramatic passion play nonetheless unfolded under the terms of a logic easily grasped by those within the Roberts community. To outsiders, this latest effusion, following on the heels of his 1979 claim of having spoken with a 900-foot-tall Jesus in the sands of Palms Springs (where else?),[123] was one more sign of advancing senility within evangelicalism. The guy had lost his marbles. Yet, insiders knew better. The Palms Springs Jesus had directed Roberts to raise monies for a medical center complex which immediately went belly-up financially for lack of demand; and there were other disappointments. The later fundraising episode was evidence of Roberts's growing desperation, that he had somehow or other misplaced the spiritual market mandate from heaven. He was struggling to rejuvenate his fundraising prowess. Send in money as a sign of his continuing value to God.[124]

Televangelists employ an expression, "seed faith," that conveys the moral market thrust of these new theologies. Viewers are asked to forward their dollars to an importunate ministry as a gesture of faith in the long-term solvency of the enterprise of Christ. This spiritual investment, this "seed faith," in the corporation of God will bring a return many times the sum of the original outlay. The pleas are usually sandwiched between videotaped accounts of believers who have received staggering returns—an increase of *ten-fold* the most exalted expectation—upon their initial investments, sometimes referred to as "love gifts." An unemployed couple sends in half of their final benefit check to the station and *voila*, are offered jobs at double their former salaries. A struggling businessman declares 30% of his monthly

[123] *Newsweek*, 31 January 1983.

[124] More recently, Jerry Falwell Jr. used the same moral market standard in appraising the candidacy of Donald Trump. "He took Trump's business success as a sign that the candidate was in tune with the needs of American Christians, a sentiment shared by many advocates of the prosperity gospel who offered Trump their support. Mark Burns, an African-American pastor, declared at a Trump rally, 'Jesus said, above all things, I pray that you prosper [not exactly]. . . . I think that is what Donald Trump represents.' " (Bowman, *Christian: The Politics. . .*, 225.)

profits for the ministry and *voila*, is awarded a contract quadrupling the net worth of his company. A senior citizen sacrifices a large portion of her social security check to the ministry and *voila*, wins the state lottery. One after another, the rewards for this form of spiritual industry are recounted. Viewers are presented a God who evaluates the ingenuity and worth of spiritual effort on his behalf and repays industrious believers many fold their original contributions.[125]

And what of "the world?" Does not a contamination of sorts occur here? Do we not observe an exploitation of urges and motivations all too *secular* in nature and origin? A veil of righteousness draped across a tableau of rank materialism? Deception and greed? Hypocrisy? While the indictment rings true at times, there is nonetheless a logic in operation here as genuine and coherent as anything we have encountered, or will encounter. For we must understand that while moral market evaluations of character in the larger American social and economic context hinge upon performance in the market arena, spiritual market assessments within the evangelical community are even more expansive, pivoting upon points of invidious (Christian/secular) distinction as well. *And so the diligent evangelist rationalizes his behavior with an additional logical distinction: there is good Christian money and there is bad secular money.* Judgment turns upon the motivations of the steward and the investor. Does the televangelist appeal for money in order to advance the kingdom of God—i.e., is his motivation "God-centered"—or is he driven by a purely "man-centered" material interest. Does the viewer remit her "seed faith" as a demonstration of commitment to the enterprise of God or does she do so in order to make some easy money. An invidious line of demarcation then separates the spiritual *Christian* investor from the material *secular* investor. The one is Christian, "God-centered"; the other secular, self- or "man-centered." And God knows the difference and rewards the petitioners accordingly. Invidiously distinguished by the terms of this calculus, prosperity, in and of itself, serves then to identify and confer genuine spiritual value and

---

[125] Upon his return to California from a year in Denmark, Phil Zuckerman recounts a hilarious conversation he overheard while standing in line at his bank, wherein the bank manager (in a very loud voice so everyone could hear) was counseling a client in his office who had fallen deeply into debt:

> You need to gather up your debt statements . . . and put them in an envelope. Then you need to take that envelope to my pastor. He is a real man of God, and he has a special power when it comes to removing debt. . . . he will pray over it and bless it and anoint it. Then you just need to give $50 a month to his ministry, and within a year, God will see to it that your debt is all gone. I promise you. He is powerful. I have given this advice to so many people and it works every time. (*Society Without God. . .* , 167.)

worth. The evangelical Christian embraces a consecrated materialism *in, but not of, the world.*

Of course, motivation rarely assumes so one-dimensional and undiluted a form. Surely the average evangelical harbors within himself a jumble of often conflicting urges; surely an element of "man-centered" aggrandizement enters into any transaction of this sort, however transcendent the embroidering rhetoric. This is undeniable, but any practical evaluation of the sincerity of this form of belief proves a formidable undertaking and is perhaps in any event not all that important for our purposes.[126] For surely a historical and cultural phenomenon of the range and resilience of evangelicalism cannot survive—let alone thrive—upon hypocrisy and deceit alone. (Although the same cannot be said of some organizations and governments which speak with one voice.) Those who survey the values, beliefs, and conduct of contemporary evangelicals and find everywhere the evidence of "hypocrisy" or "accommodation" or vestiges of European "ethics" had better look again. The employment of a particular logic of invidious distinction in the moral market contexts above is but part of a larger cultural pattern. Values and behaviors that appear on first glance to mirror those of the larger American society nonetheless reveal upon closer examination a deeper logic or structure of discrimination. What may appear on the surface a "liberalization" in particular beliefs or behaviors—or, indeed, "contamination"—nonetheless adheres to the terms of an unrelenting calculus. What may appear, for example, to most observers an ordinary American shopping center or mall— the institution itself an icon of conspicuous mass American consumption and materialism—becomes transformed by a wave of the southern California evangelical developer's wand into a *Christian* shopping center, *Maranatha*

---

[126] But Lisa Keister raises any number of fascinating related issues that are worth mentioning. In a piece of work that even Weber would admire, she taps into an extraordinary data set to explore the relationship between four categories of religion in America and wealth accumulation. Among the factors that she argues discourages wealth accumulation among "conservative Protestants" are some largely culturally invidious distinctions concerning family size ("fertility" rates), educational attainment, investment and inheritance strategies, and social contacts, among others. Key to these differences are of course the evangelical logic disparaging certain aspects of "the world," this resulting, for example, in attitudes ". . . . overtly hostile toward secular education." Or, more generally: ". . . . the frequent recourse to prayer and trust in God among conservative Protestants may reduce their inclination to invest." (as seen in the preceding footnote.) So that a host of social and cultural factors place evangelical (and other "conservative Protestants") Christians far below Jews, mainline Protestants, and Catholics in wealth accumulation comparisons. Hence the irony of internally contradictory invidious distinctions, as we will see. ("Religion and Wealth: The Role of Religious Affiliation and Participation in Early Adult Asset Accumulation," *Social Forces*, Vol. 82, No, 1, September 2003, 177-78.)

Village, replete with a Christian board of directors, Christian supermarkets, and Christian boutiques; all for an avowedly Christian purpose.[127]

Accommodation? Liberalization? Or a *sacred* materialism?[128] *Our* distinct, *sacred* version of modern American consumerism, as opposed to *their* corrupt version; a *sacred Christian* worldliness, as oxymoronic as that might seem. Observe here an integrated economy of spiritual market motivations, behavior, and outcomes designed to advance the interests of God's chosen community; interests perceived, defined, and advanced in terms of what I refer to as a logic of invidious distinction, a dynamic serving to sacralize all things Christian and damn all things secular, no matter how interchangeable they may appear on the surface. For indeed, as someone once wrote, *opposites are those things alike in all ways except one.*[129]

These kinds of spiritual transplantations occur over the length and breadth of the evangelical community landscape. A wholesale declension of persons, objects, and relationships in Christian and secular terms unfolds right under the noses of uninitiated onlookers. Over the years (but primarily since *Roe v. Wade* and the *ERA,* as these dynamics are triggered by changing apprehensions of cultural danger) evangelicals have developed a competing Christian equivalent (better yet: opposite) for nearly every secular phenomenon or institution. *They* have Disneyland, *we* have Heritage Park[130]. *They* have the Ivy League and the Big-Ten, *we* have the Christian College Coali-

---

[127] American academicians occasionally stumble upon these dynamics and treat them *descriptively,* failing to grasp the larger implications of a cultural pattern: "Though believers argue that Christian prosperity differs from worldly acquisitiveness, these Christians recognize that their message inscribes materiality with spiritual meaning. Inverting the well-worn American mantra that things must be seen to believed, their gospel rewards those who believe *in order to see* . . . As an [Christian] academic, writing in a scholarly world dominated by the upper-middle class, it is not unusual to see prosperity read pejoratively as indulgence or fetish instead of a humdrum part of everyday living . . . . when many people say 'prosperity,' they mean survival." The two tiny slivers of understanding here refer to what I call the *sacralization* or *complete reversal* of secular phenomenon. (Kate Bowler, *Blessed: A History of the American Prosperity Gospel,* Oxford University Press, 2013, 8.) {emphasis in original}

[128] This more general *cultural* process is by no means unique to American evangelicalism. As Marshall Sahlins writes of initial Hawaiian encounters with foreign capitalisms: ". . . . Western goods and even persons have been incorporated as indigenous powers . . . assimilated to indigenous ideas of social 'valuables' or sacred kinds. . . . It is cultural self-realization on a material scale. . . ." ("Cosmologies of Capitalism: The Trans-Pacific Sector of 'The World System'," Radcliffe-Brown Lecture in Social Anthropology, *Proceedings of the British Academy,* LXXIV, 1988, 73, 7.)

[129] As George Marsden writes of American fundamentalism: "Dispensationalism itself was strikingly ant-modernist. In many respects it looked like the *mirror image* of modernism." (*Understanding Fundamentalism and Evangelicalism,* Grand Rapids, Michigan: Eerdmanns, 1991, 41.)

[130] Which, prior to the Bakker scandals in the 1980s, "had become the nation's third most visited attraction." (Kate Bowler, op. cit., 77.)

tion (changed to the Coalition for Christian Colleges and Universities in 1995), the Christian College Consortium (1971), and the Council for Christian Colleges and Universities (1976).[131] *They* have the Mall of America, *we* have Maranatha Village. *They* have Barbie and Ken, *we* have Grace, the Pro-Life doll who sings "Jesus Loves The Little Children." *They* have the Columbia Record and Tape Club, *we* have The Word Family Record and Tape Club ("Any 4 *Christian* cassettes or compact discs for only $1 each"; including Carman's "The Resurrection Rap"). *They* have *The New York Review of Books*, *we* have *Books & Culture: A Christian Review*. *They* have Metallica (a "hard-metal" rock band), *we* have Stryper. *They* have Halloween haunted houses, *we* have Nashville's Judgment House. *They* had Liberace, *we* have Dino. *They* have Great Expectations (a video dating service), *we* have Equally Yoked. *They* have ABC/NBC/PBS, etc., *we* have TBN/CBN/Hillsong Channel. Indeed, profane simulations dot the TBN (Trinity Broadcasting Network) schedule: instead of "secular" television's long-running *Dating Game*, we find *Maker's Match*; instead of the secular daytime soap opera *Another World*, we have *Another Life*. Keeping abreast of new technologies, TBN even boasts its own web site on the Internet.[132]

Idle cash on hand? Two mutual fund options are William Van Alan, Jr.'s *Noah Fund* (started 1996), and Arthur Ally's *Timothy Plan* (1994), with $19 million in assets.[133]

---

[131] Alan Wolfe, "The Opening of the Evangelical Mind," *The Atlantic*, October 2000.

—To break this category down even further: ". . . within the last ten or fifteen years Christian psychologists and historians and literary scholars and philosophers and visual artists have all founded their own organizations and established their own journals. . . . all of this would have been inconceivable before the Second World War. . . . clear evidence that we are now in a different stage." (Nicholas Wolterstorff, "The Mission of the Christian College at the end of the 20th Century," *Faculty Dialogue*, no. 1 [Fall 1984], 43.)

[132] Observe the monumentally successful *Left Behind* apocalyptic adventure novels series (now 12 in all), conceived by the evangelical televangelist warhorse Timothy LaHaye and written by Jerry Jenkins, which has sold 50 million copies. With respect to Christian mobilization to the Antichrist in the form of the "The Tribulation Force," "We see then a 'new' Christian emerging in this fiction. No longer ostracized, alienated, and old fashioned, the new Christian is wealthy, technologically savvy, and exerts a powerful cultural influence." Whereas "The Christian heroes of. . . earlier [rapture fiction] are a small and embattled minority. Christians are depicted as simple, often rural people who do not function well in the modern world." Not so now with their own Christian prototypes playing off secular opposites. (Amy Johnson Frykholm, *Rapture Culture: Left Behind in Evangelical America*, Oxford University Press 2004, 34-36.)

[133] See Jacob Heilbrunn, "Moral Capital: The prophets of Biblical investing," *The New Republic*, 10/6/97, 20-21.

Sacred/profane declensions are the current rage within evangelicalism.[134] Travelers passing through Miami's airport may even encounter the planes of a local Florida company calling itself *The Lord's Airline*. Heritage Park hosted a "Conference of Christian hairdressers."[135] Perhaps this is what one member of a Christian rock band had in mind during an appearance on a Christian talk show (also produced in Florida and broadcast nationally by TBN) by the flip observation and prediction that "You know, pretty soon we're going to be pumping Christian gas at Christian gas stations into Christian cars."[136] Perhaps the smart money's on sooner than later?

---

[134] The only other journalist or academician to come even remotely close to an understanding and account of this phenomenon within evangelicalism is Chris Hedges in *American Fascists: The Christian Right and the War on America* (Free Press 2006). See his discussions of "logocide," or their deadly use of opposites, and the overall authoritarian conception of "dominionism." Re: ". . . . the Christian Right and radical Islamists, although locked in a holy war, increasingly mirror each other." {in virtually all ways except one, of course.} (10-14, 24); and the ". . . . gradual establishment of new standards for very aspect of life . . . . Families and friends are divided into groups of 'saved' and 'unsaved.' " (55)

[135] Fitzgerald, 77.

[136] Joey Taylor, southern California avant-garde rock musician, on Bob Hoskin's *Feedback*. No doubt his band went on to perform later in that decade in "the Alive Festival. . . . the Christian equivalent of Woodstock." (Hanna Rosin, op. cit., 32.)

—Out in the marketplace, sacralized hybrids continue to proliferate: a Christian mutual fund ("The Timothy Plan"), "Christian Shoppers card-a-log" (bulk-mailed Christian product and service company cards), a Christian Chocolate factory (California), *Shirley and _____ Christian Tour Co.* (operating out of North Carolina, with the *T* enlarged and elevated on the side of the bus to suggest the Calvary cross), Christian comics (esp. the Charles Colson ones), and *Lifeline*, a Christian long distance phone company. Instead of the *Nike* sports cap, "Fear not," evangelical merchandizers counter with a "Fear God" alternative. Pat Robertson's spin-off enterprise, KaloVita, The Good Life Company, hawks vitamins and "Sea of Galilee" face creams and mud masks. Closer to *my* home: a Christian Karate Association (CKA) and independent landscape workers who advertise their services in the neighborhood commercial paper as "Christian Gardeners."

—More recently, academician Richard G. Kyle does well to recognize and describe a few of these Christian/secular declensions, but fails to understand that they do not issue forth out of acculturation, or evangelicals becoming more mainstream, unable to ". . . . tell the difference between the two", but from a cultural dynamic of distinction, a turning out of inferior sacralized evangelical versions of secular originals that pack an ideological message of Christian/secular difference. E.g., "During the 1970s, the lines between contemporary Christian and secular music became indistinct." (*Popular Evangelicalism in American Culture*, London: Routlege, 2018, 177.); yet here is a Patrick Henry University student reflecting on ". . . . contemporary Christian artists such as Steven Curtis Chapman and Mercy Me. . . . 'yes,' Derek added, 'the gospel message is clear. Unlike some secular songs, which leave you with an empty feeling.' " (Hanna Rosin, op. cit., 15.)

—Susan Harding's own list and account of these kinds of sacralizations only slightly misses the mark: "There were conservative Christian bookstores, novels, comics, concerts, movies, singers (rock 'n' roll, heavy metal, and rap, as well as gospel), actors, sport stars, coaches, psychologists, and public intellectuals. Many towns had a Christian Yellow Pages so that Bible-believers could find like-minded plumbers, car salesmen, veterinarians, and dentists. . . .

And in arguably the greatest stretch of all: "Upon opening in 2017, Museum of the Bible will become the Christian Smithsonian."[137]

These parasitical simulations often pop up where least expected, as Jeff Sharlet reported in *The Family*, his account of a secretive Christian political organization operating out of the now notorious Ivanwald mansion in a D.C. suburb: "More recently, [United States] Senator Sam Brownback told me that the privacy of Family cells makes them *safe places* for men of power—an appropriation of another term borrowed from an enemy, feminism."[138] The dynamic properties of such declensionism become even more apparent and crucial, again, in the almost exponentially ideologically-charged application of *complete reversals*, wherein the pivotal qualitative distinction disappears altogether. What Sharlet calls the "the bait-and-switch exegesis of American fundamentalism" goes so far as to obliterate even the acknowledgement of any glimmer of difference between sheer opposites. "Hate equals love; obedience is freedom. . . . The Family believes it values the 'least of these,' the poor; which is why it [the poor] must serve the powerful, those blessed by God with the authority to dole out aid to the deserving . . . . We've reached the point where piety and corruption aren't at odds but are one and the same." At times then we can even jettison "in all ways except one" as too constraining.

The general pattern here is of a kind of creeping up on phenomena ostensibly secular and rendering them either sacralized or replicated, as Garry Wills observes:

> . . . . [for] the religious Right, the flag is *not* a secular symbol. That was guaranteed for them, during Dwight Eisenhower's presidency, when 'under God' (Lincoln's phrase from the Gettysburg address) was added to the Pledge of Allegiance. In fact, in independent Christian schools a Christian Pledge of Allegiance is recited that reveals the full impact of the two words that matter most to these believers in

---

Whether explicitly or implicitly, born-again Christians were being aggressively trained in techniques of interpreting and remaking the modern religious and secular worlds from a Christian point of view. The cultural walls of separation were torn down but not destroyed in the 1980s. They were miniaturized, multiplied, and internalized." Well, sort of, as we will see. (*The Book of Jerry Falwell: Fundamentalist Language and Politics*, Princeton University Press, 2001, 151-52.)

[137] Candida R. Moss . . . *Bible Nation*. . . , 61.

[138] *The Family: The Secret Fundamentalism at the Heart of American Power*, Harper Perennial 2009, 20, 63, 81, 89. And how typical that the origins of The Family trace to 1935 Seattle, where it begin "as a businessman's anti-labor alliance" under its eventual Washington D.C. founder, Abraham Vereide. (61)

the more generally recited pledge. This one begins: 'We pledge allegiance to the Christian flag, and to our Savior, for whom it stands . . . .' [139]

In fact one discovers an early trial run of such reversions in the Biblical juxta-positioning of the ancient fallen Eve and the resurgent Virgin Mary: "Traditionally in Christian writing [Justin Martyr, Tertullian, and Irenaeus], the Virgin is given as a new Eve, a woman whose *yes* in God's offer to participate in the salvation of humanity effectively *reverses* Eve's instigation of original sin."[140] {emphasis added}

The reader may have noticed a kind of collusion between the two ostensibly different kinds or levels of logics introduced above. My account of the televangelist's rationalization of his conduct draws upon both the moral market notion of fundraising as one major market indicator (the sheer number of conversions is another) or evaluator of spiritual character and prowess (a more culturally specific, national trait) *and* this invidious Christian/secular distinction of a higher "God-centered" purpose (a more general, "deeper," sacred/profane dynamic). The evangelist seeks money from viewers as a demonstration of the success and value of his ministry, a sign of God's approval, all the while putting distance between himself and any malingering "secular" connotations by casting his motives in purely other-directed, "sacred" transcendent terms. *Thus he joins the moral market logic of his aspirations with the invidious Christian/secular distinction of his aspersions.* Despite the apparent different levels of generalization and significance, the one nicely dovetails into the other. Both prove indispensable to any explanation of his conduct. Indeed in the cultural world I have inhabited and now describe there are no insular or independent logics; all mesh tightly with one another.[141] Such is a fundamental property of these dynamics.

---

[139] *Under God . . .* , 81. {emphasis in original}
—And as Michael L. Butterworth reports, even the national pastime, baseball, has undergone evangelical "re-branding," becoming another sacralized item on the ever-expanding lexicon of declensions. ("Saved at Home: Christian Branding and Faith Nights in the 'Church of Baseball'," *Quarterly Journal of Speech*, Vol. 97, No. 3, August 2011.)

[140] Elizabeth Bruenig, "Jesus, Mary, and Mary," *The New York Review of Books*, 11/21/2019. {second emphasis added}

[141] There is another sense in which interaction occurs. We tend to assume, for example, that the apparent commercialization of holidays—Christmas, in particular—has arrived at the modern end of a secularization process of sorts. Leigh Schmidt contends, however, that the historical interaction between the sacred and secular proves a good deal less linear and more complex than any simple secular trend model suggests. Rather, Christmas in the 18th and 19th American centuries was an exceedingly "secular," gustatory affair, becoming sacralized in the course of movement into the twentieth, refashioned into a more pious alternative to

Now this apparent linkage not only calls our attention to a cardinal feature of these kinds of cultural dynamics—their interpenetration and synchronization—it also suggests an approach to a nagging question: Why exactly do these moral market ideas resonate so deeply and strongly within evangelicalism? And why, by extension, have they come to exert so compelling a hold over the American moral imagination in general?

There are two contexts to consider here: the environmental and constitutional history of the nation *and* the internal structure and dynamics of evangelicalism itself. A very brief examination of the former suggests that the constitutionally created de-monopolization of religion (with the First Amendment to the Constitution in 1791) encouraged the larger social forms congenial to moral market dynamics and thought. For in banishing any general formal "establishment" of religion (and discouraging any government promotion of religion in general)[142] in the new nation Jefferson and Madison did more than simply promulgate religious toleration; they created the world's first genuine free market of religion. This de-regulation of religion effectively unleashed the energy and force of market dynamics in a manner the world had never seen before.[143] We shouldn't then be surprised to find that so many of the entrepreneurial tools, phenomena, and patterns of thought associated with economic markets began making an appearance in the new religious market arena.[144] Now although the 1787 Constitution and the subsequent Bill of Rights may have simply formalized and institutionalized a disintegration of the various colonial religious cartels already in process,[145] the document indubitably hastened these developments. Indeed the forty or so years following the ratification of the Establishment Clause saw the expansion of those Christian denominations—the Methodists and Baptists, in particular—whose spiritual and organizational ideas were more attuned to the new market conditions than the older colonial churches. Their

---

pagan market versions. (*Consumer Rites: The Buying and Selling of American Holidays*, Princeton University Press, 1995.)

[142] Leonard W. Levy, *The Establishment Clause*, New York: Macmillan, 1986.

[143] William Lee Miller, "The Seminarian Strain: Church and Statesmen in the Democratic Party," *The New Republic*, 9 July 1984, 19.

[144] A classic sarcastic treatment of which can be found in Thorstein Veblen's "Note to Chapter XI," in *Absentee Ownership and Business Enterprise in Recent Times: The Case of America* (Boston: Beacon Press, 1967). A special thanks to Professor J. S. Fuerst for this reference. See also Veblen's "Christian Morals and the Competitive System" (1910), reprinted in *Essays in Our Changing Order* (New York: Augustus M. Kelley, 1964). For more recent scholarly accounts, see R. Laurence Moore, *Selling God . . . .* (1994) and Frank Lambert, *"Pedlar in Divinity" George Whitefield and the Transatlantic Revivals, 1737-1770* (Princeton University Press, 1993).

[145] Butler, *Awash In A Sea of Faith . . .* , esp. chapters 7 and 9.

agents peddled spiritual wares in a manner similar to any merchant or itinerant vender; they competed in open air markets for the approval of their clientele and for the blessings of God; they measured themselves spiritually in terms of success in these ventures. (And the harsh, demanding environment, and the migrational, transient nature of the population, separated from traditional European family supports and culture, certainly increased their clients' receptivity to artificial evocations and substitutions for fading traditional sources of meaning and feeling.) In these crude beginnings of American denominationalism, in the creation of a free market of religion, can be found the cultural and historical origins and context of this evangelical affinity for moral market ideas. Economic and spiritual markets—with all their attendant ideas and dynamics—established some sort of elementary syncretic relation with one another.[146] But—and huge *but* it is—as we saw earlier, economic, rational actor models cannot simply be dropped down into or imposed upon this historical context as an explanation of the uniqueness of American evangelicalism. Disestablishmentarianism represents or provides a mere context, not a cause; such an explanation was advanced earlier.

Our concern becomes then, given their origins in respective emergent cultural sensibilities, what precisely do *moral* market and *spiritual* market dynamics have in common? Why might the one prove congenial to the other?

Quite simply, the nature and occasion of the evangelical spiritual experience parallels the kind of moral testing that Americans are thought to undergo in the economic market arena. Observe that the supplicant achieves

---

[146] As far as I can tell, Peter Berger was one of the first to recognize this link between economic and spiritual marketplace dynamics. See *The Sacred Canopy: Elements of a Sociological Theory of Religion* (New York: Anchor Books, 1969), 138.
—Lydea Bean has a slightly different take upon this affinity:

> . . . . Why is the U.S. evangelical tradition tied to laissez-faire economics? Most sociologists would answer the question by looking at the internal dynamics of the religion field itself: for example, looking for relationships between theology and economic individualism, or tracing how evangelicals have re-defined their subcultural boundaries over time. By contrast, I find that evangelical conservatism and evangelical identity became linked in the United States after two groups of organized elites recognized their shared interest in building a new partisan coalition. Starting in the 1940s businessmen who opposed the New Deal forged an alliance with theologically conservative Protestants. Together, these two groups built new institutions to socialize evangelicals as loyal 'conservatives' to fight big government and defend America's Christian identity. . . . linked laissez-faire economics to traditional morality. (Lydea Bean, *The Politics of Evangelical Identity: Local Churches and Partisan Divides in the United States and Canada*, Princeton University Press, 2014, 225.)

grace or salvation in a "personal relationship" with her God, generating by her own efforts a "born-again" conversion experience (in spite of evangelical claims that grace flows freely from God—is a gift), without benefit of ritual social supports to directly lift her from a fallen condition (as in Catholicism). Although not everyone undergoes the classic regeneration experience and there are certainly supports and pressures of a social nature present, clearly the supplicant performs with a measure of independence in a market atmosphere of sorts. Before, during, and after the proverbial conversion experience (and even, as is often the case, in lieu of it) he undergoes spiritual testing and monitoring, both in his own eyes and under the scrutiny of his family and community. He strives to produce evidence of spiritual achievement, what I will call "signals of difference." The quality and duration of his performance, he understands, will serve as the basis for ongoing evaluations of his spiritual character and worth. With these considerations in mind, perhaps the ease with which the modern televangelist grounds his own spiritual evaluation in the monetary performance of his ministry becomes more apparent. Both dimensions of his performance appear grounded in a moral market calculation of personal worth.

It is instructive that both the transmission of faith and the transmission of wealth to offspring pose the identical kind of evaluation problem. There is an almost immediate erosion of the moral *significance* of the original achievement, as though, in the case of the latter, the passing of wealth from one generation to another undermines the calculus of evaluation. Traditionally, Americans assume some kind of lineal relationship between ability, effort, achievement, and success in the marketplace. Market performance and the accumulation of its rewards are, by and large, deemed a reflection or outcome of character and diligence. The individual who places himself in the arena is thought to have undergone a moral examination of sorts. Our mythological American moral market Adam arrived with nothing but the shirt on his back and proceeded to make mountains out of molehills. He proved himself in the arena. Those who fall by the wayside are judged to be lacking the requisite moral market virtues; they become marginal characters in a moral market dramaturgy. And yet problems arise as each succeeding generation skews the original calculus of evaluation. Cain and Abel, offspring of our market Adam, merely inherit the firm. Upon what do we now base our judgment of their character? Even a five-fold increase in profits can scarcely retire the lingering doubts: could they have made it on their own? What sort of traits do they really possess? What might they have achieved if dropped into the shoes of the old man in that original economic jungle East of Eden? These moral market ideas form the basis of an enduring American ambivalence (and occasional expression of resentment) toward inherited wealth. Will the idle enjoyment of the fruits of our labors—the rewards for our industrial virtue—poison the wellsprings of that virtue? Will the transfer of wealth to offspring skew the moral market calculus?[147] An air of inauthenticity hangs over the succeeding generations of inherited privilege. The average American both reveres the process of testing in the marketplace and yet harbors suspicions of the potential impact the accumulation and transmission of its rewards—the suspension of moral testing—will have upon the formation of character among future generations. No wonder Donald Trump sought to minimize the attendant moral market aspersion by claiming that he had only inherited one million from his father rather than the actual enormous sum of four hundred million—a good deal of that transferred by illegitimate means. But why go to such lengths to conceal it? Although he lost virtually all of it through sheer incompetence and has declared innumerable bankruptcies still he clings to a veneer of moral market respectability by reformulating the calculus. Now virtue resides not in clear economic market success but in the new benchmark of *debt*, mountains of it in fact.[148] Debt rationalized away as the new moral market indicator of achievement, the more of it the better. And the greater the mounting pressures of debt, the continual postponing or rolling over of due dates, the greater the ripple effect, or the more likely the delinquent deal-making addict would be sent careening into the succoring arms of authoritarian plutocrats—the Putins, oligarchs, and crown princes of the world—all too willing to bail him out with laundered black market money, keeping him solvent through one rollover after another, artificially propped up, continual staying one looming financial execution after another, all of it ultimately coming due in the quid pro quo form of international political paybacks. For he who lives by the moral market dies by the moral market. And so kiss Russian sanctions, the Ukraine, Saudi journalists, and Yemenese children goodbye.

A similar ambivalence troubles the evangelical family.[149] The ideal conversion experience follows a prolonged period of wandering through the

---

[147] Scions of "old money" have felt a similar pressure to demonstrate virtue. "Ordeals" are sought—perhaps even orchestrated—and then celebrated as evidence of genuine intrinsic merit. See Nelson Aldrich, *Old Money: The Mythology of America's Upper Class* (New York: Knopf, 1988).

[148] " 'I'm the king of debt. I love debt.' Trump told CNN's Wolf Blitzer on Wednesday, seemingly trying to explain the comfort level he has with debt after a long business career that included four bankruptcy filings by his companies." (Matt Egan, "Donald Trump: 'I'm the king of debt,' " CNN Business, May 7, 2016.)

[149] The similarity between the two kinds of transmission problems first occurred to me while reviewing Randall Balmer's brief account of spiritual inheritance angst in his *Mine Eyes Have*

secular wastelands of America. From these peregrinations emerge the spiritual Horatio Algers of evangelical legend; their stories make for the most riveting, gut-wrenching testimonials of any revival season: "I was lost, but . . . then I found God. . . . I now owe my life to Jesus." They extol a faith tempered and annealed in the fire and brimstone of secular dissolution and sin. These are generally supplemented with the customary Biblical examples of challenge and triumph. The forty days and nights of Jesus in the wilderness, the quintessential spiritual moral market experience. But the average evangelical son or daughter rarely undergoes any such trial. Most are spoon-fed their religious beliefs. When asked about spiritual turning points in their lives, most relate only a vague, gradual growing in their faith. Belief turns more readily upon routine and repetition, upon the accumulation of a seemingly interminable number of weekends in church buildings, Youth For Christ meetings, and summer Bible camps; all depositing well-worn spiritual grooves in their souls. Yet given a choice between the direct imbuing of religious beliefs in their offspring and setting them adrift to discover and acquire Christianity on their own, parents invariably (understandably) opt for the greater certainty of routinization. One unavoidable consequence is the occasional feeling of inauthenticity dogging both parents and offspring, as though a faith grounded in rudimentary instruction pales in comparison to any faith borne or hammered out of experience. The parent who can actually reflect back upon periods of agnosticism or atheism, of delinquency and despair, in her own life before a born-again conversion may come to question the depth and resilience of her own children's shallow faith. A pedestrian religious existence suspends the spiritual market evaluation of genuine belief. Parents seek to pass on these hard-won spiritual earnings to offspring and yet lament the consequences of a too easy inheritance. And children in turn feel the pressures for spiritual performance; some are almost driven to apology for the absence in their own lives of a period of testing followed by conversion or triumphal recommitment. They long for some sort of genuine cauldron experience or act of spiritual heroism to relate. The inertia of routine wears heavily upon their sense of self-worth and virtue. At times, simply to rouse themselves from lethargy, some improvise or manufacture situations of spiritual market testing. As we will see in the accounts to follow, they learn to simulate conditions of spiritual struggle, delivering polished accounts of trials and tribulations before fellow students, relating perilous encounters with a profane secular world of opposition, dramas designed to demonstrate or enhance their ultimate spiritual market credentials and standing in the community.

Seen The Glory: A Journey Into The Evangelical Subculture In America (New York: Oxford University Press, 1989), 94, 106.

All told, moral market thinking occupies only a modest portion of the mental territory of the modern evangelical. By no means does it represent the defining feature of evangelicalism, although it does assume great importance for us in another closely related respect: indeed we might better conceive of it as one of the four or five distinctive elements of the larger American society, one of a few cardinal cultural properties serving to differentiate the American condition and experience from those of our closest European cultural ancestors.[150] An exploration of the role and meaning of moral market thinking and phenomena in the larger American culture—beyond the precincts of Evangelicalism—would carry us far beyond the aims of this study. But a few more contemporary examples may help European readers understand what is for them the almost inexplicable resistance in the United States to European-style universal healthcare coverage. That the English would, for example, celebrate the British National Health Service at the opening ceremony of the 2012 London Olympic Games must have baffled a large portion of the American television audience. That it was linked so closely to children's literature and the Great Ormond Street Hospital reveals the enormous sentimental cultural gap between the two societies.[151] Across

---

[150] These moral market calculations represent the nuances of a more general cultural distinction, as is evident in the observations of one emulative Norwegian: "The most prominent spokesman of this [reform] movement is a blunt 44-year old businessman named Carl Hagan, who as leader of the Norwegian Progress Party [10-20% in polls] argues the welfare state has undermined traditional values. . . . 'Why is it, when everyone wants to be rich, that it can be wrong for someone to succeed?' he asked. 'If someone makes it in Silicon Valley or in American business, he's considered a good man and you look up to him. In Norway, it's the other way around—you get a negative reaction.' " (Tyler Marshall, "Scandinavia Today: Too Much Togetherness?" *Seattle Times*, 26 February 1989.) Why indeed?

—Then there's the English, who in the '60s and '70s made a folk hero out of Albert Thorogood, "Idle Albert," the "able-bodied father of five who had managed to live on the public dole for nearly all of his adult life. . . . and graciously allowed the government to pick up the tab for his three-bedroom home in the Essex city of Southend. . . ." (*Newsweek*, March 5, 1976.)

—I suspect also that moral market sentiments lie behind an assortment of American exceptionalisms, e.g., the tardy appearance on the scene of the largely European phenomenon of "bencoms," local community financial cooperatives: "In the United Kingdom, the law enabling bencoms to use withdrawable shares is more than a century old, but it was only in the 1990s that it was rediscovered, and only in the 2000s that enterprises began using it in any meaningful number. . . . The community shares model is unfamiliar in the United States. . . . regulations have been too stringent to permit it. . . . But the law is changing slowly in such a way that it might, one day, accommodate bencoms." (Samanth Subramanian, "A Port In A Storm: A community's quest to save its harbor," *Harper's Magazine*, April 2018, 70-71.)

[151] The implications of these cultural ideas are evident in the resistance of red state politicians and their conservative Republican (largely evangelical) constituencies to European-style single-payer healthcare systems, and to even the more limited Affordable Care Act version of them. As Christian Smith notes in a broader context: "In her book *Poverty and Eternity: How*

the Atlantic, by marked contrast, Republican governor Rick Scott of Florida, frustrated by Congress's inability to overturn the ACA, the Affordable Care Act, or "Obamacare," instructed his attorney general to join an ongoing lawsuit that would "eliminate protection for pre-existing conditions." Paul Krugman quotes Scott's rationale in his op-ed column:

> "Scott declared, 'We've got to reward people for caring for themselves.' "

Krugman concludes: "Right, because if you get cancer, or arthritis, or multiple sclerosis—all among the pre-existing conditions for which people used to be denied coverage—it must be your own fault."[152]

The evangelical moral market attitude towards illness resists empirical capture or quantification. Here is Kate Bowler's (the "Christian Joan Didion") rich description of one version of it among prosperity theology believers:

> In a spiritual world in which healing is a divine right, illness is a symptom of unconfessed sin—a symptom of a lack of forgiveness, unfaithfulness, unexamined attitudes, or careless words. A suffering believer is a puzzle to be solved. What had caused this to happen? As I walked around with slings and braces on my arms, I heard whispers and caught looks, some sympathetic, some disproving, some gravely concerned. In the small church where I did most of my research, I knew I was loved. I was prayed for. I was ministered to. But when, week after week, I returned with the same droop in my arms and weakness in my hands [from an as

---

Religion Shapes Assistance to the Poor, From Early Church to Modern Welfare States, Sigrun Kahl investigates the origins of striking cross-national variations in beliefs about the deservingness of the poor. . . . Conservative welfare regimes, in other words, which most people assume to be recent secular inventions, in fact have their origins in early modern religious reformations and the deep culture trajectories they generated." (*Religion: What It Is. . .* , 116-7.) Smith fails, however, to discern, address, or attempt to explain the *deep* current American-European differences that persist. Perhaps a more general *religion absconditus* in Europe has something to do with our sharply diverging approaches to social welfare?
—"During the failed effort to repeal the Affordable Care Act in March, Kansas congressman Roger Marshall, citing scripture, said, 'The poor will always be with us . . . There is a group of people that just don't want health care and aren't going to take care of themselves.' Utah congressman Jason Chaffetz ranted to CNN: 'And so, maybe, rather than getting that new iPhone that they just love and they want to go spend hundreds of dollars on that, maybe they should invest it in their own health care.' " (Jeff Madrick, "America: The Forgotten Poor," *The New York Review of Books*, June 22, 2017.)
[152] "GOP to Americans with health problems: Drop dead," *The Seattle Times*, June 17, 2018.
—Fintan O'Toole persuades us that President Donald Trump embraces these kinds of moral market motivations as ". . . . *virtues*. If you despise the food stamp program as a disincentive to the shiftless poor to buck up and take responsibility for themselves. . . . then the easiest thing to do is nothing." ("Saboteur in Chief," *The New York Review of Books*, 12/6/2018.) {emphasis added}

of yet undiagnosed malady], I thought I saw their lips close and their arms cross, and I felt like faithlessness personified.[153]

And so one is either socio-economically feckless or spiritually faithless, caught between a rock and a hard place. Just imagine the ideological intensification that occurs when this relatively benign internal insinuation of invidious distinction is categorically projected out into the hostile external secular world. Observe here how intramural failures of faith fold rather seamlessly into the closely related casting of larger moral market aspersions of individual social and economic unworthiness. This internal cultural idiom proves but a hop, skip, and jump away from broader extensions, wherein a national health care system would undermine this finely calibrated moral market calculus. Where the lottery of health has been rigged in favor of the anointed ones. Otherwise, the categorical invidious distinction of secular social sin is removed from the moral market arena. A categorical absence of faith should bring categorical consequences. Religious-Right politicians could care less that mortality rates—infant and general—are the highest in the modern Western world. The moral market system is merely sifting the Christian wheat from the secular chaff.

Ah, then there is the Tea Party, another political force tugging on the coattails of the Religious Right, reacting to the sheer gall of a black president who might undermine the moral market foundations of "moral hazard"ism:

> The Tea Party movement took off on February 19, 2009, when a CNBC business editor, broadcasting from the floor of the Chicago Mercantile Exchange, excoriated Obama's plan to help homeowners avoid foreclosure by refinancing their mortgages, accusing the government of 'promoting bad behavior' by supporting these 'losers' and suggesting that the Chicago bond traders create a tea party and throw all the derivatives of the mortgages into the Chicago River. . . . Within a year a thousand Tea Party committees had sprung up all over the country calling for a reduction of the national debt, lower taxes, and an end to 'wasteful government spending'. . . . [154]

---

[153] *Everything Happens For a Reason and Other Lies I've Loved*, Random House 2018, 16-17.

[154] Frances Fitzgerald, *The Evangelicals: The Struggle to Shape America*, Simon & Schuster, 2017, 593.
—" 'Tea Party members rarely stressed economic concerns to us—and they never blamed business or the superrich for America's troubles. The nightmare of societal decline is usually painted in cultural hues, and the villains in the picture are freeloading social groups, liberal politicians, bossy professionals, big government, and the mainstream media.' Illegal immigration is a particular anxiety—not because employers give low-wage jobs to illegals or outsource them to China and India, but because those who slip over the border, or their children, crowd schools and hospitals. *They are the 'undeserving,' who drain the federal treasury and imperil the benefits due to birthright citizens.*" (from Sam Tanenhaus's review of Theda Skocpol and Vanessa

Luckily, calmer, less moral-market-inclined heads—and Keynesian principles—prevailed, averting an economic apocalypse, but such is the perennial political challenge and struggle in America to ground the social and political future of the society in an empirical, evidence-based here and now.

Up to this point it has been my intention merely to introduce the theoretical terms and structure of my presumption of an American cultural difference and to do so in a manner which simultaneously illuminates the role these various cultural logics and dynamics play in American evangelicalism; accordingly I have sought to provide a few elementary features distinguishing an indigenous moral market ethos from European antecedents and some even more finely-honed principles for distinguishing the evangelical embrace and application of that ethos from that found in the larger American society. The nature and pattern of the interaction of these deeper kinds of cultural logics and dynamics will become even more apparent, oddly enough, as we move on to an exploration of some of the shallower regions of evangelical culture. In the juxtaposition of these deep and shallow elements lies the analytical rewards of their remarkably stark points of contrast.

National Currents and Moods

It is upon a third, much lower level of generalization that I will concentrate for the remainder of this chapter. Along this particular vein we discover all manner of social moods and currents that appear to pass through the community, leaving no permanent markings (hence: shallow history). There is, however, more to these apparent smooth passages than meets the eye. Their importance for us lies not so much in the particular issues or matters of historical content they raise as in the additional light they may shed upon how this community comes to adopt the ideas and standards guiding the conduct of its members. Does all behavior flow predictably from the authoritarian structure and terms of an inherited cultural logic? The "inerrant" commands of scripture? The traditions and routines of a particular sect or denomination, such as Free Methodism? Or are there not other influences which may momentarily supplant conventional codes of conduct or habits of thought? And what sort of relationships might these apparently more ephemeral elements assume with the two major logics introduced above? Does their appearance on the scene bring a suspension or supplantation of these deeper sources of thought and behavior? What sort of dynamics link "deep" and "shallow" phenomena?

Williamson's *The Tea Party and the Remaking of Republican Conservatism* in *The New York Review of Books*, 3/8/2012, 8.) {emphasis added}

The possibilities are manifold. Observe that these more ephemeral cultural moods often appear to incorporate or borrow meanings and imagery from the aforementioned two logics (hence: deeper history), or generate variations upon themes, or may even exhibit relatively autonomous origins of their own, sporadically appearing and then disappearing, only to reappear once again. I have found this an oscillating, hot and cold community: the example of a school swept up in the euphoria of a uniformly popular venture—as during the latter stages of World War II—easily juxtaposed to moments of glacial coolness to national trends and the icons or movements which embody them. Periods of receptive, almost giddy social expansiveness set against brooding, rancorous moments of withdrawal and social isolationism. And how terribly evangelical *and* American this is.

At this juncture a few concrete examples will help flesh out the nature of these relationships among the various levels of cultural and historical phenomena.

A Radical, Progressive College

Consider, for instance, the career of one of the rather more interesting characters in the early history of Seattle Pacific College, Miss Candis Nelson, who served in the 1920s and '30s as the Normal School director. Given her ability to force out a standing college president, Orrin Tiffany,[155] one might assume that she was a powerful, influential woman and that the views she embraced and espoused represented conventional, orthodox evangelicalism, at least as we have come to think of it in our modern period, and that they aligned closely with those of a rigidly fundamentalist or conservative board of trustees. Indeed this is the impression that the (internally-published) Centennial history of Seattle Pacific University, *Seattle Pacific University, 1891-1991: A Growing Vision*, conveys to the innocent reader: that she was prim, proper, and devoted to her profession, espousing views and values that however socially old-fashioned (in the good sense of the term) they might appear to jaded modern eyes, were nonetheless reasonably similar (especially in political and theological areas) to those embraced by the modern evangelical academician. Indeed the assumption fairly permeates the (ironically, terribly *unhistorical*) Centennial history: that however occasionally bombastic, stilted, fustian, or quaintly archaic these early college leaders, their ideological inclinations roughly paralleled or precursed the "vision" of the modern period. That the earlier "vision" represents nothing more than the later modern ver-

---

[155] Due to unrequited love, we understand: "She got extremely jealous and did her best to get him [President Tiffany] ousted. She was a troublemaker before she came here and while she was here . . . she did her best to undermine him. . . . Well, this undermining went on for several years. . . ." (C. D. Demaray interview with Cyril Hill, 10/18/79.) {Archives}

sion in its embryonic form, the two merely callow and ripe versions of the very same "growing vision." The history of the school accordingly becomes then an account of the simple gestation, maturation, and amplification of this original dispensation of light. Unfortunately, in order to make the teleology work whole regions of historical experience are all too conveniently expunged.

In many respects, the case of Candis Nelson (and the early Seminary and college community) duplicates the findings of an increasing number of revisionist studies.[156] These early evangelicals were quite different from their more modern descendants. Miss Nelson, for example, although she shared and expressed a typical late-nineteenth, early twentieth-century Protestant anxiety over the influx of immigrants and "heathen religions," nonetheless voiced some aggressively feminist opinions on the equality and prominence of women in America life and railed frequently at political malfeasance and graft in public office holders, descrying the influence of wealth upon politics, admonishing that although "Education gives power . . . power in the hands of an *immoral class* is a menace to the public good."[157] {emphasis added} Later, in the 1930s, Nelson was cribbing notes to herself:

[156] Two papers in *Religion and American Culture: A Journal of Interpretation* offer a wealth of references: Richard C. Goode, "The Godly Insurrection in Limestone County: Social Gospel, Populism, and Southern Culture in the Late Nineteenth Century," 3, no. 2 [Summer 1993]; Douglas Firth Anderson, " 'A True Revival of Religion': Protestants and the San Francisco Graft Prosecutions, 1906-1909," 4, no. 1 [Winter 1994].

[157] Prior to her arrival at Seattle Pacific, the few articles Candis Nelson placed in local North Dakota public school district journals and newsletters during the 1910s are pretty standard fare, one largely xenophobic in tone, arguing for the compulsory attendance of Christian religious exercises in the public schools in order to stem the "invasions" of "heathen religions" from abroad. And yet lodged in a portion of this particular piece, amidst an enumeration of the cultural sins of these alien religions, is an arresting idea:

> Do any of them stand for morality, as we count morality? Do they try to uplift womanhood which makes for the sobriety and strength of any land? Do they raise up institutions to care for the unfortunate and the fatherless? Do they recognize the brotherhood of man and what it stands for in a unification of a great idea? No, they do not. On the contrary, for the most part, they stand for the degradation of women, in their methods of "sacred prostitution" and systems of slavery. That alone should debar them from a Christian land. "What is civilization?" was asked of Emerson and he replied, "The power of women."

Another piece from North Dakota, the "Moral Aim of the School," found an audience via the *Midland Schools* newsletter:

> What mean these headlines, "The Corrupt Machine," "The Bribery of Public Men," "The Franchise Graft," "The Public Land Graft," "Exploitation of National Resources," et cetera, found in almost every magazine and daily

Our classrooms cannot be dominated by fear. The cur. must be everchanging. Schools need to study labor, communism and all other controversial problems. American distress [the Depression] had stirred us to question traditions and bring many things in the open for discussion.

. . . . [the] doctrine of self-interest now has the field, more extreme and sinister than ever before.

We have been Jefersonian[*sic*] [scribbled insertion: "guaranteed by <u>nature</u> (natural social order?)"]   are we turning Hamiltonian? [scribbled: "gov't by special +privileged class"] *We profess "equal opportunity" as a philosophy but if anyone points out the discrepancy in our economic and industrial order we are outraged and suspect he is financed from Moscow. It is our task to build a new social order. The schools cannot be content with transmitting the cultural traditions of the past. They must open up a new frontier.* It means we must reorganize our schools, a perplexing and appalling undertaking equal to the reorganizing the [*sic*] social structure itself. (Isn't the school a part of the Social Structure. Nelson.) Perhaps the time is at hand when we must cease to be Jeffersonian or Hamiltonian and become Educators. The <u>call to education is</u> <u>claer</u> [*sic*] we must lead and not follow. {italics added}[158]

Nelson published several articles in a New York journal, *School and Society*, among them a 1933 piece quoting Socrates and Plutarch (but no scripture) and championing the redistribution of wealth:

At the present, 90 per cent of the wealth is held by 13 per cent of the population. This cannot continue at the expense of the nation's greatest asset—its children.[159]

---

paper? Does it mean that men have had a healthy conscience up to the present era of graft and have now suddenly become exploiters of public office and public means; or does it mean that there has been in the last score of years a gradual letting down along moral lines so that under the pressure of modern conditions the moral conscience in public agents cannot or at least does not withstand the strain? The latter seems more probable.   {Undated items from the Archives}

[158] From a collection of typewritten notes on articles and books that had exerted influence on her thinking. {Archives}

[159] (29 September 1933); and juxtaposed to her 1934 article, "Some of Today's Educational Problems," the text of an address presented to a New York City conference on education which cites and draws upon the ideas of John Dewey, is a smaller, boxed report of the pro-suffrage speeches she had delivered to "women's meetings" in the New York area. (28 July 1934)

Perhaps it was this pattern of vigorous political activity that caused Cyril Hill, a member of the community at the time, to later remember Nelson as " . . . a troublemaker at the school where she taught . . . before she came here and while she was here." (C. D. D. / Hill interview) {All Archives}

Characteristically enough, the Centennial history makes no mention of any of this: within its pages we encounter a denatured Candis Nelson, an ideological eunuch preserved in a jar of historical formaldehyde, on display along with all the other bloodless specimens from a static, irretrievable community past.

But was she alone in her Progressive enthusiasms?[160] Fortunately in this instance we have some other rather more generous sources to draw upon, whose examination leads to the conclusion that before and during Candis Nelson's tenure at Seattle Pacific these ideas—and closely related variations, elaborations, and applications of these ideas—had come into the possession of nearly everyone on campus.

The 1916 school yearbook, the *Cascade*, for example, begins with a fairly gushing paean of a dedication not to an esteemed teacher or administrator but to the idea of "progress":

> To the spirit of the great West—that noble discontent which ever drives men forward to better things—to that spirit which has made possible the West as we know it, and as it will be—we reverently dedicate this annual.[161]

There immediately follows an account of "Progressive Legislation in Washington," a piece commemorating such memorable breakthroughs in Olympia (the state capital) as the Women's Suffrage Law of 1910 (later re-

---

[160] To extend the observation even further, consider that Anna Louise Strong, a "leading voice" and chronicler of the Seattle General Strike (1919), radical sojourner ("one of the few Westerners to gain and keep the admiration of Mao Tse-Tung"—Sale, *Seattle: Past to Present*, 133), and later expatriate to the Moscow of an imagined great Soviet experiment, hailed from a rigorously evangelical background; that her father, the Reverend Sydney Strong, was Pastor of a Congregational Church; and that in one early work she sought to persuade her readers of *The Power of Prayer*? (ibid., 113) How apparently natural and fluid this movement from piety to social revolution.

[161] {Archives} One finds also in the 1925 *Cascade* the title page poem, "The Spirit of Progress."

—An Anna Louise Strong editorial appeared in the *Union-Record* two days before the commencement of the Seattle General Strike, declaring that the workers were " . . . undertaking the most tremendous move ever made by labor in this country, a move that will lead—No One Knows Where! We do not need hysteria! We need the iron march of labor." She later reflected upon the interpretation of that provocative phrase advanced by both the prosecution and defense at her subsequent trial, concluding that "Neither gave the real essence of those words. *They appealed to the faith of the pioneer in inevitable progress; they stirred the passion of the march to the undiscovered West.* Yet they carefully avoided battle."

Similarly of George Cotterill, about whom Roger Sale writes, "Eight years later [1927] George Cotterill was still saying the northwest was 'the world's outpost of outlook and opportunity, the place of vision and achievement.' " (Both from Sale, *Seattle: Past to Present*, 130.) {emphasis added}

-86-

pealed) and the Minimum Wage Law and Workman's Compensation Act of 1913. There was much to celebrate.

> Another great victory for the voters of this state was the passing of the Initiative and Referendum Bill which took effect in 1912. Besides this, forest reserves have been established, good roads built, pensions granted to widows, hospitals built for the insane, schools erected for the feeble-minded, and numerous other reforms have been made by legislation within the last few years.
>
> However, all of these late reforms mentioned above step into the background of prominence as we consider the last great reform bill [yet to be] passed by the people. This is prohibition. . . .

Egalitarianism and prohibitionism, social reform and personal piety. Like oddly assorted birds of a feather, these apparently contrary concerns fly easily together.[162] Indeed we will find time and again that to the progressive evangelical mind these apparently unrelated issues represent mere complementary dimensions of *both a local and national* struggle to raise the common man up from under the burden of his exploitation by the "Interests," whether from the intoxication of liquor or the unequal distribution of wealth and political influence. Those associated with the temperance movement were a good deal more sophisticated and broadminded than popular historical memory might allow.[163]

---

[162] A good illustration of this fusion of piety and progressivism comes from a *Falcon* report (3 March 1935) of the conclusions or recommendations adopted by the 1935 Washington Youth Conference:

> 1) Personal Religious Living.
> 2) Personal Evangelism.
> 3) World Peace: The group favored joining the World Court and League of Nations, and protested the plan of maneuvering the U.S. Navy in Japanese waters (The protest was endorsed by the entire conference).
> 4) *Solving the liquor question* : Education against liquor is insufficient. The need is for education plus *legislation*.
> 5) Building a Christian Economic Order: The capitalistic system is largely at fault for modern social and economic disorder. The problem is not over-production but rather lack of distribution.
> 6) Constructive use of leisure time. . . . The move for *decency in movies* was endorsed.
> 7) Christian attitude toward other racial groups: each race should have equal opportunities of education and occupation, and equal social privileges.
> 8) Marriage and Home Life.
> 9) Christian Patriotism.   {emphases added}   {Archives}

[163] For example, during the great labor unrest of the mid-1880s the

In December of 1912, the *Cascade* reported the results of a mock presidential election conducted a few weeks earlier on campus:

> First Choice: Eugene Chafin (Prohibition) 51 / Theodore Roosevelt 19 / Woodrow Wilson 15 / Eugene V. Debs 4 / William Howard Taft 1
> Second Choice: Woodrow Wilson 46 / Theodore Roosevelt 17 / Eugene Chafin 11 / Eugene V. Debs 8 / William Howard Taft 6 / Pierce 1.

Recall that William Howard Taft, *attracting only one first choice student ballot*, was the incumbent Republican president, Wilson the Democrat challenger, and that Roosevelt had bolted from the Republican Party to form his own Progressive Party and run as a third-party candidate; Debs was of course the Socialist Party candidate. The appeal of Eugene Chafin goes without saying.

> ....WCTU [Woman's Christian Temperance Union] revised its explanation of the relationship between drunkeness and poverty. Having argued previously that drunkeness caused poverty among working people because laborers squandered their pay in saloons instead of supporting their families, the WCTU began to see drunkeness as the result of poverty. Before 1886 Willard [Frances Willard, president of WCTU] herself had believed that the burning issue for labor was not so much higher wages as "how to turn present wages to better account"—i.e., how not to waste them on liquor. After the Great Upheaval, however, the WCTU newspaper, the *Union Signal*, ran a series of articles on child labor and the use of alcohol as a consequence of overwork and deprivation. By the 1890s the *Union Signal* was writing that "men and women, overworked, with a state of low vitality and innumerable difficulties to meet, naturally turn toward anything that will afford temporary relief. . . . In the midst of misery, drinking is almost inevitable."

The WCTU established numerous social programs and services which they deemed "municipal housekeeping," and with respect to suffrage: "During the latter part of the nineteenth century, however, the broadest support for woman suffrage was to be found not in the divided suffrage movement but in the Woman's Christian Temperance Union (WCTU)." In fact, Frances Willard considered herself a socialist, not a reformer. (Nell Irvin Painter, *Standing at Armageddon: The United States, 1877-1919*, New York: W. W. Norton, 1987, 63, 105, 232-33, 267.)

Then again, there is the other side, another skeleton, rattling about in the closet of history:

> Frances E. Willard, whose Women's Christian Temperance Union played an important role in organizing the activities of boys and girls in small towns of the Middle West, established [John Harvey] Kellogg as the Union's director of physical education. . . . In 1885 the WCTU established a department of social purity, headed by John Harvey Kellogg and his wife, and thus linked itself to a campaign which, beginning in the 1870s with isolated attempts to prevent state legislatures from licensing and regulating prostitution, swelled into a national crusade aimed at purification of the entire society through the advocacy of premarital chastity. (Kett, *Rites of Passage . . .* , 171, 193.)

Later in the depression years community disenchantment with industrial capitalism would understandably reach a climax of sorts. A 1934 *Falcon* editorial sought (and apparently failed) to dispel some of the gloom that had descended over the campus, invoking FDR in its title, "Fear Not":

> From somewhere a stern hand rules the United States—originally "the home of the free, the land of   the brave." The religious and democratic foundations are being shaken; life has low values; depression crushes our lives to the ground, takes away our property, puts hatred in the hearts of our neighbors, causes "greed" to stalk the land, casts away our confidence, and cuts our anchor of hope.[164]

---

[164] *Falcon*, 19 December 1934.
—Ibid., 14 November 1934: An ad for a meeting of the Young People's Missionary Society listed discussion topics: "Midnight and Calvary" and "Is America Doomed?"
—A 1935 *Falcon* column reported that in an annual meeting of the Inland Empire Teachers Association the members produced resolutions on the economic crisis denouncing the exorbitant "profits" of business and industry and championing programs enhancing "human welfare." (10 April 1935)
—Professor Walter Helsel spoke before the campus International Club on the relationship between "The Church and Labor," arguing that American society ought to treat workers with as great a consideration as "capital." (13 May 1936)
    Throughout the 1930s the *Falcon* reported debate topics of local high school and college tournaments and forensic societies that indicate a domination of the agenda by progressive social and political issues: "Federal . . . equal educational opportunity grants . . . ."; "Social Insurance?"; "Socialized Medicine"; " . . . minimum wage and maximum hours for industry"; " . . . minimum wage affirmative wins"; " . . . National Labor Relations Board . . . empowered to enforce arbitration . . . industrial disputes."
—12 December 1934: Debate topic: "Resolved: That the federal government should adopt a policy of equal educational opportunity throughout the nation by means of public grants to the several states for public, elementary, and secondary education."; 2 October 1935: Forensic Society debate topic: "Social Insurance?"; 11 December 1935: High school debate topic (Seattle Pacific still ran a high school): "Socialized Medicine."; 3 November 1936: Debate tournament topic: "Resolved: That Congress shall be empowered to fix minimum wage and maximum hours for industry."; (17 November 1936); 16 November 1937: Year's debate topic: "Resolved: That the National Labor Relations Board should be empowered to enforce arbitration of all industrial disputes."
    Indeed with but one minor exception ("Resolved: That the government should regulate the labor unions." 24 October 1941) the train of progressive issues extended clear into the early 1950s:
—Radio debate: "Should American youth support the reestablishment after the war of competitive enterprise as our dominant economic system?" (17 November 1942)
—Topic: "Resolved: That labor should be given a direct share in the management of industry." (13 December 1946)
—Speech dept. debate topic: "Resolved: That the United States should abandon free economy in favor of a system of economic controls. . . . These controls would include prices, wages, credit, production, profit, rent, and planned economy." (19 November 1948)
—Topic: "Resolved: that the United States should nationalize the basic non-agricultural industries." (3 February 1950)

The *Falcon* reported upon the conclusions or recommendations adopted by the 1935 Washington Youth Conference, whose fifth point concerned "Building a Christian Economic Order: The capitalistic system is largely at fault for modern social and economic disorder. The problem is not overproduction but rather lack of distribution."[165]

There is every indication that faculty members shared the political ideas and sentiments aired in the student newspaper. On election day in 1936 (FDR's first re-election) the *Falcon* ran a piece ("Political Views of Faculty Exposed") surveying the opinions of the faculty on statewide Initiative measures:

> It seemed that the general opinion was that an income tax is desirable revenue for the state. . . . The desirability of an old age pension seemed to be accepted by all.[166]

It is instructive that I encountered not a single letter to the editor or commentary in my review of the student newspaper suggesting that such utterances were in any way heretical or uncommon. Not one. Progressive ideas appear to have dominated the discussions of the period.[167] It is also

---

[165] Indeed as late as 1939 the staff of the *Falcon* appended a subtitle to the logo of the student newspaper, defining itself as "The Progressive College Newspaper of the Northwest." In 1941, this was changed to "The Torch of Truth"; in 1942, "Builder of Character, 1889-1942"; in 1946, "The Fear of the Lord is the Beginning of Wisdom"; returning in 1948 to "The Progressive College News. . . ." before expiring a final time in 1950, replaced once again by "The Fear of the Lord. . . ." These shifts in the logo may reflect a kind of ideological identity crisis, the school searching for itself, all the while depositing wandering but meaningful cultural footprints in the snow, clues to be read by those tracking the community's eventual transition from Progressivism to modern political conservatism.

[166] (3 November 1936). The first initiative must have failed (a two-thirds majority is needed in Washington State to override a provision in the state constitution forbidding income taxes) because to this day Washington State has no income tax.
—An article in the same issue recounted a presentation of Dr. Lyle Post before the perennially activist International Club, during which he advocated the extension of domestic political and economic ideas to international relations and foreign policy:

> Cooperative associations can be an important factor in removing the causes of war . . . and because the cooperatives tend to eliminate the middle-man, diversify wealth, and offer an opportunity for the common man to better his position, cooperatives may be a deciding advance in the fight for world peace.

[167] While progressive ideas and issues may have dominated the discussion it is quite possible that adherents may not have held a numerical majority over, say, moderate or conservative Republicans in the community. I found one article (only one) which suggests just this: In

"Election Returns Gain Speculation" most students and faculty who were interviewed expressed a preference for Landon over FDR in the '36 election. As one respondent explained, "I'm for Landon. I'm looking forward to an old age pension." Notice the confusion here: voting for Landon because he thinks he advocates a kind of New Deal social program. Which may have been precisely the aim of Republican party strategy that year, for although as Samuel Eliot Morison writes, the "clamour against President Roosevelt so increased both in pitch and volume that many political seers believed that the New Deal was doomed" and an overconfident Republican party luxuriated in H.L. Mencken's judgment that the Republicans could beat FDR "with a Chinaman, or even a Republican," the fact remained that if Landon were elected "he would have continued the New Deal under another name." In spite of all the Roosevelt bashing at the '36 Republican convention ("despotism," "universal bankruptcy," etc.) "the platform promised to do everything that Democrats had done, without destroying 'free enterprise, private competition, and equality of opportunity.' " The conventional wisdom ("A poll conducted by the *Literary Digest* predicted Landon's election.") had already turned Roosevelt out of office when, "in one of the greatest landslides in political history, Roosevelt received 60.7 percent of the popular vote." (Samuel Eliot Morison, *The Oxford History of the American People*, New York: Oxford University Press, 1965, 975-76.)

The point here is that one has to keep the historical context of this likely 50/50, FDR/Landon community split in mind. Consider that in 1952 a (30 October 1952) *Falcon* presidential straw poll reported the results, Eisenhower 353/Stevenson 80/MacArthur 13/Hambler 10, and that in a 1960 poll in which nearly half (550) of the student body participated the numbers were Nixon 453/Kennedy 52 (*Falcon* 26, no. 6: "70 percent of the students said they would not vote for a Roman Catholic Presidential Candidate."). Four years later the (6 November 1964) *Falcon* reported the results of campus polling: Goldwater 64%/ Johnson 36%, virtually the reverse of the national outcome. *So that in the course of thirty or so years we observe a considerable shift in political sentiment that is unrelated to national trends.*

Nationally, the depression experience figured prominently in the evangelical leaders' views of capitalism: "While statistics indicate that the bulk of the Protestant clergy voted against Franklin Roosevelt, nevertheless, in 1934, 95 percent of 21,000 ministers responding to a questionnaire said that they favored 'a cooperative commonwealth' over a capitalistic system, and 51% favored a 'drastically reformed capitalism.' This was obviously a great shift in clerical opinion from its almost unanimous support of laissez-faire in the years 1865-1890." (McLoughlin, *Revivals, Awakenings, and Reform* . . . , 172.) Unfortunately, McLoughlin's categorization scheme is confused at best, referring as it does to this particular clergy group as "many conservative liberal Protestants." One gets the impression he has no idea of the actual size of these respective groups; and I question his sweeping appraisal of the 1865-1890 period as ideologically all of a piece. Also, 1890-1929 is a long chunk of history. What occurred then? Did evangelicals support capitalism then?

—And inevitably, one supposes, the mood of critical social and cultural introspection began to spread beyond the bounds of these original polemical bones of contention, drawing attention to internal community inconsistencies, on one occasion prompting an unusually assertive student to challenge the nature of authority at Seattle Pacific, this student launching a rare attack upon the Watson administration:

> . . . . But again, there is another "influence" in S.P.C. which is beyond dictatorship. It is a sort of Louis XIV form of government. We as students are more concerned with this kind of "divine monarchy." It seems that signatures and suggestions . . . "do not mean anything". . . . (*Falcon*, 20 March 1935)

instructive that no account of these matters intrudes upon the official published history of the school. We find no trace of this extended period of radical disenchantment with the social and economic order in this community's collective memory, a grievance extending clear into the 1950s.[168]

The Labor Movement

Now these various disenchantments with the players and conditions—the owners and managers, the inequality, regimentation, and inebriation—of the emerging industrial order were by no means confined to Progressive reformers of the early twentieth century or the later depression years; neither were they primarily located nor given sole expression within these odd fusions of personal piety and radical politics prevailing among some of the higher-bred and -educated, urban middle-class reformers. Indeed in a 1966 paper rarely cited by scholars, "Protestantism and the American Labor Movement: The Christian Spirit in the Gilded Age,"[169] Herbert G. Gutman laid waste to a prevailing view of an American Christianity largely enamored of industrial capitalism.[170] Returning to original sources and documents of

---

[168] There were, however, local Methodist ministers who did not follow the lead of the SPC faculty and rose to defend the status quo. During this very same period of local political unrest the Methodist minister, Abraham Vereide, reflecting upon a meeting four years earlier with Franklin Roosevelt, wrote the new president a complimentary letter as "our Moses" but later grew sour on the worth of any "private charity or public welfare." He used whatever national reputation ("having won over political leaders in Washington, D.C., Vereide used their influence to establish even more prayer breakfast groups across the nation. . . . 'The big men and real leaders in New York and Chicago,' he wrote his wife, 'look up to me in an embarrassing way.' ") he had amassed to rally local businessmen (not labor or unions), encouraging city councilmen Arthur Langlie to "let God use me" to become mayor and governor—"a sweeping victory for conservatism"—to put down the radical elements. Unlike the SPC faculty, Vereide's "Biblical principles" were grounded in the one-sided recognition that "economic reconstruction must begin with an individual recovery from within." (Kruse, *One Nation Under God. . .* , 39-45.)

[169] Reprinted in *Work, Culture, & Society in Industrializing America* (New York: Vintage Books, 1977).

[170] Covering the same period, Martin Marty makes only scattered reference to labor movement issues, concentrating upon the tenuous connections between Social Gospelers of the formal churches and radical organizations, dismissing the Social Gospel as theologically memorable but largely ineffectual, more important for "vision" than effect. Characteristic of most of his work, he is not looking for Biblically-based and inspired rejections of the socio-economic order, tending to repeat traditional formulas of the relationship between capital and Christianity, while pursuing more diffuse interpretive themes—"irony," "modernity," "transmodernism." It is instructive that Professor Marty's most recent work makes no mention of the Gutman paper. See "Social Christianity as a Recovered Wholeness," in *Modern American Religion, Volume 1: The Irony of It All, 1893-1919* (University of Chicago Press, 1986). As we will see in other penetrating works in this area besides the Guttman paper and the piece by Richard C. Goode (cited in a subsequent footnote), in particular, one gets the impression of an

the last half of the nineteenth-century, he unearthed evidence of complex Biblical arguments tendered in support of the rights of the working classes, discerning among them a reliance upon scripture for an understanding of the workers' personal experiences of the tumultuous transformations of industrialization and urbanization. In various union and labor-related journals and newsletters spanning four decades, workers, editors, union officials, and even the wives of laborers vented an unmitigated ire against these economic developments, framing their grievances in terms of an industrial capitalist violation of Biblical principles. A Railway union commentator, a Massachusetts ship joiner, a contributor to the Denver *Labor Enquirer*, an Indiana coal miner's wife, a United Mine Worker president—all these and many more—rained a chorus of execrations down upon the heads of robber barons, financiers, and their fellow conspirators in government.

The appeals to Biblical models and precedents spanned the entire political spectrum of labor organizations. Even the journal of the more conservative American Federation of Labor (*American Federationist*, 1895) issued calls for "A living Christ moving, living, breathing and dominant in the hearts of people, not a dead Christianity, dreaming of a dead Christ, but live Christians as live Christs, scattering the table of the money changers in the temples . . . going down in the poverty-stricken alleys of the robbed industrial slaves, and raising up its victims." This kind of Christianity, claimed the author, was *"the real article."*[171]

Christian imagery flowed hot and heavy not only onto the pages of the labor journals and newsletters but indeed found its way into the rhetoric of many well-known political activists and reformers, the Socialist Eugene V. Debs most notably. Debs, following the Pullman Strike debacle, penned a Labor Day oration from his prison cell likening his incarceration to that of Daniel under the Persians. He celebrated the holiday as one which "would stand first in Labor's Millennium, that prophesied era when Christ shall begin in reign on the earth to continue a thousand years."[172] And George E.

---

abundance of local primary source documents that have simply been overlooked by conventional historians of American religion.

[171] Louis Nash, "Is This A Christian Civilization?" *American Federationist* 1, January 1895. Quoted in Gutman, 93.

[172] Ibid., 98; although Debs's appeal was nationwide, he was a particular hero to southwest socialists, whose movements betrayed a similar interaction of class and culture:

> Religious influences were powerful enough, all right, and these radicals were as thoroughly Protestant as they come. But their churches had divided along class lines and they were segregated in those beyond the railroad tracks. Debs observed that "holiness people make good Socialists." Pentecostal churches were full of poor people. As Green puts it, they "integrated

McNeill, an abolitionist turned American Federation of Labor trade unionist whom Gutman regards as the most eloquent labor reformer of the era, often introduced himself to audiences with the disarming salutation, "I come here tonight as a Christian." Furthermore, in the *Labor Leader* (1890) he observed that

> . . . . The influence of the teachings of the carpenter's son still tends to counter-act the influence of Mammon. In this movement of the laborers toward equity, we will find a new revelation of the old Gospel, when the Golden Rule of Christ shall measure the relations of men in all their duties toward their fellows . . . by the free acceptance of the Gospel that all men are of one blood. Then the new Pentecost will come, when everyman shall have according to his needs.[173]

The Nature and Structure of Community Disenchantment and Identity

The contemporary evangelical likely will find the social and political views of these ancestors alien and disquieting, if not altogether repelling. Indeed in one respect the yawning ideological gulf separating the two periods ought to remove political conservatism from any consideration as one of the defining features of evangelicalism. Yet observe that each of the foregoing examples reveals a kind of disenchantment with an emerging industrial order that although grounded in and differentiated by the particular class positions and historical moments borne and experienced by the various protagonists—and further distinguished by the promulgation and deployment of divergent political stratagems—nonetheless shares *a larger abiding cultural grievance.* Indeed that lumberjacks, dock hands, mill workers, and labor activists could momentarily link arms with merchants, engineers, ministers, and schoolmarms in a common cause spanning decades and a host of social and economic disparities offers testimony to the power of a shared ideological

---

socialism into a religious world view," and he quotes a Texan saying, "Give us Socialism and the religion of our Lord and Savior Jesus Christ." Comrades faithfully attended weeklong "protracted" Socialist camp-meeting revivals and "Holy Roller" revivals as well, and heard the same preachers at both. "Red Tom" Hickory of Texas came on as a fire-and-brimstone revivalist preaching a second coming "lighted with the lamp of socialism." (C. Vann Woodward, "Home-Grown Radicals," a review of James R. Green, *Grass-Roots Socialism: Radical Movements in the Southwest, 1895-1943*, LSU Press, 1979, in *The New York Review of Books*, 5 April 1979.)

[173] Gutman, "Protestantism and the American Labor Movement . . . ," 100.

vision.[174] But what of the nature, condition, and occasion of this cultural disenchantment?

As we have seen, the insurgents commonly voiced an often bitter and nostalgic denunciation of the direction and social consequences of urbanization and industrialization in the late nineteenth- and early twentieth-century America. However occasionally incongruous the public programs and rhetoric of the labor radicals, Progressive reformers, and other malcontents, their grievances could be reduced to some variation upon a jaundiced assessment of what capital, wealth, bosses, the "Interests," and all their attendant epiphenomena had wrought upon the fabric of American social and economic life.

On the one hand, middle-class reformers located the festering sores of social infection—whose betraying symptoms were the trade and self-indulgence in liquor and prostitution, and the corruption of government officials—in the moneyed "Interests," often downtown Republican businessmen and occasionally the Democrat party bosses also, who prospered from the

---

[174] Consider, for example, the suggestive (though often contradictory) parallels in this account of voting behavior:

> The missionary appeals of Lee Benson, Samuel P. Hays, and others have combined with the computer and the diligence of quantitative historians to generate a startling revision of assumptions about electoral behavior in the late nineteenth century. The quantifiers have permanently altered our perceptions of the political landscape of the Gilded Age and chartered fresh road maps for the rest of us to travel by. The major finding of Paul Kleppner, Richard Jenson, Samuel McSeveney, and other scholars of like persuasion is that the mass of American voters, from the 1870s down through the early 1890s, from New England and New York across the Middle West, were prompted in their voting behavior primarily *by ethno-cultural values, mostly religious and sectarian in their roots.* This finding is not only important in itself; it confirms a sense that despite frequent provocations to the contrary, class-consciousness and economic radicalism were shallow and ephemeral characteristics in the electorate. It also reinforces an awareness of decentralization and pervasive localism in the political horizons of most voters. (Geoffrey Blodgett, "A New Look at the Gilded Age: Politics in a Cultural Context," in D. W. Howe ed., *Victorian America*, Philadelphia: University of Pennsylvania Press, 1976, 89.) {emphasis added}

I would caution, however, that the reading of "ethno-cultural values" into voting patterns is fraught with uncertainty. Even more so in any attempt to use them as measures or indicators of a cultural ethos or worldview.
—Even in the twelve-volume work generally regarded as signaling the emergence of conservative American fundamentalism, *The Fundamentals*, a series produced from 1910-1915, one author acknowledged without apparent controversy that the "church leaves its members free to adopt or reject socialism as they deem wise." (Nancy T. Ammerman, "North American Protestant Fundamentalism," in Martin E, Marty & R. Scott Appleby eds., *The Fundamentalism Project, Vol. I: Fundamentalisms Observed*, University of Chicago Press, 1991, 22.)

moral deterioration of the laboring classes; they abhorred the "impurity" and unfairness of the disproportionate influence of wealth upon government and the usurpation of public resources by self-aggrandizing private parties, among other things. On the other hand, labor radicals diagnosed and defined social maladies in terms of the depreciation of the personalities, skills, and value of traditional manual laborers and labor, the increasing dependence of workers and families upon bosses and owners, the seemingly unlimited extension of work hours, and the sheer regimentation and depersonalization of factory labor itself, all having their ultimate source in the unbridled power of capitalistic ownership, the accruing wealth of which ensured a corresponding disproportionate influence over the elected representatives to whom the workers and their advocates turned for ameliorative legislation.

Above and beyond these understandable differences in outlook and method arising from often widely divergent social and economic positions and experiences, both workers and reformers carried with them into the fray an anti-capitalistic, pre-industrial ideology that sanctioned and legitimated the terms and focus of their protest. Of the many approaches (and compromises) that were adopted to account for the often inexplicable *discrepancies* between the new industrial order and traditional pastoral Biblical models of charity, craftsmanship, egalitarianism, and communalism,[175] it was this evangelical-grounded version that proved the most evocative and effective (for these particular groups), deriving as it did from some of the most cardinal assumptions animating both evangelicalism and America culture. As Herbert Gutman wrote of nineteenth-century workers who clung to a pre-industrial worldview:

> But some, especially trade unionists and labor reformers and radicals, discovered that preindustrial ideology heightened rather than obliterated the moral dilemmas of a new social order and that the Protestantism of an earlier America offered a religious sanction for *their* discontent with industrial laissez faire and the "Acquisitive Man." A pre-industrial social order had nurtured particular religious beliefs that did not disappear with the coming of industrialism and did not easily or quickly conform to the Protestantism of a Henry Ward Beecher or a Dwight Moody and the secular optimism of an Andrew Carnegie or a Horatio Alger.[176]

---

[175] Similar in many respects to Lincoln's borrowings from scripture to condemn slavery in his second inaugural address: "Both read the same Bible, and pray to the same God; and each invokes His aid against the other. It may seem strange [therefore] that any men should dare to ask a just God's assistance in wringing their bread from the sweat of other men's faces; but let us judge not that we be not judged." Imagery lifted from Genesis 3:19 and Matthew 7:1.

[176] Gutman, "Protestantism and the American Labor Movement . . . ," 84.

As we have seen, the emerging industrial society became for many of these malcontents a terribly *fallen*, terribly *un-Christian* social, political, and economic "world" of disenchantment, as thoroughly decadent and despoiled as any Sodom and Gomorrah. The emerging economic order came to represent a world of profanity and sin; the pre-industrial past, or the democratic, egalitarian vistas of the future, by contrast, assumed the mantle of God's chosen societies.

The contemporary Seattle Pacific student will doubtless find disconcerting the guiding animus of student themes printed in the April 1913 Seattle Seminary *Cascade* yearbook, particularly those addressing the topic of "Our Twentieth-Century Civilization." For his collegiate ancestors documented and uniformly execrated the seemingly inexorable parade of "slavery," "misery," and other ill-effects and epiphenomena of the "merciless oppression of political and industrial progress," a metastasizing cancer spreading throughout the formerly healthy body of Christian "culture." The modern evangelical will find in these words a rather strange and *exotic* kind of speaking in tongues, belonging to and evoking an altogether different time and place.

What then proves most characteristic of the nature and structure of this ideological interpretation or galvanizing worldview (as I mentioned earlier and will return to again and again throughout the course of the study) is a dualistic apprehension of the persons, objects, and forces composing the evangelical's social and political world. It is a dynamic process that thrives upon the perception of impending cultural danger. As is the nature of ideology in general, the tendency is to simplify and reduce the components of society into the elementary opposing forces of absolute right and wrong, good and evil, the sacred and the profane—and most germanely for our purposes, the Christian and the secular. So that when we encounter the surviving transcriptions of these movements' wholesale rejections of the world which industrialization and the "Interests" had wrought, we find that they were often framed in these familiar bi-polar terms.[177]

---

[177] Although the primarily southern Farmers Alliance Exchange and subsequent People's Party may have had evangelical Christian elements within it, Lawrence Goodwyn, in perhaps the standard work, suggests that genuine Populism (not the William Jennings Bryan variety) was more properly the result of the havoc the Civil War wreaked upon the southern banking system and agriculture, and the resulting exploitative crop-lien system that impoverished farmers and eventually appropriated much of their land. (See *The Populist Moment: A Short History of the Agrarian Revolt in America*, New York: Oxford University Press, 1978.)
—More recently, Richard C. Goode has unearthed compelling evidence that radical, religiously-motivated social gospelers played a major role in the Farmers Alliance in Alabama, his findings leading him to call for a major reappraisal of traditional understandings of southern religion. (See "The Godly Insurrection in Limestone County: Social Gospel, Populism,

The evangelical cultural dynamic of a sinful, deteriorating *world* out there threatening a virtuous, wholistic *community* of remembrance in here, offered a coherent, unifying vision to so many other individuals and groups who felt similarly threatened and confused. For so ubiquitous were the experiences and consequences of industrialization and urbanization that nearly everyone could in some manner identify with the logic and emotions of this cultural lamentation; one's own peculiarly expressed cultural grievances could serve to buttress and reinforce the complaints of others, often melding into a seamless web of cultural disenchantment. What this ultimately suggests, above and beyond addressing why these different individuals and groups embraced and employed similar imagery at various moments in their histories, is that the form of evangelical social and political ideas (and a closely-corresponding community identity) *receives its particular impression or configuration with direct reference to some conception of a threatening world out there*—i.e., assumes a particular coloration in direct reaction or opposition to some looming profane or secular presence.[178] It was just such a recognition and designation of the emerging capitalist order as an erroneous, fallen *world* that sent so many Christians leaping into the welcoming arms of radical populists and socialists who could offer their fellow malcontents succoring community and social models not unlike those of the imagined early Pauline sects. Notions of from each according to his abilities, to each according to his needs, evoked a nostalgia in

---

and Southern Culture in the Late Nineteenth Century," *Religion and American Culture: A Journal of Interpretation* 3, no. 2 [Summer 1993].)

[178] The perception of clear and present dangers is not an exclusive American concern; it seems in fact particularly characteristic of nationalist religious ideologues. It is not surprising then that Vladimir Putin's guiding philosopher, Ivan Ilyin, came to imagine and promulgate "a Russian Christian fascism. Born in 1883, he finished his thesis, on God's worldly failure, just before the Russian Revolution of 1917. . . . the Russian Federation of today resembles the Russian Empire of Ilyin's youth in one crucial respect: it has not established the rule of law as the principle of government. The trajectory of Ilyin's understanding of law, from hopeful universalism to arbitrary nationalism, has been followed by the discourse of Russian politicians, including Putin. Because Ilyin found ways to present the failure of the rule of law as Russian virtue, he helps today's Russian kleptocrats portray economic inequality as national innocence. By transforming international politics into a discussion of *spiritual threats*, Putin has used Ilyin's ideas about geopolitics to portray Ukraine, Europe, and the United States *as existential dangers to Russia.* . . . Christianity [for Ilyin] meant the call of the right-seeing philosopher to *apply decisive violence in the name of love.* To be immersed in such love was the struggle '*against the enemies of the divine order on earth.*' Thus theology becomes politics. Ilyin blurred 'democracy,' 'socialism,' and 'Marxism' into a single continuum of corruption, and maintained that politics that did not oppose Bolshevism opposed God. He used the word 'Spirit' (*Dukh*) to describe the inspiration of fascists. The fascist seizure of power, he wrote, was 'an act of salvation.' " (Timothy Snyder, "God Is a Russian," *The New York Review of Books*, 4/5/18, 50-1.) {emphases added}

many for a Christianity in its most genuine, unadulterated (pre-industrial) form.[179]

Identity & Transition

The value of these historical digressions lies not so much in the demonstration once again of the interaction of these major cultural logics in the ideological framing of these groups' disenchantment as in what this all can tell us about the process of the formation of and transitions in community identity. For in both local and national arenas we observe in the course of nearly three-quarters of a century *a gradual transformation in the nature of this perception of a fallen, encroaching world: from one of a crass Gilded-Age commercialism dominated by the wealth of the "Interests" and driven by the organizational imperatives of capitalism to an altogether different one of an elitist, secular humanistic liberalism (concentrated most heavily in the news media, entertainment industry, intellectuals/academia, and the federal and large metropolitan governments) underpinning the ascension and expansion of the modern welfare state.*[180] Purely in terms of the sheer ideological distance covered from the inception and early days of the Seattle Seminary to the

---

[179] Such as, for example, Acts 4: 32-35: "The whole body of believers was united in heart and soul. Not a man of them claimed any of his possessions as his own, but everything was held in common, while the apostles bore witness with great power to the resurrection of the Lord Jesus. They were all held in high esteem; for they had never a needy person among them, because all who had property in land or houses sold it, brought the proceeds of the sale, and laid the money at the feet of the apostles; it was then distributed to any who stood in need." And 5: 1-12: One couple who withheld earnings from the apostles and "lied to the Holy Spirit . . . dropped dead" in their tracks. (*NEB*)

[180] One of the more intriguing ironies here is the role these progressive ancestors of modern evangelicals played in the creation of the modern welfare state that the latter now so thoroughly detest:

> . . . . the progressives produced a vast literature against laissez-faire. In fact, an ordered linear exposition would have shown that their attachment to voluntarism became increasingly nominal and their commitment to interventionism increasingly real as the period advanced. Whatever its long-range consequences, the irreversible transformation of government from a relatively inactive entity to a progressively interventionist agency was a surpassing achievement. And so, just as emphatically, was the progressives' formulation of the intellectual rationale for much of the modern welfare state, including Social Security, unemployment insurance, public works, and medical care. "Whiggish" though the notion surely is, one cannot resist suggesting that *the New Deal left such a dearth of social and political thought partly because its policies reflected values, concepts, and theories already in the public realm—put there by progressive settlement workers and social scientists.* (William H. Harbaugh, "A Climate of Creativity," a review of Robert M. Crunden, *Ministers of Reform: The Progressives' Achievement in American Civilization, 1889-1920*, New York: Basic Books, 1982, in the *New Republic*, 7 March 1983.) {emphasis added}

present University community, the transition proves almost breathtaking in scope. (No wonder the official Centennial history passes over these events without mention.) Yet however sweeping this change from early twentieth-century radical Populism and Progressivism to modern political conservatism—an ideological conversion of near glacial velocity and scouring thoroughness—*it nonetheless appears to have left the nature and essence of evangelicalism largely unchanged.*

How can this be? One compelling explanation is that what these nearly opposite social and political period pieces have in common is not so much appeals to scriptural precedents or *exemplum fidei* as an equally sharpened and pronounced bi-polar vision and apprehension of an errant, irredeemable world, particular variations upon which in their respective eras provide the central loci or rallying points of their bearers' cultural disenchantment. Indeed as the external object of aspersion—the "world"—has changed, the terms of invidious Christian and profane distinction *and* the nature and structure of internal community identity have also changed.[181]

Why the transformation or transition from one to the other? Was it inevitable? Perhaps so, then again perhaps not. Indeed although the preconditions and causes were manifold, complex, and exceedingly difficult to unravel, there are some obvious contributing elements. A good deal is explained by the almost natural course of economic development, industrial growth gradually raising the living standards of the country, expanding the size of the middle-class, this swelling tide of national income lifting all boats, although certainly heaving the larger vessels and yachts disproportionately higher along the shore than the diminutive dinghies of the lower echelons.[182]

---

[181] Although, lacking *direct* knowledge of and exposure to the evangelicals of the earlier period, I am perhaps unavoidably burdened with my own biased sense of the *much greater* application and refinement of these invidious distinctions in the modern period. Indeed, had I been forced to rely solely upon similar kinds of "historical" materials for my reading of the contemporary community an altogether different impression might have emerged.

[182] By 1894 the total value of U. S. manufactured products equaled that of Great Britain, France, and Germany combined. (Gutman, *Work, Culture, & Society* . . . , 33.) During 1896-1901 alone (following the 1893 depression) the national GNP jumped from $13 to $21 billion. (Painter, *Standing at Armageddon* . . . , 171.)

William H. Harbaugh, although fully cognizant of the darker (crusading, violent) side of Progressivism and of this period in American history, nonetheless acknowledges that "This burgeoning army of bureaucrats—or public servants—made society a shade more equitable and considerably more livable. . . . By 1920 or thereabouts urban life had become healthier in some respects than rural life." A managerial revolution spurred economic productivity and ". . . reduced the work week in manufacturing almost a full day, raised real wages markedly, and generated much of the private and public capital for the nation's mushrooming social overhead: schools, parks, libraries, hospitals, museums, roads, bridges, water and sewer mains, police and fire departments, and an embryonic state and local welfare system. By the mid-1920s, indeed, it had created what Ellis Hawley aptly terms the world's 'first industrial

As legislation was enacted to lighten the burden and consequences of labor—shortening the work week, stabilizing the wage structure, legalizing and protecting the collective bargaining power of unions, enhancing the safety of the workplace;[183] as more laborers were drawn upward into the ranks of property owners and consumers; as families began to reach accommodation with the new regimens of work—the routines of labor, domestic life, and leisure becoming social and industrial habits; as nearly everyone was in some manner or other drawn into the consumption and enjoyment of the fruits of the once execrated system, the formerly well-burnished edge of discontent began to dull, and once pronounced feelings of resentment and *discrepancy* began to fade.[184]

---

economy geared to the production of consumer durables and cultural fare for the masses.' " (Harbaugh, "A Climate of Creativity.")

[183] During the earlier Populist period Herbert Gutman found that workers had begun to hold their own against management:

> Not all strikes and lockouts resulted in the defeat of poorly organized workers. For the years 1881 to 1887, for example, the New Jersey Bureau of Labor Statistics collected information on 890 New Jersey industrial disputes involving mostly workers in the textile, glass, metal, transportation, and building trades: 6 percent ended in compromise settlements; employers gain the advantage in 40 percent; strikers won the rest (54 percent). In four of five disputes concerning higher wages and shorter hours, New Jersey workers, not their employers, were victorious. (Gutman, op. cit., 48.)

The 1914 Congress passed legislation exempting labor from antitrust prosecution (Clayton Anti-trust Act). And there were Woodrow Wilson's Three Reforms (also 1914) of the "New Freedom": reduction of the tariff, restrictions on the trusts, and overhaul of the banking and currency system, including the introduction of a moderately graduated income tax. Yet Wilson resisted other Progressive legislation, blocking "a bill to establish a system of long-term rural credits that would have made low-interest mortgages available to farmers [although much less radical than Charles Mancune's Sub-Treasury Plan of the People's Party of the 1890s], and he refused to support a child labor bill that he considered unconstitutional interference in the conduct of private business," as well as withholding support from the suffrage amendment on the grounds of states' rights to define their own electorates. (Painter, *Standing at Armageddon . . .* , XXXIX, 278.)

—"The high point of the reform movement was reached in 1915 with the legislation of mother's pension, aid to the blind, and workman's compensation [Clayton Act], the first social insurance program in the United States." (Kirsten Grønbjerg, David Street, & Gerald D. Suttles, *Poverty and Social Change*, University of Chicago Press, 1978, 40.)

[184] There is an almost implied uniform gradualism here in my presentation that is somewhat misleading. Growth, although rapid, came in sporadic bursts, as evidenced by recurring economic depressions, especially those of 1893-1897, 1907-1908, and 1914-1915 (Grønbjerg et al., *Poverty and Social Change*, 37). And tremendous total economic growth by no means ensured social and political tranquility during these expansions. In fact the Alexis de Tocqueville principle of unrest coming during periods of rising expectations certainly came into play here. These years were punctuated by the complex expansions and contractions, twists and turns, in all manner of social, economic, and political phenomena and trends. *It is only in looking at the*

Particularly out west, as the conditions and consequences of labor grew more humane and routinized, as reformers savored their many political successes (all the while having gained a greater appreciation of the irrepressible, un-reformable nature of certain individual and social vices), as the number of single itinerant men declined, many going on to marry and begin families—reducing the demand for saloon liquor and prostitutes—setting down roots, swelling the ranks of a burgeoning middle-class, the once pressing agenda of the middle-class reformer also began to lose much of its urgency.

Memories of a pre-industrial innocence—the independence and integrating wholeness of labor, shop or farm, and family—gradually lost their poignancy and motivational appeal and pull. The explosion of economic growth and opportunity following World War II, in particular, propelled many of those among the disenchanted laboring classes into the ranks of the upwardly-mobile middle classes. Evangelicals were swept along with other Americans, carried from the margins of economic respectability to the broad center of modern prosperity. Indeed, they have long since become so completely absorbed into the mainstream of American *economic* life, representing some of the most ardent defenders and apologists for an American version of *laissez-faire* capitalism, that the once pejorative connotations of "mammon," or the insidious material rewards and possessions of the "world," have become all but drained of their damning ideological force, lingering now only as quaint anachronisms (i.e., invoked primarily, as we saw above, for the purpose of routine—often hypocritical—denunciation of the "man-

---

beginning and the end of the process of transition that any uniformities among the properties of the before and after periods suggest themselves.

Also, I do not mean to leave the impression that the large majority of evangelicals were either radicals, populists, or progressives during this period (or that they stayed put ideologically from the very beginning to the very end). Among those groups that might be called "fundamentalist," George Marsden argues that a "Great reversal . . . took place from 1900 to about 1930, when all progressive social concern, whether political or private, became suspect among revivalists, and was relegated to a very minor role." By the 1920s the unifying factor would become "political conservatism." (Marsden, *Fundamentalism and American Culture* . . . , 86, 92.); ". . . .evangelical participation in progressive reforms . . . except . . . for prohibition . . . dwindled sharply." (George Marsden, *Understanding Fundamentalism and Evangelicalism*, Grand Rapids, Michigan: Eerdmanns, 1991, 30.) William McLoughlin agrees, detecting an enthusiastic embrace of laissez-faire capitalism during the first thirty years or so of the 20th century. Yet, as suggested earlier, more recent work has called these earlier judgments into question, as William Lee Miller notes: ". . . . you could argue that both of the major American movements on the 'left,' before the New Deal—populism in the late-nineteenth century, progressivism in the early twentieth—were given their shape and much of their impetus by the Protestant churches." ("The Seminarian Strain: Church and Statesmen in the Democratic Party," *New Republic*, 9 July 1984, 19.) Again, we can define evangelicalism so narrowly as to reduce the phenomenon to fundamentalism alone. Yet it seems to me that in light of the accumulating historical evidence a broader, more inclusive category more accurately captures the nature and identity of these religiously-inspired partisans.

centered" materialism of the "secular" world). For as we have seen, evangelicals, perhaps with greater enthusiasm than any other sector of American society, embrace the assumptions raising individual economic performance in the marketplace to the heights of a leading indicator or barometer of intrinsic moral character (with all the attendant social and political ramifications). And what a marked shift in political economics this represents.

But what then serves to distinguish contemporary evangelicalism from its late nineteenth-and early twentieth-century counterparts is not so much this shift in political economic ideology as an even more compelling correlated change in the form and composition of what appears to threaten it from outside, what it means by *the world*. The average evangelical now fears and apprehends a worldly beast—better yet, a Leviathan—of an altogether different nature and dominion, whose full identity and properties (and the social and cultural conditions underlying and sustaining its seemingly inevitable appearance upon the scene) will be explored throughout the remainder of this study.

Principles of Community Identity

Unfortunately, the above presentation may leave the reader with the impression of a relationship between these respective evangelical conceptions of an *external* world of venality and an *internal* community of virtue that is a good deal simpler and more direct than is actually the case. In fact, there occurs an exceedingly complex interaction here between three (or more) elements: the actual Biblical text, precedents, and traditions that are adopted or accrue to any church or denomination or even to the larger American evangelical community as a whole; the general evangelical formulation of the properties of an external *secular world*; and evangelicalism's conception of its own internal community characteristics (with due consideration, once more, for the variegated nature and texture of each of these phenomena). But by no means is this contemporary evangelical conjuration of a threatening secular world, with all the attendant bi-polar distinctions (yet to be fully enumerated and examined), something which uniformly emerges prior to some purely opposite evangelical vision of an ideal Christian community or world, one already fashioned out of whole cloth; rather, we will find that both prove syncopated reifications, and are nearly always conceived of or elaborated upon *in terms of the other*.

Then too both of these finely calibrated configurations or characterizations of *the Christian* and *the secular* assume some kind of additional relationship with the more stable, formal Biblical and doctrinal elements underlying the European Protestant and American evangelical traditions. For although it is by now apparent that I would impugn any evangelical claim of the direct, unaccommodating application of Biblical principles and models in their family and community lives, by no means am I suggesting there is no link whatsoever between scripture and individual and community behavior. Far from it.

An example can help here. Recall our earlier discussion of the evangelical attitude towards work and wealth. In the seemingly never-ending debate over the role and meaning of money within the evangelical community both the proponents of "prosperity theology" and their social internationalist (my term) critics may take comfort in scriptures which would appear to corroborate diametrically-opposed positions. Obviously these Biblical passages and their embrace and citation by various partisans within evangelicalism (and indeed throughout history) long predate their contemporary polemical uses. So that neither of these conceptions (God wants you to accumulate, enjoy wealth *versus* God wants you to share, redistribute wealth) of the arrant nature of a worldly materialism are purely reactionary products or reflections of the phenomenon they decry. There is some basis in scripture and in the various evangelical and Protestant traditions for these positions, some prior form or historical context and structure to the range of possibilities from which they sprang; there may have been a kind of logical affinity operating between them. Similarly, I detect no exclusive one-to-one *causal* relationship between the robber baron capitalism of the last half of the nineteenth century and the models of an altogether different Christian workers' utopia championed by some workers and union activists. The former was not the sole cause of the latter. Hence, scriptural rationalizations for all sorts of social schemes abound, and vice-versa.

The example of sexuality may prove even more useful. One can hardly argue that the contemporary evangelical position upon sex solely owes its existence to, or represents a direct reaction to, modern sexual latitudinarianism. Formal sexual prohibitions were in force within the adolescent precincts of evangelicalism long before the sexual revolution of the '60s and '70s brought a host of threatening new possibilities; recall the divided staircase of the early years of Seattle Pacific. What I would instead argue is that the evangelical community seizes upon these decidedly different approaches to sexual behavior, work, wealth, and other potentially contentious matters as *points of departure, deploying out in all directions from these central antinomies a series of correlated distinctions, the entire framework of which becomes incorporated within even more comprehensive codifications and schematizations that also owe their origins to similarly fundamental logical oppositions, all ultimately linked to or derived from—in one manner or another, however far removed—some observable (though often illusory) property or feature of these respective antithetical Christian and secular social worlds.* The nature and content of these interactions will become a good deal clearer once we move from this unavoidably abstract theoretical introduction to a consideration of the actual day-to-day life of the community. There the reader will find these dynamics less obscure, or as the anthropologists put it, somewhat less *exotic*, more readily grasped.

Obviously then there are some real departures in attitude and behavior between the evangelical Christian and his non-Christian counterpart which can neither be reduced solely to the evangelical community's apprehension of (and reaction to) those differences nor attributed to any elaborate formulation of the depraved nature and constitution of a threatening secular world, especially one which is held as the ultimate source of a diametrically-opposed community self-definition. To avoid a *too* spurious reification of these dualistic ideas into ideological creatures bearing inordinate causal powers of their own, one must exercise extreme caution and always take into consideration the complex interaction of logics, communities, and social worlds, and their ongoing relationships with inherited Biblical and doctrinal traditions.

Prince of Peace, God of War

During the same aforementioned period, the community underwent another transition that was similar to the movement from political progressivism to political conservatism but which resists the kind of explanation advanced earlier—indeed, may be inexplicable in those terms. For whereas the earlier political transition was in large measure the outcome of a range of social and economic factors brought into play by industrialization and urbanization, developments which ultimately transformed the focus and object of the evangelical's cultural disenchantment, no such preconditions appear to underpin this second transition, a rapid evolution from pre-World War II passivism to militarism and post-war anti-communism. More likely we encounter here the kind of general cultural osmosis I mentioned earlier: the spread of national influences or moods through the breaches of the often highly-defined-and -celebrated ideological bulwarks of the community, in this instance faculty and students awash in the flood of an all-consuming and mobilizing nationalism that fairly gushed following the attack upon Pearl Harbor in December of 1941.[185] Then again, we may find the inherent structure of evangelical ideas amenable to this brave new world of war. Perhaps once more we observe in operation here the principle that although the objects of aspersion change, the general cultural principle and dynamic remains the same.

---

[185] In this respect the college was like most other small American towns or communities which clung to and then jettisoned an understandable reluctance to once again enter the international arena of war.

In the mid 1930s Seattle Pacific students, faculty, and guest speakers frequently decried the manufacture and exportation of armaments by the great powers to less stable regimes and countries around the globe. Miss Agnes Butler appeared before the International Club, warning of "Munitions in Latin America": " 'The traffic in arms,' Miss Butler said, 'is purely an international syndicate which is manipulated by the financial loans of the exporting munitions country.' " She called upon her listeners to support an "arms embargo."[186] It was an issue that was on everyone's mind, as seen in that year's debate topic of the Forensic Club, "Resolved: That the nations should agree to prevent the international shipment of munitions."[187]

References to the domestic munitions industries which stood to profit from an expansion of overseas markets are ubiquitous throughout the 1930s. Aspersions cast upon the motives of munitions entrepreneurs reflect the lessons drawn from the First World War, when workers and reformers watched with rising resentment as private industries gouged a strapped national government for unconscionable levels of war profits. Yet this debate over the international shipment of armaments represented but one dimension of a larger, more comprehensive indictment of the Roosevelt administration's conduct of American foreign policy. Critics detected a relentless pressure from industry to expand American capitalism's theater of operation. The cardinal theme here is one of anti-imperialism.[188]

Dr. J. J. Hansacker, associate secretary of the Society for the Prevention of War, warned the Seattle Pacific community of impending

War! World Suicide! Is this to be the climax of twenty Christian Centuries? But why war with Japan?[189]—three possible reasons: a war between Christianity and

---

[186] *Falcon*, 28 November 1934.

[187] Ibid., 19 December 1934.

[188] We often overlook the other side of William Jennings Bryan, from his *Memoirs* (1925):

> If true Christianity consists of carrying out in our daily lives the teachings of Christ, who will say that we are commanded to civilize with dynamite and proselyte with the sword? Imperialism finds no warrant in the Bible. . . . Love, not force, was the weapon of the Nazarene; sacrificing for others, not the exploitation of them, was His method of reaching the human heart. (quoted in Harvey Cox, *Religion in the Secular City. . .* , 60)

[189] Japan proved a particularly sensitive subject for most west-coast evangelicals due to their special missionary relationships with China, Japan, and the rest of the Far East. These extensive experiences tended to blind evangelicals to even the suggestion of a nascent Japanese Fascism and expansionism, compounding an inherent Progressive reluctance to condemn smaller powers. (I thank Professor Guenther Roth for pointing this out.)

Paganism (which side fights which we don't know), desire for an open door into China (since we won the Philippines by two wars this struggle may mean another), and of course "war for peace"... In the last war 6,500 men were slaughtered daily for four years in *an attempt to get the markets*....[190] [emphasis added]

In April of 1937, the *Falcon* published the results of a campus-wide poll, the unambiguous nature and content of whose questions prove as instructive and revelatory as the tabulated results:

Students Vote Pacifist in Opinion Poll [191]

1) Do you favor government ownership of the munitions and [*sic*] industry and a 100% tax on all war profits? Yes 121 / No 20

2) Do you favor embargos on both sides at war? Yes 120 / No 21

3) Do you favor America's present official naval policy of "maintaining a navy in sufficient strength to defend our interests, commerce, and overseas possessions?" Yes 65 / No 75

4) Would you refuse to support the government in war except possibly to repel an armed invasion of Continental United States? Yes 123 / No 16

5) Do you believe that an adequate national defense requires an immediate increase in the size of our army, navy, and air force? Yes 9 / No 131

6) Do you believe that economic imperialism is a major cause of war and heretofore that its abolition is necessary for a permanent peace? Yes 108 / No 29 [emphasis added]

In the same *Falcon* issue one receives a sense of the power and urgency of these sentiments from a column ("Students for Peace and Democracy") reporting on a Congress of American college students convened at the University of Illinois:

We are the youth of America and the most disillusioned youth in history. You can't kid us, the nations value their gold more than they value their sons.... We don't want your white crosses.... They insist that youth is sick of reading

---

—Miss Lillian Pickens before the International Club: "Japan really has a friendly attitude to world affairs, she stated, but it is not to be judged by the belligerent moves of the uncontrollable army maneuvers." (*Falcon*, 8 December 1936.)

[190] Ibid., 6 March 1935. However crude the foregoing analyses, readers familiar with the work of William Appleman Williams (especially *The Roots of the Modern American Empire: A Study in the Growth and Shaping of Social Consciousness in a Marketplace Society*, New York: Random House, 1969) will no doubt appreciate the guiding animus.

[191] *Falcon*, 27 April 1937. 300 questionnaires distributed; @ 150 returned. (S.P.C. total enrollment: 310, 12 October 1937 *Falcon*)

—An account of Tutome Fuchiyama's views in "Freedom of Seas is Debate Topic": "This nation, he averred, is far too greedy for land and money to allow any amount of organized peace work and propaganda keep her out of war...." (ibid., 22 April 1936.)

editorials and hearing speeches to the effect that preparation for war is the only way out of war.[192]

As in probably any American academic community of the period we discover among the often impassioned execrations of imperialistic motivations both sophisticated, realistic understandings of the historical background to the European predicament and superficial, facile apologies for the conduct of Germany and Japan.[193]

---

[192] Ibid., 27 April 1937.

[193] These were not uncommon sentiments during this period, both on the national and international levels:

> While dictators stormed, the Western democracies were swayed by a profound pacifism, which may be defined as a somewhat doctrinaire insistence on peace regardless of consequences. Many people now believed, especially in England and the United States, that the First World War had been a mistake, that little or nothing had been gained by it, that they had been deluded by war-time propaganda, that wars were really started by armaments manufacturers, that Germany had not really caused the war of 1914, that the treaty of Versailles was too hard on the Germans, that vigorous people like the Germans or Italians needed room for expansion, that democracy was after all not suited to all nations, that it took two to make a quarrel, and that there need be no war if one side resolutely refused to be provoked—a whole system of pacific and tolerant ideas in which there was perhaps the usual mixture of truth and misunderstanding. (R.R. Palmer & Joel Colton, *A History of the Modern World*, 3rd ed., New York: Alfred A. Knopf, 1965, 818.)

—Some local observers, echoing the judgment of John Maynard Keynes in *The Economic Consequences of the Peace*, located the source of impending world-wide conflagration in the terms of the 1919 Versailles treaty, repudiating the cynical, self-aggrandizing manipulations of the West European parties. The *Falcon* reported the remarks of the college's "Student Volunteer Secretary" to the effect that England and France harbored ulterior motives beneath the surface of their apparently high-minded promotion of the League of Nations: "The League is just a screen behind which the nations want to arrange the map of Europe." (16 October 1935)

—As late as 1941 a Dr. Bowman reaffirmed his pacifism:

Know politics, says Dr. Bowman: Advocates action

> Denmark's splendid educational system has not been destroyed, and, in Dr. Bowman's opinion, Denmark did wisely in not offering resistance to German aggression.
> Dr. Bowman is an ardent advocate of cooperatives, and he feels that their success in meeting American economic needs is borne out by this mushroom increase in the last two years. (ibid., 31 October 1941.)

For many S.P.C. students and faculty the question of war and peace represented much more than a mere ideological debating point; opinions and attitudes translated into purposeful behavior within and without the community. They established committees, circulated petitions, posted letters to Washington, and organized often day-long conferences, summoning nationally-known anti-war activists to the Seattle campus.[194]

The evangelical rejection of war turned upon the loathsome memory of World War I—a sentiment held in common with most other Europeans and Americans, a social internationalist revulsion towards imperialism, a history of missionary associations with Japan and the Far East, and the exemplary personal pacifism of Jesus in the Gospels.[195] (And these represent, as I have suggested before, the typical range of general, national, and local

---

[194] Among the plethora of items appearing in the *Falcon* throughout this period, an October 16, 1935 piece announced: "Peace Program Launched: Faculty and Students Organize Executive Peace Council" and reported the visit of the Reverend B.H. Pearson, General Superintendent of the Young People's Organization of the Free Methodist Church, who brought

> . . . . the request that 50,000 signatures be obtained to a peace pledge within the next two weeks.
> The pledge read as follows: "God helping me, I purpose [*sic*] not to cross the border of any nation voluntarily except in friendship, nor to support my country in such action."
> After the 50,000 signatures have been obtained throughout the nation, according to Rev. Pearson, they will be sent to President Roosevelt as an expression of public opinion.

[195] Typical is a column reporting a meeting of the "Young People's Missionary Society" in which a ". . . . Mr. Walton Ackley presented the two points of Christ's attitude towards wars, using the scriptures as reference." (ibid., 23 October 1935)
As late as 1940, we find these observations in the *Falcon*:

> —I cannot picture Christ running a bayonet through his brother man or tossing a hand grenade in his face. And He is my example. How then can I do what I know *He* would never do??
> —War is not only sin; it is the ultimate sin. It means the complete denial of love-the heart of Jesus' Gospel. How can I be a disciple of His if I deliberately deny the very essence of that discipleship?
> —Someone said long ago, "Love your enemies, bless them that curse you, do good to them that hate you." I believe He meant what He said. Need I say more? (ibid., 19 March 1940)

Here is the only pre-Pearl Harbor justification for armaments (however indirect) and a warrior Christ that I came across—one, I should add, thoroughly steeped in *non sequitur*: "Rev. Pearson speaks on Evangelism . . . . Later Christianity ruled the world. There were Christian rulers and Christian armies, but as time went on Christianity began to fade and they lost sight of Jesus, the Christ of Christianity. . . . the best thing that they could have done was to stay true to Jesus. . . ." (ibid., 14 March 1939)

sources of the attitudes and conduct of this community.) We find then a consensus in force upon the campus—and indeed throughout the country at large—regarding the origins and appropriate response to the gathering storm of European war. Anti-imperialism, isolationism, and pacifism offered a soothing tonic for gun-shy, world-weary Americans. Furthermore, a good many evangelical Christians believed that out of the weakness of appeasement would emerge the strength of a Christian transformation; it was a diffidence grounded in the inversion logic of the Gospel teachings of Christ. From capitulation would come an ultimate triumph of principle and good will.

Even as late as January of 1940, with Germany having consumed Czechoslovakia and Poland and both England and France having declared war in September of 1939, the *Falcon* issued "A New Year Resolve," a lead editorial claiming to have divined the source of the European conflict, although relying upon an old and familiar theme:

> Ostensibly a battle for the preservation of European democracy, the roots of the present conflict are nevertheless deeply imbedded in imperialistic designs.
> Outstanding in this New Year should be a steadfast resolve of American youth to keep America free of foreign embroilments. A resolve for peace is compatible with our American heritage, and is a noble effort toward a steadying influence in a world of turmoil.[196] {emphasis added}

The Gospel of the Stars and Stripes: Inversion or Infusion?

The summer of 1940 brought the collapse of France and the consolidation of Nazi control over an area of land roughly equivalent to that held by Napoleon. Yet only with the torching of the American Pacific fleet by the Japanese armada exactly one month later at Pearl Harbor did a truly stunned campus shake itself awake from a deep, irenic slumber. As for many Americans, Pearl Harbor was the last straw. Perhaps more than anything it was this strike against a benevolent, paternalistic America by a formerly passive object of American missionaries that sealed the fate of evangelical passivism. For indeed Hell hath no fury greater than that harbored within the breast of the bearer of an offer of salvation and grace that is subsequently spurned.[197] The evangelicals dove into the war business with a barely-con-

---

[196] Ibid., 9 January 1940.

[197] Some of the almost personal nature of the offense or affront comes through in the following *Falcon* article (24 March 1944): "Dr. Warren Gives Data on Japanese Conquests in War. . . . Since their sneak attack on Pearl Harbor the Japanese have stolen 114,000 square

cealed relish. Years of accumulated vexations and frustrations appeared to vent themselves upon the newly discovered enemies of Christian America. In an unprecedented surge of energy, the community actually began to exult in the emotional release of vengeance and retribution, indulging feelings that were formerly regarded as invidious, reprehensible sins.[198] Swept away by the rising tide of nationalism were the Jesus models and the appeals for the preservation of civilization.

Understandably, the college began to re-tool its ideological and spiritual infrastructure, to re-shape its academic form. "Armistice Day Chapel" became "Patriotic Chapel"; Selective Service Broadcasts replaced the Missionary Hour; the "Star Spangled Banner" and "God Bless America" supplanted the hymns of Charles Wesley. Over the course of a few months, the Prince of Peace had superannuated, grown unfashionable. Gone were the principles of *inversion* radiating from the New Testament teachings of Jesus[199]—particularly the application by Jesus of love and passivism against the overwhelming physical force of enemies and evil (in anticipation of an eventual spiritual transformation); enter the *infusions* of a national society mobilizing its armies and emotions for war.

Upon commencement of a new school year in October of 1942, the *Falcon* welcomed students with a front page editorial, "Once Again," a piece that appeared to draw together a summer's worth of brooding reflection upon the reality of war, promulgating a revisionist evangelical agenda, one grounded in a new "realism."

> It was, perhaps, a commentary upon the entire year's work ahead that our first all-college assembly was a "War Assembly." *We are living in a new order. Times have changed.* Of necessity plans must be changed. . . . War is costly in culture, research, and *sometimes in character* as well as in money and human life. You are to be commended for the *realistic* and contagious way in which you are facing the future. *To truly face life with Christ means to live in His Word, with no compromise whatsoever with sin and in full commitment to His will and leadership.* Then, too, we must dedicate ourselves anew to our country . . . [we should demonstrate a] willingness to serve. It means less criticism and more cooperation; it means less selfishness and more patriotism; it means to do the job ourselves which we require of other professed

---

miles [Oregon?] from the United States . . . and have enslaved 16,000,000 people in these areas . . . [the Japanese] must be defeated in a battle to the end."

[198] This displacement or projection of internal anger onto others has a long history. See, in particular, "Soldiers for Christ: Anger, Aggression, and Enemies," in Philip Greven, *The Protestant Temperament: Patterns of Child-Rearing, Religious Experience, and the Self in Early America* (New York: A Meridian Book of the New American Library, 1979).

[199] Matthew 5:5—the "Beatitudes"; and Mark 9:33: " 'If anyone wants to be first, he must make himself last of all and servant of all.' " (*NEB*)

Americans. . . . By this dedicating ourselves anew *to God* and *to country*. . . .[200] {emphases added}

Indeed, with no apparent recognition of incongruity or internal contradiction: welcome to a Christ of an altogether different nature and form, to a new age sanctioned by the all-absorbing atmosphere of nationalism.[201] Then again, perhaps we shouldn't be surprised to find that a community so adroit at the internal application of peer and social pressures, having generated well-worn and -exercised paths and methods for the inculcation of values in its own students, should suddenly find itself vulnerable to waves of national emotion that flowed along these very same avenues of transmission, overwhelming the normally resilient ideological defenses of the community. And then too it was a transition greatly aided by the apprehension of an altogether different kind of external peril: a tangible, militant nation-state, marshalling armies and brandishing the actual concrete weapons of war, threatening to breach the borders of the sacred homeland; a rather more immediate danger than the more diffuse, almost theoretical bugbear of corporate imperialism.[202]

During the course of the war, the campus newspaper, the *Falcon*, recorded but a single dissent to this great reversal, one faint but persistent voice echoing ideas and sentiments of a bygone era of innocence, one last gasp before a consensual silence descended upon the campus. In a long letter to the editor, Irving W. Sylvia launched a devastating attack upon the new nationalism of the college, rendering the revisionist posture scripturally indefensible. The current mobilization for war, he argued, paralleled the paganization or secularization of Christianity under the warrior, Constantine, the first Christian emperor of Rome:

---

[200] *Falcon*, 6 October 1942.

[201] President Watson no longer spoke of the "God of Peace," instead referring to those earlier sentiments as "the *peace propaganda* of a few years ago." ("President's Annual Report: Golden Jubilee Year, 1941-1942": "Section F. The War Emergency. . . . Brief Summary.") {emphasis added} {Archives}

[202] I should add, however, that a similar transition occurred during World War I. In that particular instance we observed the irony of liberal theologians leading an attack upon premillennial fundamentalists for their opposition to the war, insinuating that they were funded "from German sources. . . . [Further] In 1917 the California-based [pre-millennial] journal [*The King's Business*] had warned against the disastrous and demoralizing effects of war and urged Christians to 'love our enemies,' even if they were Germans. . . . By April 1918 the war was becoming a godly cause. . . . By May 1918 they [the editors were] . . . relating the Kaiser directly to the devil." (Marsden, *Fundamentalism and American Culture* . . . , 147-51.)

Today the same thing is being done: We hear all about us the roar of the patriot, shouting America's cause is Christ's cause. When we enlist in the army we are told we are enlisting under the banners of Christ. Christianity has been made analogous with materialistic, proud America. . . . How can we attempt to identify Christ with war? Why should a Christ who refused to lead the Hebrew people in a war against Roman tyranny, who healed the wounds of a Roman soldier, who cried in the midst of his suffering on the cross, "Father forgive them for they know not what they do," who spent His life in a ministry of Love amid the brutal wars of His day, condone war in our day; a war which is every bit as brutal and selfish as the wars of His day?

We hear men say, "Now that we are in this war, we must fight or be conquered." This to me is a denial of Christ's whole teaching of faith in love. When the evil presses round about us we lose faith in the efficacy of love and say that Christ is not sufficient unto our day. Christ is all right when peace reigns, but when the forces of darkness become powerful, we either forsake Him, or identify Him with the forces of darkness. . . . [Yet] His way of love will conquer all evil. . . . [203]

No more incisive internal critique of the inherent contradictions of the new evangelical realism was ever penned. But perhaps more intriguing than the mere fact of an anachronistic opinion of this sort surfacing during this rapid emotional and ideological preparation for war was the response of the *Falcon* editor. No doubt put on the defensive by the inescapable logic and veracity of the argument, lapsing into a condition of spiritual amnesia that appeared to nullify or deny all the paper had heretofore extolled and promoted, he replied, "Dear Mr. Sylvia: Amen!.......The Editor."[204]

In this particular instance, Mr. Sylvia's powerful indictment of the evangelical compromise must have produced considerable consternation, for a

---

[203] *Falcon*, 5 April 1943. Actually, there was one other: The *Falcon* in March of 1943 reported with perhaps a trace of sarcasm that the local U.S. Navy chapter had conducted an S.P.C. chapel session, presenting what the paper called "Movie Propaganda." Underneath, a "Commentary" cautioned that

> . . . . a great number of Christians in our country love to think that God has laid His hand upon them and their nation to deliver them from all evil. They feel they are fighting on God's side when they strike against the Axis nations. But God does not always work that way. Jesus said, "If my kingdom were of this world, then would my servants fight." But though He and His followers represented the cause of right, He strove not to vindicate them but rather submitted unto Satan and all his works, even the cross itself . . . it became the Central Purpose of Lord Jesus to die in the hands of evil ones. (*Falcon*, 1 March 1943)

[204] In time the reader will come to recognize the role "Amen" occasionally performs among evangelical clientele: it ushers the congregation past those seemingly interminable, disquieting moments when ideological etiquette has been breached, when the contradiction between logic or ideals and reality has been laid bare for all to see.

discernable lapse of concentration and a hiatus in the publication of war-related materials ensued, as the editors paused to regain their composure and momentum, putting some time and distance between themselves and *the letter*, only then moving on, gingerly, as though nothing had happened and no contradiction would result from the simultaneous trite affirmation of the meaning of the letter and the full-throttle effusion of nationalism and militarism that followed.

Some six weeks passed before the *Falcon* resumed the war business as usual, publishing a large section with pictures and captions which read, "Serving Christ and Country," "Be Strong, Be Brave, Be True," and a column, "We're Patriotic 100% and over the Top in Pledges." These were followed later in January by the headline exhortation, "Fight . . . Defeat Satan."[205] With considerable *élan*, the community completed its headlong rush into the militarization of the Christian spirit.

Seattle Pacific claimed 220 names in active military service.[206] All told, by war's end, SPC President Watson had buried a son-in-law and performed memorial services for eleven fallen students. How to explain and rationalize the carnage?

The Mysterious Will of God

A *Falcon* editorial in March of 1950, three months before the invasion of North Korea into the South, ruminated upon the deeper meanings of the Pacific war and the occupation of Japan:

> God has opened the door [for missions, etc.] to Japan through the means of a devastating war which has made many of the Japanese people to see that their gods cannot help them.[207]

Even more instructive: the man who supervised the occupation of Japan (1945-1952), General Douglas MacArthur, however he may have viewed the transcendent purposes of the recently concluded war, conceived of his particular task in largely evangelical terms:

> . . . . whose sacred duty it became, once the guns were silenced, to carry to the land of our vanquished foe the solace and hope and faith of Christian morals. . . .

---

[205] Ibid., 27 May 1943.

[206] *S.P.C. Bulletin*, January 1944; also, *Falcon*, 1 March 1943: Gospel League Revival: "Give Us Reality. . . . he gave up his ministerial expectations and loved ones to join the Navy."

[207] *Falcon*, 10 March 1950.

I decided that this was to be, for the first time in history perhaps, a *Christian* occupation.[208]

By 1946, we observe then the culmination of this transition from the progressive Christian internationalism of the 1930s to the nascent cold-war nationalism of the post-war epoch, a transformation which had produced, as an exuberant Dean Walter Helsel so baldly phrased it, a newly revised evangelical "Gospel of the Stars and Stripes."[209] Perhaps it was only natural that new enemies would appear on the horizon, the experience of identifying, mobilizing against, and ultimately defeating a clear and present foreign danger making the transference of the pattern of ideas and emotions which emerged during the Good War all that more fluid.

The Red Menace

A 1952 *Falcon* editorial promoted the motivational value of Christian faith for American soldiers in Korea, urging the community to heed

> The words of the militant Christians. . . . The military and President Truman are backing this program; they are beginning at last to realize that the soldier needs Christ . . . the soldier needs something more than free beer to bolster his spirit when he is sent to fight. . . . Servicemen have been exploited long enough. . . . [We need] not merely soldiers carrying the flag of our country, but Christian soldiers carrying the flag of our Christ as well—young men who are not only going to fight—but young men who are going to be goodwill ambassadors to keep Asia from going Communist.[210]

A decade later in 1961, a year of mesmerizing anxiety which generated such campus editorial comforts as "Faith in a Troubled World" (Christians need not overly concern themselves with nuclear war: ". . . . it should be [faced] with straight backs and erect heads.")[211] and recommendations for students to rush in droves to campus screenings of such paranoid "red tide" gems as *Communism on the Map*,[212] we encounter an unapologetic nationalism buttressed by scripture, as in one student's "Thoughts about Service":

> . . . . facing every able-bodied male student is an obligation to his country. These same students can talk glibly about dedicating their entire future to Christian service and try to escape by all means possible a term of service in the uniform of

---

[208] {emphasis in original} Quoted in Samuel Eliot Morison, *The Oxford History* . . . , 1062-63.
[209] *Falcon*, 21 February 1946.
[210] Ibid., 25 January 1952.
[211] Ibid., 27 October 1961.
[212] Ibid., vol. 26, no. 14—no date.

their mother country. High intelligence and personal Christianity does not absolve anybody from his obligation to his native land. "Render unto Caesar the things which are Caesar's."[213]

We observe then both the continuing embrace and application of de-monological imagery—the division of the antagonistic parties into absolute good and evil terms—and an additional element of *ideological acceleration*, in the sense that the particular nature and content of the threatening com-munist systems developed for most evangelicals—and indeed for most Amer-icans—into an even more menacing specter than the recently vanquished fascism.

Why this additional impetus? I would argue that in many respects the *similarity* of many elements and dynamics within communism and evangeli-calism (as well as the more obvious differences) *and* socialism's clear indiffer-ence and irreverence for the moral market order and meaning of American capitalism lies at the heart of much of the modern evangelical's extreme aver-sion to the Soviet Union and to his fear of the spread of communism around the globe (and, I might add, to any domestic political program or venture with even the faintest tinge of socialism associated with it).

For an illustration of the first, the *dynamic* similarities between the two, recall a film released during the early 1960s, *The Manchurian Candidate*. In it Laurence Harvey plays a disturbed young Korean war hero just returned from Asia. His father, a Soviet mole, has risen to political prominence and is about to receive the nomination for vice-president of one of our major par-ties. Through flashbacks we learn that Harvey has undergone an excruciat-ing series of brainwashing sessions while in captivity in North Korea and become programmed to shoot the presidential nominee during his conven-tion acceptance speech, the assassination serving his father as a dramatic prime-time launching pad to the presidency. As I discuss later in greater de-tail in chapter 10, this cinematic ideological genre reflects and triggers a cer-tain anxiety prevalent among evangelical Americans (and perhaps in less concentrated form throughout the rest of the culture), what I call the *fear of complete reversal*. (Indeed as a youngster, I found the film particularly troubling, a source of many nightmares.) For you see it is the evangelical's widespread experience of and respect for the conversion experience in his own life, among both brethren and targeted unbelievers, that renders him particu-larly—almost morbidly—vulnerable to this anxiety. He both explicitly and subliminally understands the potential power of total conversion, the change from black to white, from good to evil, and vice-versa, often within the course

---

[213] Ibid., 8 December 1961.

of a single evening. No one is immune to it. And so what could be more threatening than an adversary wielding a similar kind of life transforming power? Hence in this one respect it was the similarity between evangelical conversion narratives and communist indoctrination or brainwashing narratives that comprised one source or dimension of a larger cultural antipathy towards communism. The other respect concerns a more obvious difference: the respective theistic (religiously tolerant) and atheistic (religiously intolerant) proclivities of their official political cultures.

The second, as indicated above, concerns the Soviet rejection of the very moral market nature and condition of the American social and cultural order, a few tenets and expressions of which we have already examined. Taken together, these two cardinal idioms comprise, I would contend, the very core of a seminal American cultural identity. To impugn or deny them—to be both anti-Christian and anti-moral market—is to embody two of the most anti-American principles imaginable;[214] and to do so in so brazen and aggressive a manner is to trigger an extensive ideological reaction and mobilization, as we saw throughout nearly three decades or so of the Cold War period.[215]

With respect then to the Seattle Pacific community, there was, in short, an *ideological infrastructure* already in place (drawing upon all three levels of logics discussed in this chapter) which made for a smooth transition to the virulent anti-communism of the 1950s. It is an inveterate animosity to all things socialistic which continues undiminished to the present day.[216]

---

[214] As Frank Fortner, a social studies teacher at Bethany Baptist Academy warned his students during the 1980 elections: "Our biggest threat is communism. Carter's philosophy supports the SALT II treaty. How many of you believe Russia will comply with a treaty? They're liars and atheists. Russia is anti-God, anti-capitalism, anti-democracy, and anti-anything we do. . . . ." To a student who complained of his calling President Carter "anti-American," Fortner replied: "I have a right. I have a right as an American citizen to say what I want. . . . . I'm trying to teach you about Americanism." (Alan Peshkin, *God's Choice: The Total World of a Fundamentalist Christian School*, University of Chicago Press, 1986, 138-39.)

[215] There are of course other sources of the American aversion to communism, such as the defense of liberty and democracy—two cardinal American political values. Unfortunately, *these tended to be the first principles relinquished—both at home and abroad—during the Cold War fight against communism.* It has been our chronic proclivity, for example, to support and tolerate repugnant military régimes for their endorsement—however lukewarm—of economic and religious freedoms, all the while overlooking the extinguishing of political freedoms.

—Perhaps a more global (or, in evangelical terms, *dispensational*) interpretation comes from David Brion Davis, wherein the Russian revolution and the Soviet State represented a threatened usurpation of the American destiny as the "vanguard" of history. (*Revolutions: Reflections on American Equality and Foreign Liberations*, Cambridge: Harvard University Press, 1990.)

[216] It is instructive that with the fall of the Soviet empire evangelicals had lost the preeminent profane *bête noir*, many televangelists, such as Pat Robertson, then re-directing their attention

A Final Word: On Cultural Depth and Intensity

In this chapter I have explored a range of properties and dynamics inherent in the phenomena I—and certainly others before me in their various ways—have referred to as cultural logics. A good deal more will be said about them in more concrete ways in the chapters which follow. However, presently, in anticipation of the eventual presentation of these more tangible community details, a few additional theoretical observations are in order.

The reader may have noticed, for example, that these phenomena assume all sorts of internal logical relationships with one another. As we have seen, with respect to measures of range or scope it makes sense to systematically arrange or distribute the three aforementioned cultural phenomena along a continuum running from a very high level of generalization (sacred/profane distinctions characterizing virtually all cultures) to a very low level of generalization (national currents and moods and the even shallower particular denominational codes and partisan Biblical interpretations). Now although this way of thinking about these logics may have been initially useful in establishing some familiar landmarks in an unfamiliar terrain of historical persons, groups, events, and theoretical claims, unfortunately these measures of generality yield ever-diminishing returns when pressed to the limits of their explanatory power. Earlier we saw in the case of particular cultural disenchantments how their ideological expression and political prosecution could draw together a confusing array of logical elements from all levels of generality, creating a variegated stew of social discontent, with little apparent regard for the more precise, constraining theoretical boundaries of my presentation. Occasionally, on the surface at least, there might appear little rhyme or reason, little order or structure—indeed no underlying logic or pattern—to these crisscrossing ideological webs and alignments. To leave the reader with such an impression would be somewhat misleading. The following brief concluding discussion may prove helpful then in suggesting some other systematic ways of thinking about these phenomena and the relationships they may assume with one another.

There is, I would contend, a discernable continuum of ideological intensity inherent in the very nature and structure of these cultural logics. By this I mean that individuals and communities are inclined to adopt and employ these conceptions (e.g., sacred/profane demarcations, moral market evaluations, shifting theological, political currents and agendas) more *or* less in-

---

to other threats, such as Eastern religions and especially the "New Age" movement. (January 1990 CBN broadcast)

tensely in accordance with varying perceptions or apprehensions of a range of internal and (primarily) external environmental conditions. Put simply, the more heightened the perception of a clear and present cultural danger the more pronounced the embrace and employment of these invidious distinctions. And conversely—and in purely abstract terms—the higher one ascends these imaginary continuums towards ever more severe sacred/profane divisions of the persons, objects, and relationships in a social environment the greater the *potential* ideological charge which may issue from their actual deployment.[217]

We have observed these kinds of ideological intensifications in the histories of the sundry individuals and communities so far discussed. Recall both local and national labor activists venting grievances with early twentieth-century capitalism that many other individuals and groups beyond the social ken of the laboring classes could embrace. A reasonable consensus upon the nature and source of cultural danger emerged that transcended class. Hence at particularly telling moments in these unfolding histories elements of both high and low orientation, defined and contrasted in terms of their distribution along these different theoretical levels of generalization, came to buttress and reinforce one another in the generation of a movement ideology. We might think of this as yet another variation upon the aforementioned dynamic of *ideological acceleration*: in this instance formerly diverse local phenomena become drawn together into a kind of cultural vortex, propelled *and* swept to a higher level of cultural interest and urgency, all the while retaining the local features of their social and economic origins. Such is the often *socially heterogeneous* nature of cultural disenchantment and opposition; although perhaps even more frequently individuals and groups express a discontent more congruent with their social, political, and economic moorings and life experiences. (This proves one major reason, as suggested in an earlier chapter, why sociologists deploy so few of the tools necessary to understand

---

[217] I emphasize *potential* here because the generation of ideological intensity is never assured solely by the level of generalization along which these logics operate; for so much depends upon the considerable variation in an individual or group's perception of imminent danger to the integrity and longevity of the values and standards of the community or nation. Oscillations in this relationship between threat perception and ideological intensity may then occur somewhat independently of movements up or down these various descriptive levels of generalization.

—By no means are these kinds of dynamics confined to the American scene alone. The fundamentalist Islamic uprising in Iran was clearly an ideological reaction to the clear and present danger of the westernization introduced by the Shah and his "Satanic" American government accomplices. *Contrary to the sociological "proximity" thesis, the closer traditional forms of religion are to "modern" systems the greater the potential perception of cultural danger and the more intense the ensuing reaction.*

evangelicalism.) Moreover, I would contend there is indeed a logic and order to the appearance and apparent centripetal power of these often fleeting moments of shared cultural discontent, a dynamic architecture which may be systematically scrutinized and measured and which holds some relevance for us in other less momentous contexts as well.

This notion of ideological acceleration in its simplest form may contribute to the explanation of less ideologically (and less theoretically) convoluted historical transitions. With this theoretical device it becomes possible to discern and measure degrees of ideological acceleration among assorted logically-ordered cultural components and hold these differences responsible for the considerable variation in outlook and conduct we observe among individuals and communities over time. One might argue, for example, that it was the difference in the depth and intensity of the respective political positions which underlay and explains the remarkably fluid, un-problematical transition from the international pacifism of the Seattle Pacific '20s and '30s to the conservative anti-communist nationalism of the '50s and beyond (with due consideration given, certainly, to the shifting perceptions of external danger). The former position drew its ideas and legitimation from many different levels and sources of influence: the inversion principle of the teachings of Jesus, the internationalist perspective of a political Progressivism which social and economic developments would eventually undermine, and perhaps most importantly, a somber, skeptical national mood of isolationism that grew out of the disgruntling experience of World War I. Yet these consolidated experiences and ideas proved no match for the concrete provocation of Nazi German and Japanese aggression and the highly effective casting of the conflict and the antagonistic nation-states in much deeper demonological terms. The evocation and portrayal of monolithic systems of good and evil arrayed against one another in irreconcilable conflict and the association of a virulent, irredeemable Satanism with the Axis powers (in conjunction with quite natural urges to defend the motherland) virtually ensured the triumph of a new, more *ideologically-accelerated* evangelical realism. However scripturally dubious, the motivational power and appeal of this revisionist ideology had grown virtually irresistible, sweeping aside all lingering opposition. In this instance, the sheer ideological velocity and power of this form of sacred/profane invidious distinction overwhelmed a lower order of political, theological orientation. (And it seems only natural that as the Fascist demons were ultimately exorcised and the threat of Soviet expansionism became more apparent in the post-war period, these by now well-exercised and -established cultural infrastructures would be recast with new demons to further torment the recuperating Christian nation. Indeed a Cold War of nearly forty-years duration serves to remind us of *the deeply imbedded cultural nature and resilience of this antagonism.*)

These examples prompt the consideration, finally, of an even more general principle that may come into play here. I have in mind the neo-Marxian conception of changes in the *quantity* of certain socio-historical elements within a society producing changes in the ultimate *quality* of the social-cultural phenomenon in question.[218] In our particular instance, measurable differences in the *quantity* or the degree or level of the ideological intensity of these apprehensions of cultural danger and their closely correlated systems of invidious sacred/profane distinctions may tell us much about respective differences in certain related *qualities* of these very same individuals, groups, and societies. Quantitative differences in ideological intensity may then be highly related to qualitative cultural differences. More of the same may in time produce more of something of an altogether different nature. *So that although this notion and practice of sacred/profane demarcation represents a very general (deep) dynamic present to some degree and in some form in nearly every religious community and society, systematic variations in the levels of perception, promulgation, and deployment of these dualistic distinctions may prove a major defining source of social and cultural distinction.* Indeed, a good many apparently inexplicable social and cultural phenomena (e.g., McCarthyism, the Cold War, the "Pro-Life" movement, attitudes towards government interventionism, etc.—topics to which I will devote future attention) may be explained in terms of appreciable systematic variations in this kind of ideological intensity.

All told, we find that changes in the degree or the intensity of the perception of cultural threats or danger—and/or changes in the very objects or sources of the apprehensions and aspersions themselves—are directly linked to oscillations or transformations in the nature and form of social, political, and theological ideologies. The aforementioned transitions from Christian radicalism to modern political conservatism, and from Christian pacifism to militarism, largely reflect the workings of this cultural dynamism, both sharing a deeper infrastructure and historical momentum, however divergent the respective conditions, durations, and outcomes of each.

---

[218] Max Weber was acutely aware of this dynamic as well:

> Such a balanced presentation would almost always have to add other features and occasionally would have to give greater emphasis to the fact that, of course, all *qualitative contrasts* in reality, in the last resort, can somehow be comprehended as purely *quantitative differences* in the combinations of single factors. ("The Social Psychology of the World Religions," in Gerth & Mills eds., *From Max Weber . . .* , 292.) {emphases added}

And finally, and perhaps most importantly for our purposes, the domination of the moral market ethos within both evangelicalism and the larger American society—the permeation of market thinking throughout virtually every nook and cranny of American culture—more than any other single factor explains the historical presence, persistence, and (especially) the contemporary fluorescence of evangelicalism within American society. Evangelicalism thrives in the American environment as it does in no other comparable modern society because moral market thinking dominates American life in a manner unseen in any other society. *The quantitative embrace and promotion of the moral market ethos—discerned and measured in terms of degrees of ideological intensity and acceleration—has created over the course of our national history a qualitatively unique American cultural condition.* In conjunction with other less cardinal contributing elements, this flagrant cultural idiom has produced a market-driven, lowest common denominator consumer society whose cultural vacuity (and I emphasize here culture with a lower case *c*) has proven highly amenable to evangelicalism. *It is this condition and affinity—not internal characteristics of, or differences in, class, education, region, or the more general advance of, and/or reaction to, "modernity"—which largely underlies and defines the American expression and experience of evangelicalism.* (In this sense 20th-century American culture has reproduced in a different, more sophisticated form the culturally unsettling conditions of the shifting 19th-century frontier communities and society, an environment which proved so conducive originally to evangelicalism.) Together, these two elements—moral market thinking and an enduring appetite for invidious sacred/profane-like distinctions—occupy the ideological heart of American culture; in them can be found the ultimate source of a cultural distinction which sets American society so far apart from even her most immediate European ancestors.[219]

---

[219] In making this claim, I realize that I am cutting against the grain of a strong school of thought that places *equality* at the center of American ideology. As Gordon Wood writes of David Brion Davis, " . . . it is for him, as it was for Tocqueville, 'the fundamental theme and characteristic of American civilization.' " (review of Davis's *Revolutions: Reflections on American Equality and Foreign Liberations*, in *The New York Review of Books*, 27 September 1990, 33.) So be it. *They now stand corrected.*

—See also J. R. Pole, *The Pursuit of Equality in American History* (Berkeley: University of California Press, 1978).

—Max Weber caught but a bare glimmer of this American difference during his trip to the United States in 1904, attributing much of what he saw and experienced solely to Calvinist Puritanism, particularly the decline of high culture: ". . . . America had become what it was because of the 'democratic traditions handed down by Puritanism as an everlasting heirloom.' The United States, he declared, was 'the great creation of the Anglo-Saxon spirit,' and the 'Protestant asceticism' of that spirit 'laid the historical foundation for the special character of the contemporary *democracy* of the nations influenced by Puritanism, as distinct from that which is based on the "Latin spirit" ' Second, Weber argued, Puritanism nurtured a hatred of fine arts, frivolous amenities, and indulgent luxuries. For a good Puritan, Weber said, all sensual pleasures were suspect. Wherever Puritans ruled, they put an end to good theater, great lyric poetry, all plastic arts, and any hint of beautiful music." (Engen, *City on a Hill* . . . , op cit., 211.) {emphasis in original}

PART THREE

ACADEMIC CULTURE

CHAPTER 4

INTRODUCTION

Despite a seemingly insignificant role in contemporary higher education, religious or sectarian colleges have not always occupied so obscure and neglected a position in American academic life. Indeed, ecclesiastical orientations figured prominently in the development of early colonial American colleges and universities. Reviewing the histories of our most distinguished eastern institutions, we may be surprised to learn how many owe their origins to some avowedly sectarian purpose or affiliation. Harvard (1636), for example, emerged from the land grant of a Puritan landowner, John Harvard, whose aim was to bring closer the day when " . . . every student shall consider the mayne end of life and studies, to know God and Jesus Christ, which is eternal life. . . ." [220] A host of colonial academic institutions—now going by the names of Brown, Columbia, Syracuse, Princeton, Rutgers, Pennsylvania, William & Mary, and others—all bore similar sorts of relationships with an evangelist, an established church, or minor sect.[221]

Indeed by 1795, when the doughty evangelical, Timothy Dwight, assumed the presidency of Yale University (founded 1701), the hold of evangelical Christianity over the institutions of higher learning in colonial and early national America was firmly established. Throughout this early period, sectarian evangelical interests dominated the development of higher education in America and, indeed, as one author claims, "in the spread of education throughout the [non-European] world." [222]

These early American academic institutions were largely patterned upon English models. Chartered by the crown, these colleges were supported by colonial administrations and ultimately controlled by sectarian churches. Clergymen held all positions of authority: trustees, administration, and faculty. Collegial members pledged fidelity to official doctrine. Students attended compulsory Bible courses, chapel, and Sabbath observances. For the most part they rose every morning at 6:30 a.m. for chapel sessions: the presi-

---

[220] C. Robert Pace, *Education and Evangelism: A Profile of Protestant Colleges*, New York: McGraw-Hill, 1972, 9; quote in David L. McKenna, "Bless God, Beat Yale," Spring Arbor College Commencement Address, 5/23/76. {Archives}

[221] Martin E. Marty, *Pilgrims in Their Own Land: 500 Years of Religion in America*, New York: Penguin Books, 1985, 151, 125, 58; Leon O. Hynson, "The Savor of Evangelical Salt," *Faculty Dialogue*, no. 7 [Fall-Winter 1986-87], 101.

[222] Pace, *Education and Evangelism* . . . . (1972).

dent read aloud the scriptures and "a faculty member asked forgiveness for all of the sins committed by the students since yesterday's sunrise."[223] The privilege of matriculation was, of course, extended to males alone.

This period of early colonial higher education was scarcely characterized by uniform, unbroken piety. As always in American religious history, we observe a sporadic waxing and waning of enthusiasm for things spiritual. Revolutionary era students, perhaps reflecting the indifferent and unrepentant populace from which they were drawn, proved loathe to be tread upon; they emulated the wider colonial rebellion percolating all around them. Absorbing the infectious brio of the times, colonial students rebelled against the regimens imposed upon them by the various church denominations. Students of Williams College convened a mock communion, while other perhaps more scripturally attuned fellows established a H.E.O.T.T. society, after Isaiah 55:1, "Ho, every one that thirsteth," thus mirthfully sacralizing a drinking club. At Princeton, the solemnity of chapel was undermined one morning when the dean opened the lectern Bible only to observe a pack of playing cards unceremoniously pop out onto the floor, industrious students having worked late into the night cutting card-sized holes in the individual pages of the Holy Writ to accommodate the deck of evil. Of this period, Lyman Beecher, a Yale sophomore in 1795, wrote:

> College was in a most ungodly state. The college church was almost extinct. Most of the students were skeptical and rowdies were plenty. Wine and liquors were kept in many rooms; intemperance, profanity, gambling, and licentiousness were common. . . . [224]

Modern evangelical academicians look back upon the era with some distaste, a period mired in decadence and decline, an interregnum between pre- and post-revolutionary periods of academic sanctification and reverence. As a recent SPC President David McKenna judged: "the colleges became enclaves of Deism and infidelity." And there was the inevitable *persecution* that seems to haunt the imagination of modern evangelicals, as in McKenna's dramatic account:

> Chapels were disrupted, Bibles were burned, and presidents were driven from office by anti-Christian protestors. Believe it or not, Christian students were forced underground and kept their minutes and their members in secret code. Around

---

[223] McKenna, "Bless God, Beat Yale."
[224] Pace, *Education and Evangelism* . . . , 10.

1800, a pastor who visited the dormitories of a Christian college in Ohio wrote in his diary, "They are secret preserves of every vice and cages of unclean birds." [225]

And yet inevitably, after the waning came the waxing. Somehow or other, the early colleges survived the onslaught of pagan latitudinarianism, preserving the memory and example of orthodoxy with sufficient fidelity to limp into an ensuing period (roughly 1800-1830) of renewal.[226] Williams College, once dismissed as a seedbed of infidelity and Deism, produced a small coterie of students known as the Haystack Group, campus evangelicals who reinvigorated a lapsed student body and then dispatched emissaries with the contagious message of revival to other colleges up and down the coast. David McKenna claims that Alexis de Tocqueville, touring the states during this period, observed that " 'Deism and infidelity are in retreat, evangelical churches are in the ascendancy.' "[227] President Timothy Dwight of Yale seized upon the evidence of expanding religiosity to launch a relentless drive for the total conversion of the student body. Spiritual insurgence spread beyond the collegiate compounds, church coffers swelling in proportion to the

---

[225] McKenna, "Bless God, Beat Yale." As will become all too apparent throughout this study, claims of persecution are nearly impossible to assess given the tendency of evangelical authors to take the sympathy of an internal evangelical audience for granted, seldom providing the documentation that would allow independent appraisal of incidents and sources. These claims of "persecution" derive more than anything from an evangelical need to feel persecuted or threatened by the "world"—thereby legitimating their claims of "otherness" by those feelings of persecution—which proves difficult to effect given their often prominent and prosperous positions within American society.

By contrast, consider Martin Marty's rather benign passing reference to these sorts of phenomena in one college of the period:

> When the time came for more conservative Congregationalists to look back for a father and founder, they seized on Samuel J. Mills, Jr., who in 1808 first organized a society for missions while at Williams College. Mills and his "Brethren" favored secret codes and clandestine meetings, both at Williams and after they moved on to Andover Seminary and started a Society of Inquiry on the Subject of Missions. No one but reborn of evangelical Protestants with a passion for missions were allowed. (*Pilgrims in Their Own Land . . .* , 182.)

As the reader can attest, there is no hint in this account of persecution. It would appear that collegiality or solidarity was the primary aim of this secrecy.

—Now as for genuine persecution of Christians, for example—in Iraq following the overthrow of Saddam Hussein and as a result of the decline of "secular regimes in Egypt, Algeria, and Turkey"—see Janine di Giovanni, "The Vanishing: The plight of Christians in an age of intolerance," *Harper's Magazine*, December 2018.

[226] William G. McLoughlin designates this period of 1800-1830, the Second Great Awakening. (*Revivals, Awakenings, and Reform . . .* , chp. 4.)

[227] McKenna, "Bless God, Beat Yale."

size of their rapidly expanding congregations, fomenting among formerly pecuniarily-pinched church elders the dreams of pursuing the great commission abroad; soon after came the formation of the first American foreign missions society.

Riding the cresting wave of an evangelical resurgence, seventeen theological schools were founded between 1807 and 1827.[228] Indeed some 129 Presbyterian, Methodist, Baptist, and Congregational colleges were established before the Civil War. This undeniable link between Christianity and the American higher learning prompted Arthur Holmes, perhaps the leading promoter and apologist of the contemporary Christian college, to conclude that "American higher education was the child of religion, and the history both of church denominations and of westward expansion can be traced through the history of America's colleges and universities."[229]

With absolute denominational affiliation and control written into the charters of these virgin institutions, the enthusiastic religions and churches redirected their attention from the older colonial colleges, where in spite of occasional rejuvenations their authority had grown increasingly uncertain, to this newly established group of colleges, thus providing the first instance of a shift of interest westward that would repeat itself throughout the century; indeed some (although a much smaller percentage than in the first transition) of these institutions would in turn loosen or jettison altogether their denominational affiliation early in the next century and be succeeded by yet another generation of church colleges—Seattle Pacific, notably, among them.[230]

We observe then the gestation of an entire order of private Christian liberal arts colleges, institutions which Arthur Holmes contends are "largely American in innovation, unknown in Europe and even in Canada."[231] It is perhaps only natural that a good many evangelical academicians look back upon these earlier periods with fondness as the golden ages of American higher education, when private denominational colleges exceeded public institutions in size, number, and perhaps even quality, a domination and then

---

[228] Pace, *Education and Evangelism* . . . , 11. To cite just a few of the more familiar: Baptists: Denison; Congregationalists: Oberlin, Western Reserve; Disciples of Christ: Antioch, Hiran; Episcopalians: Kenyon; Methodists: Ohio Wesleyan.

[229] D.G. Tewksbury, *The Founding of American Colleges and Universities Before the Civil War*. Cited in Arthur Holmes, *The Idea of the Christian College* (Grand Rapids, Michigan: Eerdmans, 1975), 19.

[230] This pattern of denominational establishment, maturation, and denominational independence represents one of the few times I would accept the generalization of a secular trend process in operation here of "secularization."

[231] Holmes, *The Idea of* . . . , 21.

a parity that would erode with each succeeding college generation, particularly upon entry into the twentieth-century.[232]

The Modern Evangelical Christian College

Today, approximately 250 to 300 American colleges and universities claim some sort of religious affiliation. In 1966, such institutions accounted for nearly 5% of the total collegiate enrollment in the nation, a marked increase from the 2% of the 1950s;[233] nearly sixty years later, the proportion has not changed appreciably.[234] The Carnegie Commission had these institutions clearly (and depreciatingly) in mind with its 1972 report on *The Invisible Colleges*.[235]

Some purely quantitative comparisons with other kinds of academic institutions prove instructive. Take, for example, the number of books in their libraries. With respect to the American Library Association's minimum standards for library collections, 33% of strongly religious colleges meet such standards as compared to 50% of nominally church-related colleges and

---

[232] In 1900, David McKenna asserts, the total student populations of private and public colleges were nearly identical. ("Our Surprising Christian Colleges," *Action*, Winter 77, Official Publication of the N.A.E., The National Association of Evangelicals.)

Also: "As late as 1931-32 the enrollments in the two types of institutions were about equally divided. Today that division has markedly changed; about four of every five students are enrolled in publicly supported colleges and universities." (Earl J. McGrath & Robert S. Webber, "Effective Functioning: A Study of Fifteen Successful Independent Institutions of Higher Education," *Faculty Dialogue Special Edition*, no. 3 [Spring-Summer 1985], VII.)

[233] Manning M. Pattillo, Jr. & Donald M. Mackenzie, *Church-Sponsored Higher Education in the United States* (Wash. D.C.: American Council on Education, 1966), cited in Robert F. Sandin, *The Search For Excellence: The Christian College in an Age of Educational Competition* (Macon, Georgia: Mercer University Press, 1982), 3.

—"The fact is, that of the 12 million university and college students in the United States only about 90,000 are enrolled in the 77 member-schools of the Christian College Coalition. What's more, over 97% of evangelical Christian young people attend not Christian but secular universities where today they find little incentive to align intellect and faith even on campuses that once heralded an explicitly Christian origin. The total number of college students enrolled at religiously affiliated campuses is no larger than the student enrollment of two state universities. Only about 3% of the college students in the United States attend Christian colleges that reinforce their faith commitments." (Carl F. H. Henry, "The Crisis Of The Campus: Shall We Flunk The Educators?" *Faculty Dialogue*, no. 11 [Spring 1989], 38-39.)

[234] Although the proportion of Christian colleges and universities has remained reasonably constant (as has the number of all such institutions), an altogether different pictures emerges for primary and secondary education. Robert Wuthnow reports a 47% *increase* in the number of Christian schools and a *doubling* of the number of students since 1971. (*The Restructuring of American Religion: Society and Faith Since World War II*, Princeton, New Jersey: Princeton University Press, 1988, 198.)

[235] Alexander W. Astin & Calvin B. T. Lee, *The Invisible Colleges: A Profile of Small, Private Colleges with Limited Resources*, New York: McGraw-Hill, 1972.

90% of non-religious colleges. The sectarian college library collection averages approximately 75,000 volumes, a mere fraction of those of many non-religious colleges.[236] Strongly religious colleges charge lower tuition, hire fewer Ph.D.'s, pay employees less, and maintain a much cheaper, less complete physical plant. The claim often advanced to explain away the impact of these deficiencies (especially in salaries)—that they are easily overcome by the greater motivation of staff and faculty—fails to persuade even Robert Sandin, a prominent defender and apologist (albeit often realistic critic) of the evangelical Christian college: "by and large greater competence and higher compensation are correlative." Reluctantly, he concludes that in general "By all the quantifiable benchmarks of quality, therefore, the colleges of the more marked religious orientation tend to be more measurably weaker than similar colleges of less sectarian orientation . . . the facts of the comparison are undeniable."[237] Indeed an American Academy of Arts and Sciences report on the Baccalaureate origins of successful doctoral candidates from 1920 to 1966 found that only one identifiable evangelical college, Wheaton (Illinois, and member of the Christian College Consortium), was among the top 300 undergraduate institutions in the production of future Ph.D.'s.[238]

By and large the consensus of all these studies is of an unmistakable *progression* from low academic standards and results in strongly religious colleges to high standards and results in non-religious colleges. Throughout the entire spectrum of private liberal arts colleges, this relationship holds. For many, this comes as no surprise. Yet again, these represent mere quantitative symptoms or measures of difference; later, we will introduce and appraise the more intangible *cultural* qualities and conditions underlying these differences.[239]

---

[236] Sandin, *The Search For Excellence* . . . , 5. The 1984-85 Seattle Pacific University catalog reported a total collection of approximately 115,000 volumes in its Weter Library (@ 2,800 students).

Compare these figures to those of some small American colleges issued nearly *ten* years earlier: Amherst—506,255 vols. (1,291 students); Antioch—216,729 vols. (1,761 students); Carleton—251,845 vols. (1,640 students); Lawrence—197,011 vols. (1,360 students); Swarthmore—402,065 vols. (1,256 students); and closer to home, Reed College—243,947 vols. (1,132 students). ("A Recommendation on Learning Resources to the Academic Policies Committee," May 20, 1976.) {Archives}

[237] Sandin, *The Search For Excellence* . . . , 6.

[238] McKenna, "Bless God, Beat Yale."

[239] One prominent evangelical academician, Alan Wolfe, director for Religion and American Public Life at Boston College, argued in 2000 that a Renaissance of sorts was occurring in formerly backward-looking evangelical colleges and universities that was "revitalizing" the more academic dimension of these institutions. Unfortunately he comes up with no more than a handful of scholars who have even published in conventional university press formats, let

Now with respect to our more immediate object of study, Seattle Pacific University, is the school representative of this group of strongly religious evangelical Christian colleges? It is my impression that the school is larger, more liberal politically, theologically, and socially, and more professionally-oriented than the average Christian college. An urban location may explain much of this. By and large its faculty, administration, and students consider their school to be, along with Wheaton, the leading evangelical college in the country; more than once I have heard it extolled or celebrated as the "Wheaton of the West." President David McKenna claimed just prior to his departure in 1982 that the school was the leading evangelical professional school in the nation.[240]

Hence one preliminary conclusion is that Seattle Pacific is unrepresentative of the other Christian colleges in the land. We might more appropriately think of it as an elite institution, a self-proclaimed and elsewhere acknowledged best of the genre, a quintessential Christian institution whose example other less distinguished and successful evangelical colleges seek to emulate.

Seattle Pacific belongs to an association of the most prominent Christian colleges known as the *Christian College Consortium*.[241] A brief survey of the

---

alone upon non-religious topics. (Alan Wolfe, "The Opening of the Evangelical Mind," *The Atlantic*, October 2000.)

[240] "Academically, I believe Seattle Pacific can lay claim to being the leading Christian university for professional studies. Just look at our faculty . . . [they] are gaining national, even international reputations in their respective fields." ("Interview: David McKenna Surveys SPU's Centennial Decade," *Response*, September 1981.)

—To these two should be added a more recent candidate, Patrick Henry University in Virginia, which first opened its doors in 2000. See Hanna Rosin's up-close-and-personal journalistic account (unfortunately marred by some questionable sarcasm—see p. 71) of *God's Harvard*, op. cit.: Yet "The average SAT score is at a tier below Ivy League—1230-1410—the equivalent of the University of Virginia or Rice." (46-47) Then again, a sizeable (unspecified) proportion of the student body was home-schooled.

[241] Thirteen in all. Their location and approximate full-time enrollments (as of 1984-1986, if available): Asbury (Wilmore, Kentucky: 1,075), Bethel (St. Paul, Minnesota: 1,900), Gordon (Wenham, Massachusetts: 1,100), Greenville (Greenville, Illinois: NA), George Fox (Newberg, Oregon: NA), Houghton (Houghton, New York: 1,200), Malone (Canton, Ohio: NA), Messiah (Grantham, Pennsylvania: 1,500), Taylor (Upland, Indiana: 1,500), Trinity (Deerfield, Illinois: 600), Westmont (Santa Barbara, California: NA), and Wheaton (Illinois: 2,400). [SPU: 2,800]

Among its many activities and services, the Consortium commissions or conducts marketing studies of potential student recruiting pools, oversees Washington D.C. legislative internships for students of the member colleges, sponsors periodic conferences on Christian higher education, and at one time published a journal, *Universitas*, which ran for a few issues and then expired.

For all the self-promotional accolades Seattle Pacific is prone to bestow upon itself, it nonetheless remains the general consensus among evangelical academicians that of all these colleges Wheaton occupies the spiritual and philosophical center of serious evangelical academia

promotional catalogs of these institutions and whatever anecdotal accounts of them I accumulated during my stay at Seattle Pacific leave the (our second preliminary) impression that except for minor differences in size and a greater or lesser emphasis upon professional schools these colleges are in the areas of curriculum and ideology largely indistinguishable from one another. David McKenna, for example, in a commencement address delivered at North Park College in 1972 acknowledged that "When we made an initial survey of the [then] ten colleges of the Christian College Consortium, we found that they tended to be carbon copies of each other. Even their innovations were imitative."[242] So that although, as I intimated above, Seattle Pacific and Wheaton are in the minds of many evangelicals the prototypal Christian institutions of the West and Midwest,[243] their emulation by other less distinguished schools and the apparent consensus among the faculties, administrations, and students of these schools upon the fundamental assumptions guiding the structure and mission of the Christian college produce a remarkable homogeneity.[244] Indeed it is the profound ideological uniformity of these colleges in particular[245] and of evangelicalism in general that prompts the claim that not only is Seattle Pacific highly representative of this collection of Christian colleges but that, beyond this, it also contains a *remarkably representative slice of the larger contemporary American evangelical community and*

---

and has indeed produced many prominent evangelical leaders, Billy Graham perhaps the most renowned among them.

—Another similar but larger organization, the Christian College Coalition, was founded in 1976 and claims 71 members (including all the members of the above Consortium). It is based in Washington D.C., which was also the original location of the Consortium until it moved to St. Paul, Minnesota.

[242] David McKenna, "Freedom Now," Commencement Address, North Park College, 5/28/72. {Archives}

[243] I should add that an east coast college, Gordon, although one-third the size of Seattle Pacific, advances equally strident claims of academic prowess, and does indeed—by evangelical standards—boast an accomplished faculty.

[244] By contrast: ". . . . Notre Dame, the quintessential American Catholic university, has many evangelicals on its faculty, including its provost, whereas Wheaton has no Catholics." (Alan Wolfe, op. cit.)

[245] A slightly different regional slant on the origins and growth of these evangelical institutions: "Finally, we discover the third dimension of the southern evangelical errand in boardrooms and classrooms where a small but influential group of entrepreneurs worked quietly behind the scenes to build a network of schools from Southern California to South Carolina. Meant to instill Christian values in young Americans, these institutions were also conceived as conservative counterweights to state-sponsored colleges, which evangelical entrepreneurs held responsible for the New Deal's state-controlled economy and society's slide toward secularism." (Dochuk, op. cit., XXIV.)

culture, as will become apparent later when we more closely examine the nature and composition of the student body.[246]

---

[246] I invite the reader to compare my account of Seattle Pacific University with *New York Times* religion editor, Kenneth Briggs's, report of a visit to Grace College, Winona Lake, Illinois, ("Evangelical Colleges Reborn," *New York Times Magazine*, 14 December 1980), a comparison of particular relevance for the three chapters which follow.

CHAPTER 5

THE LOGIC OF THE EVANGELICAL CHRISTIAN COLLEGE

E vangelical academicians and administrators expend an inordinate amount of time and energy thinking and writing about their institutions. Offhand, I would venture that the bulk of materials published by the faculties of Christian colleges dwell in some manner or other—however tangentially—upon the enterprise itself: rationalizations, justifications, apologias for the very idea of a Christian college.[247] Over the years, something of a cottage industry has sprung up. For example, two "Faith and Learning Institutes" (to be discussed) in 1972 (North Park College, Chicago) and 1973 (Wheaton, Illinois) convened assorted faculty members from Christian College Consortium institutions. Through assorted papers delivered to the conference participants attempted to formulate a distinctive Christian view or approach to their specialties. They met once, twice, in successive years, and then disbanded, not to reconvene again for several years.[248] A brief survey of the topics covered suggests that with the production of some 30 or 35 papers per meeting the subject matter had been exhausted and participants then retreated to their home institutions to get on with the more pressing (and rewarding) duties of undergraduate teaching. Aside from the matter of the quality of these papers (a discussion of which will follow later), what proves so striking is the radical departure, both in scholarly rigor and subject material, from what might be regarded as the routine scholarship and research activities of a liberal arts academician. There is virtually no attempt here (other than in passing) to address the central concerns of a discipline or the more general issues and themes of the humanities and the social and natural sciences; no sustained attempt to produce either a summary or a

---

[247] Concerning the "Integration of faith and learning . . . clichés," Ted Ward writes: "The eager embrace of the seemingly endless series of *Faith and Learning* seminars, conferences, and workshops suggest zeal and hope [of its realization]—whether or not faith is well placed." (Ted Ward, co-editor, "So What?," *Faculty Dialogue*, no. 6, [Spring-Summer 1986], 1.) {emphasis in original}

[248] Between 1973 and 1986 there must have been another conference of this sort because I have in my possession the Spring-Summer 1986 issue of *Faculty Dialogue* containing several papers delivered at a "Second National Conference on Faith and Learning: Visions for the Christian College Community," Bethel College, North Newton, Kansas, April 17-19, 1986.

seminal contribution. In time, we will discover that this approach to scholarship proves all too characteristic of the evangelical academician and college.

Although I find that in general the Seattle Pacific faculty moves more easily from the home institution into the larger academic world of research and ideas (and employs one or two members who have distinguished themselves in their disciplines) than do most of the other faculties of the Christian College Consortium schools (which represents, after all, the Ivy League of Christian colleges), it too devotes an inordinate amount of time to institutional introspection and self-analysis. The self-absorbing questions of who and what we are, and where we are going, appear at times to monopolize intramural discussions. This is, however, not to argue that such reflections or considerations are inappropriate or unwarranted. Indeed, when Christian academicians broach the subject of a mission or "calling" they often preface remarks with reference to various "Idea of a University" themes residing in the public domain and that have "secular" as well as sectarian scholars and thinkers for their origin. Nearly everyone would agree that it is the duty of a university president to radiate a vision of the role and purpose of higher education in a society. That this is so seldom accomplished by the leaders of large public universities offers testimony to the buffering distance that has grown between the contemporary realities of curriculum, the motivations and aspirations of students and faculty, the demands of the public, and the philosophical origins and legitimations of classical Western notions of higher education.

In what follows I will emphasize (though not exclusively dwell upon) one of the more celebrated of the many philosophies of the Christian college that have emerged from this flurry of introspection. Indeed of all the works designed to provide a Biblical and philosophical foundation for the contemporary American Christian college none has proven more influential and enduring than Arthur Holmes's *The Idea of a Christian College*, a book I think it no exaggeration to call the *other* Bible of the modern evangelical academician.[249]

Any apology for the evangelical Christian college encounters an immediate practical philosophical problem. Why separate Christian and "secular"

---

[249] Grand Rapids, Michigan: Eerdmans, 1975.

—At Seattle Pacific, a packet of pre-registration materials was sent to each matriculating freshmen; usually included was a note suggesting that the prospective student read *The Idea of the Christian College* before his/her arrival on campus.

— "*The Idea of a Christian College* by Arthur Holmes has probably been more influential than any other single work in inspiring our thinking about the nature of a Christian college." (Michael L. Peterson, "Thoughts On The Future Of The Christian College," *Faculty Dialogue*, no. 10 [Winter-Spring 1988], 85.)

colleges? Not just a college or university system in which students may prosper as Christians, freely and un-self-consciously participating in extracurricular activities such as the "Campus Crusade For Christ" or a "Christian Student Union," but *separate, demonstrably different Christian and "secular" institutions.*

Many evangelical academicians simply take for granted a series of fundamental Biblical principles underpinning the Christian college,[250] often subsuming the institution under the general legitimating rubric of "secondary creation,"[251] a conception that would appear to justify the retroactive implantation of a host of anticipated modern ideas and institutions into the original mind of God, belated second thoughts and terrestrial tinkering that could not all be squeezed into those first seven frenetic days in Genesis.

Looking back, these principles assumed their most pure and concrete expression in the European Middle Ages, wherein we discover a homogeneous Christian medievalism, an academic pinnacle from which all subsequent academic history degrades. As writes Arthur Holmes:

> The medieval university was governed by a unifying religious perspective but education today is rootless, or at least governed by pragmatism and the heterogeneity of viewpoints that makes ours both a secular and pluralistic society. The result is a multiversity, not a university, an institution without a unifying worldview and so without unifying educational goals. . . . Christian perspectives can generate a worldview large enough to give meaning to all the disciplines and delights of life and to the whole of liberal education.[252]

---

[250] *SPC Bulletin, 1976-78* (Quoted in David McKenna, "Eighty-five and Doing Well," undated manuscript): "This community has been guided by the scriptures. In fact, because they continue to provide guidance for our individual and institutional lives, they hold an important place in our curriculum. . . . I can say that we are closer to a Biblical community on our campus today that at any other time in my experience." {Archives}

[251] David McKenna, "Concept for the Christian College" (Undated manuscript; probably from his tenure as president of Spring Arbor College, 1967 or earlier): " . . . the concept for the Christian college must begin with the Person and Work of Jesus Christ . . . . Secondary creation may be a solitary act or process of God alone or it may be a mutual act or process of God and man . . . the Christian college, a secondary creation." {Archives}

[252] Holmes, *The Idea of* . . . , 19-20.

—Dr. Robert Webber of Wheaton College urged SPC chapel students to achieve a greater appreciation of the medieval Christian world view, a unified vision which produced a comprehensive "Christian understanding of art, music, literature, architecture, and city planning." ("Education in the Context of a Christian Worldview," Chapel series, 10/27-28/80.)

Unity & Permeation vs. Division & Compartmentalization

The medieval university wove the elements of knowledge into a seamless web of wisdom and truth. Unity, synergy, and circularity reigned supreme, generating intellectual fields of gravity that held disciplines in tight relation to one another, all revolving within the orbit of a larger, all-encompassing worldview. For while rigid barriers separate disciplines from one another in the modern university, the medieval cloister erected few such hurdles. A general climate of "permeation" prevailed, expressed more recently as the "integration of faith and learning": all subject matter drawn into direct relation with central Christian beliefs; no discipline insulated from the larger infrastructure of life. Celebrating this almost intoxicating medieval universalism, the aforementioned Arthur Holmes is led to a seemingly ineluctable conclusion: "All truth is God's Truth."[253] Any and every piece of knowledge or insight, wherever it is found and by whomever it is uttered, bears some sort of immediate, integral relation to the whole of knowledge, whose ultimate origin is God.[254] No stray dogs of truth wander outside these hallowed epistemological confines.

---

[253] Holmes, *The Idea of* . . . , 25; also: "The truth is a coherent whole by virtue of the common focus that ties it all into one."

[254] In both my library research and fieldwork on the SPU campus (and upon perusal of more national materials as well) I did not, and have not yet, encountered a single serious intramural debate over, or objection to, these basic assumptions. I did not encounter a single student who in any way found these ideas problematical. Just two of many possible examples:
— "For approximately three decades, the Christian college's strongest philosophical argument has been the *Integration of Faith and Learning*. While state schools may often have superior facilities, well-known faculty, a nationally ranked football team or better proximity, they cannot deal with the integration of faith and learning which is crucial to the untutored believer in a world of hostile or conflicting ideas. . . . We correspondingly place a heavy burden on this concept and find it perennially to be a common topic of collegial discussions, few of which seem to be directed towards the validity or merits of the concept itself. Most discussions simply begin with it as an axiomatic concept and proceed to demonstrate how it should operate in one's professional or institutional life." (Mel R. Wilhoit, "Faith And Learning Reconsidered: The Unity Of Truth," *Faculty Dialogue*, no. 9 [Fall 1987], 77.) {emphasis in original}
—Were students absorbing the same message?: One quarter the SPU faculty conducted a short essay contest (with a cash prize) on the meaning of a liberal arts education. *They received but a single entry*, an essay entitled "The Role of a Liberal Arts Education in a Professional World" (10/11/2002). The essay, praised by the faculty and authored by possibly the most competent, intellectually gifted student I encountered at Seattle Pacific, although it eschews the easy division of the world into Christian and secular counterparts in its adoption of a general conception of the liberal arts, nonetheless regurgitates predictable, shop-worn McKenna and Holmes themes:

> [A liberal arts education] . . . shows us the unity of many diversified fields of knowledge; it brings together the truths necessary to understand ourselves,

"Secular" colleges and universities, by contrast, lack any comparable center of gravity, drift aimlessly, fracturing and "compartmentalizing" knowledge. Free-floating disciplines fly apart from their anchors in elemental God-centered truth. The parts of knowledge relinquish their very special relationships with the whole of knowledge. All told, this "secular modernism" produces "linearity" instead of "circularity," "intellectual polytheism" instead of "intellectual monotheism," and the "rootlessness" and lack of enduring purpose of a "multiversity" instead of the cohesion and unwavering direction of a medieval cloister.[255] Into the vacuum left by a retreating Judeo-Christian worldview rushes the synthetic values and meanings of the bogus modernist religion of "secular humanism," with her attendants, unbridled reason and "scientism,"[256] close beside.

Open vs. Closed Systems / Unity of Truth vs. Parcelization of Truth

The quintessential Christian academician labors in an open, "exploratory" environment. Unfettered by the "closed" system of secular instruction and research, wherein certain areas of truth are quarantined from scholarly investigation, she luxuriates in an atmosphere that encourages the discovery of "more and more of God's truth."[257]

---

our world, and our relationship to it; and . . . promotes a wholeness of persons . . . [We] learn to reconcile reason and emotion, mind and spirit . . . [as opposed to] our compartmentalized professional society . . . specialized subject areas . . . [offering instead] a holistic concept of the human being . . . [allowing us] to perceive truth as a unified whole . . . a greater, unified body of truth . . . unifying the splintered pieces of God's truth.

[255] David McKenna, "A Vision of Wholeness," three-part Convocation Address, 9/28-30/70.) {Archives}; Holmes, *The Idea of* . . . , 57-58.
— "[American higher education is characterized by a] . . . potpourri of disciplines . . . hopelessly fragmented . . . disregards the unity of truth." (ibid., 34) / "This is a schizophrenic day that desperately needs an integrated understanding, a world-view that can stick fragmented pieces together." (ibid., 58) / "The libertine interprets 'education for democracy' to mean one that ensures absolute equality, no viewpoint can be more true than another: all stand on the same level and are to be presented with a benign and uncritical relativism." (ibid., 84)

[256] Writing in *Faculty Dialogue*, Holmes offers "scientism" as the second of three definitions of "secular humanism": "(2) For many this implies scientism, the claim that the methods of natural science provide us with the only reliable knowledge we can have, and that the application of scientific knowledge (i.e., technology) affords us the best hope for resolving our problems, whether physical, psychological, social, political, or whatever." (54) (Arthur F. Holmes, "Christian Intellectual Community and the Challenge of Secularism," *Faculty Dialogue*, no. 6 [Spring-Summer 1986].)

[257] Holmes, "Christian Intellectual Community . . . ," 58-59.
— ". . . . a world view is exploratory, not a closed system worked out once and for all but an endless undertaking that is still but the vision of a possibility. . . . It explores the creative and

It naturally follows that if God is an undifferentiated whole, then truth and knowledge are also all of a piece—an un-vitiated, unified whole.[258] Since this whole derives from God, the physical and social natures, orders, and relationships of all things are known perfectly to Him. God embodies the "perfect knowledge of everything man ever sought to know or do."[259] Upon acknowledgement of the origin of truth and knowledge and the reality of sin, and the acquisition of redemption in his own life, the Christian scholar gains potential entry to this all-encompassing, all-inclusive world of illumination and insight. Although secular scholars may catch occasional partial, fleeting glimpses of truth and knowledge, occupying as they do virtually the same physical and social worlds as Christians, any mature appreciation of the relationship of the parts to the whole eludes the pagan scholar. Inevitably, they confuse and mistake parts for the whole, trees for forests, true statements for *The Truth*. Rejecting the revelation of Christ and the daily instruction of the Holy Spirit, the secular scholar labors fruitlessly in the "closed" vacuum of the secular liberal arts university, shuffling aimlessly from one isolated morsel of knowledge to another, eyes trained down upon his own busy terrestrial feet, incapable of gazing upward to apprehend a higher divine source of truth and light. S/he simply hasn't a clue how it all fits together.[260]

The Christian scholar, by contrast, luxuriates in an "open system" of scholarly inquiry that erects no barriers to the free play of his intellect. He

---

redemptive impact of the Christian revelation on every dimension of thought and life, and it remains open-ended because the task is so vast that to complete it would require the omniscience of God. . . ." (ibid., 59)

[258] In his 1978 Weter Faculty Award Lecture, Seattle Pacific History Professor, William Woodward, urged his colleagues to " . . . apprehend the wholeness and unity of truth . . . [and reject] the artificial fact-faith dichotomy. . . . To achieve unification of thought is to become like an integer, a whole number. . . . the wholeness of truth: all truth is in fact God's truth . . . the whole of reality. . . . Since all truth is God's truth, truth discovered (in any field) amplifies truth revealed." ("Becoming: A Historian's Prospectus for Integrated Learning.")

[259] Holmes, *The Idea of . . .* , 25.

[260] "Scripture refers to fallen man's mind as being 'darkened' (Ephesians 4:18, Romans 1:18-23). Darkness here refers to a skewing of one's perception of reality rather than to a lowering of his I. Q. . . . Therefore unregenerate man (and to a lesser degree Christian man) comes to only partially correct answers in his quest for knowledge. . . . The non-Christian cannot understand Scripture apart from the Spirit's witness (I Corinthians 1:18, 2:14, 3:19) although he can perceive God to some degree in nature. The Christian has the benefit of understanding, though never in a complete sense, both natural and special revelation. . . . Training obtained in the Christian college will necessarily be different from that offered in the university but not inferior to it. . . . To quote Gaebelein, 'Our task is not only to outlive and outserve those who do not stand for God's truth; *it is also by God's grace to outthink them.*' " (Gerald D. Hess {Biology—Messiah College}, "Practicing What We Preach," paper delivered at the Faith/Learning Institute, Wheaton College, August 13-24, 1973.) {emphasis added}

may explore the relationship between religious beliefs and academic disciplines. As he fashions himself into an "empty vessel" he may become filled with otherworldly illumination, jettisoning the fetters of the human condition, the hampering "relativity of human perspectives and the fears of human concern."[261] He grows exponentially in his freedom to explore the world around him.

All told, this may strike the innocent reader as a rather unusual conception of intellectual and academic freedom.[262] Arthur Holmes defends the notion with a retreat once again into the Middle Ages:

> The fact is that faith liberates rather than enslaves the mind. . . .
>
> According to Russell Kirk, the medieval universities enjoyed academic freedom not despite but because of the framework of Christian belief in which they operated. Insofar as their scholars were Christian, this framework did not restrain them. Rather it protected their dialog, it guaranteed them liberty to pursue the truth in detail and in totality and to lead their students into the same enterprise of committed scholarship. "The teacher was a servant of God wholly, and of God only. His freedom was sanctioned by an authority more than human. . . . In medieval times, it was precisely their Christian framework that gave masters and students this high confidence. Far from repressing free discussion, this framework encouraged disputation of a heated intensity almost unknown in universities nowadays. . . . They were free from a stifling internal conformity, because the whole purpose of the university was the search after enduring truth, beside which worldly aggrandizement was as nothing. They were free because they agreed on this one thing, if on nothing else, that the fear of God is the beginning of wisdom." [263]

---

[261] Holmes, *The Idea of . . .* , 84.

[262] This notion of Christian academic freedom is part of a larger evangelical conception of the personal liberation which conversion and redemption bring; for example:
— "Faith is that trust, not hope, but trust that Christ accepts us as a person and that we then become a free man. Free in the way a bird flys [*sic*] and soars but still flys with the season. The direction of the Christian life is led by the Holy Spirit in the path that He wills . . . . 'Freedom is what we have—Christ has set us free! Stand then, as free men, and do not allow yourself to become slaves again.' (Galatians 5:1). . . . the freedom to be a Christian person. . . . It works for me and I have been able to evolve very freely in this framework." (Monroe Olson {North Park College—Music}, "Faith, Freedom, and Knowledge," a paper delivered at the Faith/Learning Institute, North Park College, Chicago, August 14-25, 1972.)
—At the secondary school level, here is Art Swanson of Bethany Baptist Academy: " 'My goal as a teacher is to shape students' mind [*sic*] to one pattern. I think that one pattern would give society the freedom to be a free society. Individuals have the freedom to reject that system, to choose as they see fit. I can't make them choose; I can only teach them.' " Also: "In [Headmaster] McGraw's words 'Bethany is a closed system within the Biblical framework. We would say that that opens it to everything. The world, of course, would disagree.' " (Peshkin, *God's Choice. . .* , 266, 59)

[263] Russell Kirk, *Academic Freedom*, quoted in Holmes, *The Idea of . . .* , 79-80.

Given these antiquarian pedagogical interests we shouldn't be surprised to learn that Holmes retreats even farther in history to locate another even more appealing model for the Christian college community—the utopian, authoritarian state of Plato's *Republic*. It is in-

Freedom & Truth

Does this total embrace of transcendent truth jeopardize academic freedom? Why no, answers then SPC President David McKenna. Just look at those marvelous early colonial colleges! Their founders shared similar medieval convictions about "Truth." Even though only ministers could be presidents, teaching positions were reserved for Christians who signed "creeds" professing absolute fidelity to orthodox Christian belief, and students were recruited directly from the families of church congregations and the less demonstrably devout among them were relentlessly proselytized by their more zealous peers and elders, a more genuine intellectual freedom prevailed. The modern academy has got it all wrong, argues McKenna: absolute truth breeds academic freedom, not the reverse, although he concedes that in the colonial colleges "Freedom of ideas and behavior was severely restricted under the name of truth."[264]

The colonial American system of colleges derived largely from the English example. Only much later, with the intrusion of German university elements into the new world colleges, was the medieval heritage usurped and the modern passion for an ersatz intellectual freedom indulged:

---

structive that he finds much in Plato's regime to admire: " . . . we are impressed with his concern for society, with his emphasis on unchanging values, with his integration of the curriculum around the disciplined mind, with his emphasis on critical thinking. We note the diversity of viewpoints discussed, the lack not only of unanimity but also of dogmatic indoctrination. [Although] Admittedly he censored some of the literature of his day because it detracted from intellectual and moral growth. . . ." (80). Indeed one searches the Holmes account in vain for any indication that there is anything amiss in this Platonic / Christian wonderland, that there may be serious moral fissures and flaws in the facade of Plato's ideal community and state, and even more perplexing historical problems with the actual martial city-state, Sparta, from which Plato drew so much inspiration and borrowed so many elements for his own model.

My judgment of Plato's *Republic* as authoritarian (if not totalitarian) rests upon Karl Popper's classic treatment of the much misunderstood treatise in *The Open Society and its Enemies, Vol I: The Spell of Plato*, 5th rev. ed. (Princeton, New Jersey: Princeton University Press, 1966). In Plato we find themes similar to those examined throughout this study, in particular his law of social entropy: " . . . *all social change is corruption or decay or degeneration.*" (19) {emphasis in Popper original}

[264] "In the academic world, truth and freedom are usually at opposite poles." ("The Christian Mind: Freedom," Chapel address, 4/25/75.) {Archives}

—D. Elton Trueblood, who in 1946 left Stanford with much fanfare for diminutive Christian Earlham College, regards the presidency of evangelical Timothy Dwight at Yale the high point of colonial academia: "[Yale] became alive with both intellectual and spiritual vitality. I suppose that under Dwight, Yale was the most hopeful place of learning on this continent." ("The Idea of a College—Revisited," in W. Frank Hull IV, ed., *The Christian College: Some Thoughts and Reflections*, Center for the Study of Higher Education, Toledo, Ohio: University of Toledo, 1974, 9.)

Truth was now to be sought, not found. Freedom was now to be objective, not committed. Thus, a new orthodoxy for higher education was established. Christian scholars became heretics and Christian colleges became outcasts.[265]

Freedom emerges from the Christian scholar's devotion to revealed truth[266]; the secular scholar, by contrast, engaged in the blind pursuit of ungrounded conceptions, ultimately squanders *both* liberty and truth. Like oil and water, the one proves immiscible, irreconcilable with the other. Quite simply, truth can never emerge from absolute freedom.

The ramifications for scholarship and teaching are profound:

> . . . . the truth that sets us free is the revelation of Christ through the self-transcendent mind. . . . The Christian mind is free from the sins of the mind. . . . Intellectual idolatry is to make one level of the mind the only way of thinking. For instance, some advocates of the scientific or logical mind contend that reason is the only way to know truth. When they take this position, they are no longer scientific; they are worshippers at the shrine of scientism. . . . The Christian mind does not make an idol of any level of mind. Rather, it is free to learn the whole range of the ways of knowing. . . . The Christian mind is freer because it entertains no idols. . . . A secular mind . . . is a "mind of dread". . . . A Christian mind, however, is free from that fear because faith fills in where knowledge cannot go. Rather than demanding all of the answers at once, the Christian mind can live at peace with ambiguity and uncertainty. Freed from the sin of the mind, we can now contend that *the Christian mind is intellectually freer than the secular mind*. . . . the secular mind cannot afford to confront ultimate questions in his search for truth.[267] {emphasis added}

Intellectual Integrity & Academic Superiority vs. Intellectual Expediency & Inferiority

It naturally follows, once again, that if the Christian scholar by dint of his confession of faith gains a foot in the door leading to the sacred hall of knowledge and truth, thereupon undergoing a virtual transformation of his faculties of perception and lucubration, we ought then observe a corresponding jump—perhaps even a quantum leap—in the quality and profundity of his scholarly output. His teaching and relationships with students ought to scintillate and sparkle, dazzling onlookers with his grasp of the whole

---

[265] "The Christian Mind: Freedom."

[266] The standard Biblical reference is John 8:31-33: ". . . . you dwell within the revelation I have brought, you are indeed my disciples; you shall know the truth, and the truth will set you free." (*NEB*)

[267] David McKenna, "The Christian Mind: Freedom."

panorama of knowledge and truth. Calvin College historian, Ronald Wells, avers that

> As Christians we have *an extra set of lenses*, which perhaps allows us to see what others see, but also *more then they and perhaps more clearly*. Indeed, as Nicholas Wolterstorff has argued, these extra lenses can act as "controls" on what we see through ordinary lenses, insuring that common sense beliefs will not contradict special beliefs. . . . As Christians we say we see not the antithesis of what non-Christians see, but *all that they see, and more*, because we have an extra set of lenses. Further, that extra set of lenses helps us to see not only more; it helps us to order and to control our understanding of what comes to us through the ordinary lenses. . . . Perhaps like our dual gestalt picture [*Young Lady or Old?*], if it is pointed out that the nose of one is the chin of the other, *ordinary people* will see what we mean. . . .
>
> Of course, it needs to be said in closing that Christians must act Christianly towards others in discussing these matters. We who say we have *the best view of reality* must not come to others in triumphalism.[268]

Also, the experience ought further heighten his appreciation—if not virtual adoration—of truth. Hence the faith of the Christian scholar not only renders more probable infinitely greater intellectual, academic, and scientific discoveries and syntheses of knowledge, but additionally fosters an academic milieu that fairly exudes intellectual honesty and integrity.[269]

This devotion to truth imbues the academic milieu with *a transparency of motives*, a phrase here meaning the routine confession of all underlying assumptions and beliefs that serve to guide and determine scholarly activities and results. All scholarship and teaching routinely begin with *admissions* of adherence to the evangelical Christian worldview. Faculty candidates are rigorously examined by Christian college presidents for evidence of transparent Christian qualities. How open and easy is the expression of faith? More often than not, individuals with superior academic credentials are found wanting because of unconvincingly crabbed or guarded disclosures of

---

[268] "The Vocation of the Christian Historian," *Faculty Dialogue*, no. 5 [Winter 1985-1986], 37-38. {emphases added}
—Headmaster McGraw of Bethany Baptist Academy remarked at the first chapel meeting of the year: "To a Christian, all things should become new. This is really being said in a spiritual sense. If your spiritual outlook becomes different, it will change everything about your life. A Christian ought to be able to do everything a sinner can do, better; if the Christian and the sinner have the same ability, the Christian ought to be able to outshine the sinner in any area of life." (Peshkin, *God's Choice* . . . , 52.)

[269] "If I were teaching symbolic logic . . . my Christianity would come through in my attitude and my intellectual integrity. . . . Elton Trueblood has said that the Christian scholar is likely to be a better scholar for being a Christian than he would be otherwise . . . . The reason, says Trueblood, is motivation, for the Christian faith is the sworn enemy of all intellectual dishonesty and shoddiness." (Arthur Holmes, referring to Trueblood's *The Idea of a College*, in Holmes, *The Idea of* . . . , 50.)

personal beliefs. Spurned applicants fail to project the clear *signals of difference* which ought to distinguish the Christian scholar from his secular counterpart.[270]

The secular scholar, by contrast, harbors a multitude of "hidden prejudices." Beneath the more formal surface claims of "objectivity" and "value neutrality" lurk disingenuous motives that may allow for lapses into deception and deceit. We have no idea what drives or motivates him. What are his ultimate loyalties? He may celebrate objectivity and open-mindedness and yet labor under the thrall of assumptions of which he may be only vaguely aware (or which he knowingly masks and conceals), preconceptions which skew or corrupt the direction and content of his teaching and research. He smothers the reality of eternal values in a relentless blather of "relativism," wherein man becomes the "measure of all things." And it is precisely this rejection of a greater transcendent source of truth that encourages in the secular scholar pretensions of intellectual grandeur, as he arrogates to himself the kind of wisdom formerly reserved to Gods. He may then become arrogant in his demotion of other more spiritual ways of knowing.[271]

Hence a formal scientific impartiality camouflages the institutional reality and strategic promotion of an exclusionary "secular humanistic" worldview.[272] The secular university's celebrated ideals of toleration and

---

[270] In a chapel talk, then SPC president David McKenna recounted an interview with a faculty candidate. The applicant, designated "the fellow" by McKenna, was a "well-published scholar" and was at the time being considered for employment at other "secular" colleges in the area. Concerning Christian beliefs, the "fellow" confessed having grown up in a church although he conceded that he was not a Christian, asserting that "his faith would make no difference in his style of teaching." Without further ado, McKenna reported with relish, he terminated the proceedings: "Needless to say, the interview was short; this guy is not a member of the faculty today." ("Take Ten Twice Again," Chapel, 5/18/77.)

[271] The Christian scholar, by contrast ". . . . gives his striving after excellence the balance of humility. In light of this the Christian teacher is not pompous, condesending [*sic*], proud of his scholarship in an arrogant manner but has a sense of reverence in respect to the total wisdom of God in Christ." (Richard Osberg {Huntington College—Christian Education}, "The Christian Teacher—An Authentic Person," a paper delivered at the Faith/Learning Institute, Wheaton College, August 13-24, 1973.)

[272] "For more than a decade these premises—diffuse dependency, total transiency, radical relativity, and absolute autonomy—have dominated the university classroom more influentially than any and all other alternatives. They have become the *masked metaphysics, the covert conceptuality of modern liberal learning*. Almost every sampling of student reaction to liberal arts studies in the mainstream colleges and universities in the last decade evokes the overwhelming verdict that these students considered themselves intellectually constrained to shape their worldview by these *controlling emphases*. This naturalistic outlook notably differs from the atheistic communist view only in secondary details rather than in basic assumptions." (Carl F. Henry, "The Crisis of Modern Learning," *Faculty Dialogue*, no. 1 [Fall 1984], 11.) {emphases added}

pluralism serve to produce (ironically, in the Marcuse sense) the perhaps not so unintended consequence of repression. The evangelical academician observes that almost everything may be discussed in the secular university except that which is most central to his own life and work. In what sense then can one speak of academic freedom?

David McKenna, who received a Ph.D. in psychology from the University of Michigan (and briefly held a position on the faculty) before moving on to the presidency of Spring Arbor College, the first of three such evangelical college offices he would come to occupy, warned from experience that

> . . . . secular religionists [are] . . . wise as serpents. . . . . Their technique is to teach without revealing their "hidden assumptions." Converts are won and disciplined without losing their innocence. Secularists will seldom argue with Christians because their creed makes room for evolving religions. Christians, however, must learn to argue with secular religionists in education because our creed makes no room for other gods.[273]

Better to openly acknowledge one's assumptions, one's religious commitments, as does the evangelical Christian college with its confession of a "bias for truth," than wallow in the "hypocrisy of moral neutrality."[274]

---

[273] McKenna, "Secularism: Coverup [*sic*] in Education," op. cit.

[274] McKenna, "The Christian Mind: Freedom," op. cit.

—Political Science Professor William Harper of Gordon College urges the practice of a kind of mental hygiene in order to liberate the mind from "all overriding temporal loyalties to party, ideology, regime, nation, etc." Even though the so-called impartiality and objectivity of the secular university conceal an underlying adherence to "temporal loyalties" that distort scholarship, not all commitments should be spurned. Rather it is a matter of encouraging "commitments that are Biblically shaped versus all others." The adoption and persistence of these prior "explicitly scriptural commitments" improves the "Christian quality of one's work," enhancing the Christian scholar's ability, once more, to "uncover political reality as it really is." This intellectual expurgation, or mental flushing away of the debris generated by the secular academic mind and his enveloping institutions, fulfills then a necessary precondition of genuinely impartial scholarship, or as Harper calls it, "Disengagement . . . my professional equivalent of being 'in the world but not of it.' " Better to repudiate all claims of objectivity and follow the lead of the Marxists, who "openly acknowledge their faith," and thereby lay the foundation for a "true scientific pluralism, where each scholar can work on the basis of his freely expressed faith." ("Scriptural Priorities vs. Temporal Loyalties," *Universitas*, May 1974.)

Homogeneity & Wholeness & Balance vs. Heterogeneity & Brokenness & Imbalance

Homogeneity is a most highly desired academic and social condition. The ideal (and in many respects, the actual)[275] Christian college community flavor is vanilla—literally everywhere. The rationale and apology is firmly grounded in the earlier notion of the fundamental metaphysical and epistemological unity of all material and social life. Diversity, by contrast, reeks of error and dissolution. Academic communities bereft of an integrating Christian worldview are riddled with discordant ideologies and pseudo-religions. The social chaos of their student bodies reflects the chaos of a fragmented "secular" worldview. Religious errors beget social errors. The appearance and preponderance of diversity masks the underlying conformity of secular relativism. Christian colleges need not then apologize for the uniformity of their theology or the racial and social backgrounds of their students, for these have direct links with a larger legitimating unity of all truth and knowledge; they merely reflect or evoke a transcendent reality.

> A college where there is an open advocacy of conflicting opinions by persons who individually espouse them is not necessarily a place of freedom. . . . Freedom in the sense of seriousness of inquiry is often most feasible for students in an academic community which is socially and religiously homogeneous, provided that the faculty understand and implement a dialectical method of instruction. Sometimes the clash of ideas is more explosive at a sectarian Christian college with selective employment and admission policies than at an ideologically heterogeneous public university. . . . Unrestrained commitment to the gospel truth is no compromise of freedom. It looks like a compromise of freedom only to the person who does not think of the gospel as true.[276]

David McKenna debunked the revered academic quest for "diversity" as just another secular "sacred cow." The Christian college simply "must have selective admissions," must hire only professed Christians for full-time

---

[275] Earl J. McGrath and Robert S. Weber document both the perception and reality of homogeneity in their survey of fifteen sectarian colleges: "The church influence in attracting and serving students is evident in the scores of the institutions on the *Human Diversity Scale* of the *Institutional Functioning Inventory*. On this scale the scores indicating the ratings made by faculty members in eleven of the colleges were below the national average; in some, near the very bottom of the scale. These figures reflect an ethnic and religious homogeneity atypical of most other institutions of higher education." ("Effective Functioning: A Study of Fifteen Successful Independent Institutions of Higher Education," *Faculty Dialogue* Special Edition, no. 3 [Spring-Summer 1985], 22.)

[276] Sandin, *The Search For Excellence* . . . , 37-39; also 157: "Our contention is that the creation of a religiously and morally homogeneous campus community may be educationally appropriate because it establishes a social context for an unbiased intellectual and personal reappraisal."

faculty positions, and must apply gentle but firm pressure upon the professional staff to demonstrate fidelity to Christian norms and practice: ". . . . the community should be homogeneous enough to set a prevailing tone of personal commitment to Jesus Christ."[277]

Wholeness

The pursuit of "wholeness" dominates the Christian academic mind and agenda. More than any other, this notion draws together the various strands of evangelical thought into a comprehensive, interrelated academic worldview. It rests upon a number of assumptions about the nature of human personality, foremost among these being that each individual human being receives a particularly unique, sacred imprint or impression from his creator. Arthur Holmes refers to this inherent personal property as a "God-given, God-preserved, God-restorable potential, a potential to be developed, disciplined and invested in response to God."[278] To bring human potential to fruition becomes then a sacred enterprise, the Christian college performing a sacred function, perhaps the most important post-adolescent one in terms of the overall program for the development of Christian personality and intellect. In almost post-millennialism terms, David McKenna goes so far as to claim that the education offered by these evangelical institutions fulfills an ordained "Holy purpose . . . . *It is the Kingdom of God.*"[279] Secular universities, by contrast, fail to grasp the sacred inner structure of human personality, ignorantly severing the soul from the body and the mind, rendering themselves incapable of bringing the student's human potential to its fullest realization. They instruct and cultivate the various parts of the personality, yet fail to nurture the whole.

Human "wholeness" demands the equilibrium of mind, body, and spirit. A genuine whole person maintains a "balance" among the three elements, none imperialistically expanding to supplant or dominate the others. Disequilibrium occurs when one or two of the three achieves an exaggerated influence over thought and behavior, plunging the personality into an unwholesome imbalance, a condition one observes, for example, in those persons guilty of the sins (as different from one another as) "scientism" and "sen-

---

[277] David McKenna, "A Community of Learners" (undated typescript, prob. @ 1970). {Archives}

[278] Holmes, *The Idea of . . .* , 23.

[279] McKenna, "Concept for the Christian College." {emphasis added}
—Also: "To educate the whole person, to encourage disciplined learning and the quest for excellence is a sacred trust." / "To imagine God in the fullness of our humanity is our highest calling. A liberal education that develops our humanity therefore implements God's calling, and *the creation mandate finds expression in the educational process.*" (Holmes, *The Idea of . . .* , 23, 35.)

sualism," maladies arising in the first instance from the malignant growth in the obsessions of the mechanical, unreflective rational mind and in the second from the over-indulgence of the sundry desires of the body, the expansion of either's domain resulting in a corresponding diminution of the spiritual dimension.

The "secular" university churns out students with imbalanced, impoverished personalities. They may demonstrate highly refined skills in the employment and manipulation of abstractions and data, but an entire realm of personality—the supernatural field of the soul—has throughout their education lain fallow and uncultivated. The secular monument of reason looms largely uncontested overhead, blocking the warm, illuminating rays of the soul and spirit. In this climate, then, of refined, sophisticated incoherence, education unfolds in a random, sporadic fashion; student personalities pass by unappreciated and unregenerated, their inherent depth and breadth gone unplumbed and unexplored, their human potential unfulfilled. Upon graduation, the secular university releases listless, fragmented student personalities into the world and thus further accelerates the pace of depersonalization and fragmentation, which follow in the train of the ineluctable secularization of culture.[280]

Holistic Education & Intrinsic Values & Eternality vs. Specialized Education & Instrumental Values & Temporality

The secular university student encounters a bewildering array of partial elements of reality, fashioned into course units, bereft of a larger, unifying perspective. He shuffles from classroom to classroom as though passing from

---

[280] "Underlying both the emotivist and the rationalist fallacies is an outmoded faculty psychology that divided man into intellect, emotion and will. As a result one or another of these faculties vies for supremacy . . . the mistake is evident. . . . The cognitive and the affective are inseparably united in the structural unity of the whole person." (Holmes, *The Idea of . . .* , 71.)

—". . . . Christian truth deals with the whole person . . . the total need of man. . . . Secular man can be confronted with the awareness that the secular cannot claim wholeness for itself. The Christian educator must interpret the dimension of the spirit, as known and understood in Jesus Christ, as the only dimension which offers man meaning and the fulfillment of his own essential personhood." (Dr. Myron S. Augsburger, "Education and Evangelism for this One World," address delivered at the International Congress on World Evangelism, Lausanne 1974, reprinted in *Universitas*, January 1975.)

—"The Christian college or university must propagate the Christian world view and, as its prime goal, promote a true integration of faith and learning. The goal is in sharp contrast to the secular institution and many Christian schools in that it addresses *the whole man—body, mind, and spirit.*" (David J. Masoner, "What 'Christian' Higher Education Means: Philosophy, Process, And Product," *Faculty Dialogue*, no. 9 [Fall 1987], 9.) {emphasis added}

—Just outside the entrance to Oral Roberts University one finds a six or seven foot high tiled structure with the logo: "Educating The Whole Man." (Kat Bowler, op. cit., 63.)

one secluded region of life to another, growing increasingly perplexed and skeptical, perhaps even coming to the conclusion that life has no larger purpose or meaning. At best, he graduates from the large public university with a smattering of independent talents and insights. Arthur Holmes characterizes him as "a connoisseur of the fragments of life. But a jack-of-all-trades is a master of none: he is a fragmented individual. What today we label as general education requirements do not themselves make for the unified understanding that education desires."[281] Upon graduation, the pagan student emerges a hopeless dilettante, directionless, potential squandered, while the Christian college graduate, an emboldened "master," having apprehended and understood the unity of truth and knowledge, accelerates and elevates the pursuit of her God-given potential onto a higher plane of personal aspiration. Consolidating all that she has experienced and learned, she moves on to "think Christianly, to participate in history in thoroughly Christian ways, and to value as Christians should."[282]

Not only do the respective graduates embrace fundamentally different broad and narrow conceptions of the nature, source, and composition of truth and knowledge, and follow disparate developmental paths, indeed they diverge sharply as well over the eventual applications to which their education and training are to be put. The Christian student discovers greater satisfaction in the *intrinsic* value of his just concluded formal education, while the secular student prizes its more *instrumental* value. Upon graduation, the former celebrates the acquisition of a solid foundation beneath his feet, from which he can launch a lifelong pursuit of truth and personal authenticity, while the latter carries more pragmatic, egocentric concerns,[283] anticipating the kind of high-paying job that will support a fast-lane lifestyle and the uninhibited acquisition of consumer goods. The secular student develops and hones marketable skills and plans for a career, a vocation, a profession, all

---

[281] Holmes, *The Idea of* . . . , 34-35.

[282] Ibid., 44.

[283] "Presumably the Christian will have a different sense of motivation in studying as a God-given task instead of making knowledge an end in itself or a means to such ends as personal development or professional competence, but his inner compulsion will not necessarily look any different from the outside than any other pursuit of excellence." (Jeannine Bohlmeyer {Bethel College—English}, "Position and Supposition," a paper delivered at the Faith/Learning Institute, North Park College, Chicago, August 14-25, 1972.)
—"The overused cliché 'whole person' represents an inescapable reality. Social accountability requires an institution to accept responsibility for its net effect upon people, not just the well-intentioned particulars of its major agenda. Thus when the net effect on the graduate is an acquired tendency toward selfish uses of knowledge and the acquisition of personal power through academic meritocracy, something is very wrong." (Ted Ward, "Service: An Endangered Value," *Faculty Dialogue*, no. 4 [Fall 1985], 5.)

grounded in terrestrial time; the Christian student cultivates a "wholeness" and a body of unified knowledge and insight that will endure for all time:

> In that sense I can take with me [to heaven] some of the benefits of a liberal education, while the benefits of vocational training last only for the duration of the job for which it equips me here and now. Christian liberal arts education has an eternity in view.[284]

These are the *primary logics* underpinning the evangelical Christian college and informing nearly every dimension of personal and social life in these academic communities. They are in many respects analogous to, or even derivative from, the kinds of *cultural logics*—particularly the sacred/profane dualism—introduced earlier in chapter three. With the appropriate modifications and permutations taken into consideration (e.g., the greater conservatism—both political and theological—and anti-intellectual animus of the average American evangelical), they are also largely embraced and implemented in evangelical churches, families, and communities across the nation. In the course of the unfolding discussion and as the nature and situations of the narration warrant, I will add logics that elaborate or expand upon these more fundamental conceptions and will introduce altogether new ones that flow logically from them. As with my ongoing developing definition of evangelicalism, I will depend upon the full disclosure and amplification of the contents of this study to make clear what I have in mind by the terms *cultural* and *social* (particularly chapter 11), although obviously they involve an approximate difference between *patterns of ideas* and *routines of behavior* with which

---

[284] Holmes, *The Idea of . . .* , 45.
—The secularist has "squeezed all of eternity in this moment"; they "deny the past." By contrast, "Christ [has] . . . redeemed our sense of timing." The secularist pursues "defensive" living in the present, while the Christian seeks the Will of God. The secularist is uncertain about the future and therefore formulates elaborates plan for it, since "this is the kind of surprise that the secular mind can't take"; the Christian "has the faith which includes the surprises. . . . [We] Celebrate the past, fully experience the present, and eagerly anticipate the future." (McKenna, "The Christian Mind: Timing," Chapel address, 1/7/74.) {Archives}
— "The Greek translation of the Bible employs two principle terms to speak of time. *Chronos*, an invention of humanity, divides existence into segments that serve as markers of human activity. In our day, schedules and calendars and clocks have become tyrants to be manipulated and tamed by 'one-minute managers.' There is another dimension: *kairos*, divine time, the urgent and pregnant instant when Providence arrests the heart and conscience of the faithful with a spiritual vision and call for responsibility in a broken world. There is no option for manipulation; one must take a leap of faith or suffer the moment to pass.
This article . . . opened with political, cultural, and evangelical voices crying in a contemporary wilderness for a vision of moral coherence and social responsibility; searching for a *kairos*, a revealed moment to press forward as instruments for reform and renovation of the social order." (E. Joe Gilliam, "Vision For Life: Values And Moral Goals In Christian Higher Education," *Faculty Dialogue*, no. 10 [Winter-Spring 1988], 107.) {emphasis in original}

many are familiar, however imprecise or conflated the distinction may appear at times. Thick, rich description and common sense understanding take precedence here over theoretical precision.

Now as for the matters of origin and application, the same sorts of dynamics discussed earlier in Chapter 3 apply here as well. There I ventured the observation that these logics—or, more precisely, the various declensions of persons, objects, relationships, and institutions in diametrically-opposed Christian and secular terms—are scarcely the product of a pure aversion or reaction to "secular" phenomena alone. Instead they emerge from a motley blend of current ideological imperatives and historical influences and precedents. The medieval university model (however erroneous the evangelical's depiction of it), for example, was hardly conjured out of thin air in order to provide an academic foil to the large modern public university (although certainly *seized upon* as a provocative *point of departure*); the evangelical academic vision of itself does not then turn *exclusively* upon the real (or imagined) characteristics of a secular nemesis. Institutional self-conceptions have always been generated and sustained in conjunction with many other contributing elements. Throughout the following presentation this understanding of the complex, often untidy origins of these apparently simple and precise invidious logical distinctions must be kept firmly in mind.

Let us now turn our attention to the daily routines of academic life on this particular Seattle Pacific University campus for evidence of these logics and dynamics in operation.

CHAPTER 6

ACADEMIC STRUCTURE

The late nineteenth-century founders of Seattle Seminary could scarcely have foreseen the sprawling urban behemoth that has grown to envelop their offspring on all sides. Neither could Bishop Francis Asbury, the guiding spirit of primitive American Methodism, who was said to have displayed "a genius for locating schools in out-of-the-way and inaccessible places," the ultimate aim of his ingenuity being, of course, to " 'shield students from temptation',"[285] a knack (and not so ulterior motivation) he for the most part shared with other evangelical educational pioneers, Free Methodists among them.

Presently, the campus lies sandwiched between commercial and industrial urbanism. West of the Fremont district along Nickerson avenue, the approximate path Alexander and Adelaide Beers traipsed to reach the fledgling seminary nearly a hundred years earlier, unfolds a strip of service and manufacturing companies that evokes the mood of one of those closely-cropped industrial "parks" of south Seattle: plastics, construction, glass, tugboats, lumber, restaurant equipment, electronics, the ubiquitous 7-11 convenience store and, farther on, a myriad of indistinguishable four- and five-story apartment buildings that butt shoulder to shoulder along Nickerson clear until the Ballard Bridge on-ramps appear, the low-slung bridge shuttling cars downtown to the south or into Ballard to the north over what some of the antiquarian locals still think of as Salmon Bay. Rising steeply to the south above this incongruous mixture of busy commercialism and verdant, motionless campus are the charming Victorian cottage and bungalow neighborhoods of Queen Anne Hill proper, a topsy-turvy region whose physical peaks and valleys reflect a similar social and economic topography, juxtaposing as it does occasional pockets of utterly ordinary middle-class squalor with the vestigial splendor of the urban plantations of early industrial and business magnates and their later progeny of the "Highlands."

If indeed evangelical fathers and mothers across the land are motivated in large measure by a desire to arbitrarily preserve or prolong the innocence of their offspring when they banish sons and daughters to the social and cul-

---

[285] Alexander W. Astin & Calvin B. T. Lee, *The Invisible Colleges: A Profile of Small, Private Colleges with Limited Resources*, New York: McGraw-Hill, 1972, 17.

tural tundra of America where most evangelical colleges can be found,[286] it is perhaps just as likely that others of comparable outlook dispatch them with equal conviction instead to institutions like Seattle Pacific, hoping to introduce them—albeit under closely monitored conditions—to the distractions and temptations of modern urban society and to the trials and tribulations of fashioning an occupational niche for themselves in an arrant national culture. *In loco parentis*,[287] above all, grants an institution like Seattle Pacific license to lightly sully the noses of these adolescents in the dirt of the real world, so that toes are stubbed, nerves exposed and jangled, and even wounds inflicted, but all in a gentle, nurturing, and, ultimately, recuperative atmosphere. Evangelical parents—as is true perhaps of the majority of American parents—want their children trained for a decent job or profession in a salubrious environment that leaves them pretty much as they were before.[288] They prefer, in a word, no surprises.

The initial impression is of a Seattle Pacific student body considerably more conservative religiously and politically than its counterparts in state universities and this is generally borne out by opinion surveys conducted over the years by both the college and national educational polling organizations.[289] As I will argue later in much greater detail (when comparing student

---

[286] An editor of *Faculty Dialogue* asked the students, faculty, and administrators at one college what made their Christian college different?: "Its students, especially, seemed pleased enough with themselves that they had made the right choice—their faculty could be trusted more, could be expected to be more interested in them, and they expressed the idea of being *intellectually and spiritually 'safe'* through various sorts of statements. They were comparatively better off than their cousins and former playmates who had gone into the *less safe* forms of higher education." (Ted Ward, "The Too-Well Hidden Agenda," *Faculty Dialogue*, no. 9 [Fall 1987], 2.) {emphases added} And so, somewhat before secular academic political correctness, observe the "safe apace."

[287] Holmes, *The Idea of* . . . , 93. (i.e., prolonged paternalism)

[288] "The basis for this suggestion is a little honesty about why students come to Christian liberal arts colleges for undergraduate education. . . . All too often the primary motivation is to find a congenial Christian atmosphere where one can prepare for a comfortable niche in middle-class America. . . . It is difficult, at best, to encourage students to call such structures into question when their overriding ambition seems to be to fit into the structures. And if the student demand is for an emphasis on vocational preparation within the present structures, then that's what most of our colleges will provide, despite our rhetoric. . . ." (Harold Heie {Dean, Messiah College}, "Bursting Educational Wineskins," *Faculty Dialogue*, no. 11 [Spring 1989], 128.)

[289] The Astin 1980 college student survey: Political Orientation

	National Norm	S.P.U.
Liberal	19.6%	11%
Middle-of-the-Road	60	50
Conservative	17.1	37

and national survey data), the students are remarkably representative in religious and denominational terms of the anywhere from 1/5 to 1/3 or so of Americans who deem themselves born-again, Bible-believing, and witnessing evangelical Christians, although as is characteristic of the more highly educated persons in any community, they exhibit a good deal more toleration and appreciation of the social, political, and religious beliefs of others; on selected litmus test issues such as the E.R.A., federal social welfare programs, and capital punishment, they are generally more liberal than the average American evangelical.[290]

The Academic Program

As we have seen, Seattle Pacific claims distinction for the manner in which formally separate subject areas are drawn together into broader, more comprehensive "schools" of inquiry, reversing the tendency in the research-oriented secular universities of a continuing differentiation of academic regions into ever-shrinking (albeit proliferating) disciplines. Indeed given the smug tone of this presumption of having somehow or other transcended the conventional limitations and boundaries of academic knowledge,[291] the

---

(Source: *A Profile of Students at Seattle Pacific University*, published by the Office of Student Affairs, 1980-81.)

[290] Although students are drawn to Seattle Pacific from all over the United States (the school maintains "area representatives" in ten other states) and, indeed, the world, nearly 3/4s or so of the student body hails from within the state of Washington. During the 2003 school year there were some 150 or more foreign students out of the approximately 2,800 total, the majority of whom came from Canada, Asia, and the Middle East. These students learn of Seattle Pacific from the many students and alumni who become full-time foreign missionaries, from the members of "outreach" teams which are dispatched to special overseas missions for periods of up to a year at a time, and from their fellow countrymen in the states who have become knowledgeable of American colleges and universities, some matriculating at schools such as Seattle Pacific simply because of low admission standards, discouraged by the higher English fluency and standard competency requirements of state universities, such as the University of Washington (as I discovered through conversations with Iranian students at SPU).

[291] ".... what is it that you can see and hear that is different at a Christian college? ... What is unmistakably different about the way Christians think, learn, and behave? ... The centrality of the Bible should result in a peculiarly Christian style of learning, something visitors can witness in classrooms and hear in the dormitories, and observe among graduates of Christian colleges. That learning style includes awe and wonder and *eschews arrogance*.... It takes the ineffable seriously, and *does not pretend that theories, concepts, numbers, and facts alone will capture reality.... Clerks at the bursar's desk should not be rude as many are at state colleges or universities.... Friendliness should be rife, and should be democratic, with cafeteria workers, janitors, and secretaries viewed as real persons who get invited to campus plays or sporting events.*

I have personally seen this respect for persons at a few Christian colleges, and *it is like being in another world—a world where harshness and coldness have been banished.*" (George Keller, "Faculty Response: The Four Distinguishing Features Of A Christian College Education," *Faculty Dialogue*, no. 10 [Winter-Spring 1988], 113-17.) {emphases added}

reader may be unprepared for the perfectly ordinary designations the nine Seattle Pacific "schools" have been apportioned in practice: Business and Economics, Education, Fine and Performing Arts, Health Sciences (Nursing), Humanities, Natural and Mathematical Sciences, Physical Education and Athletics, Social and Behavioral Sciences, and Religion. One might have anticipated something a good deal more audacious—a "School of Universal Knowledge" perhaps.

Two major periods of academic reorganization produced the current academic program. The first arrived with the new administration of President David McKenna in 1968. Following an initial year of observation, McKenna unveiled in the spring of 1969 nine proposals designed to overhaul an anachronistic curriculum and send the college on a "Quantum Leap"[292] into the modern age of higher education. Of the nine, only two or three survive today in anything like their original form, and these were simple structural modifications of teaching loads, student course requirements, and the system of credits. Proposals for weekly Collegiums, an Institute of Research, and other related endeavors to stimulate campus discussions and research projects among the students and faculty gained approval, but within a year of their introduction petered out for lack of student and faculty interest, eventually disappearing altogether. The net effect of this reorganization was to bring Seattle Pacific into conformity with the formal academic structures of the large public universities, such as the University of Washington or Michigan, the latter from which McKenna received his doctoral degree. It sought both to concentrate the student's attention upon a smaller number of more substantial subject areas and (the claim of a greater Christian college faculty involvement with students to the contrary notwithstanding) to reduce faculty contact with students so as to leave more time for original research. With respect to scholarship, the outcome was predictable, the faculty's reluctance to enlarge their conception of their own role upon campus anchored in a familiar ideological inertia denigrating the pressure to "publish or perish" as an insidious, corrupting emanation of the large secular public universities. Understandably, some ambivalent foot-dragging greeted the reforms of this aggressive new president.

Ten years or so later, McKenna tried again, this time floating a more ideologically-explicit series of proposals designed to address and hopefully institutionalize the vague, abstract ideals of the "integration of faith and

---

[292] "Nine Reform Proposals: Public Trustee Session Hears 'Essential' Plans: McKenna Offers Distinctive Claim," *Falcon*, 9 May 1969.

learning" and the "Christian scholar-servant model."[293] The result, a "Foundations and General Education Program Based on the Christian Scholar-Servant Model" of 1980,[294] mandated basic mathematics and writing qualifying "competency exams," a series of Biblical "foundations" courses, and produced an array of distribution areas with intriguing titles: *Individual in Society . . . the Aesthetic World*, etc. In effect, the program discouraged students from fulfilling what are generally known as "distribution" requirements at most large public universities (which, I would concur, are meager simulations of a genuinely eclectic liberal arts education) with courses chosen from a single discipline.[295]

This "[all-] encompassing and revolutionary"[296] curriculum was celebrated with characteristic hyperbole and invidious reference to distinguished "secular" universities.

> After reading of the failure of the Harvard faculty committee to come to consensus on the substance for their curriculum in general education, I am convinced that our faculty is on the verge of a leadership "breakthrough" in curriculum development. My enthusiasm for the work was reinforced again when I participated in the National Congress on Church-Related Higher Education. Vainly, I sniffed and searched for some clue to the influence of the Christian faith upon curriculum. . . . the faculty at Seattle Pacific University is far advanced in the task of putting flesh upon the Faith and Learning skeleton which has rattled around in our curriculum closet for so many years.[297]

---

[293] M.: " . . . . time and time again we've been presented with the Christian scholar-servant model. . . . [the ultimate goal of Christian education is] to seek truth." (Student Government Chapel, 11/16/79.)
—Marsha: " . . . . the cliché, the 'integration of faith and learning,' has been used to death, but it is the major difference between us and the U. W." (ASSP Election chapel, 4/14/80)

[294] The title is from a later 1984-85 University catalog. David O. Dickerson (Vice-President for Academic Affairs), "General Education at Seattle Pacific and the Christian Scholar-Servant," *Seattle Pacific University Review*, Spring 1980.

[295] Each "area of knowledge" requirement could be retired by selections from lists of "core" and "options" courses that number anywhere from three or four to fifteen and twenty. (Yet those in special pre-professional programs are advised to select certain optional sequences.) All told, a student could then receive an introduction to the fundamental unity of truth and knowledge that underlies the *Individual in Society* (10 credits) by selecting *Colonial America* (5 credits) for the "core" course and *Fundamentals of Economics* (5 credits) for the "options" course, or coupling the *Nature of Cities* (5 credits) with *Survey of Sociology* (5 credits). Those students looking for any kind of interdisciplinary or "common core" introduction to notions of the "individual in society" will be sorely disappointed.

[296] Dickerson, "General Education . . . ."

[297] David McKenna, "State of the University, 1979-1980," address to the faculty Senate, 9/18/79.

As always, an invidious evangelical *signal* of distinction or difference—the ability to effect curriculum consensus or "unity"—becomes juxtaposed to a secular sign of dysfunction, to secular academic division and fragmentation.[298] *We* have consensus; *they* have dissensus, disjunction. And yet, do *we* really? Let us explore some of the potential problems of this academic venture.

To what degree, for instance, does the inherited body of assumptions and preconditions the Christian college brings to its task in fact—ironically, ultimately, ineluctably—undermine any such endeavor? And I mean this in the very practical sense (as opposed to more abstract philosophical problems I will raise in the next chapter) of: does the background, training, motivation, outlook, and structure of the academic duties of a typical Christian college academician prepare her to produce or assess the full range of human experience and academic research and scholarship that would provide the foundation of any such universal body of truth and knowledge? Similarly, does the average Christian college student possess the experience and intellectual maturity to appreciate, assimilate, and ultimately make sense of this kind of academic presentation?

Under the aegis of these (both ideological and institutional) expectations, the typical Christian college teacher-scholar is placed in an unenviable position. Aside from the immediate problem of whether or not the above curriculum in and of itself even allows the kind of synthesis McKenna (and others) had in mind, the logic underpinning the program demands that the scholar, above and beyond his own area of specialization (e.g., dissertation or publications), draw together the various fields and subfields of his own discipline, relate that discipline to the larger school of thought to which it conventionally belongs (e.g., School of Social and Behavioral Sciences, etc.), add a unifying epistemological context of human and natural knowledge, and then finally demonstrate the manner in which his Christian faith (one usually couched in terms of a particular Biblical tradition or exegesis) informs and illuminates every dimension of this larger given, immutable universe of truth and knowledge.[299] That most Christian scholars issue preliminary lion-

---

298 "Among Christian liberal arts colleges are motifs which suggest common strengths—both real or potential: . . . [we can produce] communities each with a corpus of shared values where the faculty just might be able to agree on a core curriculum. . . ." (Robert S. Kreider {Administrative Vice-President, Bethel College}, "The Recovery of the Academic Vision," *Faculty Dialogue*, no. 6 [Spring-Summer 1986], 99.)

299 "The atomization of the arts under the influence of science is not remedied by team-teaching that merely offers plural perspectives on one problem. Such an approach models the opposite of integration. Instead, scholars in the liberal arts need to explore, publicly, the meeting points or [of?] disciplines, to develop and employ commonality rather than to define and justify exclusivity. Thus, for example, the literary critic will work with the theologian to

hearted exhortations at water's edge, and then, upon having plunged ankle-deep into this cold cosmic ocean, pull back upon the scholarly reins, retreating to higher, drier ground, all the while lapsing into belated, fainthearted apologies over the prospect of even sketching the outlines of such a daunting intellectual (and spiritual) undertaking, is not at all surprising.[300]

---

discover the dynamic between style and historical context in order to ascertain the transferability of, say, the Biblical principle of non-retaliation. . . . The challenge here is an even greater one to proponents of the liberal arts: *we must hold ourselves accountable not only for the integration of our discipline into a coherent world view but also for the integration of our entire lives—and our life as a group—into that world view.*" (Thomas E. Schmidt, "Cowboys Of Community," *Faculty Dialogue*, no. 8 [Spring-Summer 1987], 84, 86.) {emphasis added}

—"The Christian higher education community must effectively address itself to the importance of its call, to be the salt and light to the world. It must accomplish this goal in an excellent manner and it must point those involved toward the *Truth*, by integrating, in specific and meaningful ways, the Christian faith and all academic disciplines. (And by His Grace and call, it can be done!)" (David J. Masoner, "What 'Christian' Higher Education Means: Philosophy, Process, and Product," *Faculty Dialogue*, no. 9 [Fall 1987], 3.) {italics in original} [underline added]

—"Just as the Enlightenment in its revolt against Biblical theism sought to explain law, religion, science, ethics, and all aspects of culture without reference to miraculous revelation and redemption, so Christian supernaturalism *must bring into its purview every sphere of reality and activity. It will involve all the disciplines of a liberal arts education—the whole range of philosophical and moral thought, the sphere of education, literature and mass media, politics and economics, physical and biological sciences, psychology, leisure and the arts, and much else.*" (Carl F. H. Henry, "The Christian Worldview Imperative," *Faculty Dialogue*, no. 11 [Spring 1989], 30.) {emphasis added}

[300] These efforts are usually put on display at specially convened gatherings of Christian scholars, most having the phrase "faith and learning" somewhere in their titles. Although I am inclined to think (and have been informed) that these kinds of conferences probably meet every year somewhere in the Christian college community, I am only familiar with (and have read the papers of) three: "Faith & Learning Institute," North Park College, Chicago, August 14-25, 1972; "Faith & Learning Institute," Wheaton College, Wheaton, Illinois, August 13-24, 1973 [both Archives]; and more recently, "Second National Conference on Faith and Learning: Visions for the Christian College Community," Bethel College, North Newton, Kansas, April 17-19, 1986 (papers published in *Faculty Dialogue*, no. 6 [Spring-Summer 1986]). Since this 1986 conference was designated the "second" national conference, there must have been a first, so I can report an awareness of four actual conferences on this subject. The latter conference is interesting in that it represents one of the few times that those academicians I will call "social internationalists" received equal billing with other participants (at least in the subsequent publication). It is also instructive that those authors either of foreign origin or who work outside the usual Christian college network or public relations circuit approached the conference topic in a manner quite different from their colleagues, one which would confound the average Christian college community member. In this respect the contributors represent an unusually odd assortment; two or three might arouse considerable consternation if allowed to address the typical Christian college chapel audience.

I should mention also that Eerdmanns, perhaps the most prominent Christian publisher, has begun a series of ten proposed volumes on just these academic questions titled *Studies in a Christian World View*, sponsored by the Institute for Advanced Christian Studies and edited by that old evangelical war horse, Carl F. H. Henry. I am aware of two volumes: Arthur F. Holmes, *Contours of a Christian World View* (1983) and Keith E. Yandell, *Christianity and Philosophy* (1983), and have read the former.

As Eugene Lemcio, one of the most accomplished professors in the school of religion (Ph.D. Cambridge University) who was directly involved in the McKenna curriculum discussions reluctantly acknowledged, notions of "integration" are "all too easy" to bandy about in the abstract:

> Yet, somehow, it seems extremely difficult to integrate our experiences and perceptions of the external world. Anyone who has attempted to teach an interdisciplinary course or integrate faith and learning knows what I mean.[301]

The role any faculty member of a Christian college traditionally performs, emphasizing as it does a grammar school-like cadence of class meeting schedules and a debilitating press-the-flesh, the higher the number of hours spent with the professor the higher the quality of education mentality, would by itself (irrespective of any philosophical/logical considerations) tend to extinguish whatever creative scholarly fires may have been smoldering within the breasts of their academic hosts. Indeed the pressure for intense teacher-student interaction, however laudable in and of itself, was partially responsible—at least in the earlier periods of its most dogged implementation—for

---

The Christian College Coalition has co-sponsored a series of paperback introductory texts published by HarperSan Francisco (a division of HarperCollins). Eight volumes are projected, with titles such as *Literature Through the Eyes of Faith, History Through the Eyes of Faith, Biology Through the Eyes of Faith,* and so on. As David O. Moberg writes of the series in *Faculty Dialogue* [Fall 1991]: "Painstaking planning and careful production of the manuscripts characterize each of the books. A task force of five to eight experts in the discipline works with the author(s) and editor, and a nationwide conference with up to 120 professors, mostly from Coalition member colleges, critiques the manuscript and plans its use prior to final pre-publication revisions. Narrow sectarianism is impossible under the impact of their dedicated, competent, multi-dimensional scrutiny." This puts one in mind of the old Soviet science and scholarship—particularly this arriving at a pre-publication consensus.

Generally the authors of these attempts to sacralize academic disciplines hail from a handful of the elite Christian colleges.

[301] Eugene Lemcio, "The Scholar as Priest and Advocate" {first delivered at a faculty retreat, 9/14/79}, *Seattle Pacific University Review*, Spring 1980.

—"Let me illustrate from my recent experiences in two seminars on faith and learning, the integration of faith and learning. *In neither of these seminars have I discerned any general agreement as to how the teacher is to exhibit and promote faith and learning in an integrated way*. . . . And one can find theological professors arguing that theology and Christian faith ought not to impinge upon the academic integrity of non-theological disciplines. . . . such attitudes of suspicion, of jealous guardianship. . . ." (Donald M. Lake {Wheaton College—Bible Studies}, "Should Theology Be the Queen of the Sciences?," a paper delivered at the Faith/Learning Institute, Wheaton College, August 13-24, 1973.) {emphasis added}

—And at the secondary level of Bethany Baptist Academy: "Fundamentalist Christian educators use the term 'integration' to designate their need to merge Scripture and subject matter in their daily classroom routine." (Peshkin, *God's Choice* . . . , 56.)

producing Christian "scholars" who had virtually no experience (other than the long forgotten thesis or dissertation) with actual scholarship.[302]

What lies behind the reluctance to modify these pedagogical views and practices are traditional missionary conceptions of Christian service, a closely-related ministerial view of adult-juvenile relationships, and, perhaps more importantly in the contemporary period, an ideological reaction ("point of departure"—outlined earlier) to the predominance of research and publication in large "secular" universities. As prior (and by no means ancient) incidents at Seattle Pacific have demonstrated, the faculty member who reduces his office hours, committee memberships, class hours, or involvement in extracurricular student activities in order to devote more time to research is severely leaned upon by the administration.[303] Indeed, nationwide one rarely finds an evangelical academician who will come forward bearing formal, public testimony to the virtues of independent, original scholarship and research and who understands the value, and exuberantly expresses the importance of, such endeavors for the enhancement of every dimension of academic life: personal competence and confidence, teaching, faculty discussions and collaborations, and public service.[304]

---

[302] And the old habits and assumptions die hard: "I. *The levels of academic integration:* (a) *The level of scholarship.* Scholarship is what most people understand 'integration' to be all about; that is, the in-class work of professors <u>teaching</u> at Christian colleges." (Richard Perkins, "The Place Of Ideology In Christian Liberal Arts: Why We Need More 'Ought' And Less 'Is'," *Faculty Dialogue*, no. 7 [Fall-Winter 1986-87], 55.) {Underline added}

[303] As one former faculty member recalled: "In fact there are a couple of faculty members there now who when they first came were severely criticized because they did not want to become involved with the students, they wanted to do more publishing and research. I know in both instances they were reprimanded." (Dr. David Terrell interview, 2/5/2003.)

[304] For example, although the journal, *Faculty Dialogue*, was ostensibly begun in 1984 to encourage Christian academicians to write and submit papers for publication, there have appeared within its covers few thoughtful discussions of the value of research and scholarship, again most likely because so few Christian academicians pursue it with enough diligence to become acquainted with its multifaceted rewards. Consider a rare exception:

> Few teachers at Christian colleges write books or articles. There are many reasons for this including insufficient time, inadequate background, lack of motivation, and absence of rewards. . . . In addition to contributing to the world of scholarship, faculty who get their writings published can increase their popularity, prestige, income, and speaking opportunities. . . . Faculty, through writing, will discover voids in certain areas of their knowledge, even in subjects where they are considered proficient. For many years I taught a course in New Testament survey, but it was not until I decided to write some background material that I realized my ignorance. I had been avoiding some topics and treating others lightly because of my inadequate knowledge. (Richard Ruble {Trustee Professor at John Brown University}, "Teaching and Writing," *Faculty Dialogue*, no. 4 [Fall 1985], 89-90.)

Perhaps no internal ideological conception has proven more damaging than this devaluation of independent scholarship and research.[305] Given the seemingly endless stream of invectives launched against distinguished public and private non-sectarian colleges and universities[306]—the persistent *projection* of both scholarly insignificance and educational ineptitude onto secular counterparts, in particular—the lingering sway of anti-intellectualism remains one of the most striking and ironic features of this academic community.[307]

Yet by no means has a consensus emerged among evangelical academicians on the proper relationship between theology and academics in either activities of teaching or scholarship, however diminutive the role of the latter.

The editors of *Faculty Dialogue* have had so much difficulty scraping together publishable material that by the Spring of 1989 the number of issues per year was reduced from four to three (although circulation had grown from 2,000 to 12,000). Number Ten reprinted three papers from the inaugural issue, two of which had already appeared in other journals or in books, and also boldly announced a series (#11 through #14) of "heavily thematic issues" that have so far failed to materialize.

[305] "Publishing, often seen as an extraneous burden distracting the professor from the 'more significant' task of teaching, has fallen on bad times. . . . the willingness to openly share the responsibility and accountability in print is usually left to a handful of philosophy and education professors." (Ted Ward {editor}, "Faith, Love, Hope—The Remaining Mission of Christian Higher Education," *Faculty Dialogue*, no. 1 [Fall 1984], 3.) / "Especially among the Christian colleges, the number of academic books reaching the academic marketplace other than through the 'Christian publishers' is disproportionately small. In relatively few catalogs of academic and scholarly books does one find major material from the Christian colleges. . . . *can writng be so repugnant a nuisance?* . . . For many more, the crux of the issue is whether to be a scholar or a school teacher.

Excellence in teaching is a popular claim among Christian colleges—and so it should be—but such claims are often little more than a smoke-screen for financial constraints that disallow productive scholarship and contribution of the professor to the discipline." (Ted Ward, "Teaching and Writing," *Faculty Dialogue*, no. 2 [Winter 1984-85], 12-13.) {emphases added}

[306] SPU Professor Ronald Boyce, reflecting upon his previous career across town at the University of Washington, assured chapel students: "SPC is better than the U. W., that Sodom of the east." ("My Spiritual Journey," Chapel, 11/17/76.)

[307] Then again, there is every indication that those faculty who have responded to the exhortations of their more academically competent colleagues to attempt to write and publish would have been better off heeding their own instincts and forgoing the venture into print, as any innocent reader of these two papers can attest, the authors here displaying academic skills that would be found unacceptable in many of the best *undergraduate* programs of the nation's public universities:
—Arthur W. Nelson, "Mendicant Individualism," *Faculty Dialogue*, no. 8 [Spring-Summer 1987].
—Les Blank, "Finding The Balance: Academic Freedom And Accountability," *Faculty Dialogue*, no. 11 [Spring 1989]. Where Les is, indeed, truly *not more.*

In this rare instance all sorts of tenable approaches have been advanced.[308] Some Christian academicians eschew the idea of thoroughly Christianized disciplines—psychology, history, and the like—and yet embrace diffuse notions of an all-embracing evangelical academic knowledge unifying the various fields of knowledge. So that while the secular scholar may indeed perform the vital service of discovering or planting individual trees, only the Christian scholar is capable of leaning back and appraising the entire length and breadth of the mature forest of universal knowledge. Others, perhaps more numerous, adopt a simple pejorative stance, disparaging secular universities, acknowledging their conventional academic prowess but claiming a system-wide epidemic of academic dishonesty and interpersonal insensitivity.

Evangelical academic *signals of difference* surface in all sorts of unexpected ways and places, as is evident in the following example.

Christian Basic Skills

Is there a distinguishable *Christian* approach to grammar and composition? Yes and no, answered SPC English professor Joyce Erickson in a brief two-page treatise appearing in the faculty journal, *Seattle Pacific University Review*. Responding to curriculum discussions then underway, she sought to clear the air about these notions of the "integration of faith and learning."[309] Beyond the obvious disparities of attitude and effort—". . . because we are Christians we act in loving ways toward each other and we 'do our best' "—are some rather more subtle areas of distinction. Granted there is no discernible Christian syntax, sentence structure, or essay form; no particularly Christian mechanics of reading or studying a book or text. The presentation and acquisition of basic skills betray no obvious division into the kinds of contrary Christian and secular idioms we have observed elsewhere in this community. The difference can be detected, rather, in "expressionism," or how a thing is said, a dimension of writing, she contends, upon which Christian assumptions may have some bearing. But by "expression" ("choices about how it is said") she implies much more here than a mere aesthetics of style and form. Indeed, the innumerable compositional decisions writers

---

[308] Robert Sandin writes admiringly of the non-instrumental value of the liberal arts for the development of personality, etc., and continues on that "There is no such thing as 'Christian sociology' or 'Christian economics,' but there is such a thing as viewing the social sciences Christianly, that is viewing them as a tool for purposes of Christian ministry." (*The Search for Excellence . . .*, 92-93.)

[309] Joyce Q. Erickson, "Some Notes on Teaching Writing from a Christian Perspective," *Seattle Pacific University Review*, Spring 1979.

make have some unforeseen moral consequences, triggering a *moral aestheticism* of sorts, a revisionary critical calculus in which the motivations and intentions of authors carry far more weight than the beauty and felicity of their prose.

Judgment turns then upon the motivations and intentions of an author. Does she attempt to dupe or manipulate the reader or does she "care" for and "love" the reader, investing her imagined audience with "dignity and intrinsic worth"? Herein lies the Christian/secular rub. All those binary Christian and secular qualities we encountered earlier in chapter five are deployed in predictable juxtaposition:

> Therefore, one respects the other, one is honest with the other, one does not try to control the other overtly or covertly through manipulation. In writing, this means that one does not talk down to an audience. . . . It means that the authority or superior knowledge of the writer is not used destructively. It means that the writer does not manipulate through dishonest or fallacious arguments or appeals. It means that any necessary self-disclosure by the writer hides nothing which bears on the case or on the relationship. It means that anger or points of conflict are not hidden, denied, ignored, or glossed over, but that disagreements are stated clearly with respect for the person of the opponent.

By now this sort of declensionism has become all too familiar (with still more to come): the Christian virtues of love, integrity, honesty, equality, respect, and transparency set in direct opposition to pagan deceit, power-dependency, opacity, and neglect. Erickson acknowledges that although non-Christians have throughout literary and intellectual history also aspired to such conduct and many have, in certain limited respects, achieved it, this represents the mere inauthentic aping of behaviors whose origins lie elsewhere. For evangelical Christians simply radiate difference. As we will see in the next chapter, she effectively *monopolizes* these highly-prized virtues: "The point here is that it is *a basic Christian understanding* of the world which undergirds these imperatives of human relationships." {emphasis added} The non-Christian may conduct herself in an overtly "Christianly" manner yet remain completely ignorant of the ultimate transcendent source of her own virtuous behavior.

The Christian teacher encourages then the development of basic skills of speech and composition in her students, laying a foundation for the enhancement of a "caring" for God's creatures (the audience) and a sacred *secondary creation* (the "universe of discourse") that are to follow. She also performs the duties of a literary moral sentry, shielding her students from the intrusion of insidious secular habits, instilling and cultivating the critical aptitudes so essential for the winnowing of the good habits of "caring" from the bad habits of "carelessness." The student's literary education represents then a kind of journey along a developmental continuum: a movement from an arrantly profane "carelessness" towards one's audience at the low end to a more Christ-like "caring" or husbandry of one's skills and the larger community of discourse at the high end. She has become a *Christian* author of *sacred* works, however mundane the immediate form or practical purposes of her literary creations.

The Milieu of the Evangelical Academician

In addition to the pressures of fashioning academic courses decidedly different from their equivalents in secular universities and the routine tasks of assembling the materials of a subject area or discipline for presentation, there are other more peripheral considerations that often influence and even cast a pall over the content and conduct of classes. Among the many factors coming into play here are the anti-intellectualism of the national evangelical community (reflected most directly in the Board of Trustees), traditional notions of Christian service, and perhaps most importantly and intriguingly, *the logic of an organic Christian egalitarianism set in opposition to secular inequality and bureaucratic hierarchy.*

Obscurantism

In time it becomes increasingly apparent that the Seattle Pacific student body is a shade (if not a good deal) more conservative politically and theologically than the faculty,[310] students bearing opinions and behaviors largely inherited from their more doctrinaire families and churches.[311] Along with the more obvious, often unshakeable belief in the inerrancy (infallibility) of Biblical scripture and traditional paternal "family" values, many exhibit—oddly enough for matriculating college students—an equally entrenched

---

[310] One should not conclude from this, however, that "liberals" (theological or political) constitute majorities on the faculties of Christian colleges. Far from it: ". . . . *most evangelical Christians are ideological conservatives.* Our evangelical colleges are full of conservatives—wall-to-wall conservatives." (Richard Perkins, "The Place Of Ideology In Christian Liberal Arts: Why We Need More 'Ought' And Less 'Is'," *Faculty Dialogue*, no. 7 [Fall-Winter 1986-87], 60.) {emphasis in original}

[311] One of the brightest female students commented: ". . . .there's a lot of people at SPU . . . their Christianity is . . . more shallow . . . a part of their lives they've inherited from their parents . . . but [in contrast to these people] I'm drawn to people [usually outside SPU] who think about deeper issues on a deeper intellectual level . . . prefer other people who don't just get their faith spoon-fed to them." (Wanda, *SSI*, May 2003) [Note: In all quotations drawn from the interviews of Seattle Pacific student senators—henceforth (*SSI*, May 2003)—I have taken the liberty of modifying syntax to improve fluency and have corrected the more glaring grammatical speech errors.]

animosity towards intellect and the liberal arts.[312] This divorce of *reason* from *emotion* represents a well-known, much-discussed theme in American enthusiastic religion.[313] That which distinguishes the contemporary evangelical variation from earlier American (and European) antecedents is an antagonism more thoroughly grounded in the by now familiar ideological foundation of conspicuous invidious distinction: the *imbalance* of an overweening intellect is not so much viewed as a sin as a *contaminating secular contusion*. Students are fluent in this logic and language of aspersion; tales of intellectual temptation and woe visiting the unwary Christian are standard fare in chapel.

Joe, a student, recalled his own realization of the inherent contradiction between a high-brow academic philosophy and simple Christian faith:

> Most people have enough philosophy so that they're really screwed up. . . . I have enough so that not only am I screwed up but I can screw up other people too. . . . Somebody said, "Hey Joe, don't you notice that when people read the scripture and hear the scripture their lives are changed?" I sat there, wow! . . . I had all the really good arguments Satan put in my head to keep from believing.[314]

Ken Hutchinson, a former Seattle Seahawk professional football player, advised students that

> . . . . you never know God through intellectual intelligence . . . intellectual mind . . . the Bible wisdom is emotional.[315]

---

[312] This frequently surfaces as a more general anti-aestheticism:

—Picture: girl throwing (spinning on a potter's wheel) a pot, with the caption: "Why Should a Christian Study the Arts?" (*Response*, October 1976.)

—"Student: *Of what value to the Christian is this knowledge of composers, being able to hear what is going on in their music, and similar technical matters, when I feel the compulsion of carrying out the great commission?* . . . Perhaps the reason for a strongly defensive attitude by some students is because this primacy of emotional response goes unquestioned." (L. Everett Sanders {Greenville College—Music}, "Meaning in Non-Verbal Music: Implications for One Christian," a paper delivered at the Faith/Learning Institute, Wheaton College, August 13-24, 1973.) {emphasis added}

[313] This is, of course, a tendency much older than the American experience. For as Francis Bacon introduced his *Advancement of Learning*: "The effort in the first part is to refute once and for all the ancient charge that learning undermines piety and civility." (Quoted in Lawrence A. Cremin, *American Education: The Colonial Experience, 1607-1783*, New York: Harper & Row, 1970, 93.)

[314] "Be Not Wise," Student Chapel, 11/24/78.

[315] "False Images," Chapel, 11/19/77. Also:

— ". . . . your symptoms are by no means rare among Christian students. Given your intelligence and active personality, your refusal to study literature can only be a willful exclusion on your part to consider material that you find to be threatening. You have a fear of knowledge, a fear of knowing . . . you . . . draw a line between faith and learning . . . you perceive learning

And finally there is Bob Cull, an itinerant Christian singer and musician who travels the evangelical college chapel circuit, appearing in chapel to recount his earlier experiences on secular university campuses:

> Nothing was more of a bummer than trying to talk to intellectuals who didn't have any brains . . . were just trying to throw out the right words. You know what I mean? Intellectual jive talk was all it was . . . makes me really sad. I see Christians that know the words but don't know the person. . . . [Later, fumbling for words:] I can't even remember how to talk correct English grammar. . . . [316]

To be weak, or even break down, in the ways of worldly expression becomes then a badge of honor, a sign of spiritual distinction, a celebrated signal of difference. Mr. Cull, tongued-tied, bereft of schooling and erudition, yet brimming with resentment and emotion, effectively purges himself of the tainting corruption of secular coherence and intellect; with much fanfare, he dons the liberating mantle of an evangelical Descartism: I don't think terribly well and often wax inarticulate, therefore I am holy.

Attempting to lighten the burden of ideological baggage with which many students arrive laden, the faculty counters with a veritable barrage of "the mind is sacred also" salvos. Religion professors appear before chapel to assure a minority of fundamentalist students that it is "OK to think," to reason, analyze, and contemplate things; after all, one argued, did not Christ implore his followers, "let us reason together"?[317] What is more, the college

---

to be a '*this-worldly*' *activity*, and as a result you often see it to be a threat to your faith. . . ." (From an imaginary dialogue between a Christian college English professor and a student: Samuel Sherrill, "Fear of Knowing: A Literature Student Finds Out What's In It for Him," *Universitas*, April/May 1974.) {emphasis added}

— "To begin with, we must recognize that Schloss's uncomfortableness [?] with the category of excellence is not as rare as some might think. He simply has the courage to voice what many of us feel. As I reflect on the times when I was honored for academic achievement (excellence?), I can recall clearly that my sense of joy and self-satisfaction was *always* tinged by a sense of uneasiness, embarrassment, or even guilt. Now, as I fill the role of teacher bestowing such recognition, I notice the same reaction in my students." (Randy L. Maddox, "Faculty Response: Exorcising The Guilt Of Excellence," *Faculty Dialogue*, no. 10 [Winter-Spring 1988], 121.) {emphasis in original}

[316] Bob Cull, "Love Songs to the Father," Chapel, 1/23/76.

[317] Professor Daniel Berg of the religion department spoke to a specially convened freshman chapel to the effect that the entering students' evangelical backgrounds had engendered in them "lurking doubts about the life of the mind. . . . Why is it that we separate knowledge and the spiritual dimension?". . . [You will face] "a world of Christians ahead of you who negate the mind." ("The Idea of a Christian College," Chapel, 11/19/80.)

—Professor Frank Spina, from the same department, cautioned students that "anti-intellectual strains have no place here." There should be no stigma laid upon the "Christian's

sponsors frequent week-long lecture series, bringing prominent national Christian scholars and academic figures to campus, often for the singular purpose of persuading skeptics of the value of a liberal arts education, parading these visitors before the student body as role models, some self-professed "Christian humanists," men (primarily) who have successfully cultivated faith *and* intellect and who are unashamed of the results.[318]

At issue here in this apparent rift between evangelical academicians and students drawn from the larger evangelical community are two contending formulations of Christian / secular antagonism. Most academicians distinguish a sacred Christian *balance* (mind<->body<->spirit)—with which the Christian college seeks to imbue her students—from an opposing secular *imbalance* (particularly an exaggeration of the mind or intellect); accordingly, when they censure students for a neglect or fear of intellect they are seeking the restoration of *an equilibrium among these three elements of personality*. Likewise the more rigid fundamentalist or charismatic students who otherwise impugn the cultivation of intellect also trigger the terms of a logic, this one juxtaposing a sacred Christian spiritualism (transcendent: God-centered) which so often accompanies the experiences of conversion and faith with the dry, mechanical, unsentimental exercise of reason (terrestrial: man-centered), the latter condition plaguing the "secular" academy. This second invidious distinction is of course the more broadly drawn, yet both conservative students and liberal faculty derive their imperatives from the ideological demands of a more general logic, fashioning their own particular diametrically-opposed Christian and secular derivations and aligning their sympathies accordingly.

As is so often the case, students are then understandably torn between *competing logical imperatives*—the one (of the faculty) encouraging and the other (of the national community) denigrating the cultivation of intellect (and we will see more of this kind of internal contradiction). It has been my experience that the latter exerts the more pronounced influence over students, as evidence in this one respect by a uniform lack of interest in the general liberal arts.

Hence the Seattle Pacific professor often finds himself before freshman students a few of whom are academically and temperamentally unprepared for college studies. Fortunately, most are not, the majority coming instead

---

application of critical thinking to every facet of human knowledge . . . let's all declare war on the mediocre and second-rate . . . let's declare war on bad music, bad poetry, bad art. . . ." ("Christianus Sum, Ergo Cogito," Chapel, 10/23/81.)

[318] Dr. Kenneth Kantzer (four chapel addresses, Christian Commitment Week, 1/11- 14/77), anticipating criticisms that the content of his lectures might be too academic or intellectual, introduced the first with the remark, *"I assumed that you didn't check your brains on the way in,"* and then proceeded to deride evangelical "anti-intellectualism," encouraging the use of "the mind." {emphasis added}

from literate middle and upper-middle class families whose parents send their sons and daughters to reputable private and public high schools and who demand respectable academic performances for their time and/or money.[319] Although one observes an apparent genuine interest in academic studies in these students, it is an enthusiasm and curiosity of an abbreviated sort, one which rarely blossoms into the kind of visionary liberal arts "wholeness" the college celebrates. Understandably—and perhaps even more so than their counterparts in large public universities[320]—Seattle Pacific students are narrowly focused in their studies upon a future profession or a career in the altruistic service occupations of the ministry, education, and health care, among others.[321] For the vast majority of Seattle Pacific students

---

[319] The average high school GPA of entering Seattle Pacific freshmen compares favorably with other Northwest universities, as we see for autumn quarter, 1981: SPU 3.39, UW 3.4, University of Puget Sound 3.3, Pacific Lutheran University 3.4, Seattle University 3.24. (from *A Profile of Students at Seattle Pacific University*, Office of Student Affairs, 1980-81.)

Yet I should add that with respect to attracting the very best students produced by Washington high schools each year, Seattle Pacific lags far behind the others. For example, out of 530 Washington state high school seniors chosen "Washington Scholars" ("Using grade point average, Scholastic Aptitude Test scores, leadership and community service, the Washington Scholars program taps three top students from each legislative district, invites them to a luncheon in Olympia and hands them a four-year tuition waiver worth $1,650 a year.") from 1982 through 1987 who matriculated the next year at a Washington college (@ 340 went out of state), only six went to Seattle Pacific.

The six-year totals: UW[1] (225), WSU[1] (77), Pacific Lutheran[4] (51), University of Puget Sound[5] (37), Whitman College[4] (35), Central Washington University[1] (21), Western Washington University[1] (16), Seattle University[3] (14), Gonzaga University[3] (13), Whitworth College[2] (11), Eastern Washington University [1](6), Seattle Pacific[2] (6), Evergreen State College[6] (5).

Legend: [1]Public/[2]Evangelical-Protestant/[3]Catholic/[4]Mainline Protestant/[5]Sectarian origin, now non-religious/[6]Experimental Public.

(Data and quote from Jody Becker, "Trying to keep the bright ones here," *The Seattle Times*, 19 June 1988.)

—Yet again, Christian colleges would appear to excel at producing acceptable medical school applicants: " . . . nearly all [of the four-year schools in the Christian College Coalition—@ 50] average 90 percent success rate for students seeking admission to medical school." (Kenneth Briggs, "Evangelical Colleges Re-born," *New York Times Magazine*, 14 December 1980.)

[320] Comparative data available in Appendix D of the dissertation.

[321] A cursory glance at the numbers for declared majors reveals a liberal arts program on the verge of extinction. Those majors with 20 or more students: Business Administration & Economics (352), Education: Christian, Physical, Special, Music, Administrative, Counseling (344), Nursing (241), Psychology (97), Computer Science (72), Home Economics (60), Biology (51), English (51), Engineering Science (47), Pre-med (34), Religion (33), Clothing & Textile (30), Social Sciences (28), Art (26), Chemistry (24), Language Arts (24), Sociology (23), Political Science (23), Mathematics (22), History (21), Communications (21).

this notion of the "wholeness" of a liberal arts education represents an often frustrating detour on the road to some sort of professional degree.[322] It is a predilection and pattern (Business / Education / Nursing) that is duplicated at other sectarian colleges throughout the nation.[323]

Anecdotal accounts of a general academic lethargy or indifference abound. One evening I attended the finals of a campus college bowl tournament, an event modeled on the famous television program of the '50s and '60s, wherein two teams of four students competed to answer academic and religious trivia questions. During the course of the evening I was rather astonished to observe that *not a single student* on the panels or in the audience could correctly answer any of the following three questions:

"Who was the author of *Civilization and its Discontents?*"

"Who wrote *The Old Régime and the French Revolution* and *Democracy in America?*"

"What film was [*sic*] Humphrey Bogart and Ingrid Bergman most known for?"

Not a single attempt at any of these. No one knew. Remarkable.[324]

What is more, each year the university sponsors a "Liberal Arts Week," during which nationally-known Christian academicians visit the school, a prominent faculty member delivers a keynote lecture, and a call is issued (at least the year I was on campus) for student papers on the topic of the meaning and value of a liberal arts education, the very best of which receives a cash award. This particular year the faculty award lecture, delivered in the largest lecture hall on campus, was reported to have drawn a "handful" of students. Judges of the student essay competition completed their duties with relative dispatch: the call for papers garnered but a single solitary entry, whose author, predictably enough, was awarded first prize.[325]

Total: 1624 (not counting, for example, philosophy, anthropology, and others with too few to qualify); Pre-majors: 783. (from "A Profile of Students at Seattle Pacific University," Office of Student Affairs, 1980-81.)

[322] With respect to the claim that Christian colleges promote the "wholeness" of a liberal arts education, C. George Fry (an evangelical partisan) observed a contrary trend at most Christian colleges, conceding that " . . . the theory is seldom substantiated in practice. Many church colleges are really mini-universities, including professional schools of theology, law, nursing, and education." ("Are Christian Colleges Worth the Trouble?," *Christianity Today*, 12 February 1971.)

[323] Appendix D of the original dissertation.

[324] (College Bowl, 2/3/2003)

[325] From Student Senate meeting discussion, 11/9/2002.

Anti-intellectualism poses a formidable challenge to those faculty seeking to rejuvenate the cerebral dimension of "balance" or "wholeness" and graduate Christian "scholar-servants" who even begin to approach the abstract ideal. The burden proves too onerous for many, according to Anthony Campolo, a visiting Staley Scholar, who likened the experience to that of whipping life back into a dead horse:

> Incidentally, most of them [professors] used to be alive . . . nothing kills profs more than dead students. . . . Christian students in Christian colleges are notoriously bad . . . obsessed with getting a grade for the least effort . . . Not at all like students at Pennsylvania or Harvard. . . . Haven't seen that sort of dedication to learning at any Christian college.[326]

For all their efforts, some of the more demanding professors, like the visiting Campolo, are rewarded with a familiar epithet, "faith wrecker"; yet again, others manage to earn the begrudging respect of their students, having inspired students to rise to the challenge of understanding and defining their own beliefs.[327]

One female student senator, with parents of contrasting Christian and agnostic backgrounds who had divorced, remarried and divorced others, and then remarried yet again, reflected upon her initial confusion:

> I came to Seattle Pacific because the other colleges were too big and I was afraid of losing my faith . . . yet my faith has been challenged here more than I ever

---

[326] Spoken at a chapel talkback session, 5/18/2003. Campolo was then chairman of the sociology department at Eastern College, Pennsylvania, having taught formerly at the University of Pennsylvania, and was the Staley Distinguished Christian Scholar for the week of May 16-18, 2003.

[327] "I remember one professor my freshman year who came and refuted several things that I believed in—Christian doctrine. . . . ['What?'] Oh, he went through the Old Testament and pointed out inconsistencies in the old and new—matters of time and history ['Factual errors?'] . . . or where a tribe had been left out and no reason why . . . or a lot of people think this Psalm points to Jesus Christ when there's absolutely no way they could have heard of Jesus Christ . . . that kind of thing. . . . I sat kind of stunned. He said, 'OK, now that we've refuted the Bible, let's get together tomorrow and talk about why we believe what we do. . . .' I've never had Dr. W. though . . . who is a faith ['Wrecker?'] challenger. . . . I think the professors here want to tell you their point of view and then it's up to you to decide what you'll buy and what you won't. . . . I kind of did, you know, being a Presbyterian, expect that the Free Methodists would be kind of wrong." (Jacob, *SSI*, May 2003)
—From one religion professor's lecture: "Probably the resurrection was an event in the minds of the believers and if you had a videotape whirring you probably could see nothing. The Gospels say nothing about Jesus's physical resurrection—just that they encountered him." (Class: *Understanding The Christian Faith*, 1/11/2003.)
Perhaps I join the reader (and those believing in the inerrancy of scripture as well) in wondering how one can dismiss the Biblical account of the physical resurrection of Jesus as illusory and still regard oneself a Christian?

imagined it would be . . . to the point where right now I know less of what I believe than when I entered. . . . To have a New Testament class and have the feeding of the ten thousand questioned as to whether it really happened . . . some of the miracles questioned . . . or whether they were just a moral to the story . . . it was difficult. Old Testament was even harder . . . because almost everything was questioned, all the way back to Adam and Eve. But it's been healthy because my own faith has been strengthened . . . [now I] struggle for myself instead of just adopting what I've always been taught. It's awfully frustrating. There are times when I really question what I believe. . . . One professor says this and another that, and they're both coming from the same . . . and the problem is not so much the truth or error of the passages in the Bible as trying to figure out how it all comes together. For example, what's more proper behavior: to go out and be a missionary to the world or accept people for what they are and what they believe . . . . I think it's the same for most people here: they want to discover how they fit into the giant plan. I don't think people come here to learn the story of the Bible, but rather to understand the meaning of all that, how it applies to us. . . . Everybody here thinks that almost everything is inter-related . . . . All three of my classes one quarter were so interrelated I couldn't believe it. . . . Everybody's looking for something to unify their education, looking for a focal point.[328]

Daniel, a bearded, portly fellow who delighted in my characterization of him as the campus "holy man," attained an understanding and appreciation of the strategies employed by the religion professors more quickly than others:

> When I first arrived I expected the profs to all be Billy Grahams . . . but then I discovered that they weren't quite the saints that I had imagined. In fact, some of them were faith wreckers . . . and boy was I lonely and depressed. But then I caught on to what they were doing: they were trying to shake me up so that I would think, so that I would come to know what I believe through my own struggles and efforts rather than simply accepting everything the church had taught me. . . . That made a big difference . . . [It] took me a few weeks.[329]

The strategy produces in some students the desired result of casting a momentary pall over the inherited beliefs of their parents, raising doubts and anxiety and perhaps even producing genuine moments of doctrinal introspection (I emphasize *doctrinal* here because nearly all young persons are sunk in one form or another of critical self-examination). For others, the experience proves too threatening and destabilizing, the prospect of creative, independent thought raising too menacing a specter. A good many quit, quietly slipping away from their more resilient peers, returning to their homes and families the first few weeks of autumn quarter; indeed by the second or third

---

[328] (Wanda, *SSI*, May 2003)
[329] (*SSI*, May 2003)

academic quarter, 40% of the matriculating freshman class has usually vanished into the hinterland (although probably just as many leave for other reasons, such as simple homesickness or money problems).[330] Still others batten down the ideological fortress and fend off the liberal challenges to inherited orthodoxy, comfortable with well-worn ideas and patterns of belief. (As we will see later in Part Three, some of the even more extreme defensive responses harbor a potential of further deterioration into psychologically unhealthy and even damaging patterns of thought and conduct.)

Equality vs. Hierarchy

In the late '70s and early '80s Seattle Pacific faculty grew more inclined to contest the relations of authority under which they labored or served. Many began to take seriously the notion that an "equality of faith" among community believers ought to set the Christian college community apart from the petty, manipulative, hierarchical relationships characterizing the secular university and the larger American society.[331] Yet few could deny that for such an equality to prevail in the concrete world of the Christian college those with an inordinate amount of authority or power, namely the Trustees (and often the administration), would have to relinquish a portion of it to others—to students and faculty, and in perhaps even rarer instances, the Trustees to the administration. Community members would have to become equally contributing partners in a venture of faith, equal—albeit differently functioning—appendages of a unified, organic-like "body of Christ." Perhaps it was the appearance of a kind of internal institutional politics at Seattle Pacific during the 1979-1980 curriculum reform discussions that moved Professor Eugene Lemcio of the religion department to reflect upon the appropriate role of authority and power within the Christian college community.

> Anyone who's been awake in the last half-dozen years senses the emergence of several well-defined power blocs. Traditionally, the administration has been viewed as the locus of authority and power on campus. At least, it's been most obvious there. In recent years, however, the Trustees have played a larger role in the decisions made at various levels of our collective life. Paralleling this, the faculty

---

[330] from *A Profile of Students at Seattle Pacific University*.

[331] One chapel speaker, a lobbyist for a Christian organization in Washington D.C. and regular participant in Capitol Hill Bible study groups, claimed that a "secular university" cannot be " *a body of brothers and sisters who get together as equals. . . . Leadership* [is a] *. . . secular term not a Biblical term . . .* [representing as it does] *a psychological manipulation. . . . Within the body men should not exercise authority one over the other.*" Referring to the examples of Jesus and Paul, he concluded that leadership "does not exist within the body in the secular sense." (Burnett Thompson, "Not of this World," 3/26/80.) {emphasis added}

itself has gradually emerged as a more visible, political force. Two schools have affected internal changes. A dormant AAUP chapter has been revived. I have heard the dreaded [*secular*] word "union" uttered a couple of times in response to a perception that a hierarchical, corporate model has fostered an employee rather than a colleague mentality among the faculty. . . . [332]

Lemcio judges this kind of thinking and behavior contrary to a genuine Christian ethos. Observe though how the unrealistic expectation of a purely selfless and bloodless a-political resolution of campus issues may ultimately deny community members access to the very sentiments and political tools which must be unapologetically expressed and brandished—not suppressed—in order to expeditiously generate any sort of consensus.[333] Perhaps as much energy was expended trying to conceal the political nature of the negotiations and the motivations of the interested parties as actually went into the eventual resolution of differences.

He continues, reminding colleagues that

> . . . . servanthood belongs to a framework of thought that *runs against the grain of prevailing norms and values.* Jesus contrasted the world system wherein rulers lord it over their subjects, with *the upside down structure of God's Rule*: the greatest will be the servant/slave of all. . . . the Lord of creation kneels at its feet with a towel. *All notions of power regarding God, all notion of power as it affects human relationships are turned on their heads in the Kingdom of God. They belong to that system where living comes by dying, winning by losing, filling by emptying, ruling by serving.*[334]

---

[332] Eugene E. Lemcio, "The Servant as Priest and Advocate," *Seattle Pacific University Review*, Spring 1980 (first delivered at a faculty retreat, 9/14/79). Lemcio's limited perspective of the McKenna years led him, quite understandably, to underestimate the dominance of the Trustees (and through them, the Free Methodist church) throughout the history of the school.

[333] A similar episode was reported at Westmont college: "Another example of the dissonance created by competing goods relates to the process of developing the college's mission statement. Of the four interest groups most directly affected by this decision-making process—trustees, administrators, faculty, and students—each group seems to want unilateral control over what makes up our mission while hoping other groups will feel valued and involved in the process of defining the mission. The situation has been more agonizing, I suspect, because *we have found it almost impossible even to agree on a process.* At this foundational level, this crucial dimension of our institutional life, we have been plagued by our unwillingness to submit our various individual and group goals to the common good." (Jonathan H. Hess, "The Transformation Of Westmont," *Faculty Dialogue*, no. 8 [Spring-Summer 1987], 124.) {emphasis added}

[334] Lemcio, "The Servant as Priest and Advocate." {emphases added} Lemcio is one of the very few evangelicals (if he considers himself an evangelical) I have encountered who understands and embraces what I regard as the fundamental logical center of the teachings of Jesus, this principle of inversion. See David Martin's *The Breaking of the Image: A Sociology of Christian Theory* (New York: St. Martins, 1979).

Observe the binary terms of the evangelical logic on naked display. Principles of *inversion*, *organicism*, and *egalitarianism* fairly abound here. Every "member" (part) of the "body" (whole) of Christ, the Christian community, performs a determined (by prior transcendent gifts) function, occupies an elemental, *sui generis* niche in the larger Christian order. All occupy different positions and perform unique duties, yet are equal in the distribution and reception of community esteem and ultimate redemption. No one exercises "authority" or employs "power" as is commonly understood; no one—acting either personally or corporately—compels an involuntary behavior from another, for the members of the community are the willing, un-coerced slaves of one another. Each volunteers time and energy to satisfy the needs of the other; each sacrifices or "empties" himself of inner-direction in order to fill himself with the will of the other. Sentiments, I might add, altogether alien to those celebrated by Satan in Milton's *Paradise Lost*: "Better to reign in Hell, than serve in Heav'n."[335]

Again, we encounter here principles that prove deceptively easy to pronounce and rhapsodize over and yet exceedingly difficult to follow or institutionalize,[336] as was demonstrated in the course of one dynamic chapel speaker's discourse upon these matters. Regarding personal relationships, this speaker instructed a chapel audience to the effect that "For Christians,

---

[335] I 262, 263.

[336] The above egalitarian sentiments are belied by the reality of divergent social interests and roles, all too evident, for example, in David McKenna's short introductory remarks to a faculty-staff "mixer" held in Gwinn Commons, the Seattle Pacific campus cafeteria. He began with the observation that once everyone had collected their donuts and coffee both staff and faculty immediately drifted apart, clustering at opposite ends of the cafeteria. He urged them to try to get to know one another, for the sake of "community." (David McKenna, "A Simple Meal," undated typescript.) {Archives}

That these sentiments of spiritual equality prove equally resistant to implementation in the relationships of professors, students, and the professional staff is made evident by the convening of separate "staff devotionals" in Alexander Hall (*Response*, March 1978) and the appearance in the early 1980s of separate "Faculty Chapels." These faculty chapels may have existed earlier, but the first reference to them I came across was in the February 1981 issue of *Response*.

Consider evidence from another Christian college: " . . . [Asking of his own college, Westmont] Why do so few faculty consort with staff or administration with faculty? Why do we faculty think the college should aspire to be an academically elite institution? *Why are staff workers not allowed in the faculty dining room? All these conditions reflect implicit assumptions about power, ambition, social obligation, individual and community worth, and all reflect an existential world view.*" (Schloss, "Social Ecology And The Nominally Religious World View . . . ," 119.) {emphasis added} / "The faculty dining room brouhaha is an example of this tension. (Should the faculty have their own dining room? Who should have access to that room?) While almost no one believed that the pro or con of a faculty dining room in and of itself was high on our educational agenda, it consumed time and effort and caused widespread division quite disproportionate to its intrinsic importance. . . . each side tended to blame the other for the escalation." (Jonathan H. Hess, "The Transformation Of Westmont," 124.)

there should be no domination, [we ought to be] just servants to one another." In Christian marriages, for instance, both partners ought to sacrifice their hopes and aspirations for one another, "each being submissive to the other"; this mutual subjugation producing relationships which, contrary to appearance and expectation, are rich and rewarding. Indeed there is something gloriously sacred about this kind of "servanthood," because the "world" worships "masterhood" instead. Furthermore, extending the principle beyond purely personal relationships, the consistent Christian ought then, for example, reject the political approach of such groups as the "Moral Majority" as a worldly aberration contrary to the example of Jesus, since these movements " . . . try to change the world with the power methods of the world."[337]

Here, once again, *internal community logics collide.* For how many Christian communities have seen the egalitarianism of their dreams vanish under *ideological pressures to generate invidious Christian/secular distinctions and to aggressively project and radiate these logical meanings and understandings outward into the fabric of a larger threatening secular society?* Once more we observe one particular reading or expression of the logic of difference jostling with another equally compelling, equally antagonistic to the example of "the world." We must be leveled, powerless, mutually submissive in our faith,[338] yet we must also make some sort of dent in the world (must make the United States a thoroughly Christian nation). We must produce the latter and yet somehow or other preserve the former.

In his conclusion, Lemcio wonders, "How will we broker our power differently? What changes in administration, style, teaching, curriculum, research, student and staff relations will need to be made so that we can at least approximate the servant community / institution?" And then again on second thought, he catches himself, lowers his sights, and reluctantly concedes

---

[337] Anthony Campolo, "About the World," Staley Lecture Series, 5/16-18/2003.

[338] For some, these leveling principles ought to apply even to the assignment of grades for coursework. Jack Norton, Associate Professor of Christian Education at Houghton College, argues that "Much of our current grading system seems to be *in fundamental contradiction to the gospel.* . . . Are we consistent when we affirm, even with applause at graduation, those who graduate with one degree of cum laude or another, when in fact, the 'C' student who graduated on the five-year plan may have grown more and achieved more personally? My students have become used to my occasional speech about the priority of learning over grades, but their responses indicate the system places them under law, not gospel. I will admit that I seldom hear 'A' students complain about that system. . . . [Give all students A's?] a naive response. . . . [But] What if at least some of our general education requirements were offered on a pass-incomplete basis?" ("Response to Thomas Wolbrecht," *Faculty Dialogue,* no. 4, [Fall 1985], 87-88.) {emphasis added}

The irony here is of course that such Pass-Fail options in general education have been in place in large "secular" universities since the early 1970s.

that "the possibility seems remote indeed."[339] How indeed does a professor both affect *spiritual equality with the very same students who have come to him for instruction in this matter of wholeness?* Therein lies the ideological rub. The dynamic force of the logic places him in an unenviable position.

For all the self-promotional talk of an institutional gift for producing wholeness in its students, this particular academic community falls considerably short of its liberal arts pretensions and aspirations. We observe here an academic philosophy and curriculum largely (though not exclusively) fashioned in opposition to an imagined secular antithesis (with numerous unacknowledged borrowings). The promotion, defense, and elaboration of these principles are all too often advanced in purely negative terms; they represent mere foils to their secular counterparts;[340] they betray weak theoretical and practical foundations (as we shall see), wobbling and tottering when forced to stand on their own substance and power. In spite of occasional loudly advertised forays into the "integration of faith and learning" the evangelical academician hasn't got much to show for all the posturing and commotion. The more ambitious academician struggles and strains to bring these invidiously inspired principles to some sort of practical realization. In this chapter we have explored some of the more tangible impediments strewn in his path by the larger national evangelical culture and the institutions in which he labors; in the following chapter we will explore some even more fundamental problems inherent in the very structure of the ideas themselves, ones which may render them untenable even as guiding theoretical principles of education and scholarship.

---

[339] Lemcio, "The Servant as Priest and Advocate."

[340] Consider journalist Monique El-Faizy's account of a visit to Virginia's Patrick Henry College:

> But a Christian education such as the one offered at Patrick Henry is not about exploration but about fortification. Students here are being trained to take their ideas and influence the world with them, not to go out and learn what the world has to teach. That imperative elevates the importance of debate and moot court in conservative Christian schools—life is about convincing those who disagree with you and about defeating your opponents. Almost a third of the students at Patrick Henry are involved in debate and the school has a formidable team that routinely wins national tournaments. In evangelical politics the courts [re: Roe v. Wade] are seen as the key to turning the country around, so it is critical that the Christian community be armed with talented lawyers. . . . In the days before the 2004 presidential election the school stopped holding classes since so many students were working on campaigns. . . . (op. cit., 184-5.)

CHAPTER 7

TRUTH, IDEOLOGY, AND SCIENCE

A
t times it seems as though truth and knowledge are for the evangelical academician almost tangible objects independent of human perception and thought, hovering somewhere in the stratosphere until God deems the time appropriate for their appearance on the human scene, when they come tumbling down, all of a piece, from the sky. The Christian scholar becomes then like a beachcomber scouring the seashores for heavenly driftwood, searching for little bits and pieces of truth and knowledge dotting the sands of evangelical academia.

Truth and knowledge come then to represent not abstract ideals or conceptions—assumptions, statements, propositions, generalizations, interpretations, inductions, deductions, probabilities, physical laws and processes—employed to make sense of a wide range of phenomena, but are rather more like *natural objects* in their own right, assuming a form and substance apart from any interceding human cognition and thought. They become, in effect, the metaphysical, epistemological *givens* of the natural and social universe, as concretely real as any stone or tree. The *Truth*, by dint of a conversion experience and an ongoing "personal (*and*, we might add, *social*) relationship" with the creator, falls into the *possession* of the believer; it represents a "gift" of an *a priori* given, however unseen or other-dimensional the transaction may appear on the surface to the uninitiated. Although the believer must certainly achieve a kind of spiritual mood and condition for its reception, in no sense does she fully earn or deserve any subsequent revelation. Only as the aspirant molds herself into an *empty vessel* may she experience the other-worldly filling of her yawning internal human cavity. The myriad elementary particles of truth and knowledge comprising this larger monolithic system of truth are similarly given; unimpeached by active human hands and minds, they are passively discovered, sighted, unveiled.[341]

---

[341] Lest anyone infer from the foregoing discussion that the author somehow or other believes that the physical objects of the natural and social world are illusory, I would remind the reader that the discussion has to this point dealt primarily with the issues of epistemology, not metaphysics or ontology. I do believe that both kinds of objects are real, have weight and mass and all the properties we commonly associate with tangible objects, and do in fact *exist* apart from the perception and understanding of human beings. But this is quite different from saying that their *form, identity, meaning,* and *significance* exist independently of any such understanding, which is the evangelical claim.

We would then be hard-pressed to think of these evangelical students and academicians as in any way related to the kind of John Dewey human actors who virtually create and transform objects in the very act of their perception. One discerns no such interpretive slack in the taut ropes of evangelical cognition. Rather, regenerated Christians are *tabula rasa* receptors of the deep, enduring structures of a universal truth and knowledge. Turning to their daily tasks, Christian college scholars and scientists routinely embark on voyages of exploration, epistemological treasure hunts, seeking the given cosmic code underpinning all inorganic and organic matter, the ethereal imprint governing the form and development of all human and natural life. They discover facts that are extant and whole, yet tightly woven into the primeval fabric of the universe.[342]

There are immediate implications for the origin and nature of human values. Genuine (*true*) values are inherent in the given facts themselves and never emerge or develop independently—never through the evolution, say, of particular human communities or societies.[343] Cultural progression or

---

[342] "From a Biblical standpoint the crucial consideration is that the sum total of the best of secular learning in unregenerate man culminates in a human wisdom which is not only void of the true knowledge of God but worse, may be antagonistic thereto (I Cor. 1:19-21; 2:5,6). The essential goal of learning from the Biblical standpoint is *a crowning wisdom and knowledge which is not produced by the human mind but whose treasures are rather hidden in Christ* (Col. 2:3) and *which comes from above* (James 1:5; 3:17) *as a gift*. Thus the unique quality of Christian learning is *a vertical dimension* whereby the whole range of human learning at the horizontal level is opened to enlightenment, shaping and directing from above through the infused presence of the Holy Spirit. This creative and quickening infusion is *highly limited by human free will* . . . the process of formal learning can be integral to that *divine alchemy* whereby the love of God opens a dimension of knowing totally beyond the means of purely human manufacture. . . . a received body of knowledge is re-worked and so to speak, redeemed as it becomes the Christian scholar's own learning and thus *subservient to his relation to Christ.* . . . facilitates a *unity of comprehension* not otherwise open to human experience. . . . The beacon of light shed by God's word marks the path pursued by the Christian scholar." (George L. Bates {Westmont College—Physics}, "Integral Christian Learning for Engaged Living [Being a Tribute in Miniature to Christian Higher Education]," a paper delivered at the Faith/Learning Institute, North Park College, Chicago, August 14-25, 1972.) {emphases added}
—"The Christian must find meaning and truth in all that he does. He must affirm that the Word (Jesus Christ) 'was with God at the beginning, and through Him all things came to be; no single thing was created without Him.' (John 1:3, *NEB*) It seems then that the Christian must reject the extreme formalist school and *insist on meaning in his mathematics*. This meaning need not be related to physical reality but emphasizes the faith that Jesus Christ adds meaning to all aspects of life. *If mathematics is a gift of God to man, then man discovers mathematics rather than creates it*, even though the discovery involves a high level of creativity." (D. Wayne Cassel {Messiah College}, "Are There Any Truths in Mathematics?," a paper delivered at the Faith/Learning Institute, Wheaton College, August 13-24, 1973.) {emphases added} These two just a small sample of possible examples.
[343] On the equation of facts and values:

variation produces nothing original or unanticipated under the sun. *All emergent human forms and values are concretely sunk in the original given structure of human personality and society.* The most highly-prized human virtues and attributes are but terrestrial versions or approximations of the immaculate formal properties of God; in no sense are they seminal human creations or appropriations. All told then, truth, facts, values, and knowledge are grounded in the given order of the natural world, in the immutable nature of the *potentially* regenerated human being; they are essential, indivisible.[344]

Truth and Knowledge in the Bible

Consider the Biblical justifications typically advanced to support these notions. John 8:32 is popular: "If you dwell within the revelations I have brought . . . you shall know the truth, and the truth will set you free."[345] Observe two distinct, but closely-related claims here: the latter we encountered earlier as the decidedly exotic evangelical conception of academic freedom (conformity enhances personal liberty); the former, which concerns us now, would appear to suggest the ability of the believer, having exerted the necessary effort of "dwelling," to fully comprehend the New Testament teachings of Jesus and grasp "the truth." But in what sense? In this instance, if I may be allowed a momentary transgression, the speaker of record, Jesus, lapses once more into characteristic ambiguity. Considerable latitude is accorded the believer in the determination of the scope of these revelations. Does he mean *all* of the truth possessed by God the Father? Or just that much anchored in the actual words of these prophetic utterances? And is a

---

—It is this "alienation of facts from values and rampant relativism that has deprived academic man the power to discern and judge." (Fry, "Are Christian Colleges Worth The Trouble?" 7-8.)

—"Positivism with its insistence on empirical verifiability reinforced it [the "bleakness" of a "world of bare facts"]. Fact and value thus are divorced. Whatever our place in nature, neither nature nor science support the values we pursue. . . .

A relation exists, therefore, between what 'is' and what 'ought' to be, between fact and value. The physical world is not without purpose, value-free or value-neutral, to be manipulated at will for whatever we might desire, nor is its worth altogether relative or anthropocentric. *Fact and value are united* by God's purposes in creating." (Holmes, *Contours* . . . , 26, 161.) {emphasis added}

[344] In this regard, it is instructive how many of the chapel speakers I heard both on tape and in person began their talks with a brief definition from *Webster's* of a particularly crucial word or concept. I found the practice a derivation of this assumption that the facts of the world are concrete and unchanging, as though words have no etymologies, are not human creations which have evolved and will continue to evolve over time. No doubt Webster was an evangelical Christian.

[345] *NEB.*

conception of *knowledge* included within this more general epiphany of *the truth*?

A similar kind of ambiguity, for example, nettled SPU president David McKenna, who struggled to rationalize the apparent moral ignorance of Adam and Eve in Genesis 2:16-18 ("He told the man, 'You may eat from every tree in the garden, but not from the tree of the knowledge of good and evil; for on the day that you eat from it, you will surely die.' "):

> Again, God has separated himself from his creation at the point of truth. The restriction was not against knowledge—this would be contrary to the conscious and intelligent person whom God had created in His own image. But this was a warning for man to remember that he was not infinite as God is infinite. As a man, he could not absorb the ultimate truth about good and evil that God knew. . . . From the Genesis story, we learn that the search for knowledge is not the same as the search for truth.[346]

I share the reader's confusion. There are some simple facts in the Genesis story that McKenna appears to neglect.

First, it is important to recognize that Adam and Eve did not necessarily possess *eternal life* prior to their fall. The reader may be surprised to learn that mortality for the species was not one of the ramifications of original sin, but an *a priori* condition of the original couple. Recall that in the second creation story of Genesis (the first runs from 1:1 to 2:4), God places Adam in Eden " . . . and in the *middle* of the garden he set the tree of life *and* the tree of the knowledge of good and evil." (2:9—emphases added) Now although God surely warns Adam to stay away from the second tree (2:17), he makes no mention of the first. (Although it is conceivable that both may have been included in the prohibition, for as Eve answers the serpent: "We may eat the fruit of any tree in the garden, except for *the tree* in *the middle* of the garden. . . . " However the ambiguity is resolved—one tree or two in the middle—neither Adam nor Eve ate from the tree of life.) Presumably, Adam or Eve could have eaten from the tree of life and immediately gained the immortality of a god. In fact, the serpent is quite correct and sincere when assuring the couple that the consequences of eating fruit from the tree of the knowledge of good and evil are not nearly as severe as God predicts: "Of course you will not die. God knows that as soon as you eat it, your eyes will be opened and you will be *like gods knowing both good and evil*." (3:4-6—emphasis added) Recall that God warned Adam "*on the day* that you eat from it, you will certainly die" (2:18—emphasis added), a *specific* caution (and prediction) that makes no sense if one clings to the common assumption that death for

---

[346] "God Doesn't Know All The Answers," undated typescript. {Archives}

the human species was a major consequence (along with the introduction of sin) of the Fall; for indeed Adam and Eve were already mortal in their pre-lapsarian innocence. (They could have eaten from the tree of life prior to the Fall—it was not expressly forbidden—but there is no indication they chose to do so. If they had so eaten, would not the consequences have been *irreversible*, as were those of eating from the other tree?) Confirmation of this follows in 3:21-24:

> The Lord God made tunics of skins for Adam and his wife and clothed them. He said, "The man has become like one of us, knowing good and evil; *what if he now reaches out his hand and takes fruit from the tree of life also, eats it and lives forever?*" So the Lord God drove him out of the garden of Eden to till the ground from which he had been taken. He cast him out, and to the east of the garden of Eden he stationed the cherubim and a sword whirling and flashing to guard the way to the tree of life. {emphasis added}

There are, I suppose, many possible renderings of these ancient verses, ones which discern in these simple words a plethora of often incongruous meanings and implications. My own not so imaginative review of one distinguished translation yields some admittedly simple-minded conclusions. Apropos this notion of a unity or oneness of God, observe in the space of some three to four pages of scripture the number of intimations of a *pluralistic* nature and form of God: "Then God said, 'Let us make man in *our* image and likeness to rule the fish in the sea, the birds of heaven. . . .' " (1:26); the serpent claiming indulgence will make Adam and Eve " . . . like *gods* knowing both good and evil." (3:6); the above (3:22): "He [God] said, 'The man has become like *one of us*, knowing good and evil . . . .' "; and "When mankind began to increase and to spread all over the earth and daughters were born to them, the sons *of the gods* saw that the daughters of men were beautiful; so they took for themselves such women as they chose." (6:1-3; emphases added)

And this other notion of a "knowledge of good and evil" proves intriguing in that its rather uniform, undifferentiated character in the Edenic setting—an apparently indistinguishable talent or awareness characterizing both the gods and fallen man—suggests that God (or the gods) may harbor elements of moral ambiguity or evil within his (or their) nature and condition. Notice the absence of any formal description of God in these verses. The believer obtains a sense of God's character through the record of his proclamations and actions. Nowhere in the origins verses of Genesis does one encounter the claim that God embodies a kind of absolute goodness, perfection, or sinlessness that one finds, for example, in the New Testament. There is every indication here of a prelapsarian Garden riddled and riven by ambiguity, and evil. Does not the "crafty" serpent exist prior to the disobedience of Adam and Eve? Does not evil itself exist prior to the Fall of these mortals? (Although there is no early mention made here of Satan, the fallen angel, who appears later.) Does it make sense then to think of evil as a phenomenon apart from or independent of God's pre-human creation? Presumably, when the two of them acquire the knowledge of good and evil, becoming "like one of *us*," the consequences of shame (over their nakedness) and a newly discovered capacity to sin come from somewhere; they scarcely emerge *ex nihilo*. After all, only God is a creator of things. Inherent in the very meaning of the appropriation of the knowledge of good and evil is an assumption that the acquisition bore some sort of relationship or acquaintance with a common, pre-existing source. In other words, there is no indication in these passages of a jealously guarded secret knowledge of good and evil which is for "the gods" a qualitatively different possession or experience from the one newly acquired by Adam and Eve; instead what appears to distinguish the unfortunate snake-bitten couple from the gods is that they have not eaten from the tree of life (are mortal) and they are relatively powerless (God moves them around at will). Indeed, for all the references that are made to these first few chapters of Genesis (usually in illustration of the evangelical's conception of the nature of God and his creations), the actual text betrays a God (and gods) with features rather more vaguely reminiscent of Zeus and the Greek deities and other Levantian antecedents.[347]

Perhaps more importantly for our purposes, the chore of naming all the living creatures—upon which some evangelicals stake a monopolistic claim for the Biblical origins of scientific thought—was performed by Adam *before the Fall* (in the second creation story of Genesis 2:19-21, and *before the appearance of Eve*: which, if one is inclined to literal interpretations, could just as easily warrant the licensing of science to men alone). Here, as elsewhere, scripture offers no consistent pattern, no definitive precedent establishing the qualities of Adam and Eve that are to survive their brief rebellion (why a capacity for science and knowledge and not some other attribute?), particularly for those who would like to see this scientific spirit follow Adam and Eve into the post-lapsarian age. Precisely which attributes were actually lost in the Fall? The ambiguity inherent in the Genesis account poses a problem

---

[347] A comparison with Hesiod's *Theogony* (trans. and intro. by Norman O. Brown, Indianapolis: The Bobbs-Merrill Company, Inc., 1953) is instructive. Of the mediums and expressions of revelation, Norman O. Brown writes: "[Hesiod] tells us how the Muses once appeared to the shepherd Hesiod and told him to sing. This claim to divine inspiration is not a mere literary artifice. 'The word of the Muses' came to shepherd just as 'the word of Jehovah' came to the herdsmen of Tekoa. The poet is a prophet of religious truth, and Hesiod is conscious that the truth revealed to him conflicts with much that passed as truth in his own day: the Muses tell him that they 'know how to tell many falsehoods that seem real,' as well as to 'utter truth' when they wish to (lines 26-27)." (35)

requiring some interpretive gymnastics—from David McKenna, above, for example, who makes what must appear to many an artificial distinction, essentially arguing for a tree of life (immortality) replete with special properties (or that God's own source of being and lifespan is of a qualitatively different nature) which elevate God's knowledge of good and evil far beyond man's. Adam's mortality bars comprehension of the "ultimate truth about good and evil that God knew," a lesson "from the Genesis story" McKenna eventually incorporates into the conclusion that "the search for knowledge is not the same as the search for truth." In other words, McKenna demotes the appearance of "knowledge" in the (2:16-18) phrase to an error of usage and semantics; what God actually meant, he claims, is the tree of "the [nearly] *ultimate truth* about good and evil." This slight revision adheres more closely with his ulterior ideological motives, that of disarming any suggestion of an obscurantist bent in the nature of God (in his withholding of a kind of "knowledge" from man), and thereby sacralizing the role of the Christian college in the "search for knowledge."[348] God means only to discourage the blind pursuit of this "ultimate truth," of which only he is privy, not impede the Christian student and scholar from discovering the essential givens of truth and knowledge, from grasping as many of these facts as have been made available to the redeemed believer. Listen! McKenna can be heard exhorting the pensive, anti-intellectual, anti-scientific evangelical student, scripture supports what we're doing here: God has revealed to us the nature and source of truth and knowledge and how to go about acquiring them! And that, he insinuates, renders us superior in potential insight and knowledge to secular academies.

Again, the ambiguities inherent in the text render any such claim problematical. The Bible slumbers in a deep reservoir of other possibilities. One can just as easily cite passages that would appear to disparage any understanding of the world in these terms—the musings of Koheleth, author or compiler of Ecclesiastes, a book Northrop Frye referred to as "The center of the conception of wisdom in the Bible. . . ."[349], for example:

---

348 Indeed, since the recognition and full comprehension of original sin is perhaps the cardinal assumption of, and pivotal operational element in, Christian scholarship—as we have seen, constantly invoked in disparagement of secular academia—this Genesis notion of God shielding man from the "knowledge of good and evil" strikes too near a sensitive evangelical nerve to be allowed full unrevised reign. By association, it potentially casts a negative divine aspersion upon a vaguely similar kind of knowledge the Christian scholar must have if s/he is to perform sacred academic duties. McKenna accordingly labors to modify its apparent meaning.

349 *The Great Code: The Bible And Literature*, New York: Harcourt Brace Jovanovich, 1981, 123.

So I applied my mind to understand wisdom and knowledge, madness and folly, and I came to see that this too is chasing the wind. For in much wisdom is much vexation, and the more a man knows, the more he has to suffer. . . .

I applied my mind to acquire wisdom and to observe the business which goes on upon earth, when man never closes an eye in sleep day or night; and always I perceived that *God has so ordered it that man should not be able to discover what is happening here under the sun. However hard a man may try, he will not find out; the wise man may think he knows, but will be unable to find the truth of it* . . . .

One further warning, my son: the use of books is endless, and much study wearisome. (Ecclesiastes 1:17-18; 8:16-17; 12:12, *NEB.*) {emphasis added}

In a moment of candor before a chapel audience, David McKenna conceded that he "picks and chooses" the portions of the Bible he prefers (and as the reader has become all too aware, there is much to choose from). And so here, once again, we observe *current utility* determining the pattern of scriptural selection and historical evaluation:[350] scripture is employed to defend and enhance the claim of privileged access to a sacred fount dispensing the holy waters of truth and knowledge; hence modern rational exegesis disarms or deflects any insinuation of obscurantism in the Biblical being and character of God. Rest easy, fellow evangelical academicians, way back then God had already presciently bestowed a sacralizing imprimatur upon the contemporary evangelical college. He had anticipated our current agenda and epistemology.

This notion of a given, *a priori* world of truth and knowledge, of pre-formed ideas and objects, has scarcely confined itself to some of the more strident proponents of an evangelical Christian academic worldview. Indeed it gives the author no pleasure to acknowledge that one of the major figures in the emergence and development of sociology, Émile Durkheim, expounded virtually identical views of the nature of social phenomena in his central methodological work, *The Rules of Sociological Method* (1895), and later in a more anthropological treatise, *The Elementary Forms of The Religious Life*

---

[350] Stephen Jay Gould observes a similar kind of paralyzing present-mindedness, or the confusion of "current utility" with historical inevitability, at work among certain scientific schools of thought, dubbing this outlook " . . . the Panglossian vision. . . . Panglossian adaptationism makes history irrelevant . . . the same error that sinks human sociobiology—the equation of current utility with historical origin, or the idea that we know why a structure evolved once we understand how it works now. . . . [An appreciation of this error] invalidates, for example, the so-called anthropic principle now preached by some physicists and cosmologists who do not understand the lessons of history. The strong version of this principle holds, roughly, that since human life fits so intricately well into a universe run by nature's laws (current utility), these laws must have arisen with our later appearance in mind (historical origin)." ("Cardboard Darwinism," *The New York Review of Books*, 25 September 1986, 54.)

(1915).[351] In the course of the following I will draw upon examples of problems in Durkheim's epistemology and indicate their relevance for our understanding of this evangelical vision of truth and knowledge.

The Role of the Scholar and Scientist

Two or three primary misgivings are invariably triggered by this claim of having fashioned an approach to scholarship and teaching that is grounded in a conception of *given* objects, facts, and values, and the laws governing their composition and behavior, independent of, and indeed largely impervious to, human perception and thought.

In the first place, these assumptions *diminish the active heuristic role of the individual scholar or scientist*. For if the objects, facts, values, and meanings of life exist prior to human thought and interpretation in no way originates, recasts, or transforms their being and significance, then scientific investigation becomes reduced to the mere discovery of these *a priori* phenomena; analytical thought contracts into the mere description and elaboration of the features of primordial essences. Observation, experimentation, conjecture, theorization, verification, falsification, and the like would appear then extraneous to the actual creation or apprehension of truth and knowledge. As David McKenna once explained: "Education, even Christian education, is still *a quest for truth within the framework of having found the truth.* . . . total learning begins with revealed truth, it is extended by discovered truth and it is tested by applied truth."[352]

Paul Q. Hirst demonstrates the play of similar assumptions in the epistemology of Durkheim, surmising that if conceptualization is summarily reduced to the simple appreciation or apprehension of given facts, knowledge becomes

> . . . . displaced into the real . . . is made the order of the real itself. . . . Thus science can only be a cognition that reproduces the order of the real itself and the order of the real must be knowledge in itself. Science can only uncover or discover a knowledge that already exists as a given in the real. Knowledge is displaced into "things." The scientific subject becomes little more than an accurate sensory apparatus which receives the true "message" from reality.[353]

The evangelical version of science merely re-circulates presuppositions as explanations, the *given* underscoring and reinforcing the *given*, the former

---

[351] See Paul Q. Hirst's seminal work, *Durkheim, Bernhard and Epistemology* (London: Rout-ledge & Kegan Paul, 1979).

[352] "The Three Cultures," undated typescript. {Archives} {emphasis added}

[353] *Durkheim, Bernhard and Epistemology*, 100, 104.

forever, and redundantly, serving as the cause and consequence of the latter. Indeed, when one takes into consideration both a cultural ambience of intellectual and scientific obscurantism within which most evangelicals are reared *and* this conception of the origins, nature, and practice of science and scholarship, is it any wonder the average Christian scholar approaches original research and scholarship with such ambivalence, if not outright trepidation? Indeed what doth it profit a Christian scholar to raise theoretical temples to the sky if they ultimately rest upon the shifting sands of human ephemera? All told, these are powerful mutually-reinforcing and -retarding cultural and epistemological assumptions, depositing a subtle, nagging inertia in the deeper recesses of the imagination of even the most enthusiastic (often secular-trained) evangelical academician.

These assumptions permeate virtually every field of inquiry within evangelical academia, from economics to zoology, and spill over into everyday thought and *praxis*. Elemental, God-given facts and governing laws are commonly accepted as the matter-of-fact building blocks of the natural and social worlds.

In the bald expression of one chapel speaker: ". . . . the Bible says so because it's true. . . . [for example:] stealing is wrong," in violation of a commandment, because God built into the universe such principles as the "right of private property." Observe that in the beginning, God formulated a set of "inborn norms" that when broken unleash an "inborn prosecutor who punishes." Those who "go against God's laws"—as is so often the case in "secular" society—"go from analyst to analyst," blindly seeking the ephemeral, abortive cures of "man-centered" psychological therapies, ignorant of certain principles, among them that mental health has spiritual requirements which can be derived only from the given structure of human personality.[354]

The notion that truth and knowledge ought more appropriately be regarded, in the words of Paul Q. Hirst, as "intra-scientific products," largely human improvisations, and that "we know what . . . [they are] through the procedures of analysis and synthesis. . . ." and not through the blank reception of representations emitted from given natural and social objects and relationships, must appear an oddly foreign outlook and approach to the evangelical academician who seriously adheres to dogma. For it would instead appear that science discovers or creates knowledge in the form of images or models—scientific metaphors—that are employed in the understanding or illumination of the likely natures, properties, and structures of natural and social phenomena. The form, composition, and veracity of these under-

---

[354] Leslie Parrott {President of Nazarene Olivett College}, "Attitudes That Can Make or Break Your Life," Chapel, 4/11/78.

standings are continually evolving. Many evangelical academicians (though probably fewer Christian college physicists) will likely find disorienting the following description of the kind of phenomena that engage modern physicists:

> It is good to realize that when physicists talk about spaces they don't always mean spaces that are physically real. They are usually artificial spaces devised to simplify calculations. No physicist thinks that the curves he uses to graph functions on two-dimensional paper are "out there" in physical space, or that probability waves of quantum mechanics (they are waves in imaginary "phase spaces" of high dimensions) are out there, like water or sound waves. Probability waves exist only in the minds and discourse of physicists. [355]

The Hidden Bias of the Given

Recall the earlier accusation that secular universities are riddled with "hidden prejudices"; that contrary to the rhetoric of "value-free" scientific objectivity secular academia promotes a religious world-view as coherent and compelling as anything found in the evangelical Christian college.[356] So

---

[355] Martin Gardner, "Physics: The End of the Road?" *The New York Review of Books*, 13 June 1985, 33.

Actually, this is a bit too simple, for while the "waves" used to represent the probability distributions of elementary particles are indeed only imaginary (theoretical), *probability itself is something more*. As Jacob Bronowski writes of Karl Popper's discussion in Popper's *The Logic of Scientific Discovery*: "Probability on this view is *a concrete property of physical systems in which the events overall fall out in a consistent way*, but not in a unique way. In such systems, probability is an inferred or theoretical entity which we do not ourselves observe directly, much as an electron is—and it is real in the same sense. I share this view of probability as a physical property, and so I think do most physicists now; though I prefer to express it by saying that probability can only be ascribed to events which have a distribution, and must be read as a symbol for the distribution as a whole. On Popper's view and mine, then, probability is not a description of a state of mind, or a subjective expectation of how a future event will fall out: and in fact these personal experiences cannot be marshaled as distributions." ("Humanism and the Growth of Knowledge," in *A Sense Of The Future*, Cambridge, Massachusetts: The MIT Press, 1977, 85.) {emphasis added}

[356] There is an irony here in that the scholar, Michael Polanyi, in whose work evangelical academicians often find confirmation of parallels between religious and scientific experiences and belief systems [e.g.: "When Polanyi (1967) says 'we know more then we can tell' the Christian does not find this 'tacit dimension' completely surprising." (Kenneth E. Tuinstra {Westmont College—Biology}, "Incarnational Integration," a paper delivered at the Faith/Learning Institute, Wheaton College, August 13-24, 1973.)], discerned these very same assumptions underpinning Soviet science. In *Personal Knowledge* (University of Chicago Press, 1962, 235-239), for example, he recounts the development of a philosophy and history of science, or the official "neo-Marxian theory of science," under Stalin in the 1930s. This program produced an initial revision of the history of science, party scientists reaching consensus upon the principle that the gradual accumulation of scientific knowledge came in "response to practical needs." Any notion of a "pure science" independent of class interests or material

formulated, the sole difference between the two reduces to an openly acknowledged bias versus a concealed or camouflaged one.[357] Our second

exigencies earned advocates charges of "bourgeois" elitism and false cosciousness. The Soviet
Academy successfully "unmasked" science for what it actually was: "technology." And since
technologies were essential to a growing material welfare the cultivation of science became
linked with an advancing socialist prosperity and eventual utopia.

Not only was the history of science reformulated into more amenable mechanistic terms;
Soviet ideologues went even further, launching campaigns against some of the most brilliant
products of modern "bourgeois" theoretical science—"relativity, quantum mechanics, astronomy, psychology," among them—intellectual pogroms that reached a frenzied peak with the
direct attack upon the earlier genetic work and system of Gregor Mendel. With respect to the
latter, in August of 1948 the revised position went into effect when "Lysenko triumphantly
announced to the Academy of Science that his biological views had been approved by the
Central Committee of the Communist Party and members rose as one man to acclaim this
decision."

In essence, *Soviet science impugned as deceptive, class-bound ideology the notion that "bourgeois" science
had successfully fostered an impartial, universally applicable phenomeno-technique capable of generating theories
and evidence at once testable and reproducible.* Polanyi observes that "The claims of bourgeois science
to objectivity and universal validity are unmasked as false pretences on the grounds that *no
affirmation of science, history, or philosophy can be objective and that in reality they are always partisan.*"
{emphasis added} True objectivity, in the Soviet formulation, comes with the unabashed embrace of "partisanship," producing in the case of politics, for example, "a science that bases
every political action on a strictly objective assessment of the social conditions in which it has
to operate. . . ." As with modern "creation science," these competing bourgeois and Soviet
conceptions were viewed as mutually exclusive, their Soviet adherents assuming that an expansion of the latter automatically ensured a diminution of the former: ". . . . the doctrine
that all science is class science served simultaneously both to discredit bourgeois science and
to accredit socialist science." What of course steadied the hand of apparatchiks drafting promulgations of scientific truth was a congealed confidence in the "inherently righteous and therefore historically inevitable victory of a future Communist world government." Polanyi, reflecting upon the nature, design, and implementation of the Soviet vision of scientific thought
and knowledge, is led to conclude that "The strict application of this theory of knowledge
would suppress natural science. . . ." as we now know and practice it.

[357] Consider one example of how this allegedly works in a subfield of sociology, the "sociology of religion." Professor David Claerbaut of North Park College in a "Special Report" to
Universitas reviews the treatment of religion in twelve sociology textbooks. He finds particularly
disturbing the practice of lumping all the world's religions together under a single rubric,
"religion." This notion that all religions are basically alike conceals a *hidden value judgment,* he
avers, "one that masquerades under the guise of objectivity but is actually agnostic in nature.
The more one studies sociology, the more evident this agnosticism becomes. . . . There exists
a sociological frame of reference or view of reality which is more influential than any religion
as a perspective on life, for even spiritual matters must yield to this world view. We shall call
this view *sociologism.*" Perhaps the most objectionable feature of sociologism is its cultural relativism, having the effrontery to suggest that "Religion is a culturally relative matter with one
culture's notions being as good as another." In fact, Christianity is "supracultural." In these
textbooks, "That one could live his life with Christ at the center is scarcely considered. . . .
[and although the possibility of God is not ruled out] The idea of an almighty God Who both
rules all of society and concerns himself with each individual member seems to be considered
completely untenable. . . . sociologism . . . does not seem to regard the option of the existence
of a living, creating God, Who is the source of all truth, as a viable one." Once more, if the
transcendent truths of Christianity were truly understood and absorbed it would become

misgiving concerns an irony—better yet, an inherent deception or theoretical subterfuge—implicit within this claim.

Are the two kinds of biases (even assuming for the moment the accuracy of the evangelical characterization) comparable? The evangelical academician complains of a "secular" academic bias that is at heart anti-Christian, one disavowing the kind of transcendent spiritual evidence and experience so integral to his perception and conception of the world at large. The bias and all its attendant quasi-scientific paraphernalia are dismissed as "man-centered," thoroughly prejudiced human improvisations. Now although the Christian academician confesses to an even greater urgency in the promotion of his Christian beliefs—his version of bias—among students (which the secular academician performs in his own right—albeit in a deceitful manner), *notice the altogether different foundations of these respective biases*. The Christian academician's bias is not grounded in human ephemera, but derives rather from a trans-human source. Indeed, if he is just a blank receptor of the divine transmission of genuine *a priori* givens, having no say in their formulation, then he essentially grants himself immunity from the indictment of human-centered prejudice he has levied upon his secular counterpart. As such, he effectively lifts the burden of ideological responsibility from his own shoulders. He is not *really* biased because his recipe for the real contains no artificial human ingredients; his vision embodies a prejudice of an altogether higher order. In the words of C. S. Lewis:

> [The] Christian literary man, [by stark contrast to his secular counterpart, exults] . . . in being as little as possible ourselves [sic], in acquiring a fragrance that
>
> is not our [sic] own. . . . Ah, there is a preeminent difference.[358]

As an *empty vessel* drained of profane pollution, the evangelical academician stands ready to be filled with the anointing fluid of truth and knowledge.[359] With no flawed human interpretations clouding her direct perception of the real, she embraces a bias of an altogether higher order.

---

possible for social science to illuminate seemingly intractable social problems, since "For the Christian, these immediate causes [of, for example, the social problems of poverty and ghetto riots] can often be linked to ultimate causes and cures concerning the nature of man and his need for redemption." ("How Sociology Texts Treat Religion," *Universitas*, April 1974.)

358 Cited by David McKenna in "Where Will You Stand?" Ivy-Cutting Address, 5/23/80. {Archives} {emphasis added}

359 The "empty vessel" metaphor has throughout Christian history served as political leverage in the adjudication and legitimation of spiritual claims. For example, Sabina Flanagan argues that Saint Hildegard of Bingen overcame bias against her sex and won papal endorsement of her prophetic visions in part with the assertion that she was but an innocent transmitting medium of epiphanies, eschewing any personal responsibility for their ultimate

Divine Intervention

Another misgiving concerns this matter of the role of "God's will" in the affairs of human beings and societies, or the age-old Calvinistic-tinged "determinism" question. A common view among evangelicals is that while not every minute detail of personal and social life unfolds according to a divine script, virtually all the major events in a person's life and in the life of a society are so directed; God is "in control," guiding both the life of the believer and his community.

Perhaps no other theological issue arouses as much consternation within the academic community. What are the implications for the individual disciplines, say, of sociology, political science, history—or even, for that matter, biology and physics?[360] How does the average Christian scholar reconcile his own particular understanding of determinism with a traditional arts and sciences approach to higher learning? Can science and scholarship genuinely prosper under the guidance of these assumptions?

Consider, for example, the attempt of Seattle Pacific history professor, William Woodward, to come to terms with these issues in his 1978 Weter Faculty Award Lecture upon a Christian vision of history.[361] Speaking before his colleagues, Woodward acknowledged that "Most of us will readily allow our faith commitments to shape the methodology of our scholarship." Secular historians embrace similar kinds of assumptions, what might be called "ultimate concerns . . . such as [among others] . . . the grounds for human values and morals judgments, the possibility of objectivity, and the role of Providence or chance in human events," fundamental outlooks that, for the most part, remain unspoken and concealed, but which determine the direction and content of their work. Borrowing a phrase from another evangelical academician, Woodward labels these personal "control beliefs" and claims they derive largely from the "naturalistic, positivistic, and evolutionary orientation of much of modern thought." Upon the shoulders of the Christian historian falls the burden of "expos[ing] and critici[zing] the control beliefs underlying contemporary historical analysis," and further, the even heavier burden no less, of producing in its stead a positive, distinctly

---

substance or origin, a humility serving to dampen the potential threat she may have posed to her male church superiors. (*Hildegard of Bingen, 1098-1179: A Visionary Life*, London: Routledge & Kegan Paul, 1989.)

[360] "The significance of Christian higher education lies in *scholarly handling of data from the natural and special revelations.*" (Ted Ward, "Faith, Love, Hope—The Remaining Mission of Christian Higher Education," *Faculty Dialogue*, no. 1 [Fall 1984], 5.)

[361] "Becoming: A Historian's Prospectus for Integrated Learning."{Archives} In 1988, Woodward served as vice-president of the Pacific Northwest Historians Guild.

Christian view of the ebb and flow of history. "How then can history serve faith?" he asks.

History represents the "matrix both for God's sovereign acts *and* for God's self-disclosure." It comprises a record of divine intervention in human affairs and the illuminist epiphanies of individuals and groups. Woodward's Christian beliefs "instruct" him that "God is in control of events," that history is "teleological, a meaningful whole," and that faith offers the medium through which is revealed "the ultimate purpose underlying the course of human events."[362]

The Christian historian employs the techniques of historical investigation in an altogether novel manner, allowing his faith to guide the selection of topics, the collection and handling of evidence, and the eventual form and content of historical interpretations. Indeed, faith gives Woodward an "edge" over the conventional secular historian. From it flows an enhanced ability to empathize "with personalities in the past, since he knows the *essential* character of man: fallen yet redeemable." This deep understanding (of original sin) emboldens the Christian scholar and historian: with great assurance he can then dismiss distorted evolutionary theories of the "perfectability" of man, assumptions inspiring futile attempts to ameliorate "complex social and political problems."

How the Christian historian actually detects the intervention of God in the affairs of men is a matter of some concern. Woodward employs a familiar *monopolistic* solution:

> . . . . where God's character and God's purpose are evident in the unfolding affairs of mankind, there God is directly and visibly exercising his Providential care.

In other words, if it matches our expectation of how God's manifestations ought to look, well then it is God's handiwork. As for God's character and its identification and expression in particular events and situations, he assures his brethren once again in breezy tautological fashion that

---

[362] Woodward's elder colleague in the history department, professor Roy Swanstrom, concurs: ". . . . the Christian believes that God is sovereign over his eternal purposes beyond the limits of time, as well as over specific, concrete events, both great and small, in recorded history." (*History in the Making: An Introduction to the Study of the Past*, Downers Grove, Illinois: Intervarsity, 1978, 13, 18.)

Woodward acknowledges the following authors for his view of Christian history: John McIntyre, *The Christian Doctrine of History* (Grand Rapids, Michigan: Eerdmans, 1957); Arthur F. Holmes, *Faith Seeks Understanding* (Eerdmans, 1971); George Marsden ed., *A Christian View of History?* (Eerdmans, 1975); Nicholas Wolterstorff, *Reason Within the Bounds of Religion* (Eerdmans, 1976).

In short, where justice and mercy prevail, God's hand is at work; by implication, where justice and mercy are violated, God will intervene to judge, eventually if not immediately.

Hence how easy and almost matter-of-fact becomes then the researching and writing of history. Prior to the observation, collection, and collation of historical evidence and experience, we are given a divine Mover who by definition can produce only just and merciful interventions, corroboration hanging on a tenuous thread or string of assumed historical events and developments which simply document the assorted whims and wishes of God. Everything of value in history (in this instance, the plethora of possible events and meanings evinced by the simple terms "mercy" and "justice") emerges from design; whereas everything damaged or evil bears independent—largely satanical or secular—origins.

Woodward concludes:

This view allows for God to harden the heart of Pharoh, to direct the annihilation of the Canaanites, to raise up Cyrus, and yes, to raise up a Hitler and secure his downfall, *without portraying him as arbitrary or history as deterministic.*

Say what? In this have-your-cake-and-eat-it-too world of Christian history, Woodward produces for us a Humpty Dumpty-like God in whose name words and meanings are fashioned to fit any contingency or occasion, who embodies diametrically-opposed properties within his own being without apparent internal contradiction: a God who is "in control" yet permissive of human serendipity and iniquity; a God who freely and independently determines all events in history (and is therefore perhaps the only genuine moral actor) yet whose divine intentions and methods are removed from moral scrutiny. Although the waters of human history flow continuously from his hand, the moral tributaries would appear to have a mind of their own, trickling down independently from their ultimate divine source. This is David McKenna's omniscient and omnipotent God, in sole possession of a superior brand of knowledge of good *and* evil, and yet neither acquainted with, nor soiled by, the origin, expression, and persistence of the *latter* both in the original creation and all subsequent history.

It is in this sense that the evangelical view of history employs a lower standard of evaluation for God than those routinely applied to his fallen creatures. By means of a pervasive moral *monopolization* the evangelical shields his creator and the author of all history from the consequences of his creation and his ongoing manipulation of the events of history. *Thus is preserved the aura of an impeccable, unified moral deity so integral to the evangelical mood of personal and community separation and difference, of conspicuous invidious distinction.* For to cast aspersion upon the wholeness and goodness of God is to cast an equally insidious aspersion upon the parallel claim of a community-wide "wholeness" of being and purpose.[363] Indeed, the (metaphysical and epistemological) case for evangelical moral *apartheid* (as well as for other quite different conventional Christian *theodicies*) is founded upon the perfectly unblemished nature and condition of a sovereign God.

Which still leaves this nettlesome problem of the actual detection of God's intervention in history. For even Woodward acknowledges that all these monopolistic skirtings round the difficult issue of verification, especially those which define such interventions as immediately self-apparent and categorically all of a piece, simply beg more questions than he feels equipped to answer. Indeed, the larger paragraph from which earlier quotations were lifted provides ample evidence of indecision and ambivalence, the author caught in an ideological tug-of-war, when the focus shifts from vague general assumptions to the consideration of concrete examples.

> Faith also instructs the Christian historian that God is in control of events, sovereignty acting as sustainer and judge of the universe. *The specific application of this concept of Providence becomes a very delicate matter, however.* To what extent can I presume to perceive God's active and direct intervention to alter the course of history? It becomes a meaningless truism to say that God works in every event, but to deny that Providence exists is to repudiate the efficacy of prayer. *Yet do I as a scholar dare to decide where God's actions specifically shape human events? I confess I have not resolved this dilemma.* But at this point in my thinking I want at least to affirm this: where God's character and God's purpose are evident in the unfolding affairs of mankind, there God is *directly and visibly* exercising his Providential care. In short, where justice and mercy prevail, God's hand is at work; by implication, where justice and mercy are violated, God will intervene to judge, eventually if not immediately. . . . Admittedly it is a profoundly difficult problem, one which has been answered in vastly different ways by different Christian historians. {emphases added}

Woodward's conundrum is resolved by an all too easy lapse into evangelical monopolization, into tautology, and also into what someone once referred to as the *infinite regress of qualifications*. Simple definition replaces the observation, collection, and analysis of historical evidence.[364] All things good

---

[363] "Evil is both allowed for good purpose and is made by God's mighty acts to serve those ends. In the final analysis, history and the entire world-process, for all the evils that arise, are not dysteleological but teleological." (Holmes, *Contours* . . . , 89.)

[364] Consider one rare internal objection to aspects of this notion of an elevated Christian perception of history: "Integration of faith and history is impossible. No person has a sufficient grasp of reality to make valid statements about it. The process of history is so complex, the causes and results so vast, the cross currents so swift and deceptive that only a man with great temerity would venture to say 'thus saith the Lord'. . . . One cannot know at what point God

spring from God; all things evil originate elsewhere, yet remain subject to ulterior divine manipulation and transmogrification.[365]

_____

will again intervene in human affairs to alter the course of history. . . . Who has the courage to suggest that elsewhere in the past (apart from revelation) God intervenied [*sic*] in human affairs? Or that he will do so again at some point in the future. Those who have set a date for the Lord's return should be a warning to us [not to make "predictions"] as should the Lord's own words that no man knows the time or the hour of His return . . . .

[And yet having issued these sensible cautions, the author nonetheless too easily falls back onto reigning epistemological assumptions of the passive, "given" nature of Christian truth and knowledge:] The process of integration must be done by the student himself. . . . [The teacher] can only provide a shadow of a shadow of reality in the mind of the student. *The Holy Spirit has to make the connections between facts, viewpoints, interpretations, and the truth, the reality of events in the life of each student.* . . . Validity will include at least the idea that history has a beginning and an ending; that it is purposeful; that God may have allowed the Evil One to intervene in His creation but that God is still in control. At certain time-segments God has intervened miraculously and will do so again." (Professor Frank Hieronymous [no kidding] {Westmont College}, "Paradoxes in Faith and History," a paper delivered at the Faith/Learning Institute, Wheaton College, August 13-24, 1973.) {emphasis added}

[365] The monopolization of virtue and dis-appropriation or redistribution of vice is a common ploy of evangelical apologists intent upon sanitizing or purging odious features from the evangelical record. See Michael Gerson's particularly amnesiac effort in *The Atlantic* (of all places), "The Last Temptation," April 2018.

—It should take only a quick stroll through Carolyn Renee Dupont's *Mississippi Praying: Southern White Evangelicals and the Civil Rights Movement, 1945-1975*, to dissuade anyone of the notion that the average white southern Christian layman/woman were mere passive bystanders to Jim Crow and white supremacy.

—From an evangelical publisher: "It is important not to forget the enormity of this evil or the extent to which evangelicals condoned it. But it is also important not to forget that evangelicals played a greater role than any other group in taking the gospel to the slaves and treating them as their spiritual equals." (Douglas A. Sweeney, *The American Evangelical Story: A History of the Movement*, Grand Rapids: Baker Publishing, 2005, 108.)

—Re: the Green family Museum of the Bible in Washington D. C: "Steve Green is convinced that the Bible is the source of unmitigated good—and that any bad that has been done with it is a result of bad people with bad interpretations . . . . [e.g., Pagan Rome and Christians and American slavery:] Victory for the abolitionist movement is construed as a victory for the Bible: 'Ultimately,' reads the signage, 'it can be argued that the Bible and its followers were among the most important and instrumental influences in the abolishment of slavery in both Europe and the Americas.' " (Candida R. Moss. . . , *Bible Nation*. . . , 129-32, 161.)

—Such *infinite regresses of qualifications* will no doubt be employed when evangelical Christians look back upon the Trump administration years and try to explain away discomfiting data: "Percentage of white evangelical Christians who think the United States has a responsibility to accept refugees: 25./Of religiously *unaffiliated* Americans: 65." ("Harper's Index," *Harper's Magazine*, June 2018, 9.) {emphasis added}

—One prominent Christian ought to know better than to continually commit the sin of monopolization regress:

". . . . my thesis is always the same, and it is very simply stated, though it has two parts: first, contemporary America is full of fear. [*But why, pray tell?*] And second, *fear is not a Christian habit of mind*. As children we learn to say, 'Yea, though we walk through the valley of the shadow of death, I will fear no evil, for Thou art with me.' We learn that, after his resurrection, Jesus told his disciples, 'Lo. I am with you always, to the close of the age.' Christ is a gracious, abiding presence in all reality, and in him history will finally be resolved." Hence, fear is

What sort of bearing might these assumptions have upon our modern theory and practice of the arts and sciences? More specifically, what implications might follow for even a mildly rigorous conception of verification in scholarship? The inescapable reality is that once any form of preter-natural causation or influence in any field of inquiry is seriously entertained then as a matter of course *all the various claims or forms of such illumination or intervention are rendered equally plausible.* We simply do not have—even within the terms and contexts of the major world religions themselves—any common, demonstrable, reproducible method or procedure of detecting, demonstrating, and assessing the existence and impact of other-dimensional influences upon natural and social life. To put it mildly, we possess no general yardstick or standard of measurement by which the competing claims may be set off— the one against the other, the more substantial and veracious winnowed from the less substantial and veracious. For what is the actual substance of an evangelical Christian historian's claim to have discovered the workings of God in the events of history other than the assertion of a uniquely personal (or group) spiritual experience or impression? Upon what grounds, for example, do we evaluate the claim of a Shia or Sunni Islamic scholar to have discovered an equally powerful logic operating in history? Even within the narrower theological confines of the world's established religions, how do we compare Joseph Smith's divine illumination and reception of the golden tablets of the *Book of Morman* with the epiphany of Paul on the road to Damascus? The resurrection story of Jesus with the one of Apollonius? The prophet Muhammed's spiritual reception and recording of the revelation of the *Quran* with the Reverand Sun Myung Moon's instructions from God? The six years of spiritual discipline underlying the supreme enlightenment of Siddhartha Gautama with the illumination of the way of the universe and the path of all natural events set down by the legendary Lao-Tze in *Tao Te Ching*? And let us not pass too summarily over Oral Robert's vision of an eighty foot tall Jesus rising out of the desert near Palm Springs (again, *of all places*). All told, these represent irrefutable claims of once-in-a-lifetime, never-to-be-repeated, other-worldly spiritual illumination or event.

If these general evangelical assumptions held sway, how could one justify the exclusion of any heartfelt—no matter how vagrant or exotic—spiritual understanding—Jewish, Buddhist, Islamic, Rashnesh, Rastafarian, Moonish, Taoist, etc., etc.—from the discussion of almost any natural, social, political, psychological phenomena or subject matter in a university curriculum? These respective legendary accounts of religious figures and occasions (and whatever metaphysical, epistemological, and social imperatives go with

---

instead a *pagan* cast of mind? A purely *secular* cast of mind? (Marilyyne Robinson, "Fear," *The New York Review of Books*, 9/24/15.)

them) are *unfalsifiable*, unverifiable, and irreconcilable, and for these reasons cannot (and ought not) serve as the guiding axioms or first principles of any institution of higher learning (although certainly made the subject of study in the various disciplines as appropriate) nor direct the scholarship or science of any truly serious academician. These *almost too obvious*, largely *reductio ad absurdum*, objections appear to have occurred to very few evangelical academicians, or at least are rarely discussed in these terms.

Science as Belief

The idea of science as just another kind of belief system has gained considerable currency among many evangelical academicians. Although it is undeniable that residing deep within the various ways of human feeling and believing are common denominator emotions and experiences fundamental to any apprehension of the world around us—characterizing both religious and scientific thought and behavior—the evangelical claim extends far beyond these simple parallels. Here we usually find two—often confused—variations upon a central defensive theme. There is the Christianity and science are similar forms of subjective belief apology; and there is the Christianity and science are scientific birds of a feather apology, the latter approach largely confined to the extremist "Creation Science" movement (and will be mentioned only in passing),[366] although on occasion they have been known to borrow elements from one another.

David McKenna provides a version of the first in his account of the religiosity inherent within experimental science:

> The scientist demonstrates the self-transcendent mind when he prepares an experiment, controls the variables, and then withdraws from the experiment to watch it work. He is literally in ecstasy—standing beyond to appraise what he sees. Revelation and miracles do the same for the self-transcendent mind. Through faith, we stand aside to judge life from an eternal perspective. Once we have seen, we can never be the same. Like the scientist, we are obligated to reappraise our

---

[366] See Laurie R. Godfrey, 1) "The Flood of Evolutionism," *Natural History* 90, no. 6, 1981 and 2) ed., *Scientists Confront Creationism* (New York: Norton, 1984); Nile Eldredge, *The Monkey Business: A Scientist Looks at Creationism* (New York: Washington Square Press, 1982); Philip Kitcher, *Abusing Science: The Case Against Creationism* (Cambridge, Massachusetts: The MIT Press, 1982).
—Some idea of the strength of creation science among evangelical academicians can be gleaned from Albert J. Smith's survey of the science faculty members attending the Christian College Consortium's 1972 Faith/Learning Institute. He reported that a majority of respondents would just as soon ignore the creation/evolution controversy and surely rejected the rigid scientific creationism position. It should be noted, however, that the institutions in the Christian College Consortium are among the most liberal Christian colleges in the nation. ("Creationism and Evolutionism as Viewed in Consortium Colleges," *Universitas*, March 1974.)

position and reorder our priorities on the basis of our new knowledge. Obviously, then, through the self-transcendent mind, *God is proven,* Christ is known, and man is redeemed.[367] {emphasis added}

Mathematics professor David Neuhouser:

> . . . . the process of understanding and coming to have faith in divine revelation is very much similar to the process of understanding and coming to have faith in a scientific model. I realize that revelation must be a gift to us from God but our evaluation of it and acceptance of it may be the result of a reasoning process very much like the scientific method. And, we should remember that scientific models are obtained in various ways, perhaps even sometimes by revelation, but in any case, must be checked by the procedures in the scientific method. . . .
> . . . the behavior of the scientist will depend, at least in part, on which model he believes in and the degree of that belief.[368]

For lack (and ignorance) of a more elegant Latin phrase, we might designate this notion that lying at the very heart of any scientific observation or judgment is a simple profession of belief in what the scientist is experiencing or measuring that is essentially indistinguishable from any other common form of belief, religious among them, *the fallacy of reduction to indistinguishable fundamental elements,* or *reductio ad absurdum.* David McKenna once even extended this leveling principle to include almost everyone in the Christian community: "Each of us is a natural scientist. We have a drive to know, a need for logical proof, and evidence of results which we can test with our senses."[369]

---

[367] "The Christian Mind: Freedom."

[368] David L. Neuhouser {Taylor University}, "Divine Revelation and the Scientific Method," a paper delivered at the Faith/Learning Institute, Wheaton College, August 13-24, 1973. Also:
— "This involves the basic philosophical questions of how one comes to know something; and this involves belief; and this in turn involves faith. Strange as it seems, *mathematics involves a kind of faith.* It is imperative that a Christian mathematics teacher understands and communicates to his students the power and limitations of this kind of faith—the difference between faith in absolute truth in a mathematical context and faith in ultimate truth as it may affect one's whole life." (Steven R. Lay {Aurora College—Mathematics}, "Relating Mathematics and the Christian Faith," a paper delivered at the Faith/Learning Institute, Wheaton College, August 13-24, 1973.) {emphasis added}

[369] "The Christian Mind: Freedom." Also:
—"With the realization that the scientist is essentially analyzing data in the same manner as all people process data, even though it is in some instances with a more formal methodology, it becomes very hard to distinguish science from other areas of human knowledge." (Samuel L. Dunn {S.P.C.—Mathematics}, "Toward a Christian Theory of Probabilism," a paper delivered at the Faith/Learning Institute, North Park College, Chicago, August 14-25, 1972.)

I am reminded of a conversation several years ago with an undergraduate student who had come fresh from an introductory lecture upon Einstein's theory of relativity. Somehow or other she had received the impression from her astronomy professor that radio and light waves are virtually indistinguishable, indeed that radio signals might better be conceived of as just another form of light. As with our evangelical academicians above, she was guilty of a reductionism of sorts, for although the two phenomena may indeed be reduced to the elementary particles—electrons, photons, etc.—of electromagnetic energy, there still remain fundamental differences between them, such as the different vibration rates of their constituent atoms and the color spectrum produced by the greater oscillations of the particles of light. For as is the case with many of the properties of natural and social phenomena, somewhere along any continuum of electromagnetic energy, changes in the quantity or frequency of the vibration of atoms produce changes in the quality of those vibrations, providing us with a beacon of light instead of FM symphony broadcasts, Beethoven instead of annoying howling cats.[370] To maintain that radio signals are just another form of light is to ultimately reduce all transmissions of electromagnetic energy to subtle, commensurable variations upon light, and as soon as all such energy becomes a version or form of light, then nothing is light, since the notion of light as a distinguishable phenomenon has been rendered meaningless.[371]

The evangelical equation of science and faith suffers from a similar reductionism. (To argue that science is just another kind of faith is essentially to argue that science as a distinct way of knowing does not exist. For if everyone is a scientist, as McKenna suggests, then no one really is a scientist; we are all just believers of sorts.) Marked, irreducible differences remain: not only does the religious believer produce or evoke within himself a greater *quantity* of belief than the average non-evangelical scholar (this is, after all, what the evangelical means by a "leap of faith," since he is dependent for corroboration and sustenance of his faith upon phenomena largely un-

---

[370] Those familiar with Marx (Hegel also) will of course recognize the analogous proposition that in particular social and economic developmental continuums quantitative changes bring about qualitative changes. (*Das Kapital*, Vol.1, 4.)

[371] This student may, however, have been thinking of the phenomenon known as *sonoluminescence*, wherein sound waves passing through water "generate an eerie blue glow in the liquid." Explanations vary from the simple (heat "generated by gas in a tiny bubble that is alternately expanded and then crushed by passing sound waves") to the complex ("virtual photons popping out of the quantum vacuum"). (Matt Crenson {Dallas Morning News}, "Weird Phenomenon seems to make light of laws of physics," *The Seattle Times*, 12 May 1996, A21.)

measurable and unseen),[372] but does indeed in the very process of such exertions of faith produce genuine *qualitative differences* as well. The resulting differences are perhaps most poignantly illustrated by the evangelical academician's own *exotic* expressions of his understanding of the principles and practice of science.[373]

Predictions

Consider, for example, this matter of "prediction" in science and scholarship. For many evangelical academicians the term evinces a host of prophetic connotations, as though anyone who formulates a prediction is engaged in an oracle-like forecasting of impending events or processes—that is, hankering after, assuming, or projecting God-like premonitions, omniscience, and, ultimate, "control."

As one Seattle Pacific senior explained to fellow chapel students, the natural and social sciences harbor ulterior motives, their practitioners coveting absolute control over their human and material objects of investigation:

> This is because, actually, the goal of science on the surface is to predict; the underlying goal of science is to control. What scares the scientist is that he can't predict human beings much less control them.[374]

David McKenna, on another occasion, sharing a personal family conversation with chapel students, concurred:

> When my son, Doug, and I were talking about his graduate study in psychology, he said, "Our professors remind us again and again that the purpose of psychology

---

[372] ". . . . faith which depends on scientific evidence is no faith at all." (David McKenna, Chapel Address, 4/16/80.) {An ironic refutation of his own argument that scientific and religious beliefs are virtually indistinguishable.}

[373] "To these two principles, naturalism and anthropocentrism, Kurtz adds two others on which some but not all humanists agree. One of these we shall call *scientism*, the view that *scientific knowledge can be applied to the solution of all our problems, as well as to the testing of all human beliefs and moral judgements*. . . . a suppressed premise is at work, that everything in existence exhibits the same kind of relationships and processes and so can be subsumed under the same model. And this is the thesis of monism, in this case of philosophical naturalism. Such a scientific world view is therefore more 'scientism' than science; it is in reality a naturalistic philosophy. . . . The tension is between theism and imperialistic, scientific reductionism. *It is 'scientism,' not science, that confuses science with metaphysics and universalizes a theory of limited scope.*" (Holmes, *Contours* . . . , 18, 41, 79.) {emphases added}

[374] S.S., a student "reader" of a report at a science colloquium, "Religion, Science, and the Future of Man," Chapel, 10/19/67.

is to predict and control human behavior. . . ." [More generally] Science analyzes the pieces of life and matter in order to predict and control.[375]

Yet predictions as they are actually formulated and employed in the natural and social sciences can—and often do—mean nothing more than the simple specification of the kinds of empirical evidence that should be brought to bear upon a particular research problem or claim—in the testing of a theoretical structure, proposition, or historical reconstruction.

This is precisely the sort of elementary understanding that one finds so conspicuously absent from the "work" of perhaps the most egregious practitioners and apologists of these Baconian conceptions of science,[376] the so-called "creation scientists" (with whom, to be fair, many Christian college academicians are loath to be associated). For instance, in his discussion of Gary Parker's (*Creation: The Facts of Life*) rejection of the Darwinian notion of "a single, nested pattern of similarity interconnecting all life" in favor of "a mosaic pattern . . . suggesting creation according to a common plan," Niles Eldredge recounts searching in vain for any specification of the concrete features or elements, or any pattern to the collection of physical evidence, that might support and illuminate the structure and substance of this larger "plan." Coming up empty-handed, he concludes that

> Parker's "mosaic pattern" allows absolutely no predictions about the distribution of similarities in the organic realm. . . . We need look no further into creationist notions of biology for signs of true science: *if you cannot make predictions about what you might expect to find when you look at an organism, you cannot be doing science with that organism.*

---

[375] "The Christian Mind: Freedom."

[376] Baconian/Scottish Common-Sense Realism was, in a nutshell, an outlook grounded in the notion that the "facts" of any science should be obvious to the primary senses. (See Marty, *Modern American Religion: Vol. 1.* . . , 35-36; Marsden, *Fundamentalism* . . . , 55-62, 111-112.) The Common Sense approach to science was/is, above all, anti-theoretical. For example, Duane Gish, a prominent Creationist author, was recorded before a friendly evangelical audience arguing that he "had yet to find a scientific fact which contradicts the Bible. . . . Now you and I are both aware of many scientific theories and opinions of scientific people that contradict the scriptures. When we separate that which is merely opinion or theory or ideas from that which is established fact, there are no contradictions." (Tape of a lecture to the Lutheran Evangelistic Conference in Minneapolis, January 23, 1978. Quoted by Robert J. Schadewald, "The Evolution of Bible Science," in Laurie R. Godfrey ed., *Scientists Confront Creationism*, New York: Norton, 1983, 294.)
—"What I find disturbing about *Habits* [*of the Heart*] is the similarity between it and the reams of theoretical discourse in my own field. Such protracted expressions of *theory*, regardless of the veracity claimed for the respective methodologies involved, are suspiciously self-serving exercises in the needs of academic guilds to authenticate their own existence." (Steve Cook, "Peter Pan In Hell," *Faculty Dialogue*, no. 8 [Spring-Summer 1987], 41.) {second emphasis added}

So, in the end, there is as little of substance in the scientific creationist treatment of the origin and diversification of life as there is in their treatment of cosmological time. They pose no testable hypotheses and make no predictions or observations worthy of the name. They devote the vast bulk of their ponderous efforts to attacking orthodox science in the mistaken belief that in discrediting science . . . they have established the truth of their own position.[377] {emphasis added}

This reluctance or inability to set the boundaries of acceptable empirical evidence or to establish common standards of measurement and verification within which scientific inquiry is to unfold (and the taking of a barely disguised relish in the denigration of "secular" scholars who do) appears a common failing of those who claim an appreciation and understanding of the intervention of God in the natural and social worlds. It encourages a reliance upon such questionable theoretical ploys as the *monopolization of positive qualities* and accounts for the annoying vagueness and generality of so many of these arguments and positions.

For most evangelical academicians, the Bible represents a theology and a religious history, not a collection of scientific monographs or a textbook. Indeed if there is any unwritten genteel code within the precincts of evangelical academia, it is surely that *specific tests are to be avoided at all cost.*[378] Under no circumstances actually specify the kinds of physical, personal, and social

---

[377] Eldredge, *The Monkey Business*, 138.

[378] In this respect, perhaps the most egregious error committed by anyone of the faith in the last two centuries was that of the fervent leader of a sect foolish enough to actually publicly establish a date for the second coming (which, as the reader may have gathered, came and went without undue commotion). William Miller and his "Millerites" unsuccessfully anticipated the Second Coming in 1843. (See Sidney E. Ahlstrom, *A Religious History of the American People, Vol. 1*, New York: Image Books, 1975, 579-80.) More recently, Nashville's World Bible Society published 3 million copies of Edgar Whisenant's, *On Borrowed Time*, a tract setting the date of September 11-13, 1988 for the impending "rapture" or return of Christ. (Carl Suplee, "Enter the Doom Boom," *The Seattle Times*, 7 January 1990.)

— "Perhaps more importantly for our purposes, diversity can show the varied appeal of a Christian view of things and will *prevent us putting all our eggs in one intellectually fragile basket.* To vary the metaphor, *theological options* provide *backup systems should undue problems develop with one particular formulation.* After all, the formulation is man made; only the Biblical revelation itself carries unqualified divine authority. . . .

We must therefore distinguish between claiming that the unifying perspective is true and claiming that every part of a specific elaboration is true. *A stronger truth-claim may be made for the perspective than for its detailed elaboration. . . .*

Nor is the origin of biological life a Biblical issue, except in that God is ultimately Creator of all, Creator of every kind of thing [an exquisite *non sequitur*]. 'Life' in the biological sense may well be a function of highly complex chemical processes, rather than something over and above them. Nor is the antiquity of the earth an issue. *None of these are Biblical concerns."* (Holmes, *Contours . . .* , 36, 49, 79.)

evidence which can be brought to bear upon particular points of the evangelical vision of the world.[379]

All of this produces a kind of lukewarm fuzzy-mindedness in those apologists still clinging to the belief that any sort of genuine scientific thinking and experimentation can survive these assumptions. Robert Sandin claims

> . . . . for example, that there is no contradiction between any fairly interpreted statement of the Bible and any established principle of social or natural science. Any contradictoriness that might appear is explainable, I believe, as due either to the misinterpretation of the Biblical statement or the unreliability of the scientific principle. Neither is there any contradictoriness within the system of Biblical truth itself. . . . The content of Christian faith is not inconsistent with any finding of rational inquiry in any area of human experience. . . . [380]

And in an earlier discussion of the Genesis account of creation, he suggests that

> . . . . honesty requires him [the Christian scientist] to recognize that *the specific method and duration of the creation are not disclosed*, either in the scriptural account or in the findings of science.[381] {emphasis added}

Yet Genesis 1 and 2 clearly specify both the "method and duration" of the creation:

> Thus heaven and earth were completed with all their mighty throng. On the sixth day God completed all the work he had been doing, and on the seventh day he ceased from all his work. . . . This is the story of the making of heaven and earth when they were created. [382]

The method was creation by divine fiat, out of nothing; the duration was six days. Of all the possible scientific predictions that could be culled from scripture this is one of the most unswervingly specific and clear (and surely one with which all evangelicals are familiar). No wonder Sandin squirms to extricate himself from under the concrete terms of the Genesis account. And no wonder also—because of its embarrassing specificity—that the exact Genesis account of the origin of the world (and the age of the world,

---

[379] Even the apostle Paul had a more advanced scientific outlook than many modern evangelicals: "Do not stifle inspiration, and do not despise prophetic utterances, but bring them all to the test and then keep what is good in them and avoid the bad of whatever kind. . . . Put everything to the test; keep hold of what is good and avoid every kind of evil." (I Thessalonians 5: 19-22, *NEB*.)

[380] Sandin, *The Search for Excellence* . . . , 224.

[381] Ibid., 94.

[382] Genesis 2:1-4, *NEB*. Need we add, puckishly, what about the universe?

traditionally estimated at around four—six thousand years old from an extrapolation of the generations of "begets" in later verses) is one of the first parcels of theological baggage the serious evangelical Christian academician will jettison from his own "introduction to science" class discussions of the geological age of the physical world, offering instead what has become known as "theistic evolution." Nearly all would have preferred an origins myth or theology bereft of incriminatingly concrete details.[383]

The Infinite Regress

At some point even the most polished methods of procrastination or evasion fail to brush aside an accumulating body of disconfirming evidence and, as just seen, a good many evangelicals fall back upon an invocation referred to earlier as the *infinite regress of qualifications*. Typically the approach produces a constant changing of the terms or claims of arguments in midstream to rationalize or explain away unexpected findings or even manages the inclusion of every possible outcome within the range of the original prediction, thereby anticipating potentially damaging future evidence. (We might even think of these techniques as comprising the internal theoretical mechanics or dynamics of the more general practice of monopolization.)

No better illustration of the infinite regress in operation exists than a chapel address of a later Seattle Pacific president, David Le Shana, on the subject of prayer. On this particular occasion, a final formal presentation to students upon the conclusion of his first year in office, Le Shana offered instruction upon the ways in which an educated Christian should think about the need for, and carry out the systematic assessment of the results of, prayer.

Prayer, for Dr. Le Shana, is no simple matter. The supplicant must exercise as much "spiritual discernment" in the understanding of answers to prayers as he does in their original formulation. For "God doesn't answer our prayers in exactly the form in which we present them to him." As a matter of fact, there are three or more probable, discernable "answers" to prayer. Among the possibilities: 1) First, that "God may change the situation about which we pray." The examples are numerous: Peter in prison; the roadside conversion of Paul to reduce the persecution of the church in Acts 4; and Paul in prison, as reported in his letters to the Philippians. "He can do things, even miracles . . . the body can be healed. . . . I've experienced it over and

---

[383] The medieval church, for example, would have been wise to exercise equal caution: "The theological authority of the Medieval Church was severe and specific to a degree which seems intolerable today. As late as 1700 a good Catholic educated in France would be taught and would believe that our first ancestor Adam died on the 20th of August of the world year 930." (Michael Polanyi, *Science, Faith, and Society*, University of Chicago Press, 1964, 75.)

over again." 2) Secondly, "God may show you and me how to change the situation while we pray." Usually these are "Do it yourself" commands from God. "Success" arrives after we meet prior conditions of some form, God here recognizing that many Christians substitute prayer for "duty," reluctant to impose the discipline of obedience upon themselves. 3) And finally, the "most difficult": "There are times when God may leave the situation as it is, but change the person." Again he mentions Paul in prison, concluding that God "changes us in the middle of the circumstance. . . .You see, *it doesn't really matter how God answers prayer. We know that he does, and that is enough.*"[384]

Now, the believer may find petty and annoying the critical question of how one actually knows that God has answered prayer, or can distinguish a particular answer from among a host of apparent answers, *when virtually every probable outcome of prayer* (and many Christians would count more than the three of Le Shana) *automatically confirms the intercession of God? Indeed, no matter what the substance, form, condition or occasion in and upon which the prayer is uttered, no matter what the chain of events preceding or following the prayer, God has in some manner or other answered prayer. The Le Shana scenario anticipates nearly every aim and outcome of prayer.*[385]

Is there any conceivable outcome here which might contradict the foregone conclusion that God answers prayer? Obviously these are matters involving purely individual "leaps of faith," of personal spiritual awareness and experience (though often performed together in groups), which may very well occur and hold true: God may indeed answer prayer in the manner Le Shana describes. And surely his method of thinking about prayer proves innocuous enough when confined to the apprehension or understanding of the results of prayer alone. Furthermore, the average reader may find incomprehensible the idea of anyone confusing the above outlook with anything like science or scholarship. Yet as we have all too often seen, the above assumptions and methods of handling this kind of spiritual "evidence" permeate the various disciplines in the Christian college, producing similar kinds of infinite regress.[386] They are readily apparent in the Woodward award lecture upon

---

[384] Chapel address, 4/22/83. {emphasis added}

[385] See also: Shane Sharp, "When Prayers Go Unanswered," *Journal for the Scientific Study of Religion*, 2013: 52, 1-16.
—Weber's take on a related matter: "Weber observes: 'Priests may find ways of interpreting failures in such a manner that the responsibility falls, not on the god, but on the behavior of the god's worshippers.' " (Christian Smith, *Religion. . . .* 2017, 174.)

[386] Among many possible examples:
— ". . . . large and frequent discrepancies discovered between actual experiences of Christians in prayer and the teaching of Scripture will not easily deflect the committed Christian from the normative guidelines of Scripture, any more than a scientist would seek to change his data base in the physical world to relieve conflict between his theory of physical behavior

divine intervention in history and in the various other examples of evangelical academic disciplines I have introduced throughout this study.

Again, although it is undeniable that a scientist or scholar harbors an elementary kind of belief in the procedures he employs and in the phenomena he has observed and documented, surely any evangelical college student ought to realize that what distinguishes scientific reasoning from the kind of apprehension above (in addition to many other qualities) are procedures of testing and verification that can be shared or duplicated by other scientists not immediately privy to a particular experiment or discovery, as well as general rules of engagement designating the kinds of evidence relevant for the ratification or falsification of arguments and predictions. Devout Muslims, for example, cannot really verify or understand—nor, it would seem, do they wish to—the particular spiritual experiences and claims of American evangelicals, and vice versa. Generally, each simply assumes the total error of the other. Indeed, when all is said and done, science and religion remain fundamentally different ways of comprehending the world around us.

All too often the notion of "testing" means nothing more to the evangelical student and academician than the orchestration of milquetoast sessions

---

and the hard evidence of facts.[??] Rather will deference be made to the over-riding integrity and authority of Scripture so that *corrections to human practice of prayer will bring experience into line with scriptural norms.* Without presuming that the nature of Christian higher education ranks anywhere near prayer in truth value, the same conclusion applies by analogy: regardless of any apparent failures in Christian higher education, the Scriptures never-the-less provide reliable guidelines so that corrections to educational practice to better achieve Scriptural norms will bring truth and liberation to the experience of learning, *which will never come by modification or rejection of the truth of the Scriptures."* (George L. Bate {Westmont College—Physics}, "Integral Christian Learning for Engaged Learning (Being a Tribute in Miniature to Christian Higher Education)," a paper delivered at the Faith/Learning Institute, North Park College, Chicago, August 14-25, 1972.) {emphases added}

— ".... as the science of psychology continues to develop there will not be a true contradiction [*sic*] with the special revelation of God. However, two problems may arise that appear to leave the Scriptures and psychology in conflict. *Firstly, there may be a misreading or misinterpretation of the data collected and analyzed, and secondly, there may be a misreading or a misinterpretation of the special revelation of God....*

Where the Scriptures speak clearly about the nature of man the Christian Psychologist *can unhesitatingly reject any data that is in direct conflict with Scriptures and accept for integration any data that is in direct agreement with Scripture....* Behaviorism in the form of programmed learning may work but for reasons entirely different than [*sic*] those suggested by the behaviorists. Christian psychologists *might do well to determine some alternate explanation* for the effectiveness of programmed learning.... The best position that a Christian can take at the present time is to accept that which is in unquestionable harmony with Scripture, reject that which is in direct opposition to the Scripture and to wait for further truth where no clear harmonization is presently possible." (Leland Forest Asa {Trinity Western College—Administration}, "Psychology and the Christian," a paper delivered at the Faith/Learning Institute, Wheaton College, August 13-24, 1973.) {emphases added}

and cauldron experiences—fabricated challenges or crises, usually, placing students under momentary duress—whose sole purpose is the strengthening of faith in anticipation of the trials and tribulations awaiting their eventual release out into the secular world. In the words of Robert Sandin, the ultimate aim of Christian education is to "enable a reflective person *to become settled in his ethical, aesthetic, and religious convictions.*"[387] Upon this point there is widespread agreement. Writing in *Faculty Dialogue*, another evangelical academician confirms and elaborates the principle:

> If these techniques [empiricism, value-free presentations] are carefully placed in a Christian context they can be employed with great effectiveness. At the simplest but most important level the Christian context is the fact of a Christian instructor and a Christian institution. *As role playing is used, and as values which might even be antithetical to Christianity are played out it should be clear that everything is "safe," because of who is doing it and where it is being done. It is just an intellectual game* to enhance understanding and provide insight into worldly value systems. If it is understood—and it should be made clear early in the course—that all truth is God's truth, *even empiricism* can be used in the Christian classroom. . . .
>
> This is not to say that this process is entirely danger free. As students are caused to peer intently into alien values, *there is always a concern that they might find something compelling or irresistible about them.* It is important that the instructor know his students and that, *although inquiry is kept open and honest, it is controlled and monitored, and that the antidote of God's answers be kept close at hand.* . . . Although this essay seeks to speak against the Christian college as an intellectual hothouse, *it is surely preferable to grapple with the enticements of competing value systems in the relative safety of the Christian institution.* . . .
>
> After consciousness raising, and being confronted by the dissonance of a particular national value when compared to the truth of God, the student must make his own decision. [388]

The Integrity of Science and Scholarship

We are by now familiar with the sundry aspersions cast upon the integrity of "secular" academicians and scientists by their evangelical counterparts. Some have been blunt and bilious in tone; others more charitable, their plaintiffs employing veiled allusions and tempered insinuations, the often barely visible or detectable signs of an underlying invidious assumption (*we are more honest than they*), animadversions largely fashioned for internal community consumption.

---

[387] Sandin, *The Search For Excellence* . . . , 177. {emphasis added}

[388] William Mullins, "The Character and Social Behavior of the Educated Christian: A Historian's Approach to Acculturated Christianity," *Faculty Dialogue*, no. 2 [Winter 1984-85], 73-74, 79. {emphases added}

One of the more polished of these, a position paper delivered at a 1979 Seattle Pacific faculty retreat discussion of the "Christian Scholar-Servant Model," proves instructive in this regard. Associate professor of English Janet Knedlik's (Ph.D. Harvard) " 'Restoring a Lost Breathing': The Tradition of Scholarship,"[389] takes for its point of departure a passage from Dorothy L. Sayers's, *Gaudy Night*, a mystery novel set in Oxford University of 1935.[390] The plot centers upon a "falsified footnote, a footnote which camouflages the existence of a document which would otherwise undermine the premise" of a scholarly work in question. The thematic point here concerns the nature of personal and academic integrity and the opportunity it provides for a series of invidious comparisons. In her account of the trials and tribulations of Lord Wimsey and Oxford academician Harriet Vain we encounter the recurring motif of an internally placid, genuine, transparent Oxford—the *inside* —set in opposition to the commotion, duplicity, cynicism, and opacity of Peter's worldly diplomatic duties—the encroaching *outside* world.

> Here's where the real things are done, Harriet—if only those bunglers out there will keep quiet and let it go on . . . how I loathe haste and violence and all that ghastly, slippery cleverness. Unsound, unscholarly, insincere—nothing but propaganda and special pleading and "what do we get out of this?" No time, no peace, no silence; nothing but conferences and newspapers and public speeches till one can't hear one's self think. . . . If only one could root one's self in here among the grass and stones and do something worth doing, even [if] it was only restoring a lost breathing for the love of the job and nothing else.

As we might have anticipated, a whole series of finely-calibrated binary qualities fall into predictable alignment. The *internal* properties of Oxford are on display in "values and habits of mind each of them betrays with every word and gesture." That is to say, Lord Peter and Harriet exude a wholeness, maintaining a perfect symmetry between character and action, between the *inside* of personality and the *outside* of behavior (anticipating Chapter 11 to come). They are guilty of none of the dissembling vices—affectation, mannerism, the harboring of ulterior motivations—that so vitiate the ways of the world around them. Accordingly, Peter has a "talent for keeping to the point and speaking the truth"; and Harriet's honesty demands that she face "the facts and state a conclusion. Bring a scholar's mind to the problem and have done with it." For her, an unselfish devotion and "service" to the transcendent ideals of one's scholarly craft becomes a "perfect freedom." Whereas

---

[389] *Seattle Pacific University Review*, Spring 1980. The paper was also, I believe, presented in chapel.

[390] The selection of this particular novel was by no means solely a matter of personal taste. Sayers, along with C.S. Lewis, is one of the patron saints of evangelical academia.

those *outside*, where the "self has so many guises," examine the "facts" with great difficulty, are unduly swayed by the arguments of "authorities," and ultimately succumb to the comforts of uncertainty and doubt, lost in an "indeterminate search" that yields no conclusions.[391]

As for the origins of the ideals of Oxford, of scholarship, these "principles of honor of mind have been enduring absolutes, like those of love and joy and honest labor—*divinely imbedded from the beginning within the natural order* for its sustenance, and never wholly extinguished by human folly." {emphasis added} Mindful of her partisan audience, she ponders aloud the difference between the Christian and secular scholar, laying the ground work for the much anticipated ideological payoff, the seemingly inevitable culminating *them and us* comparison:

> I would say, "yes," there is a *potential* difference—not in our goals and ideals, but perhaps in the consistency of our adherence to those goals and values and ideals. Just as there exists for every Christian the potential—often unrealized but potential nonetheless—for a higher nobility than that of the natural sphere, so too there exists for the Christian scholar the same potential for a higher, more consistent cleaving to the ideals of scholarship. In *the sphere of grace* we may hope to experience a scholarship less marred by envy and pride, somewhat less crippled by self-interest and subjectivity than is the common experience. . . . [representing as it does] another order a life. . . . The scholar's goals of *objectivity and balance of mind,* rescued from the push-and-pull of frenetic desires, are *finally achievable* [well, perhaps more than mere *potential*] through the Christian's privilege of walking in the spirit, for when we walk in the spirit we "do not fulfill the lusts of the flesh". . . . *All these prerogatives of union with Christ* are ours, through the yielding of our attention to the tutelage of scripture and *its supernatural transforming of our minds.* . . . {first emphasis in original; others added}

Extending the principle of invidious distinction, of academic transcendence, she anticipates that a "new way of being. . . . set[s] apart" an academic community in which "we may hope, I think, to bring to our disagreements a greater objectivity and generosity of soul than may be the common lot of university communities."

Aside from the familiar casting of aspersions upon secular academia, these are noble sentiments. But in what sense does the typical evangelical academician consistently achieve this kind of moral distinction? And are the

---

[391] I should point out that Knedlik does not actually employ the binary terms, inside/outside, in her presentation; they make their first and only appearance in the initial *Gaudy Night* quotation that begins this section. It is, of course, my interpretation that this attitude of division nonetheless permeates her argument and accordingly characterize it in this almost geographic manner.

moral issues and challenges the same for "secular" and "evangelical" academicians? Consider one example.

The occasion is a class on medieval European history, a very popular introductory course taught by one of Seattle Pacific's most highly regarded young male professors—let us call him professor Hume. In this particular lecture, professor Hume is discussing the process by which canonical (or approved) Biblical writings were passed down from the early Christian church and achieved a position of orthodoxy. He avers that conventional characterizations of the campaigns to eradicate "heresy" in the early church as spasmodic "fits of intolerance" fail to appreciate and address the problems besetting the young church. During the first few centuries myriad groups and movements designated themselves "Christian"; they adopted and promoted some extraordinarily "peculiar views of Christ." The Levant was literally flooded with "all sorts of writings out there." Hence the efforts of Paul and others in the early church are more appropriately viewed as attempts to winnow "untrue" or "incorrect" peripheral teachings from more authentic texts. One such rejected body of pedagogy derived from a group called the Gnostics. Referring to Elaine Pagel's book, *The Gnostic Gospels*, Hume provides a very brief summary of these "peculiar" doctrines, a complex system of religious thought that in his account becomes summarily reduced to simple spiritual/material dualisms—celestial and terrestrial realms divided between a good spiritual God and a bad material God. He then scurries past the Gnostics to take up the process of the eventual selection of orthodox texts, assuring students that contrary to what "some of us" grew up believing, the early church fathers, not God, separated the canonical wheat from the heretical chaff: "Man had to decide what was true and orthodox." And as for the sort of motivations and criteria propelling the selection process, the evidence, according to Hume, strongly indicates that the church elders chose from among the various extant, competing "gospels" the ones written by those persons "closest to Christ." The guiding principles were those of "inspiration" and "authority"; they sought to distinguish the "true" and "authentic" reports from among all the other spurious accounts that both preceded and followed the genuine Gospel tradition. Having delivered this assurance, he moves on, devoting the remainder of the period to the subsequent developmental history of the church.

Now, the above account appears innocent enough. Professor Hume has advanced a position that certainly may be supported by appeal to historical evidence. So what is so troubling with this presentation?

Unlike professor Hume's students, I was familiar with the contents of *The Gnostic Gospels* and can report that although Pagels's provocative work is regarded by a few scholars as *too creative* in certain respects (and is by no means considered the definitive account by everyone), I can think of no study which offers a more decisive refutation of the Hume version of the canon selection process. Indeed, the cardinal theme of the book is that partisan political and organizational interests dominated the controversies over canon selection. Each of the first four chapters demonstrates the political and institutional ramifications of the eventual orthodox positions upon doctrine, Pagels discussing in succession the triumphant versions of the resurrection, monotheism, God the Father, and the crucifixion and persecution. She argues that in each instance canonical selection served to reinforce the hierarchical, male-dominated structure of power in the developing church.[392]

For our purposes the moral bone of contention here has little to do with the veracity of these respective accounts, for surely either one could be true and the other false, or they both may ultimately prove erroneous (or, more likely, incomplete). Rather, it concerns the responsibilities of a scholar and teacher when before a classroom of largely innocent, often credulous, young students. In this instance, we witness one of the most highly regarded members of the faculty, a young man with an almost boyish ingenuity about him, compromising his academic integrity (however unwittingly) in the "service" of "special pleading" (the Knedlik phrase). The ideological intention is clear and unmistakable. For whatever reason, he aims to shield his students from potentially disturbing evidence, choosing to uniformly affirm and reinforce a more palatable traditional evangelical view of the composition of the Bible (that he may very well believe) while ignoring or suppressing a prominent contrary argument.

This relatively minor incident, in and of itself, prompts a final observation, which is perhaps all too obvious. Weak, questionable, or egregious character and acts of folly—and even "sin," for that matter—are by no means confined to the members of any one community, region, or strata of society. As personal traits and behaviors, they are randomly distributed among the population at large. This seems to me an incontestable Biblical principle and/or empirical reality. Furthermore, different academic institutions and communities place different kinds of pressures and burdens upon their members. Hence although bad character, and bad faith, may be randomly distributed among the academic population at large, *particular kinds of academic environments invariably encourage and produce, however unintentionally, particular kinds of dishonesty*.

The average private or public university scholar labors mainly under an imperative to publish a certain quantity and quality of work and to

---

[392] Elaine Pagels, *The Gnostic Gospels*, New York: Random House, 1979.

demonstrate a certain level of competency and popularity in the classroom. The average evangelical Christian college teacher, by contrast, feels a pressure (however welcome or internalized) to mold himself into a particular kind of paternalistic role model; his primary duties and contributions seldom extend beyond teaching and counseling students and making himself an integral part of the social life of the college community. The demands of the institution—and by implication, the larger evangelical constituency—are in large measure for the smooth transmission of an ideological cultural heritage. In this sense, the imperatives under which the Christian academician labors encourage the kind of routine partisanship observed in the class of professor Hume.[393] The evangelical academician likens herself to a "slave" or "servant" in the preservation and promotion of a larger (than herself, and life) God-given vision of the meaning of her own existence and of her college and church community and of the body of truth and knowledge imbedded within that vision, and only secondarily or tertiarily as an independent mind engaged in the creation of original science and scholarship. As such, the traditional norms and values of the latter are often misunderstood, if not actively compromised and violated. Often, and without hesitation, the claims and responsibilities of the latter are enthusiastically relinquished in the service of the former.[394]

So that while the deviant secular scholar, straining under the burden of his duties, may ultimately succumb to temptation, fabricating or exaggerating some portion of his research or scholarship in hopes of advancing his career (or, perhaps more commonly, in order to bolster a particular school of thought[395] or enhance his reputation among peers), his evangelical

---

[393] According to Robert Sandin, the Christian social scientist above all seeks "harmony," tries to smooth over the rough edges of apparent contradictory evidence: "Social scientists inevitably find analogies to human behavior among sub-human animal species, and the Christian scholar will need to show how the implications of these resemblances can be harmonized with the Biblical view of human nature." (*The Search For Excellence . . .* , 92.)

[394] "Conciously [sic], he conforms to the essential assertions of Scripture all those assumptions most basic to and constitutive of his scholarly study; they must be consonant, consistent, coherent with the central themes of Biblical theology . . . . " (Wayne McCown {S.P.C.—Religion}, "The Use of the Bible in the Integration of Faith and Learning," a paper delivered at the Faith/Learning Institute, North Park College, Chicago, August 14-25, 1972.)
— "As Christians, we must use *appropriate methods* to solve problems that are *chosen on the basis of whether or not their solutions are redemptive*, will make people more like God. We must be *careful to collect appropriate data from appropriately chosen samples . . . .* [and then appending a sop to scientific objectivity, as though the preceding in no way contradicts what follows:] we must report negative as well as positive results. . . . " (Kotesky, *Psychology from a Christian Perspective*, 25, 42.) {emphases added}

[395] See David Joravsky, "Unholy Science," *New York Review of Books*, 13 October 1983; Harriet Zuckerman, "Deviant Behavior and Social Control in Science," in Edward Sagarin ed.,

counterpart experiences equally insidious moments of moral amnesia, indulging in routine acts of scholarly inattention, indolence, omission, or outright distortion, usually in furtherance of a conventional theological wisdom or institutional agenda, a cumulative pattern of behavior which may serve to advance his own position or standing within a department and among the larger college community. In every academic and scientific setting, then, are generated the kinds of demands and pressures which foster individual acts of intellectual partisanship and scientific mendacity.[396] Yet it is the evangelical academic community's particularly strident pursuit, embrace, and celebration of conspicuous invidious distinctions *vis-a-vis* its secular university nemeses which often blinds its apologists to the inevitable moral breakdowns experienced by its own members.

Plus ça change, plus c'est la même chose

The reader has been made privy to the cultural assumptions or logic underlying the theory and practice of evangelical higher education that rarely see the light of day outside evangelical academic cloisters. Most American academicians will likely find them rather otherworldly. As is appropriate to the anthropological ethnographic drift of much of this book, the term *exotic* surely applies here.[397] Very few would conceive of the traditional role of science and scholarship in American academia in such a manner. And yet in thirty years or so of research upon these matters the author must confess not having unearthed a single "secular" account or exposé of such esoteric evangelical ideas, let alone an internal evangelical academic reckoning. Perhaps one reason for this dearth of scholarship—and journalism also—is that the preponderance of academic journal articles and books about evangelical religion are authored by Christians. It might seem that few non-religious scholars, and I can think of only a handful at most, find the topic worthy of

---

Deviance and Social Change (New York: Russell Sage, distributed by Cornell University Press, Ithaca, New York, 1977).

—A shorter, more concentrated dose of the pessimistic view (and examples) of the scientific community as a whole can be found in Nicholas Wade's "Madness In Their Method: Why scientists find fraud so seductive," *New Republic*, 27 June 1983.

[396] And in other arenas as well, as we see with David Green's attempt to draw Biblical scholarship into the evangelical fold of his D.C. Museum of the Bible: "What Green's statement [about a scholastic issue of Jesus's wife] reveals is a bias against any scholarship that might challenge the traditional Christian understanding of the Bible and the Biblical story." (Candida R. Moss. . . *Bible Nation.* . . , 68.)

[397] Sort of what Micaela di Leonardo had in mind by the title of her book, *Exotics at Home: Anthropologies, Others, and American Modernity* (University of Chicago Press, 1998).

study.[398] Indeed there are at best only a few public free-range intellectuals who dare publish critical works on the topic of religion at all.[399]

Has anything really changed? Come along then as we briefly dip our toes in the supposedly ever-changing flow of the river of evangelicalism or, more particularly, the treatment of religion in both evangelical and secular academia. What are the vital life signs? In this regard I am not at all surprised to report that not much of anything has changed and that the reader of the earlier part of this chapter will have come away fully-prepared to predict and understand the current condition and context of matters religious in America, at least as discussed and written about by openly Christian academicians.

In 2013 the Institute on Religious and Public Life, publisher of *First Things*, a journal described by some as extremely conservative or "neo-conservative," convened a conference in New York City to discuss two books by the eminent American sociologists Robert Bellah and Christian Smith. Of the fourteen participants who eventually contributed papers to a subsequent publication,[400]none identified him or herself as a non-Christian, atheist, or agnostic, whereas virtually all professed Christian beliefs or made such held beliefs obvious. One of the editors introduces their topic with a few guiding questions: Is God just a cultural creation? "Need it be so? . . . . Is social science necessarily on a collision course with traditional modes of religious understanding?" For our purposes, the timing could not have been more felicitous.

Although I would urge my readers to fully peruse this document for themselves in order to fully assess the assertions advanced by the author whose text you hold, allow me to offer a few scintillating hors d'oeuvres to whet the appetite.

The editor warms up the wary reader with the assurance that Bellah's is "an important argument [re: primitive play of our ancestors served as

---

[398] For a general overview of how religion gets treated in academia (that makes no mention, of course, of the more sensitive matters discussed here) see John Schmalzbauer and Kathleen Mahoney's "Religion and Knowledge in the Post-Secular Academy," Chapter Nine in Philip S. Gorski et al., 2012. See also Gorski's "The Return of the Repressed. . . ."

[399] E.g., Gore Vidal, Christopher Hitchens, Richard Dawkins, Daniel Dennett, Sam Harris, Chris Hedges, Jeff Sharlet, and, on the U-tube circuit, the all-too-generous-and-polite Neal Degrasse Tyson; their thin ranks easily exceeded by comedians: George Carlin, Bill Maher, Ricky Gervais, John Oliver, Eddie Izzard, Julia Sweeney, among others. All this in spite of the claims of one Christian academician that " . . . . throughout George W. Bush's second term these forceful thinkers dominated the bestseller lists." (Robert C. Jones, *The End of White Christian America*, Simon & Schuster 2016, 225.) Indeed, were it only so.

[400] R. R. Reno & Barbara McClay eds., *Religion and the Social Sciences: Conversations with Robert Bellah and Christian Smith* (Eugene: Cascade Books, Imprint of Wipf and Stock Publishers, 2015).

precursors to religious ideas and practices] that is for the most part congenial to religious people." He exhorts skeptical (presumably largely Christian) readers to avoid pre-judging the offerings: "Social scientists sometimes say true things about this or that aspect of the human condition and for that we should be grateful rather than resenting their field's limitations." Again, the reader already has some idea of what those resentments and limitations might consist. Indeed, "the heart has its reasons that reason doesn't know."[401] Fair enough.

In "Impossible Pluralism," Paul Griffiths complains that "common sociological sense" is just shorthand for "a story I like the sound of." He suggests that the shifting evidence in historical and Biblical studies complicate a "universal history like Bellah's" and yet other kinds of evidence, e.g., global warming,[402] get short shrift: "Mass extinctions are part of the ordinary rhythm of life on this planet." And so, ho-hum, not to worry. As for the possibility of a tolerant "universalism" in his own field, he can appreciate other religions only so long as Catholic Christianity's relationship to God remains *sui generis*, "given to no others."[403]

Thomas Joseph White complains in "Sociology as Theology," that "just when you thought liberal Protestantism was dead. . . .", along comes Robert Bellah. For all this social and cultural developmentalism, captured in his title, *Religion in Human Evolution. . .*, he "refuses [to engage] the larger metaphysical questions that are always in the background. . . ." Bellah ignores "the immaterial soul, with its powers of intelligence and free will. There is a principle in the core of our being that comes from God directly and that is called to return to God." Such disregard has its roots in "deep taboos of our contemporary academic culture." The secular pluralism he admires and extols proves illusory since "the partial truths we find in them take on their ultimate value when they are purified by the illuminating life of Christ."[404]

---

[401] Ibid., xi-xviii.

[402] Dan Kahan might argue that this extreme evangelical form of evidence denial is more broadly related to a benchmark dynamic he thinks of as a kind of cultural "expressiveness": for "It is only when they perceive that a policy bears a social meaning congenial to their cultural values that citizens become receptive to sound empirical evidence about what consequences that policy will have." ("What's Really Wrong with Shaming Sanctions," Yale Law School Research Paper #125 preliminary draft, undated, 12.)

[403] R. R. Reno & Barbara McClay eds., *Religion and. . .*, 10-12. One also hears traces of conservative evangelical dogma in Griffith's rant about a religious universalism. As Bellah subsequently replied: "The other thing that shocked me was Griffiths' horror at the idea of a world civil society, which he believes 'would mean the end of the church and, I think, of most other religious traditions.' " (ibid., 35)

[404] Ibid., 20-22.

Notre Dame theology professor Francesca Aran Murphy acknowledges that "It's quite impossible, of course, for an orthodox Christian theologian to buy into Bellah's narrative taken as a whole. . . . But his anthropology of freedom is important and should be assimilated into *a Christian anthropology*."405

In response, Professor Bellah is surely too kind and generous is his largely futile attempt to defend and explain the ultimately *value neutral* (the term is of course Weber's) aims of modern scholarship and science. It seems that his repeated assertion that the designation, "myths," does not necessarily imply "false" or "untrue" falls on deaf ears. That an avowed Christian might carry on with the study of religion in a reasonably objective fashion—impartially employing such tools as characterization and description— does indeed appear an impossibility to most Christian academicians. Lamentably, "The non-relativistic pluralism that I espouse is simply incomprehensible to him [Paul Griffiths], as it was to many of the symposium participants. . . . [For example, as a Christian] I've studied Navajo religion, which evokes in me insights I cherish rather than a demand that I reject it as a competing 'metanarrative.' "

What is more, this particular cast of contributors largely hails from Catholic institutions. Just imagine the critical response were there more evangelical academicians attending, whose probable contributions we got some idea of earlier.

Philip Gorski, a sociologist from Yale, the sole participant who seemed to have actually read and understood Bellah's distinguished book, opined that "the influential synthesis of [Clifford] Geertz and [Peter] Berger were partial and even superficial by contrast. . . [Bellah's] easily the best account now available. . . profoundly radical." 406

But for our purposes the discussion and critical responses to the second symposium book, Christian Smith's *What is a Person? Rethinking Humanity, Social Life, and the Moral Good From the Person Up*,407 proves even more

---

405 Ibid., 8. {emphasis added}

406 In the interest of full disclosure: Gorski's most recent book is titled, *American Covenant: A History of Civil Religion from the Puritans to the Present* (Princeton University Press, 2017). He was a student of Bellah's who unfortunately in one weak moment in an otherwise distinguished effort lets down his guard: "That dream [of a "righteous republic"] was never fully realized. . . . Nor will it ever be, by this generation, the next, or any other, because the American republic is built with *the crooked timber of a fallen humanity*, just like any other polity." (223) {emphasis added} This veiled reference to original sin is taken from Kant. And "just like any other polity"? Fortunately, there have been some rather marvelous post-WWII nations that seem to have shaken free from the shackles of sin and created god-free societies that have for a half-century or more put pious American exceptionalism to shame.

407 University of Chicago Press, 2010.

illuminating. Unlike Bellah's book, the response was overwhelmingly positive, for Smith, typical of American sociologists of religion, is a celebrated member of an overtly Christian academic tribe. The central theme of his *What is a Person. . .* is easily summarized and already familiar to the reader of this volume. Secular academic social sciences have "reduced" unique "persons" or personalities to mere abstract "rational actors" or data points. As such they have stripped human beings of their particular God-given qualities and potentialities and overlooked their universal lapsarian natures. Although as far as I know he does not emphasize or even mention original sin and other such orthodox conservative Christian talking points in his University of Chicago Press book—hence my characterization of his approach as getting Christian dogma in through the back door—the cloaking insinuations are all too obvious, at least ought be by now to the reader of this volume. Indeed as the overwhelming majority of the participants in the Symposium were from Catholic institutions I was immediately reminded of the Hilary Clinton/John Podesta e-mail server controversy, the most damning of whose revelations concerned the so-called hostility of the Clinton campaign to religion, evident in communications deriding the public faith of certain conservative Catholic Republicans. All that conventional piety was just for show, smokescreens concealing their actual evangelical Religious-Right moorings, evangelicalism proving too crude or vulgar a base religion for their rich Republican friends, who just "wouldn't understand."[408] Likewise, over the years conservative Christian academicians such as Christian Smith have learned to temper their overt expressions of orthodoxy to enhance their own claims to academic respectability. Colleagues of faith participating in the Symposium, however, are not observing or operating under such camouflaging restraints, to our ultimate benefit. Respondent David Yeago, from Trinity School, for example, won't be bound by protocol:

> Christian revelation gives believers a place to stand from which it is possible to see also the rationally accessible truth *more clearly*, and once such truth has been seen, it can be explained and defended by properly philosophical arguments. . . . models and world views that obscure the reality of the person do not typically sit lightly on the surface of the mind, ready to be dislodged cleanly by the better argument. They have complex and obscure relations to the tangle of illusion and disordered desire that resides deep in the fallen human heart.[409] {italics in original}

---

[408] Marc A. Thiessen, "Hillary Clinton is a threat to religious liberty," *The Washington Post*, October 13, 2016; Mary Beth Hagan, "Hacked emails show level of contempt for deeply religious," *The Virginian Pilot*, October 20, 2016. Op-eds that appeared also in *The Philadelphia Inquirer*, *The Seattle Times*, among others.

[409] R. R. Reno & Barbara McClay eds., *Religion and. . .* , 70-72.

David Novak chides both Smith and Vogler, the latter a philosopher from the University of Chicago, for trimming their sails in alien waters, for

> . . . . suppressing his [/her] metaphysical/theological beliefs in order to meet their entrance requirements for secular public discourse. . . . [oooh. . . . burn!]
> Discussing human dignity requires that we not suppress our belief that human dignity and human uniqueness comes [*sic*] about because we are the *imago Dei*
> . . . .
> But as a sociologist like Christian Smith knows, any society that attempts to deny the human-God connection is a society that is inhibiting (often violently) human persons from actualizing what makes us unique in the world. Even in the most secular societies, the "God Question" just won't go away, but is again and again "the return of the repressed." [410]

It is in the discussion of rational actor models and game theory and the concept of reductionism in the social sciences that we observe academicians from distant virtual parallel epistemological universes talking past one another without much sympathy or comprehension of the other's positions. Even for this social scientist, attacking rational actor models (dubious creations at best) is like picking low-hanging fruit. Of course they appear to reduce the rich complexity of individuals and societies to mere mechanical, impersonal processes. But this school of thought is just one current of a larger multifaceted academic stream of effort to comprehend the world and her inhabitants. In certain defined contexts it can provide insight into how human beings behave; the same for what Smith dismisses as "variables sociology"[411] (not always my favorite reading matter also).

It is quite predictable that a "critical realism" [euphemism for *Christian*] ideologue like Christian Smith would single out a political science advocate of game theory from a public university for the lion's share of his symposium response to critics.[412] Considerations of space forbid an extended treatment

---

[410] Ibid., 86-87.

[411] It is somewhat ironic that when Christian Smith has an ax to grind, or point to make (e.g., that evangelicals are *not* at all like the religious right, or a "disciplined charging army," as Frances Fitzgerald put it in the May 18, 1981 *New Yorker*), he debunks what he calls stereotypes by falling back upon the very same methodologies (survey data and statistical analysis— or "variables sociology") that otherwise offend his notion of "critical realism." No doubt he would claim to be saving "the person" because of the interviews he also conducts above and beyond the obligatory impersonal data collection. But one searches in vain for just how his greater grasp of "layers of personhood" generates superior insight. (*Christian America?*. . . , 193.) However, at least give him credit for acknowledging (tongue-in-cheek?) that "There's nothing quite like the Manichean threat of a desperate struggle against darkness to keep the constituents' checks rolling in." (194)

[412] Re: James R. Rogers's "The Gimlet Eye of Social Science" in R. R. Reno & Barbara McClay eds., op. cit.

of every problematical assertion, but how little Smith actually understands or appreciates social science becomes immediately apparent in his employment of the concept, "reductionism."

Initially, Smith defines reductionism in his own book as "trying to understand certain entities by reducing them to their component parts existing at lower levels." This dark side of reductionism contrasts fully with the quite different light side of *"methodological* reduction [note without an –ism]. . . (the partial decomposition of elements at one level into parts at a different level for purposes of systematic analysis) . . . an essential aspect of science when appropriately done. . . ."

> . . . .my argument rather contradicts both *ontological* reductionism, which fails to acknowledge and understand the completely stratified nature of reality, and *causal* reductionism, which routinely seeks to explain facts by more basic features and causes operating at lower levels.[413]

Again, as considerations of space forbid the complete deconstruction of Smith's convoluted, tortured explanation, consider this brief decoding of euphemisms: First, *"ontological* reductionism . . . stratified nature of reality," meaning that secular social scientists fail to take into account four or more layers of personhood: 1) original sin; 2) God-given individual personality and social determinism; 3) *imago dei*, or that human beings were/continue to be made in the likeness of God; and 4) that every human possesses a "soul" transcendent of material existence (whether or not you want one). Second, *"causal* reductionism," or the pot calling the kettle black, such that "reduction" (contrary to *reductionism*) becomes a justifiable form of argument, as when the "person" with qualities bestowed by God has those "gifts" fully accounted for in any explanation. On such occasions a *synecdoche*-like theoretical leap is quite acceptable. It is not legitimate, however, to project social phenomena out in the world with features that transcend the qualities of the constituent elements, individuals, or to isolate mechanisms—like rational actor motivational dynamics—that fail to fully take into account the complexity (the four layers) of the God-given "person."

None of this should be confused with "theoretical abstraction and conceptualization," tools that are employed by nearly "every science. . . . [and] lie at the heart of the critical realist program of social analysis." After all, even we ideological Christian academicians "think"; *we* just do it in a better, more enriched way. *We* add our deeper understanding of the "stratified nature of reality" to the mix. For how simple and obvious explanation becomes when any social problem can be reduced to the veiled dysfunction of original

---

[413] *Christian America?*. . . , 104-5.

sin. And so one Christian academician's *synecdoche* becomes another secular academician's indefensible *reductionism*. This secular straw man proves easily shredded.

> The other [secular reductionism] is about insisting that everything concerning some aspect of some entity existing at one level of reality can be fully accounted for and explained by some lower, less complex level of the same reality *(e.g., human persons are 'nothing but' their brains and bodies, which are 'nothing but' bits of matter and energy transfers, ad nauseam)*.[414] {emphasis added}

Human beings are, of course, a good deal more complex than just atoms, molecules, and tissue. Our minds have proven so limber and ambidextrous that we have conceptualized both science *and* religion, discovered dark matter and energy *and* composed sacred texts integral to the theory and practice of a myriad of religions.

Christian Smith has conveniently misconstrued the conventional understanding of reductionism for his own tribal purposes.[415] We more commonly think of reductionism in a somewhat different manner. Take Karl Marx's labor theory of value, for instance, which in its most simplistic form *reduced* the value of the products of laborers to merely the expenditure paid for the labor itself and to no other factors. For ideological reasons it *largely* ignores the contribution of other actors, elements, and dynamics (that "variables sociology" recognizes)—skilled management, innovation, aeronautical engineering, manufacturing techniques, raw materials, supply and demand, political economics, etc.[416] Indeed although Christian Smith addresses (worships?) the concept of "the person" in his book, his version of "the person" proves equally impoverished. He strains to force whatever he has gleaned

---

[414] Ibid, 106-7.

[415] One of the most egregious examples of such comes from the conservative Catholic "essayist," Joseph Bottum: "An era more comfortable than ours with religious history would have understood immediately what Occupy Wall Street was: a protest against the continuing reign of Satan and a plea for the coming of the Kingdom of God, with a new heaven and a new earth. . . . a great, incoherent cry of apocalyptic spiritual pain: We *know* what is right—true, good, real—and still the world lies in sin and error." (*An Anxious Age . . .* , xvi.) In this instance, once again, any tremor of a moral, ethical, or value-based action gets *monopolistically* explained away or reduced to some variation upon a parallel evangelical Christian theme. Obviously, he fails a very basic ethnographic test: whose words are these? Native's or observer's?

[416] Although the concept is generally attributed to Marx in *Das Kapital* and elsewhere by modern Marxists, it was widely expressed by others as well, even Adam Smith. A Seattle City Councilperson, who was a local community college teacher and claimed to be Marxist or socialist economist, argued that the workers at Boeing should assume control of the company because labor was the actual source of value, not management; as though engineers had next to nothing to do with the ultimate dollar value of Boeing planes.

from conventional secular social sciences to fit into his more "complex" version of "personhood." But alas, the borrowings are, as some of his supporters aver, designed to make his offerings "respectable" to the gods of secular academia. His "critical realism" is neither persuasive nor realistic.

> . . . . we must not confuse historically developing cultural understandings of a reality with the ontological reality itself [his God-given layers of personhood]. The widespread influence of 'social constructionism' in academia [that religions are human products, ala Peter Berger] and our [secular] culture might suggest that human beings are really not persons as a matter of ontological reality, but that we have only come to contingently think of them as persons in our context, given our particular history. . . .
>
> The real personhood of all living human beings as *an ontological fact*, whether or not any person or culture [atheists, Buddhists, Islamists] recognized it, is *similar in this way to the real existence of germs as the cause of many sicknesses and diseases, even though for most of human history people knew little to nothing about germs.* [417]

Some readers may wonder, is he serious? Prior to the scientific revolution sickness and disease were irrationally attributed by religions, Christianity among them, to all sorts of nefarious "ontological realities" that even Smith now discounts. How convenient, and ironic, that we can now legitimize original sin through the metaphor of germs. He has somehow or other reversed the chronology of the emergence and development of human knowledge and understanding; like Marx standing Hegel on his head, he's got it all backwards. For whereas in his estimation we may now be no more than only inching towards *ultimate* truths, or *the truth*, actually we have been and continue to move further and further away from ignorance and *falsehood*, and precipitously so. Due to the *social constructionism* of natural science—due to medical breakthroughs—we no longer accept a veritable swarm of superstitions as "ontological realities." More recently, for example, due to the popularizations of Spencer Wells, we no longer think of race as an actual empirical reality, or an absolutist's datum; it is indeed more of a social construction, a conclusion supported by our constantly evolving understanding of the very nature of DNA itself. But by what similar sort of developmental process will the undeniable ontological "fact" of the "real personhood of all human beings" emerge and command our attention and acknowledgment? How will all the other "partial truths" of other religions and epistemologies simply wilt or melt away under the flame of this ultimate truth? It didn't happen in the lifetimes of Cromwell or Abraham Lincoln (who foretold of George Washington rising from the grave to issue in a new American millennium) or a host of other Calvinist pre- and post-millennialists. These are of course, deep

---

[417] *What is a Person?* . . . , 115. {emphasis added}.

and abiding apocalyptic assumptions that the more respectable Christian academician cannot divulge or share with the wider academic world for fear of ridicule.[418] And no wonder. For as any decent evangelical often claims, even the devil can quote scripture. And we are all too familiar by now with the loathsome fear of complete reversals that dog this community. Better to just pay lip service to Darwin and get on with more important things, like the indoctrination of evangelical youth.

Sadly, what ideologues like Christian Smith do offer are vague, unsubstantiated claims of superior insight and understanding, eschewing any Heisenberg-like embrace of uncertainty and humility.

> What puzzles in sociology, Rogers [a secular political scientist] asks, can my critical realist personalism solve better than the extant theories? Immodestly, I say: all of them. . . . But my larger point is that my framework is better than his.[419]

Breathtaking. I cannot think of a single reputable secular natural or social scientist who has or would ever issue such a claim. And yet observe that the truly deep and persuasive critiques of rational actor models of the social sciences of economics, sociology, and political science, for just one example, have come from *within secular academia*, such as from the pen of economist Richard Thaler, who hails from the very belly of the beast itself, the University of Chicago, just awarded the Nobel Prize, who takes to task some of the sacred cow ideas of the traditional "Chicago school of economics." And we could multiply the examples *ad infintum*. Although the conventional wisdoms (the phrase is from John Kenneth Galbraith) and paradigms of academia and science are always resistant to change (Thomas Kuhn), evangelical and milquetoast conservative Catholic academic institutions are even more lethargic, having no comparable imbedded self-correcting mechanisms, because like Christian Smith's "critical realism" they reject the very notion and practice of "value neutral" natural and social science upon which such self-examination is based. Indeed any overtly "Christian" academician of any note produces papers and books primarily about religion and not much else.

---

[418] And kudos to Matthew Avery Sutton for a long overdue account of the American evangelical obsession with apocalyptic thinking, *American Apocalypse: A History of Modern Evangelicalism* (2014).

[419] Reference is to James Rogers, cited below. From "Reply to My Critics," in R. R. Reno & Barbara McClay eds., op. cit., 111-112. Readers are by now familiar with such hubris, no different from that expressed by various SPU faculty members, sheltered as they are from external peer scrutiny.

—See James R. Rogers's decisive one-page summing up, "Smith's Contribution to Doing Social Science: The Proof of the Pudding," in his paper, "The Gimlet Eye of Social Science," ibid., 98-9. To wit: so where's the evidence of your superiority? At the moment, the pantry shelves appear quite bare.

Years ago Alan Wolfe forecast "The Opening of the Evangelical Mind" in an article in *The Atlantic* but could only come up with a handful of Christian academicians of any substance.[420] We are still waiting for his predicted evangelical intellectual Renaissance. There are, of course, a multitude of American distinguished academicians who are Christians, as with Robert Bellah, Peter Berger, Francis Collins, and many others[421]; the difference being that they accept the paradigm of value neutrality which ideologues like Christian Smith so easily dismiss.

A Final Word

> The task before us is therefore clear: first, to certify *Winnie-the-Pooh* as legitimate literature by demonstrating that it contains Christian dogma; and secondly, to raise it to the level of *great* literature by showing the historic purity of its connection to the traditional sources of Christian thought, in opposition to the erroneous whimsies of latitudinarians and Enthusiasts.
>
> Let me proclaim at once that, although there are few overt citations of Holy Writ in *Winnie-the-Pooh*, the subject of the book is nothing other than the central drama of our faith: the Fall and Redemption of Man. [422]

There is perhaps no greater impediment to serious science and scholarship within evangelical Christian academia than the reliance upon traditional Judeo-Christian lapsarianism for first principle explanations of nearly every personal and social phenomenon. The practice represents the ultimate tautology, the ultimate reduction of the variegated causes and consequences of individual and social behavior to a single given, *a priori* human condition of existence—to an inert, immutable, fallen human nature. Simply stated, human beings and societies are the way they are—behaving, developing, turning out the way they do—because people are the way they are.[423] Hence

---

[420] October 2000.

[421] In fact, as briefly mentioned early on, one of the members of my committee that first received this book in its original two-volume dissertation form was described to me by our department secretary as an overt Christian. From our contact and deliberations alone I would have never guessed as much. Kudos to him for his enthusiastic support and never making it an issue. Indeed at the conclusion of the defense he urged with no hesitation: "Let's get this off to publishers."

[422] "*O Felix Culpa!* The Sacramental Meaning of *Winnie-the-Pooh*," by C. J. L. Culpepper. D. Litt., Oxon., in Frederick C. Crews, *The Pooh Perplex: A Freshman Casebook*, New York: E. P. Dutton, 1963, 54-55. {emphasis in original}

[423] Consider *New York Times* religion editor, Kenneth Briggs's, (not unsympathetic) report of a visit to Grace College in Winona lake, Indiana (which readers will recall as the headquarters

an original, *essential* human nature determines and explains all human behavior, underlying and vitiating all personal and social outcomes.[424]

As we have seen, no wonder evangelical academic scholarship appears sunk in virtual paralysis. Why people behave the way they do—or, more appropriately, why human beings and the world are so evidently flawed—is too obvious to warrant further examination. How often the myriad rationalizations and justifications for the evangelical approach to academic endeavor reduce to an understandable reluctance to improve upon an explanation that cannot be improved upon. Unfortunately, this simple, seductive idea, firmly lodged within the minds of believers, apparently explaining everything, in fact explains next to nothing. And it fails as an explanation (of particular phenomena), I might add, *even though the underlying metaphysics, ontology, and theology—God as creator and Jesus Christ as savior of humanity—may in fact hold true.* There is every possibility, in other words, that the Christian metaphysic may prove entirely correct, while the evangelical Christian epistemology—one apparently and inextricably linked with it—may prove as equally and entirely wrong. This is, after all, what Neils Bohr had in mind (upon hearing the objection that God would not allow the ambiguity predicted by quantum mechanics into the universe) when he urged Einstein to stop telling God what to do: stop projecting your own expectations, biases, visions into the universe. Read the cosmic code for what it is.[425]

---

of the Free Methodist Church): "Non-Christian, nonevangelical views are often ignored, distorted or raised like fat clay pigeons that can be shot to smithereens. . . . [Yet some of the more liberal faculty contend that] If they are going to defend themselves against *such threats* [liberal ideas and philosophies] . . . then they must truly know *their enemies* rather than sticking their heads in the sand.

A course that covers Marx, for instance, points out that he correctly criticized the greed behind capitalism. But Marx's Achilles' heel, in the interpretation of Grace's instructor, is that *he denies the doctrine of original sin by incorrectly assuming that mankind is perfectible.*" {emphasis added} ("Evangelical Colleges Reborn," *New York Times Magazine,* 14 December 1980.)

Nary a mention here of the labor theory of value, dialectical materialism, or the historical struggle between, and transformation of, classes; rather, a Marx judged delinquent for a lapsed appreciation of the fallen condition of mankind. A criticism perhaps as appropriate and damning of *Monkey Business* as of *Das Kapital.*

[424] Timothy Fitzgerald cites another profound bias animating "religious studies," the widely proclaimed assumption that ". . . . all humans everywhere are believed on this kind of theory to have a natural facility for cognizing the Infinite, and 'the religions' are particular forms or expressions by which these cognitions or special feelings are given tangible expressions. . . . [under the guise of a] liberal ecumenical theology. . . claiming that religion is a natural and/or a supernatural reality in the nature of things that all humans have a capacity for, regardless of their cultural context." (*The Ideology of Religious Studies,* Oxford University Press, 2000, 7, 4.)

[425] "Even though he [Einstein] helped to found it in its earliest years, he could not accept the quantum mechanics that evolved later and allowed 'uncertainty' to intervene in the universe. His vehement rejection of it was in part at least a consequence of his pantheistic beliefs in a

Perhaps this consideration—and others I raised earlier—lie at the heart of Peter Berger's exhortation to fellow observers of religion to lay aside personal religious beliefs and assumptions (Berger is himself a devout and, if I may use the term, "enthusiastic" public Christian) and conduct empirical investigations in a spirit of—in his perhaps too often cited but too seldom followed phrase—"methodological atheism."[426] The term, and the context out of which it emerged or was employed, represents an admission of sorts that too rigorous (or "wholistic") a belief in or application of the evangelical Christian worldview in academic pursuits can become more of a hindrance than a help in the illumination and explanation of social and religious phenomena.[427]

It is in this sense that I would further argue—with great conviction—that the veracity of the present study *scarcely depends upon the resolution of any contending metaphysical claims. Whether or not the Christian God and Jesus the Savior are the genuine articles has little bearing upon the veracity or corroboration of the arguments advanced herein.* They stand on their own two feet. What fundamentally distinguishes this kind of scholarship from the sort we have observed in the evangelical colleges is simply that the Christian scholar can rarely make the same

---

perfect universe; his mild religion flawed his reason in the end. 'God does not play dice,' he said, dogmatically. 'Stop telling God what to do!' Niels Bohr retorted." (Nigel Calder, *Einstein's Universe*, New York: Penguin Books, 1980, 234-35.)

[426] Peter L. Berger, *The Sacred Canopy: Elements of a Sociological Theory of Religion*, New York: Anchor Books, 1969, 100. Also: "Thus sociological theory must, by its own logic, view religion as a human projection, and by the same logic can have nothing to say about the possibility that this projection may refer to something other than the being of its projector. In other words, to say that religion is a human projection does not logically preclude the possibility that the projected meanings may have an ultimate status independent of man. Indeed, if a religious view of the world is posited, the anthropological ground of these projections may itself be the reflection of a reality that *includes* both world and man, so that man's ejaculations of meaning into the universe ultimately point to an all-embracing meaning in which he is himself grounded." (180)

[427] Considerations of space forbid a full examination of the internal contradictions plaguing the work of the avowed Christian sociologist, Christian Smith. The author urges readers to compare the 2010 and 2017 books listed in the bibliography and cited here in several footnotes. Although he does an admirable job in the latter of affecting a "methodological agnosticism," an insufferable hubris nonetheless creeps in all too reminiscent of passages quoted from the earlier book: "Critical realism tells us to practice science in the service of the truth about reality, as best we can (fallibly) understand it, and not in the service of ideology or narrow self-interests. That basic charge immediately tethers science to a *moral* commitment: to learning and speaking the truth. The modern divorce of fact and value is thus overturned. . . . [or that religion and science are not all that different] Again with critical realism, facts and values are reconnected. . . ." (*Religion: What It is. . .*, 133.) For evangelicals, as we have seen, there is nothing wrong with such a reconnection. Recall the earlier citations from *Religion and the Social Sciences: Conversations with Robert Bellah and Christian Smith.*

claim.[428] Since he assumes all sorts of divine interventions and relationships that are virtually impossible to observe, measure, or assess, should the metaphysics prove untenable or crumble, then nearly everything else which has built upon the theological infrastructure comes tumbling down with it—at least in theory. (An altogether unlikely intramural logical prospect, in any event, because as we have seen, the metaphysic and the epistemology have, so far, proven un-amenable to any kind of empirical investigation and verification.)

In light of these considerations, it becomes incumbent upon the scholar, of whatever religious persuasion, to shed the skin of metaphysical preconception, inducing in herself the kind of religious or spiritual amnesia urged by Berger, and step boldly into the darkness, unaided by any assumed divine guidance (relying instead upon purely *human theoretical* guidelines and *empirical* clues). For if, as the Christian academician avers, God is indeed in control of the persons and events of history, his terrestrial manifestations and agents ever-present, then any moderately accurate compilation and description of human behavior and events can only serve to document and authenticate this intervention in our world. It would seem that the best we mortals can do in light of apparent unresolved metaphysical uncertainty is offer an account of the visible phenomena in society and history and trust that some kind of verisimilitude or coherence exists between metaphysical and material realms.[429] As should be fully apparent by now to the reader of this volume, the author fully deigns to practice what he preaches. In this respect, a comparison of the scholarly and scientific products of the respective evangelical Christian and "secular" private and public academic institutions over the last

---

[428] These evangelical assumptions often surface in unlikely places. For example, James Davison Hunter (1983) closes his conventional sociological account with the admonishment to fellow investigators of evangelicalism in particular and of religion in general to take their subjects and their beliefs seriously because some day, *"to their astonishment," the skies may open to reveal Christ returning to earth in glorious fulfillment of scripture, and then what will the skeptical, dismissive sociologist have to say for himself?"* (135) {emphasis added} Aside from the sophomoric nature of the remark, the kind of thing any evangelical college graduate might toss out, notice the insinuation here that somehow or other the value or veracity of a sociological account hinges upon or is conditioned by a metaphysical truth claim. If the *Parousia* occurs, then these smart-alecky secular academicians are just out in the cold, their life work rendered superfluous or meaningless. With this unfortunate remark, Hunter confirms the impression of an all too unreflective (however dispassionate or subliminal) embrace of this underlying evangelical wedding of metaphysics to epistemology.

[429] This kind of genuine academic realism and pragmatism (an emphasis on what "works") is rarely seen in or extended to American politics. One notable exception can be found in a marvelous essay by former New York governor, Mario Cuomo: "In the American Catholic Tradition of Realism," in E.J. Dionne Jr., Jean Bethke Elshtain, & Kayla M. Drogosz eds., *One Electorate Under God?. . .* , 13-18. It should be required reading for religious politicians.

hundred years or so will prove both intriguing and instructive. We can only speculate upon the present condition of human knowledge and science had the medieval evangelical academic model been in force throughout all of modern European and American history. One can only hope that the performance of the evangelical-laden administration of President Donald Trump during the 2020 Covid-19 pandemic will serve as a sad reminder of the empirical value of such delusions.[430]

---

[430] And a reminder also of the media's ignorance of Trump's evangelical beliefs, most evident in their continual misconstrual and reconstruction of his comment in early February, 2020 that the coronavirus would soon disappear "miraculously," as "magically."
—Perhaps one explanation of the gullibility of the American public to anti-scientific quackery can be found in the dispersion of the graduates of evangelical colleges out into primary and secondary education. Raymond Eve and Dana Dunn of the University of Texas at Arlington distributed a random sample questionnaire to the nation's high school biology teachers. They discovered that "a high percentage of high school teachers profess superstitious beliefs" and that, more importantly, the "teachers seem to misunderstand 'what science is all about.' A prominent misunderstanding concerns the role of facts and theories, only 5 percent demonstrating a clear understanding." ("Superstitious biology teachers? Many believe in the supernatural, racial superiority, survey finds," *The Seattle Times*, 9/11/88.)

CHAPTER 8

SPIRITUAL STRUCTURE

In addition to the myriad individual ways in which the faculty member endeavors to bring evangelical faith into the classroom—from the simple inauguration of each class period with a brief prayer to more elaborate, systematic (and ultimately futile) attempts to formulate sacred versions of academic disciplines—there are the formal extracurricular programs designed to enhance the student's spiritual life on campus. These include the by now familiar thrice-weekly chapel sessions (@9:30-10:20 a.m.)—with special emphasis upon a "Christian Commitment Week" series, usually scheduled near the beginning of each academic quarter; "Cadre groups," small, informal bands of students who meet once a week under the tutelage of a faculty member, administrator, alumnus, or (only occasionally) independently of adult supervision; Sunday night "Celebration," an hour-long service of prayer, song, and testimonies (student accounts of spiritual struggles and victories) held in the campus cafeteria (gatherings the size of which fluctuates wildly from year to year, providing a good barometer of the spiritual temper on campus); "Urban Involvement" programs that send students to talk with street people at downtown Christian coffee houses one evening a week, participate in Sunday worship services for international refugees, visit with homeless mothers and children at skid road hotels, play cards with the elderly at nursing homes, meet with inmate prayer groups at state prisons, meet with juveniles in detention centers; and a particularly important and laudable related program, "Urban Plunge" (one designed to heighten student awareness of the plight of the urban poor), wherein volunteers spend a week in downtown Seattle with a nominal amount of pocket money and a mattress on the floor of a seedy hotel or a sleeping bag on a hardwood campus gymnasium floor as a bed for the night.

What is more, there are dormitory Bible study groups that appear to materialize almost spontaneously among students, becoming an omnipresent feature of dorm life during periods of "spiritual awakening" on campus; "Discipleship groups," smaller, more intense versions of cadre groups which meet to concentrate upon the particular spiritual goals or problems of individual students; "Action Teams," musical and dramatic ensembles that perform on and off campus, often touring around the state and to other states as well; "World Prayer groups" that convene regularly to solicit divine assistance for missions of the church and student volunteers overseas; and finally, "Operation Outreach," a program which recruits and then distributes student volunteers among various world relief organizations and summer missions and sponsors "Spring Breakaway Teams," small crews dispatched to various sites in North America for intense two-week spring-break "ministering" (to Indian tribes on reservations in Canada, for example).

Less orthodox groups emerge from student interest in various social and political issues and these are often at odds with the more conservative political tenor of the student body as a whole and are seldom encouraged by the administration. Students who supported the nuclear freeze movement, for example, received none of the official sanctions which the Office of Student Ministries routinely confers upon the conventional community "outreach" and overseas missionary programs and their spin-offs. The more politically active students, in general, tend to labor in the splendid isolation of their own virtuosic concerns—as did one of the more aggressive liberal students who conducted a "Prayer Vigil for Peace" one evening a week in the center of the campus loop, a standing candlelight discussion and prayer gathering that usually drew very few students away from the comfort of the dormitories.

Students harboring international social and political concerns (heretofore and henceforth referred to as "social internationalists") over, for example, the role of the United States in Central and South America and other human rights issues, tend to gravitate towards the few more liberal faculty members who promote unconventional—some almost radical—approaches to world problems, although these are often advanced in conjunction or sympathy with a traditional missions approach.[431]

The aforementioned programs and their numerous subdivisions and variations comprise the core of the Seattle Pacific student's practical spiritual

---

[431] For example, SPU history professor Ronald Palmer's 1980 Weter faculty Award Lecture, "Is The Current Crisis Worth Understanding? Or, A Liberal Arts Approach To The Third World" (5/6/80), offers a confused mélange of radical, liberal, and traditional evangelical themes: "Foreign aid equals a subsidy for American big businesses to secure markets for American goods and maintain Third World nations within the American orbit."/"In a certain sense, the current crisis is not in the Third World but in the heart of man."/"Perhaps the key relationship between Reconciliation Theory and the Third World centers on the concept of justice. Ronald Sider's thorough examination of the Biblical principles of justice leaves no doubt that 'the Bible clearly teaches that God wills fundamentally transformed economic relationships among his people.' "/"The need for reconciliation to God implies an active counter-force opposed to reconciliation. God is not the author of confusion. Where world events become overwhelming, we may note the presence of Satan. Just as we can recognize God's hand wherever truth, justice and love emerge, whether from the recognized Christian community or not, we can also perceive the hand of Satan wherever oppression, injustice, distortions and hate abound (whether inside or outside Christendom)." {underline in original} Professor Palmer's cadre group, "Bread For The World," was one of the largest that I visited, attracting 30-40 students.

education.[432] Since I will be dealing with aspects of, or drawing illustrations from, many of them throughout the remainder of this study, I will not provide a comprehensive discussion of them all at this time; many in fact neither require nor warrant further exploration. Rather, I will restrict my attention to one or two with which I became the most familiar, offering brief introductions and then some examples drawn from my campus experiences in order to reproduce for the reader some of the situations and moods of the spiritual life of the average student.

Chapel

Chapel occupies the center stage of spiritual education at Seattle Pacific University, as it does in nearly all serious evangelical colleges and universities throughout the nation.[433] It represents the locus of the routinization and ritualization of the cardinal cultural assumptions under-girding the college community, an epicenter from which are spun out the symbols, argots, and meanings (some foreign, some familiar) that any novice student must grasp, absorb, and ultimately master if he is to ascend to a higher plateau of spiritual maturation or "wholeness." Short of this, he must come to know them simply to prosper in his daily life; they are essential to a feeling of belonging, to becoming an esteemed and valued member of the academic community.

In fact, I will venture that one can accurately gauge the ideological intensity of any ostensibly religious college merely on the basis of the nature and role of chapel at the institution, without ever having set foot on campus. Consider this proposition: colleges which no longer conduct regular chapel sessions, or which do not require chapel attendance if they do, can be

---

[432] Another view, comparing quite different Methodist and Mennonite colleges: "At the Methodist colleges I attended, this course of study [in the denominational worldview] included fall and spring revivals, required Bible courses, and required daily chapel. At Bethel college this course of study typically includes Menno Simons lectures in the fall and Bible lectures in the spring, required religion courses, convocation, and voluntary chapel. . . . What is taught in this unannounced, uncertified, unaccredited program of study for which no professors have any formal training is probably the most important part of the curriculum, certainly the college's reason for being. This part of the curriculum purports to be a sharing of the faith, and there are no performance standards established for students." (John K. Sheriff, "Mennonites, Free Methodists, And Liberal Education," *Faculty Dialogue*, no. 7 [Fall-Winter 1986-87], 92-93.)

[433] "The spiritually vital chapel service is the heartbeat of the Christian college. No other campus activity is more characteristic of the distinctive *raison d'etre* [*sic*] of a Christian liberal arts institution than the chapel service. Embodying and extending that mission, the chapel service fulfills spiritual, academic, and institutional purposes that otherwise are not likely to be fulfilled. . . . alumni surveys conducted by the college alumni office have indicated that graduates repeatedly mention chapel as having had a significant impact upon their lives." (Rex Rogers, assistant professor of political science, Cedarville College, "Chapel In The Christian College And University," *Faculty Dialogue*, no. 7 [Fall-Winter 1986-87], 13, 21.)

designated cool in evangelical intensity (for my measures of religious intensity, see chapter 12); colleges which regularly conduct chapel but do not require attendance are lukewarm in intensity; while colleges which both regularly conduct and require the attendance of all students are usually red-hot in evangelical ideological intensity (i.e., in the usual sporadic hot and cold fashion; but note that I have in mind here something quite different from the conventional sense of revival fervor, as we will see).

During his tenure at Seattle Pacific, David McKenna regarded chapel as the "integrating core . . . [of] . . . SPU as an evangelical university," claiming that one year alone of chapel attendance, without making further acquaintance with any of the academic or other extracurricular activities of the college would allow one to "know what SPU was all about."[434]

In many ways chapel recreates in dramatic, concentrated fashion the kinds of pressures, fissures, and antagonisms present among the larger national evangelical culture. Take, for instance, the perennial campaign of the faculty to enamor students of this notion of "the integration of faith and learning," to persuade them of the value of a reasoned view of Biblical faith—an effort, paradoxically, that merely serves to illustrate the pressures pulling the two phenomena apart, dynamics readily apparent in any quarter's chapel schedule of programs and speakers. Observe the contending logics at loggerheads: the Christian student will listen to a faculty member celebrate the virtues of free thinking and the cultivation of intellect, extol the maintenance of a salubrious inner balance among the elements of mind, body, and spirit—or hear a virtually identical exhortation delivered by a "distinguished" visiting Christian scholar—in chapel one week, and the following week will sit through an altogether different presentation, often from one of the seemingly ubiquitous itinerant chapel circuit evangelists, who will with equal urgency warn of the perils of unbridled reason and science, ridicule the inflated arrogance and intellectual flatulence of "humanists," and set off alarms over the threat of liberal theology—or, as we saw earlier, will endure a similar entreaty from one of his fellow students, who rises to caution the others to remain wary of "too much philosophy."

It is primarily here in chapel—although there are equally contentious moments in the classroom and elsewhere—that the conflict between an obscurantist national evangelical culture and the serious academic arm of evangelicalism, the Christian colleges, is most painfully exhumed and displayed.

---

[434] Chapel address, 9/24/80. It should be noted that the author attended not only one full year of live chapels, but reviewed the audio tapes from the previous ten years or so, nearly 360 total chapels. The review of these tapes (and the transcription of many of them) alone consumed nearly six months of my fieldwork time; they proved absolutely indispensable.

Although the evangelical student likely hails from a family and church climate in which these contending ideas are scarcely foreign, seldom has she experienced them in such concentrated, confusing doses, and in the kind of versions or variations that compel her to make sense of, and ultimately reconcile, what would appear to be contradictory claims.

A perch in the chapel balcony above the main student congregation affords the onlooker a particularly panoramic view of the ideological concerns of the college community. For example, this notion of a breach between the larger evangelical community and the faculty over the role and value of intellect hovers as a kind of inert, abstract generalization with antecedents strewn throughout American religious history until one observes it among real life students in dramatic, concrete situations. Consider: not once did I observe a student walk out of (or protest) an "ear-banging" sermon upon the dangers of intellect, "scientism," and "secular humanism," or an address casting aspersions on the motivations of "secular" political leaders, the Democratic Congress, and public university scholars, or one heaping scorn upon the materialism and commercialism of American society, the media, the entertainment industry, and other related institutions and phenomena. Even the chapels designed to chasten and humble the students for motivational or missionary purposes invariably drew uniform, respectful responses, although occasionally some cast a remorseful, suffocating pall over the audience.

But let me tell you about the chapels they did vacate—two, in particular, wherein students behaved in an almost eerie manner I didn't immediately understand but which appeared neither to break the decorum nor disrupt the proceedings for the other students. These chapel sessions featured two of the most dynamic and accomplished Christian academicians to appear on campus that year, Anthony Campolo and Bruce Lockerbie. Both presented several lectures during week-long visits to Seattle Pacific. Both delivered one lecture in particular that leaned pretty heavily on the anti-intellectual, fundamentalist element in the evangelical community, at times ridiculing the fearful, obscurantist strains that often infest more conservative denominations. Lockerbie waxed particularly caustic in his indictment of evangelicalism for "aesthetic squalor." And, most tellingly for our purposes, during both of these lectures students here and there in the audience, one by one—never more than one at a time—gathered their belongings, rose from their seats, and quietly walked out of the church. What is more, both men appeared completely unruffled by the silent flight of these students. Although the speakers paused occasionally to watch them go, neither said anything, as though their departure were inevitable, irreversible, as though the scene had played itself out a hundred times—again and again— in Christian colleges all across the land. No more than ten or fifteen students in all drifted away, but the chapel air was redolent with the meaning and significance of their actions. Even I, the uninitiated, could sense and literally *feel* the delivery of a powerful cultural message. Each departure struck a plangent, reverberating blow for an unimpeachable social and theological conservatism. One spied a shared condolence of meaning in the eyes of their fellow students, as these silent, devoted dream walkers passed by, on a "walk with God," the immobile hold-overs ushering them out with careful, artful sideways glances that betrayed no inclination or movement of the head, no tell-tale sign that the speaker had lost control of his audience. In clear violation of the spirit, if not the law, of the university's guidelines for student conduct, these (in all likelihood) most apologetic defenders of conservative doctrine and values—whom the more liberal students refer to as purveyors of the "legalistic" approach—walked away from a terrestrial challenge and obligation. And I, the innocent observer, both mesmerized and bewildered by this unfolding drama, the events of which appeared to raise no great consternation in the students to my right and left in the balcony (due possibly to boredom, I would later discover), seeking perspective and understanding, was immediately thrown back upon the Biblical imagery attending the *Parousia* (or Second Coming): how one by one the faithful would be lifted from their worldly positions and duties ("one would be taken, another left"), each in turn drawn away to a camp meeting in the sky with the returning Christ (brrrrrrrr!). In how many others was this imagery of the finals days evoked, I wondered?

As we saw earlier, one observes then a discernible tension within the academic and spiritual programs of the university which mirrors the larger evangelical cultural divorce between head and heart, between secular matters of the mind and Christian motions of the heart and spirit. The transition from classroom to chapel or cadre group and back again is seldom performed as fluently as are the deft theoretical movements linking faith with learning that one encounters in the writings and proclamations of the faculty and administration. The inherent strain of this passage from one realm to the other is often revealed with most telling effect in chapel.

During the course of a single year the Seattle Pacific student may very well sit through a variety of chapel presentations, among them: musical and dramatic productions that students will take on tour, faculty testimonials, impassioned representatives from most of the Christian overseas relief and missionary organizations, the reports of student teams which have been sent out to "minister" locally or overseas, Christian politicians (in the past, such luminaries as Senator Mark Hatfield, Indianapolis Mayor {and later} Senator

Richard Lugar, Washington Governor John Spellman, Seattle Mayor {and SPC alumnus} Wes Uhlman, among others), representatives from the Billy Graham Crusade (once Mrs. Graham herself), student testimonials, Christian athletes, Christian college presidents and scholars, Christian family counselors (often the bestselling Christian authors), Christian college circuit riders who have no particular skill or profession other than the leadership of their own self-named or -incorporated organizations (the ubiquitous Josh McDowell, for example), itinerant Christian folk and soft-rock groups, music and drama ensembles and student testimonial exchanges from other Christian colleges, itinerant Christian inspiration storytellers ("how I overcame tragedy or a handicap and lived victoriously"), sermons and lectures of SPU presidents, alumni programs, discussion panels, local churches' day with fair-like booths and signs, recent notorious converts (e.g., Chuck Colson, Eldridge Cleaver—offering evangelical versions of the Phil Donohue show), and a good deal more.

Although the average chapel fee of $40 (for a 1/2 hour presentation) scarcely represented a living wage, there exists a particularly large and experienced contingent of chapel circuit riders (in the Methodist tradition) who shuttle from one Christian college to another in search of receptive, responsive audiences, or in promotion of a particular cause or organization or publication, and who receive considerably more than the average remuneration.[435] "Christian Commitment Week" speakers, for example, earn a thousand dollars per four-day stint, a sum commensurate with the importance the university places upon the quarterly series. The larger fee no doubt also reflects the operation of a market in the bidding up of the costs for the most dynamic, charismatic speakers, as evangelical colleges throughout the nation compete for the best talent to initiate their semester and quarter academic sequences, nearly all of which begin and end at approximately the same time, a coincidence that tends to inflate the value of the most prized speakers. Accordingly, the larger Christian colleges with greater resources, such as Seattle Pacific, can afford to pay premium prices for their most important chapel occasions.

Christian Commitment Week

Christian Commitment Week is strategically located near the beginning of each quarter's series of chapels. In order to appreciate its significance we need first understand the often tedious and monotonous nature of prayer

---

[435] Much earlier on, in the late '70s, chapel speakers earned an average of $40 per appearance and $200 maximum. ("Who Sez and How Cum?" Trustees Chapel, 5/12/78.) What it increased to in later decades is anybody's guess. I never dared to ask. The other $1,000 four-day Christian Commitment Week fee I surmised from an overheard conversation.

and worship in the evangelical community.[436] The problem of sustaining the kind of personal and collective spiritual intensity which underlying ideological assumptions (of virtuosity) would seem to demand proves particularly burdensome in light of the considerable routinization of the Seattle Pacific spiritual program. Faith is as rigorously and systematically scheduled as academics.

Accordingly, students frequently lament the condition of their "prayer life." At times, their campus lives appear to unfold at a frenetic pace: they scurry from class to chapel to class to Bible study group and then to devotional, all convened or terminated with spiritual salutations and prayers; they take their meals with a prayer hurriedly uttered over a tray while seated among throngs of other souls in the campus cafeteria; they return from an evening of study at the library or from some other engagement and begin an anticipated night-long slumber with a few formulaic remarks to God, slipping into a familiar groove, often trite and unfeeling, they realize, and woefully short of ever approaching the splendor of God, the rambling prayers identical to or slight variations upon the ones uttered the night before, and the night before, and the night before.

Clearly, these routines cloud the mind and dampen the spirit in some. At times, a torpor overcomes even the most resilient believer. She settles into all too familiar habits, merely "going through the motions," as they so often say here on campus, mired in a spiritual depression or rut from which it proves difficult to lift oneself. It visits nearly everyone sometime or other, choosing its victims with apparent indiscrimination.[437] One senses and observes this ennui particularly in chapel, surrounded by students who attend three sessions a week (perhaps 1/3 of the student body), a weekly cadre

---

[436] "I grew up among Methodists. My father was a minister, and for eight years while I was still living at home he was a conference superintendent. . . . I spent at least two weeks of every summer for the first sixteen years of my life at camp meetings. I attended so many revivals and altar calls and heard so many testimonies that the world of spirits was as familiar to me as the world of matter. I attended a Free Methodist high school and two Free Methodist colleges." (Sheriff, "Mennonites, Free Methodists, And Liberal Education," 84.)

[437] Even SPU President David McKenna confessed such a period of spiritual torpor after his initial two years at Seattle Pacific: "This may be why the dominant drive of my spiritual life since last summer has been an attempt to capture a vision of wholeness for my church, my college, my home and my life. The drive had been developing for a long time because I felt that I was coming close to being *a victim of fragmentation* [i.e., succumbing to a secular malaise]. I sensed it in the church when younger and older members almost broke relationships over a social issue. I had felt it in the college as I absorbed the shock of being mistrusted as a president just at the time that I was trying to become more honest as a man. I saw it in our home as mobility scattered our family and we had little time for prayer and Bible study. I knew it personally because I had gone through several months of low-grade depression when the joy of my work had been almost lost." ("A Vision of Wholeness") {emphasis added}

group, Sunday church, and have various dormitory and other Bible study groups and obligations. The majority of students meet their obligations without complaint, some with considerable enthusiasm; the less devout, however, attend these gatherings only sporadically and without much enthusiasm, enduring the required religious regimen as an inevitable emotional tax one pays for attending an evangelical Christian college. Perhaps it is this latter group which always seemed to occupy the balcony of chapel, for a casual glance around the second tier during almost any chapel session revealed students poring over class assignments, writing letters, filling in crossword puzzles, reading romance novels, reviewing movie schedules, or even, on one occasion, studying a book on violin bowing techniques. During congregation-led prayer many simply stare inattentively off into space; the more brazen continue to read, write, or study right through prayer and attract surprisingly few disapproving glances for so doing.

Once required of all students, faculty, and staff (with designated "officers" to "monitor" assigned student seating in the early years),[438] chapel attendance remains mandatory in principle for all full-time students (although the church chapel can accommodate barely half or so of the entire student body), but is in fact sparsely attended by upperclassmen and faculty, having evolved mainly into the preserve of freshmen, sophomores, and a sprinkling of the more devout, spiritually-active juniors and seniors. Except for an occasional special dramatic or musical presentation or a particularly riveting speaker, I rarely saw those whom I recognized as faculty or administrators attend (and as late as 1976 there was a contractual obligation to attend).

Even the most devoted students experience moments of tedium and boredom, when the absolute redundancy of the occasion and the gestures, the apparent treading and re-treading of well-worn ground, becomes more than the patient soul can endure. As rich and fascinating as this grateful observer found chapel's tri-weekly pageant of evangelical community life, the flashes of illumination came few and far between the seemly endless monotony.[439]

---

[438] Yet elsewhere: Dean Simpson, a teacher at Northwest Nazarene College in Napa, Idaho, mentioned during a chapel appearance that chapel seating charts were still used at Northwest Nazarene to enforce attendance. ("A Psychology of Salvation," Chapel, 11/11/78.)

[439] On one particularly listless morning, the campus chaplain (who regularly conducts chapel), upon observing the leaden gait of the students, the flurries of idle chatter, and the prolonged mingling among acquaintances, an indication of minds on other matters, bereft of reverent purpose, followed an unusually lackluster rendition of a hymn with the acknowledgement and admonishment: "I know it's fun to come to chapel and see people and talk amongst yourselves, but people remember where you are and your purpose for being here. Please do not talk as you enter chapel; be in an attitude of worship. Please do not respond or sing like automatons. Put some feeling into it!" ("Give Thyself," Chapel, 3/24/80.)

Christian Commitment Week is designed to routinely rouse students from these troughs of emotional and spiritual slumber. Although the title implies an intention to produce conversions in that portion (@10%) of the student body not yet acknowledged Christians, such aims are actually of secondary importance. CCW is a spiritual exercise whose purpose and consequences truly transcend the actual content of the programs themselves. Often, diametrically-opposed conceptions of evangelicalism are advanced with apparently indistinguishable results.

For example, one quarter a Christian documentary filmmaker, Mel White[440], regaled and enthralled students day after day with wit and warnings, exhorting them to work to produce greater love and compassion within the Christian "body" at home before ever considering the call to "service" overseas. Consolidate your friendships, your lifelong treasures, among yourselves, rather than compiling missionary portfolios and devising elaborate plans. In his final chapel appearance of the week, he left students with a story of his first year of teaching at Fuller Theological Seminary (Pasadena, California). He told of a colleague who weaned him that first year from purely academic obsessions, extracting him from a "success-oriented" shell, the two forming an enduring friendship, only to later sit by helplessly as his newfound friend fell victim to cancer, and was gone from his life within a month. "You know, the people I pray for always die," he conceded, voice breaking, eyes brimming with tears. He urged students to lay aside the differences that kept them from estranged friends, for one day it may be too late. Cherish and love one another now, not in some anticipated future time. He raised an imaginary glass ("of milk"), toasting the most enduring and satisfying thing in life, the bond of "friendship." Every arm in the auditorium followed his up, and he held them all there, suspended in a magical moment. Towards the front, students sobbed, clinging to, comforting, and drawing strength from one another. A tear trickled down Mel White's cheek as he lowered the arm and every other arm dropped in unison.

---

[440] "*Whatever Happened to the Human Race?* was not Francis Schaefer's first foray into film. In 1976, he and Frank [his son], with the extensive assistance from ghostwriter Mel White [who had written Jerry Falwell's autobiography], had collaborated on another film/book combination titled *How Should We Live?* That effort not only laid important groundwork for acceptance of Schaeffer's views on abortion, but helped introduce evangelicals to secular humanism, an elastic concept that would eventually supersede communism as their prime ideological nemesis. . . . White. . . was called in to rescue the project when it seemed to fall apart. . . 'Francis was all over the place,' he observed, 'philosophically, ideologically, theologically. I never could follow him. I still can't.' " (William Martin, *With God on Our Side: The Rise of the Religious Right in America*, Broadway Books, 1996, 195-6.)

"I'm going back to a world I fear . . . [and instead of retiring to the Fireside Room in the Student Union Building for another talkback session] let's just stay here now and comfort one another, reach out to our friends, spend a few quiet moments before we return to the world out there."

Caught in a moment of genuine emotional rapture, students—male and female, male and male, female and female—drifted across the stage and clasped, expressing an abiding love and devotion for one another. A student body officer embraced the campus chaplain and spoke of his affection for him and how much he had meant to him over his four years at Seattle Pacific. An organ began to play, signaling the termination of chapel. The students lingered, milling about, savoring the occasion. Those moving up the aisles walked with their heads turned back to catch a final glimpse of the stage. Other students, flushed with emotion, pressed forward to embrace Mel White. A brief and apparently perfect moment of spiritual exhilaration had ended; the world loomed menacingly outside the doors of the church.

And yet during another lecture series, Anthony Campolo, chairman of the department of sociology at a small Christian college in Philadelphia, took a different approach, with little appreciable difference in response. In contrast to Mel White's lithe, mustached elegance, attended by subtle inflections of cadence and tone, Campolo's style, although equally polished, betrayed a more aggressive exuberance and a greater reliance upon the vernacular and ethnic borrowings for effect. Indeed he often thundered his message across to the students, as though reaching out to them in their seats and lifting and shaking them by their collective lapels. Blunt as a sledgehammer, Campolo let it be known in his three lectures on "How to be different from the world" that students simply *weren't different*. Wagging his finger, he fairly bristled: "Let's face it, you're not different from the world! Don't kid yourselves!" A true Christian ethos spurns the wasteful materialism and manipulative power relations (personal and social) of "secular" American society. Gripping both sides of the podium, he screamed: "American society doesn't need you! Doesn't want you!" And yet, *you* keep wanting what the world has! By the third lecture, word had spread and all seats were filled; students were crouching and standing in the hallways and the foyer; a campus video camera was whirring away in the balcony; several prominent faculty members sat here and there among the students. The audience roared its approval of Campolo's rapid-fire verbal jabs to the solar plexus of spiritual hypocrisy and pretense. He exhorted them to go to the relief of the poor and repressed multitudes in foreign fields unless they felt called to special work here at home. Concluding his final lecture, he issued a stirring call to personal and social independence, urging students to pledge: "I'm going to live free of the expectations of others!" He continued, bellowing: "I expect a revolutionary movement to spread to all of Seattle and to the world! Now how many of you are going to stand up right now and commit yourself to Jesus Christ? How many? Stand up!" Virtually everyone leaped to their feet, thunderously, followed by a roar of excitement. Only a few students remained seated, towards the right front someone told me later, and Campolo may have had these in mind when he said, "Those of you sitting down . . . yes, you . . . you ought to feel uncomfortable . . . don't you?" Here and there, students turned and surveyed around them for those still seated. Even I felt the pressure of this scrutiny as I madly scribbled away in my notebook, recording his every word, vaguely aware of the white-hot eyes raking the pews and aisles for spiritual malingerers. How ironic, this living free of the expectations of others!

Later in the spring, I asked a few students to reflect upon the Mel White and Anthony Campolo visits[441], curious whether or not they found their approaches somewhat confusing and difficult to reconcile. Most expressed disagreement with certain provocative assertions or aspects but found the overall message compelling. How can this be?

Indeed, if one overlooks for the moment the apparent diametrically opposed positions upon foreign (Campolo) and domestic (White) service, which understandably caused some students problems, what proved so powerful and invigorating in the respective messages, producing so uniformly visceral a response in the student body, was this familiar appeal to an in-group/out-group antagonism. After all was said and done, the nub of nearly everyone's outlook upon personal and social problems could be reduced to the simple belief that there remained a fundamental difference between them and us, between the "secular world" *out there* and a genuine Christian world *in here*. However different the emphases, the shared ideological animus proves overwhelming, capable of drawing theological liberals and conservatives together in common cause against an encroaching "secular" enemy.

Accordingly, the truly successful Christian Commitment Weeks are those which reinforce in the minds of students the irreconcilable divorce between a secular *them* and a Christian *us*, invoking and exercising the ideological emotions of separatism, and perhaps most importantly, exposing internal Christian community discrepancies between ideological appearances and concrete realities, laying bare for all to see any deliberate or inadvertent accommodation, fraternization, or collusion with the things and behavior of

---

[441] See Susan Harding's account of a very similar visit paid by "Franky" Schaeffer, son of Francis Schaeffer IV, to Jerry Falwell's Liberty Baptist College: "Schaeffer's sermon seemed to be on the tip of everyone's tongue as they debated what he said, what he meant, and whether he was right." (*The Book of Jerry Falwell*, 139.)

the secular world. A Mel White will, for example, spin a captivating vision of internal Christian community love which, he contends, "secular" men and women can scarcely begin to understand, let alone reproduce in their own conventional social relationships. Set in bold relief to White's enthralling and ennobling accounts of his virtuosic friendships, the average Christian student's own relationships must appear a trifle impoverished by comparison—too pedestrian and brittle to withstand close scrutiny or the social corrosion of real life. Perhaps he returns home at night to brood upon the condition of his own personal alliances, reluctantly acknowledging the truth of the Mel White indictment: they fall embarrassingly short of this vision of ideal Christian love. The longer he compares them the more apparent the discrepancy becomes. He has been remiss, has backslidden from higher sacred ground, allowing insidious "secular" thoughts, gestures, and practices to creep into his daily life, sullying his personal relationships. The Mel White model of exemplary Christian conduct stirs his imagination; there has been so much left unsaid and undone. And so in public he joins with his equally delinquent fellow students in raising an arm to toast these immaculate notions of Christian friendship and is overcome with emotion. The chapel concludes, but, swept up in a magical moment that may never return, he spies a friend across the hall and their eyes lock upon one another; he rushes to his or her side and they clasp, embrace, exchange expressions of apology and devotion, lamenting the artificial barriers that have kept them apart for so long. Luxuriating in the warmth and love of a fellow believer, perhaps he thinks he has discovered the "wholeness" everyone talks about but seldom achieves: a truly unblemished Christian love, at long last.

When bringing this discrepancy between promise and performance to the attention of students, Anthony Campolo is a good deal less delicate and sentimental. He savages the secular American lifestyle and its ethos of manic copious consumption. It is a vaguely familiar social internationalist screed: the starving multitudes out there and the fat and sassy, "worldly" American evangelicals in here. The Christian student has heard variations upon this theme before, but seldom delivered in such a ferocious, frame-rattling—and ultimately, reasoned—manner. To the mild discomfort of some students, Campolo reveals that he shaves with an old razor blade that receives continual re-sharpening and reuse and a plain bar of soap—not the expensive "perfumed" aerosol lathers; owns and wears but a single suit; and jointly owns and shares a lawnmower and other household items with his closest neighbors. Above and beyond the simple necessities of food, housing, and clothing, what more could the average believer require? Like a modern Diogenes wandering about clothed by a drafty barrel, he seeks the reduction of life to the barest essentials, all the while searching for a few (crudely) honest men (and women),[442] those encumbered by few worldly pretensions, a condition allowing for the true radiation outward of inner personalities, potentials, and commitments (and freeing up surplus monies for redistribution among third-world relief projects).

So ideologically positioned, Campolo excoriates the Moral Majority for its adoption of the tactics of the "secular" political world. The calculating exercise of power should garner no laurels within the Christian community. Indeed, Jesus pursued the aims of God in an altogether different manner, preaching that strength emerges from weakness and capitulation, from a turning of the cheek and the surrender of a cloak to others (the "inversion" principle). These are noble, exemplary behaviors. Unfortunately during unguarded moments the "secular" American understanding of power seeps not only into the public posture of the evangelical churches, leading to the formation of secular-like political action groups, but into individual friendships and marriages as well. They become riddled by extortion and a skewed, one-sided dependency, wherein the one who needs the other the least exercises domination over the one who needs the other the most. By contrast, Christ taught the *mutual submission* of friends and comrades to one another; He would surely rail against the intrusion of the alien ulterior motive of power into personal relationships, let alone into the public behavior of the evangelical community.

This portrait of a healthy, *whole*, Christ-like personal relationship set against a corresponding unflattering secular opposite evokes some anxiety in the young evangelical student, for he may tend to recognize himself more in the latter than the former. A moment's reflection persuades that he has indeed allowed these kinds of insidious power moods to creep into his own behavior. He thinks of friends and how rarely he has elevated their interests above his own or concentrated upon furthering the greatest good in the lives of intimate others. Some are even staggered by the truth of Campolo's indictment, as though he has rubbed their noses in the truly dirty secular nature of their behavior for the first time. For these believers it becomes a moment of startling clarity and revelation, Campolo capturing the essence of the students' predicaments, naming—assigning form, substance, and meaning to—inadequacies and anxieties that until then were only vaguely felt and rarely diagnosed and understood.

The realization of discrepancy and drift motivates the affected students to purge the offending thoughts and behavior and to draw together in the

---

[442] And Diogenes was *vulgar*, regarding the observance of such elementary social courtesies as relieving oneself privately instead of publicly as a compromise upon the transparency or honesty of a person, concealing the true inner self from public view. (See M. I. Finley, "Diogenes the Cynic," in *Aspects of Antiquity*, New York: Viking Press, 1969.)

wholeness and purity of a genuinely Christian alternative. It is this periodic brush with the profane secular American society, this momentary bearing of the full weight of this logic of invidious distinction, that invokes and reinforces in the minds of the students the vast gulf separating Christian and secular social worlds and produces these precious, often genuinely moving, moments of community solidarity. Through such highly affecting (and rewarding) experiences students develop and consolidate the emotional capabilities and categories—which I call *signals of difference*—that flow from the larger evangelical cultural assumption of an irreconcilable Christian / secular antagonism.

As we will see throughout the remainder of this study (particularly in Part Three), the final stage in the progression from receptive audience of novice students to polished participants and performers in the ritual celebration of the values and meanings of the community arrives with the special chapels staged and presented by the students themselves. These "student chapels" reveal callow students fumbling with the scope and terms of the logic of conspicuous invidious distinction, struggling to fill the shoes of the departed larger-than-life evangelists who have appeared before them, novices striving to achieve and demonstrate a spiritual precocity to their peers and mentors. It is in the student chapels that one observes the most telling public *significance* of these ideological pressures upon the personalities and behaviors of young evangelical students.

Cadre Groups

The cadre group is a smaller, more intimate version of chapel designed for rigorous Bible study and confidential student discussions. Usually a professor, administrator, staff member, or even a student organizes and leads these sessions, but occasionally an alumnus will venture back onto campus to conduct one as well. It is in the distribution of students among the various cadre groups that the more formal ideological veneer of a unified community of faith, composed of interchangeable, spiritually indistinguishable parts, disintegrates into a mélange of academic, social, and activity specializations and interests, some groups developing over time into discernable cliques. This becomes all too apparent in the mere enumeration of the groups from which the student could theoretically choose: *Student Ministry Coordinators, Single Parents, Non-Traditional College Students, Prayer and Share, John (for Sociology Majors), Inter-Varsity Discipleship Training, Faith-Use It or Lose It, Organ* [donor's?] *Cadre, Women's Basketball Team, Wind Ensemble, Developing a Biblical Worldview, Running Fellowship, Russian Cadre, Women Track Athletes, Catholic/Protestant Dialogue, World Religions, Ephesians, Bread for the World, Problems Facing Today's Family by*

Dobson, Faith in a Scientific Age, Contemporary Christian Gospel Music, Chancil Players [drama], *Classical Guitar Music, Cheerleader Cadre, Basketball Players, C.S. Lewis, Hawaiian Students, Coping with Stress,* and *French Cadre,* among other more generic "prayer and share" cells. These might strike the reader as an odd assortment of exceedingly specialized topics given all the disparaging remarks from evangelical academicians upon mindless secular "pluralism" or "multiculturalism."

In the curricular scheme of things, students may substitute one weekly cadre group for one weekly chapel appearance, but it is generally the case that the more devout students attend cadre voluntarily, not merely to relieve themselves of a chapel requirement. Although some groups would appear to offer idle entertainment and relaxation (with prayer before and after), many do in fact promote serious discussions and encounters, and some even seek to advance social and political causes. Attendance can vary anywhere from three or four students to almost thirty in the more popular cells. Throughout the remainder of this study I will draw upon observations gathered from among these groups and many other less formal campus get-togethers.

Consider in closing one dimension of these claims of academic and spiritual transcendence: to what ultimate effect or significance? What sort of demonstrable impact do these programs have upon the *actual* behavior of the evangelical student? We have heard the claims of a greater academic integrity and honesty from evangelical faculty partisans. An equally strident assumption concerns the student bodies of these institutions: they demonstrate a greater integrity and honesty than any comparable secular or public university student population. Although few evangelical college community members would make such a brazen claim in a mixed public setting, internally the assumption is merely taken for granted. Let us turn then to an examination of how and to what extent these ideas are implemented in the daily lives of students.

PART FOUR

SOCIETY

CHAPTER 9

THE A-SOCIAL COMMUNITY

O ur story of everyday life in this community begins with the simple physical geography of the Seattle Pacific campus. Now, by geography I have in mind not so much the actual location of the school within its surrounding urban envelope as a more intangible and fluid notion of social and cultural boundaries, demarcations of the mind that inevitably project themselves out into the urban landscape, depositing topographical codes and clues that with the appropriate detection and deciphering can tell us as much, if not more, about the interiors of persons than about the actual lay of the land itself.

The innocent observer, wandering onto the Seattle Pacific campus for the first time, will likely be struck by the perfectly ordinary collegiate feeling of the grounds and buildings and their apparent successful integration into the surrounding commercial and residential neighborhood. The initial impression is one of easy pedestrian movement from outside to inside, the mere spatial configuration or posture of the buildings and grounds arousing no daunting feeling of withdrawal or insulation from the immediate business and residential area, no cloistering of people or buildings behind some impermeable barrier, no decompression zone through which the visitor must pass to complete the transition from a discernibly foreign outside to the more familiar inside of a campus haven.

Imagine our surprise then at a rather more ambivalent survey of the physical landscape, this one by Professor Baron, whom we encountered earlier, a geographer and chairman of the School of Social and Behavioral Sciences, who evinces an altogether different setting for a campus audience,[443] reading into the apparent disheveled sprawl of the grounds and the position and posture of the buildings an ulterior institutional motive, that of turning an uninviting "backside" to the larger urban society, producing a "barricade effect." Through the din and dim of visual clutter and blight, he discerns clear lines of intentional cleavage, of insult given and umbrage taken. Indeed of all the campus approaches, only the northeast entrance meets his approval: it "shows Seattle Pacific for what I think it is, and should be . . . an urban campus . . . *connected to the city* . . . *in but not of the city*." With the

---

[443] "The Campus Fringe" (cassette & slides), The Urban Challenge Series, Part 1, April 1978. {Archives}

invocation of the Biblical allusion, to live as though "in but not of the world,"[444] the professor effects a kind of uneasy compromise between the competing urges of inclusion and exclusion, of assimilation and separation. For in his presentation the professor surveys the landscape and architecture of a campus more successfully integrated into the surrounding urban community than most colleges and yet envisions geographic division and reproach, projecting all sorts of cultural antagonisms onto the innocent lay of the land and the buildings thereon. Allowing his geographic imagination to run wild, the professor discovers all sorts of veiled meanings in mere physical direction and form, evoking from virtually a random arrangement of grounds and buildings the imagery of medieval moats and cloisters, discerning among inanimate structures the sulking moods of withdrawal and incivility, as though the campus buildings, pouting victims of a secular urban affront, have drawn up their skirts and swung around their *derriéres* to the city in some awesome display of the collective Seattle Pacific buttocks, the college "mooning" the city, as it were.

Appreciate then the irony of Professor Baron's yearning for an institutional mood of rapprochement with the surrounding neighborhood and the secular city beyond foundering upon the rocks of these *almost subliminal concessions to the power of the evangelical logic of community cultural divorce.*[445] He strains to locate signs of invitation amidst the architectural design and landscaping of the campus but reluctantly concedes a geography of antagonism and demarcation, imagining physical barriers to social inclusion and cooperation where there are none. Against his better judgment, the professor imbues the physical structures and lay of the land of his campus with the fractious terms and conditions of the evangelical state of mind, with the meanings of contention and belligerence, of social and cultural apartheid. However much he may long for a kind of cultural truce with the secular world outside there remain irreconcilable differences that color even his perception of the arrangement of simple inanimate physical space and structures. However

---

[444] Myron S. Augsburger, President of Eastern Mennonite College, speaks of the "community of Christ" as the "new people," the "new humanity." He asks that we reflect upon Christ's "High-priestly prayer . . . they are not of the world even as I am not of the world. . . . as the new humanity, we are in the world but not of the world . . . a new people of God." ("Education and Evangelism For This One World," a paper delivered at the International Congress on World Evangelism, Lausanne, Switzerland, 1974. Reprinted in *Universitas,* January 1975.)

[445] Others concur with the more general point here: "Fellowship with each other in the church is more congenial than service in an apathetic and even hostile environment outside. Of course we make occasional evangelistic raids into *enemy territory* (that is our evangelical specialty); but then we withdraw again, across the moat, into our Christian castle . . . pull up the drawbridge, and even close our ears to the pleas of those who batter on the gate." (John R. W. Stott, "Involvement: Is It Our Concern?" *Faculty Dialogue,* no. 4 [Fall 1985], 21.)

unwitting or involuntary, he serves as a beacon or transmitter of a distinctive cultural vision.

To the nature and form of that social vision I now turn.

The Natural Platonic Christian Community

Upon the 85th birthday of Seattle Pacific in 1976, President David McKenna delivered a celebration address, in which he advanced that the college community represented something more than just another academic institution.

> This community has been guided by the scriptures. In fact, because they continue to provide guidance for our individual and institutional lives, they hold an important place in our curriculum. . . . [We live in] *a personalized community that has not changed*. . . . I can say that we are closer to a Biblical community on our campus today than at any other time in my experience. . . . [446]

And what are the distinguishing features of this seminal, unchanging, self-renewing, Biblical academic community?

Affinities vs. Interests

Members of Christian communities are drawn and held together by common *affinities*; secular men and women, by contrast, come together for altogether different reasons, assembling in institutions and cities allowing—nay encouraging—the naked, unbridled pursuit of individual *interests*. In the Christian community a common faith generates a natural gravity of consensus, producing a unity of like-minded and -motivated individuals for whom the community becomes a self-transcending end in itself, a precursor or terrestrial simulation of the much anticipated post-millennial kingdom of God.[447] In the secular city the urban order serves merely to establish and maintain a fragile balance among often antagonistic individuals, providing the vehicle or arena in which citizens pursue and realize individual aspirations to the exclusion of any larger public interest.

---

[446] "Eighty-Five and Doing Well," *SPC Bulletin*, 1976-78. {Archives} {emphasis added}

[447] As we will see, this new Christian community is constituted on a different basis from earlier "Social Gospel" visions: "But the kingdom of God is not Christianized society. It has to be 'received,' 'entered,' or 'inherited' . . . Those who do receive it like a child, however, find themselves members of the *new community* of the Messiah, which is called to exhibit the ideals of his rule in the world and so to present the world with an *alternative social reality*. . . . a *radically new and different social organization*, whose values and standards challenged those of the old and fallen community. . . . This social challenge of the gospel of the kingdom is quite different from the 'social gospel.' " (John R. W. Stott, "Involvement. . . . 14, 18.) {emphases added}

The naked contrast between the two led David McKenna to the conclusion that the Christian college community—Seattle Pacific in particular—possesses "the inherent qualities of a natural community," among them: "face to face interpersonal relationships, sufficient resources to meet basic physical and social needs, and common values and common goals." Drawing strength from this unadulterated condition, the Christian college community can then "present a solid front to the outside world," that social behemoth riddled with the by now familiar problems of fragmentation, disorientation, and, above all, urbanity. Indeed in the McKenna cultural diagnosis the developmental pathologies of secularization and urbanization trace parallel tracks of infection and affliction, the one virtually indistinguishable from the other. The "urban revolution" reaches a culminating nadir with the "breakdown of natural communities in the burgeoning city . . . [spawning] the facelessness of almost complete anonymity . . . the serious loss of social and spiritual supports . . . [and] the disintegration of common values and goals." The world-weary Christian withdraws from the tumultuous and artificial secular urban terrain into a primordial community of reinvigorating integrity and wholeness. Inside, an "unusual sense of oneness" prevails, melding the disparate backgrounds and personalities of comrades into a unified body of protection against a "hostile world."[448]

Persons vs. Roles

In the natural Christian community what the outsider may tend to think of as ordinary social behavior—the presentation of a public "self" in daily social situations which in all likelihood diverges from true inner feeling or personality—becomes an anomalous phenomenon, a form of interpersonal vulgarization and deception. Secular society differentiates individuals according to the roles they assume and perform, defining and identifying members by their approximate positions in an ordered hierarchy of positions. Individuals adhere to rules of conduct appropriate to their roles or positions in

---

[448] McKenna, "A Community of Learners." (undated typescript, prob. @ 1970) {Archives} Also: "The principle on-campus task of Christian higher education is to develop *communities of love. . . . Sound communities grow from the collective quest for righteousness. . . .* That there will always be slippage—errors, culpability, ungodliness—requires both just rules and redemptive processes. . . . Ray Anderson, Fuller Theological Seminary, puts the finger on individualism as the major anti-Christian social value that has *invaded* North American Christianity. Redemption, as once fulfilled and always fulfilling process, *brings all Christians into peer relationship* [equality of faith] and *provides the continuing basis for sound community. . . .*

The secular society today knows little about what such communities are like." (Ted Ward, "Faith, Love, Hope—The Remaining Mission of Christian Higher Education," *Faculty Dialogue*, no. 1 [Fall 1984], 4.) {emphases added}

corporate ladders of social order and significance. So ingrained are these formulas of social fabrication and performance that they tend to carry over into informal personal relationships, tarnishing these as well. As the corrosion of secular social hierarchism and fragmentation spreads, an ever-expanding circle of persons experience within themselves a widening distance between inner character and external behavior; they become increasingly *un-whole*. The larger social consequence of all these accumulating individual experiences of personal fragmentation is a growing divorce between symbolic appearances (the rhetoric of public relations) and inner collective realities (the feelings and motives of citizens). A veneer of urban sophistication and social ease conceals more fundamental subterranean intentions. Persons manipulate one another in pursuit of narrow objectives, oblivious to the longer-term social consequences of their actions; motives and intentions become suspect. Virtually no expression of emotion, no gesture or behavior, can be taken at face value. Trust and community evaporate.

Genuine Christian community, by contrast, cultivates and harbors individuals whose external countenance and behavior are directly wedded to internal personality. Moods and moves reveal the person within—whole and indivisible—and only rarely conceal them. Come hither, the evangelical apologist beckons, to a community whose members routinely mend the torn fabric of modern secular personality and society. For David McKenna, the difference between Christian community and secular society is clear and unmistakable:

> Their [Christian individuals'] mutual relationship is *highly personalized* because the Christian community is determined by *character* [of persons] rather than *characteristics* [of roles]. . . . [Christians are motivated by] *purpose* rather than *prestige*. . . . In this environment, *concept* [symbolic appearances] and *community* [social reality] are *merged into one*.[449]

---

[449] McKenna, "A Community of Learners." {emphasis added}

Also: ". . . . when a man is in Christ, he is a new creature. It is a change of heart, a deep transformation of our inner being that is required; but the wonder is that it also, in many lives, is actually demonstrated. Far from being a change which begins and ends with a man's own *personal character, this change is one which comes in the entire social order*." (D. Elton Trueblood, "A Personal Faith," *Faculty Dialogue*, no. 1 [Fall 1984], 31.) {emphasis added}

— ". . . . people when they get converted do begin *to alter the social structure*." (Tony Campolo, "New Ways of Talking About God," Chapel, 5/16/83.)

—". . . . the Christian college's distinctive [*sic*] is a fellowship of worshippers *where each is* [a] *brother and role identifications dissipate*. . . . The Christian community of confession, however, finds its goals and values *outside the situation*. . . ." (Edward Kuhlman {Messiah College—Education}, "Education for Wholeness: A Christian Alternative," a paper delivered at the Faith/Learning Institute, North Park College, Chicago, August 14-25, 1972.) {emphases added}

In a pluralistic society, the impersonalism of secondary associations tends to take over the face-to-face personality of the closed community. People communicate through specialized *roles* rather than as *persons*. . . . The open [secular] society lacks the cohesive core of the closed [Christian] society. [450]

Transparency vs. Duplicity

When all is said and done, when all the variations upon themes and the invidious comparisons with secular individuals and society have been drawn and taken into account, the goal of evangelical Christian personality development and maturation ultimately reduces to this idea of personal wholeness, to the melding of a unique God-given personality with behavior—or, as I will characterize it throughout the remainder of this study—to the aspiration and achievement of *transparency*.[451] Christian *wholeness* assumes transparency, or clarity of motive and conduct. Personal and community redemption assume and exude evidence of both. Accordingly, the ultimate goal of community development becomes then the uniform evocation and maintenance of *social transparency*. The transparent community is the ultimate expression of Christian wholeness.

In the words of one Christian college academician:

---

[450] David McKenna, "Community in the Christian College," undated typescript, probably @ 1970. {Archives} {emphasis added}

[451] For David McKenna the behavior and vehicle of an extraordinary Washington D. C. cab driver exemplified these principles. Upon getting into "the cleanest, neatest cab in the world" and hearing about his pride in his work and his cab, McKenna's "spirits being lifted by his simple dignity. . . . *The next question jumped right out of me. 'You have to be a Christian!'* I said. 'I wouldn't be anything else,' he confirmed. . . . he was a whole person, oozing dignity. . . . have you put yourself as a person in relationship to the other members of the body of Christ *so that even the stranger you meet in a revolving door may spot the difference?* " (David McKenna, "Education For Exiles," a commencement address delivered at Houghton College, reprinted in *The Wesleyan Advocate*, 5 August 1974.) {emphases added}

—J. Allen Peterson, addressing chapel on proper Christian relationships and notions of actions and reactions, contends that in "My spontaneous reaction [in any such genuine relationship] . . . *you would immediately see the kind of person I am.*" ("A Marriage Affair," Chapel, 10/17/77.)

—This notion of transparency also appears in very early Puritan imagery, as for example in the much misunderstood John Winthrop trope, "a city upon a hill." The sermon in which it is found, "A Model of Christian Charity," urges all sorts of communal, non-market feelings and behaviors upon the Pilgrims and employs the "city upon the hill" as a symbol of the *clarity* of the eventual divine judgment of their efforts. As Paul D. Erickson writes: "Christ said that *'a city that is set upon a hill cannot be hid.'* " ("Winthrop v. Reagan: The real 'city on a hill,' " *New Republic*, 20 October 1986, 15.) {emphases added}. More recently, Abram Engen takes a more conventional tack: ". . . . Catholics and Protestants believed that Jesus's 'city on a hill' referred to the true church, the communion of saints and the gathering of the godly in particular places (Protestants) or as the one universal institution (Catholics) . . . . for Catholics [in particular] Matthew 5:14 became one of the strongest bludgeons in their arsenal. . . ." (Engen, *City on a Hill* . . . , op cit., 49.)

There is a oneness, a wholeness involved in being a Christian. The believer in Jesus is an authentic person. . . . The Christian teacher is not a teacher plus being a Christian[;] he is a Christian teacher. There is an interrelationship here with regard to the unity of the person. . . . The integrity of his faith permeates his life in a total sense. . . . [He becomes] a whole man in Christ. . . . He [the Christian] *cannot switch Christ on and off depending on the demands a situation places on him or the environment in which he finds himself functioning because Christ is his life.* . . . [This ensures an] *open and honest atmosphere . . . natural because a Christian is not playing charades* but is a person who has had a meaningful encounter with God.[452]

The pursuit of wholeness and transparency can often take some precarious and dramatic turns, as was the case with Wanda, who reflected back upon a particularly compelling student senate meeting we had both attended (to be explored more fully in a later chapter):

I was shaking. . . . It was the first time I've ever been honest in a public situation on this campus. It was probably at that time, like that instance I shared about [the anxiety which prevented her from approaching some of her best friends about forming a prayer-and-share group], the discipleship group that I was hoping to become involved in, I was, really—my boyfriend and some close friends were just counseling me that, as risky as it is, *we are nothing as Christians if we are not transparent* and so I had a definite goal at that moment in my life too that—so help me—I was going to quit lying. . . . I really wanted to make some close friends and [wanted] for people to get beyond the stereotype of me.[453]

Sometime in the fall of 1970, having accumulated two years experience in the office of President, David McKenna delivered a major three-part convocation address to the Seattle Pacific community, seeking in his "A Vision of Wholeness" declaration to draw together the various loose strands of evangelical academic thought into a coherent enunciation of the principles guiding his administration. In it, he pays particular attention to the personal and community consequences of this divorce between inner personality and outer behavior:

We have had a lifetime of practice for the role of being phonies and, whether it is the institution of the corporation or the commune, everything we do tends to reinforce our falseness. *The vision of wholeness, however, projects a climate that is dangerous for phonies.* In fact, I have to admit that the closer I get to a commitment in which I seek to demonstrate the meaning of Christ in ultimate human concerns, the phonier I feel. . . .

---

[452] Richard Osberg {Huntington College—Education}, "The Christian Teacher—An Authentic Person," a paper delivered at the Faith/Learning Institute, Wheaton College, August 13-24, 1973. {emphases added}

[453] (*SSI* interviews, May 2003)

. . . . we are all "niggers" if the color of our skin, the title of our position, the level of our class, the gender of our sex, or the doctrine of our denomination locks us into a system where we are accepted or rejected because of our *roles* rather than our *persons*. "Authenticity" is honesty, openness and acceptance. But it is more than that. *It is the spirit and the power of Jesus Christ at work in human flesh.* . . . Without the incarnation in authentic persons, the word of a vision of wholeness will be abortive and even blasphemous. But with *a community of people who are peeling off the phony layers of their lives and rebuilding with honesty and love,* a vision of wholeness for Seattle Pacific College will become a continuing demonstration of the meaning of Jesus Christ for all who watch us.[454]

It is only within the confines of the "closed" Christian community that the monopolized virtues of Christian wholeness and authenticity may possibly come to fruition, therein approximating their most heightened human expression.

With a drive to be authentic persons, they are *free to be themselves, real* in the presence of other people, and ready to see the potential for wholeness in every man. . . . It is in Him that *we refuse to exploit another person for our own gratification.* It is in Him that *we refuse to force people into our molds.* . . . *Wholeness is a quality of the soul* . . . that can only be learned . . . in the adventurous presence of *other real persons.*[455]

---

[454] McKenna, "A Vision of Wholeness," three-part Convocation Address, 9/28-30/70. {Archives} {emphases added}
—And yet anyone who would hold Jesus up as a paragon of personal/public wholeness and transparency must deal with the accounts of his manner of public instruction and preaching: the delivering of lessons in parables that none in the large crowds could understand, confusing even his own disciples, to whom he revealed genuine meanings in private, away from the throngs. Throughout the gospels we observe a Jesus who is often oblique and opaque, apparently concealing his feelings and ultimate aims from even his closest and dearest associates. Recall that in the most crucial of public occasions, the audience before Pilate, when asked to explain himself, he remained largely silent, answering interrogatives with one or two simple affirmatives.
—In the words of Arthur Holmes: "Sin, thirdly, is a pervasive condition of the inner life as well as the outer. . . . The phenomenon of self-deception, of role-playing and wearing masks, is well known to psychologists, sociologists, and philosophers. . . . God, we are told, desires truth in the inward parts. . . . *if sin extends to every human relationship, grace can, too.* Reconciliation to God is followed by reconciliation to other persons in a life of love. *Barriers come down—racial barriers (neither Jew nor Greek), sexual prejudice (neither male nor female), socioeconomic aloofness (neither slave nor freeman)—all are united in Christ.* The new life in Christ, like sin, has *societal dimensions* in the kingdom he preached. . . . [Christian liberty] It renews the person, restores relationships, and *gives a present taste of what the kingdom of God was at the creation intended to be.* . . ." (Holmes, *Contours* . . . , 123-25.) {emphases added}
[455] McKenna, "A Vision of Wholeness." {emphases added}

Wholeness & Brokenness (Modern Original Sin)

Reflect for a moment upon the relationship between wholeness and original sin. Traditional notions have undergone some altogether creative evangelical theological revisions over the years. In the introductory chapters I portrayed the particularly amnesiac Free Methodist conception of "entire sanctification" or "holiness" (a view holding forth the possibility of a believer through grace and sustained effort so purifying himself as to approach Christ-like perfection) as an attempt to overcome the spiritual and social gravity of lapsarianism and put some distance between the evangelical community and the great unwashed pagan masses. These earlier promulgations[456] parallel a modern evangelical variant.

Observe, however, that the contemporary evangelical academician is uncomfortable with both lapsarianism and this earlier theological elixir of entire sanctification. He understandably shrinks from the unflattering vulgarity and determinism of the Calvinist variant, a theodicy fashioning a pit of human depravity so imponderably deep that no one—not even the virtuoso—could possibly orchestrate a theological escape. And although he (better yet, the logic) also requires some sort of transcendence of the universal human condition, the escape clause offered by entire sanctification often strikes him as too nakedly strident and self-righteous, too undisguised, jeopardizing missionary appeals to unbelievers—and, for some, altogether contrary to an equally powerful competing logic of Christian egalitarianism and humility.

Hoary notions of total human depravity prove then a bit too constraining and rigid for the more limber evangelical moral imagination, one straining under the relentless ideological pressure to widen the gulf between Christian and secular society. After all, one cannot very well embrace and promote a conception of universal human depravity and then turn right around and locate within the terms of that absolute iniquity features (or escape clauses) serving to distinguish believers from even more degenerate pagans.

Accordingly, if universal depravity proves too leveling *and* unpalatable a notion then the evangelical academician necessarily falls back upon a more defensible modern position, softening the harsh tone of original sin with a rather more mellow modern timbre, transposing it into the more amenable key or form of a break with, or separation from, the mind, sentiments, and intentions of God. In other words, a human descent into fragmentation and division—into un-wholeness. And so in a deft, intriguing revision of Genesis,

---

[456] These notions of perfectionism extended far beyond Free Methodism. Perhaps the most notable instance was the somewhat ironic Oneida community of John Humphrey Noyes. (See Marty, *Pilgrims.* . . . 192-96.)

Adam and Eve, the original *whole* persons, are found guilty of disobedience, thereby divorcing themselves from the protection and nurture of God the father and sending the species careening down the path of personal and social brokenness and ruin. How much more appealing (and manageable) this idea of the ministrations of the evangelical academic community producing not the rejuvenation of a Christ-like holiness or sinlessness in students, but rather a more plausible and marketable alternative: *the restoration of personal wholeness.* One almost detects an audible sigh of relief escaping from evangelical academicians everywhere, as though an unreasonable burden has been lifted from their shoulders. Indeed, the prospects for healing the split personality of modern man (this chronic imbalance of mind, body, and spirit) are a good deal more promising than any imagined remission of the damage wrought by Adam and Eve. And so whereas some charismatic ancestors sought invidious social distinction and elevation (in addition to the obvious personal edifications) through the extreme vehicle of entire sanctification, the contemporary evangelical academician pursues more modest objectives, dangling before his young charges the more amenable modern distinction of wholeness. And so with redemption comes a re-unification of sorts, a re-assembling of the fragments of a fallen modern personality and society.

Variations Upon a Theme

Have these ideas made their appearance in the written work of campus academicians? Consider three examples.

A "Genuine" Polity

Political science professor Bruce McKeown, responding to David McKenna's invitation to reflect upon campus discussions on the formal revision of the curriculum and an institutional name change—to "university"—expressed some disappointment with the proceedings in "Scholarship, Servanthood and the Symbols of Community," a brief paper published by the school's in-house journal.[457] Internecine departmental sparring and occasionally rancorous, divisive exchanges bothered him. Among the lessons emerging from these unanticipated experiences was the deflating realization and concession that even among the Christian faculty of a Christian college one could observe "behavior similar to national interest group politics." Equally disappointing was the undistinguished nature of the discussions themselves, and the eventual curriculum: a mere replication of those

---

[457] *Seattle Pacific University Review*, Spring 1980.

emerging on other college campuses, where similar general education schemes were under consideration. Indeed given the rhetorical flourishes accompanying the announcement from the administration, some among the faculty were understandably poised to embark upon a visionary program that might finally set Seattle Pacific apart from her secular counterparts. Yet upon reflection he concluded that "Unless we extend beyond 'mere general education' and develop a *genuine public*, then what we have is just another effort at curriculum revision which is a necessary but insufficient condition for realizing the scholar-servant model." {emphasis added} What the genuine Christian scholar-servant ought to demand from himself and his comrades in an authentic "born-again community" is something occupying an altogether higher plane of aspiration. Seattle Pacific academicians should, first and foremost, render themselves

> . . . . able and obligated, as mandated by the standards of scholarship and serv-anthood, to develop a community at Seattle Pacific University distinguished by the creation of *a genuine public and a public philosophy unique in the contemporary setting*— unique because this community could result in radically transforming Seattle Pacific to enacting a vision of scholarship and service in marked contrast to other groups [including the Moral Majority] characterized by and operating according to the politics of *group interest, private regardedness,* and *elite dominance.* {emphases added}

A rather more authentic revision would require

> . . . . in light of the Christian scholar-servant model, that we "redo" Seattle Pacific in accordance with the ideals of community *far different from secular effort characterized by self-interest.* I am convinced that the integration we are seeking, if it can be achieved at all, will begin at a place such as Seattle Pacific. We have everything in our favor: the symbols, the model, the personal involvements and commitments, and a foundation of faith. Our purpose is to understand and change the world. Let's go on with the task. {emphasis added}

City versus Community

Religion professor Frank Spina aired complementary views in his "Can the City Be a Community? The Interaction Between Politics and Religion."[458] He begins with a traditional sociological notion, namely that small communities and large cities are as different as night and day, the *gemeinschaft – gesellschaft* distinction. Communities emerge from natural affinities, from

---

[458] Originally produced for the Seattle Project Task Force in the spring of 1977 and later published in a revised version in the *Seattle Pacific University Review,* Spring 1979.

consensus, whereas cities arise from the exercise of sheer power, functioning as "social control systems" to broker the competing interests of individual citizens. No surprise then that the modern city violates God's a-political intentions; indeed the Old Testament readily documents

> .... the conviction that politics, viewed as the epitome of *human* sovereignty, is a deviation from God's intention for ordering human society—as a community. Therefore, a, if not the, main theme of the Biblical tradition is the conflict between organizing human society as a social control system or as a community. {emphasis added}

Members of God's intended natural villages accordingly develop *inner* compulsions to adhere to community norms, to treat one another with honesty and fairness, compliance requiring no external coercion. Order emerges quite naturally out of mutual affection and respect, from individually-embraced community aspirations. And since these shared values have for their source an immutable, eternal God, the community proves immune to the ravages of time, to the kind of social, political, and economic erosion and decay that inevitably undermines the foundations of the secular cities of the world.

> .... true security is possible only in the context of the community. The same goes for diversity. This is why membership in the community is not precluded by a priori identifying characteristics, such as nationality, ethnic make-up, geography or status. The community is therefore *incidentally diverse, but essentially unified.* Members of the community are *committed to everything that is good about humanness in life* [monopolyism]. Because the community is not based on political power, which is inevitably ephemeral, and because it is rooted in that which transcends both politics and history, *it is by nature a perpetual social organization—it is "eternal."*
> .... the community's commitment of values knows no limits, for the supreme value is the affirmative response to God and His graciousness [conversion], which includes a commitment to the welfare of the other members of the community. . . . Instead [of a secular survival ethic], the values of love, concern, peace and justice are ultimate, for they are based on the character of the deity who called the community into existence in the first instance and who sustains it with His presence and guidance. Such values are ultimate even to the extent that death is not resisted to manifest them.

The ideal Christian community transcends preconditions normally associated with human social groups and societies; genuine community springs from supra-cultural sources—"covenant produces social organization"—operating above and beyond the mundane principles and limitations of fallen human societies. Unhindered by routine social processes, the Christian community assumes and exhibits a fundamentally *a-social* nature. Socially transcendent "rules of God" supplant pedestrian "rules of man." The gravity and bond of redemption draw transformed Christian men and women together into anointed communities unlike the world has ever known.

And yet how to explain away any vestigial community-like values and sentiments in the *secular* city? Mere fawning appearances: the reified "city" simulates these things in order to evince greater belief in the legitimacy of the social order. The urban polis foists inauthentic presentations of belief (the promulgations of "civil religion," for example) upon an unwary public and thereby enhances the persuasion of its edicts. Furthermore, and ironically, functional benefits may accrue from this deception. Things work better, performance improves: " . . . the city functions best when it simulates or approximates the community, even though we steadfastly maintain that the city can never do more than simulate or approximate." Yet however convincing these affectations of belief, the city can never move beyond simulation to generate genuine Christian community order, as *"full appreciation* requires an understanding of and commitment to the deity who revealed Himself through Israel and Christ. *Others 'see through a glass darkly' (and, to a lesser extent perhaps, so do Christians).*"[459]

In sum, Professor Spina produces a model Christian community unburdened by the accumulated weight of ordinary human social conventions and processes. What emerges is a kind of *sui generis* phenomenon *par excellence:* the near perfectly transparent and sentimentally-unified community teeming with equally transparent and like-value-minded individuals; a community with no developmental history to speak of and bearing an apparent immunity to the mundane processes and phenomena normally associated with social maturation, aging, and decay.

The Logic of Manners

English professor Joyce Erickson, whom we met earlier ("Christian Basic Skills," chapter 6), views the novels of Jane Austen through the same transforming interpretive lens.[460] The larger institutional point?: " . . . the vision of the moral life which is projected in her novels has relevance to the vision of the moral life which should be projected in our Christian liberal arts curriculum."

What sort of moral order? To Erickson's way of thinking moral vision concerns mostly "the relation between, and integration of, private and public morality." In the Austen novels "open and easy manners" denote the more

---

[459] {emphases added} Paul, by contrast, wrote that *everyone* sees through a glass darkly, Christians included, to no "lesser extent." I Corinthians 13:12.

[460] Weter Faculty Award Lecture: "Jane Austen's Novel of Manners and the Liberal Arts in 1979—What Common Ground?"

public "visible" side of personal relationships, although they may also at the very same time illuminate some of the deeper, more fundamental sources of behavior, those emanating from inner character—"the invisible . . . motives which animate individual behavior." The apparent presence or absence of manners may reflect a similar presence or absence of moral character; *deficient external manners signify deficient internal character*. And as we might have anticipated, the *good* character underlying good manners stems from an altogether different source from the *bad* character responsible for egregious behavior.

The distinction between "conduct" and "manners" is instructive: the latter represents the "outward manifestations of the well-mannered but conduct implies both outward and inward." In *Mansfield Park*, for example, evaluative words fall into two distinct categories. On the one hand the external "manifestations" or appearances of impeccably honed and burnished *manners*, evident by such terms as "appropriate, correct, discretion, propriety, harmony, respectable, etc.," concern things of "*social or secular value*," whereas on the other hand indigenous personal *character*, emanating from a "moral or spiritual order," concerns the generation of the quite different qualities of "conscience, duty, good, principle, right and wrong." Although in this sense elements of social or secular value would appear comparably diminished in worth, this is not uniformly the case, for on rare occasions some may undergo a kind of revitalization, yet "only when they are informed by some moral order of value which *transcends the social.*" In other words, a social practice or phenomenon may attain moral seriousness or wholeness—become sacralized—upon effectively dissolving itself and re-emerging as something altogether different, something ultimately other-worldly in form. Hence *good* character displays a transcendent pedigree, while *bad* character betrays only the telltale stain of the universal fallen human condition.

And as for the actual revelation or discernment of character?

> All of her characters' basic goodness or badness, stupidity or wisdom, is inherent in them from the beginning of their appearance in the novels, but these basic characteristics are *only revealed as they interact with other human beings*. We do not *know* whether characters are good or bad until we have seen them in a range of interactions, from tête-à-têtes to large gatherings; their character is revealed not in their introspection but in their social dealings. In fact, we are generally admitted to a character's (usually the heroine's) introspection only after some public event has required the kind of self-scrutiny Emma has undergone. All this is to say that it is in their manners that human beings' morality is ultimately revealed. {second emphasis in original}

In other words, unlike the virtual opacity shrouding modern secular social relationships, there is a good deal of transparency in Jane Austen's social world; there are moments when external behavior clearly reveals internal character. The ultimate point of these modern and early nineteenth-century comparisons is the perhaps not unanticipated detection and lamentation of an ineluctable historical trend: secular society descending along that familiar slippery slope of social atrophy, whose present condition of degradation means that

> . . . . we have come to accept as normal, as perhaps Austen's contemporaries were beginning to accept, a distinction between the morality which guides our private human relationships and the morality which governs relationships in the public sphere.

Erickson seizes upon the Austen "drawing room" as a kind of redeemed social arena wherein the routines of ordinary public discourse are momentarily suspended, creating a neutral buffer zone between the demands of society and the imperatives of personality and conscience.

> The drawing room is an appropriate spatial symbol of this disinclination to separate the public and private since it is neither wholly public nor wholly private. . . . It is in the drawing room that the public is invited to co-exist with the private, both in terms of the people who meet there and in terms of the conversation they share. . . .
> In the drawing room the public and private spheres are not separate. Rather the one is collapsed into the other. The drawing room is a microcosm of the country's life *and* it is a place where the individual *may "be" himself or herself.* [461] {first emphasis in original}

The drawing room represents then for Erickson the most likely non-private realm in which character may be revealed in conversation and behavior— *where wholeness and transparency may prosper.* And, appropriately enough, this "balance" between private and public of the drawing room pivots upon an "axis" that has for its foundation the "same moral and religious base" occupied by modern Christians. Under-girding the drawing room, this "microcosm" of moral action in the world, is a larger, more "coherent world view, a unified cosmos." At this point, one imagines her pausing to wink at her assembled colleagues, as though anticipating their appreciation for having returned them to more familiar, congenial territory:

> Most of us know rather well [wink, wink] the larger lineaments of the transcendent moral and religious order which informs Austen's worldview. It is Renaissance

---

[461] But as Mark Twain once observed, " 'Just be yourself' is the worst thing you can say to some people."

Christian humanism, tempered by an Enlightenment emphasis on reason. It assumes a deity who is in control of the universe and human beings who, by God's leave, have the capacity to inhabit that universe with a degree of order and human happiness if they will exercise the proper responsibility. It is possible to know what is right and to act upon that knowledge. In fact, it is assumed, *everyone knows what is right and on this shared knowledge rests a coherent social order*. . . .

It is the *particular kind of coherence* [wholeness/transparency] on which Jane Austen builds her microcosm that makes her seem alien to many contemporary readers or which, at best, requires patient translation to contemporary students (although to us as Christians [wink, wink] it should not seem all that alien or untranslatable). {emphases added}

Accordingly, the mission of the Christian college becomes the application of the healing salve of "integration," the creation of a "drawing room" community grounded in the universally valid axioms of a transcendent moral order, and the maintenance of an a-social atmosphere in which transparent selves and conduct may flourish free from the corruption of secular social habits.

Jane Austen's vision of *an integrated moral life* is also rooted in the communal life of family and neighborhood, but as we have seen, it cannot be transferred wholesale to a society that is urban, technological, democratic, and pluralistic. Yet as Christians we share her implicit conviction that the *best human society* is based on a commitment to *principles called forth by someone or from something beyond the individual wills and desires of its members*. Part of our mission is to create an equally-compelling vision—for our students and our society—of *an integrated moral life* based on our best understanding of the Biblical witness. {emphases added}

Social Sin

So brazen a logic of invidious social distinction requires the performance of some rather ambidextrous theological gymnastics, especially in light of certain Biblical traditions. For what could possibly make these internal communities of wholeness and light, transparency and integrity, so different from their secular counterparts? Where can such principles be located in scripture? Are not all human beings, within and without the evangelical community, characterized by such presentations of the self, wherein we are all in certain situations prone to affect something we are not. We suffer through meeting and socializing with people we find intolerable. We project a sunny disposition when in fact we are annoyed, hurting, or venting inside. Mothers and fathers put on happy faces to spare impressionable children unnecessary anxiety when things occasionally get rocky within the family. These fragmentations of the inner and outer self are part of everyday life. But there would seem to be something altogether different at work here in this evangelical Christian community, or at least so they claim. Somehow or other what we might think of as a natural relationship or divorce between what one feels and thinks inside and what gets presented to others outside ought be entirely eliminated. This is what evangelical Christians mean by *wholeness* and *transparency*. What we normally think of as both the friction and lubrication of ordinary social discourse become the unchristian properties of an entirely different *secular* world. But, as suggested above, to be able to advance this sort of claim some rather novel theological maneuvers must be performed, with especial regard to this traditional Judeo-Christian concept of sin.

Hence what we might think of as the quirks or characteristics of individuals must undergo *reification*, a conventional academic term often applied to theoretical sleights of hand of questionable validity. What we might ordinarily think of as traits of individuals alone are generalized or projected onto larger social groups. Sometimes these kinds of projections are warranted, as is the case with some of the dynamics that have been explored in the field known as mass psychology, the most damaging unpredictable examples of which occur in stock market panics or crashes or more recently, as when a particular generation (millennials) are all lumped together, supposedly sharing a certain kind of economic disenfranchisement vis-à-vis their parents' generation (baby boomers).

But what I observed in this small academic community was something a good deal more calculated and ideological in nature (as defined in my introductory chapter). Take this concept of sin, for example. Ordinarily, and throughout the history of Christianity, sin has been regarded or served as a generic property assigned to individual human beings alone. As recorded long ago in the book of Genesis, one human being brought it on; and through a rather audacious theological leap of imagination, we have all somehow or other ended up carrying that original blemish or stain—each one of us, *individually*, indiscriminately, without exception. We have all taken a heavy draught from that bitter cup. Aside from a quirky "holiness movement" episode in American religious history, with their rather brazen notion of "entire sanctification," this has proven generally the case.[462] As the Bible puts it, we

---

[462] No doubt other exceptions, grounded in particular historical moments, can be found. Jonathan Blanchard, the founder of Wheaton College in 1860 (and of "several radical newspapers"), observed in a commencement address delivered at Oberlin College in 1839 that "slave-holding is not a solitary, but a social sin." (Michael Gerson, "The Last Temptation," *The Atlantic*, April 2018, 46.)
—Hence the irony of Walter Rauschenbusch, one of the major figures in the rise of the social gospel in the 1920s and thereafter, who urged "his flock. . . . 'to see sin as the treasonable force which frustrates and wrecks these ideals. . . . of social righteousness contained in the person of Christ and in the Kingdom of God. . . . and despoils the earth of their enjoyment.' Sin is not any particular action. Sin is not an action at all. It is a shroud, a 'treasonable force,' that spreads across human society. It is the *cause* of social actions." (Bottum, *An Anxious Age*

have all sinned and fallen short of the glory of God, Christians and pagans alike. Thus anchored in scripture, virtually every evangelical Christian will own up to it, accepting the universal burden: born-again or not, we are sinners all.

And yet somehow or other something rather curious has happened within the American evangelical community over the course of twentieth century, the latter half in particular. Oddly enough this traditional concept of sin, or the nature of sin, has actually changed, and radically so for a good many evangelicals. Somehow or other this lapsarian notion, uncontested literally for centuries, has as in the Marxian way of characterizing such matters, been fully turned *on its head*, sharing the fate of Hegel. American evangelicals have put their own peculiar twist or stamp upon this matter of sin.[463] We might even think of this reformulation in terms of a theological revolution on par, arguably, with that of the Ninety-five Theses Martin Luther addressed to the archbishop of Wittenberg in 1517. And perhaps we shouldn't be surprised, for such *complete reversals* are not all that unusual a feature or dynamic of the evangelical cultural experience, as we have seen.

Over the course of a year or two within this community I came to a rather startling understanding of what I had been seeing and experiencing: *sin had been given a social face*. As secular academicians might put it, *it* (sin) had been *reified* into something altogether different from what one might expect in a traditional Christian academic community. Sin could now assume social forms. Just try wrapping your head around that one! Once I had come to this almost jolting realization a good deal of what I had been observing began to make sense. Yet still I wondered: do they actually, really believe this? That sin infects and can characterize more than just individuals? That it could have a social face? That it could "go viral" as we say these days.

Simply stunning. What on earth was going on here? Perhaps it needed repeating to make it more approachable, and plausible: sin as an individual phenomenon was being *reified* into a transcendent *social* phenomenon. Satan was no longer the nefarious creature who crept into the individual hearts of Christians and pagans alike, tempting everyone to *sin*—although he could still occasionally be found resorting to his old tricks in his old neighborhood. No, Satan had now largely flown the coop, now impervious to that ancient

---

. . . , 66.) And thus the social sin of the left has evolved over the decades into the social sin of the Religious Right, just another example of the "complete reversals" that seem to occur with some frequency within evangelicalism, as we have and will continue to see.

[463] Garry Wills might trace the origins back even further, citing "What Andrew Delbanco calls 'the transformation of the idea of sin from the self-critical Augustinian meaning that it briefly sustained in pre-revolutionary England into the self-righteous form that it has chiefly assumed in Protestant America: sin as excrescence, disease—the threatening other—against which the community of purist selves builds barricades.' " (*Under God. . .* , 72.)

limitation, growing like the creature in the movie, *Alien*, once lodged in the chest of one man until he/it could no longer be contained, bursting from the breast of that one individual, becoming an insidious property or quality infesting all elements, nooks, and crannies—and of not just of any social entity—but of those of the *secular* world. The individualism of sin, of *Satanism*, gone rogue as *secularism*. Right before my eyes was occurring a *reification* that challenged nearly everything I had heretofore understood about the Christian religion. Right then and there it all suddenly began to make sense. It dawned on me: this was sort of like those primordial preliterate tribes in the anthropological literature who divided their physical and spiritual worlds into *sacred* and *profane* categories and regions.[464] It was as though I were being bathed in these exotic expressions of some very ancient cultural dynamics so contemporary in their application that their primordial human cultural origins were effectively camouflaged from my modern *rational* eyes. Readers Biblically inclined may appreciate and ruminate upon that seemingly odd, unintended commentary; reflect back upon the *Son of Man*. Culturally, we are that *Son*.[465]

No wonder evangelicals rage against a modern *secular* world. It took a recent viewing of a film of the stage play, *Angels in America*, to remind me of the original evangelical rejection and reaction to homosexuality "coming out of the closet." Recall that so many of the televangelists and their followers had literally seethed with disgust at the mere thought of a man making love

---

[464] Brent Nongbri has a rather interesting more general view about all this: ". . . . the act of distinguishing between 'religion' and 'secular' is a recent development. Ancient people simply did not carve up the world in that way." In other words, the *sacred* stuff around them was never thought of, or reified, into what we now have perhaps mistakenly conceptualized as "religion." (*Before Religion: A History of a Modern Concept*, Yale University Press, 2013, 3.)

[465] Which isn't to argue that the individualism of sin has been completely eradicated, receiving occasional lip service depending upon strategic situations: "Efforts to transform public schools, in the view of most evangelicals, must be made through individual Christians, who appear somehow different in their personal relationships with others in the schools." (Christian Smith, *Christian America?. . .*, 132.)

—A very traditional, conventional academician, George M. Thomas, generalizes the lip-service litany: "Conflicts over collective and individual identities tend to center on citizenship. Religious movements work on the self within everyday life, constructing a self-disciplined individual who acts methodically and morally. *The constituting of the modern citizen as the disciplined, rational, moral self is pressed outward across spheres of everyday life and upward to political institutions, to make nation and state morally accountable.* . . . Political action is a form of personal expression, and personal spiritualisms are powerful frames for this." Yet this is followed by the confusing "Another lesson for social theory is that actor-centered theories are inadequate to the task of understanding global religious engagements. Our analyses cannot begin with the individual, whether presumed to be rational or nonrational. Identities, rationalities, and actions are embedded in structured contexts. . . ." ("Religious Movements, World Civil Society, and Social Theory," *The Hedgehog Review*, Vol. 4, No. 2, Summer 2002, 56, 58.) {emphases added}

to another man. Recall the creeping rationalizations of this fear and loathing, accelerated by loathsome accounts of HIV and AIDS, as though a pox had rained down from heaven upon the gay community, in blanket condemnation. Nearly insufferable platitudes went something along the lines of "hate the sin, but love the sinner," uttered by those knowing full well that it was Satan who had infected an entire social community, not some random germ looking for victims, and that the individual sinner could no longer be loved in any way, shape, or form; AIDS effectively symbolizing the *reification* of God's wrath down upon an entire fallen *secular* portion of a social community. And so the social transference or displacement of grace was complete, as it is also more generally with all matters *secular*.[466]

As we have seen, institutions and societies may then be judged more or less malignant in a manner unrelated to the accumulated moral characters and performances of the individuals who compose them. They become, in effect, *sui generis* social phenomena—in and of themselves sacred or profane, Christian or secular, redeemed or damned. The stain of Eve now spreads far beyond its original boundaries.[467]

---

[466] This reversal has not been appreciated or understood by academicians, as in this ironic observation: "By the 1980s, outright public resistance to desegregation had fallen out of favor. But the individualistic flavor of Baptist theology, with its tendency to reduce racial problems to individual sin rather than systematic social discrimination, remained, ensuring that most responses to the race problem by groups like the Southern Baptist Convention were fairly shallow." (Robert P. Jones, *The End of White Christian America* . . . , 171.)

[467] There are of course particular evangelical church and faith communities' takes on this notion of sin, as writes T. M. Luhrmann of a small evangelical sect, the Vineyard: "People spoke of sin at the Vineyard, but what they meant by it was separation. . . . Sin is understood not as forbidden behavior but as an inner state of being separated from God. That may be caused by doing something of which God disapproves, but the problem is not that *God* has withdrawn. The problem is that the sinner cannot bear to be close to God. . . . the exemplar of sin is addiction. . . . 'We are all addicts!' roared a Vineyard leader at the regional conference I attended at Wheaton College in Illinois. He strode back and forth on the stage, pummeling the air with his fist, insisting that we turn to addiction *to fill the emptiness inside, to deal with loneliness, to compensate for our disappointing jobs and marriages.*" (*When God Talks Back: Understanding the American Evangelical Relationship with God*, Knopf, 2012, 104-05.) {emphasis added} When the contradiction between the ideas of individual and social sin is brought to their attention, evangelicals do not struggle to reconcile the two, just as they will easily embrace the Vineyard approach as just another way of saying the same thing. As we have seen more recently on the national political scene, evangelicals are wonderfully tolerant of internal contradictions *within* the ranks of their own, embracing whatever is set in opposition to a secular equivalent. As a researcher with her own largely psychological agenda, Luhrmann is of course looking for certain things that advance it and understandably overlooks or ignores other things that don't.
—"(What most evangelicals mean by 'hell' is a spiritual 'separation from God,' not necessarily a place of fire and pitchfork-wielding devils.)" (Christian Smith, *Christian America?* . . . , 81.) Indeed how could a warm-and-fuzzy personal Jesus countenance such a thing for even a

As the reader might anticipate, the citation of Biblical evidence upon this question is predictably mixed.[468] Dennis Hollinger, writing in *Faculty Dialogue*, seizes upon the apparent depreciation of "the world" in a New Testament letter of John as evidence of a larger conception of social structural iniquity:

> The "world" is not merely defined as *human beings* who thwart God's justice and peace, but rather *social structures and norms which distort God's intentions for humankind.* . . .
> "Do not love the world or anything in the world. If anyone loves the world, the love of the Father is not in him. For everything in the world—the cravings of sinful man, the lust of his eyes and the boasting of what he has and does, come not from the Father but from the world." (I John 2:15-16).[469]

No wonder such attributions or reifications might give traditional evangelical missionary types pause to reconsider the nature and thrust of their calling. One of the early and most effective fire-breathing televangelists of the religious right, James Robison, became so inclined, returning to the saving of souls after having dangled his toes in the world-changing stream of politics in the late '70s and early '80s. Perhaps the experience had left an uncharacteristically foul, un-Biblical taste in his mouth.[470]

Hollinger goes on to claim that Biblical scholars have in recent years capitalized on a growing exegetical prowess to expand upon and enrich the meanings of such traditional terms as "powers," "principalities," and "rulers," many now coming to the realization that the lessons of verses once deemed linked to particular Biblical characters or kingdoms are actually

---

wayward flock? Seems also an understandable fall-back position for evangelicals anxious about their own salvation.

[468] There is, for example, Yahweh's identification with and designation of a "chosen people" in the Old Testament, a clear indication of an ethnic social distinction. Also God's indiscriminate destruction (men/women/children/fetuses) of Sodom and Gomorrah surely qualifies as a social-geographic identification and condemnation of the sin of an entire group of people; certainly The Flood also. On the other hand, there are the New Testament precedents, most notably the censure of the Pharisees by Jesus, who assailed the pretensions of hypocritical religious leaders who *uniformly* rejected the religious aspirations and claims of an entire group.

[469] Dennis P. Hollinger, "World-Changing Faith: Some Cautions," *Faculty Dialogue*, no. 2 [Winter 1984-5], 106. {emphases added}

[470] Prior to this complete reversal televangelists also shared these individualistic notions, modeled largely upon Billy Graham: "In 1964, in response to the mobilization of black clergy and churches that drove the civil rights movement, independent Baptist leader Jerry Falwell delivered a famous sermon called 'Ministers and Marches,' where he justified white clergy inaction on civil rights issues, declaring, 'Preachers are not called to be politicians, but soul winners.' " (Robert P. Jones, op. cit., 170.) But sin would become a social property in due course.

more general in their reference and application, encompassing "social realities as well." He discovers in the letters of Paul (Col. 1:15-17, 2:13-15; Eph. 1:16, 2:2, 6:10-18; Romans 8:38) occasions where these expressions "seem to point beyond angelic and satanic forces to *diabolic manifestations within the structures of life* [themselves]." Although sin in the traditional view appears the singular affliction of persons, the species most fundamental flaws and propensities, such as the "penchant toward self-serving motivations and illegitimate power [are actually found] *among all societies and social organizations.*" Indeed, the "inherent nature of social structures [brings them into direct opposition with the] . . . norms of God's kingdom."

These perverse notions of individual and social sin are not easily reconciled. The distinguished evangelical academician, Arthur Holmes, for example, a scholar occasionally prone to offer sensible advice in one book only to contravene it in another, upon this particular topic indulges a familiar habit. For while he argues in his most influential earlier work, *The Idea of a Christian College*, that "A Christian college does not exist to combine good education with a protective atmosphere, for Christians believe that the source of evil is ultimately within a man, not without," later in *Contours of a World View* he concludes otherwise:

> Since relationships between people give rise to the institutions of society, relationships pervaded by sin. . . . [and] Since an institution assumes a life of its own apart from the private function of individuals, *its structure and purposes are affected by sin*, along with its day to day operations. *Sin is a social reality, not just a private affair.* The Old Testament therefore recognizes corporate as well as individual responsibility. A family, a tribe, a nation can be accountable, their corporate sin judged.[471]

As we have all too often seen, no matter the historical accumulation of theological tradition or precedent, the Biblical documentation appropriate to any contemporary occasion and purpose can be unearthed, or simply invented. In the former instance, when openness, universalism, and inclusion are Holmes's desired values and outcomes, a moral individualism—or sin *within* men—is advanced; while in the latter instance, when the logical imperative of an invidious "worldview" assumes control, sin becomes a distinguishing and separating feature of social groups, institutions, and nations— a "source of evil . . . *without.*"[472]

---

[471] *The Idea of . . .* , 47; *Contours . . .* , 124. {emphases added}

[472] It is the acceptance of this widespread misunderstanding of the role of social sin that mars an otherwise insightful account of how the cultural ideas (not social factors) of evangelicalism led to two completely opposite Dutch (Christian Reformed Church) congregational reactions (six staying/seven leaving) to the influx of southern blacks into southwest Chicago neighborhoods. "In essence, white evangelicals have been opposed to individual racial prejudice while

The adoption of any notion of social sin of course serves to grease the wheels of the evangelical vehicle of conspicuous invidious distinction, accelerating the logical locomotive of social division and separation, rendering more palatable this idea of diametrically-opposed Christian and secular social organizations and structures.[473] It also has created some confusion among conventional Christian academicians who have set their analytical watches to pre Religious-Right individualistic lapsarian time zones. That reliable Catholic warhorse and sociologist Andrew Greeley, for example, offers up a quite telling comparison of two different presidents' dalliance with sin. The attempt to impeach the first, Bill Clinton, was "The most dangerous intrusion of religion into American politics in the last hundred years. . . the effort of a largely southern, largely Evangelical, largely Calvinist cabal to cancel the election of an American president by a gross intrusion into the private life of that president. . . . I take it as self-evident that the non-criminal personal behavior of a public figure is not a justification for removing him or her from public office save in a country in which Calvinist (with the accompanying hypocrisy) equates sin (especially sexual sin) with crime. . . . To their people in their base (which is also George Bush's base) this made sense: A sinner could not be a good president. . . . To miss the religious twist—the Calvinist Puritan dimension—in the attempt to destroy Clinton is to misunderstand it completely."[474]

---

failing to understand the structural, institutional character of racism in the United States. They are, in other words, 'anti-structural.' The inhibitive factor seems to be based in the white evangelical understanding of spirituality: each person is responsible for his or her salvation through Christ and the maintenance of that relationship." In other words, if only they were sociologists, prejudice wouldn't exist within these churches and among evangelicalism more generally. *Au contraire*, as we have seen. (Mark T. Mulder, *Shades of White Flight: Evangelical Congregations and Urban Departure*, Rutgers University Press, 2015, 6.)

[473] "But it is clear in the Bible that *sin is more than an internal moral problem*—sin impacts all human beings, their endeavors, and even all the world. To make sin basically an internal and individual matter is to understate the effect of evil in this world and contradict the Biblical witness." (Anthony Frank Spina {SPU Religion professor}, "Biblical Non-negotiables," *Response*, April 1977.) {emphasis added}
—This notion of social sin is, of course, not unique to the contemporary period. Martin Marty, for example, writes that William Jennings Bryan drew from University of Nebraska sociologist Edward A. Ross "the concept of 'social sin' and applied it freely to the system that produced such men of wealth [Carnegie, Rockefeller] while others hungered." (*Pilgrims. . .*, 358-59.)

[474] "The Puritans and American Politics," in E.J. Dionne Jr., Jean Bethke Elshtain, and Kayla M. Drogosz eds., *One Electorate Under God?. . .*, 106-07.
—As Richard Wightman Fox puts it in the same forum, absent this absconded individualism of sin: "Knowing themselves as sinners allows them to withstand the temptation to turn their cause into a righteous mission on God's behalf. Awareness of sin—of their often hidden desire for fame, power, privilege, and other kinds of self-aggrandizement—can counteract religious

Thirteen years or so later, we discover that it was instead Andrew Greeley who completely misunderstood the cultural logic at work in the Clinton impeachment episode. Along comes President Donald Trump and Roy Moore to commit sexual and other actual transgressions far exceeding even the slippery-sloped imagination of Bill Clinton. But these are *categorically different* from the offenses of Bill Clinton. And, contrary to Greeley's claim, there is no hypocrisy here, only a cultural attribution and re-calibration that defines sin away into distinctly different social arenas. Observe the amazing religio-moral gymnastics that evangelicals must perform to displace sin from individuals onto the broader social category of *secularism*.[475] Apparent hypocrisies and double standards that defy belief become then quite comfortably advanced and borne. As we saw in the college community, sin becomes a social property that can only creep into and infect the interior Christian community from outside. What else can explain such apparent mind-boggling internal contradictions? Clinton represents a sin-drenched social category (liberal secularist) not a fallen individual, whereas Trump becomes a recently saved (Christian) evangelical who once allowed secularism to invade his private space.

The Students and the City

And just what sort of form do these often vague notions of social difference actually assume on campus? Let's examine one aspect. Given this steady stream of animadversions is it any wonder that one finds among the student body discernable currents of ambivalence towards the surrounding city? One observes them embracing and expressing pejorative apprehensions of (and occasional muted admiration for) the secular urban *bête noire* in a variety of often confusing ways, which is perhaps understandable given that

---

people's temptation to see themselves as chosen instruments for divine-sponsored action." (96-7)

[475] For a good example of how two Christian sociologists completely misunderstand this distinctive property of evangelicalism, arguing that what really divides Americans from one another is four different conceptions of God (since 95% of Americans actually believe in God), see Paul Froese and Christopher Bader's *America's Four Gods: What We Say About God and What That Says About Us* (Oxford 2010): "Despite what pundits on both left and right exclaim, the American public is not engaged in a battle between the secular and the religious." Of course not, the battle is instead between one-third or more of Americans—evangelicals—and those other Americans of all, little, or no faiths whom evangelicals have deemed the liberal secular enemy. The phony Christians who attack Christianity are exemplified most notably in the political realm by Barack Obama, Hilary Clinton, and Nancy Pelosi, all devote, professed Christians. The difference is not "theological," as these authors claim, but *ideological*. The authors' calling out of Christian academicians like James Davison Hunter for misguided "culture war" claims completely misconstrues (as does Hunter in his own way) the underlying cultural origins and causes—not correlated theologies—of social and political division.

slightly more than half attended high schools in cities of more than 50,000 people.[476] Those from urban families and high schools often chafe under the ideological burden of reconciling their own scarcely unpleasant personal experiences and associations with the wide net of aspersions cast by the anti-urban animus of the cultural logic. Others fall more comfortably under the sway of these largely rural/urban discriminations, as was the case with one student senator who prior to matriculation lived in a northern suburb and whose occasional subsequent encounters with the central city left some abiding impressions, a few of which he shared with a farewell "senior scenario" chapel audience.

> . . . . the rest of the world isn't like [us]. . . . [On the] news, TV, you can really see it . . . [just wait] until you really get out in it . . . riding the bus to work downtown . . . they're really different . . . they don't think there's a God lift. . . . [prepare yourself for a] guy who's one-quarter there . . . smells bad and he sits right next to you. . . . [and then there's the other extreme, the] businessman . . . briefcase full of important papers . . . movers of the city of Seattle . . . teach them . . . make a lot of friends out there . . . they're different . . . out there . . . there's a whole world out there.[477]

A random sample questionnaire distributed among the student body contained a few items which sought to indirectly explore this notion of distinguishable social habitats. In one, students were presented with a large portion of a quotation similar to the one above and asked, "Whether or not you have had the same work experiences, in general how much do you identify with these feelings?" A discernible majority (55%) expressed anywhere from moderate to extremely close identification with its sentiment.[478] Another

---

[476] 45% hailing from cities of more than 100,000—nearly all of whom from Seattle itself, although 23% came from towns under 10,000. (#22, Questionnaire)

[477] 5/9/83.

—Another student, Paul, confessed before a chapel audience his reluctance to perform service, deriding his own selfishness in a mock conversation with God: "I'll go anywhere [for you, Lord] except Africa, Chicago, New York . . . Lord, I'll go anywhere, as long as its SPC." Then came a scholarship offer from a Chicago Seminary, but once again he felt a nagging reluctance: "I heard about the cold weather and the cold people." (Student Chapel: "I Will Strengthen You," 4/3/78.)

[478] "Whether or not you have had the same work experiences, in general how much do you identify with these feelings?"

Very much identify with	[5]	(24)	11%
	[4]	(47)	22
	[3]	(48)	22
	[2]	(44)	20
Can't identify with	[1]	(53)	24

asked, "Would you say that one positive aspect of living in a large city is that one's faith is constantly tested, that one's Christian character is really challenged?" The overwhelming majority (76%) of those sampled agreed in one form or another.[479] Conversations with student senators revealed a dissonant medley of fears and appreciations of large cities that such simple questionnaire items and numerical tabulations can scarcely begin to unravel and harmonize.[480]

[NR] (1)   *
                             _
                            99%

—A closely related item:
"In general, based upon your life experiences so far, would you say that there is a real difference between life in the Christian community and life in non-Christian society?"

Yes, great difference	[5]	(57)	26%
	[4]	(96)	44
	[3]	(40)	18
	[2]	(18)	8
No difference	[1]	(4)	2
	[NR]	(2)	1
			99%

[479] On a response continuum that ran from [1] Not at all — to — [5] Very much agree, 76% chose [3] or higher, 51% [4] or higher, and 24% [5]. Though I should add that 48% of those sampled said that they would like to remain in Seattle once they graduated.

[480] When asked to compare the difficulty of maintaining Christian beliefs in a large city such as Seattle with a small town or community, student senators responded in a variety of often confusing ways. Indeed, as one follows the often unexpected twists, turns, and even flip-flops in their apprehension of the city/community relationship, the reader begins to understand why no consistent pattern or relationships emerge in the tests of the data which immediately follow in the main text. A sampling:

—Rudy: "I was really afraid . . . the schools that I was in always told you about the horrors of a public school and heaven forbid that you should go to a state university. . . . I took that with a grain of salt . . . still I was really afraid of hugeness and state universities. I wanted the community of people I could relate to and my high school was so small [Indiana farming town of 200-300 people]. . . . ["SPU a haven?"] Yes, I've felt like this is a little paradise, cut off from the real world."

—Paul: "I think it's sheltered here. . . . This really reminds me of some of the earlier communities in America when mobility was really reduced. . . . [We] don't adventure out into the rest of Seattle. Going downtown ["Is an emotional experience?"] . . . oh, it really is. I remember one gal who came from a small town and she came back from downtown and she was really shocked. ["Easier to preserve faith in a small town or a city?"] Easier in a city, because everyone knows what's going on in a small town. In the city, nobody knows you. ["But what about temptations?"] That's true . . . there'd be more opportunities, but also less accountability. . . . Well, let's see ["Go ahead and change your mind if you'd like."] . . . It is true about the more opportunities to sin ["Pressure to compromise?"] . . . I think so . . . just the idea that 'everyone is doing it.' ["But in a small community like SPU don't others help keep your faith in line?"] It's true . . . true . . . I'd say it's easier in a small community . . . and that's what I was thinking at first . . . also there's a lot of closer friendships in a small town."

—Frances, very liberal, spent much of her youth in Japan, with missionary parents, yet was quite rebellious when first arrived at SPU: "First Avenue . . . I almost hate downtown Seattle,

Perhaps a rather more compelling indication of the presence of these attitudes comes not from the bare juxtaposition and comparison of traditional notions of city and community but from more subtle social geographic declensions and modulations that occur in the students' thinking about the disparate corridors and districts within the city itself. After all, the thinly-veiled urban/rural connotations of these invidious city/community distinctions may serve merely to link evangelicals with an outlook or lineage of aspersions grounded in an extended Western (e. g., the *gemeinschaft/gesellschaft* dualism of sociology)—and especially American—social, cultural, and intellectual tradition.[481] Most everyone is familiar with an enduring American frontier mentality that has taken a jaundiced view of the "city slicker." Include also the well-documented Protestant suspicion of the teeming hordes of second- and third-wave Catholic immigrants in the large cities of the eastern seaboard,[482] and the even earlier and more virulent apprehensions over the continuing migration north of emancipated and then later disenfranchised southern blacks. Surely all these (and other more recent) phenomena have contributed over the decades to a not always generous perception of the American metropolis.

Sacred/Profane Geography

Yet is not a rather more unique cultural idiom in operation here? A more distinctive Christian/secular cultural demarcation, providing a focus above and beyond the more obvious disenchantments with urbanization that have accompanied the industrializations of modern Western societies? Just what

---

just because I don't know what to do around those people, and they are very different from me. Like riding the busses. It's very different, feel very unsafe. Shopping centers too, U-District a little. ["Cities more harmful to faith?"] I would say yes: more people, more pressures. Best times for me: when out by myself, thinking, reflecting, out in nature, closer to God. In the city you are surrounded by man and his accomplishments. You don't see people as God's creations a lot of the times, and we become separated from him. City life: pace is so fast, no time . . . ["Any positive aspects?"] Uh huh, very definitely. When I was in D. C. I loved it, and I was challenged that week a lot . . . met so many people . . . have to learn to accept them as themselves. That can be a real challenge. There're so many weird people in the world and in the city you're going to get the ones who've grown up in the most diverse circumstances . . . kind of fascinating." (*SSI*, May 2003)

[481] For example: Morton & Lucia White, *The Intellectual Versus The City* (New York: Oxford University Press, 1977).

[482] The Reverend Josiah Strong, a progressive and author of an 1885 book (*Our Country: Its Possible Future and Its Present Crisis*) that "in the fifty years after *Uncle Tom's Cabin* . . . sold more copies than any other work" except the Bible, warned of the large, diverse city, as "every serious menace to America—Mormonism excepted—lurked there. . . . The city was not only the home of roughs, gamblers, thieves, robbers, lawless and desperate men, rioters, skeptics, and the irreligious, but was also the lair of wealthy and luxurious people who did not care for the Kingdom." (Marty, *Pilgrims. . .* , 338-39.)

sort of relationship might this sharper discrimination assume with these more general devaluations of urban life?

In formulating a survey question that might get beyond the more common apprehensions, I cast about for an uncompromisingly severe test. I wondered, for instance, how many—if any—of the students actually thought of the geography within the city itself in so nakedly Christian and secular a fashion? At that point a fairly provocative scheme suggested itself: a map of the city of Seattle delineating the various neighborhoods and areas of the city, along with the instructions: "Think about SPU in relation to the city of Seattle: a) Are there areas of the city which make you particularly uncomfortable or which strike you as un-Christian in atmosphere? Conversely, are there areas of the city you consider to be particularly Christian or conducive to a Christian atmosphere? b) If you tend to answer yes, mark those areas on the map with a C for the more Christian areas and a U for the more un-Christian areas."

Frankly, I anticipated a large majority of the student sample dismissing the item out of hand, as a few surely did—one or two students, for example, responding in large, bold print that this was one of the silliest notions they had ever heard of.[483] And I could hardly disagree. Given the stress the faculty often placed upon humility and service, upon the individual nature of sin and grace, and the large number of students with urban backgrounds, I braced for a uniform, even mocking response, something along the lines of, "What on earth? Parts or sections of Seattle aren't Christian or un-Christian, only people are!"

But it never came. To my surprise, virtually half of the respondents answered 3 or higher to the first section of the item (on a continuum ranging from [1] Not at all—to—[5] Yes, very much); and in the second part nearly 30% actually marked two or more Cs or Us directly onto on the map itself.[484] (The discrepancy between the two explained by many students' lack

---

[483] It is instructive that every one of the few Catholic respondents unanimously (and derisively) dismissed the idea.

—Father William Sullivan, President of cross-town Seattle University, spoke to chapel students of a related contrary tendency within Catholicism to "internalize" potential rifts and to "re-unify," absorbing the dissident or virtuosic elements—Benedict, Francis of Assisi, Ignatius, Jesuit, etc.—in a "reformed" synthesis. ("Reformation of Catholics," Chapel, 11/6/78.) —All of this isn't to suggest that there are no such currents whatsoever within Catholicism. See, for example, Mark O'Keefe (O.S.B.), *What Are They Saying About Social Sin?* (from Paulist Press catalog #125, Sept./Oct. 1990: "The author examines how sin becomes embodied in economic, political, social, cultural, and religious structures.")

[484] "Think about SPU in relation to the city of Seattle. Refer to the map below:

a) Are there areas of the city which make you particularly uncomfortable or which strike	b) If you tend to answer yes, mark these areas on the map with a C

of familiarity with the Seattle area, which a number conceded on the questionnaire. They agreed with the sentiment but were unable to specify locations.)

Given that 45% of the sample students reported attending high schools in cities larger than 100,000 (again, nearly all from Seattle), we might suspect that the results merely reflect the divergent rural and urban backgrounds of the students. Yet a subsequent test of the correspondence between (former) city size and (present) inclination to identify Christian and secular areas of the city yielded no relationship whatsoever.[485] And what is even more intriguing, a further test of the relationship between degrees of evangelical religious intensity and this same inclination yielded only a slightly less random relationship, although students who marked extreme responses to the city item (choosing either [1] Not at all, or [4] or [5] Yes, very much) exhibited some clear differences in religious intensity and outlook.[486] (It is of interest

---

you as un-Christian in atmosphere? Conversely, are there areas of the city you consider to be particularly Christian or conducive to a Christian atmosphere?

Yes, very much	[5] (15)	7%
	[4] (37)	17
	[3] (54)	25
	[2] (35)	16
Not at all	[1] (73)	34
	[NR] (3)	1
		100%

for the more Christian areas and a U for the more un-Christian areas."

Number of C's & U's :

[5] Five or more (20)	9%
[4] Three/Four (30)	14
[3] Two (10)	5
[2] One (20)	9
[1] None (134)	62
[NR] (3)	1
	100%

One might argue, for example, that the students may have been intimidated somewhat by the formality of the question and questionnaire into answering when their instincts actually rebelled against these notions. I did not, however, encounter passivity in other areas of the survey—especially the questions on sexuality—the students often noisily refusing to answer what they deemed to be offensive items.

[485] Regression of high school city size on the two Christian/un-Christian areas of the city items yielded R^2s of .002 and .004. A regression of city size on the "Would you say that one positive aspect of living in a large city is that one's faith is constantly tested, that one's Christian character is really challenged?" item also yielded an almost perfectly random relationship of .002.

[486] I use a "Combined Religious Intensity Scale" (explained at length in Appendix A) to measure degrees of evangelical intensity. This scale regressed on the very same survey items above in ff #28 produced R^2s of .084, .060, and .136, very slight relationships. Regression tests of possible relationships between several survey measures of religious intensity and identity (academic class also) and these several urban questionnaire items yielded no significant correlations.

Now while regression tests of any *systematic* relationship yielded only very slight results there were some demonstrable differences in other respects when students who made extreme

also that the eight or so Catholics who returned questionnaires responded quite differently from their fellow students.)

The partial null results in the latter instance above, especially, suggest several possibilities. In the first place, as hinted above, the students' views of the city may reflect a larger, more general cultural outlook upon cities that is in this particular formulation unrelated to (or a distant relative of) a narrower evangelical cultural view. Secondly, the large number of students from Seattle[487] who are intensely evangelical and inclined to make severe abstract Christian/secular distinctions with respect to other phenomena may nonetheless find their home city too familiar and comfortable an environment in which to deliver such invidious discriminations. In addition, students may also, as evident in the second quotation above, feel the pull of other Christian ideals antidotal to such severe geographic divisions. In a word then, there may be more involved here than the simple translation of a strong sense of Christian/secular difference into the identification of concrete Christian and secular landmarks (although recall that at the extremes of religious intensity, as evident above, the latter discriminations were clearly made). The attempt to discern their deployment out in the secular city itself may, in this particular instance, strain these distinctions to untenable limits of ideological elasticity

---

responses to the first (Are there Christian/un-Christian areas of the city?) item are isolated and compared. For example, the 52 students who chose [4] or [5] Yes, very much, and the 73 students who chose [1] Not at all, were isolated on another item, "How would you describe your present religious philosophy or beliefs?"

			Christian/Un-Christian Areas of the City?			
Religious Beliefs			"Yes, very much"		"Not at all"	
	Total Sample		52 students		73 students	
Very Liberal	[1] 30	14%	2	4%	18	25%
	[2] 51	24	15	31	18	25
	[3] 64	29	9	18	23	32
	[4] 45	21	18	37	7	10
Very Conservative	[5] 20	9	5	10	5	7
		97%		100%		99%

(There were 7 total sample non-responses to question, 3 NRs among the 52 students, and 2 NRs among the 73 students.)

The same student groups were compared on the "Combined Religious Intensity Scale" (mentioned above) and a similar pattern emerged. The 52 students recorded slightly more intense evangelical index scores than the 73 students, although the differences were not as marked as in the above religious self-description item.

[487] Students I could not actually identify and isolate for further analysis because in order to ensure anonymity I did not ask students for names of their high schools of the cities from which they came. I know that a large number come from Seattle because of the college's own figures on entering first-year students.

and sophistication.[488] In this regard, the students' willingness to extend the logic out into various sectors of the city may simply reflect the power of the cultural ethos to project its influence into virtually every dimension of these young persons' lives, however unsystematically and randomly these apprehensions fall into place in their own minds.

Unity & Division

This notion of a communal wholeness itself warrants further examination. It represents another dimension in which the ideal Christian community is said to embody transcendent, a-social properties. Observe how the external urban society wallows in diversity and division while the internal Christian community sits high and dry, luxuriating in a unity of mind and purpose. How might this aspiration and assumption of internal unity serve the larger aims of the cultural imperative? Let us look deeper.

President David McKenna, for example, advancing a kind of "trickle-down" theory of unity, finds confirmation of these ideas in "the Biblical statement, 'Our Lord is one Lord,' [a proclamation which] confirms the oneness of reality and the wholeness of truth," and in the realization that "God . . .

---

[488] Consider that many students who responded to the item failed to even place a C over the position of their own Christian college on the map.

In retrospect, what may be needed is greater discrimination between the kind of general aversion to large cities that assumes the form of urban myths (e. g., assuming the stereotypical liabilities of anomie, anonymity, loneliness, absence of community, etc.), notions which appear endemic to American culture, from a more fundamental and specific evangelical association of urbanism with the larger decadent historical forces of rationalization and secularization and the more contemporary secular phenomena of liberalization and relativization of values, materialism, and consumerism. Perhaps a better survey item would look something like

"From the following list (or add items of your own creation) choose or specify the properties or qualities which aptly describe what you have come to understand by:

1) **Secular Society** ———————————— 2) **Christian Community**

Possible choices: Simplicity, authenticity, specialization, naturalness, depersonalization, unity, hierarchical, cohesion, artificiality, complexity, wholeness, fragmentation, urban, pretense, transparency, role-playing, immorality, values, anomie, self-sacrifice, small town, close-knit, diversity, relativism, personal, humanistic, other-directed, self-centered, power-dependent, equality, indulgence, materialism, mutually-submissive, family-oriented, liberal, singles, permanence, transience, morality, anonymity, loneliness, conservative, individualistic, conspicuous consumption, child-centered, sexual hedonism, daycare, etc."

—A different item might ask respondents to simply distinguish between "cities" and "communities." Or ask if these kinds of distinctions make any sense: "Is there really such a thing as secular society? Christian community?" Of course, the survey item in ff #23 above asks something very similar to this.

revealed the oneness and the wholeness of reality through the creation." And so the unity of God begets a united universe, which begets the unity of truth and knowledge, which in turn generates the unity of various Christian communities. Appropriately, the Christian college "retains the oneness and wholeness of the universe in truth as well as in community."[489]

The Wholeness of God

Now although as I mentioned in an earlier chapter it hardly serves the larger purposes of this study (nor am I qualified) to pause at every turn in the unfolding argument to examine the veracity of scriptural claims, in this particular instance a brief exegesis may be warranted. Take then this notion of the unity or oneness of God. One might imagine, given the finality with which Biblical citations (both direct and implied) are delivered by the adherents of this position, that no other interpretation could stand the light of day. The idea that God is one, an indivisible unity, would appear incontrovertible. Yet to this simple-minded theologian other possibilities appear legion. It may seem ignorant (of the historical development of theology and the present advances in Biblical scholarship) on my part, for example, to call attention to the traditional conception of the *Trinity*, or the division of the Godhead into Father, Son, and Holy Ghost, which on the surface at least might undermine any *absolute* notion of the unity of God. Moreover, there are the respective roles and realms of being that the various Trinitarian actors assume and occupy, and, even further, apparent moral and epistemological specializations. For instance, when Jesus is asked about the events and timing of the last days of the world and his projected second coming, he responds that he has no idea, for only the Father in heaven possesses that kind of knowledge.[490] And when in the Gospel of Mark "A man of the ruling class put this question to him: 'Good master, what must I do to win eternal life?' Jesus replied, 'Why do you call me good? No one is good except God alone,' "[491] raising the specter in the mind of this reader at least (after all, who would dare accuse Jesus of *false* humility?) of a kind of moral partition of the natures of Jesus and God, a fissure in the assumed seamless moral texture of the celestial realm.

---

[489] "Scholarship and the Rule of Christian Faith," 37-38.
—"The wholeness of truth in God is a cardinal doctrine of the scriptures." (McKenna, "A Vision of Wholeness.")

[490] "So, when they were all together, they asked him, 'Lord, is this the time when you are to establish once again the sovereignty of Israel?' He answered, 'It is not for you to know about dates or times, which the Father has set within his own control.' " (Acts 1:6-8, *NEB*.)

[491] Luke 18:18-20, *NEB*.

Even a cursory glance over these texts reveals a sprinkling of other fractious possibilities. Why this pattern of selection? How might we explain the appeal of unity?

Body of Christ [492]

The trickle-down "body of Christ"[493] unity theme lies at the heart of philosophical (and administrative) legitimations and apologies for the apparent monochrome quality of these academic communities. It would appear as if an almost vitalistic transmission of spiritual and epistemological energy occurs along these linking avenues of unity, the uniformity and receptivity of the lower human dimensions dependent upon the uniformity and accessibility of a higher order.[494] A whole God demands and breeds whole godly communities.

---

[492] By no means are these "body" metaphors unique to Christianity. Preliterate religions tended to employ similar organic, anthropomorphic tropes, referring to a temple or house as a "human body"— the "body" of the temple, the "body" of the house. (Mircea Eliade, *The Sacred and the Profane: The Nature of Religion*, New York: Harcourt Brace Jovanovich, 1959, 174.)

[493] The organic "body of Christ" metaphors are ideally suited and liberally employed by evangelical academicians to legitimate and illustrate the unity themes:

— " . . . . using the analogy of the human body, Paul says, 'God has harmonized the whole body by giving importance to functions which lack apparent importance, that the body should work together as a whole with all of the members in sympathetic relationship with one another'. . . . 'the Body of Christ,' then, became the unifying principle for the early church." (McKenna, "A Vision of Wholeness.")

—Appropriately, Bible study and prayer groups in the dormitories are designated "cell groups": " . . . cell groups belong to the students and the residence hall staff." (McKenna, "State of the University, 1979-1980.")

— "I believe that the litmus test for assaying the spiritual and transformational health of Westmont's [College] *society* may well be its commitment to a deep expression of unity. Paul's prayer and admonition in Philippians, chapter 2, is directly relevant. We must not only live together in love and harmony, we must live and work *as though we had only one mind and spirit between us!* " (Jonathan H. Hess, "The Transformation Of Westmont," *Faculty Dialogue*, no. 8 [Spring-Summer 1987], 126.) {second emphasis added}

—"The most fundamental thing to say about the Christian college is that it is an arm of the body of Christ in the world. . . ." (Nicholas Wolterstorff, "The Mission of the Christian College at the end of the 20th Century," *Faculty Dialogue*, no. 1 [Fall 1984], 45.)

[494] " . . . . the presupposition that all truth forms an orderly unity . . . based on the prior belief that all of reality was created by one being, God. . . . [leads me to] seek to approximate that real unity of all things within my own worldview. . . . In addition, both of these sources of knowledge must in turn be constantly used to critically evaluate my own worldview as I seek to bring into a harmonious whole both (and other) types of knowledge as an expression of my own belief that God is Lord of all truth and that all things find their origin and consummation in him." (Gowdy, "Theoretical Model for the Process of Integrating . . . .")

— " . . . . the route I prefer: a belief is justified by virtue of its coherence within the entire body of what one knows and believes. My underlying justification of this strategy . . . lies in what we may call the unity of truth, which is to say that truth *in toto* is itself an interrelated and coherent whole. . . .

The more mundane concrete expression of these notions of unity are severe student selection standards, as SPC President David McKenna explained to an alumni audience in 1975, announcing policy revisions: "Selective admissions would also open up the possibility of *admitting only committed Christians* to the college so that the process of integrating faith and learning could be intensified *for a greater impact upon the contemporary world*. . . . we have been building on a 'sense of community'. . . ." [495] Two or three years later, McKenna appeared before chapel to announce the further tightening of faculty hiring: the college would henceforth demand a more rigorous statement of faith from faculty aspirants, recounting with relish how he had summarily dismissed—literally showed the door to—"this guy," a faculty candidate—who failed the litmus test of faith. [496] And such policies characterize evangelical institutions nationwide. [497]

Perhaps these kinds of formal proclamations upon unity lend themselves to a mood of rising expectations, encouraging the unrealistic view among some of the more committed students that anything less than a campus poised on the verge of absolute uniformity of mind and purpose represents an untenable dilution of community aspiration. During the student body election campaign, for example, candidates delivered speeches in chapel. One presidential contender, after reeling off an impressive list of accumulated activities and campus positions, pledged to "return spiritual unity to campus . . . in order to [bring] a spiritual awakening to campus," a restoration which would allow the members to "rebuild the community we desire . . . [and] bind the student body together." The other presidential contender promised to lead the student body out of "apathy," fomenting a "return to community." Claiming to be a "relational-type leader" and citing his accomplishments as student director of one of the dorms, he offered to restore "vision" and a "sense of community" to the campus. Finally, a female vice-presidential candidate (the obvious victim of formal speech classes) rose to suggest that the students think of Seattle Pacific as "a book" ["Use simple

---

The intent is to explain the whole range of human experience by reference to what is most ultimately real. By identifying what is universal, then, in human experience, we can evaluate alternatives in terms not only of their consistency but also of the completeness with which they integrate things into a unified and meaning-giving whole." (Holmes, *Contours* . . . , 51-52.)

[495] "President McKenna brings alumni to 'SPC-1984,' " a report on the SPC Alumni Banquet, 5/31/75 (*Response*, August 1975).

[496] Chapel, 5/17/78.

[497] Of admissions criteria, Robert Sandin defends a "discriminating . . . [religious/ethical] personal test. . . . . [since] The integrity of the Christian campus community is involved . . . . [Furthermore] an admissions policy which certifies the reliability of the individuals who comprise the student body will enable the faculty and administration to minimize the arrangements for external control of student conduct." (*The Search for Excellence* . . . , 154-55, 157.)

concrete metaphors to grab and focus the listener's attention"], gliding through an overwrought rhetorical examination of the book's anatomy, the most important appendage of which was the binding: "What binds us together is the most perfect and complete unity there is, Jesus Christ."[498]

A month or so later, I spoke with one of the brighter, more liberal student senators about the election campaign; he expressed frustration and exasperation:

> "Why must we always have unity! . . . What's wrong with diversity and differences?"[499]

Internal Unity/External Division

Diversity is wrong because it undermines the *internal* community union of the sacred and profane ("wholeness") and thus jeopardizes—at least in terms of a formal philosophical argument or apology—the symmetry of divine and terrestrial realms upon which the Christian academician's claim of moral and epistemological superiority depends. (The abstract theoretical—better, ideological—connections are obviously beyond the grasp of the average student, the overwhelming majority of whom aspire to unity for all sorts of mundane social reasons—largely peer and institutional pressures to excel or conform.[500]) Furthermore, *internal unity is crucial not only for the theoretical alignment of these disparate realms of being, truth, and knowledge, allowing for easy movement from one to others (to wit, the more unified the faculty and student body—both individually and as a whole—the greater the potential access to, and flow of, this larger dispensation of truth and knowledge), indeed it proves equally indispensable for the adoption and maintenance of a community posture towards the external "secular" society.* And this latter role or function is often demonstrated most clearly, ironically enough, in critical remarks that would appear to have an altogether different thrust,

---

[498] ASSP Elections Chapel, 4/18/2003.

[499] (*SSI*, May 2003)

[500] The unity theme is reinforced in all sorts of ways. For example, one song I heard at every conceivable gathering and occasion on campus went: "We are one in the spirit, we are one in the. . . . Know that we are Christians by our love," the first phrase chorus repeating at the beginning of each verse.
—As Alan Peshkin writes of Bethany Baptist Academy: "Though Bethany is not a community in the geopolitical sense . . . it is a community in the fullest psychological terms. . . . I marvel at the unity, the connectedness of Bethany's world. . . . I could never resist the thought—and it came frequently—'How nice to belong here. . . .' [There is] strikingly little divisiveness of belief and behavior among persons charged with conducting its curricular and extracurricular activities . . . divisiveness does not exist on any matters of consequence." (Peshkin, *God's Choice. . .* , 284, 141.)

that of directly reprimanding those who would split social and epistemological worlds into antagonistic Christian and secular realms.

Consider a portion of a David McKenna convocation address exposing the errors of Jerry Falwell and the Moral Majority:

> The most obvious of the intellectual flaws is a segregated worldview in which the sacred is divided from the secular. . . . Rev. Falwell disclaims any theological underpinnings for the Moral Majority. By his own words, he states that when he speaks as the President of the Moral Majority, he speaks only as Jerry Falwell, citizen. But when he enters his pulpit on Sunday, he speaks as a minister of the Gospel of Jesus Christ. By splitting his worlds, his political philosophy and tactics do not have to answer to his Christian theology. . . . All of the issues divide into "pros" and "cons"—pro-life, pro-family. . . .
>
> A Spirit-guided, liberally-educated Christian has a holistic world view. *There can be no division between the sacred and secular in the worlds of knowledge.* When Jesus promised that the Holy Spirit will lead us into all Truth, His words made sacred all human knowledge and all ways of coming to knowledge. Consequently, a student at Seattle Pacific University does not move from a sacred class in New Testament to a secular class in literature. In the search and discovery of Truth, we are always treading on holy ground.[501]

The above passage appears to contradict nearly everything I have heretofore argued. Yet, oddly enough, *it is precisely the promulgation and promotion of these conceptions of internal unity which serve to ensure external division from, and out in, the society at large.* For when the evangelical academician speaks and writes fondly of the indivisible integrity of the sacred and the profane he actually has in mind *a kind of "wholeness" that operates solely within the confines of his own redeemed person and the Christian academic and cultural communities in which he dwells rather than some more distant general property of the external material and social worlds that surround him.* As we have seen, he means that evangelical students or academicians ought to wear their Christianity on their sleeves—brazenly, unapologetically—at every turn in the unfolding drama of their careers and lives. The intramural spiritual saturation or "permeation" that McKenna claims so distinguishes the Christian college from the "separation" (of faith and

---

[501] "Spirit of Truth." {emphasis added} In this instance, McKenna is either naive or disingenuous, since it is virtually incontestable that Falwell's theology—his ideology—did in fact determine his political program.

—Ironically: "The segregation of sacred and secular worlds is a throwback to a medieval heritage that cannot be repeated." (McKenna, "State of the University, 1981-82.")

—Similarly, from Arthur Holmes: "The 'secular' is not itself evil; in fact, in God's world it too is sacred. . . . everything about men created in God's image belongs to God—that is, it is sacred. . . . Religion cannot be compartmentalized; the secular man attempts to do so but only succeeds in fragmenting his life, unless he roots another religion at the heart of things, perhaps a quasi-religion of a humanistic or naturalistic sort. . . . *There can be no effective dichotomy of the secular and the sacred or of culture and faith.*" (*The Idea of . . .* , 23-24.) {emphasis added}

learning) of the secular University above all demands the imbuing of every thought, gesture, behavior, and relationship with the unmistakable hues of Christian coloration. The genuine Christian "scholar-servant" ideally exhibits personal unity (no partition into Christian and secular roles or occupations, nor any imbalance of mind, body, and spirit), creates and settles within unified communities (no division into Christian and secular activities, social groupings, entertainments), and establishes and maintains integrated academic institutions (no divorce of secular from sacred subjects).[502]

And it is precisely the ideological pressure to generate and maintain an impeccable unity and wholeness of the **interiors** *of persons and their communities that drives members to seek out and eliminate diversity and division* **within** *while projecting its omnipresence* **without.**[503]

The War of Worlds

So conceived, this dynamic relationship between *unity within* and *division without* advances our understanding of Christian academicians of apparent good intention and conscience who might appear on occasion caught in webs of contradiction and hypocrisy. The same David McKenna, for example, who above chides Jerry Falwell for alternately donning secular and sacred hats to advance a political agenda and who expresses reverence for the unity of truth and knowledge has nonetheless at other moments in his career, as we have seen, displayed a weakness for invidious distinctions and comparisons, routinely sundering "whole" worlds into diametrically-opposed realms of *them* and *us*.

---

[502] Among many possible examples:

—"Students and faculty must combine academics with the processes of 'ordinary life' within the college community. *Integration ought to infuse all activities throughout our school: when and with whom we talk, what we talk about, how we relate to each other, where and how we live, how we share our lives, the degree of our involvement with each other—all of these are integrative activities.* If we live essentially private and autonomous lives, presenting a public front, keeping largely to ourselves, risking little or nothing in interpersonal relationships, then integration cannot go beyond 'mere academics.' " (Perkins, "The Place of Ideology In Christian Liberal Arts . . . ," 55.) {emphasis added}

—"We need, rather, *the rigorous actualization of our faith in every avenue of our existence.* In the final analysis, we will exalt Christ in everything because 'He is before all things and in Him all things hold together' (Col. 1:17). Either we do that or we become one more component of secularized pluralism." (Leon O. Hynson, "The Savor of Evangelical Salt," *Faculty Dialogue,* no. 7 [Fall-Winter 1986-87], 106.) {emphasis added}

[503] Stanley Fish discerns a similar dynamic at work in recent proposals to expand the role of religion in public higher education, evangelical academicians urging greater *external* toleration (diversity) while seeking to preserve the internal intolerance (unity) of their own institutions. ("Why We Can't All Just Get Along," *First Things,* February 1996.)

The first example is drawn from the late '60s and leaves the impression of an irrepressible guerrilla mentality:

> . . . . that community will present *a solid front to the outside world.* . . . [But] Rather than being limited to the goal of internal self-perpetuation, the Christian community is a dynamic unit geared for *action* in the world of which it is a part. With its personalized identity among the membership, and its climate of spiritual support, it *challenges the world* with the confidence of *its higher values.* There are disciplines for its membership based upon the common values for the community, but these lines of conduct are not restrictive. Rather, they are derived from the morality of the Christian example and conducive to individuality in Christian growth. The community, therefore, becomes the *training ground for a task force of believers who penetrate the world* at every level with the Christian witness and yet, *maintain the identity, support and motive of the closer communion.* Having established a community based upon a primary relationship with Jesus Christ and having developed that community as resource center for spiritual growth, the community goal must be *an offensive thrust into the modern world.* [504] {emphases added}

A few years later in 1974, McKenna appeared before the International Congress on World Evangelism in Lausanne, Switzerland, unveiling during his presentation a complex ten-part flow chart illustrating in great detail "The Great Commission: An Integrated World System," assuring fellow participants that both education and evangelism pursued the complementary goals of making "whole men" and "reaching the whole world." Yet it was a "whole" world that might appear, upon further reflection, a good deal more divided and less united than first imagined:

> Orwell predicted that by 1984 a powerful world system would control our lives. As a *counter-system* to an Orwellian world, Jesus gave us a design for world evangelization with the power to change not control the lives of men. Even now, *these two systems are on a collision* [course]. . . . *the battle is ours for this generation.*[505] {emphasis added}

McKenna concludes, exhorting his colleagues:

> It is time for a Lausanne Declaration of commitment to *the Christian world system.* . . . [We must set to work rallying our forces for] an early and inevitable confrontation with *the pagan world system.*

How far we have come from the oneness of God and of the unity of all truth and knowledge—the union of the sacred and profane—underpinning the

---

[504] "A Community of Learners."

[505] "Christian Higher Education and World Evangelization: A Strategy for the Future," *Universitas,* January 1975.

internal solidarity, cohesion, and wisdom of a 3,000 member academic community to an apocalyptic vision of world systems marshalling forces for an ultimate unity-shattering battle over the spiritual (and material) future of the planet.[506]

A Proposition

We might even fashion this relationship between internal unity and external division into a kind of proposition, to the effect that the greater these *internal pressures for* (and orchestrations to bring about) *conformity and homogeneity* ("unity") the greater the corresponding *apprehension and perception of external division and danger*, along with a greater antagonism directed towards those external persons and groups deemed most threatening (most uniformly *unlike us*) to the bases or preconditions of this internal unity.

Then again the relation between the two phenomena may prove even more complex.[507] Perhaps we might better conceive of it as a form of

---

[506] Observe this coupling of sacred unity with secular division: Dr. Robert Webber of Wheaton College recounted for chapel students a lesson learned during his undergraduate years at Bob Jones University: " . . . everything for the Christian is sacred. . . . There is no distinction between the sacred and secular world." But later in his address he urged students to help "turn our religion outward . . . to reshape the world. . . . [We] must declare a state of war. . . . Victory of Christ . . . to destroy the ideologies of the world." Christians must take an "aggressive place in the world . . . [in] education. . . . [must] capture the major universities of the world. . . . We must go to battle . . . combat secularism and the ideologies that rule the world." ("Education in the Context of a Christian World View," Chapels 10/27-8/80.)

—"First, the living God *is the God of nature as well as of religion*, of the 'secular' as well as the 'sacred.' In fact Christians are always uncomfortable about this distinction. For everything is 'sacred' in the sense that it belongs to God and nothing is 'secular' in the sense that God is excluded from it. . . . Indeed 'everything God created is good, and nothing is to be rejected if it is received with thanksgiving' (I Timothy 4.4)." {emphasis in original}

Yet later: " 'Religion that God our Father accepts as pure and faultless is this: to look after orphans and widows in their distress and to keep oneself from being polluted by the world' (James 1. 27)." And then there is the Old Testament Yahweh condemning entire cities as uniformly evil: " 'I am against you.' (Amos 2. 13; 3. 5)." (John R. W. Stott, "Involvement: Is It Our Concern?" *Faculty Dialogue*, no. 4 [Fall 1985], 22-23, 25.)

[507] Colonial Puritanism may represent an imploding variation upon this theme. Gordon S. Wood contends that although persecution in England proved a major source of internal cohesiveness and discipline, upon transplantation to New England the absence of external enemies seemingly drove them "to impose order and orthodoxy upon themselves with an unanticipated ruthlessness. . . . [rooting out] deviants from their own midst." ("Struggle Over The Puritans," *The New York Review of Books*, 9 November 1989, 28.)

—Philip Greven explains the Puritan search for enemies as a displacement or projection of internal anger onto others. See "Soldiers for Christ: Anger, Aggression, and Enemies," in *The Protestant Temperament: Patterns of Child-Rearing, Religious Experience, and the Self in Early America* (New York: A Meridian Book of the New American Library, 1979).

—Contrast this with Arthur Hertzberg's reading of the Jewish Diaspora to America, wherein the absence of any focused, sustained threat has allowed Jews to luxuriate in a cultural haven, safe from inveterate enemies, an environment responsible for diminished religious solidarity, reciprocity or continual give-and-take between perceptions of *internal conditions* and *external dangers* that tends in time to blur the distinction between the two, the one having become integral to the nature and expression of the other. So that as we saw in our earlier chapter on deep and shallow history, apprehensions of disunion or clear and present (invariably monolithic) dangers abroad may accelerate the drive for solidarity at home with as great a frequency or urgency as the routine evocation and promotion of unity within may serve to generate internal community needs for these very same tangible external enemies. In that sense, these notions *and* perceptions of internal unity and external division surely feed upon and reinforce one another, may in fact be *locked into a kind of deep calibration with one another, the one an indispensable part of the nature and evocation of the other.*[508]

War of Words / War of Weapons

An appreciation of these cultural dynamics may advance our understanding of recent events.[509] Now while evangelical militants have surely

---

vitality, and identity. Hertzberg predicts eventual assimilation and loss of Jewish cultural and religious distinctiveness. ("What Future for American Jews?" *The New York Review of Books*, 23 November 1989.)

[508] Conventional historians often fail to understand how integral these apparently irrational ideas or dynamics are to the very nature and identity of evangelicalism. Martin Marty, for example, dismisses the notion of "secular humanism" as just another in a long line of phantom scapegoats, taking great pains to explain to us that a religion of secular humanism has few adherents or simply doesn't exist; indeed were it properly laid to rest we could all "get back to the *serious* business" ("Before *serious* Americans turn away from the issue in disdain. . . .") of genuine Protestant religion. This mild admonishment was followed, oddly enough, by letters to the editor—from University of Chicago alumni, no less—protesting *seriously* that a "secular humanistic" threat does in fact exist. ("Secular Humanism, the Religion of," *The University of Chicago Magazine* 79 [Summer 1987], 2-5, 12; Letters, 80 [Winter 1988], 45-46.) {emphases added}
—R. Scott Appleby, Marty's co-editor of the six-volume *Fundamentalisms Observed* project, answered a letter to the editor of the *University of Chicago Magazine* complaining of the derogatory all-inclusiveness of the term "fundamentalisms" with the closing remark that all these apparent negative elements of fundamentalist religion "stifle the true spirit of religion which fundamentalism purports to defend." And just what is the *true spirit* of religion? As I observed in chapter 1, Christocentric scholars embrace ideal conceptions of religion or Christianity that actual religions frequently betray. To dismiss certain unsavory characteristics or aspects of these movements as aberrations or irrationalities is to risk misconstruing the core identities and meanings of these phenomena. As with the portrait of evangelicalism I have sketched, the apparent irrationalities often prove essential to the nature of the religion itself. They must be taken *seriously*. ("Letters," *The University of Chicago Magazine* 85 [June 1993], 3-4.)

[509] Or, rather, ancient events also, as again these dynamics are by no means confined to modern evangelicalism. Elaine Pagels contends, for example, that early Christians (first three centuries CE) regularly condemned rival or antagonistic groups as agents of Satan, first the Jewish leaders of the Sanhedran (council of elders), then the Jewish Pharisees, and finally

energized and mobilized their followers with inflammatory rhetoric (e. g., Pat Robertson: "Just like what Nazi Germany did to the Jews, so liberal America is now doing to the evangelical Christians"; Jerry Falwell: "Modern U. S. Supreme Courts have raped the Constitution and raped the Christian faith and raped the Churches."[510]), unleashing steady outpourings of persecutional imagery, the level of violence has rarely escalated beyond words. For nearly a half century now we have observed a similar pattern of a knee-jerk perception of impending danger and paranoid response. What then explains the conflagration at Waco during the early years of the rise of the Religious Right? David Koresh and the Branch Davidians? The immediate academic and journalistic commentary dealt with European and American historical precedents—premillennial apocalyptic movements, internal Branch Davidian theology, and second-hand psychological assessments of Koresh.[511] Several academic compilations explored the tragedy further.[512] Perhaps most intriguing of all, the reactions to the massacre surfaced among the more established evangelical media. Paul Crouch's *TBN* (*Trinity Broadcasting Network*) and Robertson's *CBN* (*Christian Broadcasting Network*) glossed over the unsavory aspects of the cult and seized upon the event as evidence of an accelerating persecution of evangelical Christians.[513]

My contribution to the historical account of this event would include the simple observation that the Koresh Branch Davidian case represents not so much another example of an extreme apocalyptic cult—in a long line of such cults—as yet a rather more interesting and virulent expression of this central evangelical cultural dynamic—this logic of invidious social distinction. As I read it, David Koresh—for whatever combination of psychological and other reasons—merely prepared for and then executed an overt *defensive* war against the secular behemoth in real life that most respectable evangelicals

---

spreading the indictment more generally among the Gentiles as well as the nascent Gnostic movement. (*The Origin of Satan*, New York: Random House, 1995.)

[510] "Demagoguery in America," *The New Republic*, 1 August 1994, 7.

[511] Paul Boyer, "A Brief History of the End of Time," *New Republic*, 17 May 1993, 30-33; Stephen D. O'Leary, "Nuts About The End of the World," *Seattle Post-Intelligencer*, 21 March 1993.

[512] James D. Tabor and Eugene V. Gallagher, *Why Waco? Cults and the Battle For Religious Freedom in America*, Berkeley: University of California Press, 1995; Stuart A. Wright, ed., *Armageddon in Waco: Critical Perspectives on the Branch Davidian Conflict*, University of Chicago Press, 1995; James R. Lewis, ed., *From The Ashes: Making Sense Out of Waco*, New York: Rowman and Littlefield, 1994.

[513] One Jewish intellectual was not all that unsympathetic. See Leon Wieseltier, "The True Fire: A Defense of Spiritual Strangeness," *New Republic*, 17 May 1993.

dare play out only in their own minds or before captive home audiences.[514] And I emphasize *defensive*. For what distinguishes the Koresh incident from the more baneful, premeditated event that followed later in the 1995 Oklahoma City terrorism bombing perpetrated by Timothy McVeigh in revenge against the federal government for Waco was the mentality of self-fulfilling persecution. It is what anchored the Branch Davidian compound in the fertile soil of an American evangelical cultural apartheid imagination. Is it any wonder that Koresh migrated to Waco, Texas, home of one of the most respected publishing houses in traditional evangelicalism, Waco Books, locating himself in as conventional, respectable, and metaphorical a setting as an aspiring evangelical crusader could hope for. Any sensible federal law enforcement strategy would have pulled the troops back, demilitarized the zone, and starved the cult into ultimate frustration and submission. Absent the looming presence of the great secular behemoth, Koresh's *raison d'être* would have merely evaporated in the hot Texas dust.

---

[514] See, for example, the raucous November 1996 issue of *First Things*, containing a "symposium" upon "The End of Democracy? The Judicial Usurpation of Politics." "Four of the five essays contemplate with evident approval the prospect of mass civil disobedience, and [Charles] Colson—'with fear and trembling'—goes one better—he nods at Jefferson and proclaims that 'revolution can be justified from a Christian viewpoint.' " Two of the journal's seven editorial board members (Peter Berger and Gertrude Himmelfarb) resigned in protest; reports on the "fracas" surfaced in *The New Republic* and *The New York Times*. (David Glenn, "The Schism," *Lingua Franca* 7, February 1997, 24-26.) Jacob Heilbrunn's account divided the disputants into "Neocons" (conservative Jewish intellectuals) and "Theocons" (conservative Catholics), the latter grouping offering one indication of how ideas of spiritual-cultural warfare have spread beyond their Religious-Right origins: " . . . . what *was* new about the *First Things* symposium was the attempt to fashion a cogent, serious and popular intellectual framework for these ideas—to render respectable ideas that intellectuals had come to regard as the province of the radical right and the booboisie. . . . their solution is to embrace explicitly the notion of a Christian nation." (*The New Republic*, 30 December 1996, 22.) {emphasis in original}
—Over 1.4 million copies have been sold during the '80s and '90s of former Assembly of God preacher Frank Peretti's *Piercing the Darkness* (Westchester, Illinois: Crossway Books, 1989), a novel about a small-town church persecuted by liberals, part of a larger theme of growing "spiritual warfare" between the secular and Christian world.
—As Susan D. Rose writes of the Covenant private secondary school community: "They are a peace-loving people, and yet, continually speak of the need to prepare for military warfare—in the spiritual realm." (*Keeping Them Out of the Hands of Satan* . . . , 47.)

Conclusion: The American Rural Moral Imagination

It comes as a surprise, then, to discover that in most European languages, the same word can be used to refer to a 'city' and a 'town.' Some languages, like German, French, or Polish, do not distinguish between them at all; a city is a *ville* and a town is a *ville*. This suggests a view of cities and towns that recognizes continuity rather than differences, as if cities were larger versions of towns, or vice versa.. On the other hand, in English, and especially in American English, the perceived difference between cities and towns, especially between big cities and small towns, is considered paramount.[515]

Western culture and its fruits had its foundation in the Bible, the Word of God .... Communism, on the other hand, has decided against God, against Christ, against the Bible, and against all religion, Communism is not only an economic interpretation of life—Communism is a religion that is inspired, directed, and motivated by the Devil himself who has declared war against Almighty God. ... The Fifth Columnists, called Communists, are more rampant in Los Angeles than any other city in America. . . . *In this moment I can see the judgment hand of God over Los Angeles. I can see judgment about to fall.*

When God gets ready to shake America, he might not take the Ph.D. and the D.D. and the TH.D. *God may choose a country boy!* . . . *A hillbilly, a country boy!* Who will sound forth in a mighty voice to America, "Thus saith the Lord!" (Billy Graham, Los Angeles, 1949)[516]

Americans harbor an ambivalence or apprehension towards their own large cities that many Europeans find incomprehensible. Overseas, Paris, London, Barcelona and Madrid, Florence and Rome, Amsterdam, Vienna, Stockholm, Berlin, and even dirty, cacophonous Athens occupy positions of cultural authority and esteem in their respective societies. These cosmopolitan centers radiate cultural influence out into the countryside, where, for the most part, denizens—burghers and peasants alike—bask in the warming rays of these cities' cultural brilliance, however uncomprehending (or indifferent) some remain of their cultural products and legacies (rebellions or resistance stemming largely from regional, ethnic, and political differences— the Basques and Catalonians in Spain, the Bretons in France, for example— rather than from any purely anti-urban animus).[517]

---

[515] Witold Rybczynski, "The Mystery of Cities," *The New York Review of Books*, 15 July 1993, 13.

[516] Dochuk, op. cit., 139. {emphases added}

[517] This may prove less valid in the realm of higher culture. Robert Hughes, for example, suggests that the "city-rural split" or aesthetic tension drove modernism in art and other fields in 19th-century Europe. (See "The Decline of the City of Mahogany: Art, Money, New York, the 1980s: a Jeremiad," *The New Republic*, 25 June 1990, 38.)

An altogether different outlook permeates a large portion of American society. For many Americans the urban behemoths of New York, Chicago, Washington D. C., San Francisco, Detroit, Los Angeles, and others represent not cultural beacons but rather the nadir of modern liberal decadence. These urban centers—New York City, in particular—evolved in the final few decades of the twentieth-century (and in an even more accelerated fashion and pace than we saw earlier in our history) into objects of cultural fear and loathing, into the dreaded *bête noires* of an indigenous rural moral imagination. What we have observed as a major current flowing strongly and clearly within evangelicalism itself becomes rather less urgent, more diluted and muddled, as it trickles down through the tributaries of the larger majority Protestant culture.[518] At its undiluted source, we find that a city like New York represents for most evangelicals the Sodom and Gomorrah of modern secular society—a daunting secular behemoth and cesspool—attracting and compressing within its boundaries the highest possible concentrations of all those secular maladies we have encountered throughout this study.[519]

—Nathan Glazer: "But at the bottom of it all, I think, is neither automobile use nor ethnic and racial succession nor TV-watching nor housing controls, but one simple factor: that they [Europeans] love their cities more than we do." ("The Hard Questions: It's Better in Europe," *The New Republic*, 11 November 1996.)

[518] During the mid-twentieth century perhaps the most popular artist in America was Warner Sallman, whose *Head of Christ* and other mass reproductions "[exemplified] the ideology of many middle-class Protestant Christians," portraying "the evangelical ideal of family life set in rural America. . . . an antidote to the present world of decadence and disobedience. . . . Sallman never painted the modern urban world . . . only nostalgic rural towns and Biblical cities." (David Morgan, "Imaging Protestant Piety: The Icons of Warner Sallman," *Religion and American Culture: A Journal of Interpretation* 3, no. 1 [Winter 1993], 32, 36, 39.)

[519] It is in this one respect that Susan Harding's otherwise perceptive *The Book of Jerry Falwell* once again misses the mark—the larger ideological context of evangelicalism; her book ends in this manner:

> When Charlotte and her son, David, visited me in New York City on Easter weekend in 1985, I saw it as another small episode in the movement of contemporary American fundamentalists to abandon their historic separatism from the secular world. . . . [the were excited, enjoying the visit, and yet atop the Empire State Building, "distress" filled Charlotte's face, and she turned to her son to confess that] "David, you are going to laugh when you get back to Lynchburg about how your mother cried on top of the Empire State Building. I was looking down on the city, and I thought about all those people down there who've never heard the gospel. I wondered, what does God see when he looks down on New York? And it just broke my heart. All the lost, lonely, destitute people, crowing for identity, their lives empty and cold without Jesus. There are millions of people down there who have never heard the Word, who don't know how much God loves them and that Jesus died for them. I saw a cross coming down from the sky reaching right into the city. It's the channel of communication God has given us if only we will

Nearly everything evangelicals despise in secular society can be found in exceptional doses in the New York City of their collective moral imagination.[520]

---

open our hearts. So many people here, convinced they are all alone, that no one can help them. But they are so wrong. If only they would ask, the Lord will help them, he's their true friend, and he's there for everyone. . . ." Even the city's aggressive secularity did not phase them—they made no comment, for example, about the World Trade Center brochure entitled "The Closest Some of Us Will Ever Get to Heaven." But Charlotte did on several occasions "adequately depict" the city in biblical realist terms, incorporating its reality into "the one real world detailed by the biblical story." In my account of the language of fundamentalism in the 1980s, I have emphasized the similarities, the space of overlap, between fundamentalist and modern, religious and secular, Bible belief and unbelief. Charlotte always wanted me to remember the difference, specifically, between Bible belief and unbelief. [But why?????]

Charlotte caught us up in her evangelistic vision for about ten minutes, then dried her eyes and suggested we go to lunch. Before we left, she put a tract, a little pamphlet explaining God's plan for salvation, on the window ledge. (275-6)

[520] It may come as a surprise then that the most fervent evangelicals and the greatest demographic surges in their numbers have come not in rural areas of America but among suburban buffer zones separating the heartlands from secular urban cesspools. Here in this accelerated glacial rub between regions one finds the greatest expansions in the number and size of evangelical megachurches, where congregations flock together in defiance of the secularisms that surround or butt up against them. No wonder that in a study of various competing church populations in the very same religiously indifferent Pacific Northwest of my own community study, the author encountered surprising surges in evangelical religiosity. "The fervency of evangelicalism in general is something I did not expect to find until I began this research. After nearly three hundred interviews and experiencing evangelicals in many different contexts, their passion and persistence were breathtaking at times. Even against the odds, in a region where their brand of religion was thought not to work, they were neither cowed nor cautious, but indeed almost with anticipation of what 'God would do in the Pacific Northwest.' " (James K. Wellman, Jr., *Evangelical vs. Liberal*. . . . 282.) I believe the author was both a local college professor and a clergyman.

—That religion in general can thrive, not suffer, in the midst of a secular urban behemoth like NYC is richly documented, I understand, in Jon Butler's *God In Gotham: The Miracle of Religion in Modern Manhattan* (Harvard University Press 2020). A pre-publication blurb from the HU Press site:

In Gilded Age Manhattan, Catholic, Jewish, and Protestant leaders agonized over the fate of traditional religious practice amid chaotic and multiplying pluralism. Massive immigration, the anonymity of urban life, and modernity's rationalism, bureaucratization, and professionalization seemingly eviscerated the sense of religious community. . . . Yet fears of religion's demise were dramatically overblown. Jon Butler finds a spiritual hothouse in the supposed capital of American secularism. By the 1950s Manhattan was full of the sacred. . . . *God in Gotham* portrays a city where people of faith engaged modernity rather than foundered in it. Far from the world of

Consider, for example, this prescient *Newsweek* account of the 1988 presidential campaign of televangelist Pat Robertson during the week of the southern "Super Tuesday" primary:

> The New York-based Council on Foreign Relations is a favorite target. Robertson charges wildly that it has infiltrated the State Department with "one-world socialists." The New York Stock Exchange is a center of greed in which a group of rich speculators exert economic power over the little people. ["I don't need all . . . those elitists. . . . We can do without their money."] New York in general occupies a large place in the Robertson scheme. A video—"Who Is This Man?"— distributed by his campaign shows the city as a hub of the pornography trade and other evils. Spliced between shots of porno mills are scenes of the stock exchange and an ethnic-looking man walking down a city street. On the stump, Robertson castigates New York as a center of the "secular humanism" which contributes to the nation's moral rot. He also points out disparagingly that New York produced the "life experience" pedagogical techniques of John Dewey. And then there is AIDS, another sign of moral decay, which Robertson claims, contrary to medical evidence, can be transmitted in saliva. It is a demonology calculated to appeal to people who feel they have lost control over their lives—and it seems to resonate among secular and religious voters alike.[521]

Although as I suggested earlier this indictment of New York City reflects an enduring mood of cultural disenchantment which more or less permeates major portions of American society, perhaps, as directly evident above, it receives its most virulent expression in our political life. In this regard no more memorable example comes to mind than the national response to the city's fiscal crisis of the mid '70s, particularly the Ford administration's unmistakable headline message of "Ford to City: Drop Dead!" the President and fellow Republicans deftly playing the urban cultural resentment card before a receptive and appreciative citizenry.[522] Of course, although the

---

"disenchantment" that sociologist Max Weber bemoaned, modern Manhattan actually birthed an urban spiritual landscape of unparalleled breadth, suggesting that modernity enabled rather than crippled religion in America well into the 1960s.

[521] "Populist Pat's Outreach Program," *Newsweek*, 29 February 1988, 19.

—Or, more generally: Bob Lyon of Asbury Theological Seminary asked Seattle Pacific students to assume and reflect upon the long-term perspective of Western history and culture, arguing that "western culture [is a] threat to man as God intended him to be. . . . [It is] hostile to the word of God. . . . *Large metropolitan areas* . . . [are a] *product of the Fall.* . . ."; the modern Western world in general is "a monster." The secular world represents a "basic threat to your Christian life," any social links with which must be severed if "you're going to be a Christian in the real sense of the word." ("Faith That Makes A Difference," Christian Commitment Week Chapel, 9/29/80.)

[522] The October 30, 1975 front page of the *Daily News* (Ken Auletta, *The Streets Were Paved With Gold*, New York: Vintage Books, 1980, 286). The city was of course receiving the kind

present structure of American government—disproportionate, undemocratic representation in the Senate—remains the legacy of a Constitutional Convention compromise designed to palliate the fears of the smaller, less populated colonies and states of domination by the larger colonies (and thereby preserve the slave system of the South), the historically-skewed influence of the Senate has served merely to amplify (and perhaps exaggerate) these urban/rural antagonisms, not engender them. And again although one must surely acknowledge the contributing (and in the eyes of the evangelical alarmist, corroborating) reality that some of America's most chronic and intractable social problems seem an almost indelible feature of our large urban areas (unlike Europe), and also, even in comparative terms, that urban and rural political tensions (above and beyond the European regional and ethnic elements I mentioned) are a natural feature of any relationship between groups so different in size, outlook, and function—indeed, given all these additional considerations, I am wont to maintain that an irreducible core of extreme urban denigration and resentment—an underlying evangelical calculus of vilification—remains an essential endemic feature of our social and political landscape.[523] We observe here a festering ideological moral animus alien to continental European sensibilities and societies. Its most zealous apologists seize upon what in most other cultures are malleable, reconcilable regional or political differences and invest them with a moral significance that leaves little room for compromise on key issues, as Mary Ann Glendon concluded in her study of contrary European and American experiences with the abortion question.[524] (The outlook is particularly exemplified—although tempered with a good deal more surface affability and generosity—by the person and career of Representative Henry Hyde of rural Illinois.) At the very least, this moral vision adds a rancorous tenor and incivility to our politics that the nation would do better without.

In conclusion, and in anticipation of what is to follow, the cardinal assumption and claim advanced here remains one of an evangelical

---

of routine federal assistance from the Ford administration that these more symbolic political gestures (regarding a special loan) conveniently belied (see especially Chapter Four, "Is Washington To Blame?").

[523] For a more recent example of how ignorance of the core evangelical cultural logic and ethnos renders an understanding of the rural/urban split in American life problematical, see Marc J. Dunkelman, "Next-Door Strangers: The Crisis of Urban Anonymity," *The Hedgehog Review: The Meaning of Cities*, Summer 2017.

[524] *Abortion And Divorce In Western Law*, Cambridge: Harvard University Press, 1987. Several years later Glendon elsewhere embraced and reiterated this underlying cultural animus in a short piece for an evangelical journal; see "Villages and Virtues," *First Things* 56, October 1995.

community that has (or ideally should have) thrown off the fetters of ordinary social and cultural discourse, lifting both the community and its individual members beyond the normal gravitational pull of terrestrial social processes, creating and maintaining frictionless zones of personal and social being unlike any the secular world has ever known. This notion of an a-social, a-cultural transcendence represents then the ultimate *signal of difference*, occupying the centerpiece from which rises an expansive, all-inclusive evangelical social constellation, the logical ramifications of which extend into every nook and cranny of the everyday life of the college community and out into the larger American evangelical cultural galaxy.

CHAPTER 10

EVANGELICAL BONDS:
LOVE, SEXUALITY, & MARRIAGE

The relations between the sexes: perhaps no other subject receives as much attention and scrutiny from the elders of the college and community or evokes as much anxiety and confusion among students. Indeed I found it puzzling initially, given the tenor of the times, that persons in the Seattle Pacific community could dwell at such great lengths upon inter-personal phenomena and issues that are almost taken for granted elsewhere, seldom warranting the deliberate focus of a special college curriculum or program. Matters that are generally dealt with in an informal, individual fashion on other public and private college campuses become in the Christian college topics of widespread concern, addressed with a shotgun approach, every student in some manner or other nicked by the spraying buckshot of their elder's considerable angst. For example (in addition to the many chapel presentations upon the subject reviewed on tape), while I was on campus every quarter brought a series of "Open Seminars" upon some interpersonal or sexual-related issue—premarital sex, homosexuality, anorexia nervosa, etc.—conducted by the counseling center staff, along with concurrent offerings of a myriad of closed therapy sessions for particularly distressed individuals (institutional developments which, as we shall see, have rarely been welcomed among more conservative evangelical constituencies, whose members tend to dismiss psychology as a thoroughly secular field of endeavor, one incidental to genuine Christian emotional stability and health).[525]

The mere existence of these seminars and the apparent "open" approach of the counseling center are evidence of a new candor on campus.[526] As late

---

[525] A flyer from the Counseling Center: "Announcing! more Life Skills Seminars for Your Benefit and Enjoyment. . . . 1) Speaking the Truth in Love: Being Christian and Assertive. 2) Your Body, Your Self. . . . This group for women students will consider the Christian woman's attitude and beliefs concerning her body. The focus will be on perceived body image and beauty from social, media and Christian perspectives. . . . 3) How Thin is Thin? . . . especially for women who are concerned about the potential dangers of anorexia nervosa in their lives. 4) Learn to Relax. . . . learn techniques for physical and emotional relaxation. Participants will practice relaxation techniques and discuss their application to self-awareness and life enjoyment."

[526] The conventional reading of these developments is that they reflect an "accommodation" to the larger secular culture; that evangelicals are embracing large portions of the modern

as the mid 1970s, for example, a director of the counseling center who conducted a seminar for faculty members dealing with some of the sexual and other emotional problems troubling students became the subject of pressure applied upon the administration by some prominent alumni, who urged his removal from the faculty.[527] However, in spite of the apparent relaxation of a former vigilance there is every indication of some old attitudes lingering on into the 1990s,[528] for as one counseling center staff member conceded to those attending one of these more recent seminars on homosexuality, students had approached him all that week, a few perplexed by the topic of the meeting, asking "Why are you doing it?"

Authoritarianism / Egalitarianism

With respect to the fundamental relationships of love, friendship, and marriage there are two major schools of thought within evangelicalism. We are by now familiar with the first, the "mutual submission" position, a view advanced by many academicians (and more liberal social internationalist

---

American "therapeutic" culture. See, for example, J. D. Hunter's *Evangelicalism: The Coming Generation. . .* , 1987.

[527] Dr. David Terrell, from our interview (3/5/2003): "I tried to do some of that [seminars on sexual issues] a few years ago and was told, no way! ["Who told you that?"] It came from the 'constituency,' but through the administration. . . . Students approached the seminar leaders asking, 'Why are you doing this on campus?' This is what they used to say to me and yet that is a very serious problem ["Homosexuality?"] at Seattle Pacific. . . .

I used to try to bring it up in classes, cautiously. I was told by I don't know how many students, 'We just don't want to talk about this. Why even discuss this? We're Christians . . . [The problem is confined to] one or two weirdoes.' And so that was the attitude I found, you know, just forget it. I was told that I was never to discuss the topic of homosexuality, in a *Falcon* article or in any other context, if I was being interviewed by any source as a representative of Seattle Pacific. ["A vice-president told you that?"] It came directly from the president's office. ["McKenna?"] It came down through some of the other administrators. I was told not to discuss it again. I think McKenna, in all fairness to him, I feel that he had an understanding of the problem. I think he experienced pressure from the constituency. It came from people who give money to the school, the wealthy evangelicals. But I have been talked to by members of the Board of Trustees and others, quote 'influential,' people about that particular problem."

[528] Once again the school became embroiled in matters sexual with the hiring and "unhiring" to a full professorship of a Christian poet from Old Dominion, Scott Cairns, due to a poem, "Interval with Erato," recently published in *Paris Review*. More remarkable than the fact of simply being in the running to lure a poet of this stature (Cairns, a native, wanted to return home to the Northwest) to SPU, was the absolute consternation—nay *delirium tremens*— assorted administrators and faculty members were sent into over the sexual imagery in the poem, dismissed by some as "pornographic." Cairns had resigned his position at Old Dominion and accepted the SPU offer only to have it rescinded when news of the publication reached the SPU President, who feared the reaction of a conservative Board of Trustees. (Kathryn Robinson, "Sins of the Poet," *Seattle Weekly*, 7 May 1997.)

types), wherein a virtual equality ought to prevail in relationships—partners, friends, or spouses completely relinquishing self-interests in the pursuit and advancement of the best interests of others. So that in ideal relationships one participant's apprehension of his own interests rests entirely upon the perceptions and understandings of others. These loving others become the guardians of his own self-interest, while he in turn perceives, formulates, champions, defends, and promotes the interests of others. The genuine Christian friend or lover *empties* himself of inner-direction, re-fashioning himself into a hollow *vessel* to be filled with the highest, most God-centered interests of others. Such an other-directed orientation ensures that a kind of transcendent focus guides the lives of member Christians, discouraging the intrusion of *secular* ego- and man-centered values and motivations into personality and behavior. In this manner, the often contentious elements of personality—mind, body, and spirit—are more easily controlled and *balanced*, ensuring the *wholeness* of persons and the *transparency* of behavior.

Among the larger evangelical community, I would venture that although these somewhat revisionist notions of mutual submission may receive a tolerant and sympathetic hearing, a second, more traditional Pauline view (with some partial borrowings), wherein the male or father occupies a position of dominance in any relationship or family, holds greater sway (and perhaps even more so in practice than in theory).[529] The difference merely reflects a more general disparity between the views and practices of evangelical college students (and professors) and their parents and evangelicalism as a whole.[530]

---

[529] The role of women in the Bible:
—Ephesians 5:22-24: "Wives, be subject to your husbands as to the Lord; for the man is the head of the woman, just as Christ also is head of the church. Christ is, indeed, the Savior of the body; but just as the church is subject to Christ, so must women be to their husbands in everything." (Egalitarians typically emphasize the passages before and after these two sentences, those stressing mutual self-sacrifice and submission.)
—Colossians 3:18-19: "Wives, be subject to your husbands; that is your Christian duty. Husbands, love your wives and do not be harsh with them."
—I Corinthians 14:34-35: "As in all congregations of God's people, women should not address the meeting. They have no licence to speak, but should keep their place as the law directs. If there is something they want to know, they can ask their own husbands at home. It is a shocking thing that a woman should address the congregation." (*NEB*)
John Wesley, patron saint of Methodism, embraced the Pauline position, writing "that a wife must 'know herself the inferior and behave as such.' " (Greven, *The Protestant Temperament...*, 127.)

[530] These two contentious themes are readily apparent in Christian sociologist John Bartkowski's *Remaking the Godly Marriage: Gender Negotiation in Evangelical Families* (Rutgers University Press, 2001). What is missing as usual from such accounts (however much they parrot postmodernist jargon, e.g., everything is some sort of "discourse" or reflects a "discursive" intention) is a full awareness of how such idioms play off of diametrically-opposed invidious secular derivations.

So that while both the average student and evangelical perceive a yawning gulf between Christian and secular versions of personal relationships and the family, these differences tend to get formulated in disparate ways. The typical evangelical will emphasize the promiscuous, indulgent, and ephemeral nature of secular relationships and decry the breakdown of authority in secular families, explaining these developments as part of a larger society-wide permissiveness, the ineluctable consequence of a radical secular relativization of values which has followed in the train of the abandonment of rock-solid, ascetic, Judeo-Christian values. The typical student will acknowledge nearly all of the above and yet add an egalitarian spin to the indictment (as we have seen), execrating secular "power-dependence" relationships as well in a manner that may discomfit the more authoritarian conservative evangelical, the leveling ideas invoking the specter of feminism. (Although advocates of Pauline authoritarianism will in turn often temper the tone of these declarations of male domination with a telling sop to the female underclass: for, not to worry, this inequality has elements of mutual submission built into it. Ignore the secular connotations of authority and power. In genuine Christian families the husband, although dominant, actually *serves* his spouse and offspring by fulfilling the duties and responsibilities of authority, much as Christ *served* his followers and the church. Just as the wife in turn *serves* her husband through subordination. Thus the *principle of inversion* is invoked: to lead is to serve, not dominate, manipulate, or enforce. Indeed everyone *serves* in some manner or other within *the body of Christ*.)

Christian Sexuality

It is perhaps only natural in a co-ed community of young people with proverbial over-active glands and imaginations that the matter of pre-marital sexual relations generates a great deal of concern. On this basic question liberal and conservative evangelicals are virtually of one mind: total abstinence before marriage. More generally, observe in the following account of one chapel speaker's presentation of this position the appearance of elements of the above egalitarian logic and other familiar themes and variations.

Dr. Steve Haynes, young, open-minded, and exceptionally popular among students, college pastor of University Presbyterian Church at the time and later named Vice-President of Student Affairs at Seattle Pacific, delivered a Christian Commitment Week series of chapel talks upon "God's View of Sexuality." [531] Haynes begins with the "secular" approach to sex. The

---

[531] "God's View of Sexuality" (4/6/81); "Sex For Christians" (4/7/81); and one other session, 4/8/81.

"world" or the "culture" believes that "the only purpose of sex is pleasure"; outside the Christian community "sex is the central issue of life," even though it only represents a "mere biological function." Such beliefs and practices are altogether contrary to the original intention of God. For the sexual nature of human beings emerged not from any lengthy biological developmental process, but through God's simple "gift of sexuality" (" . . . yet sometimes it doesn't feel like a gift at all").

Casual, hedonistic sex divorces the body from personality and spirit, creating an *imbalance*. To regard and treat another person as a mere object of sexual gratification undermines any real identification with the long-term interests of the other, violating that individual's wholeness and integrity. To isolate the body from the spirit is to "depersonalize" a relationship and fragment personality.

At this juncture, the chapel audience, initially skittish and noisy, has fallen deeply silent. Haynes extends a pause, and then adds softly, "We get *broken* in our sexuality by sin." For it is when Christians allow the sexual distortions of the world to creep into their own lives, when they come to believe that the "restraint of impulses is harmful," that the needs of the body grow in malignant disproportion to the needs of the spirit, and of the personality. The ramifications of this imbalance are obsessive "masturbation, fetishes, sexually-abused children." His audience slips even deeper into silence. As becomes readily apparent, Haynes has seen and heard it all, relating story after story of persons who have allowed sexual drives to expand beyond the bounds of propriety and proportion, usurping the precarious equilibrium of personality, wallowing in "the blackness of our own sin."

And yet they must understand that sex is neither uniformly "all good" nor "all bad." God's intentions are plain: He created sex for more than the simple reproduction of the species. The experience should draw people together, conveying a "special expression of physical oneness," becoming a "communion of the flesh." This unique interpersonal gravity brings predestined Christian lovers together. Sexual intercourse among Christian couples thus transcends the purely physical copulations and gratifications of secular relationships, for by and within it, genuine personalities merge in an almost heavenly fusion of bodies and spirits—are made *whole*—and any biological consequence proves merely incidental or complementary to this cardinal objective of conjugal unity. The bliss of sacred sexual union, more pleasurable than anything the secular hedonist can possibly experience, is God's "gift"—

and man's reward—for the pursuit and achievement of Christian wholeness.[532]

What students need are clear, concrete delineations, such as the difference between the letter and the spirit of the law. Christians who observe the single prohibition against intercourse and yet engage in every other sexual behavior imaginable are "faking it," living by the "letter of the law," rather than by the "spirit of the law." Let's face it, he levels with the astonished students, "petting to have orgasms" violates the spirit of the law and undermines Christian commitment. A muffled, uncomfortable rustle passes through the audience.

Haynes concludes that the "whole point" is not so much the promulgation of yet another standard of licit and illicit behavior as the reaffirmation of a more general principle that is often lost sight of: the simple, familiar Christian axiom that "interior life should correspond to . . . exterior life." The spirit of the law ought to mirror the letter of the law; outer appearances ought to reflect inner realities. The individual who presents a serene external demeanor and yet harbors within a teeming host of sexual demons sunders the wholeness of personality, the integrity of Christian character. For what the Christian academician or counselor above all seeks to bring to fruition in his student charges is *the union of personality and conduct*. Create, nurture, and maintain wholeness and transparency, and all the other Christian virtues follow as a matter of course.

Drawing The Lines

These not unreasonable exhortations for students to elevate their apprehension and appreciation of the spirit and meaning of the Christian moral laws above the mere mechanical observance of behavioral codes often fall upon deaf, uncomprehending ears—or, rather, simply fail to slake the seemingly unquenchable evangelical adolescent thirst for incontrovertible lines of

---

[532] Many years later this core evangelical dynamic of a Manichean one-upmanship (wherein a discredited secular phenomenon is directly paired with, and nullified by, a far more transcendent sacralized Christian version) re-appeared in more *au courant* formulations, as reported by Jeff Sharlet: "They don't silence sex; they promise sacred sex to those who couple properly—orgasms, according to a bit of fundamentalist folklore passed between young singles, '600 percent' more intense for those who wait than those experienced by secular lovers." (*The Family. . .* , op. cit., 337.) This passage, unfortunately without a citation, is part of Sharlet's larger argument about the post-millenarian drift of modern American fundamentalism: ". . . .not a uniform ideology but a manifold *movement*. . . moving in every direction all at once, claiming the earth for God's kingdom. . . ." But as we have seen, it is both, and with just as many pre-millenarian elements wedged in.

demarcation between appropriate and inappropriate behavior.[533] In fact, I would contend that so ingrained is the need for a rigid moral infrastructure in most of these youngsters that even those who deviate markedly from its terms nonetheless ironically retain expectations that everyone at least ought to be bound by their observance.

For example, one mental health clinician, Dr. David Terrell, who worked nearly ten years or so in the Seattle Pacific counseling center recounted that in private sessions with students struggling with homosexual feelings his professional clinical manner generally elicited two very different responses. With prospective clients he would openly establish his understanding of and position upon homosexuality at the very first meeting, explaining that "I realize my feelings, my training, go against the philosophical stance of the school and evangelical Christianity and I am not trying to push this on you, but I'll be glad to share it with you if it will be of help." One group of students was typically relieved to find a sympathetic, "non-judgmental" confidant and responded positively: " 'Oh, I'm so glad, gee' . . . [these particular kids] had respected me anyway [from classroom acquaintance] or they probably would never have come in." The discovery of a combination of impartial clinical manner and avuncular lean-on-me support proved a "big relief" for many students.

On the other hand, a quite different group of students was nonplussed by the evenhandedness of his approach, perhaps anticipating—even yearning for—moral censure. These obviously troubled students responded in an almost antagonistic fashion: "Huh, well, if that's what you are, then just bag it!" In one instance a student who had been "overt in his experience" and had come seeking help spurned the counseling conditions and approach and returned to his dormitory, telling his friends that there was this clinician at the counseling center who was advocating homosexuality. He characterized the counselor's pitch to inquiring students as something along the lines of "Get with it! Everybody do it!"

In the latter instance, the student clearly sought the invocation of some unequivocal code to lift the burden of responsibility for introspection and free thought from his own shoulders. Having been raised in a world of clear delineations of right and wrong, he was unprepared for the moral ambiguity of the clinician's casual approach. He no doubt anticipated a swift pronouncement and application of inflexible moral laws, perhaps believing in the inherent power of God-given sanctions to reverse his idiosyncrasy and

---

[533] In the PBS documentary, *Born Again: Life in a Fundamentalist Baptist Church*, a youth director of the Worchester, Massachusetts church stands before a blackboard and instructs teenagers in the differences between "satanical" and "Christian" dress. He asks: "What do we mean by a satanical way of dressing?"

restore a Christian normality. To be told that there was no simple procedure of Christian expiation, purgation, and metamorphosis and that the counselor had no real interest in documenting the number of violations, must have produced considerable personal disorientation. And as so often happens in the evangelical community, a portion of this individual's anxiety and guilt erupted in the *projection* of his own homosexual inclinations back onto the clinician. For it would seem that even the ostensibly sexually miscreant student takes a peculiar kind of comfort in a stable moral infrastructure that places his violation in some sort of larger context of order and meaning.[534]

The Survey

The average Seattle Pacific student prefers clear delineations of proper sexual conduct. When, for example, the survey sample was asked, "In general, do you consider it important for couples who are going steady, as they say, and are trying to establish boundaries or limits upon their behavior when together, to be able to distinguish a) appropriate Christian sexual conduct for unmarrieds from b) non-Christian conduct or the values and norms which prevail in American society as a whole?" the overwhelming majority affirmed the importance of thinking about sexual conduct in this manner.[535]

---

[534] In a sense, this kind of yearning for punitive order may represent a more general ascetic—dare we say, *Anglo-Saxon*—cultural disposition. Consider the reflections of Mrs. Christian Annersley, aged fifty-five, magistrate and chairman of the Bench:

> And then there is this conflict of reform versus punishment. And I'm really honestly and truly, having been liberal and "psychological" all my life, coming to the conclusion that punishment is a good thing. That punishment really gets it off the chest of a great many people. They think, "Well, I've paid!" If people can accept the fact that they have paid they can either go on being a happy criminal or they can stop being a criminal. So I don't think that punishment is a bad thing. I used to think it was, but I don't now. There now, after all my years as a reformer! It is rather a cleansing thing. Certain people are destroyed—killed by the present method. Justice is not done to these people. A very wrong result comes out. . . . (Ronald Blythe, *Portrait of an English Village*, New York: Pantheon Books, 1980, 279.)

Those who harbor nostalgia for traditional *gemeinschaft* village mores and morality would do well to examine Chapter 15, "The Law."

[535] Very important to distinguish [5] (115) 53%

			[4]	(54)	25
			[3]	(25)	12
			[2]	(14)	7
Unimportant	"	"	[1]	(9)	<u>4</u>
					101%

When asked to run through a list of light to heavy duty sexual behaviors, from [1] Holding hands, to [7] Petting, to [15] sleeping together without having sex, the students produced a surprising array of responses, a majority appearing a good deal more active and sophisticated in expression and practice than I had any right to expect; 50% chose eleven or more behaviors as appropriate.[536]

Further examination of student reactions to a request for reflections upon their own premarital sexual encounters confirms a breadth of experience within the student population. The reader will detect in the very wording of the item soliciting these reflections[537] the author's skepticism of any significant level of promiscuity. My interest was frankly stated: not so much in counting the number of students who had engaged in sex (thinking the percentage would be insignificantly low anyway) as in understanding the kinds of rationalizations these (assumed) few later employed to explain the incidents to themselves.

In any event, I was unprepared for the results: approximately 36% of the sample students acknowledged a pre-marital sexual experience. We observe

---

[536] These data mirror rather nicely the more informal numbers Peter Gardella collected over the years from his own classroom students in three of four mid-west and Atlantic colleges. (*Innocent Ecstasy: How Christianity Gave America an Ethic of Sexual Pleasure*, Oxford University Press, 1985.)

[537] "We wish to examine here the subject of pre-marital sexual behavior. We are not really interested in how many of you have engaged in such behavior, but are rather more interested in the motivations and reasonings of the few of you who have. Think back for a moment those of you who have had such pre-marital experiences: how did you explain them to yourself? (Check as many as apply):

[1] The opportunity arose and I just couldn't control myself. (20)	9%
[2] I was overpowered by the other person. (5)	2
[3] If petting and other activities—thinking about doing it—are just as sinful as doing it, why not go all the way? Either way, you feel just as bad. (3)	1
[4] It's just not that big a deal to me. (11)	5
[5] Premarital sex is not adultery and thus is not a sin." (6)	3
[6] Other: _____ (21)	10
[7] Combinations (13)	6
[NR] (138)	64
	100%

Students having engaged in pre-marital sex:
[1] Yes	(79)	36%
[2] No	(115)	53
[NR]	(23)	11
		100%

(A few students indicated that they were not Christians when they had their experiences and that the behaviors ceased upon conversion, but the large majority reported the same level of commitment before and after.)

here then a sizeable minority of students for whom the expression of and commitment to the abstract logic of Christian and secular codes of sexual behavior appears only tenuously related to actual practice (although we should keep in mind that the numbers may in many cases reflect only one such incident), yet whose illicit sexual experiences, as suggested above, none-theless do little to weaken the grip of these invidious distinctions upon their moral imaginations and the high expectations they continue to hold for both themselves and other students. The impression one gets from the survey re-sponses is of a group of students whose "struggles" with sexuality[538]—

---

[538] "In general, would you say that you are presently struggling with your sexuality?"

Yes, very much	[5]	(8)	4%
	[4]	(30)	14
	[3]	(35)	16
	[2]	(50)	23
No, not at all	[1]	(93)	43
	[NR]	(1)	*
			100%

"If you are, what form do these struggles assume?

[1] Strong attraction to the opposite sex I can't seem to control.	(37)	17%
[2] Sexual identity anxiety: don't really understand my urges and feelings; don't really know if I'm heterosexual or homosexual; wonder sometimes.	(4)	2
[3] Strong attraction to the same sex—either emotional or sexual—that I don't understand and can't control.	(2)	1
[4] Other: _____"	(53)	24
[5] More than one above.	(3)	1
[NR]	(118)	54
		99%

"If you don't consider yourself to be struggling with your sexuality, would you say that you are comfortable or uncomfortable with individuals of the opposite sex?"

Comfortable	[5]	(102)	47%
	[4]	(53)	24
	[3]	(12)	6
	[2]	(8)	4
Uncomfortable	[1]	(1)	*
	[NR]	(41)	19
			100%

"If you struggle:

a) Do you feel anxiety or guilt about your difficulties?

b) Do these difficulties ever make you doubt or question whether or not you are really a Christian?"

however much anxiety or confusion attends them—rarely translate into a corresponding uncertainty over the adequacy and veracity of the logic underlying the formal prohibitions. Students who continuously violate the code of sexual thought and conduct nonetheless appear comfortable with the almost punishing load of apprehension and guilt which ensues, although there is considerable variation in the ease or difficulty with which these episodes of violation and anxiety are borne.[539] In this sense, a (secular) world bereft of the absolute guiding terms of the evangelical logic may then loom as an unimaginably barren alternative, even among those whose wanton deviance proves so intolerable to the community.

Considerable	[5]	(7)	3%		Yes, often	[5]	(2)	1%
	[4]	(18)	8			[4]	(7)	3
	[3]	(30)	14			[3]	(9)	4
	[2]	(29)	13			[2]	(15)	7
None	[1]	(15)	7		No, never	[1]	(64)	29
	[NR]	(118)	54			[NR]	(120)	55
			99%					99%

[539] Comparing the CRI2 (Combined Religious Intensity Scale) distributions of those students admitting having engaged in sex with the total student sample, I detect little difference. See Appendix A for the content and explanation of CRI2.

—A 1989 Gallup survey of college students (sample of 539 from 100 private and public institutions) revealed that while 42% of sample students said religion is "very important" in their lives and 37% said "somewhat," approximately 50% said "they engage in sex at least occasionally, and 26% reported that they participate 'regularly.' "

The poll, commissioned by Pat Robertson's Christian Broadcasting Network (CBN), elicited this response from CBN officials: who "concede that some of the Gallup findings reflect little correlation between the religious precepts of college students and their lifestyles. 'College students say one thing,' reports Susan L. Norman, senior editor at the network, 'but do another—particularly where sex is concerned.' " ("Parade's Special Intelligence Report: College Students: Sex, Religion and Lifestyles," *Parade Magazine*, 6 August 1989, 12.)

—Here is part of "Spiritual Emphasis Week" speaker Ken Poure's "pitch" to students of Grace College in Winona Lake, Indiana:

Mr. Poure's advice to women is to watch out because "guys hands are wired in a different way"—the "guy could be in lust while the girl could be in love." He goes on to parody couples who pray before having sex, adding that many good "Christian girls get pregnant by Christian guys." *Finally, the moment of truth arrives as he charts on an overhead screen a scale that ranges from "small kiss" to "sexual intercourse."*

"How far do you go?" Mr. Poure asks. "The Bible doesn't say. But on the college level, I'd draw the line at 'little kiss.' " (Kenneth Briggs, "Evangelical Colleges Reborn," New York Times Magazine, 14 December 1980.)

The Marriage Market

In addition to its many other virtues, parents often look upon the Christian college as a pool teeming with potential suitors or spouses for their sons and daughters. The prospect of Christian boys and girls pairing off with those of identical Christian beliefs enjoys perhaps the strongest Biblical support of any conception we will encounter in this study. Although it is difficult to imagine a phrase like "be not unequally yoked with pagans"[540] falling easily from the lips of Jesus, its appearance among the letters of Paul can serve as an incontrovertible sanction for connubial separatism.

As one former Seattle Pacific faculty member put it:

> I believe there was . . . ["Pressure?"] to marry a Christian. That's the only thing that matters—I'm oversimplifying somewhat—but you marry someone who loves the Lord and that's where you find them . . . . I have a good friend who graduated from Seattle Pacific and who married one of the most popular girls on that campus. . . . This was back in the late '50s. And after they were married . . . geez . . . the kinds of things that happened between them! And this girl, she was something else. I knew her too. Poor Stan! He's remarried and very happy. . . . But he told me once: "the only thing that I was taught was to marry a Christian girl." And she was a member of the same church. . . . What more could you ask for? [laughter]
> 541

A few years later, conjugal imperatives continue to motivate single undergraduates, as Alan Basham, director of the counseling center, conceded to a chapel audience: "We have a fantasy that we have to marry somebody before we leave here."[542] The evangelical imperative produces in many a rush to judgment and in a few a near desperation to fulfill its terms within the allotted four-year period. One student senator, Daniel, tall, dark, and bearded, although a shade heavy, and a fine public speaker often called upon to deliver public devotions, told of a particularly distressing recent experience.

> Started going together fall quarter. . . . towards the end I really began to have some doubts about her—about her emotional maturity. [She had] Self-esteem problems, depended too much on others.
> Winter quarter, I said good-bye, I can't take this anymore, I need space. It's been a struggle ever since to get that through [to her] . . . kept coming by. Got to the point where I said, "I don't want to see you anymore!". . . I know that sounds harsh. The very next day she came by to see what I was doing. So frustrating! Had

---

[540] II Corinthians 6:14-18 : "Do not unite yourself with unbelievers; they are no fit mates for you. What has righteousness to do with wickedness? . . . And therefore, 'come away and leave them, separate yourselves, says the Lord; touch nothing unclean. . . .' " (*NEB*)

[541] D. T. Interview, 3/5/2003.

[542] "Love And The Squirrel Hunt," Chapel.

three, four hour talks, just yelling and screaming. . . . I was so frustrated and drained. . . . I said, "OK, yell, scream, get it out!" ["Did she?"] Yeah, for a week. ["Screamed for a week?"] No, about two hours . . . and cried: "How can you do this to me? I've done so much for you!"

My mistake was that I talked about it ["Marriage?"] . . . once . . . and she went home to visit my parents. . . .

I think she's finally gotten the message. . . . It's really sad. I have friends who come up and say, "Oh, you're Christian, when you break up you should hug and kiss and everything should be OK," and I say ideally, yes, but in reality it doesn't work out like that . . . there's a lot of hurt and pain in there. . . . I learned a lot. In the future, [I've got to] be a little more careful.[543]

The pressure of the imperative can also be documented by the sheer number of intermarriages among upperclassmen. Working from announcements published in the official college magazine I was able to arrive at an admittedly crude estimation of intramural marriage rates. For example, over a one year period from October 1975 to August 1976 (the only full year for which I had relatively complete issues) 89 total marriages and 27 inter-student marriages were reported. Given a total graduating class each year of anywhere from 250 to 350 students we find then that approximately 120 or so of these graduates were marrying each year and that of this group roughly half (or from @ 1/4 to 1/6 of total departing students) were marrying a fellow Seattle Pacific student or graduate. By any standard, this represents a phenomenal rate of intermarriage.[544]

---

[543] (*SSI*, May 2003)

—In an "exchange chapel" with George Fox College (Oregon), Ron, the George Fox College chaplain joked in the buddy-buddy vernacular of the students that these colleges are just "match factories." (Ron Crecelius, Exchange Chapel, 5/8/81)

—One Christian musician, introducing a song to the first chapel audience of the year, paused to interject, "Hope you don't think I'm talking about going to school to get a husband or wife." The students laughed and broke into applause. (Chapel, 10/4/82)

—Anthony Campolo told after-chapel discussions that the reason women are here at Christian colleges is that "mother sends you to get married," and that "A lot of you kids are going to be manipulated into marriage . . . [whereas] singleness is the preferred state." (Chapel "Talkback" sessions, 5/16-18/2003)

[544] Based upon Oct. 75, Dec. 75, Feb. 76, Apr. 76, June 76, Aug. 76 issues of *Response* magazine, the official publication of Seattle Pacific College. I may have been short three issues, since the magazine during this period supposedly put out nine issues a year. The omissions may serve to balance the inclusion in the above figures marriages entered into by any SPC graduate regardless of class year (although nearly all were present students or very recent graduates).

Also: "About 40% of last year's graduates were married, as is about one student in five at Seattle Pacific this year." (Norman L. Edwards [Dean of Students], "Today's Student," *SPC Alumni*, Autumn 1965.)

The Family

Two major Christian family models rise from these respective authoritarian/egalitarian approaches to male-female relationships. Perhaps the most prominent advocate of the authoritarian family is James Dobson ("the leading Christian family relations expert in the U.S."), whose book, *Dare To Discipline*, is a perennial bestseller, but whose prescriptions depend more upon simple-minded, spare-the-rod, spoil-the-child borrowings from behavior modification psychology than upon any systematic Biblical exegesis or formulation of principles (a criticism, incidentally, often voiced within the evangelical camp by less than adoring liberal members).[545] The Dobson program is largely self-explanatory, warranting only brief mention in passing. More important for our purposes is what the champions of family authoritarianism share with the adherents of egalitarianism, and that is a familiar weakness for invidious distinctions: the former juxtaposing Christian *discipline* with secular *permissiveness*; the latter, *interpersonal equality* with *power-dependence* relations.

Throughout this study I have made occasional reference to campus guest speaker Anthony Campolo's version of Christian egalitarianism, the final portion of which now follows.

In the second of three chapel lectures, "About the World,"[546] Campolo takes an "honest look at our culture," particularly the relations between friends, lovers, and spouses. He urges students to become aware of the general principles operating out there in the world—the reality about love and power, for example: "The more power you have, the less love you have," and vice versa.

In simple relationships, this means that the one who loves the least holds the most power. It happens all the time on this campus, he contends; it "happens in your interpersonal life." How does it happen? "You all know it": it is

---

[545] Some readers may recall that Dobson was a member of U.S. Attorney General Ed Meese's Commission on Pornography and later during the gruesome media events surrounding the execution of mass murderer, Ted Bundy, in Florida, videotaped a final confession in which Bundy sought to shift much of the blame for his behavior onto the pornographic materials he perused as an adolescent, to Dobson's obvious delight.

—Similar to Dobson in approach is another Christian bestseller, Richard J. Foster's *Celebration of Discipline: The Path To Spiritual Growth*.

—Daniel, a student senator, mentioned Dobson in our conversation: " . . . . kind of a cure-all . . . cultic elements in Dobson. ["He has big meetings—last year came to the Seattle Center."] Yeah, I went. ["What'd you think?"] At the time I thought, right on, this is what we need! Where's our religion profs? . . . but now . . . they're [his followers] indoctrinated [laughter] . . . [there are] issues that he doesn't answer . . . good questions . . . I'm not into pat answers, and I don't think he can answer them." (*SSI*, May 2003)

[546] The Staley Lectures, 5/17/2003.

the "big lie." You use the big lie to "get the other person to love you more than you love him or her." And once these games of domination start they tend to wend their way into almost every conceivable relationship; none is immune. The greatest damage of all results when they seep into the very heart of the church community itself, as when Christians use the authority of the Bible to establish domineering relationships. They "withhold love" in order to manipulate and change the behavior of others; they play power games. Often the manipulation assumes the form of a rebuke: "If you were a Christian you wouldn't ask a stupid question like that." They hurt your feelings and try to control your mind and behavior.

Christians ought to be different; we should exercise "no domination" whatsoever in relationships; we ought—especially in our intimate couplings—to be "servants of one another." There is "nothing wrong with submission . . . that's Biblical." The second chapter of the apostle Paul's letter to the Philippians gives us a saint who would "empty himself" in love of others, one who "made himself of no reputation." And further, recall that God the father demonstrated his love for us not through the strength but rather the "weakness of Jesus." The "world worships masterhood instead."

Genuine Christian marriages, then, ought to feature men who love their wives as "Christ loved the church," men who make themselves into "servants" or minions of their spouses, both partners sacrificing their hopes and aspirations for the other, "each being submissive to the other." There is "something glorious about servanthood."

Now although in all likelihood this egalitarian model of personal and family relationships holds greater sway and counts a greater number of adherents within the precincts of evangelical academia, I can report having encountered not a single sustained formal objection out among the larger evangelical community. As mentioned earlier, when phrased in the manner above of Anthony Campolo, the position appears to dovetail into the other, winning the toleration of even more conservative evangelicals, whose more visible public and television leaders are occasionally caught, in moments of compromise, tempering the bald Biblical mandate of inequality[547] with more palatable and fashionable principles of mutual submission, to the great relief of some long-suffering spouses.

The Students

When asked to reflect upon these assumed differences between Christian and secular marriages: "Do you think there is in general a great difference

---

[547] This is usually done by including the verses upon mutual self-sacrifice and submission which sandwich the more offensive Ephesians 5:22-24.

between the manner in which married Christian couples treat one another (and their children, if any), and the way non-Christian or atheistic married couples behave together?" the overwhelming majority of sample students concurred; only a few found no appreciable differences.[548]

Students characterized the disparity in this fashion:

"Treat one another with respect and as equals."

"The [secular] parents only can look forward to the here and now and it reflects in the goals they set for their children."

"More patience . . . more endurance (peaceful)—although not true in all cases."

"By striving to surpass Eros (male-female love) and to love in a fashion after agapé (self-effacing love)."

"There is more of a basis in the showing of affection and love for your spouse and children through what the Bible says, than just doing what everybody else is doing."

"In the way 1) they carry out discipline and 2) encouragement."

"See the other as part of a triad . . . God/man/woman . . . same goals."

"If God is in the center of the relationship then their [sic] will be more love in the marriage. God adds a dimension to Xtian marriage that cannot be found in most secular marriages. Sad to say, though, many Xtian unions are lacking in this area."

"Christian families have more of an unconditional love + care + understanding between members. Non-Christian families sometimes seem superficial."

"More concern for the other person."

"There should always be the attitude of the other person as being more important because of their love for God and the desire they, hopefully, have to be like Jesus."

"The respect people have for one another—less 'I' and more 'we' in a Christian relationship. Less emphasis on sex."

" . . . . Non-Christians have self as a primary focus of 'worship.' "

---

[548] "Do you think there is in general a great difference between the manner in which married Christian couples treat one another (and their children, if any) and the way non-Christian or atheistic married couples behave together?"

Great difference	[5]	(48)	22%
	[4]	(93)	43
	[3]	(42)	19
	[2]	(21)	10
No difference	[1]	(13)	6
			100%

"Have a greater motivation to stay together/power hierarchy different/deal with problems 'quieter'. . . ."

"Build and encourage each other to grow in God; looking out for the other's best."

"Concern for others' feelings; not self-centered but out to help other and obey God."

"There <u>should</u> be a difference—commitment to lifetime relationship, submitting to one another out of reverence to Christ (Eph. 5:21)."

"There needs to be a difference—like continual mutual submission—but often there is little difference."

"Christian—God-centered and true Christ-like love/Non-Christian—man-centered."

" . . . . there's more of a concern for the spiritual life of one another. Love should be more characterized in the relationship rather than social stigma or repute."

"No bond of Christian love—<u>koinonia</u>."

With few exceptions, the students express in myriad ways the clear expectation of Christian and secular difference.[549]

---

[549] A couple of the more ambivalent exceptions:

—"Unfortunately, what seems to distinguish Christian couples are negative things: e.g., male dominance. Positive characteristics include the recognition of marriage as more than a common contract."

—"I think it should make a difference but a lot of times it doesn't. The children should grow up more secure and the family should get along better but many times its the opposite. I think it depends on the individuals."

The Superior Christian Family[550]

Another survey item asked students to reflect upon the kinds of personal or social advantages that faith may confer upon the evangelical community:

> . When the Billy Graham Crusade visited the Tacoma dome last spring advertisements appeared in Seattle newspapers announcing events of the week. One such ad portrayed a husband and wife with their two children; the caption read "How to keep your family together when others are being torn apart."
>
> How much do you agree or disagree with the underlying assumption here that Christians and Christian communities are characterized by unique qualities which provide an advantage in overcoming or avoiding the kinds of problems—familial, interpersonal, psychological—that plague American society in general.

The sample students expressed overwhelming agreement.[551] Dr. David Terrell, former counseling center director, recalls that his own initial reluc-

---

[550] Quite a few years after I had polished off my final conclusions upon these matters, I came across Peter Gardella's *Innocent Ecstasy: How Christianity Gave America an Ethic of Sexual Pleasure* (Oxford 1985). Although I find the background research valuable, the author drawing upon some of the same materials I cited in my earlier historical chapters, a couple of things proved troubling. Although, as we have seen, this evangelical college and the larger evangelical community advance all sorts of claims as to the superiority of their social model and reality versus the "secular world," I have never encountered more than one or two fleeting instances (one recounted in an earlier footnote about the now defunct Mars Hill Church) of the kind of sexual braggadocio he attributes to the evangelical couple, Tim and Beverly LaHaye (the former one of the founders of the Moral Majority) in their 1976 book, *The Act of Marriage*: "Pastor, I never dreamed when I accepted Christ that He would invade our sex life, but we had never been able to make my wife's bells ring until after we were converted. Now she has a climax most of the time." (150) Whether Catholicism or evangelicalism, the evidence of such celebratory concerns for ecstatic orgasms is sparse. And even among his one or two citations— Marabel Morgan in particular—he misses the point when she writes: "God is waiting and wanting to fill your vacuum, to make you complete. . . . Right now you can become a Total Woman." A few encounters with some students who are Catholic do not a representative sample make. For evangelicals, coupling is all about self-effacing *agape* love, about *wholeness*, not sacralizing orgasms. This set in marked opposition to *secular* fragmentation, the separation of lust from love, eros from spirit. Second problem: it seems rather odd to attribute the liberation of copulation from original sin to the very religion, Christianity, that imposed the original iron cage. Perhaps only a pyrrhic victory at best?

[551]

Very much agree	[5]	(73)	34%
	[4]	(77)	35
	[3]	(34)	16
	[2]	(15)	7
Do not agree	[1]	(17)	8
	[NR]	(1)	*
			100%

—Wanda: "I definitely think there ought to be a difference . . . there ought to be a difference in every single one of our relationships if we're really governed by Christ. If members of the family are living out the kind of submissive, sacrificial love that the Bible calls us to then splits

tance to accept a position at an evangelical college (having received his clinical training at a large public university) arose from precisely these kinds of assumptions:

> I didn't want to take a job that wouldn't be challenging. . . . I really honestly, sincerely believed that I wouldn't have that much to do . . . because, you know, Christians don't have problems. I knew they did and yet deep down inside I felt maybe they don't on the West Coast . . . but I wasn't sure.

The Evangelical Family Under Siege

For then President David McKenna the logic not only confers a greater resilience upon the Christian family but also, unfortunately, places the institution in a position of some jeopardy, as it becomes

> . . . . subject to attacks that may be unknown to the secular family. . . . With a floating value base and changeable guidelines, the secular family simply adjusts in areas where the Christian family may be under attack. . . . As society liberalizes its moral view of these behaviors, Christian values are called into question. . . . Professors of marriage and family in Christian colleges seem to feel as if the Christian family is being undermined by the sexual revolution. . . . According to the professors, the Christian family is in *a life-and-death struggle with secularism*. . . . Christian values may be consciously taught in the home, but secular values are communicated subconsciously by the media and peer groups. . . . Several professors anticipate the conflict between secularism and Christianity to move *from pressure to persecution* sometime in the future.[552]

An all too familiar theme: the outlook and mood within lies in a deep calibration with perceptions of peril without, the syncopated rhythms of persecution and reaction forever playing off one another, forever active and festering within the mind and community of the disenchanted evangelical.

---

are not as likely to occur; there'll be more respect between all the members of the family. Do I think that is the case? I don't know. It seems like from the friends I know here that real traditional Christian families do stay together more than ones that don't. . . . because my parents weren't real committed Christians and that was part of the reason their marriage fell apart. . . . Hmm, I don't know. I also see a lot of Christian friends who have alcoholism in their families and just these various problems. But just as a general trend I think that traditional Christian families are a little more stable . . . well . . . a little more isolated too."
—However, Jacob, a more liberal senior student senator, was less reverent: "Kinda makes you puke, doesn't it?" (*SSI*, May 2003)

[552] David L. McKenna, "Christian Higher Education and Family Development," address to the Continental Congress On The Family, Oct. 13-17, 1975, reprinted in *Universitas*, November 1975. In preparation for this address, McKenna telephoned professors teaching marriage and family courses in the twelve colleges of the Christian College Consortium. It is instructive (and he later betrays neither surprise nor concern) that not a single lecturer or professor was female.

Satanic Ritual Abuse Syndrome & Daycare

We are in a position now to understand a rather peculiar cultural phenomenon, what had become known in the '80s and '90s as the *Satanic Ritual Abuse Syndrome*. It is my strong contention that the matter can be largely explained as a logical—almost foregone—conclusion of these evangelical cultural ideas. Consider, for example, a most telling piece of data that is seldom fully examined. The most prominent, riveting cases have largely concerned daycare or daycare operators. Initially a seeming epidemic broke out during the late 1980s. There followed in rapid succession the McMartin pre-school daycare center case in a Los Angeles suburb, the Little Rascals daycare case in North Carolina, and the Ingram family "Remembering Satan" case in Olympia, Washington.[553] Since then, we have seen additional cases of varying degrees of similarity and difference.

What underpins the phenomenon? Observe how the logic drives the attributions or indictments of secular evil. Of all the institutions that emerged and expanded operations during the "sexual revolution" of the 1960s and 1970s, daycare came to symbolize for evangelicals the deterioration of the traditional nuclear Christian family. It allowed mothers to become full-time working professional women, undermining traditional gender roles. Along with the ERA (Equal Rights Amendment) and Roe v. Wade, the weight of these developments came to be regarded within evangelicalism as affronts or even attacks upon the evangelical cultural world. Legalized abortion removed the burden or anxiety of pregnancy, encouraging promiscuity and hedonism; the ERA sought to add legal sanctions encouraging the lifestyle; and daycare freed women to pursue professional, masculine careers while neglecting the full responsibilities of mothering. The very idea of daycare triggered the evangelical logic of invidious cultural distinction. It embodied all that was malignant in the secular approach to family. In both print and television media evangelicals were fed a steady diet of daycare exposés and disparaging commentary.[554] And so it followed as a matter of course that when rumors or insinuations of abuse (often grounded in simple incidents of discipline) reached parents of a certain persuasion, particularly those experiencing some unease or guilt about having placed their children in daycare, evangelical instructed or influenced minds whetted their imaginations, encouraging them to run wild, inflating small matters to malignant secular

---

[553] Brigitte Greenberg, "Jury Rejects Children's 'Bizarre' Accusations in Sexual-Abuse Trial," *Seattle Times*, 21 November 1993; Ofra Bikel, "Frontline: Innocence Lost: The Verdict," Parts 1 &2, PBS, 20-21 July 1993; Lawrence Wright, "Remembering Satan," Parts 1&2, *The New Yorker*, 17&24 May 1993.

[554] Perhaps the nadir of hysteria was reached with Marian Blum's, *The Daycare Dilemma: Women and Children First* (Lexington Books—D.C. Heath, 1983.)

proportions. The slippery-slope of the evangelical imagination descended all the way from routine pedophilic abuse (the sexual promiscuity slippery-slope) to children getting baked to death in microwaves (the pro-life "baby-killer" slippery-slope). As with New York City, everything malignant in the secular cultural world could be projected in gargantuan proportions onto the secular daycare of the fertile evangelical cultural imagination

The indictments tended to assume two forms: insinuations of *external* abuse out there in the *secular* institutions of daycare and other related services; and insinuations of *internal* abuse—charges leveled within evangelical communities or churches of the *infiltration* of nefarious *external* satanic elements. The Ingram family case offers an intriguing combination of several inflammatory elements: Sandy Ingram, the mother, ran a daycare in her home; the evangelical church the Ingram family attended presented several evangelical documentaries on the threat of satanic ritualism; local therapists brought a therapeutic agenda ("repressed memories") that encouraged the generation of imaginary incidents of abuse.[555]

Review of the resulting court cases (some extending several years) suggests that little corroborating evidence exists. Indeed, efforts by American evangelicals to spread the conception of Satanic Ritual Abuse Syndrome abroad (through world-wide media networks—TBN, etc.) have yielded equally meager results. A front-page account in the London *Independent* newspaper documented 84 investigated cases without any evidence found warranting the further attention of the government.[556]

Obviously, sexual abuse occurs daily in American society. And yet that a particular "syndrome" could be so persuasively conjured out of what appears to be *thin air* with virtually no corroborating evidence speaks volumes about the power of this almost *self-fulfilling* cultural dynamic. The evangelical cultural mystique lends a measure of ideological acceleration that is almost breathtaking in scope and influence.

The Burden of Sexuality

While the large majority of Seattle Pacific students claim to routinely establish and maintain smooth, unproblematic relationships with persons of

---

[555] Wright, "Remembering Satan . . . ."

[556] Rosie Waterhouse, "Government inquiry decides satanic abuse does not exist," *Independent on Sunday*, 24 April 1994.

—T. H. Luhrmann describes an English appetite for the occult that is profoundly different from the American, emphasizing the benign, re-enchanting elements of magic over the malignant and satanical. See her *Persuasions of the Witch's Craft: Ritual Magic in Contemporary England* (Cambridge: Harvard University Press, 1989).

the other sex,[557] day-to-day observation imparts an altogether different impression. One detects anxieties and fears lurking beneath a surface veneer of composure and confidence. Even the most innocent and idle of dalliances between girls and boys can become burdened with all sorts of social and ideological expectations, weighed down by a freight of moral seriousness that tends to put a damper on what might otherwise develop into relatively free-flowing, spontaneous encounters and relationships. There are of course, as mentioned earlier, the considerable parental expectations placed upon sons and daughters (primarily the latter) of wooing and winning suitable Christian spouses during their four-year matriculations. Often this translates into a palpable tension among couples to steer and accelerate relationships towards an anticipated climax in marriage, an expectation which can in extreme cases, as we have seen, produce an emotional desperation among young female students as they approach the senior year.

One observes among the male students a compounded, double-headed sort of anxiety, a kind of attraction/repulsion complex. Guys are for the most part inclined to seek out and establish a traditional male-dominated, a-sexual relationship with a girl (although there is much talk of "mutual submission" and equality in relationships, I only occasionally saw or heard of these), and yet those who embrace the conventional expectation often exhibit and express considerable anxiety towards girls, wary of entering into close relationships for both fear of intimacy or sexuality[558] and an understandable reluctance to lock themselves into a long-term marriage-track relationship at the tender age of twenty (although again, as we have seen, a substantial minority do precisely this). I should add, however, that I did encounter some students who were not intimidated by the conventional terms and conditions of commitment and could almost luxuriate in the a-sexual climate of expectations, establishing warm, mutual, exploratory friendships with persons of the

---

[557] 71% of the survey students answered [4] or [5] on a continuum running from [5] Comfortable to [1] Uncomfortable " . . . with individuals of the opposite sex."

[558] This fear of intimacy is certainly more pronounced among males than females for the simple reason of the *different attitudes* the two sexes bring into potential relationships. Males associate intimacy with sexuality much more so than females, who are inclined to view relationships in the more social terms of devotion, sharing, domesticity, and mothering and are thus more capable of diluting the inevitable sexual anxieties and tensions. Their natural (yes *natural*) instincts harmonize more closely with the almost a-sexual monogamous expectations of the conjugal logic. The guys, by contrast, are more biologically driven into relationships and thus feel greater amounts of anxiety and guilt over their more insistent sexual impulses. They fear relationships much more so than do the girls because of the additional increment of anxiety and pressure they would bring to such couplings; hence the greater "fear of intimacy" among most of the males. Campus seminars on sexual topics, for example, are mostly attended by females; for them it represents much more of an unthreatening academic subject than for males, who generally prefer not to discuss the matter.

opposite sex. One could surely argue that the absence of sexual anxieties enhanced these relationships. But these were not large in number, tended to be confined among the brighter, more distinguished and active students, and for the most part included the disavowal of any immediate connubial interest on the part of the female.

We get an initial feel for some of these tensions from Frances, a perky, moderately attractive daughter of missionary parents who is a feminist of sorts and the author of an article in the *Falcon* enumerating the problems of guys on campus.

> I have a lot of close friends who are guys . . . I don't know why I never get asked out . . . I do the asking ["Really?"] . . . I do what I can . . . 'round here it's not the right way of. . . .
>
> ["They're afraid of girls?"]
>
> I think they are . . . it's disgusting . . . see, that's where the hassle is, for me, like "roomie's night out": where the whole floor goes out and your roommate gets you a date . . . not supposed to know who it is. Then you get your roommate a date also—fun, then you don't have to ask the guy directly, you just tell your roommate who you'd like. We've gone skating, etc. . . . whole group goes. But you try to ask a guy out in any other way or form—for coffee, for instance, and it's no way. Most of them it's a hurt to their ego, 'cause they're not the man anymore. They look at me like I'm something else or trying to prove something, and I'm not. It's real weird . . . frustrating about this campus. I've about had it . . . I hardly scope [look at guys in the cafeteria] anymore 'cause it's not worth it . . . What do they think, that girls are all out for commitments? That they want to marry them tomorrow? Some girls yes, most girls no.
>
> ["Alien creatures to some of them?"]
>
> I believe it.[559]

It was my impression that girls such as Frances represented a very small minority. Observe, however, that social ineptitude was usually explained as the problem of the *other* gender on campus. Male students often attributed their lukewarm interest in Seattle Pacific coeds to these girls' lack of social skills: they couldn't take them anywhere off campus because they simply didn't know how to act in a wide variety of social situations; invariably, *they* became an embarrassment.

There are both benefits and detriments to this exceedingly conservative approach to adolescent sexuality. The evangelical college system of sexual injunctions and prohibitions (just one example: dormitory room doors were

---

[559] (*SSI*, May 2003)

—Ray, a student senator and son of a minister who exhibited in student senate meetings an almost glib social confidence nonetheless in private confessed harboring an altogether different persona with respect to the opposite sex: "I like girls, except that I'm terrified of them . . . I'm very shy." (*SSI*, May 2003)

to remain open during visits from the opposite sex) may ease the additional potential burden of anxiety that often attends and complicates sexual experimentation among the young.[560] Insecurities and inadequacies in this particular area may be postponed until personal maturation and a stable marital relationship render them more manageable.[561]

And yet the atmosphere of prohibition and expectation that most evangelical youth are raised under and which is largely reproduced here among these colleges may also, however, cast a pall of reluctance and anxiety of its own over encounters between boys and girls, sowing the seeds of a peculiar kind of distrust, diffidence, and fear of intimacy (and/or sexuality) that many find difficult to overcome.

All told and in general, I sense that this approach to sexuality produces three interrelated conditions or consequences for evangelical youth: ignorance, aesthetic impoverishment, and the mystification and magnification of all matters sexual. The first two are perhaps too obvious and well-documented to warrant our further attention other than in passing.[562] The third,

---

[560] Alan Basham, promoting himself as a "more evangelical" director of the Counseling Center [as opposed to David Terrell, who preceded him], during a "Sex and Intimacy" seminar (2/16/2003) offered students a simple solution to sexual temptation, recalling a practice he and a roommate employed during his college days at Biola, a Christian school in California, wherein they carried around three by five inch index cards inscribed with "Who's in control here?" on one side and "Alan's [or the roommate's name] going to want to know" on the other.

This is vaguely reminiscent of the young Nicholas Gilman, an "ardent New Light preacher in New Hampshire" who in the 1730s developed six methods or "Remedies against uncleanness," to be carried with the believer at all times:

> 1 When a Temptation assaults thee flee from it
> 2 Avoid idleness
> 3 Give no entertainment to the begginnings of Lust
> 4 Fly all Occasions of Lust
> 5 When Assaulted alone Go into Company
> 6 Use frequent and earnest prayer to the King of Purities, the first of Virgins, the Eternall God that would be pleased to reprove and cast out the unclean Spirit. (Greven, *The Protestant Temperament . . .* , 130.)

[561] Yet in this respect evangelicals are misguided in thinking that the liberal "secular world" universally condones and promotes sexual license among adolescents and young adults. For example, even Rollo May's widely-read and admired 1969 tract, *Love and Will* (New York: Norton, 1969), prophetically raised some serious caveats with a growing sexual experimentation and abandonment among segments of rebellious American youth. See especially pp. 41-42 on the pressure upon young colleges students to "like" the new sexual "freedom" in spite of quite natural personal reservations and anxieties.

[562] A selection of examples are collected in the original dissertation under "Ignorance" and "Impoverishment," Appendix I.

however, it seems to me, lies at the heart of, or proves symptomatic of, some rather cardinal internal community dynamics, to whose examination I now turn.

Mystification and Magnification

At a very early age evangelical children are discouraged from displaying their unclothed bodies on even so innocent an occasion as water play in and around a portable pool in the backyard of a family residence. A veil of shame tends to shroud the private parts of the body. Extreme modesty prevails among members of the family. Mothers conceal their naked bodies from the wandering eyes of innocent sons, as do fathers from daughters; siblings retain only vague memories of anatomical differences among themselves.

An evangelical youth[563] grows up regarding the drives of his own body with some uneasiness and suspicion. What sort of relation these bear to the apparent objects of attraction proves somewhat of a mystery. For males, the persons who might provide visual instruction in the mere elementary forms of anatomical difference—mother and sisters—are cloaked in equivalent mystery; fathers are perhaps even less instructive and accessible to females. We shouldn't be surprised to find then that the mind and imagination of many an evangelical youth is often working overtime during puberty. With the passage of time in some of the more active and fertile imaginations there occurs a rapid acceleration of interest in (occasionally growing into an almost morbid fascination with) the persons of opposite gender. Indeed the unintended consequence of such training is that a good many youths who have come to fear or distrust libidinal attractions to girls tend to find their own interest heightened, some enormously. They struggle to make sense of forbidden impulses; they feel anxiety about the girls who arouse them and yet long for the rewards of even brief encounters. As they gain the kind of incidental anecdotal knowledge of sexuality from peers that was largely denied them by solicitous parents and continue to observe the prohibitions, the more sexually charged among them surely strain to quell increasingly active imaginations. They harbor within themselves both phobias and fascinations, loathing and yearning; many come to both fear and crave the imagined sexual experience.

(I would remind those readers for whom the above may appear all too reminiscent of traditional colonial Puritanism—or, better yet, even mid-late nineteenth-century Americanism Victorianism, an outlook extending well

---

[563] For the reasons cited in a much earlier footnote that I've lost track of, females more easily diffuse sexual energy than males. Accordingly, this brief passage applies with much greater force to boys than girls.

into mid twentieth-century—that one major distinction between the two apparently similar regimens is, of course, the larger social and cultural climate. Nearly everything in contemporary American society is sexually suggestive or titillating. Sex represents a lowest common denominator marketing tool and commodity. It is omnipresent in our daily lives. The evangelical cannot easily shield himself or his family from its blandishments {nor, it might seem, do they all wish to; for example: evangelicals watch as much or more commercial television than the average American family}.[564] The colonial Puritan, by contrast, was surrounded by few overt temptations; their world was more uniformly ascetic and prohibitive.)

One ironic, unintended consequence of the evangelical campaign against sexuality is that one finds among some newly matriculating Seattle Pacific students an often incongruous mingling of phobias and fixations, a congeries of confusing, discomfiting fears and lusts. The reader should understand that I am concentrating now upon a small minority of the student body. The range of the above and following accounts is naturally limited by a normal distribution of these dynamics among these young students. Indeed for most the ideological injunction against sexual dalliance is comfortably borne (although I could be completely off base here). While most experience the everyday emotional pull of an attraction to or admiration of comely persons of the opposite sex they hardly chafe under the reins of an authoritarian sexual prohibition. Given prior religious training and present level of emotional development the simple suppression and control of sexual urges (at least *interpersonally*) ensures considerably less anxiety and guilt than even the most harmless moments of physical experimentation. Indeed most of the student sample report few serious struggles or problems of a sexual nature and an even greater number (71%) claim a high level of comfort and ease with members of the opposite sex. For these students, apparently, the code represents no great emotional or behavioral imposition. In fact, an overwhelming majority (78%) of the sample would not in any event welcome "More acceptance of sexual freedom" as one of many possible social developments in the years ahead.[565]

Granting for the moment the veracity of these findings, our attention then falls upon a rather smaller group within the student body who are less temperamentally (and biologically) inclined to luxuriate under the terms of

---

[564] Evangelicals are "heavy viewers of conventional television." (Robert Wuthnow, *The Struggle For America's Soul: Evangelicals, Liberals, and Secularism*, Grand Rapids, Michigan: Eerdmans, 1989, 138-39.)

[565] Survey questions #64, 66, & #94c.

the prohibition, for whom sexuality proves a continuing source of confusion and difficulty. Roughly, I estimate that one in every three or four students falls into this category. The sample survey delicately formulates the question of sexual anxiety into the campus vernacular of "struggling with one's sexuality." The tabulation informs us that at one extreme 18% "really struggle" and 16% "struggle somewhat," while at another extreme 43% seldom do. Additionally, 17% of the students acknowledge that their "struggles" assume the form of a "Strong attraction to the opposite sex I can't seem to control." Another quarter or so of the sample reported more intricate problems involving the relationship between love and sex, mulling over the appropriateness of its union outside of marriage, among other concerns.[566] (For example, a few students who are a good deal more sophisticated in their thinking justify violation of the code of sexual prohibition with the rationalization that theirs was, or continues to be, a loving, caring, monogamous relationship—creating and maintaining a *balance* among the elements of mind, emotions, spirit, and body—with every intention of culminating in marriage, therefore avoiding or transcending any association with the sort of *imbalanced*, purely physical, short-term, promiscuous secular relationships.)

I am then concentrating here upon a small minority of young persons who have been burdened with disjointed, insecure personalities, inordinate doses of sexual energy, and family histories of moral authoritarianism (however well-meaning) and ignorance—and even more rarely, of cruelty—for whom the struggle to maintain sexual equilibrium proves disorientating and debilitating. They are tormented by their bodies and minds. They are emotional wrecks upon their arrival on campus, graduate in roughly similar condition, and then move on, spewing assorted emotional debris in their wake. An examination of one very specific phenomenon will serve to illustrate the actual operation and ramifications of these dynamics.

Onanism

Masturbation is not a word that falls easily from the lips of evangelicals in conversation (nor, for that matter, most Americans). Yet it would appear to occupy a prominent position in the private lives of a good many evangelical youth. As the reader can imagine, the subject does not readily lend itself to academic investigation, perhaps even more begrudgingly so among communities grown defensive from the occasional derision and sarcasm heaped upon them from perceived enemies in secular media and academia. And yet in this particular instance I have in my possession some rather unusual information that originated, oddly enough, from within Seattle Pacific itself. I

---

[566] Survey question #70.

refer to a rather crude but useful survey conducted by "some psychology students" in the early 1970s, one in which 157 male students[567] from three campus residence halls responded to questions about masturbation: knowledge and practice of it, and subsequent feelings and reflections upon their experiences. Since at present I have nothing from the general population of American college students with which to compare the findings I am wary of drawing too many sweeping generalizations from just these few numbers. They are, however, nonetheless instructive for what little information they do provide.

Most of the respondents regarded the activity as a perfectly normal human behavior: 95% rejected the notion of any danger to physical well-being; 60% thought it "predominantly true" that "masturbation can be a helpful release of sexual tension for many types of persons." However, approximately one-third of the students rejected the practice as "unacceptable" under "most" or "all" conditions and another third concluded that it "may give clues" as to the "mental health" or "moral nature" of an individual.

When asked whether they had in fact engaged in the practice "one or more times," 90% admitted having done so. Here I must confess initial surprise. Pressed to speculate on the rate prior to reviewing the survey, I probably would have ventured a guess substantially lower. Even more intriguing are the numbers for "Past" and "Present" involvement. When asked, "In the past the most often you practiced masturbation has been _____ times a week," students reported the following frequencies:

Frequency Per Week	Students (90% Yes group)
0-1	10%
1-3	28
4-5	18
6-8	18
10-15	10
over 15	2
NR	4
	100%

We discover then that in their most prolific moments *nearly one out of every two or three students was masturbating daily, or even more frequently*. Since most of these participating dormitory students were either freshmen or sophomores

---

[567] 223 were "asked to fill out the survey." Of these, 216 "agreed to fill out survey" and 157 actually returned their surveys.

the reports most likely reflect the high school and family home life conditions of pre-matriculation. For these very sexually active youths masturbation would appear to have been an almost routine bedtime (or other-time) activity, perhaps performed with all the regularity of devotions or prayer. Quite understandably, the figures for "present involvement" drop markedly, given the near universal absence of privacy in the college dormitory environment.[568] (As one respondent whose practice had dropped from a rate of six times a week to two "at present" acknowledged: "It's hard to find privacy in the dorm situation.")

The amount and intensity of anxiety and guilt experienced would seem to vary in direct proportion to the frequency of practice. For while 62% reported suffering previously "from guilt from engaging in masturbation," a considerably smaller percentage (20%) responded Yes to "Do you feel guilt now?"[569]

Additional comments from respondents reveal attitudes ranging from the outright spurning of any discussion of the topic to enthusiasm for the increased dissemination of such information upon campus. One student who found masturbation "unacceptable under most conditions," "dangerous to physical health," the mere incidence of which provided "clues as to the mental health of an individual"—all the while claiming never having performed the activity himself—complained:

> Come on let's get serious around this place. Of all the things going on in this world, you guys got to pick this topic for a survey of the male student body at S.P.C. Did you guys get lost in the shuffle.

A student who masturbated daily both prior to matriculation and while on campus wrote:

> Seems to be necessary around here. More uneasy than guilty. I know it is not unnatural. Not enough others do.

---

[568]

Frequency Per Week	Students (90% Yes group)
0-1	37%
1	13
1-3	25
4-5	7
6-8	3
9-10	2
NR	13
	100%

[569] Survey figures about struggling with sexuality prior to and after coming to SPU show a similar drop.

Finally, a student who engaged in the practice two or three times a week "previously" and who then continued to do so "irregularly" one or more times a week on campus enunciated some underlying ideological principles in his (exquisitely penned) summary comments:

> Masturbation can be a release of sexual tension but I am doubtful it is helpful. The guilt it inflicts on [the] individual who practices it is greater than the pleasure obtained. Also, although there may be probably no specific Biblical command, the teaching of the scripture clearly reveals that sex is made for marriage or sex is for sharing. Masturbation, as a form of narcistic [*sic*] attitude, doesn't fulfill the Biblical concept of sex. Masturbation, in my opinion is not helpful release. If it is discussed from [a] Christian perspective, it should be viewed as [an] immature and self-centered act. And anything that distracts a Christian from being God-centered is a form of idolatry which is sin. Therefore my personal opinion is [that] masturbation, if being discussed, should carry ethical consideration not just modern psychological [read *secular*] perspective. {Underline in original}

Note the invocation of some familiar evangelical themes. The student obviously embraces the full "Christian perspective" and yet laments his inability to bring his own behavior into line with the total abstinence the logic demands. This general pattern emerges among many of the more profligate students: formal external adherence to a code of behavior incongruously coupled with the internal entertainment of a veritable smorgasbord of sexual fantasies and obsessions. How peculiar—and yet a moment's reflection ought to give us pause to consider how truly unremarkable and predictable—this pattern of conduct.

Given the generally ironic outcome of a formal community prohibition upon sexual knowledge, expression, and experimentation leading to the mystification of women's bodies and the magnification of sexual drives in a highly vulnerable minority of students, what could be more natural and anticipated than this apparent predilection for the kind of abstract, antiseptic sexuality which masturbation represents—the continual evocation, manipulation, and consumption of safe, detoxified female imagery. What could be more predictable than this apparent link between prohibition, mystification, and magnification, and obsessive repetitive masturbation, the self-reported rates of which in some instances offer every indication of youngsters locked in an insatiable onanistic frenzy.

An additional irony is that these apparent habits can in many instances serve to reinforce the logic of prohibition. One can anticipate the development in many of these students a kind of emotional dependency upon this kind of abstract sexual expression that may block further experimentation. For absent real sexual partners and occasions, the imagination is quite capable of fashioning encounters and situations that attain an almost abstract perfection that no actual experience can rival. Students who do stray beyond the bounds of appropriate sexual conduct, carrying as they do the ideological baggage of ingrained fears and magnified drives, often find their initial sexual explorations and experiences terribly sloppy, maladroit, and disenchanting affairs. The two bodies and personalities do not seem to mesh in the kind of harmony of cadence and climax which the imagination anticipates and the ideology promises. There are awkward, embarrassing moments and much higher resulting doses of anxiety and guilt than might otherwise be the case. So that, all told, many initially find the real thing a good deal less pleasurable and rewarding than the altogether more polished and routine abstract acts of imagination. One or more of these unseemly encounters with a tangible member of the opposite sex may be enough to convince the young evangelical that sex is indeed a dirty, troubling business not worth the ensuing trouble, a cumbersome and precarious undertaking whose full exploration and understanding is better postponed until marriage, a course of least emotional resistance continually recommended by faculty and community elders.

Perhaps also for some the very high community-wide threshold of shame, embarrassment, and virtual silence upon the topic itself (and the obvious reality of its private performance) and the absence of clear lines of moral and Biblical demarcation, may serve to lessen the weight and awareness of any community disgust with or discouragement of the practice. For indeed until quite recently the full brunt of public moral condemnation fell uniformly upon premarital boy-girl sexual experimentation, the larger evangelical community reluctant to address any of the other more unconventional possibilities. We may observe then in operation here what I will refer to as the principle of *the redirection of sexual energy* towards less conventional and formally prohibitive objects and behaviors. So that the process of mystification and magnification may produce among a smaller minority of sexually-driven individuals a re-channeling of libidinal energies along less obvious and publicly execrated avenues of sexual expression. (Such dynamics may lie behind the apparent disproportionate rate of incest—and perhaps homosexuality as well[570]—among more conservative Protestant families documented in some studies.[571])

---

[570] Dr. David Terrell observes that "You see a lot of fear in [these] gays toward the opposite sex . . . fear is a common thing with them." (Interview, 2/5/2003)

[571] "Some clinical accounts have suggested that men who are highly religious, with rigid conservative views about sex and the family, are among those most prone to sexually abuse." (Diana E. H. Russell, *The Secret Trauma: Incest In The Lives Of Girls*, New York: Basic Books, 1986, 112.) Unfortunately, Russell cites none of these "accounts." Her own survey of 151 victims (927 total sample) employs the religious self-descriptions of Catholic/

Then there are those students for whom even the more ambiguous area of masturbation absorbs the full taint of moral condemnation, whose lives are wracked by struggles to reconcile the powerful urges of the body with the equally insistent pressures of community prohibition. Here we find that the most tormented are those students who combine within their persons both fervent belief in the evangelical ethos and large doses of irrepressible sexual energy. As Dr. Terrell recalls:

> I still get calls from people who have struggled with this. They have learned that "if only I am close to the Lord I wouldn't have this problem," and they're still struggling. . . . One guy spent four hours on his knees praying to God to forgive his sins, 'cause he jacked off and that was wrong. He went "it's sinful to masturbate if you really love the Lord." And so here he was, and he's still a wreck and he's been out of Seattle Pacific for six or seven years.
> ["Mel White told a senate meeting of a young man in his church who'd just committed suicide because of guilt over masturbation."]
> Oh yes, I've known students who have OD'd at Seattle Pacific because of that. ["OD'd?"]
> Overdosed on drugs. There are two of them that I can think of just off the top of my head that fortunately didn't kill themselves.
> ["Hard drugs?"]
> No, aspirin or sleeping pills. They both survived, but you deal with that every day.

The 100% Mentality

Some readers may find surprising and inexplicable these examples of a near total sexual abandonment in some students and a firm, unyielding self-discipline in others. At first encounter, I too struggled to make sense of the disparity. Why the apparent swings from total abstinence to total license within this one reasonably homogeneous community? Why the extremes of feeling and conduct? The answer, it seems to me, lies within the terms and dynamics of the logic of invidious distinction itself.

The imperative for clear, incontrovertible lines of demarcation setting off appropriate Christian from inappropriate secular conduct occasionally combines with the particular backgrounds and temperaments of some students to produce totalistic personalities averse to moral moderation. The total badness or goodness of the extreme logical alternatives leaves little room for emotional and behavioral compromise. Indeed, since a little nibbling upon morsels of forbidden sexual fruit generates perhaps as much anxiety and guilt as consuming the entire cornucopia, why not just lose control and

---

Protestant/Jewish/None/Other. She finds no statistically significant differences among them. This fails, of course, as a test of the aforementioned assertion because her data allow no further breakdown of the Protestant category.

gorge oneself to satiation? As we have seen, some students behave in precisely this manner. Evan, a student senator, spoke about a dormitory neighbor who fit the pattern:

> [He's a guy] who in my opinion is not practicing Christian ethics, morals, and stuff. He goes to all the chapels and he's got eight different Bibles—eight! . . . He went to a Christian high school . . . [but] he's rather promiscuous. ["In the dorm here?"] Yeah, and I've talked to him before, confronted him: "Well, don't you think this is wrong, messing around with all these girls here?" ["Campus girls?"] Yeah, I think ones are. ["Brings them to his room here?"] Yeah. He's not here very often, but when he is, he's usually with a girl.
> I'd say, "Well don't you think that it's wrong, shallow?"
> He goes, "No."
> "Well what about where it says 'Don't covet thy neighbor's wife.'?"
> "Oh, that's just for married people and it doesn't apply."
> It's hard to get through to him because he's got this point of view that he doesn't want to let go.[572]

More likely, the student finds the extreme of sexual promiscuity no more fraught with anxiety and guilt than the broad center of abstemious moderation, with its only occasional breakdowns, and accordingly sets up camp where the sum total of personal gratification is the greatest.

As Erik Erikson once wrote (although in an altogether different historical context) of dynamics characterizing authoritarian mentalities and regimes:

> This inner split [between expectation and performance, may induce or call forth] . . . "total" solutions in life which are based on the simple and yet so fateful proposition that *nothing is more unbearable than the vague tension of guiltiness.* In transitory states, or in lasting personality formations, *individuals often try to overcome this vagueness by becoming totally good or totally bad.* . . . It is obvious that authoritarian propaganda addresses itself to this conflict by inviting man, collectively and unashamedly, to project total badness on whatever inner or outer "enemy" can be created by state decree . . . while the obedient adherent may feel totally good as a member of a nation, a race, or a class [or, we must add, a religion] blessed by history.[573] {emphases added}

---

[572] (*SSI*, May 2003)

[573] "Wholeness and Totality—A Psychiatric Contribution," reprinted in Carl J. Friedrich ed., *Totalitarianism* (Proceedings of a conference at the American Academy of Arts and Sciences, March 1953), Cambridge, Massachusetts: Harvard University Press, 1954, 167.
—Or, more recently, concerning Pentecostalism's campaigns in Africa: "The paradigm of global spiritual warfare with its apocalyptic visions, the violence of its language, and its obsession with enemies also demands that we pay closer attention to the politics of 'who is a Christian' today. . . . apocalyptic thought has long been and continues to be the weapon of the dispossessed." (Marshall, "Christianity, Anthropology. . . ," 353.)

Dr. David Terrell observes the emotional dynamics directly in evangelical clients who come seeking treatment for alcoholism. Time and time again he encounters the rationalization in his private practice: if it's just as sinful to take one little drink as a hundred drinks, then you might as well drink as much as you like—get plastered—since it's "all the same." And so instead of guiding one's conduct according to the more relaxed mores and canons governing light or moderate social drinking, these persons find themselves drawn by the uncompromising nature of the logic into alcoholism. They must feel, in a word, little motivation to restrain themselves in light of a persistent undifferentiated anxiety or guilt that appears unrelated to any modulation in drinking habits. Perhaps for them one immediate emotionally satisfying reconciliation of this unremitting tension between expectation and behavior is a surrender to "total badness." Better to lapse into the total darkness of sensual gratification—of complete inebriation—than stumble among the anxiety-ridden shadows of spiritual dusk. Contrition and restitution can then carry greater sincerity and weight. Perhaps only an iconic American pop star with emotional roots sunk deep in an evangelical faith could squeal with such ironic cultural conviction and resonance: "I'm bad, I'm bad, so bad!!"[574]

Terrell also saw a good deal of this in gay students who approached him for counseling on campus.[575] However, he discovered that differences in

---

[574] I refer, of course, to the title track of Michael Jackson's multi-platinum album, *Bad*. My then eight-year-old daughter, who loved the song, asked what it meant. Why does he want to be bad? I explained that sometimes very good, very nice people from religious families feel a need to be "cool" or just plain bad sometimes. They get tired of being good all the time. It's kind of a dream or fantasy to be mischievous or even nasty, just for the fun of it. These were feelings to which she could definitely relate. Of course the revelations, after his death, only enhance the irony here.

[575] Although only 6 out of the 217 Seattle Pacific students returning the survey questionnaire reported any kind of sexual identity anxiety or homosexual inclinations that they "don't understand and can't control," there is every indication of a silent underground of such students in rough proportion to the population at large.

Dr. Terrell recalls that during his tenure at Seattle Pacific he was seeing approximately five individuals a week, and of that weekly average usually three or more were students coming to him for the first time.

> I found that a lot of the gays I knew on campus were very neat people in every sense of the word. They were more open-minded . . . they were really thirsty for knowledge and understanding. A lot of them that I knew were very bright, some of the better students. Some of them were in the student body administration, some in the residence hall staffs—they were RAs. They had positions of leadership on campus. (Interview, 2/5/2003)

—Mel White, a Christian Commitment Week speaker, informed a small chapel talkback session that at a "larger" Christian college he recently visited an intramurally approved and conducted survey revealed that 20% of the student body acknowledged "struggling with"

religious upbringing and training became very significant later in therapy. For example, the students who could frame their experiences in terms of *personal consequences*—imaginatively projecting the short and long-term ramifications of present behavior—and could appreciate and learn from the experiences of others, elevating their moral vision beyond the stark and simple moral regimen of absolutely right and wrong behavior, were more successful in bringing some order, value, and meaning—some sense of proportion—to their young lives. They learned to control indiscriminate urges and thus lessened the eventual impact of internal censure and guilt. Typically, they gained a maturing understanding by a direct concentration and reflection upon the often gut-wrenching personal consequences of promiscuity: "OK, I went the promiscuous route and that was devastating to me. I didn't like that: it was destructive and I chose not to follow that direction." Then again there were others, never or not yet promiscuous, who pondered possible courses of action in terms of ultimate personal happiness, perhaps focusing on more rewarding types of personal relationships: they "read or observed that it just wasn't the best way to go . . . they wanted a relationship that was really meaningful." Unfortunately, for the most part Dr. Terrell encountered these kinds of clients outside of Seattle Pacific, in the community at large (i.e., they were referred to him by other mental health professionals both while he was at Seattle Pacific and then later)[576]; whereas during his tenure he largely dealt with students from more conservative evangelical backgrounds who had great difficulty, as he put it, "really developing a strong value system." The inability of these young people to frame their past experiences and future choices in terms of some overall long-term value structure proved seriously debilitating. For in spite of an often full embrace of the evangelical logic execrating such conduct, which ensured heavy doses of internal anxiety, censure, and—ultimately for some—trauma, they went out again and again, engaging one lover after another, night after night after night. Terrell recalls his attempts to break through these cycles of obsession and indulgence and introduce some sense of moderation and responsibility into their lives:

---

some form of homosexuality. Once the administration reviewed the results a very popular professed (although non-practicing) homosexual dorm counselor (who had earlier been voted "best faculty member" on campus) was immediately removed from his position. (SUB Fireside Room, 1/10/2003.)

[576] Dr. Terrell: ". . . . these people were mature, they were able to put that in perspective, and I know some of them in Seattle now who went that way who have a strong set of values, who are functioning very well, who are very successful, who may still be out of the church. I know several . . . who go to the Episcopal church, because they're comfortable with it. But they have lovers, and some of them have lived with these lovers for eighteen years. They have good relationships."

What I like to do with my patients, if they're young and looking . . . [is this]: "OK, let's look at the options . . . let's look at pros, let's look at the cons (I'm over-simplifying). What is it that's important? What do I need to ask myself? What kinds of things do I really need to look carefully at?" *But they would have none of that: it was all wrong. . . .*

The [drubbing] they were getting was just psychologically devastating to them. ["Guilt?"] Primarily guilt, because it is absolutely wrong. You're going to Hell. You can find change; if you really commit your life to the Lord, this will be changed. And they were looking for an 180 degree turnaround. ["They felt they weren't Christian?"] They felt they weren't Christian because they had this feeling and if they were involved—I've seen them come in before any overt experiences and I've had them come in after an experience and want to kill themselves—they knew that their parents would reject them: "What is there left for me, Doc?" You know, I've been asked that in so many words scores of times. . . .

So if you were [a little bit] gay, then let's go the whole way. And you know [in a similar context], drinking was wrong . . . so if you take one drink, why not go the whole way? Alcohol [abuse] is prevalent in evangelical groups, I have found in my experience. . . . Probably see it in other patterns of human behavior too—where it's black and white. So if you go into the black, you might as well go the whole way and enjoy the whole thing.

The ensuing anxiety and guilt in this rigid moral context might very well prove as intense for one or two experiences as for a hundred, so why not enjoy the full measure of sin? And so they went out night after night, hungry for intimacy, sex, and love, and, ultimately, longing for some form of punishment upon their return to campus, perhaps hoping to elevate Terrell into some kind of therapeutic God who would plunge the knife of moral retribution deep into their hemorrhaging hearts, performing a spiritual coup de grace upon their apparently inextinguishable impulses, exorcizing the sexual demons.

Their self-esteem is very strongly affected: I'm weird, I'm queer, I'm strange, and even though for me this works and I get a certain amount of fulfillment out of the relationship with a member of the same sex—a lot of fulfillment in many in-stances—this is wrong, you know: "How can I enjoy this? How can this be mean-ingful to me when the Bible says. . . ?" And "What's going to happen to me? Maybe I can do this for now but, boy, I'd better get with it before I die. When do you think I should do that, Doc? Should I wait 'till I'm forty? Will I burn out? Will I wanta change, will I wanta become straight when I'm forty? Or should it be thirty?" Just pitiful! Some of the things that these people are dealing with. . . .

[They were] just torn apart, day after day after day, in some cases literally. I know people in Seattle right now who graduated from Seattle Pacific who are psychological wrecks because of some of the early experiences that they had, not knowing how to deal with this. Just devastated! [577]

Such is one consequence of an evangelical imperative casting the disparate realities of sexual feeling and behavior into diametrically-opposed moral regions of darkness and light.

The Fear of Total Reversal

While on campus I encountered numerous examples of an anxious antagonism towards homosexuals.[578] Dr. Terrell recalled a couple of the more heartbreaking incidents:

> I [recall] one instance of a young fellow who was gay who'd been very successful as a youth pastor here. He was feeling guilty, even though he was not promiscuous—he'd had a few overt experiences—and decided he'd better sort of share with the pastor, because he was struggling with some things and thought the pastor could help him . . . and so he went to the pastor. The pastor called the chairman, or whomever, of the prayer chain, you know: pray for so and so. In two or three days the pastor called the student back and said come over I need to talk to you. He went over and was told by the pastor that he was being stripped of his duties and position. "You're still welcome to come to the church, but. . . ."
>
> I think that kind of epitomizes [what goes on]. . . . He said, "Here I thought of all the people in the world that I could share myself with would be my pastor and the people that I worship with that are Christians, fellow Christians. I've learned very painfully that . . . never again."[579]
>
> . . . . Just pitiful! Some of the things that these people are dealing with!
>
> In [another] instance, where a guy shared in his Bible study group with his roommates—they lived off-campus in a house, and they'd lived together two years—and one night he shared with them that he was struggling with his feelings, could the guys please pray for him? He wanted to be different, to change. This

---

[577] The devastation was sometimes total. Terrell told of another young gay student who sensed the time was nigh to unburden himself and confide in other Christians. He "shared" his feelings and history with roommates and family and, according to Terrell, they just "wrote him off." The young man dropped out of school and moved to San Francisco: "He wrote the school, he wrote Christianity, he wrote his family off: 'If this is love, if this is Christianity, forget it!' " Approximately a year later, having become involved in a triangle of gay lovers, he was murdered. Terrell and those others who knew the young man found this an ignoble and wrenching outcome, he lamenting that "if we could have helped him deal with this, helped him put it in perspective, he probably would never have done what he did . . . [but] we were just pushing them aside and ignoring them."

[578] See the original dissertation for a larger collection of examples: "Homosexuality," Appendix I.

[579] No wonder some students might remain wary of Mel White's advice during his visit: "Bonhoeffer wrote that 'sin wants us isolated and alone'. . . . *When I was in a Christian college I was so afraid and alone with those things I was struggling with. . . . Talk with the campus counselors and pastors. They will keep your secret.*" (Chapel, 1/12/2003.)

was in the evening. The next day he got up and went to class and came home later and found all his belongings on the front porch of the house. They told him to get lost. That guy came to my office and just sobbed and sobbed and sobbed.

And what of the mood among gays themselves? Perhaps understandably, Terrell found them discrete and furtive: "very paranoid about anyone finding them out." He tells the story of two male students sharing the same room for two years in a campus dormitory. One roommate sought counseling from Terrell for what turned out to be homosexual tendencies. They met in regular sessions for a few months and then occasionally after that. Sometime later the other roommate also approached Terrell for help with the same problem and regular counseling sessions followed. Yet neither had knowledge of the other's "problem"; neither had informed the other of his sessions with Terrell nor discerned any sexual irregularities in the other. "Kind of the epitome of secrecy," observed Terrell.

Why the unusually strong visceral reaction to homosexuality among evangelicals?[580] I would contend that "homophobia" is very much related to a dynamic operating within the 100% mentality, most likely a derivation or outgrowth of this yearning for totalistic solutions to personal and social problems.

Perhaps lying at the heart of this phobia and reaction is something I would characterize as the *fear of total reversal*. And by this I have in mind an anxiety and uncertainty grounded in the *similarities* between the evangelical conversion experience on the one hand and completely opposite kinds of insidious and precipitous secular lifestyle changes on the other. Even if the believer has not undergone the classic born-again conversion experience himself, instead coming into gradual possession of his faith in a conventional evangelical family environment—as many do—with no single riveting moment, there nonetheless lingers an ever-present recognition of the potential for total personality transformations. She hears it all the time from friends and acquaintances and in the public testimonies of other believers who may have experienced such complete reorientations. Spiritual rags-to-riches stories are the main attraction of any revival season: "I was lying drunk in the gutter one week and then Jesus came into my life the next; I'm a new man in Christ," or so goes the familiar refrain.

And so evangelicals often warn their fellow believers of the recruiting ploys and techniques of gays—as though the gay community proselytizes in

[580] For an insightful academic study that benefits from the author's personal experience, see Mark. D. Jordan, *Recruiting Young Love: How Christians Talk About Homosexuality* (University of Chicago Press, 2011).

a manner similar to evangelism or other cult religions[581]—implicitly conceding the vulnerability of members to the blandishments and appeals of these deviant sexual outsiders, thereby steeling themselves against the kind of total sexual transformation which might occur at any moment, triggered by the kind of conversion preconditions and occasions with which evangelicals are all too familiar.[582] For as we see over and over again in evangelicalism, opposites are those things alike in all ways, *except one*.

In an altogether different historical context, Erik Erikson was led to marvel

> .... how strong and systematic are man's proclivities and potentialities for total realignments, often barely hidden behind one-sided predilections and convictions, *and how much energy is employed in inner defenses against a threatening total reorientation in which black may turn into white and vice versa.* Only the affect released in sudden conversions and in sudden aversions testifies to the quantity of this energy.[583]

Contributing to this ingrained fear or threat of total reversal is an ambivalence some evangelicals harbor toward their own sexual orientations. For indeed individuals who have shrouded quite natural sexual drives and impulses—and the topic in general—under a cloud of suspicion may have added an element of ambiguity to the larger logical sexual distinctions they are expected to make, perhaps increasing anxiety and fear over possible vulnerabilities to homosexual tendencies. It is an area of great uncertainty. Overt hostility to gays may then serve to mask inner doubts. (The often highly emotional, "feminine" nature and tone of public evangelical behavior—the weeping, singing, and carrying on—may contribute to these uncertainties; and yet the encouragement of "feminine" expressions of emotion would at the same time also seem to indicate no inordinate fear of actually becoming *too* feminine.)[584] Furthermore, among more traditional

---

[581] "Or, as a solicitation from Anita Bryant Ministries opposing homosexuality illustrated, moral deviance was not simply a matter of private choice but was creeping into all the society's major institutions: schools ('they want to recruit our school children'). . . ." (Robert Wuthnow, *The Restructuring of American Religion*, Princeton, New Jersey: Princeton University Press, 1988, 213.)

[582] "In the 'sexual revolution' of the past fifteen years, many an individual has undergone an almost complete personality change as a result of sexual advertising which marked a radical departure from previous standards of behavior." (James Hitchcock, "Competing Ethical Systems," *Faculty Dialogue* no. 2 [Winter 1984-85], 38.)

[583] Erikson, "Wholeness and Totality . . . ," 161. (This capacity or propensity for complete reorientations might appear then an even more endemic property of the evangelical personality, perhaps triggered by certain social conditions. Recall the near total reversal of the Seattle Pacific community—from pacifism to militarism—during and after World War II.)

[584] Consider also Philip Greven's treatment of the issue among the early Puritans:

conservative evangelicals, untouched by some of the more liberal feminist-leaning ideas of "mutual submission" in relationships, there may linger concerns over the sufficient demonstration of masculinity in the family and community (and certainly an interest in the preservation of male domination), an additional potential source of antagonism to any hint of unconventional tendencies and practices.

All told, the evangelical community views and approaches the issue with an ambivalence that appears at times to border upon fear and loathing, and for this the emotional dynamics inherent within the logic of invidious distinction—one of whose major derivations is the 100% mentality—are largely responsible.

The Sexual Wild Card

If and when the evangelical eventually becomes "equally yoked," vestiges of these ingrained anxieties—the attraction/repulsion complex, in particular—may very well linger on into the marriage itself. Those individuals or couples who fully embraced the original terms of sexual prohibition then confront the familiar *dispersion or differentiation problem* of now encouraging the very same impulses and performing the very same behaviors which were until the moment of their official union discouraged or vilified.[585] Imagine the emotional transition; imagine the emotional torque the young evangelical couple must experience in their fumbling attempts to raise these formerly discredited feelings and behaviors to altogether transcendent levels of sexual aspiration. For the ideal Christian couple is now all of a sudden expected to

---

The profound discomfort that some evangelical males experienced with regard to sexuality, and the necessity they felt for the denial of many aspects of their own masculinity, suggest that they may have both identified with and felt intense hostility toward women, and their own mothers in particular. . . . The "feminization" of these young males began in infancy and early childhood, but the continued conflicts which persisted throughout their adulthood suggest strongly that they continued to be plagued with unresolved doubts about their own identity as males. Some sources make sense only if latent homosexuality is assumed. To become the bride of Christ certainly carries this as one of several possible meanings. (*The Protestant Temperament. . .* , 132.)

[585] This ambivalence is by no means unique to modern evangelicals. Mircea Eliade writes of Indian tantrism: "As the tantric text expresses it: 'The true sexual union is the union of the supreme Shakti with the Spirit (*âtman*); other unions represent only carnal relations with women' . . . . a transfiguration of carnal experience occurs. 'By the same acts that cause some men to burn in hell for thousands of years, the yogin gains his eternal salvation.' The *Bṛhadâranyaka Upanishad* already declared: 'He who knows this, though he seem to commit sin, is pure, clean, ageless, immortal' (V, 14, 8)." (*The Sacred and the Profane. . .* , 171.)

effect a kind of immaculate other-directed spiritual-sexual fusion[586] which in some evangelicals' accounts ought to simulate the believer's anticipated re-union with Christ.[587]

Imagine also the additional potential complications of this great unknown of sexual compatibility, the bare outlines of which can usually be only dimly perceived or anticipated prior to any actual prolonged sexual engagement. We might refer to this as the *sexual wild card* of evangelical marriages. For while in many cases one can surely concede the benefits of sexual abstention before marriage, particularly the concentration upon purely emotional and spiritual liaisons it may afford and encourage, there are some seemingly ineluctable costs which are also incurred. These may in all likelihood include, for example, the initial (and then often prolonged) shock of the realization of the actual sexual profile of the other. How ingrained is the legacy of anxieties and phobias in the respective partners? In extreme cases, one can imagine the sexual anxiety, reluctance, or disinterest of one spouse combining with a history of sexual obsessionism on the part of the other spouse to create a relationship fraught with tension and frustration, perhaps even characterized by an eventual regression to earlier juvenile habituations or an extramural search for sexual outlets.

The Swaggart Spectacle

I can invoke no better illustration (among many possible) of these dynamics in operation than the trials and tribulations of the once prominent southern evangelist Jimmy Swaggart. Perhaps more instructive than the mere fact of his wanton pursuit of sexual titillation and release among the prostitutes of New Orlean's Airline Highway is the particular condition and expression of his lust. How terribly (and consistently) evangelical that this preacher sought his highest form of sexual pleasure not from sustained bodily contact and eventual copulation with prostitutes but rather instead from the performance of masturbation in the presence of an illicit partner who "talked dirty" and assumed all sorts of provocative postures.[588] Swaggart's recurring

---

[586] Once again, as Marshall Sahlins reminds us of native Maori ritual: "For Maori, ontogeny 'recapitulates' cosmogony. The human sexual act recreates the original union of male Heaven (Rangi) and female Earth (Papa)." (*Islands of History*, University of Chicago Press, 1985, 59.)

[587] The earlier version of this, for colonial Puritans and evangelicals, was the notion of becoming the "bride of Christ. . . . For Whitfield, as for so many other evangelicals, marriage to Christ was the role that gave the most comfort and that he felt described best the union of the regenerated Christian and the Savior." (Greven, *The Protestant Temperament. . .*, 137.)

[588] *The Seattle Times*, 28 February 1988, A13.
Also: "One prostitute who works the area and identified herself only as 'Peggy' told *Newsweek* that 'Swaggart asked me to take down my pants so he could feel my [private parts] while he masturbated.' But because he offered her only $10, she refused. 'The girls he used were real

behavior most likely reflects and derives from these aforementioned compulsive juvenile habits or patterns of immaculate copulation: the ingrained, habitual fear of intimacy and direct physical contact combined with an abstract, imaginative eroticism [589] (although fear of AIDS may have been a contributing factor here). Obviously, Swaggart sought this form of arousal and gratification outside of his own marriage, a development many observers may have found incomprehensible given that Mrs. Swaggart is (at least in the author's estimation) a good deal more physically attractive (and shapely) than the prostitute whom Swaggart routinely engaged (and the two express much affection in public for one another). It seems immediately apparent that neither the acknowledgement nor the gratification of Swaggart's obsessions was a possibility within the terms of the evangelical code of marriage (for whatever combination of interpersonal and ideological reasons).[590] Christian spouses simply do not don black lace and garters and coo provocative come-ons and then lounge back to observe the spilling of un-

---

dirt,' Peggy said, 'addicts who wanted the 10 or 20 bucks he gave them for drugs.' Another prostitute, Debra Murphree, who claims she is the woman with Swaggart in the compromising photographs that prompted the scandal, told New Orleans's WVUE-TV that she regularly met with the religious leader but never had intercourse with him. She said she considered him 'kind of perverted.' " (*Newsweek*, 7 March 1988, 51.)

—"When they were in her room at the Travel Inn he would get her to use a dildo while he sat in the green fiberglass chair and masturbated." Lawrence Wright nicely captures the irony of sacred and profane dynamics (the principle of inversion; fear of complete reversal) in his account of Swaggart's downfall. Recall the earlier observation that opposites are those things alike in all ways except one: "Only once, she [Murphree] says, did Swaggart ever enter her. 'I was on my knees, doggie-style, with my feet hanging off the bed.'. . . She has been reduced—'doggie-style'—to animal status. But isn't there, in her subjugation, in the very lewdness of this scene, something sacred? Her utter surrender is perversely like the surrender of the *penitents* who abase themselves before the majesty of the Lord. The shame, the submission, the degradation of the ego, are the same, and in this sense we see how obscenity both mocks and mirrors the divine." What is more, in Swaggart's "noble urge to destroy himself," to purge the bad Jimmy, he debases himself before the electronic world, before God, and thereby draws the notion of the submissive, self-obliterating "bride of Christ" full circle, to an absurd logical conclusion. (*Saint and Sinners*. New York: Knopf, 1993, 82-83.)

[589] The late David Koresh, leader of the ill-fated Branch Davidians in Waco, Texas, was notorious for his sexual promiscuity. Less noticed was the time he spent among the Branch Davidians in their earlier Mount Carmel retreat, where he was said to have seduced the 67-year-old widowed leader of the group in order to seize power and fathered two offspring by a 14-year-old girl. More to our point of interest, upon his initial arrival at Mount Carmel, "*He confessed to the group that he worried about his excessive masturbation.*" (*Newsweek*, 15 March 1993, 56.) {emphasis added}

[590] Those who would dismiss the scandals as products of the insidious modern secular sexual revolution would do well to consider the career of John Wesley, founding father and patron saint of American evangelical Methodism, who upon a visit to the colonies was forced to flee "back to England under indictment for defaming a young woman he had foolishly pursued." (Wright, op.cit., 18.)

procreative seed. Presumably for that one must venture a very long ways into pagan sexual territory.[591]

Although at this point in time I have no formal documentation to offer I think it likely that the sexual wild card gets played in the early stages of evangelical marriages and is responsible for much of the marital turbulence some particularly vulnerable couples experience. These youngsters often meet at a college like Seattle Pacific and perhaps come to regard the mere fact of their engagement and subsequent marriage having begun in such an institution as a strong indication of divine favor or predestination. This joining in

---

[591] Is Swaggart alone?: "The latest issue of *Leadership*, a journal published primarily for evangelical church officials, carries a one-word cover title: Sex. . . . In the first article, *23 percent* of 1,000 ministers polled said they had done something sexually inappropriate with someone other than their spouse, and *61 percent* said they fantasized about having sex with someone other than their spouse at least a few times a year." (Laura Sessons Stepp [*Washington Post*], "Denying sexuality can be preacher's problem," *Seattle Times*, 17 April 1988, 33.) {emphases added}

—In *The Book of Jerry Falwell*, op. cit., Susan Harding discovers in these events some rather less obvious traditional Biblical themes and imagery in operation that are of great interest, exemplifying some of her larger theoretical claims about Fundamentalist "rhetorics" and "narrative instability." However, the suggestive notion that these episodes, scandals, lapses, get explained away and justified within evangelicalism by their strategic grounding in a Biblical rhetorical dynamic of great moral breakdowns generating even greater dispensations of divine forgiveness and redemption and therefore may advance "flexible," creative prophetic agendas as of yet unknowable to the flock, strains our credulity at times (as does the absence of the word "ideology" in her index).

> The narrative generation of sin in order to extirpate it—of gaps in order to close them, discrepancies in order to harmonize them, excesses in order to regulate them, indeterminacies in order to fix them—is a piece of a specifically fundamental Protestant populist apostolic tradition. The character—and often the ministry, as well, of many great fundamentalist preachers—is dual in nature. The pattern of repeated undecidability-which-demands-decisions produces intense narrative relationships between the preacher and those who would follow him. Believers must decide to believe in him over and over, must ceaselessly read the gaps not as ploys or lies or sins, but as little miracles, as signs of election, as the travails of a monumental man, and in so doing, join him in a kind of divine complicity. (104)
>
> In sync with the Arminian pulse of reversible, hence repeatable, salvation, pentecostals Swaggart and the Bakkers punctuated their autobiographies with episodes of moral backsliding, devil wrestling, and deep spiritual crisis. . . . From the beginning, Heritage troubled many Christians who noticed the internal countercultural message—its suppression of sacrifice theology—but few guessed how far the Bakkers had gone in the direction of antinomian heresy, of rejecting all earthly restraints. At the time of their fall, the Bakkers not only promised their partners material abundance and well-being *but were refining a gospel of infinite forgiveness, a folk theology that seemed almost to sanction sinning by guaranteeing God's perpetual forgiveness in advance.* (261) {emphasis added}

faith represents the preeminent foundation of interpersonal joy and fulfill-ment; all other considerations, they are constantly reminded, pale in com-parison and can in any event be more successfully dealt with under the legit-imating aegis of this larger structure of faith. Matters such as sex (and the unforeseen, often nettlesome business of daily co-habitation, of long-term emotional and behavioral compatibility) are deemed incidental to this sacred process of the discovery and selection of a life-long marriage partner. Once more, Dr. Terrell reflects upon his experiences:

> The divorce rate is high among Seattle Pacific graduates. I don't know what the figures are, but the alumni association a few years ago was so concerned about it that they asked me, along with several other people, to conduct some seminars on relationships and so forth. You look at some of the graduates and I could name a bunch just right off the top of my head that I know personally who have been that route. . . . In the last year I've been contacted by six couples that have talked to me professionally who are now divorced. All of them Seattle Pacific graduates, and some of them very influential students when they were there. Every single one of them from evangelical backgrounds.
> ["Pressure to marry a Christian?"]
> Marry a Christian, that's the only thing that matters—I'm oversimplifying somewhat—but you marry someone who loves the Lord and that's where you find them. And as you said, they find out after the fact all these things about themselves, but gee whiz. . . .
> I have a very good friend who graduated from Seattle Pacific and who married one of the most popular girls on that campus . . . and after they were married the kinds of things that happened between them! And this girl . . . she was something else! I know her too. . . . Poor Stuart; he's remarried and very happy. But he told me once, he said "The only thing that I was taught was to marry a Christian girl." And she was a member of the same church. What more could you hope for? And so they go ahead and it is so hard for them, when they realize, you know, boy there's something really screwy here. They struggled like you wouldn't believe! [592]

---

[592] Chapel speaker, Jimmy Di Raddo, confessed his own considerable experience with "many Christian couples who find their marriages falling apart." He diagnosed the problem as one of "What happens when God doesn't seem to suggest a direction?" ("Where Do We Go From Here?," Chapel, 2/6/78.)
—"Marriage-mending: Churches slowly assuming greater role in keeping marriages alive." (Seattle Post-Intelligencer, 23 February 1997, Focus E1.)

The American Sexual Malaise

A good many Europeans find the American approach to sexuality baf-
fling. Phenomena treated in a casual, light-hearted manner and with some
humor by Europeans become the source of considerable anxiety and confusion among certain of their American counterparts. In my own mind there
is some question as to whether these phenomena retain the same essential
properties or ingredients of their European equivalents, whether they do not
in fact become transformed by the sheer *quantitative* nature of the differences[593] into something *qualitatively* different (a general dynamic principle,
the reader may recall, I employed earlier on in support of the claim of the
overall uniqueness of American evangelicalism). I wonder, for example,
whether puberty is not an altogether different experience for the average
American adolescent—much different than for, say, the average French,
Scandinavian, or Dutch child. I wonder if at each stage of these apparently
universal sexual and cultural transitions[594] the American does not carry an
additional load of ideological emotional baggage, the burden of which the
European has largely been spared.[595]

The French, as Laurence Wylie demonstrates in his charming portrait
of a *Village in the Vaucluse*, harbor a fundamental distrust of persons who become too *sérieux* early in life, advancing a totally different view of personal
"wholeness":

> If the people of Peyrane unanimously took the side of the rebel against his father
> in this case [for failing to provide his son with enough money to "have a good
> time"] it is because they believe it to be the right of a young person to have a good
> time. More than that, they believe it is the *duty* of a young person to have a good
> time. And it is the duty of their parents not only to tolerate, but to abet their ado-
> lescent children in the quest for pleasure. An adult who has in some way been

---

[593] One consequence of the American approach to sexuality is an almost breathtaking ignorance. See June M. Reinisch and Ruth Beasley, *The Kinsey Institute New Report on Sex: What You
Must Know To Be Sexually Literate* (New York: St. Martins Press, 1990), an account based upon
extensive survey research.

[594] See again, for example, Colin Turnbull's *The Human Cycle* (New York: Simon and Schuster, 1984).

[595] And Jon Butler, after surveying a host of historical studies of gender in America, concluded more generally that "Those books depict an interaction between women and religion
that sets American women's experience apart from anything in the history of western Europe. . . ." ("Jack-in-
the-Box Faith. . . ," 1365.) {emphasis added}
—Then there's the infamous, horrific "American Plan" of the late 1910s, as recounted in
Scott Wasserman Stern's *The Trials of Nina McCall: Sex, Surveillance, and the Decades-long Government Plan to Imprison "Promiscuous" Women* (Beacon 2018).

deprived of pleasure during his adolescent years is considered to a degree an *in-complete* person. He is looked upon with pity, or even suspicion.

Far from cosmopolitan Paris in a simple rural village, nearly a decade-and-a-half before a sexual revolution of sorts was to sweep across America, we find that

> Emile Pian's attitude toward his first sexual experience is typical of the attitude most people of Peyrane display toward sex. . . . They believe that since the sexual urge is a natural part of our existence, little may be gained by fighting against it. It is like all the inevitable aspects of life; since nothing can be done about them, they might as well be accepted. In this instance, acceptance happens also to afford one of life's greater pleasures. One would be stupid to deny oneself pleasures that come so naturally and that are so readily available. However, one must learn to control one's sexual urges because if they get out of control they may harm us. . . .
>
> When I talked to men in a confidential, relaxed situation they freely admitted that they practiced masturbation as children, although they said they did not remember at what age they began or how frequently they indulged. If a boy was caught by his parents, he would be scolded and threatened with a light punishment but the punishment was never carried out. . . .
>
> As children grow up they become aware that there is a discrepancy between the ideal and the real codes regulating sexual behavior. According to the ideal code no one should have intercourse out of wedlock. Probably few adults in Peyrane really believe this injunction. No one, however, believes the majority of the people of Peyrane adhere to it. It even conflicts with another rule of the social code which says it is good for a man to have intercourse before he is married. In the first place, it is believed that no man should attempt to settle down and accept the responsibilities of life until he has had the opportunity to release his passions. Furthermore, it is generally believed that marital sexual relations can be more successful if the man has had sufficient experience before marriage. . . .
>
> . . . . having a good time is a serious affair in Peyrane. . . . It is simply stated that "young people must have a good time," and all possible financial aid and tolerance are given to them.[596]

---

[596] 3rd ed., Cambridge, Massachusetts: Harvard University Press, 1974, 103, 113, 116-17, 119. {emphasis added} Also:

> If an unmarried girl becomes a mother, then, it is not a tragedy because of the moral issues involved or because the girl is permanently dishonored or because the child will bear the stigma of his birth. It is a tragedy because it places an unexpected economic burden on either or both of the families involved. It is tragic also because the birth of a child may prematurely end the adolescence of both the mother and the father. They may have to settle down and accept adult responsibilities before they are ready, before they have had their good time. (119)

—Then again, consider the explanation of Kerry Mumford, member of Australia's national arts-funding agency, on the group's decision to help finance a training video for prostitutes:

In marked contrast, one observes in the American nation at large the kind of schizoid extremes we found among these Seattle Pacific students: fear, anxiety, and total abstinence mingling uneasily, often antagonistically, with titillation, obsession, and total wantonness.[597] The yin and yang of the American sexual condition writ small, yet with large implications: a curious, typically incongruous mixture of Puritanism and paganism, of phobia and fixation. Two apparently contrary worlds of sexual expression and experience—ascetic evangelicalism and secular hedonism—antagonistic, hostile, separate, and yet inextricably linked with one another, jostling one another for cultural breathing space, the one often parasitically feeding off or reacting to the other (again similar to other such interactions encountered throughout this study.)[598]

Even among popular American cultural forms we can discover the deep play of these idioms. Take the seemingly innocent fairy-tale based films of Walt Disney:

> Jewett and Lawrence also identify a peculiar aspect of the personification of evil in many films-it is often linked with "curvaceous femininity": "The 'curves' of the wicked Queen are played off visually against the pure, straight lines of Snow White. A similar effort to associate curvaceous femininity with evil is made in 'Night on Bald Mountain,' [*Fantasia*] where demonic hags are presented with bare

---

"What they do for a living is not our concern. It's whether the project has good community outcomes." (*Newsweek*, 5 July 1993, 13.)

[597] The French must have found bewildering the sexual scandals that plagued the administration of President Bill Clinton. It was common accepted knowledge, for example, that Françoise Mitterrand had throughout his public career maintained a mistress. So legitimate was her position in his private life that she was conspicuously present at his funeral. (*New Republic*, 9/22/1997, 28.)

[598] In this respect American academic knowledge and appraisals of Moroccan maraboutism (Geertz, *Islam Observed…*, 48, a notable exception), or Sufism, in Islam prove instructive: "Although read in this country largely as a literature of self-help [or of asceticism], Sufi poetry is a playful and intellectually virtuosic tradition. It delights in paradox, making the sensible world a metaphor of the spiritual realm, and vice-versa: the figure of the beloved *is an object of at once carnal desire and mystical longing*; the wine is a token of both worldly pleasure and otherworldly purity. 'Our spirits are a wine and our bodies a vine,' as the poet Ibn al-Farid writes in his famous *khamriyya*. . . . Another attraction of Sufi poetry is its easy and explicit ecumenicalism. If the heart of the religion is the believer's experience of the divine, then the ritual and institutional trappings of faith become less important. *Even secular pursuits may serve one's spiritual needs*. . . . The Sufis' fusion of worldly and divine objects of desire. . . . blend the sensual with the sacred. . . . The Andalusian philosopher Ibn al-Arabi, who died in 1240, represents a grand synthesis of Sufi thought. Ignorance of his works in the West is one of the great scandals of intellectual history." (Robyn Creswell, " 'An Enthusiastic Sect'," in *The New York Review of Books*, 3/7/2019, 8.) {emphases added}

breasts and extended nipples. . . . the phallic symbolism of the demonic ruling over all the dark, fiendish activity is equally striking. . . . [599]

Witness the sex scandals that occasionally ripple through the television ministries of evangelicalism; witness also the flood of aggressive sexual Puritanism washing through the ranks of (largely academic) radical feminism.[600] Two apparently disparate ideological persuasions and protagonists who nonetheless derive a not insignificant portion of their personalities and outlooks from a common American cultural source.

There is much more to the story of the American sexual exceptionalism than I can even begin to fully address in a brief after-note. I sense that the American difference in nearly all matters sexual (including the illicit and/or criminal—particularly sociopathic and homicidal—dimensions) derives in some manner from this fundamental evangelical cultural inheritance. American serial sexual killers, for just one extreme example, a criminal personality type largely unknown in other cultures, may arise out of a complex mix of debilitating individual developmental histories and a larger complicating common core of puritanical cultural assumptions and dynamics.[601] I suspect that these *guys* represent just one more in a long line of uniquely American phenomena that can be traced back to their ultimate source in the toxic cultural cauldron of evangelicalism.

---

[599] Gary Laderman, "The Disney Way of Death," *The Journal of the American Academy of Religion*, No. 1, March 2000, 40-41.

[600] The exchange between Camille Paglia and Naomi Wolf (and others) over Paglia's "The Joy of Presbyterian Sex" (*New Republic*, 2 December 1992) is particularly instructive. See Naomi Wolf, "Feminist Fatale" (*NR*, 16 March 1992) and "Correspondence" (*NR*, 13 April 1992).

[601] And to further illustrate how directly the legacy of American sexual dysfunction has impacted nearly everyone, during the 1970s the author, while a student at the University of Washington, lived next door to Linda Ann Healy, one of Ted Bundy's early victims. Her roommates, upon discovering her missing and noticing evidence of intrusion through a side basement entrance door to her room—and blood on a pillow and bed sheet—used our telephone the next day in order to keep their own line free. The image of Ted Bundy sitting in his Volkswagen Beetle out front of the house the previous day, has been permanently seared in my memory, as are the pleading voices and faces of her roommates. If only I could have presciently known and done something—looked out the window at just the right moment. Well, perhaps, only with this chapter and book—however belatedly and modestly—I have. *L.A.H.*, and the many others, *RIP*.

CHAPTER 11

FALSE CONSCIOUSNESS:
EVANGELICAL CHRISTIAN MASKS

Man is least himself when he talks in his own person.
Give him a *mask* and he will tell the truth.[602]

As we have seen, evangelical academicians and students yearn to free themselves from the nagging inertia of mundane forms of social behavior and institutions. They conceive of ideal personal and social relationships in which appearances and realities merge, in which a kind of fusion of personality and behavior occurs, a convergence reducing conventional dramaturgical "presentations of the self " to a bare minimum.[603] Redemption and grace then bring, in addition to an anticipated personal salvation and eternal life, the much celebrated (and seldom understood by outside observers) re-unification of fragmented modern personality, whose attainment in turn ensures the re-invigoration of community. In atomistic, building-block fashion, the construction or achievement of personal wholeness brings a larger kind of a-social community wholeness and transparency. We observe members of the ideal evangelical Christian academic community aspiring to a clarity of motivation and action in which the distance between inner character and outer social expression and conduct contracts to virtually nothing.

Yet just what sort of impact do these ideas have upon the daily lives of these students and faculty? To what extent do students actually think and behave in this manner? To what extent do they succeed?

The Smile
Seattle Pacific students refer to those individuals who present a pious, joyous exterior to friends and fellow students while harboring an altogether

---

[602] Oscar Wilde, from W. H. Auden and Louis Kronenberger eds., *The Viking Book of Aphorisms*, Dorset Press, undated.

[603] These aspirations are by no means unique to modern evangelicalism. Perhaps the most notable precedent: Jean-Jacques Rousseau's *Discourse on the Origin of Inequality* (1754, in *The Social Contract and Discourses*, London: J. M. Dent & Sons, 1978) lamented the divorce of modern civilized manners (appearances) from natural personality and social form (realities). In fact, Jean Starokinski's definitive study of Rousseau is titled *Jean-Jacques Rousseau: Transparency and Obstruction* (University of Chicago Press, 1988).

different set of feelings and motivations within as bearers of "Christian masks." Indeed anyone familiar with the seemingly ubiquitous door-to-door salesmen and women of faith—the Jehovah's Witnesses perhaps the most indefatigable of the lot—or the street corner vendors of gospel tracts, or even the occasional pushy airport representatives of the more esoteric charismatic cults, are invariably intrigued (and/or discomfited) by the seemingly irrepressible smiles upon the faces of these proselytes. The projection of smiling, blissful exteriors has become such a trademark of these often nettlesome forms of enthusiastic religion that outsiders perhaps too readily dismiss their demeanors as in-authentically "plastic," "frozen," or "glassy-eyed," and the continual external eruptions of other-worldly glee seized upon as evidence of all kinds of internal turbulence and dementia. Yet to do so is to misconstrue the genuine underlying ideological meaning and significance of the smile.

For some the smile does indeed reflect joy and peace of mind. However, in the overall scheme of things it also performs a rather more dynamic ideological role: it represents a cardinal *signal of difference*, a beaming beacon of invidious distinction, a facial carriage transporting denizens of the radiant internal Christian community of joy a considerable distance from the dour external secular city of social convention and gloom; further, the expressions and gestures of joy establish an internal code of recognition and solidarity, a common body language of the redeemed.[604]

In this vein, Seattle Pacific President David McKenna once told a chapel audience that within the sacred perimeters of the Christian college community a social climate and mood altogether different from the "joyless wastelands" of the secular public university ought to prevail: a "sense of joy" should become apparent to all who enter. By contrast, even a cursory glance over the faces of passing "secular" students—at Berkeley, for example—yields an immediate telling glimpse of difference: "their eyes are hollow, they shuffle about with their heads down." Joy, he claims, is not an end in itself, but a "consequence of experience and behavior, a gift of the spirit." Whenever visiting another Christian college, for instance, he looks for evidence of these "gifts of the spirit." Walking across a campus, he conducts an informal survey, on the lookout for the "signposts of joy," observing "how they treat me, as a stranger." Conversing with the faculty and students, he searches for a deeper meaning and significance in the "gleam in their eyes." These

---

[604] Evidence of these idioms occasionally surfaces in the work of scholars looking for or emphasizing other themes, as in T. M. Luhrmann's account of the Vineyard sect, one of whose members counter-posed the example of the proverbial "flight attendant," or airline stewardess, whose trained "plastic smiles" are a performance only, similar to other secular world job routines. Within the Vineyard community one finds instead an altogether different kind of smile: we ". . . . *feel* them spontaneously and automatically." (*When God Talks Back . . .* , 108.)

indicators, among others, contribute to an eventual culminating assessment, helping him to locate the "center of meaning" and reach a final determination of the amount of "joy" generated by each institution.[605]

And just what sort of impact do these various expectations have upon the students? At first glance it would appear that the Seattle Pacific student confronts a challenging array of social gauntlets, whose crisscrossing, contradictory layouts—and ambiguous, often bewildering, emotional demands— are indications of some confusion on the part of their social architects. One feels for the faint-hearted student, for example, who must produce and maintain within herself, and provide external corroboration of, *both transparency and joy*, a daunting task for even the most stable, virtuosic believer.

Dr. David Terrell recalled an episode with one student:

> I used to get so sick . . . the word phony is a word I've used an awful lot—and I hope it's not unfair—but I think there's an awful lot of that in some of these groups. "Do you love the Lord? Praise the Lord!"—you know, all this stuff and they smile and they look great.
>
> One time I said to a girl who came in [for counseling]—she was always smiling when she came in: "Oh, praise the Lord! Isn't today wonderful?"—she sat in the office and I said, "We're probably not going to get anywhere until you tell me, what's behind the smile?" You know it hit her right here [thumps chest] and pretty soon big tears came to her eyes . . . she went on to say that she was "miserable and lonely. I'm so sick of this damn Christianity." She just spilled her guts and we began to get somewhere in therapy. Kate made a decision to leave Seattle Pacific. She went to the University and has just really blossomed as a girl.[606]

Is it any wonder this particular young woman was wracked by anxiety and confusion, by feelings of inadequacy and suppressed anger? The logic demands the production of *both* of these often contradictory signals of difference. Inevitably, the student who strives to consistently achieve and maintain the one (*joy*) eventually jeopardizes the other (*transparency*). My own experience among the students suggests that in fact the pressure for the demonstration of joy is the greater of the two, and that in the heat of a particularly telling social moment transparency tends to be relinquished first. There is, in other words, considerable community pressure to affect the countenance of a joyous, fulfilled Christian (although certainly not as extreme as in some groups), pressure to conceal inner doubts, fears, and the occasional

---

[605] "Spirit—A Sense of Joy," Chapel, 4/27/77.
[606] Interview, 2/5/2003.

emotional lapse or depression from the often censorious scrutiny of fellow students.[607]

The Rite of Openness

Yet one also observes an equally relentless pressure for transparency, oddly enough, that often indirectly confirms and documents the presence of these unanticipated social consequences (façades, affectations, presentations) of the demand for visible signals of a joyous Christian difference, producing very similar moods and occasions for the *violation* of transparency, often within and during the very same moments deemed conducive to the evocation and demonstration of personal transparency. The nature and form of this initially confusing paradox will become more apparent as we examine in considerable detail the student chapels during which are performed what I call the *cult* or *rite of openness*.[608]

In the course of my campus research I listened to nearly ten years of chapel tape recordings, the majority from the early '70s to the early '80s.[609]

---

[607] "Most of us have a fear of honesty, a fear we will show our weaknesses. We resort to wearing masks . . . even in a Christian community masks are evident. What's so unique about a Christian marriage is that we have to accept each other's weaknesses, faults, and be honest. . . . Christians should tell each other when they hurt, instead of putting up walls of isolation." [modified slightly] (Al Kovats, "Speak The Truth In Love," Chapel, 3/24/75.)

[608] This business of the wearing of masks has ancient roots. With great insight, Lawrence Wright links his own spiritual and journalistic investigation to cultural antecedents:

> I have to admit that part of what was powering this quest was my need to strip away masks and find the hidden truth. Of course, masks have always been a feature of religion. In primitive societies, which are useful mirrors of our own, masks are frequently associated with shamans and religious ceremonies. When a Zuni puts on a mask of a kachina spirit, he is thought to be transformed into the kachina itself. Similarly, among the Onondaga tribe of the Iroquois, there was a False Face Society, a shamanistic group that put on masks in order to acquire the power of the deities the masks were supposed to represent. They used these masks in their healing ceremonies. Each of the people whose lives are described in this book is a mask-wearer; indeed, one of the fascinating motifs I discovered is how much artifice goes into constructing the public personas of our religious leaders. The more recognizable the mask is to our subconscious—that is, the purer the archetype—the more power the mask-wearer will have. (*Saints and Sinners*, New York: Alfred A. Knopf, 1993, xvi.)

[609] I believe these cassettes were recorded through an additional microphone located on the lectern of the church chapel rostrum. Although not every chapel of each year was recorded (and then the practice was later discontinued), a considerable number were, and I reviewed most of these (301 total). The recordings were intended to give students who were unable to attend certain chapels the opportunity to hear them later in the library.

"Student chapels" were special versions, generally convened once or twice a quarter (at times more often, their frequency tapering off, it seems to me, in the '80s), and usually included several "testimonies"—student reports of "what the Lord is doing in my life"—or a program upon a particular theme, or even an occasional "open mike" session during which students might come forward from the audience to speak as the spirit moved them. I think it no exaggeration to say that of the student chapel tapes I reviewed a seemingly inordinate amount of time was devoted to this question of just what it means for a Christian to be "real," to bring one's outward appearance and conduct into line with one's true inner condition. A small sample of what I heard follows.

Consider Dick's testimony in the winter of 1977:

> I hope you all can be receptive and prayerful and supportive. I've struggled and fought . . . I just don't like myself much of the time . . . [There are] times when I'm so down on myself that I can't understand how anyone could like me . . . and that's when the loneliness pervades. I say to God, "You say you love me . . . you're kidding . . . how could you love this?" I feel it most strongly those times that I fail. I scream inside, "How stupid could you have been to do that?". . . bawling myself out for human frailties and weaknesses . . . entered into a supreme form of egotism, because I've set a standard for myself that I don't expect from anyone that I love or anyone that I know . . . I keep getting down on myself . . . disguise my pride in things that appear so noble and good. I don't want others around me to see those weaknesses or problems in my life . . . try to hide those weaknesses . . . and you know the most frequent form that I use is . . . putting a mask on. Try to be something that I'm not—a façade, a front. I've got a picture of myself: the great healer—reaching, touching. My front: I have the answers . . . the healer . . . make you whole. The masks I put on are masks of conformity, of some sort. Fundamental evangelical standard or even liberal, all kinds of types in between. Little games that we play, and saying the right language, making sure that we sound just right for the group we're around . . . oh Lord! . . . What I really hate are the masks and façades! . . . How many times I've ignored what God has to say about my weaknesses and problems. It's similar to Paul's analogy of Moses's use of the veil in II Corinthians 3:16. We just can't believe that God might know more than we do about ourselves.
>
> With Christ we no longer need those masks to hide our weaknesses. He gives you the freedom to be yourself. I'm not responsible for my growth—God is. Let him take the veil away. They rob me of God working in me. Too much time on masks, no time for God. It's neat . . . I can stop struggling.[610]

---

[610] "Mount Up With Wings," Student Chapel, 1/19/77. This is not an exact quotation. Some connectives—conjunctions and pronouns—have been added and some sentences have been slightly realigned to smoothen the delivery.

Vaunting, self-centered pride; the donning and stripping away of masks: phrases and themes that recur again and again.[611] Are these spontaneous outpourings of the spirit, the vague and inarticulate speech of the heart, the baring of the genuine anguish of a tortured soul, or rather an integral part of a well-orchestrated and -rehearsed performance, a slick and soothing rendition and affirmation of the evangelical idiom? Indeed all the appropriate elements are drawn together here in seemingly too nuanced and polished a package, in anticipation of too predictable an outcome. Whatever confusion and doubt plagues the student from the outset of his confession conveniently vanishes by its conclusion. Does he really loathe himself in so abject a fashion? And has the solution merely fallen to him out of the transcendent blue? Relinquish control of your own destiny to Christ (the *sacred* opposite of *secular* autonomy) and become open, whole, and, above all, experience the *internal reclamation and external expression* of your true self. We encounter here a student leader who exercises too steady a control over and an awareness of his own predicament, too adroitly diagnosing and remedying his own spiritual shortcomings, climbing too nimbly from the depths of despair and depravity to the heights of wholeness and transparency. "It's neat," all right; perhaps too neat. In a moment we will explore the origins and dynamics of such apparent assurance.

Here are Paula and Andrew, two student government leaders:

> [Paula]: The subject for this quarter ought to be authenticity. Now that's a real McKenna word. That's the very most impressive quality about Christ: no pretence. I'm truly attracted to it. 'Cause it's easy to be not authentic in a community this size. My analyst and I were talking about this very thing the other day at the counseling center. You've got all these accepted images and you turn on that tape when you don't want to be real. The Lord's calling me to stop playing games. My excuse usually is that I'm too busy. What a cop-out! What a sad situation if we're all playing those kinds of games. . . . [Concludes, leaves podium]
>
> [Andrew]: Can't honestly say I was struck by a lightning bolt to get up here in front. I have to sit down because I'm shaking. *I'm not as casual as Paula . . . I have to practice* [laughter] . . . I'm sorry but I'm really in . . . I just feel pretty bad at the moment. A friend of our family just committed suicide. His mother was an alcoholic and had remarried, but the new father was unwilling to help him out. I've been talking about it with my sister at the U.W. . . .
>
> We know people are in trouble, but we're not really willing to reach out to them . . . because I didn't . . . didn't feel that bad . . . my sister locked herself away

---

[611] As Alan Peshkin writes of Bethany Baptist Academy: "Students sometimes put on a false Christian front, motivated by the desire to gain acceptance from fellow students and teachers. . . . Wendy describes a 'make-believe spirituality' that has the effect of making other, less imbued classmates act more spiritual than they really are." Nicknames include: "Holy Joe," "Mr. Righteous," "Miss Pious," and "Miss God," among others. (*God's Choice* . . . , 157.)

in her room for two days. She wasn't willing to share that with me. Why not? I guess it's fear. I don't want to expose myself . . . afraid of someone telling the whole world. . . .

I guess that's why I'm always smiling: I don't share my problems with others. It's kinda confusing . . . I meet people on campus who are quiet and reserved and can't understand . . . we're not willing to share ourselves with other people. Probably lots of people on campus who need to talk, not just to tell me that you're fine. If people would just take five or ten minutes to share . . . I'm sure there are a lot of people here on this campus who would be willing to share themselves . . . if someone really cared . . . those are the individuals you're going to find locked in their rooms because that's the only thing they have to do with their life. . . .

It's hard to be me, Andrew Wilde . . . everybody expects something out of you . . . expects you to act a certain way. . . . Don't just say fine when people ask how you are . . . I'm tired of that. Maybe just grab hold of them and scare them even![612]

As is evident perhaps even in the bare text reproduced above, Paula spends a good deal of time in front of the chapel microphone. She is president of the student body and comfortable before a crowd. The remarks upon authenticity roll off her tongue with all the slick charm of a Broadway production. Her glib, self-effacing hipness (the very chic "My analyst and I") peremptorily disarms any lingering skepticism among her fellow students, lulling them into a confessional ease. And they are receptive because it is a familiar, well-honed message, delivered with characteristic aplomb. Andrew's introductory quip, "I'm not as casual as Paula . . . I have to practice," is pregnant with meaning, perhaps inadvertently shredding whatever pose of spontaneity or depth of feeling Paula has managed to evince. As the assembled students share a chuckle, perhaps she squirms in momentary discomfort, *her authenticity* indirectly, unintentionally impugned. Although it is apparent that Andrew speaks more from the heart, displaying both anxiety and anguish, the quip is too good, too felicitous, demonstrating too exquisite a sense of timing to come from a frightened student genuinely floundering before his peers. Perhaps he is indeed nervous and weak-kneed, but he appears to work his way through any initial physical panic, summoning internal strength, gaining momentum, and eventually hitting a loping stride. He has, after all, been here before in this pit or arena of spiritual testing. As with Paula, Andrew's is a familiar voice that I immediately recognized from other chapels. He is what we might call a BSMOC, a Big Spiritual Man On Campus. This and other chapel appearances will serve to enhance his visibility and prominence on campus, ultimately leading to his election as a vice-president of student government and a regular schedule of chapel appearances in the future. Hence,

---

[612] "He Guides," Student Chapel, 3/1/78.

in retrospect, this particular testimony might be placed in a larger motivational context. One wonders, for example, why it is easier or more important for Andrew to publicly flail himself for personal inadequacies and to publicize a particularly tragic episode in the life of his family than it is for him to marshal the emotional resources needed to effectively succor and communicate with his sister and the other members of the family? We can only speculate upon the degree of exaggeration in Andrew's account of his own emotional paralysis in dealing with the tragedy. But surely one has to wonder which episode—Andrew's attempts to deal with the suicide and his family or the chapel confession of his failures—produced the greater quantity of transparency, the more genuine gestures of "openness." In which arena was Andrew truly "being himself?": during the moments of confusion and frustration and anger with his sister and family or during these few brief moments of trembling—but successful—contrition before a large chapel audience? In which arena did Andrew exercise the greater control, engaging in formulaic revelations and expressions of the unguarded inner self? In which was he the most *real*?

A month or so later, the students convene another chapel, with ten or more students coming forward to speak. The first, Rick, strums a guitar and leads the audience in song, then speaks.

> I'm a little nervous about this. You know if I wrote a letter to myself, this is what I'd say: Dear Sunday Christian, How ya feeling? Hard for me to tell anymore with your glassy eyes and painted-on smiles . . . I'm not really sure if you're really happy or thinking about the basketball game last night or the soap opera you saw last Friday. Don't try to con me . . . I used to play the same game. I can see it. I had everyone fooled—the pastor and my friends . . . [but I] couldn't fool God. The game is fixed. God knows . . . when I'm speaking from my heart. Don't try to change the rules . . . I tried that. Only God's laws count in the end. The game is over and you call out to Christ. The gate is closed, the light will fade. Left with one card—maybe your trump card. Simply says: "Go straight to Hell. Do not pass Go. Do not collect $200."

And, mixed game metaphors aside, not a single laugh erupts from the audience. Rick strums his guitar and sings:

> I used to play the games of the world. [Then stops, adding:] Once you've recognized you're playing the game . . . sometimes we play so well we've got ourselves fooled. How can you tell? When you're praying, you use footnotes—footnotes to God: "Lord, I'll go anywhere [in your service] except Africa, Chicago, New York. . . ." Have you taken the footnotes out of your prayer?[613]

---

[613] "I Will Strengthen You," Student Chapel, 4/3/78.

So we learn that back when Rick was a *faux*, disingenuous Sunday Christian he played games with God—the artificial, self-concealing secular "games of the world"; whereas in his newly redeemed condition he speaks directly from the heart, has become the genuine article, a transparent whole character, able now to speak of a Christian's relationship with his God in terms of a game of Monopoly, complete with cards, dice, and token trips around Park Place. Presumably, he is now *whole*.

Rick lays aside the guitar and relinquishes the stage to subsequent speakers. A few utter a brief sentence or two only—some to the effect that Rick's testimony has really hit home, where they live—and depart. One after another, they pay homage to this imperative of transparency.

Indeed, to come forward into the arena of openness and confession is to strip away the mask of pretension and lay bare one's genuine identity. Students luxuriate in the knowledge that they have now ascended a higher spiritual plateau; for the moment they have purged themselves of corrupting worldly guises and dependencies, have spurned the phony "games that people play."

Sanctions

Perhaps one indication or measure of the enduring power of these assumptions are those rare moments of breakdown, when their routine celebration is momentarily suspended and prominent spiritual mandarins of the student community intervene to enforce and reaffirm the code.

In one student chapel, for instance, Doug, the student director and moderator of chapel programs, receives effusive praise and thanks from fellow students whom he has helped. Richard had some problems with his family and Doug just "showed up to help him with his parents. God can bring someone right to your door who you need. I can guarantee you that he will."

Judy relates an even more incisive experience:

> This is public thank Doug day.
> I'm someone who's fellowshipping constantly with other Christians. I'm a cadre group coordinator. Some people probably think of me as "Miss Spiritual". . . . Doug and a couple other friends took it upon themselves to finally stop . . . and . . . stop letting me play my game and faking all you other guys out long enough to say, where are you? And what are you doing? And who are you trying to kid? . . . I just want to say, thank you. That if you see somebody that you love and that you really care about, sometimes it takes sitting down and kicking them in the seat of the pants. [For] some of us it takes about three or four kicks to stop and really say

I do want to live for God and I really want Jesus Christ to make all the difference in my life.[614]

Observe the gentle but forceful application of peer pressure, all framed within the larger context of the demands of the logic; observe the confluence of both *social* and *cultural* dynamics. Two contrary imperatives are in operation here: there is the (social) pressure to conceal *and* there is the (cultural) pressure to reveal. And if that weren't enough to complicate matters, consider that the generic pressure to conceal, to present a socially-constructed mask, may be further amplified or extended by the cultural "smile" imperative. In the first instance, for a variety of possible reasons, Judy has donned a "Christian mask." It seems likely she fears the potential social consequences—rejection by her Christian friends and mentors—of exposing her personal and spiritual frailties, or perhaps simply is troubled by or unwilling to acknowledge and live within her own spiritual limitations, the lukewarm quality of her talents. She appears highly committed and engaged socially, yet in fact conceals her true outlook and feelings beneath a thin veneer of apparent devotion, a surface gloss bereft of resonating depth—or so it seems to Doug and her other "friends." And so she compensates. Unable to consistently muster the requisite unity of feeling and behavior, and unwilling to jeopardize her imagined social position on campus, she simulates the prized gestures of devotion and piety, of glee and fulfillment; she becomes a spiritual workaholic. Public professions and a frenzy of activity substitute for an authentic wholeness.

Operating on an altogether higher plane of spiritual awareness, Doug and the "friends" of Judy recognize the tell-tale symptoms. They have seen it all before: the hyper-involvement, the cheery gloss, the games, the masks—surface appearances devoid of any corresponding internal substance and depth. They come down on her in a hard, but "loving" manner. The truth of the indictment is apparent to everyone: "Miss Spiritual" is a walking bundle of contradictions, the creation of an over-eager, too-willing-to-please *social* imagination. Pressing the flesh, and spirit, they exhort her to "peel off the phony layers" of social convention (the David McKenna phrase) and "get real." And indeed, surrounded by friends who genuinely "love" and "support" her, who have stripped away the accumulation of props and camouflage, calling her social fabrications into question, only a monumentally secure and self-confident ego could withstand the pressure, could hold fast to an imperturbably pious front, however well-constructed. It should come as no surprise then that the error of her former ways suddenly dawns upon

---

[614] "Think of these Things: Whatever Is Right," Student Chapel, 11/28/77.

Judy. She concedes the pained and divided condition of her inner life and successfully purges the false consciousness of an overweening, damaged *social* self. Later, she rises before chapel peers to present the formal confirmation and reproduction of this process of self-purification, affirming the logic of wholeness and transparency, bearing one more testimonial offering to the cult or ritual of openness.

What is false? What is real? What is affectation and pretense? Perhaps only Erving Goffman knows for sure? Indeed, who approaches, let alone opens, this social-psychological can of worms with much enthusiasm or *savoir-faire*? [615] The indictment rings true because it is an accusation or observation that surely holds for everyone. Only the truly foolish or vain would cling to any kind of transcendent innocence, for we are all social creatures to some degree or other. And so when the ax of peer judgement falls upon the shoulders of some notorious *poseur* the community as whole shudders in recognition of the universality of the indictment. All feel the pressure to get one's disheveled house of personality in order. And for these students no better forum or opportunity exists for coming clean of social corruption, for performing anxiety- and guilt-relieving rites of social purification, than during these dramatic moments of testimony and confession in the student chapels, delivering performances ranging from the slick and polished to the painfully halting and maladroit. Here, all manner of malodorous personal spiritual defects and foibles are routinely exhumed and exposed to the sanitizing, purifying gaze of fellow students and God.

Public Prayer

The characterization of these moments of student confession before peers as a kind of ritualization of openness and transparency applies with equal force to another practice in community worship, public prayer before a congregation (and, with respect to the larger, ever-expanding evangelical electronic universe, before a television camera and a studio or auditorium audience).

Anthony Campolo, guest speaker and social internationalist, explained his own refusal to pray in public to students at a chapel talkback session:

> What is . . . so phony about groups that are praying? Ever notice that? How phony public prayer can be? Prayer is more intimate than sex . . . I seriously doubt whether Jesus ever led a group in prayer.[616]

---

[615] Re: Erving Goffman, *The Presentation of Self in Everyday Life*, New York: Doubleday, 1959.
[616] "About Yourself," Chapel Talkback Session, 5/18/2003.

Public talk with God, often woven in and around these confessions of spiritual bankruptcy, represents yet another projection of piety which may assume a highly ritualized, routinized form. Public prayer (in this particular evangelical context) in effect derives less from Biblical principle or example than from the cultural accretions generated by the ideological imperative to constantly produce, demonstrate, and celebrate discernible Christian/secular differences. It fosters the kind of ideological occasion and arena in which these signals of difference may be broadcast and re-affirmed, a role which private prayer simply cannot perform. And as with any such public presentation the performances may vary anywhere from genuine, heartfelt expressions of devotion or acknowledgements of error to maudlin affectations of faith and accounts of spiritual struggles.

It is not often in the discussion of such issues that a definitive, unambiguous scripture can be produced which ought to settle the matter once and for all; this is one of those rare moments. From the Sermon on the Mount:

> Again, when you pray, do not be like the hypocrites; they love to say their prayers standing up in synagogue and at the street-corners, for everyone to see them. I tell you this: they have their reward already. But when you pray, go into a room by yourself, shut the door, and pray to your Father who is there in the secret place; and your Father who sees what is secret will reward you.[617]

Seldom has so direct an instruction from Jesus been so wantonly, conspicuously, and even brazenly violated by modern disciples. Obviously, in this instance, adherence to the teachings of Jesus would undermine the ideological intention and purpose of these public demonstrations and weaken much of the spiritual infrastructure of the evangelical community, putting a damper upon the ideological agenda of modern evangelicalism. Signals of difference depend upon public demonstrations of difference—upon visible social corroboration of the adoption and application of the terms of the cultural logic. As such, secret meetings with the Father in secret places, although certainly encouraged, are of secondary importance in an a-social community of public transparency and wholeness.

The Trivialization of the Sacred
Finally, Campolo perhaps inadvertently calls attention to one intriguing feature of these attempts to generate public signals of piety and/or

---

[617] Matthew 6:5-6, *NEB*. Then there is Paul's letter to the Colossians 3:2-3: ".... fix your thoughts on the higher realm, not on this earthly life. You died; and now your life lies hidden with Christ in God." (*REB*)

transparency, particularly when that which is for him so private and "intimate" a behavior is given so public, and by implication, so trivial an expression. The *trivialization* and *vulgarization* of faith are two major consequences of the community's drive for unity in every dimension of personal and social life, for the Christianization of nearly every element of personal and social behavior. For in the very act of rendering transparently public and uniformly sacred what is for some the most profoundly personal and insular of experiences the community virtually assures the profane trivialization and impoverishment ("phoniness") of the prayer act. Hence a potentially profound, elevated form of conduct becomes reduced to yet one more rudiment of pedestrian public behavior, as though—in terms here of Campolo's scale of intimacy—the married couples of the community were to routinely perform sexual intercourse on the dais before the initially shocked, but eventually jaded, eyes of the congregation.[618] Have you no shame? Campolo asks, with some justification. No appreciation of the difference between the sacred Christian and the profane secular? A distinction, ironically enough, that the community has organized itself in the first place to *internally* overcome.

The evidence of a rampant trivialization and vulgarization within evangelicalism perhaps becomes even more noticeable in the attempts to influence the external secular culture. Witness the seeming plethora of John 3:16 and other banners decorating the balconies of American football and baseball arenas and the now routine moments of huddled prayerful devotion down on the field among former combatants following the conclusion of these athletic contests. This invariably followed (especially upon the conclusion of playoff or championship games) by locker room testimonials from sweaty, champagne-soaked athletes who simply must thank "Jesus Christ," among others, for their moment of triumph. (Can the reader recall a similar testimony from a member of the losing side?) Yet in the life of an athlete so integrated, focused, and "whole," is there actually a discernible point at which the profane leaves off and the sacred begins? Is there a particularly Christian manner of throwing or dropping a pass? Of slapping one another on the buttocks? Of showering down following the game? Or does not the distinction between the two simply become lost in the indiscriminate commotion of the spectacle itself? Perhaps there are no longer any such lines of demarcation, as was made evident by coach Bill Parcels of the Giants after his second Super Bowl win in 1991, when he gushed that "Sometimes I get the feeling God is playing in these games." Ah, unity, *wholeness*—and most

---

[618] We are perhaps reminded, once again, of colonial Puritan Cotton Mather's attempts to elevate the terrestrial act of urination, exhorting himself to think noble, divine thoughts while relieving himself. (Greven, *The Protestant Temperament. . .* , 67.)

importantly of all, *significance*. God as a blitzing linebacker. The turning of meaning into its appropriate correlated effect and validation. Is it not ironic that in the rush to inject the profession of faith into nearly every activity something deeply reverential may be lost? Might that not include a kind of genuine sense and feeling for the sacred? [619]

Sample Students

The student sample was asked to respond to the following item:

> Often times objections are directed at certain individuals who seem to be just going through the motions, trying to get by with the mere appearance of faith without a deeper spiritual commitment; some students refer to this as wearing "Christian masks."

When asked, "Do you notice this phenomenon?" the overwhelming majority (71%) responded that they had very much noticed these students. Asked if they were bothered by the practice, an even greater number (78%) expressed considerable irritation. Yet when asked, "Do you ever feel that you are yourself just going through the motions, as described above?" only a small percentage (20%) admitted consistently engaging in such behaviors, most confessing to only occasional lapses into inauthentic conduct. Nearly 80% of the sample regarded this a very important issue to "struggle with."[620]

On the surface, it would seem then that this business of "masks" is on nearly everyone's mind and, further, that many students are prone to point the finger of disapproval in someone else's direction. They would appear surrounded by *poseurs* in an environment that David McKenna deemed inhospitable to phonies.[621]

---

[619] In this respect, as mentioned in chapter one, my views differ markedly from those of Stephen Carter, who locates the source of trivialization in the larger secular culture's rejection of a serious public role for religion. See *The Culture of Disbelief* (New York: Basic Books, 1993).

[620] Student Questionnaire items #99a-d.

[621] Some examples from the student senator interviews:

—Jeff: "I have friends here who put on this false joy . . . all the time . . . but it doesn't take much to snap them out of it . . . ["Masks?"] The circles I travel in 'aren't like that.' I run into it most in the Singers [SPU traveling choir], and it's most distressing because we're representing something that it is not . . . for me it is not anyway."

—Paula: "Oh yeah . . . God . . . you know the thing is, it's kind of built in, I think. There's a systematic thing going on here where to opt into the system you've got to maintain that aura of 'I know what I'm doing' and really 'Ah hah! Hah! I know!' It's real interesting . . . ["Lots of pressure?"] yeah, oh yeah . . . I don't opt into it, but many do, you know . . . I don't put the smile on—'leave me alone!'. . . yeah, gosh, it's an interesting thing. . . . The thing that's sad is that people are walking around with smiles on their faces and they're hurting and they don't have it . . . they really don't have it and nobody knows, and they don't want to know. It's a sad thing. ["Ever see them with their guard down?"] That happened more in the dorm

How these young students actually deal with all the various converging imperatives of joy and transparency will become more apparent in the following account of a particularly dramatic week in the life of the Seattle Pacific community.

The Mel White Revue

I have made occasional reference to the week-long visit of Christian filmmaker Mel White to campus. Let us now examine his appearance in much greater detail, an account which benefits, I would hope, from my own observation of and participation in nearly every event or occasion I recount.

Mel White is described in the promotional tract announcing his "Christian Commitment Week" visit as "one of America's leading Christian filmmakers," the writer and director of "20 motion pictures," the author of six books, and an associate professor of communication and media ministries at Fuller Theological Seminary in Pasadena. His topic for the week-long series is "Fighting The War Between Worlds," a theme explained by an underlying caption: "Pressed between the values and pressures of two distinct ways of life—the world's and God's—how does a Christian respond?" A quandary for which, the tract assures us, Mr. White has "answers." Few could anticipate the kind of answers and example Mel White would offer.

Students catch their first glimpse of Mel White in Monday chapel. Slender, mid 40s, mustached with receding sandy blond beach boy hair, nattily attired in a dark blue business suit, he sits in a chair on the rostrum, a slim briefcase at his side; few notice that he fails to sing a single lick of the hymn that begins the chapel. Introduced, he moves to the lectern, unsmiling, appearing mildly ticked and pained. He begins with a story about scuba diving, one of his "obsessions" (brine, danger, testing, exhilaration). Too far away in the balcony (the students have yet to settle in), I catch only the words barracuda, tame fish, and St. Croix. Then he makes his point, looking out at the students, observing that *you* "have a marvelous way of putting on a mask and acting like you're listening."

... because you see them walking around campus with the smile on their face, and you know—because you stayed up to twelve talking to them the night before—you know they're not all there."

—Daniel: "Don't kid yourself . . . I think there are a few who are just really faking it—just a few. They're visible . . . I guess they're some who are really involved . . . I would say most who are phony are really trying but don't totally realize what the implications are . . . more than just going to church or chapel three times a week."

He pauses, allowing the full thrust of the accusation to connect and sink in. The students grow immediately silent. Nary a squirm or a cough. White grips the lectern with both hands and looks out at them.

"Everybody I pray for dies . . . everybody."

The admission electrifies the silence. Students begin to cast surreptitious sideways glances at one another, as though to ask, "Who is this guy?"

"I just spent a week with Arafat . . . Begin . . . shooting a film in the Middle East . . . Been everywhere there were dead bodies . . . I'm sick and tired of 'Youth For Christ,' promises of good times, etc. . . . The city of man will always die . . . is dying . . . is not going to last."

He lifts up the "City Guide," from his hotel room:

"The city of man versus St. Augustine's *The City of God* . . . God . . . taking us to this land we have been promised. In the Old Testament there were constant prods to move the people on, to give up on the city of man.

How do you keep from buying in?

Don't get me wrong here . . . I think Christians should be number one in academics.

When you accept Christ . . . you're free to care about others . . . you're not afraid to die. We're free to live since we're no longer bound to this world."

The students warm to these more familiar themes. They nod and anticipate more.

White invokes the example of Jesus wiping the feet of his disciples as they sat around at supper. He "makes us free to be a servant." More recently, Archbishop Romeo of El Salvador comes to mind, his "favorite model" of this kind of servanthood. Just before they gunned him down, he instructed his congregation to "Remember the dream."

"What a way to go!" exclaims White.

He closes with a brief prayer, the final word of which he instructs to students to repeat in unison ("Say it together now . . . Amen."). He sits down and a student comes forward to dismiss the audience, reminding them that only one person had signed up for the Christian Commitment Week prayer chain: "Half-hour prayer slots are available for the entire week."

And so the week began on a sobering note of ambiguity. As White moves from one prayer meeting, disciple group, and class to another, he proceeds to violate all expectations of an "inspirational speaker": discounting miracles, faith healing, the electronic church; rebuking religious authority figures; appealing for clarity, compassion, and vision. Students encounter an apparently tragic figure riven by inner anxieties, sorrows, and contradictions, burdened by the inhumanity of the human species, ill-at-ease with himself and with the facile platitudes and nostrums of his religious background and be-liefs. This week the veil of Christian complacency would drop away, reveal-ing an anguished and tortured soul, a man bent upon self-revelation and truth-telling, however discomfiting or painful.

As word spreads, each succeeding chapel or campus appearance attracts more students than the one before. White delivers his opinions with a dis-arming, mesmerizing panache. Students crowd the foyer of the chapel audi-torium; standing-room-only spillover in the foyer hears the message piped in through overhead speakers. Discussion sessions in the Fireside room of the Student Union Building double and triple in size. Students sense that some kind of weird "revival" is gaining momentum; they follow him around in droves.

Recounting many close encounters, he confesses to a discussion group: "It's the adrenaline flow . . . I'm slowly destroying myself . . . I'm a Christian who's struggling . . . we're all struggling. Don't take me as an authority fig-ure. Call my bluff."

A girl finds all this honesty inspiring: "You're so refreshing!"

A guy wants to know "Why do you do this?"

He answers, "You guys are the only hope of the church."

Still another asks, "What motivates you?"

"That's really intimate," he responds and then pauses for a moment, considering his answer.

"The first thing is sexual lust. Most of my activities serve to divert my hormones. Secondly, are the problems with grace. I've always thought I could never be loved by God. Now I think it, but I don't really believe it. I'm from an Arminian family tradition and I keep running because in my heart I can't believe that God loves me as I am. . . . Finally, it just seems that eve-rything I do turns to gold, and so I am motivated to go on and on. . . ."

Later, Mel White prefaces one of his chapel talks with an acknowledge-ment of the confusion over his unorthodox approach:

"I understand that some of you are asking one another and you have asked me 'When does this become Christian Commitment Week?' You want to see individuals coming forward, down the aisles."

He surveys the audience: "How many Christians are in the hall?"

Virtually everyone raises a hand.

"How many agnostics?"

One person raises his hand.

"How many atheists?"

Not a single hand. The students are silent.

"I'm tired of corny songs and thinking we must weep and bring people to God at the altar . . . not that it isn't necessary. But nearly all of us are Christians. So we can go on to other things."

In discussion after discussion Mel White comes across as somber, blunt, direct; he promises no rose garden and tenders no apologies: take me as I am. For the duration at least, transparency, not the mask, is the order of the day.

The Student Senate Meeting

On Thursday afternoon, twenty or so student senators, two or three faculty advisers, and myself are seated around an oval table in the Trustees Board Room, just across the hall from the office of the president. Portraits of founders and past presidents of the college gaze down upon us. Students are poised on the very front tips of armless, brown Naugahyde-grained swivel lounge chairs, anxiously awaiting the arrival of Mel White, who is scheduled to deliver a brief "devotional" talk. Anticipatory banter flies back and forth over the table.

White arrives 30 minutes or so late. The students greet "Mel" with a barrage of scuba diving quips that appear to put everyone at ease. He bids them to lower their heads for a few words of prayer and, concluding, continues to stare down into his clasped fingers, apparently lost in thought.

Stuart, sitting directly in front of him on one side of the oval table, interrupts his reverie, raising a hand and volunteering:

"I just want to thank you for being so real this week."

There are supporting "yeahs" and a general nodding of heads. Mel looks up at him and then to each face around the table in turn, staring an uncomfortably long time into each.

> I'm not real . . . What does it mean to be real?
>
> [Stuart, lamely: "Amen."]
>
> To lower the mask for a while? . . . If you're real for a little bit of the time, if you lower the mask, they shake their fists at you [He wags a fist in front of his face] . . . They want their leaders, their pastors to put on the masks, to preserve their illusions, images, idols . . . to assure the weak ones . . . comfort them and give certainty and stability. The real story is that I feel as much ambivalence and doubt as anyone . . . But they don't want to hear that. They want to be shored up, comforted.

He pauses, searching from face to face, in apparent anguish.

> Last night I spoke with my wife over the phone. . . . There's a young man we know quite well in our Nazarene church . . . they found him the other day hanging from the rafters of his apartment. There was a note left behind that told of his terrible feelings of guilt over his urge to masturbate. . . . Someone needed to tell him that he wasn't the only one in the world struggling with masturbation . . . let him know that he wasn't alone in the world . . . but there was no one in the church

to talk to . . . no one who could understand . . . so he hung himself . . . torn apart by something that isn't even a sin. . . . . Why not hang yourself for sneezing or blowing your nose?

A gush of air rushes out of the students. Punctuating the stunned silence is the barely audible sniffing and sobbing of one of the female students; a fellow on the other side of the table exhales and then whines softly, as though venting a secret wound. The students are disoriented, reeling from the telling blows that have been delivered. Given the unpredictable atmosphere, all must wonder, what is to follow? Will he throw himself from the third-floor window? Or simply burst from too great a spiritual compression and expansion, from the spiritual bends?

White looks around at the senators with sad, weary eyes and nods:

> You're the best of the bullshitters . . . the bullshitters of the bullshitters . . . the cream of the crop . . . . If you want to rise to the top in the church business, keep on your masks . . . otherwise you'll end up dead bones. . . . Jesus Christ lowered his mask and they shot him.

An unrelenting tension grips us, broken only by an occasional sniffle and sob. No one knows exactly what to do or say.

"So what do you think? What do you have to say?"

For one or two very long minutes he looks from face to face and no one speaks.

Finally Doug, vice-president in charge of the senate, ventures a response:

"I don't agree that we must keep wearing the masks . . . we've got to lower them to minister effectively. . . ." He rambles on incoherently about "leadership" and other themes which seem to dominate the emotional agenda of a student government officer, falling back upon well-worn phrases and clichés, displaying an incomprehension and conventionality almost as stunning and numbing in their own predictable banality as are White's admissions compelling for their brooding, gratuitous irony.

White endures this patiently, silently, looking out at the other students as though nothing has been said. He waits.

Then Wanda, the rather remarkable young woman we met earlier, raises her hand; White nods in her direction.

> You touched upon some things that have been bothering me recently . . . having to do with my own feelings of inadequacy . . . inability to break through to other people.
> I've been struggling . . . feeling a need to talk about things with a few other people in a devotional group. I've felt a need for such a group for some time but I never seem to manage to get one organized . . . . Well, finally I decided I just had to go up to these three or four people I know and ask . . . but I just sat and stewed

for three or four hours, trying to get up the courage to ask them . . . I just sat and sat . . . I couldn't move . . . I screamed at myself: Why can't you do this!! . . . They're your friends! . . . but I couldn't do this simple thing. . . . They would be shocked to hear me say this.

People seem almost afraid of me . . . think that I don't need anyone . . . I know almost half the people on this campus and yet I've come to realize that I don't really know anyone . . . or have one really true intimate friend.

The other students can barely comprehend what has happened. Most are astonished, embarrassed, as though some poor unfortunate soul has been drubbed and stripped naked before their very eyes. Another girl, Marit, nearly flushed beyond the redness of her freckles, voice trembling, follows Wanda's courageous lead, although unable (or unwilling) to match the detail and depth of her *cri de coeur*:

I feel the same way sometimes . . . some of my friends think of me as nearly perfect. They scoff at the idea that I'm imperfect . . . that I have problems too . . . my imperfections would fill a long list . . . I could go on and on.

The others sit silently; not another confession will escape their lips. Surely most find the tenor and substance of Marit's confession a good deal more familiar and palatable than the mind-boggler Wanda has laid on them.

Mel White waits a minute or so and then briskly concludes:

You've been talking about the kinds of individual problems of balance that must be dealt with in your own lives. What you should concentrate on from this point forward are the kinds of corporate endeavors that can further the accessibility of one another's private, real lives to other real lives . . . to share these inadequacies . . . to help reduce the distance between leaders and congregation.

He looks to his watch and indicates an escort waiting by the door: "I'm late again and must go." Gathering his coat and briefcase, he slips out the door, and then, as though sensing that his abrupt departure has left everyone in an emotional limbo, pops his head back in the door and says, "By the way, you've got a wonderful school; I've been very impressed with you."

The door finally closes and everyone in the room heaves a sigh in unison.

"What an enigma!" one girl whispers, under her breath.

A faculty adviser assures the students around him that "He's the greatest Christian speaker I've *ever, ever* heard."

An enigma perhaps, but surely also, upon later reflection, a major let-down and disappointment. Observe how White creates an occasion and mood for the most gut wrenching and draining of personal revelations, evoking from Wanda one of the most courageous moments of personal integrity and candor I had witnessed on campus, and then as though somewhat unnerved (or bored?) with the volatile ambience he has wrought, with the group poised on the verge of some genuine truth-telling, pulls back from the brink, assuming an air of detached objectivity, and then walks away from the resulting emotional cauldron, refusing to "reveal" himself further. Wanda's enthralling moment of self-revelation is characterized as one of those "individual problems of balance that must be dealt with" in her own life, on her own time, not his. He offers a nostrum expressed in no more original or lucid an idiom than the conventional campus clichés uttered by Stuart and Doug. But, understandably, the students are numb, mesmerized, unable to concentrate upon the actual content of the thought.

They all—and especially Wanda—had a right to feel somewhat cheated. Here was a rare opportunity to get to the heart of the problem of being an idiomatically-correct a-social Christian, of being laden with personal and social burdens difficult to reconcile with the imperative of transparency; here was an opportunity—with Wanda leading the way—to peel away the "phony layers" of social appearance and examine the realities of unvarnished personality, a chance to bring together all these stripped-down genuine selves and discover what sort of revelatory heat might be generated. White summarily dismisses the fear of expressing one's feelings or sentiments to others as a "problem of balance"; perhaps he fails to grasp the degree to which Wanda has identified the very nub of the problem confronting any Christian who yearns to bring the ideal transparent Christian personality and social ambience into being.

Does it occur to anyone that Wanda and her peers have launched themselves on a quixotic quest to overcome the indelible nature and structure of human social interaction, Wanda repeatedly, vainly throwing herself against the very mechanisms and lubricants which ultimately make community and society possible, and tolerable?

From the above account it is readily apparent that Mel White has revealed things about himself that few evangelicals dare admit even to themselves. Yet there lingers a nagging suspicion that a good deal more of him lay buried beneath the brooding surface than he let on, that much was in fact held in reserve. In the Senate meeting he refused to be dragged down into the dirty, unseemly trenches of extemporaneous self-examination. Wanda *truly* bared her soul and Mel White scurried away—apparently untouched, unmoved, undiscovered—with an easy parting prescription for the perennial problem of establishing the appropriate distance between leaders and congregations. At that moment, Wanda and the others may have wondered with some justification: What are *you* feeling now, Mel? Boredom? Homesickness?

Irritation? Insecurity? Crisis? Superiority? Lust? Do you actually like, love, hate—or merely tolerate—us? Wanda spilled her guts and you left her lying there in the gutter, emotionally spent and vulnerable, while you slipped away.

A few months later in the spring, Wanda recalled the moment (a portion of the following having appeared earlier):

> I was shaking . . . it was the first time I've ever been honest in a public situation on this campus . . . . It was probably at that time—like the instance that I shared about: the discipleship group that I was hoping to become involved in—I was really . . . my boyfriend and some close friends [not SPU students] were just counseling me that, as risky as it is, we are nothing as Christians if we are not transparent. And so I had a definite goal at that moment in my life too that—so help me— I was going to quit lying . . . I really wanted to make some close friends [she was a senior] and for people to get beyond the stereotype of me.
> ["Mel White?"]
> I was a little bit bothered by his cynicism . . . it kind of offended me. I really liked what he had to say . . . thought it was true . . . but he personally, I didn't know what to make of him at all.
> ["What did you feel after the session?"]
> Kind of weird—no, I felt really naked, really vulnerable . . . it was like they knew that I had these needs . . . I felt like, here I was, I exposed myself and they could either respond or ignore it.
> ["And did they ignore you?"]
> Well, there, pretty much; but I kind of shared some of the same feelings at this leadership retreat [she couldn't remember if it was before or after the Senate meeting] . . . it was there that I really opened up in front of some people about some ways I'd been feeling and I had two people come up to me and say, "I never would have thought you ever felt that way . . . I would love to be your friend . . . I would love to become close friends with you". . . . Knocked my socks off . . . you know I just felt so grateful and I was really glad that I'd been honest . . . I wasn't disillusioned. There really are people that care . . . but there are a heck of a lot [in front of whom] you can bare your soul and they will leave you laying there . . . right here.
> ["Just like anywhere else?"]
> Oh yeah.[622]

And then there's Paula, a black senator (appointed by her peers to fill a vacancy) from Los Angeles, who remembers:

> God, that was so funny! . . . I love that guy . . . [but] you know the only thing is that I think that people spent the whole time he was there speaking trying to figure out why this Christian said an obscenity in their senate.
> ["What'd he say?"]

---

[622] (*SSI*, May 2003)

He said bullshit . . . No! No! He said, you guys are the bullshitters of the bull-shitters . . . Wash my mouth out! . . . What was funny about my situation was that I probably spent the rest of the time laughing at the people who I thought were probably concentrating on that he said that.[623]

What did I think about it? . . . I thought the responses were typical . . . and kind of like, OK, now this is what I'm going to say now, so I'll say it.

["Did you know Doug was going to say that?"]

Of course . . . well, either Doug or Jacob could have said the same thing. As for Stuart [the fellow who said, "Thanks for being so real"] you know [makes a sarcastic gesture with her finger on her tongue inside her mouth].

Wanda was about the only person that surprised me . . . because usually Wanda's not vulnerable.

Just as no one in his own church reached out to assure a struggling young man that he wasn't the only one in the world who experienced anxiety and guilt over masturbation (how could anyone know?), Mel White also failed to assure Wanda that she wasn't the only one in the world who felt emotionally blocked or handicapped in her desire to break through and initiate relationships with others, neglecting in his haste (or ennui) to offer something along the lines of, for example: "I know what you mean" or "How many times have I felt the same reluctance!" or "Here are some approaches I've found useful." Indeed, any sentient person knows precisely what paralyzed Wanda;

---

[623] The accuracy of Paula's reading of the probable responses of a few fellow senators is corroborated by another senator, Chip's, reconstruction of the session:

["You remember Mel White's senate devotional?"]
Yes.
["Fresh in your memory?"]
I can still see him standing up and saying what he did [actually: he was sitting] . . . and me cringing . . . Even though he might have had grounds for saying what he said, I don't think he should have used the words he did . . . I was mad at him . . . I would say that you could better say that without using those words . . . I agree that we all wear masks, but to use that language.
["What language?"]
Some four-letter words . . . He used . . . I hate to even say it . . . I hate to . . . BS the BS'ers . . . He said the words . . . I don't like to even think about those things.
["Fellow senators' responses?"]
Got real quiet . . . You could have heard a pin drop . . . Everybody's mouth just popped open . . . I was sitting by Jacob . . . he goes, after Mel White, "Well"—meaning there's a lot of pressure.
["What about Marit, Doug, and Wanda?"]
I don't remember what they said . . . I don't even remember those people talking . . . I just remember thinking about what he said and being frustrated."

we have all experienced the same sort of anxiety or ambivalence; we have all succumbed to it.

White left Wanda lying in a pool of her own confessional blood not because he is an insensitive, uncaring person but, in all likelihood, because the social context and structure of the occasion and the sheer exhaustive nature of his schedule discourage the kinds of repeated "hands-on" personal interaction and self-exposure that the terms of the logic (and White's own contribution to heightened expectations) would seem to demand. Few persons can expend the kind of emotional energy we observed in Wanda's confession day in and day out, week after week, at every watering hole along the evangelical college circuit. To be constantly caring and convincing, to be consistently open and sharing, to wear one's heart and personality on a sleeve and hold nothing in reserve: all told, these represent emotionally-draining (and ultimately self-destructive) enterprises for most people.

White acknowledged as much during one talkback session, relating his own experience of counseling a particularly disturbed member of his church congregation, who suffered from periodic fits of despondency and depression. Although White provided counseling sessions, the man's condition failed to improve. He began to grow increasingly dependent upon him for emotional relief, demanding more and more of his time and energy. Finally, he decided that the relationship had become so unhealthy and unproductive that it should be terminated. Thereafter he received occasional desperate calls for intervention from the member, to some of which he initially felt obliged, as a Christian, to respond. The man continued to manipulate his feelings of guilt at being unable to help him and for any reluctance to respond to his pleas for assistance. Finally, one holiday weekend, as White prepared to sit down to a Thanksgiving meal with friends and relatives, the member telephoned him once more requesting support. He confessed great anguish and despair, imploring him to come to his house, to which White responded with suggestions of alternatives, places to go, and offering brief reassurance. Sobbing and pleading, the fellow then threatened to take his own life if White failed to join him immediately. "There was no way I was going to leave my family's Thanksgiving dinner . . . we learned the next day that he had stuck his head in a gas oven and was found dead."

The point was about emotional economy and the kind of realism one must carry into actual relationships: "You just can't keep giving yourself away . . . every selfless act of martyrdom is really a selfish decision."

And so it would seem that here among the students Mel White gave himself away in much more sparing a fashion than might appear at first blush. ("I'm not real.") Surely over the years as he has moved from one spiritual venue to another he has learned to pace himself, to ration out this sort of emotional energy. In other words, he has to approach these appearances as performances, employing the kinds of histrionics that are likely to elicit the desired response from audiences and yet do the least damage to the values and ideas he genuinely holds and would like to promote and his ability to continue on the next week's or month's engagement.

One can only speculate on the "true" feelings of Mel White during his appearance on campus. Yet some inkling of his motivations comes from a conversation with Jacob, student body president, who spent some time with him.

> I had lunch with him that day [before the student senate meeting] and I remember talking with him, and he said:
> "I really hate these."
> I said, "The lunch?"
> "No," he said, "Going to college campuses."
> "Why do you do it?"
> "Well, I make a thousand bucks." He gets a certain commission.
> "No, why do you do it?"
> " 'Cause it's important," he said, "but I hate it . . . I hate being away . . . What it is is that I'll come in and do my little evangelical dance and it's like Richard Pryor coming to campus."
> ["He said that?"]
> Yeah . . . there are some people who are just open and honest.
> ["Really."]
> Well, "it's just like Richard Pryor coming to campus and everybody says, 'Hey, he was great,' and nothing will change."
> It was like Campolo [who had just completed a week-long visit that spring] . . . lot of people enjoyed him . . . he was great, but . . .
> ["What about White raising the imaginary glass of milk at the end of chapel to toast friendship? Was he putting you all on?"]
> That's what I thought too . . . only I expected him to say, "Hey! You're all dead! You just drank cyanide!". . . Jim Jones and the cults . . . I thought he was building up to that . . . some of us were talking like that, in our house, we were all wondering.
> Campolo: I understood why everyone stood up [to pledge third-world service to Christ] . . . didn't want to be the only one sitting down.
> ["Mel White?"]
> He told us he was going through mid-life crisis . . . it's real difficult, a "depressed point in my life; that's the way I am." What do you say to that? He revealed some things, like "I take valium when I go from here to Tahiti."[624]
> I said, "That's not very good for you."
> And he said, "I know, I know, it's addicting, but that's where I am."

---

[624] The reader may recall that White concealed this little detail from the earlier talkback audience, then saying only that he drank a glass of wine (or a beer) on flights to Tahiti. Indeed, what would have been the response had he confessed to taking valium? Was he lying? Or just selectively unforthcoming?

> The more he talked the more I wondered why he's doing all this stuff, and yet I appreciated it.
>
> ["Senate devotions?"]
>
> I was more thinking he's right: we don't spill our guts enough ... but then there's the other extreme: how much do you spill?

Perhaps what ultimately irked or even tormented White was that after all is said and done, after all the exhortations to lower the masks of social fabrication, for closing the distance between unrealistic perfectionist expectations for Christian leaders and the realities of flawed human spirits, for exposing anxieties, inadequacies, and becoming transparently real, for breaking through the artificial forms of relationships and creating genuine love—after all these displays of the brooding, petulant, tortured, authentic man of Christ, the demonstrations of spiritual bloodletting and soul baring—after all of this, his visit could be reduced to just one more evangelical "dance," he just one more in a long line of itinerant evangelical performers who traipse from gig to gig, peddling their vaudevillian evangelical wares. The Mel White Revue comes and goes and "nothing will change."

But then again, all things considered, perhaps this is not such a surprising, unwarranted, or un-welcomed outcome.

Later, we discover the real man hiding behind the mask of Mel White. Mid-life crisis? An unusually depressed period in his life? Just another Christian struggling with the demands of his faith in a heartless secular world, he searching for the appropriate private/public *balance* in his own evangelical celebrity life?

Before a national television audience on *Sixty Minutes*, Mel White confessed to Morley Safer that he had been living an intolerable lie for years: he was gay, and that he had ghostwritten books for Jerry Falwell and other gay-bashing evangelicals: *mea culpa, mea culpa, mea culpa.* Years later he competed on the CBS reality television program, *The Amazing Race,* with his avowed homosexual son. It is now public record that he struggled with homosexuality throughout his career, seeking out Christian therapists and other treatments, electro-shock among them, that proved unable to extinguish his sinful lusts, leading to two attempted suicides.[625] Unable to live with the internal contradictions, he finally came out of the closet, amicably divorced his wife and went on to live a genuinely fulfilling life with a gay lover.[626]

---

[625] One eerily reminiscent of guardian angel Clarence and George Bailey's first encounter in *It's a Wonderful Life.* Aside from that week together on the SPU campus and a few other things that evangelical religion has done to us, what Mr. White and the author have in common is the serious thought and planning devoted to ending our own lives.

[626] David Colker, "In a State of Grace ... ," *The Los Angeles Times.*

Here is White's own account of his appearance on the SPU campus from his autobiography, *Stranger at the Gate: To be Gay and Christian in America*. He writes of only one such visit in the entire book. It was sandwiched between whirlwind layers of activity: an ocean liner cruise to England with the *Mike Douglas Show*, film projects abroad, teaching at Fullerton, and agonizing episodic conflict with his wife over his rushing back and forth to be with Thomas, his Chicago lover, the then current object of a "crazy" infatuation.

> Finally, after a year of endless painful struggle, I decided to move to Chicago to be with Thomas permanently. I sent books and clothing on ahead and flew to Seattle where I was scheduled to lead the faculty and student body of Seattle Pacific University in a week of spiritual emphasis and renewal. By then I was an emotional basket case, but somehow, I was still producing films, writing books, and traveling across the country lecturing at Christian colleges and seminaries.
>
> I prayed every day and every night that in spite of everything, my loving Creator would be present in my life and honored through it. And God answered those prayers. In the darkest night of my soul, God never failed me. When I was consumed by guilt and driven by infatuation, God was there, understanding me, loving me, forgiving me.
>
> After five standing-room only lectures to the student body of Seattle Pacific University, the teaching staff asked me to spend an hour that last afternoon talking to them about the art of communicating with young students. They didn't know that in just a few hours I would be leaving my wife and family and flying to Chicago to begin a new life as a gay man. Suddenly, the university president's secretary interrupted my lecture to announce that Dr. Billy Graham wanted to speak to me on the telephone. "It is urgent," she said, and the whole faculty looked surprised and impressed.

After determining that the call was no prank on the part of any of his friends who knew that Graham was his childhood hero and because he had met the televangelist once at Fuller Seminary, where Graham had dropped by his office to solicit criticism about his preaching, White continued the conversation.

> "My publisher says you can help me, Mel," Dr. Graham began. "Can you join me in Acapulco, Mexico tonight and work with me on completing an important book?"
>
> The serendipity of that call took my breath away. I was certain that God was using Dr. Graham to change my plans about flying to Chicago, moving in with Thomas, and leaving my family. I staggered from the telephone, finished the lecture, left a long, sad message on Tom's answering service, called Lyla, told her that after a time in Mexico I would be coming home, and got on a plane for Mexico.[627]

---

[627] Mel White, *Stranger at The Gate. . .* , 171-72. See also Chris Hedges's mention of White in *American Fascists. . .* , op. cit., 107.

Following a long flight during which he found himself "popping valium pills like candy and sobbing bitterly," Billy Graham met him in a little jeep, dropping him off at a Holiday Inn in Acapulco where a pile of unfinished manuscripts awaited and then sped off to an emergency meeting of his "executive committee." White called the airlines and discovered that he could fly to Chicago and back "before Billy knew that I was gone." The planned windy-city celebration was over by the time he reached the Lakeview Drive condo. Tom wouldn't let him in, the two of them reduced to "weeping and shouting through the locked door." He arrived back in Acapulco in the middle of the night and met Graham for breakfast the next morning. The job completed, he returned to Pasadena and over the next few weeks descended into a depression, thinking constantly of death as the only alternative. Fuller faculty friends and Lyla, his wife, sent him back north to a Christian psychologist practicing near Tacoma, Washington, where he spent nearly three weeks in isolation, the experience driving him to the brink of madness and suicide, notes to his family composed and enveloped as he went out in the evening to end it all. As Mel White climbed the Fox Island bridge for a final swan dive, he heard a voice: "It's a mean night for fishing, but come on down and we'll talk." Just below him sat an old fisherman on a boulder, tending his line, all this scarcely a dime's worth of coincidental dramatic difference from Clarence waiting on George Bailey in *It's A Wonderful Life*. The old man shook his head and fiddled to light his pipe. "Don't know why I chose to fish tonight."

But Mel White knew why. God was keeping him alive for some purpose known only to Him. He dismounted the bridge, helped light the old man's pipe, and then returned again to Pasadena intent upon slaying his homosexual demons, determined to effect an Augustinian-like taming and reversal of his biological drives. And so, continuing to ghostwrite books for televangelists and produce speeches for Ollie North, he allowed Jerry Falwell and Pat Robertson to fly him around the country in their private jets; the ultimate personal reckoning postponed yet again, the can of an evangelical reckoning getting kicked a few more yards down a dusty unforgiving road. Indeed when Mel White concluded the final chapel hour at Seattle Pacific University, many students were reduced to tears at the thought of his impending departure. He consoled them, saying "I am going back to a world I hate and fear." We are left to wonder, *which world* exactly, Mel White, did you have in mind?

The Lonely Mask

Oddly enough, I gathered these observations and reached the above conclusions regarding wholeness, transparency, and masks in the reverse order from that which I now report them; for what caught my attention initially (and most surprised me) were the seemingly inexplicable reports of loneliness and isolation among a sizeable portion of the student body. Perhaps these findings loom larger or cast a greater shadow than they might otherwise because prior to my experiences on campus, I (like many other outside observers of evangelicalism), tacitly accepted this claim (although in a much more general form) of a kind of personal and social superiority over the rest of secular American society. I must confess that although I anticipated encountering a student body sheltered from the rigors and realties of the outside world, I had already almost routinely conceded the value of such an insularity, expecting to find what is popularly thought of as a "Christian" atmosphere—a place teeming with students and faculty who were genuinely caring, gentle, virtuous, honest, and emotionally content (although somewhat cranky and naive), and certainly much more so than their counterparts in large public universities. All the more my surprise to come across repeated references to student loneliness on campus. (And as I have indicated elsewhere and wish to re-emphasize now, *virtually everything* I observed or experienced upon this campus surprised me in some manner or other.)[628]

The first hint of problems arose from a review of old student newspapers. An article in the March, 1972 *Falcon*, "Loneliness: We Live With It Yet Deny It," cited a report from the Keaton Research Group of Antioch College, an outside team commissioned by first-year President, David McKenna, in 1969 to critically examine the condition of Seattle Pacific College, the reporter selecting from it one observation that emerged following but a single week of study:

> You advertise yourself as a small college, but in fact, although you have an unusual sense of community, which we think derives probably from the religious and family backgrounds and style of life, *there is a singular loneliness among many students.*[629] {emphasis added}

The student author comments: "Loneliness? At S. P. C.? . . . ironical that what many see as the hallmark of Seattle Pacific—love and fellowship—has

---

[628] Perhaps we should have anticipated that loneliness, like sin, would also prove much more than some randomly distributed feature of individuals, that it had taken root here—flourished even—because of a broader cultural agenda and scheme of things. It would seem then a particular idiomatic expression of what John Cacioppo found more generally in one of his small study samples of Americans: "The present research shows that what might appear to be a quintessential individualistic experience—loneliness—is not only a function of the individual but is also a property of groups of people. People who are lonely tend to be linked to others who are lonely, an effect that is stronger for geographically proximal than distant friends . . . ." (w/James H. Fowler, Nicholas A. Christakis, "Alone in the Crowd: The Structure and Spread of Loneliness in a Large Social Network," *Journal of Personality and Social Psychology*, 2009, vol.97, no. 6, 985.)

[629] 30 March 1972.

been seen as the very area of shortcoming." Those who have done routine psychological testing on campus, such as Dr. David Terrell, Director of Counseling, whom we've met, later confirmed the accuracy of that diagnosis:

> I am personally amazed with the number of kids here feeling personal loneliness and alienation. In my 4 1/2 years here, of the personality tests we have run, roughly one-fourth of the students tested seem to have a real problem giving and receiving love. In this time there have been no suicides, but there have been several attempts. [630]

The *Falcon* author concluded:

> A quiet, reserved loner may feel alienated, but so can the society pacesetter, as evidenced by thoughts of suicide on the part of some of the most popular and spotlighted students. . . . "The 'whole person' can be just talk," observes Dr. Stevens, in a moment of clinical candor, " . . . a lot of so-called Christianity appears to prepare us for recluse."

A year later an article on student emotional problems began with the questions, "Depression at S.P.C.? Can it be true that Christians actually get depressed?"[631]

Loneliness Chapels

Indeed sometimes it would seem that is easier for students to come before fellow students in the performance atmosphere of chapel and wallow in their apparent isolation and loneliness than to directly break through to others in personal relationships.

---

[630] Unfortunately, earlier in 1979 one such attempt had in fact succeeded, the school losing a sophomore girl from California. (*Falcon*, 16 February 1979)

[631] Martin Bush, "Depression at SPC Caused By Frustration, Failure To Reach Goals," *Falcon*, 30 November 1973.

Examples from the *Falcon:*

—Dennis Krantz, "Psychological Problems Are Increasing at S. P. C.," *Falcon*, 8 February 1974.

—Dr. Dan Motet (SPC Psychology Professor and Counselor): "A dangerous misconception in some Christian circles says that somehow the Christian should be completely immune to depression. . . .

I recall one student who felt that as a Christian he should not be depressed, but permanently filled with joy. His depression was interpreted by him as a sign of not being a true Christian and this thought was pushing him towards an even deeper depression. . . .

I am concerned that there may be some student who, although deeply distressed, rejects the idea of seeking professional help, thinking that prayer alone should solve all of his problems. I would be the last to deny the power of prayer and the need for it. . . ." ("Others-orientation Can Help Combat Common Depression," *Falcon*, 28 February 1975.) {emphasis added}

One girl confessed to fellow students that her life at Seattle Pacific had been filled with "more downs than ups" and that occasionally the whole thing became so oppressive that she had to rely upon "small miracles . . . [just to] get through some classes." Apparently the message was that if the chapel listener wanted to avoid the kind of emotional pit she once occupied, deepen your faith in Christ. She strums her guitar and sings, "I'm having a pity party . . . all we do is pity me and cry." Throughout her testimony one hears ripples of recognition and laughter passing through the audience, and upon its conclusion she receives the loudest, most sustained applause I had ever heard in any chapel.[632]

In another chapel devoted to reports on a week-long Illinois conference of Christian college student government leaders, Elizabeth reveals some rather unanticipated findings, prefaced by a reference to her own inclination of always waiting for life-directing signs from God before proceeding with anything:

> . . . . Maybe God could give me a clear sign . . . maybe a large deposit in a Swiss bank. [laughter]
>
> You know I thought that [to] live the victorious Christian life among 500 people in a Christian community you were happy . . . yet I was terribly lonely [at the conference] . . . I'd been programmed to think that if you lived in a Christian community of 500 people that you were joyous and everything was wonderful . . . left no room for tears, loneliness . . . or being misunderstood.
>
> Christian community is not necessarily a remedy to loneliness. Jesus was lonely too, even when surrounded by a crowd . . . Don't be afraid of your loneliness or think that something is wrong with your walk with God . . . I sense a lot of loneliness and hurt in this community.[633]

A Student View

More recently, I spoke with student senators about their own experiences with establishing relationships and friendships and this phenomenon of loneliness. For some, the forming of deep and lasting friendships comes easily; the ideological imperatives prove either helpful (there is, after all, a mandate to love one another) or no obstacle to a healthy, vigorous social life. For others, the emotional links to fellow students are difficult to establish and

---

[632] "In All Your Ways," Student Chapel, 11/13/78.

[633] "Urbana Conference," Student Chapel, 1/40/80.

— "I look around SPU and see a lot of people who are hurting and lonely and dying for some kind of contact . . . [Prays:] Let's meet the needs of people on this campus . . . people are hurting and it ought not to be." ("Spring Breakaway Teams: 20/20," Chapel, 4/11/83.)

become tenuous or brittle at best.[634] The proverbial mask conceals inner confusions and doubts and, in some instances, a genuine fear of other students.

Daniel, campus "Holy Man," perhaps alone among all the students I encountered had achieved an elementary understanding of this connection between ideological expectations, social scrutiny and censure, and the incidence of student emotional problems and depression. Asked about a Billy Graham ad's assumption of a Christian superiority in matters of personal and family emotional health, he responded, drawing upon his considerable experience with male students in the dormitories:

> I disagree with that and maybe go the other way . . . that there are more problems . . . because we put each other under a microscope and we put a lot of pressure on each other and its darn hard to be there . . . a lot of pressure . . . and that leads to loneliness.
> ["How manifest?"]
> I see friends who are very lonely and I think they need psychological help—counseling help . . . They're quiet . . . they don't visit others . . . no one visits them . . . keep to themselves.
> ["Difficult to talk to?"]
> Well, not really . . . well, so so . . . but it's kind of awkward, especially when you hit a quiet spot . . . real awkward.[635]

The Rationalizations

Perhaps the most prevalent interpretation of problems of loneliness and depression on campus is the monopolistic one, wherein loneliness represents just one more of God's tools (i.e., betraying no social origin or context or disproportional representation among certain kinds of temperaments) for ensuring that individuals seek one another's company and solace, ensuring community (and performing a role similar then, as we saw earlier, to a de-

---

[634] And not always for lack of personal attributes, introspection, and effort. Consider the gifted, attractive, popular Wanda: "That's something I've had a lot of disappointment about since I've come here: I've never had an easy time making close friends . . . I've always had a million acquaintances . . . and I don't know if it's because of SPU or what. I think I've had a harder time making friends here than in high school. My best friends are still pretty much the people I was closest to in high school. Here, I would say I've probably made—it's so hard to say because my definition of a close friend is someone to whom you bare your soul—people like that I've met here, maybe one or two . . . A lot of people that I feel comfortable with that are good friends but not very intimate . . . ["Boyfriend?"] Didn't meet him here . . . I've struggled a lot with that. I've asked, why is that? I see a lot of people around me who I think—or at least it's my impression—have a lot more close friendships than I do. I don't know if it's me or the environment or what . . . it's a question I haven't answered." (*SSI*, May 2003)
[635] (*SSI*, May 2003)

natured, ascetic sexuality).[636] Indeed, over the course of twenty or more years, the community understanding of this phenomenon has reiterated some by now familiar themes.

Linda suggests that the Christian ought to

> . . . . thank God for your temporary loneliness. This is one of the hardest things I've been learning the last couple years! We as Christians have this unique attitude . . . [It] brings us into a closer, more intimate relationship with Him and this reality provides joy, not happiness, but joy and comfort . . . [And with regard to one's fellow students] It also gives one the ability to look beyond himself and his need to see others and to be able to reach out to them without even striving for something in return.

Kathi regards loneliness as a positive time of spiritual introspection:

> Think of your feeling in terms of "alone-ness" rather than a "lonesome-ness." And in that frame of reference, consider then a possibility: this "alone-ness" was prearranged for you—a divine gift of divine timing—an interim all your own.

Joan recalls that when she first came to SPC

> The loneliness was almost unbearable, but I knew God wouldn't put me through something unless I was able to handle it. I was able to rid myself of the homesickness and loneliness by turning to my Lord. Even now I get lonely at times and I go seek out a friend and talk about what's on my mind. It's good to open up to people.

And finally, Dean associates loneliness with a secular-tinged self-absorption:

> I become lonely when I start to look inside myself, and be more concerned with myself, rather than centering my concern to others.[637]

By and large we find then that behind every apparently disconcerting human experience—in this instance, loneliness—there lurks a benign divine intention, which when fully understood or framed within its appropriate transcendent, a-social context ultimately ensures a positive outcome. In this manner, cause and consequence of feeling and behavior cast off the fetters of terrestrial personal or social moorings and assume a sacralized position

---

[636] How both ironic and instructive that the experimental psychologist John T. Cacioppo singles out this very same emotion as one of nature's evolutionary tools selected to enhance the survival prospects of early human communities. (with William Patrick, *Loneliness: Human Nature and the Need for Social Connection*, Norton 2008, 7.)

[637] All from the *Falcon*, 22 October 1972.

among the other monopolized elements of evangelical Christian distinction.[638]

A Clinical Perspective

Along with other Seattle Pacific clinicians who preceded him, Dr. David Terrell found the incidence of loneliness on campus surprising and perplexing. His many years of counseling some of the loneliest of these students allowed him to offer some generalizations. The first concerns the presence of "socio-pathetic personalities" among the student body. These are young people, he explains, whose

> . . . . value system is really pretty flimsy. They may have a quote, "conscience," un-quote, that appears to be very strong in guiding their life, but it's based more on external kinds of things, like if drinking is wrong because mother says it's wrong then that's all there is to it. They might have some qualms if they do that [drink], but if they do other things that are much more significant in terms of morality . . . doesn't phase them. . . .
>
> [The more important characteristic, though, with respect to loneliness is that] it is very difficult for them to form meaningful relationships with other human beings. They are really incapable of loving, giving, or receiving . . . they're incapable of healthy, intimate relationships. They're very capable of promiscuity. They're very capable of physical relationships, often using those to keep people at a distance emotionally. So you see that type of loneliness. I have seen many of them there who, some of them, have been married two or three times since they've graduated.

He locates a second potential source in the authoritarian atmosphere of many evangelical families and churches.

> I think you find—and this is a really strong statement and I hope I'm not generalizing unfairly—sometimes that people who tend to be real unstable find the fundamental tradition very meaningful because it does take over, it does provide a sense of direction, it does tell you what's right and what's wrong, and so people who are unstable maybe migrate towards that. And people who are unstable many times have difficulty maintaining meaningful relationships.

Finally, he links loneliness with the seemingly proverbial evangelical problem of self-loathing, arguing that

---

[638] To its credit, the Office of Student Affairs once devoted a three-page section of its "Profile of Students at Seattle Pacific University 1980-81" to a discussion of "Psychosocial development," therein demonstrating an appreciation of the emotional adjustment problems created by some of the students more conservative sectarian backgrounds.

.... people who feel that God doesn't love them probably aren't going to love themselves. And in order to love other people you must first love yourself, and that is very Biblical . . . I find in my experience that a number of the people I worked with, that was a problem for them: their self-esteem was almost zilch. They hated themselves, and they were trying to be good, trying to do what God wanted them to do, and because they were such creeps they had nothing to offer other people, so they'd withdraw . . . literally. They don't want people to get to know them because they're imperfect and wicked, and they're extremely lonely. I used to sometimes tell my classes in counseling that I perceived loneliness as a very big problem and it was always kind of interesting that you could be surrounded by human beings and die of loneliness.

Although the above are plausible enough explanations, the first two in particular strike me as perhaps overly clinical in tone and substance, representing too great a departure from the kinds of perfectly normal students I observed, invoking pathologies that afflict perhaps only a very small minority. The second notion, for example, of evangelical communities emitting a kind of authoritarian scent that naturally attracts unstable personality types may explain converts from the general population who are drawn to charismatic cults and churches but fails to take into account the great majority of students who involuntarily grew up in evangelical families and churches; there was certainly little initial choice involved.[639] The third is a bit more helpful and general, and I did encounter some evidence of it throughout my fieldwork. But again, it is perhaps inevitable that a clinical perspective yields a view skewed in the direction of the darker regions of personality, an understandable slant on things that can benefit from a rather more rounded view, one which, as the reader may have anticipated, emphasizes the larger *cultural* context of these struggles with wholeness, transparency, and masks.

The Ambiguity and Angst of Unity

One rare chapel session proved instructive in this regard: a freshman-only gathering addressed by Professor Daniel Berg of the School of Religion, a faculty member often criticized by campus fundamentalists for theological liberalism, who on this occasion sought to navigate a flotilla of callow matriculating students through the Scylla and Charybdis of their transition from evangelical home life to evangelical college life.

---

[639] It remains unclear to what extent "unstable" students might choose a more authoritarian college like Seattle Pacific over other alternatives. There seem too many other variables and considerations involved to be able to reduce the selection decision to just this motivation. I suspect, for example, that unstable personalities could just as well be drawn to large public universities to get away from the family-like scrutiny of a tight-knit academic community like Seattle Pacific.

I want to discuss problems some of you freshmen might be having here in your first year on campus. Let's look at some areas where we might become sensitive to our own selves. . . . Can you find someone with whom you can really be open, can trust? Who am I? What ought I to become? These are difficult identity problems on a Christian campus. In high school, you were different from other students and could more easily tell you were a Christian. Now, where nearly everyone is a Christian, it becomes a great problem. You say to yourself, "I wonder if I'm a Christian at all."[640]

Professor Berg is on to something here. In this uniformly Christian atmosphere, formerly obvious signals of difference distinguishing the Christian from the non-believer often dissolve into a confusing congeries of competing conceptions of and variations upon a "true" Christianity.[641] Indeed for evangelicals so heavily dependent upon clear signs of demarcation for both self- and community identity, any prolonged suspension of the codes of Christian and secular difference may prove a disorienting experience, at least until the more academic, abstract, internal versions begin to take hold of the student's imagination, stabilizing and re-calibrating the logics and signals of difference. Among some of the more conservative students, for whom the academic formulation of logical differences can never recreate the more stable authoritarian structures of their families and churches, ambiguity breeds a certain anxiety and confusion, and is perhaps responsible not only for weak and volatile self-identities[642] but also for some of the more "judgmental"

---

[640] "The Idea of a Christian College," Freshman Class Chapel, 11/19/2003.

[641] From the student questionnaire:
"We all have moments of self-doubt and anxiety about what we believe and our own behavior. It is difficult sometimes to know just exactly what is a true or good Christian. With this in mind, are there moments in your life when you feel uneasy about whether or not you are in fact a true Christian really fulfilling your potential? Wonder if you really are?"

Often	[5]	(15)	7%
	[4]	(49)	23
	[3]	(65)	30
	[2]	(53)	24
Never	[1]	(26)	12
	[NR]	(9)	4
			100%

[642] These observations parallel in many respects a vaguely similar sort of interpretation advanced by Philip Greven of colonial evangelical Puritans:

> For people whose wills had been broken early in childhood, and whose sense of self had been suppressed and denied by the powerful controls and governance of parents, the emergence of a sense of self and self-will in youth, which could stretch from the early teens to the mid- to late twenties, proved impossible to accept. Their temperaments had been shaped in ways which made selfhood too dangerous, too frightening, too difficult to be sought and

personal attacks one occasionally observes on campus. This sort of angst lies at the heart of aggressive *projections* of the student's own insecurities and doubts (as to whether or not she is in fact a good, genuine Christian) onto other spiritual suspects. Taking into consideration the normal variations in temperament and background, we may find that anxiety/withdrawal (loneliness) <———> anxiety/projection (censoriousness) represent two *extreme* personal and social responses to this new environment of independence, ambiguity, and the growing (often spurned) rationalization of formerly concrete signals of Christian and secular difference (although the two reactions can be mutually reinforcing as well).

The newly matriculating student enters a spiritual arena in which her identity as a Christian will undergo thorough examination by herself and nearly everyone else. Those few who find the terms and goals of the cultural logic unachievable and the resulting scrutiny unbearable withdraw into more private worlds defended by a panoply of masks and other interpersonal screens and insulation. Wary of revealing an uncertain heart beating lukewarm in the breast of a tepid Christian, they keep to themselves, reluctant to share anxiety and pain with potentially critical peers or elders; they sink into isolation and loneliness, and some even further into despondency and despair.

As Daniel, one of the most highly regarded students on campus, confessed in a moment of exasperation:

> I'm getting to the point where some of the people I hate the most are Christians.
> ["Is that an adequate term, hate?"]
> No . . . dislike . . . it really bothers me because of that judgmental attitude.
> What makes it so hard is that it's done just with no feeling.
> ["Personal attacks?"]
> Yeah . . . you admit that you're struggling with something and immediately it's "Sinner!". . .
> Get the cross out! . . . That's what hurts.[643]

I raised the possibility of a more general, less pathological link between the ideological pressure to don masks and radiate an ideal Christian personality and the incidence of loneliness with Dr. Terrell, who responded:

---

attained. Their consciences left little room for the freedom of experience and uncertainty. And when they felt, as most did, that they were beginning to become separate, independent, and self-governing individuals, *they also began to feel intensely unhappy and anxious*. (*The Protestant Temperament* . . . , 60-61.) {emphasis added}

[643] (*SSI*, May 2003)

That used to really frustrate me because it would seem to me . . . well, it's a fact that the whole basis of Christianity is love . . . love of self . . . love of others . . . love of God certainly.

But people that I worked with, that's precisely what happened to them! I don't know how many times I was told, "Well, I couldn't share this with people in the church."

[Recounts several incidents, after which clients would say] "Here I thought of all the people in the world that I could share myself with would be my pastor and the people that I worship with that are Christians, fellow Christians . . . I've learned very painfully that . . . never again."

I've had couples tell me, who are having marital problems, you know, "No way could we share these problems with people in the church. What would they think of us?" There's that question, again and again: "What would they think of us?" I think that's precisely why a lot of people are lonely. They are scared to death to be themselves, to be genuine around other Christians, because others might think that they don't love the Lord.

Perhaps then smoldering in the heart of the loneliness and isolation of a good many perfectly normal students is a simple fear of exposure. The angst-ridden student employs an elaborate series of cloaking devices to shield the delinquent self from the often critical examination of others. No wonder we encounter students who due to temperament and/or background skirt the periphery of the ideal forms of personality and conduct, at times seeking to deflect potential condemnation or social repercussions either through the fabrication and presentation of a model Christian self, donning the mask of the joyous evangelical scholar-servant, or by fading away into the spiritual woodwork, into the painful, self-preserving security of isolation and loneliness.

But are these kids really any more lonely or depressed than the average American college student? Are they any more emotionally disturbed or even pathological? Again I think the difference here is rather more one of quality than quantity. To frame the difference in more comparable general terms, I suspect that loneliness arises in the evangelical college situation, as has been demonstrated, from *too much* rather than *too little* community; that in the evangelical college setting we observe a loneliness that is largely the ironic, unintended consequence of too great a pressure upon students to generate rarified, distinctly *Christian* kinds of personality, behavior, and camaraderie, whereas in the public university we encounter a student loneliness that derives from too much independence and anonymity, too little institutional emphasis upon the formation and maintenance of personal relationships, too few institutional social supports. In other words, we find in the public university an academic ambience that is certainly too much like the condition of the *secular* society at large for the taste or comfort of most evangelical academicians and their eventual graduates.

A Final Word

One genuinely feels for the individuals of a community who so desperately yearn to make sense of themselves and their religion, who strive to fashion unimpeachable identities and outlooks, who continually struggle to bend the tangible, problematical world of social relationships into the impeccable shape of an ideological cultural idiom and ethos. Aspirations for both an invidiously distinguished personal joy, peace, and Christ-like perfection *and* the a-social union of personality and behavior—the creation of *wholeness and transparency*—perhaps flounder in a sea of social and cultural turbulence, the two tossed and torn from one another by the irrepressible swells of human social dynamics. All told, the spectacle of young people engaged in these so apparently tragic (and ultimately futile?) emotional trials and tribulations was at various stages in the unfolding drama painful, amusing, bewildering, and yet almost enthralling also to watch. *For it would seem that one can employ all manner of measures to remove, isolate, and distinguish the human creature from secular society, but one can scarcely remove the ineluctable dynamics of society from the creature and his creations.*

Observe here a larger theoretical point: the interaction and convergence of social and cultural dynamics. We followed along as Wanda struggled to overcome the *discrepancy* between cultural expectation and social reality, attempting to transcend the interpersonal dynamics governing most relationships. Mel White, by contrast, older, seasoned, and glib, yet disgruntled and sour, has learned to live with the ever-present compromise of internal contradiction. He is not—*we are not*—what we seem . . . but so be it. Wanda takes the formal presentation—him, the logic—at face value and strives to realize and embody it: the complete evisceration of the social façade, the total union of the personal and the social. It proves a futile quest. What is false? What is real? The ironies of transparency and masquerade can swell to a critical mass and overwhelm our conventional modes of understanding. For our purposes as observers and interpreters, any complete representation of these events—indeed of the larger national evangelical community[644]—turns upon an

---

[644] As writes Paula White, Donald Trump's favorite televangelist, said to have presided over his conversion: ". . . . 'As long as I wear a mask, then I am playing the role of a character. And God is not interested in my [secular] role-playing or in yours. He wants to deal with you, the real you! He wants to know the you that struggles with secret issues of the heart. The you behind the fake smile and pretty clothes.' " (quoted in Shane Lee & Phillip Sinitiere, *Holy*

appreciation of this interaction between the social and the cultural: how they ebb and flow, the one continually and alternately folding into, reinforcing, conspiring with, confounding, and/or contradicting the other. The convergence (and the antagonism) of the *social* and *cultural*, in bold, naked relief.

What might be the larger, macro-level, cultural ramifications of some of these micro-level dynamics? Much earlier I suggested that Johann Hari's account of the relationship between tenuous, weak, or non-existent social connections and the incidence of depression might prove more applicable to a particular American context than to "our [Western] culture" more generally. Similarly the international survey data points to a profoundly unhappy and lonely American populace even in comparison with other modern Western societies, let alone the natives of French Tahiti. Given these few micro-level glimpses of the student population and their seemingly ambivalent, if not tortured, relationships with other students, interactions that suggest some sort of connection between religious ideology and personal loneliness, perhaps there is something here of significance for our interpretation of American evangelicalism in general. So that if indeed, as I claimed in the introduction, this pool of students represents a representative sample of American evangelicals, and I believe it does, what might these micro-level dynamics have to tell us about evangelicalism in general?

John Cacioppo, the experimental psychologist upon whose work Johann Hari drew heavily, traces a good many seemingly modern emotional qualities and complexes back to their early evolutionary roots, as mentioned earlier, where the individual need for connection made a good deal of sense in terms of group survival. But there are problematical as well as beneficial dimensions to such an evolved personality scheme; a host of complicating factors and contexts can intervene, as Cacioppo cautions us:

> The person who starts out with a painful, even frightening sensation of being alone may begin to see dangers everywhere in the social landscape. . . . The fear that can force us into a defensive crouch can also cost us some of our ability to self-regulate. When loneliness is protracted, impaired regulation, combined with distorted social cognition, makes us less likely to acknowledge someone else's perspective. We become less able to evaluate other people's intentions, which can make us socially awkward, but can also make us vulnerable to manipulation by anyone trying to conceal ulterior motives. At the same time, fear of attack fosters a greater tendency to preemptively blame others. Sometimes this fear makes us lash out. Sometimes it makes us desperate to please, and sometimes it causes us to play the victim. . . .

Mavericks: Evangelical Innovators and the Spiritual Marketplace, New York University Press 2009, 110.)

Again, forming connections with pets or online friends or even God is a noble attempt by an obligatorily gregarious creature to satisfy a compelling need. But surrogates can never make up completely for the absence of the real thing. In a culture built around disconnection, the better move is to work that much harder to reach out to those with whom we share even the most superficial contact in the everyday world.[645]

---

[645] Cacioppo (2008), 15-16.

PART FIVE

CONCLUSION

CHAPTER 12

THE DISENCHANTMENT OF AMERICAN EVANGELICALISM

The Outlines of an American Culture

I conclude with a reaffirmation of the claim which began this study: evangelical religion occupies the ideological heart of American society in that the inherent logic of its cultural ideas underlies nearly all aggressive promotions and defenses of American society, domestic and international.[646] As we have seen, evangelical meanings and values are largely grounded in two cardinal idioms: a dualistic vision cleaving the elements of society into neat, exclusive Christian and secular categories, and the "moral market" imperatives of an individualistic ethical calculus, the two merging to form a matrix of symbols and expectations—a cultural logic, if you will—which is then employed in the creation, identification, and evaluation of persons, objects,

---

[646] We observe just one foreign policy dimension in the controversy over "Christian rights" in China. As writes Jacob Heilbruun: "The shifting alliances of China policy have been commented on in the press as if they represent a new and strange post-cold war phenomenon. In fact, there is nothing particularly strange or new going on here. The new anti-China lobby is consciously modeled on the old anti-Soviet one that brought together hawkish Scoop Jackson democrats with trade unionists and traditional Christian conservatives. Just as the AFL-CIO, evangelicals and Jewish neo-conservatives joined forces against the Soviet Union, so the same groupings are teaming up against China." What is more, the China initiative accompanies wrangling over the legacy of Reaganism: "The Christian right and Jewish neoconservatives retort that Reaganism wasn't just about opening up foreign markets. It was primarily about morality: the defeat of communism was a sacred mission, not just an imperial one. . . . [the conservatives have] started to openly challenge the domination of American foreign policy by corporations—the same corporations that fund and dominate the Republican establishment." ("Christian Rights: The Next Big Conservative Issue," *The New Republic*, July 7, 1997, 20.)

A bit later, the U.S. State Department released a report on the persecution of Christians worldwide, responding to a demand of Congress. (Norman Kempster {Los Angeles Times}, "Christians Persecuted, U.S. Says: Agency to Clarify Immigration Policy," *The Honolulu Advertiser*, 23 July 1997.)

—Sara Diamond explores the connections between Pentacostal "Gospel Outreach" organizations and right-wing insurgents and military dictatorships throughout the Third World in her *Spiritual Warfare* (South End Press, 1989).

—Reagan's National Security Council operative, Oliver North, was driven to and then justified his illegal activities in support of the Nicaraguan Contras in largely Biblical terms, consistent with his rabid Pentacostal background. See Norman Atkins, "Oliver's Twists," *Rolling Stone*, 16-30 July 1987.

relationships, and even societies. The first of these idioms—the logic of invidious Christian and secular distinction—has been the primary focus of the present study;[647] the second was discussed at some length in an earlier chapter and will comprise the central topic (along with an analysis of moral market dynamics in American society in general) of a subsequent volume.

Now although it seems to me that these two idioms occupy the centerpiece of a peculiarly American personality and history—representing that which most clearly distinguishes the American experience from assorted European cultural antecedents—by no means do they alone exhaust the wellsprings of American distinction. Indeed there are several other social, cultural, and historical properties which set the American experience apart from that of even our closest European ancestors.

At present, I discern five additional sources, conditions, or features of an uniquely American identity.

1) The covenant theology and community of Puritan New England. I have in mind here both the relative (but by no means total) union of church and state in the early colony, with an attending pragmatic Arminianism of good works as central to the divine dispensations of individual salvation and community prosperity, and (perhaps more importantly) the social-psychological tradition of ascetic Puritanism—with particular emphasis upon sexuality and patterns of child-rearing.[648] From this early sense of a historically unique and transcendent apocalyptic mission emerged a continuously reaffirming national teleology or an *exceptionalism* deemed to set the American experiment and experience apart from all previous nations or civilizations, a new Jerusalem towards which all of human history was divinely directed.[649]

---

[647] A critical test of the main proposition follows in Appendix A, Evangelical Apartheid: The Statistical Tests.

[648] The definitive account is Sacvan Bercovitch's *The Puritan Origins of the American Self* (New Haven: Yale University Press, 1975). What is more, it seems to me, for example, that the American reluctance to deal with illicit drug use as a medical-social problem, and explore creative solutions such as legalization, rather than a moral-legal problem stems in part from a malingering observance of traditional notions of Puritan self-denial and their Victorian descendants. As Stanley Meisler, *Los Angeles Times* London correspondent, reports: "The British have trouble understanding why Americans treat addicts as satanic enemies in a war on drugs." ("Returning to Find a Scared America," *The Seattle Times*, 6 August 1989.) The sexual dimension of this was discussed earlier in chapter 10.

[649] For Alexis de Tocqueville the key to "a unique, purposive identity" could be found in the location of its origins, or cultural birthplace: "And where was America born? For Tocqueville the answer was obvious: Puritan New England." (Engen, *City on a Hill . . .* , op. cit., 102-103. —Reaffirmed most conspicuously (and Calvinistically) in Lincoln's second inaugural address. Yet other national enterprises have had their own iterations of *chosenness*. Vladimir Putin has embraced such themes from the Russian philosopher, Ivan Ilyin: "Russian innocence. . . . As

2) The institution and legacy of slavery. This obviously includes the plantation culture of the South, black family slave culture, the Civil War and subsequent malingering regional animosities, and the ongoing consequences of black migration over many decades to the large urban centers of the North.[650] Recent work has demonstrated that discriminatory federal housing policies following the Second World War have largely been responsible for black-white segregation and income inequality that continue to disadvantage and undermine black families and communities.[651]

3) The philosophical and constitutional legacy of the generation of the Founding Fathers. For our purposes the most important element here being the creation of a free market of religion with the "Establishment Clause" of the First Amendment.

> . . . . constitutional separation. . . . That, more than anything else, made the United States a new thing on earth., setting new tasks for religion, offering it new opportunities.. Everything else in our Constitution—separation of powers, balanced government, bicameralism, federalism—had been anticipated both in theory and practice. . . . We combined a number of these features in a way that was suitable to our genius, as the drafters put it—to what Montesquieu called the national *esprit*. But we invented nothing, except disestablishment.[652]

4) The Frontier. The continual movement west created a cultural fermentation and mood of many dimensions: independence and violence,[653] an almost visceral impatience and uprootedness, and social egalitarianism, among many others. Indeed the westward movement fostered the kinds of unstable, migrational populations so amenable to the cultural vacuum-filling entreaties of evangelicalism.

5) Continual immigration and social-cultural pluralism. Perhaps a good deal of the "paranoid style" in American society and politics stems from the

---

a concept, it completed his fascist theory: They had lost its 'divine totality' and 'harmonious unity.' Only Russia had somehow escaped the evil of 'history' or 'the fragmentation of human existence.' Because it 'drew the strength of its soul from God,' it was under perpetual attack from the rest of the malevolent world." (Timothy Snyder, "God Is a Russian," *The New York Review of Books*, 4/5/2018, 51)

[650] In this regard, still unsurpassed is W. J. Cash, *The Mind of the South* (New York: Knopf, 1941).

[651] Richard Rothstein, *The Color of Law: A Forgotten History of How Government Segregated America*, Liveright 2017.

[652] Wills, *Under God. . .* , 383.

—Jose Casanova agrees, calling it the "great American religious invention." ("Rethinking Secularization: A Global Comparative Perspective," *The Hedgehog Review*, Spring & Summer 2006.)

[653] Richard Slotkin, *Regeneration Through Violence: The Mythology of the American Frontier, 1600-1860*, Norman: University of Oklahoma Press, 1973.

seemingly never-ending influx of new ethnic populations, the ongoing struggle to fashion genuine American identities, and the resulting insecurities and resentments which are then often projected back upon even more recent arrivals by second, third, and even earlier generation ethnic natives. Then again, in broader historical terms, it would seem as if the evangelical/fundamentalist/mainline Protestant cultural core has also always braced itself against succeeding waves of ethnic and religious immigration, continually perceiving new threats to an eroding cultural authority.

Now by no means is every one of these features a unique indigenous feature of the American social and political landscape. As David Hackett Fischer demonstrates in excruciatingly fine detail in *Albion's Seed: British Folkways in America*,[654] many of the distinctive cultural regions and groups of America can be traced to British antecedents. The plantation society of the South, Appalachian enthusiastic religion, and, of course, New England Puritanism all have their origins in various regional folk cultures of mother England. The Founding Fathers drew inspiration from the Scottish and French Enlightenments; revolutionaries were emboldened by *Cato's Letters*. Slavery had both old and new world ancestors and contemporaries. These and other continuities are indisputable. Americans have scarcely re-invented the wheel at each stage of their cultural evolution on the new continent. But whereas, for example, English Puritanism reached a cultural boiling point with the beheading of a monarch and the reign of Cromwell only to eventually recede into a vaporous mist following the conclusion of the Civil War and the coming of the Glorious Revolution of 1688, New England Puritanism lumbered on for many decades, depositing an enduring legacy; similarly for the British cultural vapors of evangelicalism and the southern plantation society. Their offspring have prospered in the rich American soil, whereas indigenous English forms either withered and expired in the depleted soil of the mother lode, lapsed into stagnation, or evolved in altogether different directions.[655]

The originality of these idioms derives not only from their continuing vitality in the new world but from their complex interactions with one another as well. All have proven integral to the creation of a peculiarly American cultural condition and personality. But certainly some more than others,

---

[654] New York: Oxford University Press, 1989.

[655] "The segment of British society identified with bourgeois evangelicalism is usually thought the 'most characteristically Victorian,' and to it the origins of British Victorianism have been traced. In England such people lived at the periphery of polite society and political power; in America they dominated economic, social, and political institutions." (Daniel Walker Howe, "Victorian Culture in America," in D. W. Howe ed., *Victorian America*, Philadelphia: University of Pennsylvania Press, 1976, 4.)

for above and beyond their myriad, multi-dimensional contributions it seems to me that the particularly potent idioms of evangelical religion and a moral market ethos occupy special positions at the very beating heart of an almost ironic American cultural exceptionalism.

Causes and Conditions

Reflecting back upon the phenomenon in question, I think it worthwhile now to speculate upon a range of possible factors and conditions responsible for the emergence and resilience of evangelicalism in American life. There are as I see it a number of both personal and social-cultural *causes* and *conditions* of this American affinity for evangelical forms of religion, although surely at times the individual and the cultural might appear indistinguishable from one another.

On an individual level:

1) An exaggerated or obsessive fear of death; or a less histrionic reluctance to accept the finality of death, often coupled with a yearning for some form of personal and communal transcendence. As always, there is a normal distribution of these temperaments, this sort of angst, in any population or culture. Yet what is demonstrably an individual trait, randomly distributed, can receive a disproportionate expression or encouragement in certain kinds of family and cultural climates. In particular, the fear of death is more pronounced in those societies lacking the kinds of cultural forms and traditions—rituals of loss and transition—that can serve in less modern or market-dominated cultures to lessen the pain and disruption of death. Among Protestant societies generally,[656] death becomes all the more unsettling and

---

[656] We might enlarge this to include the entire Western Christian tradition. Caroline Walker Bynum argues that the fear of death lay behind the Western obsession with the conception of the resurrected (material) body, as depicted in fantastic iconography produced throughout four different historical periods. See *The Resurrection of the Body in Western Christianity, 200-1336* (New York: Columbia University Press, 1995).
—Martin Marty records the rare confession of pastor J. H. Brookes, devotee of premillennial dispensationalism and teacher of C. I. Scofield, producer of the *Scofield Reference Bible*: "On a conference verandah in 1895 Brookes revealed an inordinate fear of death and pleaded, 'Can't you leave me the hope, after all these years have passed away, that I may live to see my Lord come, and escape the clutches of that awful enemy, death?' " (*Modern American Religion, Volume 1. . .* , 227.)
—More recently, consider the life and career of a cultural icon, Walt Disney, for whom conservative Christian faith underlay a morbid obsession with death:

> It is often, though not always the case, that in Disney films the threat of death is framed in millennial terms-that is, powerful forces in the cosmos that bring death and destruction are overcome with virtuous heroic action, unyielding optimism in a better world, or miraculous intervention. . . . His films depict a millennial vision of the universe, where absolute good battles with absolute evil, with death usually imagined as the result of evil

traumatic an experience because theology and culture have removed the meaning and significance of death from the more natural cycles and rhythms of living and dying and regeneration that one finds among preliterate and other religious traditions.[657] I think it no idle exaggeration to claim, for example, that some spin-off version of this cultural anxiety or apprehension in part lies behind the unprecedented American push for medical innovations and the enormous technological infrastructure that has emerged as a result. The specter of death seems to haunt the American imagination.[658]

2) A need for certainty, continuity, definition, and concrete external direction arising from personal anxiety and insecurity, from discomfort with ambiguity; an unhappiness with an independent, self-guided existence, a fear of personal autonomy. Again, a range of these traits are distributed among

---

intentions, or as a justified fate for the unredeemable. . . . like many religious expressions, they acquire weight because they are so intimately tied to a desire to triumph over death. . . .

In many ways the Disney way of death is a critical reason the "Disney Doctrine" has so much cultural capital. As modern-day fairy tales, his films both reflect and shape religious sensibilities across the grain of American culture—they are popular meditations that rely on a cultural system of religious meanings to make sense of death. . . . Without this preoccupation with death Disney would not have had the cultural impact he did in twentieth-century America; if Americans in this period did not have similar pre-occupations and similar strategies for imagining meaning in the face of death, his films would have held little public interest. (Gary Laderman, op. cit., 40, 37, 44.)

—Then there's Billy Graham: "Even when I grew older, I used to lie awake at night and wonder what would happen to me if I died. It upset me to pray, 'If I should die before I wake, I pray the Lord my soul to take.' " (Andrew Delbanco, "The Church of Appearances," a review of *Just As I Am: The Autobiography of Billy Graham*, in *The New Republic*, 10/6/97.)

[657] This point is made to great effect in Colin Turnbull's, *The Human Cycle* (New York: Simon & Schuster, 1984).

[658] Indeed even in a more modern, almost thoroughly secularized society like Denmark, Phil Zuckerman discovered that, absent succoring traditional folklore idioms, let alone Christian phobias, fear or anxiety about death proves quite "atypical": "In sum, societies in which most people don't believe in life after death are not characterized by widespread despair, but just the opposite. The typical Scandinavian orientation to death is relatively positive, life-affirming one." He recounts an interview with Anne, a 43-year-old hospice nurse from Aarhus: "I was completely surprised when she told me that in her many years of experience working with the dying, she found it was generally the *atheists* who had an easier time accepting their impending fate, while the Christians often had the hardest time . . . often being wracked with worry and anxiety."

As we will see in Appendix B, a full understanding of this issue suffers from *an inherent disciplinary bias*: "*Thus, when sociologist of religion William Sims Bainbridge asks, 'How can humans deal . . . with the crushing awareness of mortality?' I think he is committing a mistake that many scholars of religion commit: assuming that his own fears and worries about death are universal, when clearly they aren't.*" (*Society Without God. . .*, 66, 4-5, 64.) {emphasis added}

the population at large but they may certainly become heightened within particular kinds of families, communities, and societies.[659]

Now in the above two personality dispositions one locates the source of a good many individual affinities for the evangelical religious experience; they are often characteristic of converts who are drawn to these communities from outside; in extreme cases they can be held responsible for some of the more pathological characters and currents in evangelicalism.

To these may be added conditions rather more social and cultural in nature:

3) The dislocation from the movement of populations through migration or immigration. So-called "settler" colonies or societies may prove particularly amenable to these forms of religion; as we've seen, the frontier populations of early nineteenth-century America.[660] Newly disenfranchised doctrinarian societies, such as the former Soviet Union, and societies in transition, such as China, may offer a similar kind of shifting, uncertain, albeit fertile ground.

4) A perception (and/or the reality) of a clear and present external danger or threat to the integrity, security, longevity, and/or identity of a community or society. One can discern in the level of intensity of these particular perceptions—fears, resentments, feelings of persecution—the particular ideological tone or thrust of a community, the degree of internal mobilization in the defense or promotion of a guiding cultural ethos.[661]

5) The formal, constitutionally-established and -protected free market condition or "disestablishment" of religion, often also characterized as the

---

[659] As with Erik Erikson's point about totalitarianism in chapter eight, what may make certain strains of evangelicalism attractive to emotionally-unstable persons is the simple economy of its demonization processes, successfully collecting, concentrating, and projecting anxiety or frustration onto a single object of resentment, be it Jews, Satan or the "secular world."

[660] Recall our citation of the study of Jon Butler, *Awash in a Sea of Faith*.
—William Lee Miller observes that so many of the later religious groups from Europe—Catholics, Jews, Anglicans, Dutch Reformed, etc.—brought along with them a "sense of a continuous non-American history," an inheritance conspicuously absent from the emerging evangelical communities. ("The Seminarian Strain," *The New Republic*, 9 July 1984.)
—Another take on it: "A genius for absorbing peoples of varying national and ethnic backgrounds has earned for her the reputation of being a melting pot; but in weakening the traditions that immigrant groups brought with them, the United States has not provided them with a compelling replacement. This leaves the nation perhaps the most traditionless society history has known." (Huston Smith, *The World's Religions: Our Great Wisdom Traditions*, HarperSanFrancisco 1991, 163.)

[661] "Even as late as 2006, after a quarter century of rising national prominence and power, *more than two-thirds* of evangelical Protestants in our Faith Matters survey said that they felt their values were 'seriously' or 'moderately threatened in America today,' a sense of embattlement greater than in any other major religious tradition." (Robert D. Putnam & David E. Campbell, *American Grace. . .* , 114.) {emphasis added}

uniquely American development of "denominationalism," wherein faith became a matter of personal choice in an expanding marketplace of competing religious offerings, rather than an assumed family or community inheritance.

6) Finally, and most importantly, the domination and expansion of market dynamics throughout society. *The greater the market domination of a society the greater the usurpation and replacement of more traditional cultural forms and products with lowest common denominator cultural forms and products, the greater the usurpation, commodification, and trivialization of culture.* So that contrary to some claims that evangelicalism thrives in those regions or "demographic categories" upon farthest remove from "modernism," *precisely the opposite obtains.* (Adherents of the "modernism" position would do well to reflect for a moment upon the singular prominence of evangelicalism in the most "modern," most market-driven society on earth—the United States—and its virtual absence among the more traditional regions and cultures of Protestant—let alone Catholic—Europe.[662]) Indeed the stimulation and periodic resurgence of evangelicalism derives both from the immediate presence of and contact with modernism (perceptions of the clear and present danger of "secularism" emanating in the most concentrated doses from the entertainment industry—news media, television, Hollywood, and Madison Avenue—the intelligentsia, public and higher education, the medical establishment, liberals at all levels of government, and feminism; in a word, persons and institutions largely urban in orientation who aggressively embrace and promote all the threatening profane secular logics and values enumerated throughout the study)[663] *and* from the cultural consequences, the various forms of personal and social

---

[662] The most prominent of such claims was advanced by Robert Bellah in *Beyond Belief: Essays on Religion in a Post-Traditional World*, but whose actual contents tend to occasionally undermine the implication of the title.

[663] Another way of thinking about this sort of cultural disjunction or juxtaposition comes from Harvey Cox:

> One wonders also why the conservative critics fail to see that it is possible for people to live amid social disintegration and still be religious. Indeed there are some classical saints who believed that no one could achieve true holiness without extended periods of isolation, loneliness, dark nights of the soul, and the experiencing of a certain lag of spiritual substance. One might even construct an argument, perhaps based on St. John of the Cross, *that the hardiness and chilliness of the modern world decried by the conservatives should elicit a deeper and more authentic spirituality* than the imagined warmth of the Christian Middles Ages. (*Religion in the Secular City. . .* , 79.) {emphasis added}

In this case the "should" here appears a bit of wishful thinking given what we have observed and documented. Contact tends to elicit something entirely different from "authentic spirituality."

disenchantment, of the free reign of market dynamics over the national land-scape.[664] The spread of these market dynamics is further advanced and

---

[664] That Pentecostalism is showing a global surge in some third-world societies is due to other factors largely social, not cultural, in nature. American proselytization more successfully sells the religion as a path out of poverty and not so much in terms of salvation from death or encroaching modernism and secularism. Although many American evangelical globalizers also seek to advance the Religious-Right "culture wars" agenda against abortion and promote other conservative dogmas, "On the issue of capitalism's putative benefits, however, the Evangelicals themselves appear divided." (Joseph J. Yates, "American Evangelicals: The Overlooked Globalizers and their Unintended Gospel of Modernity," *The Hedgehog Review*, Vol. 4, No. 2, Summer 2002, 79.) See also the more complex, albeit apologetic account of Allan Heaton Anderson that largely concurs: *To The Ends of the Earth. . .* , op. cit.

—Finally towards the end of her tortured review of anthropology's approach to Christianity, Ruth Marshall reaches paydirt in her accounting for Pentecostal missionary successes in Africa, acknowledging that ". . . . it could be argued that Pentecostalism constructs close affinities with neoliberal finance capital as well as contemporary ideas of debt and prosperity and thus acts in many ways as a handmaiden of capital and empire rather than an antidote to it. . . . Nimo Wariboko, a Pentecostal theologian, speculates that the spirit of Pentecostalism today may be nothing more than the spirit of the latest form of capitalism." ("Christianity, Politics. . . , 353.)

—Brian Stanley provides an illuminating account of the spread and/or odd fusion of "prosperity theology" (Norman Vincent Peale and, later, Oral Roberts), "liberation theology," and the more indigenously culturally-cued "deliverance ministry" of Derek Prince in Ghana. Prince explained away "why even fervent Christians were falling into sickness and failing to escape from poverty. . . ." Affliction and possession by demons observed no boundaries, "a claim that meshed closely with African beliefs about the ancestors." Compatible with traditional notions of sin, all could become victims and require "deliverance." Yet, as portrayed in *Hotel Rwanda:* ". . . . an approach that urged Christians to be constantly on the hunt for inherited malevolent influences that might account for their problems inculcated not trust in the power of Christ, but enduring fear and mutual suspicion." Elsewhere, aside from the Pentecostal message having "a particular attraction [for] working-class women. . . . For the poor in Latin America, as in so much of the developing world, religion is about utilizing all available spiritual resources to meet the pressing everyday needs of survival, and engaging in contractual relationships with the spiritual patrons who appear to promise the desired benefits." Yet he concludes that "so many of the Latin American poor" prefer "The promise of the spiritual power here and now . . . . [or] Pentecostalism over liberationist solutions to their predicament." (Brian Stanley, *Christianity in the Twentieth-Century: A World History*, Princeton University Press, 2018, 170, 296-309.) Hence, in keeping with our general theme: *different cultures, different Christianities.*

—David Smilde offered an equally nuanced earlier account of the socio-economic appeal of Pentecotalism in Venezuela and the rest of Latin America in *Reason to Believe: Cultural Agency in Latin American Evangelicalism*, University of California Press, 2007.

—Or Alex de Tocqueville more than century ago: "This explains why religious nations have so often achieved such lasting results; for while they were thinking only [??] of the other world, they had found the great secret of success in this." (*Democracy in America, Vol.2*, Phillips Bradley ed., Alfred A. Knopf 1945/1972, 149.)

—And Peter Berger: ". . . . 'Max Weber is alive and well and living in Guatemala.' You look at these people, and they speak Spanish or even Mayan, but they act like the Puritans that Weber was describing. Pentecostalism now is a worldwide phenomenon. . . ." (in Mathewes. . . , 158.)

legitimated by a moral market ethos that encourages evaluations of individuals in terms of their performance or non-performance in this market arena.[665]

Three Types of Cultural Response

All told, there are perhaps three or more distinctive *collective* reactions to the kinds of disenchantment, ambivalence, and/or feelings of persecution or intimidation that have arisen or emerged from these uniquely American social and cultural conditions.

Passive Separatism/Withdrawal

A community may express or respond to cultural disenchantment in a largely *non-ideological* fashion. It is the lack of any sort of heightened perception of immediate external danger, for example, which sets the Amish so clearly apart from their evangelical cousins. To my mind the Amish are traditional ascetic Protestant communities, but not "evangelical" communities; they are not ideological in any comparable sense. Their beliefs are not *accelerated* or mobilized into a defensive or offensive posture; they have not been nor are they now deploying forces on an imaginary field of battle against some clear and present danger. Religious and other beliefs guide the nature and form of their communities and the behavior of their members, but they have largely withdrawn from any sort of routine, active engagement with the object of their discontent—the modern, technological, market-driven American society.[666]

Militant Separatism

Communities may also turn acts of ideological imagination (often delusional perceptions of clear and present dangers) into tangible confrontations with the object or source of apprehension, in this instance the various forms or incarnations of the great secular Leviathan—be it the more nebulous monolithic social and cultural presence of "secularism" or the myriad nettlesome agents and representatives of "liberalism" and the liberal state. These

---

[665] Americans, for example, routinely initiate or extend a conversation with a stranger by asking, "What do you do?" (for a living), an inquiry regarded as bad manners in many other societies.

[666] Which, unfortunately, may nevertheless fail to shield them from some of the aggrandizing dynamics of the larger market culture, as R. Laurence Moore reminds us: ". . . . anyone who has traveled east from Lancaster [Pennsylvania] on Route 30 and viewed the manufactured Amish attractions that draw tourists by the thousands to the area will recognize the futility of attempted isolation. If you do not commodify your religion yourself, someone will do it for you." (*Selling God. . .* , 11.)

can be self-fulfilling gestures of mobilization and defiance directed towards secular authorities (baiting gestures that authorities often fail to understand: e.g., David Koresh at Waco) or paranoid acts of self-initiated flight and self-inflicted violence (Jim Jones and the People's Temple in Guyana). They prove intriguing as instances in which the cultural war that the average evangelical ideologue carries around in his head—displayed throughout this study—expanded or accelerated way out of proportion to any real world danger, with devastating consequences. While SPU President David McKenna and many others like him—academicians ensconced within the safe, comfortable confines of established institutions—sketched the theoretical outlines of a holy war with the "secular world system," David Koresh, the genuine outcast article, a Jesus with guns, hunted down by the secular empire, actually turned on his imaginary tormentors and fought back. He is remarkable for carrying out what many evangelicals can, and have, only fantasized about. And his were actions which few national evangelicals—understandably, given their ideological complicity—rushed to condemn, reserving damnation instead for hapless federal authorities.

Symbolic Separatism
Finally, a community may respond to apprehensions of social and cultural danger by creating a *parallel cultural universe*, as has been documented throughout this study. It is in this sense that American evangelical communities have implemented with delicious and ironic effect the injunction of living "in but not of the world." Observe the ingenious solution to an apparently intractable logistical and moral problem: spurn the decadent materialism of the modern secular American world and yet retain all of the material rewards that it has to offer. Perform a characteristically American rite of cultural epistemological casuistry: sacralize the contested objects and acts of consumption and fashion a parallel moral market universe in its stead. Sacralize, monopolize, internalize that which is worthy and good; secularize, demarcate, and demonize that which is unworthy and bad. Reify a nemesis with benefits. Indeed, for all too long this rather ingenious evangelical cultural program has been misconstrued as just another installment in a long line of developmental secularizations or sheer hypocrisy.[667] They're fat, they're wealthy, they're garish; they're living in the suburbs; they're becoming just like everybody else; they will eventually disappear into the gaudy

---

[667] Such was the case in 1947 with prominent evangelical Carl F. H. Henry's *The Uneasy Conscience of Modern Fundamentalism*, whose example "an editor of *Christianity Today* (the flagship evangelical magazine Henry started)" cited, encouraging him to preposterously claim that the "devastation of two [world] wars" could be lain on the doorstop of the "failed theology of liberalism." (Jeff Sharlet, *The Family. . .* , 153.)

mists of American normalcy. These and other rigid, a-historical, hand-me-down sociological conceptions deserve to be summarily dishonored, dismantled, and retired. Evangelical religion has always occupied a central position in the marketplace of American culture,[668] and will continue to do so far into the foreseeable future. It has served to define and create—and has in turn been defined and created by—the moral market arena of American culture. *It thoroughly embodies both the moral market impetus and the moral market disenchantments of our culture and will not go quietly into the night, as prophesied by some our most prominent academicians.* The resilience of evangelical religion reflects the resilience of the moral market: sinuous, flexible, adaptive, enduring, and, above all, quintessentially American.

The Future of American Evangelicalism

Predictions of the assimilation, absorption, or demise of evangelical religion have proven as premature and erroneous as those foretelling the end of the world. Allow me to advance instead some rather more sobering mundane rules or guidelines governing the movement of evangelical tides within the American ocean—their more or less likely ebb and flow.

One way to think of the various probabilities and possibilities is in terms of a series of linked propositions, to the effect that

→ the greater the hollowing out of cultural vacuums due to the continued expansion of a culturally bankrupt suburban cul-de-sac mentalities and materialism, and the associated widening of a depersonalizing, anomie-generating social media swamp, in combination with

→ the greater the perception of external social and cultural danger (the threat from "secular" society or other imperilments)[669]

---

[668] Again, see R. Laurence Moore's provocative *Selling God . . .* , 1994.

[669] And *either* the perception *or* the reality of a danger or threat will suffice. As someone once said, even paranoids have enemies. For in spite of evangelicals' seemingly perpetual persecution complex, sometimes the anxiety is warranted. Robert P. Jones writes that "White Christian America's critics could also stand up for churches when government officials overreach and threaten conservative pastors' freedom to preach openly, as happened in Texas in the fall of 2014. In a case that quickly gained national attention, the office of Houston mayor Annise Parker, the first openly lesbian mayor of a major American city, subpoenaed the sermons of five local pastors as part of a lawsuit related to Houston's Equal Rights Ordinance (HERO), which included protections for LGBT people. The subpoena demanded 'all speeches, presentations, or sermons related to HERO, the Petition, Mayor Annise Parker, homosexuality, or gender identity prepared by, delivered by, revised by, or approved by you or in your possession.' " (*The End of White Christian America*, Simon & Schuster 2016, 233.)
—As always, personal contact with perceived enemies tends to temper perceptions of animus. Christian Smith writes that "Some evangelicals explicitly recognize that their personal experiences differ from what they read or hear about, most often in Christian media. . . .

→ the greater the acceleration of evangelical ideological intensity (felt need for defensive and/or offensive postures or strategies erected and/or aimed against the "secular" world).

And so as a probable consequence of the foregoing, we might accordingly expect and observe

→ the greater the tendency to formulate and employ radical categorical distinctions between (internal) evangelical Christian and (external) profane secular persons, objects, relationships, and even societies (the expansion of the logic of invidious distinction—*signals of difference*),[670] and

→ the greater the (internal) community pressure to produce the individual demeanors, behaviors, and community ambiances consistent with the (often internally contradictory) vision of radical evangelical Christian distinction (smile and transparency logics) and

→ the greater complexity (and potential acceleration) of conjunctions and disjunctions with more general social dynamics (peer pressures/allocations of rewards and sanctions/presentations of the self/allusive interactionism), and *most importantly*

→ the greater the seeking out or creation of evangelical worship communities to succor, ameliorate, or neutralize the combination of social, economic, cultural *insecurities* that both appear to, and actually, threaten the equanimity, stability, and happiness of individuals and families.

Perhaps a simpler way of putting this is to suggest that *the greater the feeling of comfort and acceptance on the part of the local or national evangelical religious community vis-à-vis the surrounding, so-called secular world, the less antagonistic and ideologically*

Occasionally, our interviewees even self-critically conceded that evangelical perceptions of hostility may involve some degree of paranoia about a largely nonexistent conspiracy against Christians." (*Christian America? What Evangelicals Really Want*, University of California Press 2000, 71.)

—With the election of Donald Trump evangelicals who have trouble with his brand of Christianity have recovered episodes from the Old Testament where pagan leaders of questionable character were temporarily used by God "to enact his will and *protect* his people." (Meghan O'Gieblyn, "Exiled: Mike Pence and the evangelical fantasy of persecution," *Harper's Magazine*, May 2018, 26.) {emphasis added} Problem is, behavior aside, Trump's no pagan but born-again through and through. (See my "For What It's Worth. . . .") A nagging question persists, however: doesn't it ever occur to evangelicals that Donald Trump, not Barack Obama, may indeed be the "Anti-Christ." (See Christian Smith, *Christian America?. . .*, 112.)

[670] Most deliciously as in Trump aide, Kelly Anne Conway's, revealing invocation of "alternative facts."

intense the internal cultural focus and animus; whereas the greater the perception of external cultural intimidation and danger (however delusional and "self-fulfilling"), the greater the internal ideological mobilization, with all the various attendant consequences we have described.

And so a host of often contradictory dynamics become swept into a vortex of social and cultural fermentation, levels of intensity and social execution (e.g., the pressure or urge to publicly shred the "mask" of secular duplicity and embrace "transparency") rising or falling in collusion with a host of other accelerating or decelerating variables. We have observed how cultural dynamics permeate social dynamics, shaping more general dynamics into characteristic community and national forms; and we have observed, conversely, how social dynamics (re: Hari, Turkle, Harrison et al.) permeate cultural dynamics, establishing a motivational infrastructure of possibilities and limitations, of probable personal and social paths of least resistance, sluicing the social channels along which community behavior is more likely to flow. We have observed here the individuals of a community—commensurably autonomous *and* entranced—caught in a *more or less* deep calibration of personal, community, social, and cultural dynamics, evolving and oscillating through a history of many twists and turns, of ideological intensifications and relaxations, of expansions and contractions. Such is the convergence of the social and the cultural—and the local, national, and international—in a small American evangelical academic community.

We may then anticipate that when these two personal and four social/cultural conditions become drawn together at some point in time, in some hypothetical society, such a coalescing may very well tend to encourage or even *cause* the emergence of evangelical forms of religion. I certainly hold them responsible for the original appearance and continuing resilience of evangelicalism in American society. They may not all be essential and certainly two or three in particular situations may prove sufficient to produce or sustain the phenomena; and yet all of these in similar versions in an entirely different cultural context (i.e., absent the six or seven other defining features of American history and culture) may fail to generate or sustain a similar kind of evangelical religion. Furthermore, the routine transfer of evangelical faith from parents to children may proceed along the lines of some altogether different principles; as we have seen, there are all sorts of other interpersonal and family dynamics which may come into play here. I am not altogether convinced, for example, that the first two personal causes and conditions do much to advance our understanding of the everyday strength and appeal of evangelicalism among the families, churches, and communities in American society. By and large, the children who grow up in evangelical families—the majority of students at Seattle Pacific—overlooking for the moment some of their more exotic qualities, strike one as perfectly normal young people, exhibiting the full range of personality dispositions characteristic of any similar group of students. Emotionally, psychologically, intellectually, they appear all of a piece. Be assured that the average individual may certainly find the social and cultural contours and guidance of evangelicalism rewarding and enriching. However, whether or not the accumulation of all these apparent individual enrichments in their sundry collective forms produces a larger social and cultural normalcy or even enrichment is another question altogether.

Academicians who are Christians tend to raise the happiness issue[671] in their studies of religion in America. In this respect, I have briefly raised the issue of *cultural vacuums* as an essential factor in the emergence and persistence of evangelicalism in America. For there is a very good reason why evangelical mega-churches have largely sprung up and thrived in suburban cul-de-sac America, in the transitional borderlands separating urban and rural America. To my way of thinking, as we saw earlier, they have done so to fill the vacuum of such American cultural wastelands. Academicians who report and celebrate the evidence of a greater general "happiness" among believers rarely delve deeper into the matter beyond survey data representations, and even more rarely attempt to locate and contrast such data with those of European societies. Consistent with everything I have presented so far is my contention that evangelical religion serves as an artificial cultural substitute in America, an ersatz "connection"[672] or happiness drug that Europeans find so unappealing and unnecessary given their more "godless," culturally-rich, existentially secure, less moral market-driven societies. So I am not at all surprised by T.H. Luhrmann's claim: "There is good evidence that those who believe in a loving God have happier lives. . . we know that people who believe in God are less lonely. . . we know that those who go to church live longer and are in greater health."[673] But, compared to whom?

---

[671] As do Putnam and Campbell in their monumental account, *American Grace. . .* , 443, 490-91, based, once again, largely upon survey data, concluding that religion does indeed appear to make Americans happier than those without religion: ". . . . religious people are more satisfied with their lives mostly because they build religious social networks. . . . [Yet] A person who attends church regularly but has no close friends there is actually unhappier than her demographic twin who doesn't attend church at all." Unfortunately, Putnam and Campbell neglect to delve further into the matter.

[672] As Johann Hari might put it. See *Lost Connections: Uncovering The Real Causes of Depression and the Unexpected Solutions* (Bloomsbury 2017).

[673] *When God Talks Back: Understanding the American Evangelical Relationship with God*, Knopf, 2012, xvi—and see her footnote #10, 330-31. That there are other more ironic subterranean

Other Americans who do not do so? *Precisely. They* struggle on, un-medicated by the bromides of evangelicalism, because they are stuck in an American social regimen whose emotional compensations pale in comparison with virtually all quality of life indicators and metrics posted by modern European nations.[674] Our European friends gaze across the Atlantic moat at the proverbial American internecine war of all-against-all, at our continuing trials and tribulations, at this wall of seemingly dissonant cultural noise, and no doubt have cause to wonder: What on earth has gained possession of these Yanks? What indeed? Were it only the devil instead.[675]

Perhaps an even more important distinguishing feature of these assorted causes and conditions are the various durations of their cultural impact and influence. Here the most crucial distinction is that between *the longer-term cause*

---

currents in play here can be seen in her own inadvertent account of other matters. (Recall an earlier footnote on this matter.)

[674] See Dan Buettner, "The World's Happiest Places," *National Geographic*, November, 2017.

[675] As did our greatest social scientist, Max Weber, presciently anticipating the American cultural malaise:

> If Weber denies the applicability of the radical ethic of brotherliness to the modern economy and state, we may be sure that he would similarly deny the possibility that the organic social ethic could be resurrected to meet our current need. One can imagine the skepticism with which he would greet the present effort in the United States to offer so-called private-sector volunteerism, family values, and a renewal of local community as ways of providing the safety net, such as it was, that is no longer publicly provided. The gated, guarded 'communities,' which have in recent years been springing up in American suburbs, nowhere more frequently than California, would surely seem to Weber to be *the complete antithesis of genuine organic community*. (Robert Bellah, "Max Weber and World-Denying Love. . . ," 298-99.) {emphasis added}

—For an equally compelling depiction of a general cultural dynamic that applies with even greater force to the American experience see Robert Pogue Harrison's almost harrowing *Juvenescence: A Cultural History of Our Age*, cited earlier. He contends in general that rich, life-enhancing cultures maintain a vibrant relationship between youth (novelty, imagination, innovation) and age (wisdom, tradition). Healthy cultures ease their young charges through "the most crucial maturation process of all, for it turns self-love into world-love. . . . *amor mundi* both suffuses and sustains the world . . . its withdrawal leaves the world ever more vulnerable to the forces that provoke its withdrawal in the first place." Even more importantly in the particular cultural context of this book: ". . . . education's unofficial currency is love . . . its mission is to educe a love of the world [esp. its history and achievements]—the kind of love without which there could be no love at all." Instead, we have found among these students and evangelicalism at large an "*odium mundi*. . . a world loathing." Indeed nothing proves more diminishing, more personally and socially impoverishing, than *odium mundi*. Perhaps the greatest irony of all is that such fear and loathing of the larger world—the *secular* world—ultimately robs one of *wholeness*, supposedly the *conditio sine qua non* of an evangelical Christian college education. (118, 127-8, 132)

and consequences of market dynamics (the *disenchantment* trigger) and *the shorter-term impact of perceptions of clear and present danger* (the *ideological* trigger). The *former* explains the enduring presence and resilience of evangelicalism over an extended period—approaching two centuries—of American social history; the *latter* accounts for the episodic woof and wane in the intensity of its apprehensions and trepidations, in the periodic shifting of objects of cultural aspersion, in the cycles of decline and resurgence. Indeed it is the heightened perception of a clear and present cultural danger to the cultural integrity of evangelicalism (in both defensive and offensive postures), which more than anything else explains the current strength of evangelicalism in the various social and political arenas of American society. This ebbing and flowing merely plays itself out within the larger cultural context of disenchantment.

The disenchantment of evangelicalism has then assumed many different guises and forms over the decades, and yet evangelicalism itself always seems to carry forward into each succeeding period just enough of the nature and structure of its anchoring cultural being to continue performing its role as the ideological foundation and heart of American culture, one of the prime beneficiaries of the larger disenchantment of American society and culture.

Epilogue

I end on a personal note, this followed by one brief final, somewhat belated, general observation.

First, to my way of thinking this notion of the disenchantment of evangelicalism—a more concentrated dose of the cultural dysfunction and demoralization one finds in the larger American society—represents more than a mere theoretical abstraction or generalization; indeed it captures and expresses a good deal of tangible human experience and sentiment. I see it, sense it, feel it nearly every day. It bears a distinctly American face.

Richard, a thirty-year-old grocery clerk at our local QFC (Quality Food Center), is one such face. For several years he checked and bagged my groceries. One day, driving by my house and spotting me out mowing the lawn, he pulled over to chat. We spoke briefly. Before pulling away he lifted a blank white envelope from his glove compartment, handing me the following "letter":

Coming Home[676]

1 Chronicles 28: 9, this particular passage sticks out rather vividly as I sit down and write this letter to you. David the King of Israel is talking to his son Solomon, "As for you my son Solomon, know the God of your father, and serve him with a whole heart and a willing mind; for the Lord searches all hearts, and understands every intent of the thoughts. If you seek Him, He will let you find him; but if you forsake Him, He will reject you forever."

As I sit back and reflect upon my life this last decade I see a young man about twenty years old, going to college full of alot of hope and ambition, but a life filled with a rather large void. I had a good job while going to school, a new car, plenty of money, a fancy condominium I had just bought with a friend, but despite all these things an emptiness existed inside of me. I thought that maybe the happiness I was looking for could be found in a relationship. So I looked for that person to make me happy and fill that void in my life, all I found was more discontentment and despair as I bounced from one relationship to another. Many of these people were beautiful you might even say gorgeous, yet I found myself getting very involved emotionally and sexually, only to be hurt when the relationship ended.

Hurt soon turned to hate and anger, bitterness soon began to dominate my life and consume me. Prior to this my father had been sick with cancer for some two years and eventually passed away, all of this made for more unhappiness. All of this unhappiness led me up to Bellingham to live with my brother, I had visited Bellingham many a times, I loved its parks and rivers, yet I was still unhappy, this was in the summer of 1981. Despite my unhappiness I knew that there was a

---

[676] I reproduce the text here, as is, adding the obligatory [*sic*]s only for misspellings.

reason for going to Bellingham, I wasn't the type to just pick and move, something inside of me urged me to go something I didn't understand.

That summer I played on a baseball team with my brother and his friends who were living in the fast lane of life, sensing I was unhappy my brother sent me to a church down the street, little did I know that the pastor of the church was the second baseman of our baseball team Fred. Fred and I talked a little bit and asked if I wanted to give my life to Jesus Christ, I didn't really understand at the time what it meant but I went ahead and did it anyways.

After I had given my life to Christ that day I went home, a couple of days later I felt a peace come over me, for the first time in my life I felt a real joy inside of me something I had never felt in my life. After being in Bellingham for only a couple of months, something inside of me told it was time to move back to Seattle. I resumed many of the same relationships I had moved to get away from. God began to show me that these old relationships were bad for me.

God began to pick up the pieces and put them back together, he began to heal the hurts and the bitterness that had all but consumed me. I didn't know it then but I know it now, God had and was calling me to come home and find his peace and forgiveance [*sic*] for all my sins and transgressions. God so loved the world that he humbled himself and became flesh, a human being know[n] as Jesus Christ who being fully God and fully man died on the cross for our sins, both yours and mine. It says in the Book of Psalms 104: 11-14, God removes our sins as far as east is from west. In the Book of John in chapter 3: 16 God promises eternal life to those who believe in His son Jesus Christ and confess their sins.

Even if you don't believe in God or that Jesus was God, or don't believe you have the faith call out to God with all your heart he will anwser [*sic*] your cry. You to [*sic*] can become apart [*sic*] of the Kingdom of God, Jesus offers this opportunity in the Book of Revelation in chapter 3, verse 20-21.
God loves you and loves me despite our failures, past, present and future, turn to God and you will find peace, hope and joy, being a Christian isn't easy in this world but it beats living a life without Christ!

Richard

Second, as I have intimated throughout this book, my project has broader implications and applications. Take the tragic, bread and circus phenomenon of Donald Trump for one final instance. Hopefully the reader will not be surprised to learn that the author has *only* one thing in common with this gentleman beyond our obviously shared species and gender. For years it seems we both watched a good deal of evangelical Christian television. As mentioned earlier, no doubt we were both up late at night, mesmerized by the same programs (a practice he continued in the White House)— he in his gilded New York tower mansion and I scribbling away in my notebook on the opposite coast.

Just recently I took a refresher course, tuning in once again. And lo and behold, as the French would say, *plus ça change, plus c'est la même chose*. There it all was—on full display, complete with bells and whistles. Yet I must also acknowledge that the re-acquaintance raised some concerns, particularly for the diligent reader who has just completed this book. Such that I now wonder if said reader were to randomly flip through the channels, would s/he recognize the landscape? Has this book proven a valuable tourist guide? Would any of it now make more sense? Or would s/he still find these sites inexplicably foreign at first glance, perhaps even contradictory of what I have advanced here? For indeed even with repeated viewing s/he may not observe and hear the language and terms of an evangelical cultural logic come tumbling out of the mouths of babes in precisely the same form and manner I have presented it. And so about this potential dissonance or confusion I was concerned, *initially*. But the more I watched into the wee hours of this one particular Sunday night, the more my concerns lessened, and the more I began to appreciate once again, oddly enough, the cultural marketing genius of American evangelicalism. Yes indeed, an *exceptional* kind of *genius*. And I am now also reassured that the reader will find this parting vignette completely consistent with—indeed verifying of—what has gone before.

In Seattle, where I now sit, once again, writing this, there are five or more independent stations broadcasting locally (channels 20 to 20.5) through these largely California-based evangelical networks. One in particular, the *Hillsong Channel* (of Australian origin, I believe), is a subsidiary of the decades-old *TBN*, or *Trinity Broadcast Network*, the largest Christian network in the world. They offer a wide variety of programming, but of particular relevance for us are the large auditorium "conferences" wherein the most dynamic pastors or preachers from around the country perform before huge audiences (one show broadcasting from Sidney, Australia, where a hip, cowboy-booted, 50-year-old single mother, Lisa Harper, from Nashville, Tennessee trots out her tiny adopted black African daughter, to the "ooooooo"s of the crowd, and then addresses a largely female audience about how it's ok with the young-un strapped in the back seat of the car to inadvertently let fly an expletive—that rhymes with "Brit"—after you've spilled your Starbuck's mocha all over your lap at the drive-through.) Proselytizing these days is, of course, all about authenticity, "just keeping it real." Which might give us pause: if that were truly the case, why then can't she just say "shit" out loud to the audience and be done with it? *Too real?*

Although occasionally one observes the traditional secularism bashing, as during one episode of a pastor-led tour of Israel where the group stood before the Mount of Olives in the distance while their guide exhorted them to see through the current Democrat/Republican squabbles for what they really are—a war of worlds: Christianity (Trump Republicanism) versus Satanism (AOC Democrats)—by and large the message is now packaged and presented with a good deal more sophistication and impartial *élan*.

Quite frankly, these more recent get-togethers are amazingly rousing spectacles, brilliantly conceived and produced (good enough to charge an entrance fee! Imagine that!). Although the speakers usually run the gamut of types, this particular evening one speaker, a young pastor of a local LA congregation, appeared to have come straight out of Malibu beach central casting: crew-cut blond, lean and buff, casually dressed in t-shirt and tennis shoes. He speaks equally casually without notes or prompters, as though to a bunch of beachcombers gathered round a driftwood fire. Typical veteran speakers tend to organize their presentations around a particular Biblical verse to which they instill new life and relevance for a contemporary audience. This young firecracker, by contrast, forgoes the usual preliminary exegesis and jumps right into his sermon, if one could call it that. Alternately chatty, funny, relevant, sincere, earnest, self-effacing, flip and hip, he sets everyone at ease, quite literally holding the audience, *casually*, in the very tanned palm of his hand. As for sin or sinners, no one inside that auditorium gets painted with such a broad brush. Instead, they are all assumed to be, and are addressed as, victims of a difficult, uncaring world. Indeed, aren't we all? Most importantly, he's not there to talk about "religion" or fire and brimstone. No way, man. Instead, it's all about commiseration—about the poor hand we/they have all been dealt. The world's a mess, many of your—*our*—lives are a mess: opiate addiction, loneliness, failed marriages, two-faced so-called friends, broken families, stressful jobs, insufferable harassing bosses, unemployment, homelessness, alcohol abuse; the lamentations go on and on. You name it, the world's got it in for us. "Raise your hand if you know what I'm talking about." Virtually half the audience of thirty or forty thousand do so. Of course, the effect is electrifying.

"My beautiful wife, Ruth, over there (she waves from the side of the stage), we've struggled like you wouldn't believe, just to be here."

"You are all hurting. . . *we are all hurting*. . . . [But] What's missing here???"

The crowd murmurs.

"What's missing, people? What do we lack?????"

"We are not talking about religion, about going to church—are we now? . . . . No, no, we are talking about the relationships that just aren't there . . . that have gone south, gone AWOL if there ever were any. . . we can drown in all the religion there is and still come up empty inside, missing the only relationship that truly matters, that personal relationship with the only friend who really counts and can be counted on. . . .

There's only one true relationship that can turn it all around . . . that personal relationship with Jesus Christ. . . . Only He can bring that inner peace."

Now he's pushing all the right buttons. (Accordingly: the next hour brings another young preacher who drills home his own additional points about "empty vessels." "God wants broken empty vessels to fill with anointing oil," like filling up all that the emptiness at some sort of spiritual gas station.) The crowd truly feels the emotional aches and pains of which he speaks; none would appear to have anything like the relationships he describes. There's a big hole that needs filling with what's missing, a redeeming *personal relationship* with this ultimate "friend."

You can just feel it in the air: the controlled frenzy of a climax towards which he is building. For he's hit the nail directly on the head. Everyone's yearning for that missing connection, that completion; everyone wants to be made *whole*. Out in the congregation, believers old and newly anointed alike embrace and then cling to one another. Swirling arms and hands are raised towards a God who's hovering somewhere above them in some sort of celestial auditorium ceiling. Yet not a word is spoken this evening about *salvation*; that perhaps too distant and delayed a gratification. No, we are talking here about a this-worldly succor and elevation: Lord spare me, spare us our current trials and tribulations; lift us up! Out of this mess! And then, the cauldron of emotions effectively stirred, as it inevitably must be, there arrives the modern altar call moment (a vestige of Billy Graham?), only it is lubricated not by the deep baritone of Cliff Barrows but by Taylor Swift-like anthems from a rock band pumping out infectious melodies and rhythms. The mosh pit front of the stage swarms with deliriously happy worshippers. The speaker moves in to inject a prayer here and there and then a cadence of chorusing voices resumes. All are jumping up and down in unison with the beat, like NFL players before kick-off. How could anyone resist the pull of this seething mass of rapturous relationships? Forget the cultural wasteland of America; forget tomorrow's dog-eat-dog workday reality. Tonight the vacuum is filled and we are healed.

When Jonathan Haidt published *The Righteous Mind: Why Good People Are Divided By Politics and Religion* in 2012 I am sure that nothing could have proven more surprising or ironic to him than what followed with the election of 2016. Although he writes of an American political society torn between individualism and "groupishness" one senses a lingering uncertainty as to what actually determines or moves his fellow Americans' moral intuitions. Are we capable as generic human beings, "conditional hive creatures," of throwing a "hive switch. . . . to transcend self-interest and lose ourselves (temporarily and ecstatically) in something larger than ourselves?" Or, rather, does this more general propensity break down into a choice between *either* (negative) transactionalism and spectacles (fascism) *or* (positive) transformationalism and festivals (hives/social capital/*bowling together*)?

For herein lies the interpretive rub, which hinges, as I outlined earlier, on a *bias* of sorts, an almost culturally-embedded *preference*, in the starkest binary terms or formulation, for one kind of community or society over another quite different one. As the reader now well knows, this author finds both the Haidt and Robert Putnam depiction of, and/or enthusiasm for, a traditional American social and cultural exceptionalism seriously wanting on so many levels. Indeed Haidt's only mention of the "godless" Nordic, Scandinavian social experiments is tentative at best, the whole business and region summarily dismissed in passing.[677]Hence his somewhat muddled and confused assessment of the American prospect, still as equally fraught with civilizational tribulations as the one posed by Jon Butler in Appendix B that follows later:

> When a single hive is scaled up to the size of a nation and is led by a dictator with an army at his disposal, the results are invariably disastrous. But that is no argument for removing or suppressing hives at lower levels. In fact, a nation that is full of hives is a nation of happy and satisfied people. . . . A nation of individuals, in contrast, in which citizens spend all their time in Durkheim's lower level, is likely to be hungry for meaning. If people can't satisfy their need for deep connection in other ways, they'll be more receptive to a smooth-talking leader who urges them to renounce their lives of "selfish momentary pleasure" and follow him onward to "that purely spiritual existence" in which their value as human beings consists.[678]

---

[677] "Asking people to give up all forms of sacralized belonging and live in a world of purely 'rational' beliefs might be like asking people to give up the Earth and live in colonies orbiting the moon. . . .If you live in a religious community, you are enmeshed in a set of norms, relationships, and institutions that work primarily on the elephant to influence your behavior. But if you are an atheist living in a looser community with a less binding moral matrix, you might have to rely somewhat more on an internal moral compass, read by the rider. That might sound appealing to rationalists, but it also a recipe for anomie. . . . When societies lose their grip on individuals, allowing them to do as they please, the result is often a decrease in happiness. . . . *Societies that forgo the exoskeleton of religion should reflect carefully on what will happen to them over several generations. We don't really know, because the first atheistic societies have only emerged in Europe in the last few decades. They are the least efficient societies ever known at turning resources (of which they have a lot) into offspring (of which they have few).*" (*The Righteous Mind*, 307, 313.) {emphasis added} However questionable this framing of the social and cultural issues and context, the reader now has at his or her disposal the means by which render some sort of judgment. The disenchanting *spectacle* of Donald Trump's evangelical model for America or the re-enchanting *festival* of the *Nordic theory of everything* (a larger partial exploration of which follows in Appendix B)? These are the extreme, but *actual*, empirical alternatives.

[678] Ibid., 282-3.

As I write this, we are more than three years into the presidency of Donald Trump, an acknowledged born-again evangelical Christian who has aggressively sought to implement the vision and agenda of the evangelical Religious-Right. That Jonathan Haidt got it mostly wrong in his description and formulation of the moral foundations and cultural contexts of the righteous mind as it might apply to Donald Trump, the whole crew of accomplices within his administration, Republican Party enablers, and others like him and them is understandable. As Mary Douglas cautioned us initially, the assumption that religion performs a largely positive, culturally-beneficial role in society reflects an ingrained, Pentecostal-like *binding and blinding* bias that infects, conflicts, and compromises too many American Judeo-Christian academicians, as will be examined and dwelled upon more directly in Appendix B. It has proven a lingering impediment to an understanding of the role evangelical religion has actually played, and continues to play, in American life.

All told, with many notable exceptions, we can look over an American landscape littered with an assortment of both quietly and noisily desperate individual lives (as Thoreau partially, presciently observed), a fragile citizenry busily, alternatively, competing, thriving, commiserating with and destroying one another within a smattering of precariously-composed, predominantly culturally-vacuous communities. It ought inspire some sadness and regret that we can gaze out over a larger, overarching Gilead-aspiring (in fits and starts) Leviathan of a society of disenchantment and all the while also catch fleeting glimpses and retreating images of a truly wholesome democratic paradise squandered and lost. In this respect, we Americans, parroting Luigi Barzini one last time, are quite alone in the world. We are a distinctive people, with insecurities and phobias, aspirations and genuine achievements, all our own; in a sense, we do indeed live *in the world but not of the world*. And yet we are indeed also imprisoned within an iron cage of a society and culture of our own making.

Appendix A

Evangelical Apartheid [679]
The Statistical Tests

Some might argue that the kind of community portrait and analysis I have offered is lacking in rigor, relying as it does upon the observations and impressions of a single investigator, one in whose integrity and power of discernment the reader is asked to subscribe, as the evangelical academician might put it, on faith alone. To some extent I share these concerns and have attempted throughout this study to supplement my impressions and ruminations with more objective kinds of measures and materials. I do so not simply in anticipation of the inevitable (often justifiable) criticisms of the lacunae in my methods of observation and analysis but because of my belief that any study benefits from the application of this kind of discipline. I do believe, as argued in chapter eight, that any academician working in the social *sciences*—or any other related discipline, for that matter—must be able to define and predict the specific kinds of evidence or phenomena that will support or undermine particular contentions and arguments. I think we should be prepared to demonstrate, ala Karl Popper, that theories and explanations of social and cultural phenomena can be falsified in principle, if not always in actual practice; only then can we honestly claim to be working within the arena of the modern social sciences.[680]

---

[679] With the appellation "apartheid," I invoke more than mere descriptive parallels. As writes John W. DeGruchy, Professor of Christian Studies, University of Cape Town: " 'Bantu education' has been one of the foundation stones of the apartheid system, and it has meant that blacks have been purposely educated for servility. The rationale for such segregated and inferior education was contained in what is called '*Christian National Education*,' which ideally meant that education should be integrally related to the 'culture' of each ethnic group." ("Education at the Cape of Storms: Some Random Personal Reflections," *Faculty Dialogue*, no. 6 [Spring-Summer 1986], 42.)

[680] But as we have seen, some Christian academicians like Christian Smith dismiss "variables sociology" as riddled by a depersonalizing reductionism; other only mildly academically proficient pundits like David Brooks throw all sorts of social scientific models—Marxist, rational actor, conflict of interest, behaviorism, and whatnot, perhaps even Durkheim and Weber too—out the window as inadequate to the task of understanding and interpreting anything remotely sacred (to him/them):

> . . . . none of these models can adequately account for religious ideas, impulses, and actions because religious fervor cannot be quantified and standardized.

Which isn't to argue that hypotheses and evidence must, or indeed should, always be formulated and presented in the form of natural scientific-like "critical tests" that aim to substantiate or confute a theory in one fell swoop of experimentation (a too rarified notion of the nature and conduct of scientific testing in any event). Indeed it has been my experience that often a greater caution and appreciation of the limitations of the application of scientific methods can be found among philosophers, historians, and practitioners of science than among many of their fawning social scientific imitators.[681] In all too many instances, and in some pretty ill-suited contexts, we have been asked to accept mechanically-derived propositions and numerical data in lieu of sustained personal experience, contact, insight, and thought. I have striven in this study to produce both, although I must confess a greater sympathy for and confidence in the latter. The ultimate goal of any work, of course, remains to persuade first the immediate reader and then later a larger imaginary audience of the value (if not the veracity) of one's unavoidably personal interpretations of the phenomena in question—be they numbers, persons, communities, or cultures; that in one's fieldwork and scholarship one has, in effect, come close to getting it right.

Accordingly, how might we approach the central themes and arguments of this study in a more objective manner? One would hope that in the course of the preceding presentation a good deal of the verification and validation of its cardinal claims has been achieved, the final evaluation of which rests ultimately with the reader. But in addition to a reliance upon the (much longed for) sheer force and logic of a developing narration and the eventual emergent community portrait there remains something more that can be said in a decidedly critical, statistical manner.

Let us take, for instance, what the reader should have come to regard as a central theme of this study, namely that there is a widespread inclination among American evangelicals to fabricate or discern, and defend invidious

---

(from "How Niebuhr Helps Us Kick the Secularist Habit," in E.J. Dionne Jr./Jean Bethke Elshtain/Kayla M. Drogosz eds., *One Electorate Under God? A Dialogue on Religion & American Politics* (PEW Forum Dialogues on religion and Public Life. Wash. D.C.: Brookings Institution Press, 2004, 70). Which is, of course, a convenient way to shield his own religious models from critical inspection.

—More defensible, in my view, is Jonathan Haidt's take on his own academic field of moral psychology, for indeed ". . . . theories are cheap. Anyone can invent one. Progress happens when theories are tested, supported, and corrected by empirical evidence, especially when a theory proves to be useful—for example, if it helps people to understand why half of the people in their country seem to live in a different moral universe." (*The Righteous Mind*, 149.) But, as we have seen, the rub comes in the *appropriate* framing of social, cultural, and historical contexts in all their multi-level (his term) splendor.

[681] See especially Michael Polanyi (1962).

distinctions: to produce declensions of persons, objects, and relationships in baldly-opposite Christian and secular terms. The most pronounced claim here being that those individuals who regard themselves as evangelical Christians—with special reference to students in evangelicals colleges—tend to make and embrace these systematic Christian and secular differences more readily and deeply than do non-Christians or even non-evangelical Christians (i.e., mainline or lukewarm Protestants and Roman Catholics). Many readers have within their own powers of observation and experience the means of appraising (in this specific respect) just how different in outlook the evangelical community encountered in this study is from the more general non-evangelical national population. But this is an empirical comparison, in any event, which is at present beyond my means to attempt, and one which is also perhaps the least interesting (and the most predictable) of all those I might choose to perform. Perhaps a good deal more intriguing and challenging claim would be that *not only is there a great difference between these two populations over their respective penchants for invidious Christian and secular declensions, indeed within the evangelical population itself one can detect greater or lesser degrees of intensity in evangelical belief directly linked with or related to greater or lesser inclinations to make these sacred and profane distinctions.*[682]

Let us then turn to the student sample in order to see how such a proposition might be more concretely appraised, particularly in terms of volunteered responses to survey questions.[683] A lack of confidence in all previous

---

[682] If I had the chance to access the original sample population again I might have incorporated some of the statistical techniques that Lisa A. Keister employed in her marvelous study, "Religion and Wealth…," such as, for instance, "dummy variables" (186), to isolate or rule out certain factors—sex, rural/urban background, parent's religiosity, family income, grade point average, etc.—that might have impacted the results. However, looking back, as confident as I was that the data would confirm my hypothesis, I am equally confident that such additional data manipulations would not have undermined the original findings.

[683] A fine, more recent example (cited earlier) of how one addresses "cultural" issues and indicators by the sole use of original survey questions, indexes, "continuous scales," and the resulting data analysis can be found in Dan M. Kahan's quite illuminating "Cultural Cognition as a Conception of the Cultural Theory of Risk," originally located online (see p. 10, in this particular instance) but now found in Sabine Roesner et al. eds., *Handbook of Risk Theory: Epistemology, Decision Theory, Ethics, and Social Implications of Risk* (Springer Publishing 2012). Here is a great model of how to identify, isolate, and conceptualize certain cultural "indicators" and formulate and test legitimate propositions based upon them. Rarely has so much understanding been extracted from almost experimental-like questionnaire data. My only issue is the extent to which his "cultural" indicators ought be characterized as more generally *social* in nature, though one might surely argue that any observed "significant" quantitative differences or profiles within an indigenous American sample may reflect deeper cultural idioms that do not generalize to other cultures. In other words, Kahan's set of binary categories or continuous scales, hierarchical/egalitarian and individualist/communitarian, may be

sampling definitions and measures of evangelicalism[684] prompted the creation of my own indices—four individual and two cumulative—for the description and measurement of these phenomena.[685]

Three individual indices—*[SE] Standard Evangelical Index / [RP] Religious Practice Index / [I] Ideology Index*—combine to form the *[CRI 1] Combined Religious Intensity Scale #1* and (with the inclusion of one more item, survey question #47) the *[CRI 2] Combined Religious Intensity Scale #2*. Below I reproduce the survey questions composing these indices, including a tabulation of the student frequency distributions on individual items and a brief graphic summation of the index at the bottom of each.

---

culturally constrained themselves, let alone the particular survey questionnaire situations and items that would obviously have to be entirely reformulated to reflect altogether different cultural samples drawn from, for example, an Ethiopian, Fijian, or Indian population. As we will encounter in the forthcoming Nordic example, an even closer Western cultural frame of reference, Finns have come to regard the communitarian thrust of their national social-democratic welfare-state government as reflective and supportive of an historic, deeply-ingrained cultural individualism. These would not represent binary concepts for them. Hence I might contest his claim that "cultural worldviews, *as measured with our scales*, explain variation better than other individual characteristics, including education, income, personality type, and ideology." (22) {emphasis added} Then again, there is the additional issue of actual behavior patterns versus survey opinions, however insightfully analyzed from a distance.

[684] For a discussion of some of the more general issues regarding the categorization of religious groups, see Brian Steensland et al., "The Measure of American Religion: Toward Improving the State of the Art," *Social Forces*, Vol. 79, No. 1, Sep., 2000.

[685] Although for the purpose of making comparisons with national populations I did include in two of the indices a few exactly-worded items from Gallup's 1982 poll on religion in America. (*Religion in America, 1982*, Princeton Religion Research Center. Princeton, New Jersey.) Virtually all subsequent Gallup polls apply these same indices.

—See Froese, Paul & Christopher D. Bader, "God in America: Why Theology Is Not Simply the Concern of Philosophers," *Journal for the Scientific Study of Religion* (2007) 46(4), for some interesting comparative findings from their own national survey on related indices and issues, an analysis conducted at a much higher level of sophistication.

[SE] Standard Evangelical Index [687]

49) Here are three related questions regarding Christian faith:

a) Would you say that you have been "born-again" or have had a "born-again" experience—that is, a turning point in your life when you committed yourself to Christ?	[1] Yes (165)		76%
	[2] No (42)		19
	[3] Don't Know (10)		5
			100%

b) Have you ever tried to encourage someone to believe in Jesus Christ or to accept Him as his or her savior?   [1] Yes (184)   85%
  [2] No (33)   15
  100%

c) Which one of these statements comes closest to describing your feelings about the Bible? (Check One):

[1] "The Bible is the actual Word of God and is to be taken literally, word for word."   (25)   12%

[2] "The Bible is the inspired Word of God but not everything in it should be taken literally, word for word."   (182)   84

[3] "The Bible is an ancient book of fables, legends, history, and moral precepts recorded by men."   (8)   4

[NR]   (2)   *
  100%

[SE] Index score (of 49a-c): (possible score 1—5)

Score / Students choosing:

[5]	Two Yes+Literal	(22)	10%
[4]	Two Yes+Inspired	(135)	62
[3]	One Yes+Inspired	(32)	15
[2]	Two No+Inspired/One No+Don't Know+Inspired/ Two Yes+Fables	(21)	10
[1]	Two No+Fables	(7)	3
			100%

Score Range: *Low evangelicalism [1] ——— [5] High evangelicalism*

---

[686] In order to ensure a consistent standard of measurement, I compensated for the failure to answer individual items [NR] within a particular index by taking an average score for all the other items and assigning the [NR] item the average score. Rarely were more than a couple of items on an entire survey adjusted in this manner. In a couple of instances, where the pattern of responses was consistent and predictable and the written comments of the student explaining his reluctance to answer an item clearly indicated a predisposition, I took the liberty of interpolating more than just one or two missing responses. I rejected a few sporadically-answered surveys that showed no discernable pattern.

[687] Questions 49a-c come from *Religion in America 1982*, which reports the results of a national poll conducted by Gallup and the Princeton Religion Research Center, Princeton, New Jersey.

The Standard Evangelical Index *[SE]* questions come from Gallup's *Religion in America 1982* poll. He offers a useful but very conventional and rigid indicator of evangelicalism (not unexpectedly, as a professed Christian and member of the Trinity Church), Biblical inerrancy (the belief in the infallibility of the Bible) here serving as the preeminent litmus test for evangelicalism (which in the case of Seattle Pacific would mean that only 12% of the sample students qualify as evangelicals), a demarcation line essentially shrinking the pool of genuine evangelicals to fundamentalists alone.[688] The Gallup measure is also insensitive to degrees of commitment or ideological outlook. I have adopted Gallup's questions verbatim, but have fashioned my own scoring scale.

[RP] Religious Practice Index (#82, 83a, 84a, b)[689]
82) How often do you read the Bible?   83a) How often do you pray?

[1] Very little (41)	19%	[1] Very little (25)	12%
[2] Weekly (26)	12	[2] 2-3 times per week (15)	7
[3] 2-3 times per week (64)	30	[3] Daily (98)	45
[4] Daily (85)	39	[4] Several times daily (78)	36
[NR] (1)	*	[NR] (1)	*
	100%		100%

84) Which, if any, of these are you involved in, or do you practice?
[1] Bible study groups [2] Prayer and meditation groups [3] Charismatic Renewal Movement {primarily a Catholic phenomenon} *[4] Speaking in tongues [5] None*

a) Total number of groups		*b) How often?*	
[1] None (93)	43%	[1] Seldom (94)	43%
[2] One (84)	39	[2] Monthly (11)	5
[3] Two (34)	16	[3] Weekly (105)	48
[4] Three or more (5)	2	[4] Every 2-3 days,	
[NR] (1)	*	or daily (6)	3
	100%	[NR] (1)	*
			100%

[RP] Index score: (Four questions; possible score 4—16)
Low practice [4] ———— [16] High practice

In the Religious Practice Index *[RP]* I have once again employed Gallup's questions to construct an indicator of the actual exercise and involvement in

---

[688] Gallup acknowledges that "This is a fairly strict definition, because some evangelicals do not hold to a literal <u>interpretation</u> of the Bible, although they accept the absolute <u>authority</u> of the Bible." (*Religion in America 1982*, 31.) {Underline in original}

[689] #82, 83a, 84a & b from *Religion in America 1982*, 104, 106, 110. I have structured the responses and tabulated the results somewhat differently from Gallup.

religious practices and group activities. I did not ask about frequency of church attendance because some of the students are far from their home town churches and campus religious activities tend to replace them while at school.

[I] Ideology Index (#75a, 87a, 89, 91)[690]

75) How satisfied are you with: a) Life in this country today?

Extremely dissatisfied	[5]	(8)	4%
	[4]	(38)	18
	[3]	(88)	41
	[2]	(64)	29
Extremely satisfied	[1]	(19)	9
			101%

87a) Do you consider the United States at this moment to be a true Christian nation?

No, not at all	[5]	(76)	35%
	[4]	(93)	43
	[3]	(34)	16
	[2]	(14)	6
Yes, very much	[1]	(0)	*
			100%

89) Is the evidence of a concerted effort on the part of certain persons and organized groups in American society to, for example, remove nativity scenes from public Christmas displays, prevent prayer or religious observances in public schools, prevent any teaching of Creationism alongside Evolutionism in public schools, and to bring suit against Republican presidents for proclamations such as the "Year of the Bible," enough to make you conclude that there is a real potential threat to religious freedoms in this country?

Yes, real threat	[5]	(59)	27%
	[4]	(46)	21
	[3]	(53)	24
	[2]	(32)	15
No threat	[1]	(26)	12
	[NR]	(1)	*
			100%

91) Do you feel that through the concerted efforts of Christians all over the nation it is possible to move this nation in a more Christian direction?

---

[690] #75a from *Religion in America 1982*, 129.

Very possible	[5]	(98)	45%
	[4]	(64)	29
	[3]	(32)	15
	[2]	(15)	7
Not possible	[1]	(7)	3
	[NR]	(1)	*
			100%

[I] Index score: (Four questions; possible score 4—20)

Low ideological interest [4] ———— [20] High ideological interest

The Ideology Index *[I]* aims to measure the offensive and defensive postures and strategies adopted and employed by students both to preserve their religious beliefs within their own communities and to project them out into the arenas of local city, national, and international life. I am guided here by an underlying assumption and definition (presented in chapter 1) of ideology as an extraordinary source of meaning and motivation employed in the aggressive promotion or defense of a particular worldview, society, or social movement. I have attempted to devise items which can detect and measure a range of these ideological postures. To this end, my questions concentrate upon dissatisfactions with American society, upon the possibility of change or of the bringing to bear of concerted action for the redemption of the national society (a form of post-millennialism), and upon the perception of external threats to the evangelical community.

Cumulative Indices

[CRI 1] Combined Religious Intensity scale #1
Includes: *[SE]* (1—5) + *[RP]* (4—16) + *[I]* (5—20)
Possible score: Lowest Intensity [10] ——— [41] Highest Intensity

[CRI 2] Combined Religious Intensity scale #2
Includes: *[CRI 1]* (10—41) {above} + Question #47 (1-5) {below}:

47) How would you describe your present religious philosophy or beliefs?

Very Fundamentalist	[5]	(20)	9%
	[4]	(45)	21
	[3]	(64)	29
	[2]	(51)	24
Very Liberal	[1]	(30)	14
	[NR]	(7)	3
			100%

Possible score: Lowest Intensity [11] ——— [46] Highest Intensity

The first cumulative scale, *[CRI 1]* Combined Religious Intensity scale #1, incorporates three dimensions of evangelical religious personality (defining it in the process): reported belief and experience (*[SE]* Standard Evangelical Index), present practice (*[RP]* Religious Practice Index), and ideological posture (*[I]* Ideology Index); the second, *[CRI 2]*, adds a measure of self-definition (question #47) to form a comprehensive portrait of the intensity of the student's religious outlook and behavior.

These individual indices are not in and of themselves very reliable indicators of evangelicalism, since non-Christians may occasionally score moderately high, answering questions in a similar manner for altogether different reasons (such as, for example, former evangelicals who report their early conversion and proselytization experiences and harbor a lingering respect for scripture although they are no longer active believers; the same holding for some critical non-Christians who could conceivably answer the ideology portion in a manner vaguely similar to the zealous evangelical). Their value derives ultimately from their inclusion in a larger cumulative measure of the intensity of evangelical personality. No single index can adequately define evangelicalism; necessarily, they work in concert.

Finally, I included question #47, a self-description of religious beliefs, in the second cumulative scale *[CRI 2]* in order to draw an additional element of direct self-definition into a comprehensive, fully-rounded (but hopefully not excessively cluttered) student profile.

Sacred / Profane Index

The Sacred/Profane Index *[S/P]* seeks to determine the extent to which the students actually make these kinds of severe distinctions between Christian and secular phenomena in the various personal, domestic, social, and national arenas they frequent and occupy.

[S/P Sacred/Profane Index]
(#68, 71, 86, 96, 97a, b, 98, 100b, 101b, 103a, 104a, b, c)
68) In general, do you consider it important for couples who are going steady, as they say, and are trying to establish boundaries or limits upon their behavior when together, to be able to distinguish a) appropriate Christian sexual conduct for unmarrieds from b) non-Christian conduct or the values and norms which prevail in American society as a whole?

Very important to distinguish	[5]	(115)	53%
	[4]	(54)	25
	[3]	(25)	12
	[2]	(14)	7
Unimportant " "	[1]	(9)	4
			101%

71) Do you think there is in general a great difference between the manner in which married Christian couples treat one another (and their children, if any) and the way non-Christian or atheistic married couples behave together?

Great difference	[5]	(48)	22%
	[4]	(93)	43
	[3]	(42)	19
	[2]	(21)	10
No difference	[1]	(13)	6
			100%

86) How important is it that there be a significant difference between Christian and secular music?

Very important	[5]	(60)	28%
	[4]	(43)	20
	[3]	(48)	22
	[2]	(26)	12
Not important	[1]	(38)	18
	[NR]	(2)	1
			101%

96) When the Billy Graham Crusade visited the Tacoma dome last spring advertisements appeared in Seattle newspapers announcing events of the week. One such ad portrayed a husband and wife with their two children; the caption read "How to keep your family together when others are being torn apart."

How much do you agree or disagree with the underlying assumption here that Christians and Christian communities are characterized by unique qualities which provide an advantage in overcoming or avoiding the kinds of problems—familial, interpersonal, psychological—that plague American society in general?

Very much agree	[5]	(73)	34%
	[4]	(77)	35
	[3]	(34)	16
	[2]	(15)	7
Do not agree	[1]	(17)	8
	[NR]	(1)	*
			100%

97a) In general, should we expect a noticeable difference between behavior in the Christian community and behavior in the non-Christian community?

Yes, great difference	[5]	(111)	51%
	[4]	(68)	31
	[3]	(21)	10
	[2]	(9)	4
No difference	[1]	(7)	3
	[NR]	(1)	*
			100%

b) Specifically, should we expect Christians to be happier and more fulfilled than non-Christians?

Yes, very much	[5]	(66)	30%
	[4]	(83)	38
	[3]	(34)	16
	[2]	(15)	7
Not at all	[1]	(17)	8
	[NR]	(2)	1
			100%

98) In general, based upon your life experiences so far, would you say that there is a real difference between life in the Christian community and life in non-Christian society?

Yes, great difference	[5]	(57)	26%
	[4]	(96)	44
	[3]	(40)	18
	[2]	(18)	8
No difference	[1]	(4)	2
	[NR]	(2)	1
			99%

{Note: Only the #100b and #101b parts of the following questions are included in the S/P index}:

100a) How would you describe a person who lives a very Christian life? (Check one):

[1] a good person   [5] happy, contented
[2] helps other people   [6] charitable, giving, kind
[3] person who seeks God   [7] other: _____
[4] honest, trustworthy

100b) Now, read carefully: How possible is it for a non-Christian to be characterized by all of the above descriptions?

Impossible	[5]	(24)	11%
	[4]	(24)	11
	[3]	(34)	16
	[2]	(77)	35
Highly likely	[1]	(57)	26
	[NR]	(1)	*
			99%

101a) How would you describe a person who lives a very un-Christian life? (Check one):

[1] selfish, self-centered   [5] unhappy, sad
[2] one who does not seek or   [6] lost, without direction
   follow God's will   [7] bad person
[3] unconcerned, uncaring   [8] other: _____
[4] immoral conduct

101b) Now, once more, how possible is it for a true Christian to be characterized by all of the descriptions above?

Impossible	[5]	(60)	28%
	[4]	(50)	23
	[3]	(37)	17
	[2]	(38)	18
Highly likely	[1]	(32)	15
			101%

103) Think about SPU in relation to the city of Seattle. Refer to the map below:
{not reproduced}

a) Are there areas of the city which make you particularly uncomfortable or which strike you as un-Christian in atmosphere? Conversely, are there areas of the city you consider to be particularly Christian or conducive to a Christian atmosphere?

Yes, very much	[5]	(15)	7%
	[4]	(37)	17
	[3]	(54)	25
	[2]	(35)	16
Not at all	[1]	(73)	34
	[NR]	(3)	1
			100%

104) Often when visiting unfamiliar areas or encountering new people we have a natural tendency to think of ourselves as somewhat special and out of the ordinary, a cut above the average guy or gal on the street. Specifically, how much do you identify with some of your fellow students who made the following observations about these kinds of experiences?[691]

a) "I'm always thinking . . . I wonder what they. . . ? Well, I'm always thinking what other people are thinking, when I'm out in the world, away from SPU . . . wondering if they're Christians . . . yeah, I never did that back in high school. I was just oblivious to things like that."

Very much identify with	[5]	(6)	3%
	[4]	(31)	14
	[3]	(49)	23
	[2]	(53)	24
Can't identify with	[1]	(73)	34
	[NR]	(5)	2
			100%

---

[691] #104a-c counts for a possible score of 2-10 instead of 3-15. The average of the three items was taken and then multiplied by two. Justification: on the one hand I considered these attitudes too subtle and complex (and the introduction to the section too poorly thought out, tending to produce a defensive, affected reaction) to measure with just one item, and yet on the other hand I felt that including all three scores would overemphasize them in the index. Hence the compromise. Although "pride" in any form is considered sinful (a judgment with secure foundation in the gospels) and supposedly can be found in disproportionate quantities in secular society, nonetheless the motivations driving a dualistic vision of the world surely feed upon invidious distinctions, an elemental form of pride. Here evangelicals are torn between the logic of humility which considers such distinctions grounded in human-centered hubris and the dualistic evangelical (or "smile") logic which finds them indispensable. The above introduction tends to put one in a classical Biblical mood, dulling the more pungent evangelical instincts; it ought to have been toned down.

*b) " . . . I feel like I almost have something over other people . . . feel a little cocky
. . . you know, 'I know something that you don't know.' "*

Very much identify with	[5]	(3)	1%
	[4]	(14)	6
	[3]	(35)	16
	[2]	(54)	25
Can't identify with	[1]	(110)	51
	[NR]	(1)	*
			99%

*c) "You know it's funny . . . because I'm amazed at how acclimated I've become
to this place, to this school. I've had Christmas jobs at the Bon and at Safeway
and it just blows me away to get out there and think that the majority of the people I work with live together outside of marriage, have had a couple of divorces
by the time they're 28; the vast majority smoke, drink, you know, just the values
that simply aren't a part of my life right now, and even smelling cigarette smoke
on campus is weird 'cause you just don't do it . . . and so I'm amazed at what a
difference it is . . . culture shock . . . I feel very alone, very alienated . . . that they
could never know me or my values. It's like your some kind of archaic dino-
saur."*

*Whether or not you have had the same work experiences, in general how much do
you identify with these feelings?*

Very much identify with	[5]	(24)	11%
	[4]	(47)	22
	[3]	(48)	22
	[2]	(44)	20
Can't identify with	[1]	(53)	24
	[NR]	(1)	*
			99%

[S/P] Index score: (Twelve questions; possible score 12—60)

Lowest division [12] ——————— [60] Highest division

The Regression Tests

The regression of *[CRI 1]* Combined Religious Intensity scale #1 on *[S/P]* Sacred/Profane Index produces an R^2 of .625, which means that approximately 62% of the variation of the scores in the *[S/P]* Index can be directly explained by the variations in *[CRI 1]*. Adding question #47 to make the *[CRI 2]* scale brings an increase in the R^2 to .64. The numbers indicate a very strong statistical relationship between these two indices. These are simple regression results, meaning that I added up the various *[E]*, *[RP]*, and *[I]* Index scores from the original coding sheets to arrive at a single *[CRI 1]* score that was then regressed on a single *[S/P]* Index score. As for the potential problem of employing parametric tests on data that may not fit a normal distribution curve (as well as the other considerations of sample size, ordinal versus interval data, and randomness of the sample), I ran frequency distribution bar graphs to get some idea of the curves of the indices and other items. As I expected, *[CRI]* scales and the *[S/P]* Index are skewed slightly to the right, as is (loosely speaking) the *[RP]* Index. The *[I]* Index and #47 are roughly normal and #92, political beliefs, is skewed rightward (as is also the national population   curve). To further check, I ran the Spearman rank correlation test on most of these; the results are roughly the same except that they report a slightly weaker relationship in each case than the regression, something to be expected, I understand, given the more "robust" nature of the regression analysis. I was also curious about the influence of age or advancing class position upon this tendency to make invidious distinctions (thinking there might be parallels with a reported decline in cheating as students progressed from novices to upperclassmen). A regression of academic class and one for age on the *[S/P]* Index indicates a very slight negative relationship: advancing age (better yet, the influence of the faculty) may ever so slightly dampen this tendency to feel, see, and promote Christian and secular division.

Again, depending I suppose upon the credence one places in these sorts of measures (and one's view of the accuracy and value of responses to formal questionnaires), the results suggest that each individual index proves unreliable in detecting or predicting the dualistic mentality, but that when joined their powers of explanation increase considerably, the cumulative indices picking up the subtle changes in religious intensity responsible for variations in the inclination to divide the world into Christian and secular realms.

Finally, the point and purpose here is not so much the generation of the proof of a proposition, in the sense of demonstrating, for example, that evangelical religious intensity lies at the root of or *causes* an apartheid mentality—that the first phenomenon somehow or other varies independently from the second and is not simply joined by theoretical redundancy—as to suggest that the relationship between the two indices proves indispensable to the identification and definition of an individual as an evangelical. I am suggesting that this apartheid vision of the world is an integral, defining feature of the personality of the American evangelical, that the one is virtually indistinguishable from the other, and that any truly comprehensive analysis of the cultural phenomenon of American evangelicalism must begin with an appreciation and understanding of it.

Appendix B

Evangelical Exceptionalism:
Academic Bias, The Bankruptcy of the Sociology of Religion,
& The Disenchantment of American Society and Culture [692]

For more than a half-century social scientists have forecast rain on the parade of religion in America, either spotting or positioning thunder clouds and showers directly over the procession—the exceptional, exotic, award-winning float of evangelicalism in particular—anticipating that a flood of modernism and secularization would wash much of it away. But as with Mark Twain's observation[693] that people are always talking about the weather but no one actually *does* anything about it, such academic chatter has proven equally idle and fruitless; and, even more importantly, dead wrong. What is more, during that much anticipated period of decline two or three US Presidents have warmly embraced (and even traced their roots deeply within) evangelicalism and two of those surely would never have been elected without its votes. The most recent claimant, easily the oddest and most unlikely of the lot, had gone them all one better, having filled his administration with conservative Christians, the White House bursting at the seams with "faith-based" Religious-Right ideologues, many of whom routinely attended in-house prayer and Bible study sessions.[694] Indeed, as this

---

[692] As indicated in a footnote at the end of chapter one, this more academically directed and focused appendix originally followed that chapter as an additional introductory chapter two. Hence the more preliminary, anticipatory—perhaps even redundant—nature and tone of some of the remarks and content.

[693] Actually it may have originated with his friend, Charles Dudley Warner: "His article . . . on the New England climate is another sketch which has called out much sympathy and admiration. 'The weather in New England,' said Mr. Warner, 'is a matter about which a great deal is said and very little done.' " (from "The Author of 'My Summer In a Garden,' " in *The Book Buyer: A Summary of American and Foreign Literature*, Vol. VI. No. 2, March 1889.)

[694] Although there were several "conservative Catholics" appointed originally, one or two of whom remained on, the lion's share of the later cabinet and staff replacements or promotions came from the ranks of purebred evangelicals—Huckabee, Pompeo, Bolton, Cain, Moore et al. Trump's primary attorney, Jay Sekulow, was a perennial guest on *Praise The Lord,* the flagship televangelist talk show hosted by Paul and Jan Crouch, founders of the Trinity Broadcasting Network (TBN). It seemed as though virtually every week or so he would make an appearance, breathlessly recounting harrowing legal defenses of persecuted Christian individuals and groups.
—To get a feel for the mentalities of the men attracted to and surrounding Donald Trump, I highly recommend Jerome Corsi's *Silent No More* (Post Hill Press, 2019), a screed dedicated to

author most presciently forewarned in an earlier account: "If Supreme Court Justice Ruth Bader Ginsburg proves unable to extend her age and tenure to Old Testament proportions we may very well hover on the brink of bidding Roe v. Wade farewell, along with time-honored Madisonian principles of checks and balances, if not democracy itself. What looms on the horizon could make Margaret Atwood's dystopian *The Handmaid's Tale* look like a Sunday school picnic by comparison. Perhaps even some unsentimental Beltway veterans have begun pining for the ghost of Harry Truman, who reacted to having been conned by the crusading Billy Graham into kneeling in prayer on the White House lawn—verbatim accounts of their conversation subsequently leaked to the media—by forbidding the evangelist to ever set foot on the premises again.[695] Perhaps we can look back on that episode now with some fondness as one of the very few memorable *secular* interruptions—interventions even—peppering our political history."

And as for the infamous 2016 presidential election, observe how even the meddling Russians discerned and drew draughts from a deep well of political evangelicalism, seemingly primed and ready to pounce on any opportunity to advance their own Manchurian candidate, somehow or other immediately gleaning the meaning and significance of the purloined Podesta-Clinton e-mails:[696]

Trump, which concludes: "I have written this book in the belief that there are enough people left in this country who continue to adhere to the constitution and believe in God that Mueller and his Deep State co-conspirators will be stopped before they complete the transformation of the USA into the USSA. . . . IN THE END, GOD ALWAYS WINS! I am with God. Are you?"

[695] Kevin M. Kruse, *One Nation Under God: How Corporate America Invented Christian America*, Basic Books, 2016, 52.

[696] Just one of many Facebook items generated and spread virally by Putin's pesky little St. Petersburg cyberspace outfit. From the *US House Intelligence Committee* (Tamsin Shaw, "Beware The Big Five," *The New York Review of Books*, 4/5/2018.) It goes without saying that they *must* have had a few native co-conspirators. Just above and to the right of the flowing locks is a medallion: *Army of Jesus*.

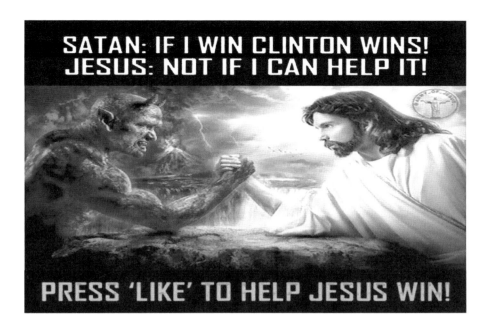

No wonder then that this likely collaboration with and/or exploitation of evangelical political angst and aims sent shock waves through the national media, although the episode merely confirmed, if not exponentially accelerated, an historic reluctance to seriously address the role of evangelicalism in American life and politics. For what was once an unstudied, inexplicable cultural embarrassment, one that former presidents like George Bush Jr. had occasionally only dabbled in or cuddled like a personal lap dog, suddenly morphed into a political Leviathan, brandishing newly sharpened fangs. No wonder liberal media recoiled and retreated even further into innocence and ignorance. No wonder few dared touch *our* lily-white evangelicalism with a ten-foot pole. That is, after all, most likely why and how Hilary Clinton lost Michigan, Ohio, and Pennsylvania: op-ed pieces flooded the national media—even the *Washington Post*—two or three weeks before the election decrying her fingernails-on-the-blackboard anti-religion screeching, sounding the alarm to innumerable klatches of disproportionately anxious, *culturally-insecure* white suburban women voters.[697] Forget for the moment locking

---

[697] That Clinton's own Methodism was pronounced—she had in fact become a "regular visitor" to *The Family*'s headquarters in Arlington (a secretive Christian political organization operating out of the now notorious Ivanwald mansion) and attended as an "active member" fellow Republican Senator Sam Brownback's weekly Senate Prayer breakfasts—could not have mattered less. The Religious Right played the secular paranoia card mercilessly. Clinton setting the record straight might have only muddied the waters, potentially unsettling her own base; so she swallowed the bitter pill of irony. (Jeff Sharlet, *The Family: The Secret Fundamentalism*

Crooked Hilary up for trumped-up imaginary crimes; evangelical resentment cut much deeper. So what if the Clinton Foundation laundered liberal monies from the likes of George Soros and his ilk? She's going straight to hell anyway. More importantly, indubitably, Democrats hate all religion except Islam;[698] *they hate your religion, they hate you.* Persecuted Christians hover precariously on the cusp of losing Christmas, of being herded off to Maoist, cultural-revolution-style re-education camps. It was all there in the e-mails, plain as day. Be thou woken, conscripts in the army of Jesus. Vote your Bible.[699]

The point is quite simple. Donald Trump is no unprecedented outlier. Long before Twitter arrived, the red-faced gargoyle spent years in his towers glued to the tube, watching televangelists, and later ringing them up to talk shop. As Susan Harding wrote so incisively years ago during the glory days of the scandals, he—like Jerry Falwell et al.—emerged from and operates in and out of a rich evangelical tradition, quite comfortably and effortlessly rolling out a thick toxic fog of *alternative facts.*

> The rule of inerrancy extends, not explicitly and by no means irrevocably (as it does to the Bible), to preachers and other "men of God." Specifically, everything Jerry Falwell authors is true. But truth is not automatic, transparent, unmediated.

---

at the Heart of American Power, Harper Perennial 2009, 272-277.) To this day, Sharlet represents the only academician or journalist who truly "gets" (at least one of) the central thrusts of evangelicalism. His two books on The Family nicely complement *Paradise Joe's.*

[698] "Marybeth Hagan: hacked e-mails show level of contempt for deeply religious," *The Virginian Pilot*, October 20, 2016. This one even made it to my hometown rag, *The Seattle Times*, 10/22/2016. And for statewide Pennsylvania: "Commentary: Clinton, team have contempt for Catholics," *The* [Philadelphia] *Inquirer*, 10/19/2016.
—Marc A. Thiessen, "Opinions: Hillary Clinton is a threat to religious liberty," *The Washington Post*, 10/13/2016.

[699] "Minimum number of times since September 2015 that Donald Trump has referred to Christmas in speeches: 23. Number of those references that suggested the holiday was under attack: 19." (from Factbase, "Harper's Index," *Harper's*, October 2017, 9.)
—Subsequent research has confirmed my own suspicions. Unfortunately, these observations were not deemed acceptable for mainstream consumption, but they are available to curious readers upon request (see Selected Bibliography): "In a new University of Pennsylvania study, political scientist Diana Mutz found that a pivotal group of voters—people who switched parties to back Trump—'were motivated by the vision of a frightening fall in social status.' *Those voters believed that the traditional primacy of 'white, Christian males' in the country was 'under serious threat.'* . . . *the Trump base was convinced that white Christians face more discrimination in rapidly changing America than blacks or Muslims.* . . . And why did a majority of white women vote for Trump? A separate study, by researchers at High Point University, found *these women also feel great 'trepidation' about the loss of traditional culture, and want to maintain distinct gender roles for men and women.*" (Tom Jacobs, "The real reason Trump was elected," *Pacific Standard*, referred to in *The Week*, May 11, 2018, 12.) {emphases added} [See the original Mutz paper: "Status threat, not economic hardship, explains the 2016 presidential vote," *PNAS Proceedings of the National Academy of Sciences*, May 8, 2018, 115 (19).]

It is the outcome of continuous exegetical exchanges between the Bible and its readers, a preacher and his people. A preacher's God-given authority, like the absolute truth of the Bible, is produced by a community of believers through its interpretive practices. It is as if Falwell, in his varied storied manifestations, were telling his followers, "Read me as you read the Bible. I appear in many versions. There are differences between the versions, and there are awkward silences and anomalies within them. My tales are troubled and they are troubling. Harmonize my discrepancies. Close my gaps. Overcome my troubles. *Make me whole.* Make me true.". . . . He produces the gaps, the anomalies, the excesses, the apertures for the uncanny, and his people produce faith by harmonizing his discrepancies. Moreover, as we shall see, these miraculous exchanges not only convert trouble into truth, doubt into certainty, deception into special election; they may, under the right circumstances, convert a poor, powerless preacher into a multi-million dollar powerhouse for God. . . . Both these stories, the story of Joshua and the story of Jerry, are "absolutely true." Indeed, they are not simply "true stories," they are "storied events." As we have seen, event and story in fundamentalist discourse have not been torn asunder. Biblical narrators, past and present, tell histories, the way things actually happened. Their stories are literally true in the sense that they do not represent history, they are history.[700]

How many times did the uncomprehending media erroneously repeat the Trump wishful thinking about the Coronavirus, substituting "magically" for "like a miracle?" Of course, they had no idea that *miracles* (of the "seed faith" fundraising kind) occur all the time within the alternative universe of evangelicalism. And most certainly, *redemptive* miracles were and remain a routine expectation within the apostolic traditions of the long suffering flocks of imperiled televangelists. For they joined in and suffered along with their prophets; an attack upon their leaders was an attack upon them. Moreover, the *greater* the mounting evidence that ought generate skepticism or disbelief

---

700 *The Book of Jerry Falwell*, op cit., 88-90, 110. {emphasis added} Again, the parallels with Trump abound, and astound:

> Below the surface of these public controversies, Falwell produced many more layers of trouble. On each of my half-dozen trips to Lynchburg from 1982 to 1989, I found that Falwell was scandalizing—was provoking the doubts of—his church people and co-workers in one way or another. Some of them were bothered by his financial and business ethics. Most of the many millions of dollars Falwell raised for his college, a home for unwed mothers, and other specific causes were used instead to support his television ministry; but such financial diversions, to the extent that they were known, were not troubling. His people were more troubled by the fact that his ministries were chronically overspent. They did not pay their vendors on time. They downsized without mercy. Moreover, some of the men Falwell hired to run the business and finance side of his ministries had criminal records. And then there were the periodic lawsuits. In 1986, for example, the Old-Time Gospel Hour was sued by an eighty-one-year-old widow for misappropriating money from her "nest egg," which she had entrusted to the ministry. (99)

in the average onlooker merely fuels the *greater* need for and invocation of additional world-confounding exceptional expressions of faith.

And so we have seen this thick veil of shtick before: *behold* Jimmy Swaggart as POTUS, rising phoenix-like from a Louisiana bayou swamp. He's back! And with a vengeance. Ideologically inebriated congregations are all too familiar with lying, cheating, stealing, and fornication[701]—the *lingua franca* and *modus operandi* of a goodly portion of alpha-male evangelicalism. And the s/cum keeps rising to the top, perennially so it seems. Like good ole boys wallowing all day long in the deep red Georgia mud of hypocrisy,[702] they still come up clean as a whistle, smelling like roses, when mama calls. Indeed, they can put shit on a platter and sell it as brownies to the faithful standing in line to worship Mr. Trump at his bread-and-circus rallies (to this day even). For many Religious Right pro-lifers affectations of piety merely provide a smokescreen, shrouding the sledgehammers looming over the heads of notoriously promiscuous secular females. Doesn't matter how many girls Brent (Bart) Kavanaugh might have harassed, deflowered, or raped; above all else, Roe v. Wade must fall.[703] For *it* remains one of the few

---

[701] *Plus c'est la meme chose:* "In recent months several high profile pastors—including Bill Hybels, the founder of the Chicagoland megachurch Willow Creek—have stepped down following accusations of sexual harassment, misconduct, or assault. . . . Paige Patterson, the head of a Southern Baptist Seminary, was pushed out after reports surfaced he had downplayed women's physical and sexual abuse throughout his years in ministry, including encouraging them not to report allegations of rape and assault to the police." (Emma Green, "Will Beth Green Lose Her Flock? . . . ," *The Atlantic*, October 2018.); Julie Zauzmer [from *The Washington Post*], "Southern Baptists debate way leader was ousted," *The Seattle Times*, 6/14/2018.
—"That saga was cited in a searing investigation by the Houston Chronicle and the San Antonio Express-News that found the Southern Baptist Convention repeatedly tolerated sexual assaults by clergymen and volunteers. The Chronicle found 380 credible cases of church leaders and volunteers engaging in sexual misconduct, with victims sometimes shunned by churches, urged to forgive abusers or advised to get abortions." (Nicholas D. Kristof, "Rapists Presented by Their Church as Men of God," *The New York Times*, 2/20/2019.)

[702] However, in general there is something much deeper going on here epistemologically than just hypocrisy, for hypocrisy tends to realize and own its own deceit or debauchery, perhaps even expresses embarrassment or attempts evasive qualifications when exposed, whereas purebred evangelicals like Donald Trump absorb their own fabrications or delusions. Hence the widespread, unprecedented "doubling-down" on obvious falsehoods throughout his administration.

[703] "Marjorie Dannenfer. . . . Since 1992, she has been at the head of the Susan B. Anthony list and has grown it into arguably the most powerful and effective anti-abortion organizing group in the country. . . . Yet the GOP candidates Dannenfelser so enthusiastically supports do little to value human life beyond limiting access to abortion. . . . When I point out some of those things . . . she talks about private-sector efforts to mediate these shortcomings. . . ." (Lisa Miller, "Marjorie Dannenfelser Used Donald Trump to Get Even Closer to What She Wants: No More Abortions," *New York Magazine*, October 15-28, 2018.)

modern bones of contention that can be picked without complete moral hypocrisy or compromise: the secular world is, after all, killing *something*. And so only at our peril do we call into question the pent-up sincerity of those issuing the marching orders of the army of Jesus. Donald Trump was/is much more than a shill of a conman, more than a spurned, spiteful Don Corleone wanna-be, more than an empty vessel into which has been poured the sour elixir of evangelicalism.[704] He's pure evangelical rat poison, through and through. If he didn't already exist, surely *they* would have had to invent him.

And so, surprise! Religion—the so-called *enthusiastic* kind—is still a very big deal, perhaps the biggest deal of all in American politics,[705] society, and culture. Has been right from the beginning, with the very first boatload of Pilgrims, followed by flotillas of slaves, the next very big deal.[706] But we will get to these larger themes, contexts, and dynamics in due course. First, we have a few smaller fish to fry.

Norteamericanos (henceforth *Americans* and *America*) seem to do and experience a lot of things—how shall I put it, *differently*? And for one last time, even more so than Luigi Barzini's beloved fellow Italians, we are truly "alone in

---

[704] Julie Zauzmer, "Acts of Faith: Paula White, prosperity preacher once investigated by Senate, is a controversial pick for inauguration," *The Washington Post*, 12/29/2016. See especially: Stephen Mansfield, *Choosing Donald Trump: God, Anger, Hope, and Why Christian Conservatives Supported Him* (Grand Rapids: Baker Books, 2017); and the particularly sycophantic, *God and Donald Trump* by Stephen E. Strang (Frontline, undated), 18-21; yet: ". . . . Christian leaders I respect have told me he is a *chosen vessel* being used by God despite his flaws." (ibid., xvi) {emphasis added}

[705] Beyond all the usual-suspect explanations for the Trump electoral victory grounded in either class, gender, race, xenophobic, Islamophobic, and other resentments was an even more significant cultural voting pattern predictor, "Christian nationalism." See Andrew L. Whitehead et al.'s persuasive analysis of a set of national post-election survey data, "Make America Christian Again: Christian Nationalism and Voting for Donald Trump in the 2016 Presidential Election," *Sociology of Religion: A Quarterly Review* 2018, 79:2. A better title might have added conservative, white, and evangelical to "Christian." Their six survey questions or "measures" of Christian nationalism are similar to items composing my own "Ideology index" in Appendix A.

[706] See Engen, *City on a Hill. . .* , op. cit.
—And in this second sense the New World white Americans are only standing upon the shoulders of European giants, as Tom Holland suggests in *Dominion: How The Christian Revolution Remade The World* (Basic Books 2019). And yet although "To live in a western country is to live in a society still utterly saturated by Christian concepts and assumptions. . . . So profound has been the impact on the development of Western civilization that it has come to be hidden from view." (13, 17) In many respects I will also claim that some very profound, albeit largely camouflaged and routinized, evangelical cultural assumptions have underlain the ideological thrust of a so-called American *exceptionalism*. They also need to be flushed out into the open and examined, as has been the intent of this book.

the world."[707] Ever since a several months-long road trip spanning the length and breadth of the USA following my graduation from college and an equally extensive first visit to Europe a few years later I have been struck by and reflected upon this difference. I remember distinctly—as though it were yesterday—wandering into an enormous park one fateful summer evening—nay, at two or three in the morning in fact—in Sevilla, Spain with some hesitation, not knowing what to expect, only to discover scores of families—and the children, seemingly no end to them, running around—feasting on paella and chattering away non-stop, seemingly lost in the absolute joys of kinship and life together in a veritable enchanted cultural world. I just sat with my travel companion (and future spouse) dumfounded, our mouths dropping wide open in amazement, as though we had been transported to another planet.[708] And then even later as I took a more academic approach to

---

[707] Barzini, Luigi, *The Italians* (Atheneum, 1964). But me thinks he doth protest a bit too much.

[708] The American sociologist, Phil Zukerman, experienced a comparable epiphany on his first bus ride into the second largest Danish city of Aarhus: "What happened during the bus ride was this: I felt a real sense of goodness. It was a sense of goodness that stemmed not from some internal endorphin rush, but rather, simply from taking in and observing the pleasant social world around me." Likewise, he also concluded: "*If only they could take this bus ride with me. . . . If only my fellow Americans could see that secular society. . . .*" (31) Morten, the husband of one of his colleagues he met while in Aarhus, had an altogether different experience when their family moved to California, near the Zuckermans. See especially 174-181. (*Society Without God: What The Least Religious Nations Can Tell Us About Contentment*, New York University Press, 2008.) Spain is, of course, decidedly Catholic, but as with the lingering remnants of Christianity in Scandinavia, it remains a largely vestigial, ceremonial "cultural religion."
—Few Americans get the chance to experience such things, as James Moscone writes of the New Victorian age that was ushered in with the '70s Religious Right: "It filtered into local communities across the nation. A suburban Colorado principal was briefly suspended for permitting junior high school students to taste a 'thimbleful' of wine during a three-hour meal in France. ('They tasted wine,' charged a spokesman for the school. 'They may have ingested alcohol.') . . . . Here in rural New Hampshire, a local high school asks parents to 'pledge to supervise all parties in their homes' and to 'welcome calls from other parents about the whereabouts of the kids.' " (*Hellfire Nation. . .* , 455.)
—In the interest of full disclosure, a more recent review of my journals from that initial European trip reveals impressions that much of Europe appeared an inauthentic tourist culture, and that for all its materialistic vacuity American society was in fact the more genuine item, at least in that one respect. Repeated exposure, and the addition of a Spanish son-in-law with all the extended family connections and implications, soon disabused me of this quite understandable erroneous first impression.
My reconsideration received further academic confirmation more recently, for as Marshall Sahlins aptly documents, such hybridizations or acculturations have occurred for centuries among non-western cultures (indeed in all cultures). The promotional self-identifications and merchandizing of culture and its artifacts, and the self-awareness of so doing, do not render such products or their sources inauthentic. "The current afterological fears that people trading in dances or artifacts, as by sales to tourists, are necessarily degrading their culture. . . . [their current stories representing no more than] 'invented traditions,' . . . . [or even] clearly

explore this apparent difference, various notions of an American "exceptionalism" continued to pop up and stick in my craw. Perhaps they originated from American academicians who had seldom or even never ventured abroad for any extended period of time. For although surely we have assumed a host of international responsibilities as the arsenal of democracy, as the modern world's frequent last best hope against the barbarians rattling the gates of civilization, there is still something claustrophobically different about American society and culture that tempers even this remarkably distinguished role on the world stage, reprises of which have begun to feel lately more like thankless burdens of our own making.

And just what sort of exceptionalism might this be?

In time it began to dawn on me that from the very onset of our colonial and then national experiment we have been riven by two distinctly flowing currents of difference. There was the initial New England Puritan venture into the wilderness,[709] a formula and project drawn from old-world Biblical prophecy, designed to create a new-world Jerusalem that would fulfill Torahic eschatologies and trigger an ultimate soteriology. Observe Puritan leaders like John Winthrop, whom we might think of not as saints but as emulative models or *figura*, exemplaries and pragmatic "appliers" of Christ, Luther, Calvin, and Cromwell in the wilderness. Soul seekers of religious freedom? Well, perhaps marginally so,[710] as they forged ahead, these divinely-burnished *exemplum fidei*, to the pitch of readiness in anticipation of the *Parousia*, or second coming of Christ.[711] This steady stream of faith juxtaposed in turn with the rivers of reason of the Enlightenment flowing through the

---

self-serving inversions of the colonizers' traditions. . . ," seriously overlooks how all societies are amalgamations of sorts, with pieced-together borrowings, even among the imagined purity of so-called pre-literate tribalisms. Indeed, beware of the long-lingering mythological invention of cultural homogeneity, however structurally rich in content. ("Two or Three Things . . . ," 411, 402-3.)

[709] "Alexis de Tocqueville's vision of 'the whole destiny of America [was] contained in the first Puritan who landed on these shores'. . . ." (Malcolm Gaskill, *Between Two Worlds: How The English Became Americans*, Basic Books, 2014, 387.)

[710] Marilynne Robinson makes a strong case for such in her "Which Way to the City on a Hill?" *The New York Review of Books*, July 18, 2019.
—By marked contrast: ". . . . this once persecuted minority of Puritans, whose 'vision,' Barry claims, 'would define—and still defines—the national consciousness of the United States,' decided that they had to impose order and orthodoxy on themselves with an unexpected ruthlessness." (from Gordon S. Wood's review of John M. Barry, *Roger Williams and the Creation of the American Soul: Church, State, and the Birth of Liberty*, in *The New York Review of Books*, 5/10/2012, 45.)

[711] Bercovitch, Sacvan, *The Puritan Origins of the American Self*, New Haven: Yale University Press, 1975.

veins of Jefferson, Madison, Franklin, Jay, Hamilton, Morris et al., leading to the world's first genuine representative democracy.[712] Both were exceptional in one tortured sense and yet only somewhat unique American hybrids, re-workings of earlier European ideas and models with a peculiar American twist; indeed the rapids, or trials and tribulations, of both can be seen coursing through the life and thoughts of their most profoundly iconic bridge or intermediary, the exemplary John Adams.[713] Much later, to thoroughly abbreviate a complex historical narrative, the latter stream of reason led ultimately to the pragmatism of FDR and the New Deal, and the other currents more directly and conspicuously to evangelicalism, conveyed and expressed in four (and now five) duly noted *Awakenings*. Not an inconsiderable number of historians looked back upon all this have located in the first stream currents of an eventual emerging so-called "civil religion," a seemingly polite, deferential, dumb-downed compromise of sorts that allows, among other things, the promulgation of the preposterous claim (and charade) of the Constitution's grounding in the Christian faith of (some of) our Founding Fathers. That the actual historical record belies any such thing scarcely matters to alternative reality evangelicalism,[714]and not even to many historians

---

[712] And yes I am aware of the oversimplification here, well documented in Michael Kammen's *People of Paradox: An Inquiry Concerning the Origins of American Civilization* (New York: Knopf, 1975), 247.

[713] "John Adams was voicing the most potent platitude of the era when he announced—as the country's self-styled Moses-Lycurgus-Nehemiah—that the *Arbella* fleet [of Winthrop's Puritans] had inaugurated the 'grand scene and Design in Providence, for the Illumination of . . . mankind over the Earth.' " (Bercovitch, op. cit., 88)

—Yet: "John Adams, the most moderate of the Founders, argued for the same position when he asserted, as early as 1786, that the thirteen states provided the first example of governments 'founded on the natural authority of the people alone, without a pretense of miracle or mystery.' " (Denis Lacorne, *Religion in America: A Political History*, New York: Columbia University Press, 2011, 144.) Leave it to a Frenchman (in the original French edition) to point this out to our own historians.

—And: "President John Adams signed a treaty with Tripoli in 1791 that stated, 'As the government of the United States of America is not in any sense founded on the Christian religion. . . .' " (Eboo Patel, *Out of Many Faiths: Religious Diversity and the American Promise*, Princeton University Press, 2018, 5.)

[714] Typical, from a seemingly bottomless well: "Liberalism is based on certain ideas, such as that of human dignity, that are actually predicated on Christianity and Biblical religion. Human dignity did not exist for the Greeks; and as we analyze the waves of modernity, it becomes evident that every attempt to anchor human dignity in something other than Biblical religion has failed. The religion of the West gave [us] . . . an understanding of obligations to that God which are also distinct from and above the obligations to society and state. . . . Together these are the beliefs that created, and grounded, the concepts at the core of the American democratic experiment." (Joseph Bottum, *An Anxious Age: The Post-Protestant Ethic and the Spirit of America*, New York: Image Books, an imprint of Crown Publishing, 2014, 288-9.)

working in evangelical academia. Certainly no reader of this book will find this surprising.

We have explored this notion of American exceptionalism in some detail, though not in the usual way, which has tended to overlook if not intentionally ignore any number of unpleasant features, evangelical religion among them. Most accounts pass evangelical religion by as an almost too embarrassing and peripheral mess of wagon-train road kill, as did Richard Hofstader in his highly-regarded *Anti-intellectualism in American Life*.[715] I instead bring it center stage, directly linking it with some rather more fundamental questions regarding the role of religion in our culture—such as, for one instance, *why is religion so seemingly important here, and relatively unimportant over there, across the Atlantic among the Europeans, our nearest cultural ancestors?* And why does evangelical religion, in particular—among all other contemporary religious phenomena—seem to cut so wide a swath, occupying so large and often troubling a portion of our collective imagination?[716]

---

[715] Long after Hofstader, Garry Wills, our most distinguished (and patient) explainer of the American experience, chastened his fellow academicians: "In a time of reviving fundamentalisms around the world, some Americans have rediscovered our native fundamentalists (a recurring, rather than cumulative, experience for the learned). It seems careless for scholars to keep misplacing such a large body of people. Nonetheless, every time religiosity catches the attention of intellectuals, it is as if a shooting star had appeared in the sky. One could hardly guess, from this, that nothing has been more stable in our history. . . than religious belief and practice." (*Under God: Religion and American Politics*, Simon & Schuster 1990, 15-16.)
—Then there's the equally distinguished Jon Butler's admonishment: "Twentieth-century Americans' supernatural beliefs and robust religious affiliation rates directly challenge historians' treatment of the modern United States as a nation that has drifted free from both personal and public religion." ("Jack-in-the-Box Faith: The Religion Problem in Modern American History," *The Journal of American History*, March 2004, 1362.)
—"In fact, until very recently religion was sidelined in most fields of modern American history. Be it the history of politics, immigration, or civil rights, religious faith was pushed to the margins when it made any appearance at all. It seemed that only historians of religion took religion seriously. . . ." (Andrew Preston, *Sword of the Spirit, Shield of the Faith*, Alfred A. Knopf 2012, 5.)
—Then again, anthropologists need to own up to their own seeming lack of interest or "repugnance" to the "unsettling" ways evangelical Christians make them "recoil." (Ruth Marshall, "Christianity, Anthropology, Politics," *Current Anthropology*, Vol. 55, Supplement 10, December 2014, 346.) Susan Friend Harding's *The Book of Falwell. . .* , is a welcome notable exception.

[716] I am happy to report that this glaring omission has been partially filled by an earlier work that I unfortunately did not come across until my own book was completed, James A. Morone's *Hellfire Nation: The Politics of Sin In American History* (2003), relevant references to which I have added after the fact. Although I don't agree with him at all that the '60s and '70s Woodstock generation represents the 5th "Great Awakening" in a largely American evangelical wax and wane spiritual cycle, I have come to think of it as a more macro-level companion to my volume. There is much to relish:

Garry Wills concludes his monumental treatise on religion in America, *Head and Heart: American Christianities,* on an ambivalent note: ". . . . for long stretches of our history, the religion that attracted most people has been Evangelical."[717] Undeniably, there have been occasional periods of what

> . . . . the American moral epic has been pushed to the side . . . rarely explored as a mainspring of American politics and culture. . . . The Puritans groped back to the tried and true—they found terrible new enemies to define them. The saints constructed their 'us' against a vivid series of immoral 'them': heretics, Indians, witches. Each enemy clarified the Puritan. . . . Political scientists have overlooked almost everything about them. . . . Great bouts of moral fervor (from the second Great Awakening that roared through the country in the early nineteenth century to the cultural wars rushing through it today) *look less like anomalies and more like the soul of American politics.* . . . The Puritan search for God organized all those pre-liberal institutions; piety drove them toward their modern forms. . . . What makes the United States distinctive? There are plenty of celebrated views, but most ignore the restless American quest for heaven. . . . (32, 101) {emphasis added}

—By contrast, unfortunately, Marilynne Robinson, the much celebrated favorite author of Barack Obama, seeks largely monopolized virtues in her highly selective reading of the Puritan errand:

> Winthrop's speech illustrates the fact that the Scriptures themselves could serve as a manifesto. Puritan interest in attempting a return to Biblical standards of life in society was not a nostalgia for an imagined past, a desire to live ancient lives, but a will to reform society in keeping with vastly more human laws and teachings of both testaments. Scripture gave authority to a vision of equity and also grace as standards of social interaction by which Christendom had not chosen to abide. . . . I am confident that our cultural investment in the image of Puritans as intolerant is vigorous enough that someone would have produced the damning evidence if it existed. ("Which Way to the City on a Hill?" *The New York Review of Books,* 7/18/19.)

Ms. Robinson: duly consult Jon Butler, *Awash in a Sea of Faith. . . ,* among others in the bibliography: "In both war and peace, the Puritans had ensured the total destruction of the Pequot nation. . . . what we would today call genocide." (Andrew Preston, 38.); John Demos, "Satan in Salem," *The New York Review of Books,* 12/3/2015; and one of my favorite's, Malcom Gaskill, *Between Two Worlds: How The English Became Americans,* Basic Books, 2014: "Edward Howes in 1632 warned John Winthrop Jr. . . . [that they] should not, for instance, cut off dissidents' ears." Indeed even Cotton Mather *then,* but not Ms. Robinson *now* seemingly, found Salem "puzzling. . . [was] troubled. . . . [urged] reparations. . . . [we ought] beg forgiveness." (125, 377)

Marxism experienced a similar corruption of original good intentions. *From each according to his abilities, to each according to his needs* has a warm and fuzzy early Christian communitarian feel to it. That the realities of the Gulag and assorted cultural revolutions so decidedly violate the scriptural ideals of Marx and Engels was neither less predictable nor more excusable as incongruous excesses than were the Puritan executions of witches and the genocide of the Pequot nation or the more recent evangelical-supported-and-celebrated campaign of hate of Donald Trump (let alone a hell of a lot in between). *They were and you are what you do, what you*

Wills calls "balance" between "enlightened" and other enthusiastic forms of American Christianity, but on the whole we have remained doggedly, consistently evangelical to the core of our religious cultural being.

Oddly enough also, in spite of all we have experienced the last half-century or so, it remains a common wisdom for some that the American is a predominately secular society. As evidence, contrasts are drawn between extremist, often state-supported fundamentalisms around the globe and our own disinterested separation of church and state. On one level at least, our *laissez-faire* denominationalism or disestablishmentarianism (which many may recall as the longest, thorniest word on mid twentieth-century primary school spelling bee lists) appears to ensure an impartiality or even indifference toward the articulations and divisions of faith, indeed in ironic ways that the framers of our Constitution scarcely foresaw.[718] And yet on another level one could argue (too much so, in the case of some academicians) that our first amendment de-monopolization of religion, along with other uniquely American features, has produced an astonishingly original, constantly fermenting social and cultural environment, one in which some rather seminal forms of religious culture have emerged and continue to reproduce themselves.[719] By and large, the most culturally significant and resilient

---

unleash upon us all. The claim that evangelicals are not responsible for *this*—for Trump and his ilk; that evangelicals are actually so much better than *this*—rings as false as any modern Marxist apology for Stalin. The devil is in the details of the implementation, in the inexcusable reality.

[717] Penguin Press, 2007, 551.

[718] According to R. Laurence Moore, the founders "believed that sectarian divisions were the unhealthy products of an established church. . . ." and not a potential unintended consequence of a free market of religion, as we might otherwise expect. See *Selling God: American Religion in the Marketplace of Culture*, New York: Oxford University Press, 1994, 81.

—Then there's Garry Wills, who finds paradox and irony at every turn: "The secular state came from the zeal of religion itself. The Rhode Island Civil Code accomplished this, as the Constitution would later do, by a restriction of the secular power's sphere. . . . It was the most religious community that produced the most religiously neutral state, just as—a century later—it would be a very religious nation that produced the first secular state." And, perhaps needless to add—a century after this—*vice-versa.* (*Under God. . .* , 352-3.)

[719] I am particularly taken by Saba Mahmood's discussion of these matters in her marvelous *Religious Differences in a Secular Age: A Minority Report* (Princeton University Press, 2016). American academicians tend to think of the problematical dynamics associated with the separation of church and state as a uniquely American feature, with Europe a largely secular phenomenon and the Muslim world too authoritarian to even trigger them. Not so, she persuades us. In fact she adds "Should the US government allow prayer in public school, or fund religious programs in prisons?" to a host of similar contentious issues that get addressed worldwide (Egypt in particular), arguing that religious freedom and public/private distinctions are fraught with "paradoxes" and "internal contradictions" that render the idea of a purely

of these has been evangelicalism. Indeed, all told, our accumulated experience suggests that the American is anything but a secular society. The survey data, as well as a host of other telling observations, lend support to the claim that we may in fact be *more religious* than at any point in our history and that, furthermore, we may be one of, if not *the most*, religious nation on the planet.[720]

As Charles Taylor acknowledges in his monumental work, *A Secular Age*:

> . . . . indeed, educated, cultivated Europeans are extremely uncomfortable with any overt manifestations of either strong nationalism or religious sentiment. The contrast to the U.S. in this regard has often been remarked. And it might help to take up here one of the most debated issues in the field of secularization theory, that of the "American exception"—or, if one likes, seen from a broader perspective, the "European exception." Put either way, we are faced with a strong even if not uniform pattern of decline [of religion] in European societies, *and virtually nothing of the sort in the U.S.A.* How can this difference be explained?[721]

---

secular, noninterventionist liberal state a chimera. (See pp. 4-5 especially.) She helps us understand and place the so-called "persecution complex" of American evangelicals in a wider context.

—Martha Nussbaum, somewhat by contrast, might argue for a bit of American exceptionalism in this regard, extremist (Tea Party) evangelicals and Trump movement to the contrary notwithstanding: "[religious restrictions] that would have gone a long way in Europe are going nowhere in the United States. . . . Nobody is calling for sweeping constitutional changes that would remove the free exercise rights in question. . . . shows a strong U.S. consensus in support of the constitutional principles I've been defending, principles that most of Europe has never accepted. . . . . On many issues our nation is divided, but the free exercise of religion is not among those issues." (*The New Religious Intolerance: Overcoming The Politics of Fear in an Anxious Age*, Cambridge: Harvard University Press, 2012, 221-23.)

[720] "In 1991, 42 percent of Americans regularly attended church, which is almost exactly the same figure as the number of churchgoers in the thirties (41 percent in 1939). . . . [whereas] in France . . . about 12 percent of the population attends church, and in England, as a recent poll in the London *Sunday Express* discovered, 34 percent of Britons do not even know why Easter is celebrated." (Lawrence Wright, *Saints and Sinners*, New York: Alfred A. Knopf, 1993, xii.)

—See Jon Butler, *Awash in a Sea of Faith. . .*, 1, 4, 283, for additional comparisons with Europe.

—"According to a 1994 survey by *Redbook*, 70 percent of Americans believed in the existence of Satanic cults engaged in ritual abuse; nearly one-third believed that the FBI and local police were purposely ignoring their crimes." (Wendy Kaminer, "The Last Taboo," *The New Republic*, 14 October 1996, 32.)

—I would remind the reader that the best-selling book in America during the 1970s was Hal Lindsey's *The Late Great Planet Earth* (Zondervann 1970), the work a telling instance of pouring old dispensational millenarian wine into new wineskins. Then there's Texas evangelist John Hagee's *Beginning of the End: The Assassination of Yitzhak Rabin and the Coming Antichrist* (Nashville, Tennessee: Thomas Nelson, Inc., 1996) which shot up the New York Times bestseller list., selling more than 800,000 copies by June of 1997.

[721] Cambridge: Harvard University Press, 2007, 522. {emphasis added}

How indeed? And yet keep in mind that none of this sprang upon us over-night, of course. Taylor rattles off a number of historical factors that may have something to do with it: the immigration experience, disparate hierar-chies of all kinds—ecclesiastical and otherwise, deference towards elites and the intelligentsia, variations upon social integration, identity, traditionalism, egalitarianism, and patriotism, all contributing to the seemingly myriad pat-terns or ways nations and civilization distinguish themselves from one an-other. And yet again, having assembled quite an impressive array of the usual historical suspects, he somewhat loses his bearings and nerve, *perhaps* unable to convince himself that he had actually done much better than it might ap-pear on the surface.

> I am only half-satisfied with this answer. . . perhaps three-quarters. . . . Here
> I confess that I am making stabs in the dark. *A fully satisfactory account of this difference,*
> *which is in a sense the crucial question facing secularization theory, escapes me.*[722]

As it has eluded quite a number of academicians—none, arguably, more dis-tinguished than Taylor—am I then foolhardy to press on? Is this too much to ask of anyone? And yet the book you hold in hand does in fact attempt to address this very "crucial question" head on, full throttle. What truly ac-counts for this American difference? What makes us unique in the world?[723]

---

[722] *A Secular Age*, 522-30. {emphasis added} Indeed I invite the curious reader to try to make any more sense of the Taylor text than I have.
—Odd then that George M. Thomas discerns little difference: "Protestantism clearly was transnational. North American awakenings and revivals, from the First Great Awakening of the 1740s through the nineteenth-century revivals through the birth of Pentecostalism at the turn of the twentieth century were all trans-Atlantic phenomena.[13] Nation-building, moreo-ver, went hand-in-hand with missionary activity throughout the world and with the constitut-ing of the indigenous person as a soul needing salvation." ("Religious Movements, World Civil Society, and Social Theory," *The Hedgehog Review*, Vol. 4, No. 2, Summer 2002, 59.)
—Yes, Pentecostalism is now spreading all over the world (see Allan Heaton Anderson, *To The Ends of the Earth: Pentecostalism and the Transformation of World Christianity*, Oxford University Press, 2013), but American evangelicalism nonetheless remains an indigenous, *culturally* unique phenomenon, no matter its particular reception and expression abroad.

[723] Of all the European sociologists of religion who have addressed this matter of exception-alism and secularization I am particularly fond of the approach taken by Grace Davie. She contends that the European churches are seen as fail-safe "public utility" institutions, com-fortable old shoes that even though not actively attended nonetheless "act vicariously" for non-attendees. Hence "religious institutions matter even to those who are not 'participants' in them. . . ." The concept of such muffled, remote, trickle-down religiosity is immediately grasped by her European audiences, but proves "not part of American self-understanding" stateside. It proves a completely foreign experience. Although this barely addresses the evan-gelical core of the American difference, I find it one useful descriptive *symptomatic* expression of it. ("Is Europe an Exceptional Case?" *The Hedgehog Review*, Spring & Summer 2006, 26-27.)

Looking back, we Americans seem to have chosen a path or direction very much less well traveled. And yet was there ever really a choice—or an "option," which is one of Taylor's prized features of what he calls this new "Age of Authenticity"—presented *us*? Was there ever a discernible fork in that original road, heading off in one direction or another? I approach this question—this conundrum even—somewhat incidentally, in the course of advancing a rather larger project and claim, the beans of which are now, once again, spilled all over the floor: namely, that *evangelical religion occupies the ideological heart of American society, is in fact that decisive hydrogen-like element on our very own cultural periodic table which so clearly distinguishes us from our European forebears.* Aside from the more remote extremist elements of Jihadist Islam, there is nothing quite like it—this *difference*, this *exceptionalism*, this *us*—anywhere else in the modern industrialized world. *This* evangelicalism business truly sets us apart.[724] The rest (European Enlightenment hybridizations largely) proves just fussy window-dressing, decorous distraction from the core architecture of our national cultural identity and distinction—dare I write, *soul*.[725] Unfortunately also, at the risk of setting Lincoln to stir in his Calvinist grave, such a distinction scarcely represents or captures the better angels of our nature. My goodness, *were it otherwise*.

In this regard the pursuit of an explanation of a particular, practical, empirically-demonstrable American difference—of an uniquely American origin, *meaning*, and *significance*—just happened over the course of its explication to morph, incidentally, into a more *general theory of difference*. As with any evolutionary scheme and much of what follows, I didn't see that train of a development or mutation coming down the tracks at all. And yet what a nice surprise when it pulled into the station! Looking back, that which reared its head out of all that steam and commotion was an idea or concoction central to this larger emerging theory, what I would like for us all now to begin thinking of and talking about as the principle of *cultural vacuums*, a conception whose appearance on the scene might seem in retrospect an almost inevitable unintended theoretical consequence of my labors. But not so back then

---

[724] Claude S. Fischer reads the matter differently, making an arguable case for "voluntarism" as our nation's unique feature. See *Made in America: A Social History of American Culture and Character* (University of Chicago Press 2010), 11, 240. Most likely the reader of *Paradise Joe's* will come away with an entirely different view.

[725] More recently, Sam Haselby tends to agree: ". . . . it was American Protestantism and not any sort of classical republicanism that was most important in shaping the development of American nationalism. . . . The post-revolutionary decades in America may have seen the greatest explosion of Christian religiosity since the seventeenth century or even the Reformation." (from Gordon S. Wood's review of *The Origins of American Religious Nationalism*, Oxford University Press, 2105, in *The New York Review of Books*, July 9, 2015.)

at the beginning of all this, as is also the case with virtually everything else that I eventually encountered or uncovered.

And so then with respect to that incidental surprise, what do I have in mind here by the expression *cultural vacuum*? Actually, it is a rather simple, perhaps even obvious, notion that will not require the hundreds of pages issued by Charles Taylor (with no apparent satisfactory outcome) to arrive at what I believe is a rather more rewarding conclusion (much as I admire Mr. Taylor's more sophisticated Herculean effort and humility) regarding what was for him only a nagging, unresolved peripheral concern.

Initial clues can be discovered in the American Puritans' proverbial errand into the wilderness, as Perry Miller first coined it. Overlooked or de-emphasized for years by scholars were virgin New World settlements *Awash in a Sea of Faith*, as Jon Butler so aptly characterized them, assemblages of common folk who brought occult idioms and practices with them across the Atlantic from their European villages. The unpacking of such cultural baggage complicated matters almost immediately. Understandably on guard at every turn, Puritan leaders descried both Indian devils lurking in the woods *without* and pagan preternatural presences animating the imaginations of their more unwashed, much less doctrinaire, fellow settlers *within*. A similar translocation occurred farther South where boatload upon boatload of slaves arrived fully steeped in African witchcraft and other spirited flights of fancy.[726]

Against these still vibrant forms and their hosts, however they may have in some ways vaguely precursed later evangelical epiphenomena, colonial authorities and masters unleashed pogroms—legislation and campaigns—to eradicate all remnants of transplanted pagan idioms from their more ortho-dox reformist dispensational communities. Although there were certainly regional and sectarian variations, by and large these purges proved most venal and destructive among southern plantation slaves, producing what Butler calls an "African spiritual holocaust" or the " 'death of the African gods' in America."[727] And so as European totems and ciphers were systematically routed from the founding villages[728] and from ensuing settlements venturing

---

[726] *Awash In a Sea of Faith*, op. cit. For example, although she cites Butler in her Chapter Five ("Suggestions for Further Reading," 191), one among several oddly sequenced sections and chapters that is vaguely related to this period, Catherine L. Albanese quite curiously passes over this important aspect of the early Puritan settlements. (*America: Religions and Religion*, Belmont: Wadsworth, 2nd ed., 1992.)

[727] Ibid., 157.

[728] There was indeed more to these developments than Butler could fully address. Once this new Puritan order was established "New England's Congregational establishment" would in time have to contend with the growing discontent of communicants who came to view their

forth to the West a *cultural vacuum* of sorts was created into which more conventional, legitimated "enthusiastic" streams of emerging evangelicalism would eventually flow, filling a yawning cultural void.[729] Observe here then the first hint of an American difference. Over time, ossification had set in among the original settlements—orthodoxy caught applying the heavy hand

---

churches as "dark place"(s) devoid of spiritual "light." Of course the New England environment was challenging enough, but there was *something* deeply *meaningful* missing from their lives. Parishioners experienced a host of joyless, tedious formal procedures, tasks, and routines that seemed to dominate their church communities, having to meet "anxiety-inducing standards for church membership." No wonder then that

> John Brown and his ministerial colleagues inveighed against the 'Emtiness of all Earthly Enjoyments,' and they enjoined their parishioners to imagine themselves as 'strangers and Pilgrims here upon earth.' Well-versed in Reformed theology, their parishioners understood that the diligent performance of religious duties would never merit salvation for them. They nonetheless persisted in the belief that their failure to observe solemn religious obligations would call down the wrath of God on their bodies . . . families . . . towns.

They were caught between a rock and a hard place. And so it was into this second socially-created void that rushed the seemingly world-lifting succor of the so-called first Great Awakening of the 1740s led by George Whitefield from England, a preacher who "repudiate[d] the idea of the godly walk," [or Arminianism] bringing new rejuvenating ideas of adult baptism and daily infusions of the Holy Spirit, among others, offering disillusioned, wilderness-challenged settlers visions of a "new religious world." What is more, "Other alienated dissenters, embittered by years of maltreatment, departed for new settlements on the northern [and eastern Massachusetts] frontier." (Douglas L. Winiaerski, *Darkness Falls on the Land of Light: Experiencing Religious Awakenings in Eighteenth-Century New England,* University of North Carolina Press, 2017, 5, 18, 28, 33.) With this monumental tome, Mr. Winiaerski has now rendered all previous accounts obsolete.

And so we see the beginning of a series of cultural improvisations that fall considerably short of their more fertile traditional European templates. A meaningful *something* is sought, but an ultimately satisfying *meaning* and *significance* denied. One vacuum after another appears, or gets manufactured, hollowed out, and then filled by the approximations of evangelical ersatz-culture, be they eighteenth and nineteenth-century western frontier towns or, much later, the ensuing two centuries of cookie-cutter suburbs. All hastily thrown together ticky-tacky vestigial substitutions for that *something* which is somehow or other unconsciously sensed or pined for as *missing*.

[729] One of the most prominent Christian historians working in a major public university, Randall Balmer, seemingly unacquainted with Jon Butler's work, attributes the evangelical surge west to one ecclesiastical document alone, "The Last Will and Testament of the Springfield Presbytery. . . . The effect of the Last Will and Testament on American evangelicalism was to reorient it from the East to the West, from a dependence on European forms steeped in tradition and toward the western frontier, which offered a kind of tabula rasa." (*Evangelicalism in America,* Waco: Baylor University Press, 2016, 15-19.)

of an increasingly tiresome intolerance too many times.[730] Taking advantage, frontier-induced and fanned Awakenings rushed in to re-enchant feral, culture-starved settlements, creating an entirely new synthetic indigenous spiritual order.[731] But what kind of cultural order?

Apparently an order no more satisfying or enriching than what the emigrants had brought over with them originally and then hastily attempted to re-inflate. Indeed the disenchantment of some New World settlers with what had been transplanted, as well as what had emerged and evolved, became increasingly manifest over time. For although the early Puritans and subse-

---

[730] Sam Haselby has an original take on this, dividing the emerging currents into "frontier revivalism and national evangelism." (mentioned in Gordon S. Wood's review of *The Origins of American Religious Nationalism.* . . , op. cit.)

[731] There were other factors as well contributing to this cultural vacuum, as Claude S. Fischer reminds us:

> Classic organic communities, in the mold of old European villages, were rare even among the earliest North American settlements. The Puritans may be an exception. . . . [but even "Those villages could not really be communities the way peasant villages were. . . . They were instead 'intentional communities' formed by contracts among a self-selected elite. . . . Even birth into a Puritan village did not guarantee full membership; choice did. . . . required people to have and describe a conversion experience."] And the present worked against strong communities. Most newcomers arrived as individuals; in the first generations, three-fourths of all white settlers between fifteen and sixty years of age came alone to America. Most came as indentured servants or deported criminals. . . . Most of the other immigrants responded to publicity in Europe claiming that America offered white men the chance to become truly independent. . . . Once having paid off their debt for passage, settlers typically moved from place to place, usually rural outposts so scattered that simply seeing other people was difficult. If they moved to towns, they usually settled among people of diverse nationalities, and trades. Many lived in villages or towns with so much turnover, turmoil, and warfare that the communities could hardly have exercised the sort of social control found in the classic peasant village. . . . [Yet, elsewhere, inexplicably] In many an emerging colonial village or town elders came to monitor residents' lifestyles, actions, and words; they were 'morally intrusive and coercively communalistic.' . . . . Then an expanding liberalism, an evolving voluntarism, broke loose in the late eighteenth century.

Although "much of that experience also dictated cooperation. . . ," it was a kind of "mutual assistance [that] entailed much more pragmatic and contractual arrangements   . . . . Cooperation rested on carefully counting favors; it was not or not simply a matter of social duty, moral obligation, or neighborly feeling." Exchange practice arose not only out of frontier conditions, it was both fostered and reinforced though self-reliance ideologies that drew upon a basic "Reformed Protestantism early on and evangelicalism later. . . ." And by no means was this the mutual aid of Kropotkin villages. (*Made in America:*. . . , 102-3; interjected quotes, 105, 108, 110.)

quent doctrinaire descendants had thoroughly convinced themselves of the satanical nature of the savages lurking in the wilderness, those who had actually been captured and whisked off to live amongst the natives soon saw things differently. As in Sebastion Junger's account:

> It may say something about human nature that a surprising number of Americans—mostly men—wound up joining Indian society rather than staying in their own. They emulated Indians, married them, were adopted by them, and on some occasions even fought alongside them. *And the opposite almost never happened:* Indians almost never ran away to join white society. Emigration always seemed to go from the civilized to the tribal, and it left Western thinkers flummoxed about how to explain such an apparent rejection of their society.
>
> 'When an Indian child has been brought up among us, taught our language and habituated to our customs,' Benjamin Franklin wrote to a friend in 1753, 'if he goes to see his relations and makes one Indian ramble with them, there is no persuading him ever to return.'
>
> On the other hand, Franklin continued, white captives who were liberated from the Indians were almost impossible to keep home: 'Tho' ransomed by their friends, and treated with all imaginable tenderness to prevail with them to stay among the English, yet in short time they become disgusted with our manners of life . . . and take the first opportunity of escaping again into the woods.'
>
> . . . . a Seneca captive named Mary Jemison . . . . became so enamored of Seneca life that she once hid from a white search party that had come looking for her . . . . [writing] at the end of her long life. . . . 'No people can live more happy than the Indians did in times of peace . . . their lives were a continual round of pleasures.'
>
> . . . . In an attempt to stem the flow of young people into the woods, Virginia and other colonies imposed severe penalties on anyone who took up with the Indians. The Puritan leaders of New England found it particularly galling that anyone would turn their back on Christian society: 'People are ready to run wild into the woods again and to be as Heathenish as ever if you do not prevent it,' an early Puritan named Increase Mather complained in a tract called *Discourse Concerning The Danger of Apostasy.* [732]

Meanwhile, back across the Atlantic, an altogether different ecclesiastical, intellectual, and peasant cultural developmental arc continued its path through what Charles Taylor calls an "Age of Mobilization," wherein traditional Catholic and Protestant institutions embedded within and occasionally contending against monarchies, revolutions, and each other, traced a unique array of Old World social, political, and cultural patterns and consequences. In marked contrast to the "New World," *ancien* cultural idioms and forms malingered on, mysteries of the occult proving in many cases complementary to, or equally yoked with, the mysteries of the Virgin Mary,

---

[732] *Tribe: On becoming and Belonging*, Twelve, Hachette Book Group, 2016, 2-3, 10-11. {first emphasis added}

although certainly experiencing episodic reminders of imperilment, interspersed with various inquisitions.

> Men and women sought out occult practitioners to 'resolve, direct, and helpe.' as an Essex Puritan, Thomas Pickering, put it. . . . The laity of early modern Europe often saw little difference between the supernaturalism invoked through magic and that pursued by the churches. . . . [And, although there were some critics, 'led principally by clergymen,' even] University-educated elites drifted toward complex, highly intellectualized forms of occultism. . . .
>
> Popular and learned occultism also shifted after 1680. Although historians, usually citing the advance of "Enlightenment" and scientific movements, have argued that magic, astrology, and divination disappeared in the early eighteenth century, they actually underwent a remarkable *folklorization*. This transformation allowed them to survive in the largely illiterate and poor segments of English society even as they did indeed often disappear from elite and literate segments of society.[733]

Among the New England Puritans, by contrast, no such folklorization of traditional enchantments occurred. True there were substantial cultural transplantations to the new colonies, as David Hackett Fischer exhaustively documents in *Albion's Seed: Four British Folkways in America*, but aside from wondrous sightings—". . . . unicorns lived in the hills beyond the Hudson . . . mermaids swam in the waters off Cape Ann . . . tritons played in Casco Bay. . . ."—Fischer primarily documents an inextinguishable "Puritan obsession with Witchcraft." Although he does note "several forms of magical obsession" common for the times, they go unnamed or unexplored; instead we largely encounter only "providential magic. . . they searched constantly for clues to God's purposes." Such concerns were by no means original, tracing back to East Anglia, "the country of Essex," but they routinely applied a new world spin to them. For as we now know, witchcraft, along with the occult, ultimately suffered the holy flame of extermination.[734] Hence the resulting

---

[733] Ibid., 22, 24-25, 28.

—As for farther north, H. Arnold Barton avers that "well into the late 1700s, the Christianity of most Danes and Swedes wasn't theologically or Biblically grounded, but simply part of a larger worldview: 'In the peasant world the Christian God and Devil coexisted with their predecessors, a host of supernatural beings—trolls, elves, watersprites, fairies, ghosts—and ultimate concern for salvation through the church was balanced by immediate needs to propitiate the spirits of farm, forest, and stream. "Wise" old men and women were charged with the cure of man and beast, and undertook a variety of other transactions with the unseen world.' " (Phil Zuckerman, *Society Without God: What The Least Religious Nations Can Tell us About Contentment*, New York University Press, 2008, 124-5.)

—Hence the greater persistence of the occult in Europe today. See Tables 183, "Belief in Astrology," and 184, "Homeopathy," in Peter Baldwin's *The Narcissism of Minor Differences: How America and Europe Are Alike, An Essay in Numbers* (Oxford 2009), 174.

[734] (Oxford 1989, 125-130.) Fischer obviously had no access the Butler's book, which was published one year later.

scorched-earth *tabula rasa* upon which the new order could sketch and foist its cumbersome, increasingly enthusiasm-bereft Puritan designs.[735]

For better or worse, a glance back then—over *there*—at an emerging European contrast reveals a virtual absence of evangelical forms of religion and a less intense but vaguely similar incremental disenchantment of the countryside and cities *and* the ensuing stabilization and ossification of traditional Catholic and Protestant institutions.[736] But why next to no evangelicalism, which went on to thrive in America?

At the risk of oversimplification, as suggested earlier, Anglo-Saxon and continental religion experienced an erosion of belief and practice in the face of the inexorable march of modernization over the newly industrializing cultural landscape but retained the lion's share of traditional cultural infrastructures—both urban and rural. *Ancien* magic *and* more formal ritualisms (dare we, these days, call them *religions*), formerly more centrally embedded, gradually evolved into mere correlated idioms and customs, a position they still occupy today in somewhat quaintly vestigial ways in countries like Italy and Spain, and perhaps even more so in Latin America. American tourists flock to their charming artifactual residues—the Vatican, La Sagrada Família, Stonehenge, etc.; whereas, by marked contrast, their equally curious European counterparts seek out Niagara Falls, the West, the Grand Canyon, etc. instead—more natural, wide-open vistas. Understandably and ironically so, as Walden Pond proves a much more alluring, civilized tourist destination than any rotting Puritan village prison stockade.

Accordingly, my argument largely hinges upon an examination of what is meant by *culture,* by contrasting visions and realities of it, and this particularly dour and somewhat critical notion of *cultural vacuums.* The one quite naturally, and conceptually, folds into the other. And so now observe here first how evangelicalism rushed in to fill the vacuum left by the eradication of the mysticisms of the early American settlement populations, in both their voluntary (Pilgrim) and involuntary (slave) community locations and

---

[735] See Malcolm Gaskill's detailed history of the overlooked relationship between Old World English cultural identities and a newly emerging American identity—the constant interplay between them—out of which was forged new American sensibilities: "American experience *flowed into the void* to make a hybrid colonial self." (op. cit., 329) {emphasis added}

[736] Caroline Walker Bynum's take on some of this might be that during the long period of Christian consolidation, from 1100 to about 1550, re-enchantment—however negligible—also assumed the form of a widespread "materialization" of the faith. Abstract theology was made more tangible, more visual and touchable through cultural artifacts. (*Christian Materiality: An Essay on Religion in Late Medieval Europe*, Zone Books, 2011.)

forms.[737] Again, to abbreviate a long developmental history, observe also the continuation of this familiar dynamic and process over the last half-century or so, wherein, by extension, evangelicalism continually rushes in to fill more modern versions of these cultural vacuums—searching out, targeting, absorbing individuals, families, small towns, suburbs. Into the void it seeped and continues to seep, or even flows for that matter.

No doubt this claim will raise the ire of some, which should come as no surprise. Indeed many American academicians, contrary to type, are uncomfortable with any appearance of elitism or condescension. And this talk of cultural vacuums will no doubt strike many as a gratuitous value judgment, perhaps properly so. Even at most public universities—believe it or not—students get routinely called out for such impertinence, for offhandedly dissing the homeland or its indigenous Anglo-Saxon residents (or at least they used to). The lion's share of academicians prefer somewhat sterilized classrooms, exemplary milieus of impartial value-free instruction and inquiry, or so they claim. But here in this particular instance we must neither mince words nor neglect performing what seems to me a rather higher duty of any genuinely thoughtful inquiry. Let us call a spade a spade and not pretend otherwise. To wit: large portions of American society are cultural wastelands—unmitigated, uninhabitable personal, family, and social disasters. In marked contrast to European villages, communities, societies, we huddle together in residential clusters that prove to be nothing short of dysfunctional cultural nightmares, and by this I mean culture with a small c—mundane, everyday, low-brow culture.[738]

---

[737] Leave it to the French to discern that something was amiss: "Alexis de Tocqueville, among others, claimed that such pursuit of happiness generated a characteristic American *un*happiness. He wrote in the 1830s that American equality, with its promise of universal success, bred sadness. 'In America I saw the freest and most enlightened men placed in the happiest circumstances that the world affords, it seemed to me as if a cloud habitually hung upon their brow, and I thought them serious and almost sad, even in their pleasures.' " (Fischer, *Made in America. . .* , 238.)

[738] American sociologists have framed any such qualitative issues entirely in traditional dualistic *gemeinschaft/gesellschaft* (rural/urban) or individualistic/communitarian terms. See Rodney Stark's culturally clueless chapter 22, "Civic Participation: Faith as Social Capital," in *What Americans Really Believe: New Findings from the Baylor Surveys of Religion* (Waco: Baylor University Press, 2008).

—Likewise, the enormously influential political scientist, Robert Putnam, appears constitutionally incapable of recognizing or addressing these kinds of cultural issues, diagnosing the current American malaise as a crisis to be understood in traditional individualistic, or nonstructural and non-cultural terms—all about restoring something that is now missing or has been uprooted or lost. For example, with respect to stalled social mobility—"the American dream"—instead of taking inequality head on "he [Putnam] is most intensely focused on increasing opportunity for individuals, and he believes the primary way of doing that is by increasing their locally available store of social capital—through improved ways of rearing

And by no means, as we will see with respect to contemporary Nordic nations, am I invoking the greater or lesser presence of indicators of modernization, however we define and describe them, as a fault line distinguishing one type of national or regional society or culture from others. The difference here transcends citations or measures of traditional village cultural charm or nostalgia. Irrespective of such distinctions, within them and it—the former, the American wasteland—to cite just one classic Paul Goodman indictment, *Growing Up Absurd* reigns supreme, and perhaps even that aspersion proves too generous an evaluation of American childhood and adolescence. Indeed even after nearly a decade of a post WWII America brimming with optimism and exceptionalist hubris, Goodman could only scan the expanding wasteland and presciently anticipate what was to come:

> Balked, not taken seriously, deprived of great objects and available opportunities, and in an atmosphere that does not encourage service—it is hard to have faith, to feel justified, to have a calling, or win honor. But what then fills the place of these? For every experience that a human being has is a whole way-of-being-in-the-world. . . . Indeed, it is a major defect of our present organized system and the economy of abundance that, without providing great goals, it has taken away some of the important real necessities, leaving people with nothing to do. . . . In such circumstances there cannot possibly be an American culture. . . . [Nonetheless] *The void is soon filled.*[739]

But filled with what, pray tell? A yawning void filled, that is, with "artificial" necessities in lieu of real, substantive things, callings, or longings. Caught up in all this, "Young fellows drift . . . looking for a connection   . . . ." Again, into the vacuum flow the pseudo-satisfactions, the ephemeral effluvia of threadbare ad agency sensibilities, spawning, culminating in the ultimate disenchantment of a "commercially debauched popular culture." It is an old story that wanders lamely towards an even more disenchanting whimper—and not a bang—of a seemingly inconclusive, reprehensible ending. And as for those who might take comfort in that which trickles down or remains peripheral to all this, "out in the countryside," he cautions: "Our poets try to move themselves by nostalgically repeating the names of towns: 'Biloxi and

---

children, and encouraging activities and associations that will increase their chances in life. . . . He calls extracurricular activities 'as close to a magic bullet as we are ever like to find in the real world of social, and educational, and economic policy'. . . ." But "extracurricular activities," like evangelical religion, are among the substitutes Americans employ to fill in the cultural void. Indeed, once traditional American social mobility—increasing economic prosperity and consumption—disappears, what remains? (Nicholas Lemman, "Unhappy Days for America," a review of Robert D. Putnam's *Our Kids: The American Dream in Crisis*, in *The New York Review of Books*, May 21, 2015.)

[739] *Growing Up Absurd: Problems of Youth in the Organized System*, Random House, 1956, 154-5, 28. Then follows 24, 109 in the ensuing paragraph. {emphasis added}

Natchez, Pascagoula and Opelousas'—*but beware of paying a visit.*" In this case, familiarity does indeed breed contempt. And all too many of us have been there, done that. Unfortunately, we do indeed swell with the discontent of contempt.

Sadly, this proves not even the half of it. Indeed, with the contemporaneous spread of social media technologies this cultural impoverishment, this hollowing out of the vacuum of culture proceeds apace, perhaps even accelerates. That Facebook, et al., were birthed in America,[740] on our watch, ought then come as no surprise. No surprise also that evangelical megachurches, those pseudo-spiritual behemoths, are located primarily in the cultural deserts of suburban cul-de-sac America.[741] To mask or ignore such

---

[740] What is more, one additional ironic, evolving consequence of the modern American "gig economy" is that it has come to resemble the family and community shattering features of Stalin's *nepreryvka,* or staggered "continuous work week." For even if there were pockets of vibrant European—like culture approximations worth perpetuating, harried work schedules discourage whatever emulations might possibly emerge. (Judith Shulevitz, "Why Don't I See You Anymore?" *The Atlantic,* November 2019.)

[741] Such geographical locations have a traceable history: "In new suburbs like Northridge and Gardena, Bellflower and Lakewood, Southern religious folk swept their neighborhoods with street witnessing and tent revivalism. . . . Once relegated to shacks on unkempt streets in Los Angeles' blue-collar suburbs, Pentecostal congregations now commanded prime meeting space on Orange County's palm-tree-lined boulevards. . . . Southern churchmen and churchwomen took command of this future by crafting a religious system perfectly suited to their new suburban home." (Darren Dochuk, *From Bible Belt to SunBelt: Plain-Folk Religion, Grassroots Politics, and the Rise of Evangelical Conservatism,* New York: W.W. Norton, 2011, 175-6.)

—Jon Butler reminds us of the Italian immigrant cultures of New York City as recounted by Robert Orsi: "Its capstone—the annual *festa* of the Madonna of Mount Carmel in Harlem—featured religion as the centerpiece of a community brought into being as much by pious laypeople as by clerics. . . . Nothing here was saccharine and sentimental. . . . [unfortunately, inevitably, they understood what was lost] when Italians abandoned Harlem for New York's Westchester County, Long Island, and New Jersey after World War II, [and] they returned to that neighborhood for decades to reenact the yearly *festa* of the Madonna of Mount Carmel. . . . Anecdotal evidence and criticism of suburban religion suggests an engagement between religion and suburbanization so strong that it accounts for the exceptional rise in church membership among Americans between 1945 and 1970. For every trip to the mall, suburban families easily made two, three, even five or more trips to suburban congregations. . . . Congregations not only participated in consumer culture but helped lead the very 'consumers' republic' Cohen describes." ("Jack-in-the-Box Faith. . . ," 1363, 1375.)

—Then again, more recently, so-called "Emerging evangelicals" have left both mainline and evangelical congregations located in culturally-vacuous suburbs, this reflecting *"the desire among Emerging evangelicals for religious lives that are more authentic. This desire stems from a gnawing sense of alienation and estrangement. Complaints circulate about life lived within bureaucratic structures and communities of relative strangers, about symbols and signifiers without real referents. So Emerging evangelicals seek to reestablish a sense of place by moving to urban neighborhoods with vital histories. They take vows of stability— the promise to remain where they live for the rest of their lives, to foster thick networks of social relations, and to incorporate, via geographical proximity, racial and socioeconomic 'others' into their lives. They seek lives of simplicity in the face of the consumer capitalist ethos."* (Brian Steensland, review of *Moral Ambition:: Mobilization And Social Outreach In Evangelical Megachurches* by Omri Elisha; *Emerging Evangelicals:*

obvious dysfunction under the mantle of an impartial, value-free social science throws down formidable gauntlets to any empirical-based, critical truth-seeking sensibility.

And here, very briefly, lies the interpretive rub. Understandably, the overwhelming majority of academicians (primarily historians and sociologists) who study religion—evangelicalism in particular—are Christians. Some wear their faith on their sleeves like an enabling pedigree. Indeed, who is better positioned to understand and analyze the role of religion in American society than a Christian academician? Just think of the barriers that almost automatically are cleared away or collapse before them. No wonder they subliminally identify with the Christian American status quo. No wonder also that they might get a little defensive about the preceding observations. They have made a lifelong cultural investment of sorts. To their way of thinking, such critiques reek of bias; they are overwhelmingly negative and elitist.

J. D. Hunter, for example, concludes *American Evangelicalism: Conservative Religion and the Quandary of Modernity* with an admonishment to fellow investigators of evangelicalism in particular and religion in general to take their subjects' beliefs seriously because one day, "to their astonishment," the skies may open to reveal Christ returning to earth in glorious fulfillment of scripture, and then what will the skeptical, dismissive sociologist have to say for himself?[742] *No kidding.* And then there's Robert Wuthnow's smug ethno-Christocentric pronouncement in *Producing The Sacred*: "A nation cannot long exist without conceptions of the transcendent to guide its destiny and sanction its highest values."[743] *Ditto.*

Observe academicians with none too subliminal attitude. I am reminded of Hendrik Hertzberg's account of a conversation at a Washington D. C. cocktail party, wherein he is discussing the Ayatollah Khomeini/Salman Rushdie affair with a young aide to a hard-right senator, who remarks: "You know, these so-called writers and intellectuals have been laughing at religion for hundreds of years. It's about time somebody blew the whistle on it."[744] *So-called?* Perhaps the reader is reminded of a twice-impeached president's identical reference to judges as "so-called." *Birds of a feather* collude together.

Faith, Modernity, And The Desire For Authenticity by James S. Bielo, *Journal for the Scientific Study of Religion*, Vol. 51, No. 2, June 2012, 388.)

[742] *American Evangelicalism: Conservative Religion and the Quandary of Modernity*, 135.

[743] *Producing The Sacred*, 3. Indeed, Wuthnow ought now go inform much of Europe that the center cannot hold.

[744] "Secular Sermon: TRB From Washington," *The New Republic*, 20 March 1989.

Social scientists who are Christian (somewhat distinguishable from Christian academicians, whom we encountered earlier) can cite mounds of survey data—Gallup, Pew, etc.—to make their case.[745] Problematical assumptions abound. Indeed, don't we all understand and accept the premise that religion makes people happy? That it produces *Father-Knows-Best* suburban bliss—better neighbors, better social outcomes? Mary Douglas be damned, end of discussion.[746] Unfortunately, rarely-cited international survey data suggest that the exact opposite is in fact more likely the case. *Indeed the overwhelming majority of the least religious nations in the world score significantly higher on life satisfaction indices than do residents of the United States.* What is more, to complicate matters even further—since this is one of the linchpins of both

---

[745] One highly praised definitive account based upon such survey data is Robert Putnam and David E. Campbell's *American Grace: How Religion Divides and Unites Us* (Simon & Schuster 2010). Some American sociologists tend to justify their existence by debunking the perceptions and experiences of ordinary lay people, journalists, and at times even fellow academicians (even Putnam and Campbell's).

—"Far from putting them into the kitchen against their wills, as critics might say, when Mom and Dad take daughters to church, *they open up the future to them.*" (Stark, op. cit., 189.) {emphasis added}

[746] "There is a large body of evidence linking religiosity to several key indicators of social health in America." (Bottum, *An Anxious Age . . .* , 286.)

—Ralph Reed of the Religious Right constantly refers to the Putnam study on talk shows as evidence of the positive value of religion in America. But again, in comparison to what?

—Douglas's fellow anthropologist, Clifford Geertz, dismissed the entire question of the evaluation of religion in general as rather pointless, for ". . . . when that [confrontation with, or acknowledgment of, cultural particularity] is done, overall questions of whether religion is 'good' or 'bad,' 'functional' or 'dysfunctional,' 'ego-strengthening' or 'anxiety-producing,' disappear like the chimeras they are, and one is left with particular evaluations, assessments, and diagnoses in particular cases." ("Religion as a Cultural System," originally published in M. Banton ed., *Anthropological Approaches to the Study of Religion*, London: Travistock Publications Ltd, 1966/reprinted in *The Interpretation of Cultures: Selected Essays*, Basic Books, 1973, 123.) As with any equally vague concept of culture, the devil is in the details, not the general notion of it, which merely serves to narrow, ironically, the focus of our particular descriptions and interpretations and any subsequent evaluations that might result from them. See also Stephen Toulmin, "Rules and their Relevance. . . ." (1971).

—Then there's the father of many American anthropologists, Franz Boas, addressing the matter of bias more generally in *The Mind of Primitive Man* (1911): "the value which we attribute to our own civilization is due to the fact that we participate in this civilization, and that it has been controlling all our actions since the time of our birth."

—Then again, to be fair, there is the opposite tendency, no doubt more pronounced among continental scholars: "For Worden, this startling [1970s] revelation ["rewriting of Ludlow's original text, from which the evidence of his passionate religiosity had been carefully stripped. . . ."] was a warning that, if scholars are to understand the past, they must constantly resist their natural inclination to rewrite history in their own image. Worden therefore takes the language of the time at its face value and firmly reminds a more secular age of the centrality of religious beliefs to the politics of seventeenth-century England." (from Keith Thomas's review of Blair Worden's *God's Instruments: Political Conduct in the England of Oliver Cromwell*, in *The New York Review of Books*, 11/8/2012, 54.)

traditional and contemporary American exceptionalisms—individual and family income levels bear little relationship to personal happiness. The citizens of some decidedly poorer countries are a good deal happier than much more affluent Americans.[747] This ought give some academicians pause.[748] Since the end of WWII European social democracies have produced some of the most envied societies and highest quality of life indicators in the world. *Ever.*[749] And yet we find among them scant religiosity and next to no

---

[747] Dan Buettner, The World's Happiest Places," *National Geographic*, November, 2017.
— "For much of the year, Finland has but few hours of light and temperatures well below 0 degrees F. Yet the Finns are the happiest people in the world, according to *the U.N.'s Annual World Happiness Report*. Norway is second, followed by Denmark and Iceland. . . . The U.S. dropped four places to 18th. . . . why does our powerful and wealthy nation—whose founding promise is the individual pursuit of happiness—consistently fall into the second tier. . . . and keep sinking?. . . . Work, and the ceaseless hunt for money, security, and consumer goods, dominate most people's lives; time for family and friends, and activities that build community and meaning, is often scarce. Loneliness is epidemic. So are consoling addictions to painkillers, unhealthy food, and technology. The most alienated among us load up on weapons and express their soul-sickness in blood. Finland, Norway, and Denmark are not without problems, but researchers say what sets the happier nations apart is *the premium their cultures place on time spent in nature, and in harmonious, intimate contact with friends and family. The Danes even have a word, 'hygge,' that describes these cozy, high-quality social interactions."* (William Falk, "Editor's Letter," *The Week*, March 30, 2018, 3.) {emphases added}
———Then again, there's always another side to the story: See Samuele Maccolini, "Finland: Hardly a Nordic Utopia," *The Week*, April 6, 2018, 14, from *Linkiesta* (Italy).

[748] Such as Claude S. Fischer, for one, whose reading of the data suggests no such social or cultural drift: ". . . . there isn't even a meaningful trend. . . . [Indeed] The rough evidence indicates a general decline in isolation. . . . the general increase in living alone has not substantially increased loneliness. . . . [in fact, "the new communications technologies" are not to blame.] Moreover, the loneliness that should worry us is not generated by a teen's Facebook humiliation, a globetrotter's sense of disorientation, or a novelist's romantic languor. It is, rather, the loneliness of the old man whose wife and best friends have died, the shunned schoolchild, the overburdened single mother, and the immigrant working the night shift to send money home. There's nothing new or headline-worthy about their loneliness. . . ." (*Lurching Toward Happiness in America*, MIT Press, 2014, 20-27.) Fischer dismisses any talk of a growing American loneliness as impressionistic, journalistic white noise, confounded by real data. Unfortunately although he does address a few European contrasts, these forays tend to dwell upon and in traditional sociological structural genres: the absence of European class consciousness, constitutional impediments to change, with references to "self-reliance," "family values," and "racial identity." (43) Indeed he mentions religion only once in passing: ". . . . people who say they are generally happy tend to be economically secure, married, healthy, religious, and busy with friends; they tend to live in affluent, democratic, individualistic societies with activist, welfare-state governments." (4) Well, that's one interpretation of the data (as if the latter isn't a contradiction in terms). Unfortunately, some largely ethnocentric-skewed assumptions override many valuable observations.

[749] It is just this kind of contrary empirical evidence that philosophers who happen to be Christians (in addition to *Christian philosophers*), such as John Gray at the University of Oxford, appear innocent or ignorant of. Mr. Gray informs us in *Seven Types of Atheism* (Farrar, Straus, and Giroux, 2018) that almost no moral progress or growth in human happiness has occurred over the centuries; that, by and large, secularization has produced little of moral or

evangelicalism to speak of. Why not? Perhaps there are clues here as to some sort of ironic, incongruous exceptionalism that lies at the root of all this, yet no American academician of whom I am aware has explored this difference *in terms of culture*. With few exceptions, they employ conventional sociological tools and techniques, locating and testing "concepts" drawn largely from within the discipline itself, "research" that invariably results in predictable findings and challenges next to nothing. But is it any wonder this proves the case, given that the majority of our academicians who study religion are themselves Christians?[750] No wonder they appear constitutionally disinclined to pursue more innovative lines of inquiry. No wonder they recycle

---

civilizational value. Yet, is anyone really surprised that the enormous material wealth of the United States has not yielded a corresponding increase in the happiness of its people? That a few secular ideologies—Marxism, Fascism, in particular—have done evil on a large scale? [But not Christianity against native Americans? The Crusades filling the streets of Jerusalem with a river of blood?] Like most Christian academicians he appears unaware, or refuses to acknowledge, that the greatest reduction in human poverty in history has occurred over the last half-century or so. That the "societies without God" of Scandinavia have produced some of the most admired and envied societies the world has ever seen. In typical monopolistic fashion he recasts the idea of progress more to his liking: "When wrenched from monotheistic religion [it] is not so much false as meaningless." Yes, our greatest challenges lie ahead. What, pray tell, does he imagine religion might contribute to any further advance?

[750] Richard Lewontin finds an equally limiting bias at work in the natural sciences, but in a contrary sort of way: "One of the problems of exploring an intellectual discipline from the outside is that the importance of certain basic methodological considerations is not always apparent to the observer, considerations that mold the entire intellectual structure that characterizes the field." Indeed, operating either inside or outside, such assumptions can prove debilitating. Sociologists of religion, in particular—of all academicians—have shown an exceedingly ironic tendency to overlook the extent to which their sub-discipline has been *socially constructed*. ("It's Even Less in Your Genes," *The New York Review of Books*, 5/26/2011, 26.)
—As when Geetanjali Srikantan summarizes his review of Max Weber's work on Hinduism: "Max Weber's scholarship on the sociology of Indian religions is analyzed to demonstrate the frame and its contents. One discovers that the idea of a Hindu religion with sacred scriptures and a Brahmin priesthood can be found not just in Weber but across all sections of European society. In interrogating the frame by which Europeans experience India, one discovers that this is *a product of categories and debates internal to Christianity*." ("Towards New Conceptual Approaches in Legal History. . . ," 125.)

tired old adages and formulas.[751] Unfortunately, they have much in common with evangelical college academicians, as we have seen.[752]

For example, there appears no sociological interest in exploring the prospect that one of the most religious societies on earth, *their own society*, is also one of the most unhappy. How odd, and somewhat grim, this observation given the widespread assumption within the sub-discipline of the sociology of religion that religion makes people happy. Who'd have thunk it?

The evidence to the contrary—from personal experience to hard empirical data—appears overwhelming. *We are for the most part a disgruntled, disenchanted society and have been so for quite some time.*[753] Imagine the unforeseen

---

[751] These tend to be couched as apologetic disavowals, such as: "When the word *Evangelical* comes up in conversation today, a variety of stereotypes are usually evoked. . . . Although stereotypes often have some grounding in truth, they are to some degree a distortion. . . . the regrettable lack of social scientific literature on the phenomenon, for research would undoubtedly clarify and qualify, if not contradict, our current understandings." (James Davison Hunter, *American Evangelicalism: Conservative Religion and the Quandary of Modernity* (New Brunswick: Rutgers University Press, 1983, 3.) *Indubitably.*

—After venting a host of understandable complaints about the sociology of religion, one well-known Christian journalist admitted that at heart the discipline might always have "a nagging sense of maybe having gotten the whole thing wrong. . . . [since] since. . . . after all. . . it cannot admit genuinely supernatural events." Hence the problem that they always want "theology itself to be consequence of something else. . . ." [i.e., social, material factors or causes.] (Joseph Bottum, *An Anxious Age. . .* , 48.)

—Or as Tomoko Masuzawa remarks about the field of "religious studies" more generally: ". . . . as some adamantly secularist scholars—who constitute a sizeable and vocal minority in the field—have observed with some displeasure, there is a higher concentration of un-reconstituted religious essentialists in this department of knowledge than anywhere else in the academy.[10] This should not come as a surprise, it is often said, given that the field is populated, and by sheer number dominated, by the representatives, partisans, and sympathizers of various religions or, more recently, by those who may be best described as advocates and sympathizers of 'religion' in general." (*The Invention of World Religions: Or, How European Universalism Was Preserved in the Language of Pluralism*, University of Chicago Press, 2005, 7.)

[752] The discipline of economics has suffered a similar self-absorption. As David Graeber writes of the field after the financial collapse of 2008: "We now live in a different economic universe than we did before the crash. Falling unemployment no longer drives up wages. Printing money does not cause inflation. Yet the language of public debate, *and the wisdom conveyed in economic textbooks, remain almost entirely unchanged.* . . . when it comes to establishing themselves [economists] in positions of intellectual authority, unaffected by such failings, their success is unparalleled. *One would have to look at the history of religions to find anything like it.*" [better yet, the sociology of religion] (from a review of Robert Skidelsky's *Money and Government. . .* , *The New York Review of Books*, 12/5/2019.) {emphases added}

[753] "Loneliness is at epidemic levels in the U.S., and could rank alongside smoking and obesity as a major threat to public health, new research suggests. In a survey of 20,000 adults conducted by Ipsos for the health insurer Cigna, nearly 50 percent said they sometimes or always felt alone or left out, *CBSNews.com* reported. Forty-three percent said their relationships weren't meaningful, and 27 percent said they rarely felt understood. While loneliness is often

implications for a discipline grounded in precisely the opposite universe of "discourse," as the current kitschy jargon might have it. Now there's an evidence-based curveball that virtually no one is taking a swing at.

At the very heart of this unhappiness, as we will see, are profound social, cultural, and economic *anxieties* and *insecurities*, what one pair of academicians have captured in a single expression, "existential insecurity."[754] This

---

associated with aging, the survey found that the worst affected were in fact young Americans between the ages 18 and 22. *[Yet]* Social media use—which some research has suggested can be isolating—had *no obvious impact on perceived isolation*." ("America's Loneliness Epidemic," *The Week*, May 18, 2018, 20.) {emphasis added}

—The latter claim about social media use is contradicted by the preponderance of the evidence, as quite poignantly reported by Eli Saslow: "She lived alone, and on many days her only personal interaction occurred here, on Facebook." (" ' Nothing on this page is real': How lies become truth in online America," *The Washington Post*, 11/17/18.)

—Maik Wiking, CEO of the Happiness Research Institute in Copenhagen, conducted simple experiments that showed that even a week away from social media connection tools produced significant drops in indicators of happiness. (TED talks, "The Dark Side of Happiness," 5/10/16.)

—It is instructive that the wealthiest, most unequal society on earth, also shows the greatest "lifetime risk of mood disorder." (Brandon H. Hidaka, "Depression as a Disease of Modernity: explanations for increasing prevalence," *Journal of Affective Disorders*, 2012 Nov: 140 (3), 205-214.)

—Flowing out of my general argument of an American cultural vacuum bereft of the family and community riches and resources present elsewhere, no wonder that: "College students aren't happy, and neither is anyone else. According to a recent study by the American College Health Association, 52 percent of students reported feeling hopeless, while 39 percent suffered from such severe depression that they had found it difficult to function at some point during the previous year." (Adam Sternbergh, "The Cure for The New York Face. . . ," *New York Magazine*, May 28—June 10, 22; re: most popular Yale course, Psych 157: Psychology and the Good Life.)

—Although Hanna Rosin reports that nationally "Adolescent suicide has dropped dramatically since the 1990s. . . in the past few years it's started to creep back up", one finds conventionally inexplicable surges in seeming hotbeds of cultural discontentment. Take Palo Alto, the community surrounding Stanford University, ". . . . a place that inspired jealousy from out-of-towners, where the coolest gadgets and ideas come from. . . ," where wealthy foreign parents buy houses so their kids could attend their schools, *but* where young students routinely throw themselves in front of the Cal train that sluices through the neighborhood, "five cars, double-decker, tearing past at 50 miles per hour. Too fast to see the faces of the Silicon Valley commuters on board", where "Twelve percent of Palo Alto high-school students surveyed in the 2013-14 school year reported having seriously contemplated suicide in the past 12 months." (Hanna Rosen, "The Silicon Valley Suicides," *The Atlantic*, December 2018.) Granted, some other countries—Denmark, e.g.—show comparable national figures, but they reflect an altogether different cultural impetus.

[754] Norris, Pippa and Ronald Inglehart, *Sacred and Secular: Religion and Politics Worldwide*, 2nd edition, Cambridge University Press, 2011.

—As an example of that insecurity, Howard Steven Friedman frames the story of a sixty-two-year-old American executive in a boxed graphic titled, "The Anxiety of the Uninsured," this just one among the many quality of life indicators—health care, guns, violence, education, and inequality, etc.—that so clearly and poorly distinguish the American social and cultural

dissatisfaction or disenchantment—and my meaning here varies slightly from Weber's *Entzauberung*, which Daniel Bell translates, awkwardly, as the "demagification—of the world"[755]—has to be acknowledged and explored if we are to understand anything about American society. And any such understanding appears inextricably linked to that perennial nagging issue: why are we so different from Europe?[756] That question alone warrants a book-length inquiry. But for now let me briefly address the first matter by recounting that there was a reason that the American sociologists David Riesman, Nathan Glazer, and Reuel Denny decades ago, in a rather epic sobering account of *The Changing American Character*, titled their effort *The Lonely Crowd*.[757] As we have seen, even today the same talk of loneliness and disenchantment constantly makes an appearance, perhaps with even greater intensity and frequency, and yet as opposed to other more topical global concerns—the rise of nativism,[758] populism, extremism, et al, for example—comparisons with Europe are rarely entertained. This proves an enormous missed opportunity, for aside from our Canadian neighbors the Europeans are the closest thing we have to a control group. They have a lot to tell us *about us*. What is more, hints or clues as to what might advance our understanding surface all the time *if only we know what to look for*.[759] Take, for

---

experience from that of other modern developed nations. (Although oddly, misleadingly titled, *The Measure of a Nation: How to Regain America's Competitive Edge and Boost Our Global Standing*, Prometheus Books, 2012, 48.)

[755] "The Return of the Sacred?" in *The Winding Passage: Essays and Sociological Journeys, 1960-1980* (Abt Books/Basic Books, 1980), 332.

[756] Not everyone agrees as to how different. See Peter Baldwin's *The Narcissism of Minor Differences: How America and Europe Are Alike* (Oxford University Press 2009). Baldwin brilliantly "parses" the existing data to make a strong case against the conventional wisdom of a marked American-European divide. He offers a splendid, nuanced, and fair argument detailing the ambiguities inherent in such claims. But again, as he vaguely acknowledges, qualitative differences often elude and belie apparent quantitative similarities (and vice-versa), as we will see.

[757] My copy is an undated Doubleday Anchor paperback, an abridgement by the authors of the original 1950 Yale University Press edition.

[758] "Asked recently what had attracted him to the far right, Frank Meeink, a former neo-Nazi, responded: 'Just the belonging. Feeling like I was part of something' . . . . what the alt-right offered was a revalorized masculinity, a sense of purpose, and a collective identity." As we will see with many evangelicals, they feel " 'red pilled.' The metaphor comes from *The Matrix*, the dystopian science-fiction movie in which the protagonist, Neo [*born-again*?], is offered a red pill that allows him to see through society's illusions and view the world in its true, ugly reality." (Angela Nagle, "Brotherhood of Losers," *The Atlantic*, December 2017.)

[759] In one comprehensive anthology of studies demonstrating all the data collection and analysis difficulties in making such international comparisons I couldn't help but notice a case study of small survey samples drawn from Columbus, Ohio and Rennes, France. Table 2.4 "Comparison of Well-Being in Two Cities" reports "Content Differences" that go beyond the

example, former president Barack Obama, who although he employed numerous "faith advisers" in the White House, would scarcely qualify as an evangelical—let alone even a citizen or a Christian according to the Religious Right—in the minds of most. Yet certain themes surface, time and again, however odd or out of place they might seem. Here is Senator Obama prior to his run for the presidency addressing

> . . . . a gathering of liberal Christians. . . . [during which he] echoed many of the complaints of the countercultists.[sic] He mused about Americans' 'chronic loneliness.' Their 'work, their possessions, their diversions, their sheer busyness is not enough'. . . . He explained that he had felt the emptiness himself in college and concluded that 'without a commitment to a particular community of faith, I would always remain apart, and alone.' [760]

Who'd have thunk it—about Obama, no less—but there/here it is, in a nutshell. Yet another variation upon an old and enduring theme, for once again into a seemingly ever-present cultural void must flow some sort of American spiritual oxygen, a vaporous something *either* anesthetizing, asphyxiating, *or* rejuvenating depending upon the inhalant's needs and perspectives, leaving no one untouched or unaffected in one way or another (this author included). And even more broadly, in terms of comparisons with other world leaders (among whom there have been only a few avowed evangelicals), observe that every American president since the end of WWII

---

usual self-reported life satisfaction questions. For example, "French women on average spend less time each day working and commuting [but the actual data on the latter appear reversed], and more time walking and reading, while the Americans spend more time in praying/worshipping [19min. versus 3 min.]. The striking difference in the time spent eating is mainly due to differences in how attention is paid to that activity. . . . confirm cultural stereotypes." But are these more than mere stereotypes? (Ed Diener, John F. Helliwell, and Daniel Kahneman eds., *International Differences in Well-Being*, Oxford University Press, 2010, 28.)

[760] Matthew Bowman, *Christian: The Politics of a Word in America*, Harvard University Press, 2018, 223.

—I believe this is the same conference, "Call To Renewal" in 2006, that Stephen P. Miller refers to in "Between Hope and Despair: Obama and Evangelical Politics," an essay in Matthew Avery Sutton and Darren Dochuk eds., *Faith in the New Millennium: The Future of Religion and American Politics* (Oxford, 2016), 202-3. Unfortunately in the attempt to draw this very long (and fascinating) speech into the orbit of mere strategic politics, Miller predictably misses the cultural disenchantment convergence.

—No wonder that Obama's favorite author is the overtly Christian Marilynne Robinson: "No theoretical language I know of serves me in describing or interpreting this era of American unhappiness, the drift away from the purpose and optimism that generally led to the development of the society from its beginnings. . . . It did create great cities and institutions as well as a distinctive culture that has been highly influential throughout the world." ("What Kind of Country Do We Want?" *The New York Review of Books*, June 11, 2020, 43.)

appears spun from this same whole cloth of religiosity.[761] Even a brief survey reveals a rogue's shooting gallery of former Sunday school pupils and teachers drawn from congregations of various whole or half-baked claims of holiness. And so I am suggesting that there is something about *us*—something decidedly different from Europeans—that appears to demand such resuscitating inrushes of faith. But there is really nothing out of the ordinary here: most Americans appear to know exactly of what Obama speaks.[762] Evangelicals talk about it all the time,[763] this almost glaringly exotic—*our* exotic—form of ennui or angst, an emotional pit in our stomachs requiring intervention, remediation, and perhaps, ultimately, *salvation*. Looking back, there was always something missing from their, *our* lives it seems. For some inexplicable reason they—we—seem to ache on an intensely visceral level, seething with what I have come to think of as a deep cultural disenchantment. But give them, and occasionally us, credit for having enough sense to realize that there ought to be *something* more meaningful and satisfying to life than what we have all more or less heretofore experienced and settled for. Something more than money and suburban cul-de-sacs; more than social isolation and opiate addiction;[764] more than lonely crowds and lone gunmen wielding

---

[761] It has been widely reported that George W. Bush attributes the saving of his life and marriage to Jesus (and Billy Graham).

[762] "In the early 2000s. . . . Perhaps one-fourth of adult Americans belonged to a churched-based support or study group. The church provided many with a social life and most of their friendships. In 1979, Sociologist Nancy Ammerman studied a fundamentalist church in a New England suburb. 'For many, almost every spare minute is spent on activities related to the church. The church *is* their leisure activity. . . . They share meals together. . . . the focus of their lives together is the church.' " (*Made in America. . .*, 153.)

[763] As Paula White, Donald Trump's favorite televangelist, put it: ". . . . the church is not for perfect saints, it's for messed-up people." (Shayne Lee & Phillip Luke Sinitiere, *Holy Mavericks: Evangelical Innovators and the Spiritual Marketplace*, New York University Press, 2009, 118.)
—Evangelical pastor, Rick Warren, author of *The Purpose-Driven Life*, the best-selling book in American publishing history, from his 2008 TED talk: "I think because spiritual emptiness is a universal disease. I think inside at some point, we put our heads down on the pillow and we go, 'There's got to be more to life than this.' Get up in the morning, go to work, come home and watch TV, go to bed, get up in the morning, go to work, come home, watch TV, go to bed, go to parties on weekends. A lot of people say, 'I'm living.' No, you're not living—that's just existing. Just existing. . . . I believe that you're not an accident. . . ."

[764] Americans accustomed to buying enormous bottles of acetaminophen at Costco are surprised to find that only small doses and quantities are available in pharmacies in Spain, although quite legally purchased without prescription. Why such pain? Why such quantities? Seemingly, everything's bigger in the U.S.
—Accordingly enough, in the heart of West Virginia, Orange County, California-based (but of course) *Celebrate Recovery* ministries have sprung up to work their magic upon the opioid crisis: "Clarksburg's traditional congregations have dwindled along with the city's population. . . . The place these churches once held in the community has been taken by new churches proclaiming a gospel of prosperity, insisting that God wants us all to be rich. And by ministries

automatic weapons; more than Walmart,[765] strip malls, Las Vegas,[766]and mass consumption.[767] A good deal more than any number of things. *Something* has been lost or been *missing* from the very beginning of our errand into the wilderness. For indeed as one of our most trusted anthropological seers and sampler of other cultural visions and contexts, Marshall Sahlins, observes,

> A people who conceive life to be the pursuit of happiness must be chronically unhappy.[768]

---

such as Celebration Recovery." (Sam Quinones, "The Penance of Doc," *The Atlantic*, May 2019, 68.)

[765] "Walmart is the biggest company on the planet. Its sales on a single day topped the gross domestic products of thirty-seven sovereign nations. If it were the independent Republic of Walmart, it would be China's sixth largest export market and its economy would rank thirtieth in the world, right behind Saudi Arabia's. . . . [Looking back] The endless round of old church-based activities, remembered an aging Ozarker were 'a form of entertainment. . . That is what you went for.' 'The church was your outstanding social function, because there you met all your neighbors you hadn't seen for a week,' another old-timer recalled of the area's farming days. But the particular strain of 'family values' Christianity that met mass consumption under Walmart's roof was the product of historically new conditions. . . . the popular faith in Christian free enterprise attracted passionate support among ordinary people. . . . for many of the nation's old agricultural periphery, the gospel of free enterprise answered some of their most pressing needs. . . . it sanctified mass consumption. . . ." (Bethany Moreton, *To Serve God and Walmart: The Making of Christian Free Enterprise*, Harvard University Press, 2009, 6, 99, 270.)

[766] Airbnb may have unknowingly provided a new kind of insight for American travelers venturing abroad. Stay at the rented out flat or extra apartment of any French couple (in Paris, our case) and become aware of the *petit* size and quantity of nearly all things domestic. Perhaps there are few plumbing snakes because Europeans extend that *petit* cultural *something* to all dimensions of life. Unfortunately, aspects of the American mentalité may be spreading abroad ("Costco kicks off European drive in Spain," *The Seattle Times*, May 10, 2014), as the New World ironically reverse infects the Old World.

[767] From "Harper's Index": "Percentage of US adults in 1978 who said that the country's levels of consumption were 'immoral': 65. Who say so today: 46." (*Harper's Magazine*, April 2019.)
—Some have argued that modern advertising and marketing techniques do not so much create wants as fan the flames of likely demands. As with the history of Henry Adams, the appropriation *and* creation of consumer objects and services tend to follow cultural "paths of least resistance." The more critical impact here stems from the spawning and encouraging of a general short attention span immediate consumption ethos. In America we chafe under the reins of lowest common denominator consumer tastes. The more freedom given market dynamics—the greater their permeation throughout society—the more popular, generic, and contrived the attending cultural products. And these, in a normative cultural sense, tend toward the least expressive, intense, and enriching of all the possibilities indigenous to our cultural reservoirs. (Gertrude Jaeger and Philip Selznick, "A Normative Theory of Culture," *American Sociological Review*, 29: 653-669.) For living in a largely market-driven culture proves an inherently impoverishing personal and social experience.

[768] " 'What The Foucault?' and Other After-Dinner Musings," *The Paris Review*, 2/5/2018.

But perhaps there is more to it than just idle pronouncements and wistful thinking?

By now it has become readily apparent to me, at least, that there is an American cultural vacuum into which evangelicalism (and other reasonable facsimiles) gets sucked *or* rushes in to fill. Sometimes like the rain, it literally pours in.[769] Or indeed, to pile on the mixed metaphors, this vacuum first spreads like a swarm of bees over the landscape, wreaking cultural havoc, decline and death emanating from a thousand seemingly unrelated stings, leaving a scorched earth ready for the ensuing planting of the seeds of evangelicalism. And as per usual, few academicians saw it either coming or going.[770] For as I have argued, the detection and understanding of it requires

---

—"But enjoyment is *not* a goal, it is a feeling that accompanies important ongoing activity; pleasure, as Freud said, is always dependent on function." (Paul Goodman, *Growing Up Absurd.* . ., 235.)

[769] As Robert Wright shows, the Apostle Paul capitalized (almost literally in a metaphorical sense) upon a similar kind of "dislocation" in the Roman Empire the century following the Crucifixion of Christ to advance his particular enterprise or brand of religion: "The familial services offered by these groups ranged from the material, like burying the dead, to the psychological, like giving people a sense that other people cared about them. . . . . early Christian churches met the needs of the day. . . . The church, [E.R.] Dodds wrote, provided 'the essentials of social security,'. . . . A church was one big family." (*The Evolution of God*, 266-7.)

[770] This and other seemingly condescending characterizations of these vacuums are also difficult for many academicians and other contemporary American professionals to grasp because of the qualitative and quantitative difference of their lives. Here is David Brooks in a rare moment of insight:

> . . . . loneliness and social isolation are the problems that undergird many of our other problems. More Americans are socially poor. And it is very hard for the socially wealthy to even see this fact. . . . [re: congressional hearing questions about privacy thrown at Facebook's Mark Zuckerberg] That's the sort of thing that may be uppermost in your mind if you are socially wealthy, if, like most successful politicians and analysts, you live within a thick web of connection and feel as if your social schedule is too full. ("Our loneliness epidemic," *Seattle Times*, 4/18/18.)

The same might be said of a good many academicians; they appear largely unacquainted with average Americans who have virtually no social schedule or "connections" to speak of, no professional networks.

—Oddly enough, one philosopher and a theologian may have unintentionally said as much while claiming that a scientific worldview is "no more or less 'testable' than the divine revelations of historic religion. . . . Alasdair MacIntyre and Jacques Dupuis. . . . [argue] that the nature of 'the good life' and 'the good society' is rationally and even objectively determinable. . . . they contend that the physical constitution and intellectual capacities of human beings are such that we can 'flourish' and achieve genuine 'well-being' only in certain sorts of contexts and not in others." (Philip S. Gorski / David Kyuman Kim / John Torpey / Jonathan Van

a bias of sorts, and a deliberate willingness to call a spade a spade. Such skewed predilections or hunches can send us hurtling off into the darkness at times, but they can also deposit us face-to-face with some unforeseen, empirically-rewarding veins of shimmering gold.[771] As Stephen Stills so presciently sang in that anthem of the anti-war *counterculture* generation of the '60s and '70s, *For What It's Worth*: "something's happening here, what it is ain't exactly clear."[772] Perhaps even after all these years we shouldn't be surprised to discover that there still lingers a gnawing, foreboding sense that for all our grandiosity and material achievements there is something fundamentally amiss, something screwy going on here—something rotten in Denmark, or troubling in Tahiti.[773] And oh, the irony of it all. Exploring the source, nature,

---

Antwerpen, eds., *The Post-Secular in Question: Religion in Contemporary Society*, New York University Press, 2012, 10.)

[771] Paul Goodman was guided by a similar bias: " 'Is the harmonious organization to which the young are inadequately socialized, perhaps against human nature, or not worthy of human nature, and *therefore* there is difficulty in growing up?' If this is so, the disaffection of the young is profound and it will not be finally remediable by better techniques of socializing. Instead, *there will have to be changes in our society and its culture*, so as to meet the appetites and capacities of human nature, in order to grow up. . . . It is not a 'psychological' question of poor influences and bad attitudes, but an objective question of real opportunities for worthwhile experience. . . . our abundant society is at present simply deficient in many of the most elementary objective opportunities and worthwhile goals that could make growing up possible. . . . It has no community." (*Growing Up Absurd*, 11-12.) {second emphasis added} And as we will see, this is not even the half of it.

[772] Even whence we might least expect it: "Republican Sen. Ben Sasse of Nebraska believes that Americans are turning to political tribalism for the sense of community they used to get from simple connection to those around them." ("Briefing: An Epidemic of Loneliness," *The Week*, 1/11/2019, 11.) That's a start, at least.

[773] I am of course not the first to call attention to such modern trials and tribulations. May I recommend the journalist Johann Hari's extraordinary *Lost Connections: Uncovering The Real Causes of Depression—and the Unexpected Solutions* (Bloomsbury Circus 2018) as a companion volume to this treatise. Although what he regards as general social disconnection I treat here as more specific to the American historical and contemporary context, the social and cultural dynamics at work are the same. For what he identifies as the general causes of personal depression I re-characterize (or even extrapolate from—some might argue *reify*) as the source of a larger American cultural depression, with all its parallel malignant social and economic consequences. Although, again, he has traveled widely, he refers constantly to "our culture" inclusively (as though there is a uniform *Western* culture), citing the massive *Bowling Alone* study of Robert Putnam as though, again, a going-it-alone epidemic of disconnection and loneliness generalizes across the board: "There are similar figures for Britain and the rest of the Western World." (80-81) I am loathe to quibble where Hari is concerned, as we concur on so much, but Putnam's focus is largely, even exclusively, on the United States; there are virtually no references to European societies (one exception a two-page account of Italian community politics, 344-46). I suspect that Hari's childhood experiences in a socially isolated, perhaps even dysfunctional, London family and neighborhood get too easily generalized. That and an initial European trip prior to heading off to college while in the midst of a severe personal depression (6) (let alone a probable lack of fluency in another language?), can tend to sour first

meaning, and significance of that illusive *something* has proven just one of the major aims of this study.

---

impressions of any new travel experience. As is readily apparent in the international data that is rarely cited or even considered germane by American social scientists, *comparative cultural contexts* tell an altogether different story. Indeed the general post-modern malaise of which Hari writes applies with an exponentially greater force to the United States:

> We do things together less than any humans who came before us. Long before the economic crash of 2008, there was a social crash, in which we found ourselves alone and lonely far more of the time. The structures for looking out for each other—from the family to the neighborhood—fell apart. We disbanded our tribes. We embarked on an experiment—to see if humans can live alone. . . . we are homesick even when we are at home. . . . (80-81) This disconnection has spread over the entire Western world. (90)

The hyperbole proves contagiously persuasive here and although overwrought, is quite understandable. As a victim and survivor of a nearly twenty-five-year chronic depression myself, I share Hari's angst. But we must issue one major caveat emptor, namely that while such emotional debilitation heightens one's empathy, such empathy invariably distorts reality. One can become *over-sensitized*. One's own depression gets read into every sad face, and occasionally also, maleficent intent into even the most innocuous gestures. The ability to detect and distinguish gradients of emotion and experience is a major causality. "Good at reading people" is not a quality I would attribute to even moderately depressed humans; more like maudlin and out of touch. To the most extremely afflicted, the world appears completely ravaged, *falling apart, broken down*, among other related misperceptions. And so this is one of the very few grains of salt I would suggest taking when reading *Lost Connections*: yes, it is bad out there, surely, but sometime in your life, if you get a chance, take a stroll through the center of Madrid some evening, or any village for that matter in most of Europe; one will quickly become disabused of any notion that we are all adrift with no anchor. Sadly, the same cannot be claimed for most American cities and towns (although some academicians will call out certain comparable rates for particular crimes that belie such assertions of difference. See, for example, "Chapter Four: Crime," in Peter Baldwin, *The Narcissism. . .* , 74-90).

One more grain of salt to swallow: "When I was a child, Margaret Thatcher said, 'There's no such thing as society, only individuals and their families'—and, all over the world, her viewpoint won." (258) *Au contraire*, for in spite of recent bumps in the road, virtually no European nation, and others elsewhere, would exchange their version of the good society for Mrs. Thatcher's. I will expand more upon this phenomenon later, wherein modern European social democracies have managed to create larger macro-national forms of the micro-tribal, community-care traditions whose passing Hari laments. Indeed if it takes a whole village to raise a child then surely why not a whole national village as well?

Then again, one wonders if societies are like individuals in another respect: "As this experiment began, one of the things they [Kaiser Permanente doctors] discovered almost immediately is that many of the [trauma victim] patients had literally *never before acknowledged what happened to them to another human being*." (242) {emphasis added} The American society, in particular, is less innocently ensnared, more guilty of a deliberate ongoing denial of the trauma it has inflicted upon its most vulnerable members, all too many of whom appear unaware of, or unwilling to, acknowledge either their own deliberate complicity or their equally unwitting victimization.

—And yet again, perhaps T. M. Luhrmann, like Hari, is right to wonder if more general social trends—urbanization, media technology—ultimately lie behind any apparent increases in mental illness. ("Is the World More Depressed?" *The New York Times*, March 24, 2014.)

So, again, what could possibly be happening here? Today, we encounter the same uncertainties,[774] approach the same fork in the road that confronted our Puritan forefathers and mothers, suspended as they were in a transitional moment in time between Old and New Worlds, unsure as to what had actually transpired—what had been or *was*, vestiges of which still nipping at their heels—and what loomed ahead perhaps even more ominously, a perilous *something* that just might appear from out of nowhere or out of nothing. With respect then to our respective roles as common actors, citizens, settlers, descendents and interpreters of a social and cultural inheritance, Jon Butler both looked back upon those original prospects *and* then framed (perhaps unintentionally anticipating) the current matter at hand, as our ancestors stared out, poised on the brink of a New World:

> The Yorkshire visitation [by church authorities] revealed the fragile adherence to Christianity [sparse attendance figures] among the early modern European laity. Despite cathedrals, chapels, legal establishments, and Christian-dominated education systems, all of Europe's Old World societies extended a most perplexing religious heritage to their New World colonies. If Virginia and Massachusetts authorities intended to expand European Christianity into the wilderness, whose Christianity would it be—that of the law, the church, the ambivalent laity? Old World Christianity had long been sheltered and supported by a complex infrastructure of theology, law, and social process. *What would happen in the New World where an ecclesiastical order had yet to be established, where the law had yet to be written or enforced, where the land lay without Christian sacralization, and where men and women were strangers to each other except, perhaps, in their longing for material gain and in their undisciplined, expansive, and sometimes ambivalent expressions of spiritual interest?* [775]

What would happen indeed? And whose or what kind of Christianity would emerge? Still we long wholeheartedly for material gain; still we remain

---

[774] Daniele Hervieu-Leger has a take on these matters worth mentioning. Although it is understandable that a distinguished French academician shies from casting aspersions upon American culture, her more general formulation of the "uncertainty" wrought by modernity proves instructive: ". . . . belief proliferates in proportion to the uncertainty caused by the pace of change in all areas of social life. . . . The most striking paradox of this situation is this: the more beliefs circulate [i.e., believers "migrate"], the less they determine tangible [more orthodox] affiliations and the more they further a desire for community liable to evolve into intensive forms of religious socialization." This correlated dynamic applies, however tangentially, to both the colonial and contemporary American cultural contexts, as advanced above. ("In Search of Certainties: The Paradoxes of Religiosity in Societies of High Modernity," *The Hedgehog Review*, Spring & Summer 2006, 59, 66.)

[775] Jon Butler, *Awash . . .* , 36. {emphasis added}
—Some of the more thoughtful of these descendents turned this New England ambivalence into transcendentalism, although Henry David Thoreau chose to focus upon more empirical observations: "The mass of men lead lives of quiet desperation." (from *Walden*, in *Henry David Thoreau*, The Library of America, 1985, 329.) Then again, we will never know how he might have compared Concord and Boston with European villages.

strangers to one another. We muddle on, a civilization riddled with unresolved tensions and paradoxes. And yet into that maelstrom of a cultural void has flowed the ameliorating succor of quite a few markedly less ambivalent expressions of spiritual interest,[776] this sweet nectar of evangelicalism most importantly and significantly. Perhaps we should have seen it coming, but more likely no one could. As Weber warned, nothing proves more predictable than uncertainty, and the ultimate *unintended* consequences of intentions gone awry, no matter how uncompromising their original source.[777]

These are large and important questions. By marked contrast, the great bulk of this study, this investigation into these matters, oddly enough, as broached much earlier, began with much smaller concerns pursued in a very small place, a two-thousand or so member evangelical academic community in the Pacific Northwest. Although my initial rationale for a small case study was largely personal and logistic, I am now persuaded there is no more valuable or rewarding approach. A few compelling reasons: 1) evangelical

---

[776] Pippa Norris and Ronald Inglehart, among numerous other insights we will cite in a moment, recognized vaguely similar kinds of dynamics at work in eastern Europe after the collapse of the Soviet Union: "Overall the publics of thirteen of the fifteen ex-Communist countries for which we have a substantial time series increased their emphasis on religion. The sharp drop in economic, physical, and psychological security. . . is what we suspect caused the resurgence of religion. . . . the collapse of the communist ideology was a central part of this, leaving people disoriented and psychologically insecure and opening an ideological vacuum that, for many people, religion fills." (*Sacred and Secular: Religion and . . .* , 278.)

[777] Following what Robert Bellah calls "evolutionary propensities," Weber also discerned in the emerging modernism and disenchantment of the world a growing tension or "conflict between religion and kinship. . . . In the place of 'the magical ties and exclusiveness' of kinship, 'within the new community the prophetic religion has developed a religious ethic of brotherliness . . . . [which] has simply taken over the original principles of social and ethical conduct which "the association of neighbors" had offered, whether it was the community of villagers, members of the sib, the guild, or partners in seafaring, hunting, and warring expeditions.' . . . The idea was 'your want of today may be mine of tomorrow.' . . . Within the group those of wealth and status have an obligation to help the needy." Marshall Sahlins calls this the "generalized reciprocity" of *Stone-Age Economics* (1972): ". . . . 'the expectation of reciprocity is indefinite. . . . Failure to reciprocate does not cause the giver of stuff to stop giving; the goods move one way, in favor of the have-not, for a very long period.' " Eventually, for better or worse, "kinship is not simply rejected; it is transformed and universalized so that it becomes the very principle of religion itself in the form of world-denying love." (Robert Bellah, "Max Weber and World-Denying Love: A Look at the Historical Sociology of Religion," *Journal of the American Academy of Religion*, 67/2, 1999.) The parallel here is that beyond the matter of how these ancient principles became transformed into a world-engaging and transforming ascetic Protestantism for Weber, we observe a similar kind of dynamic at work whereby Scandinavian kinship principles are extended or universalized into a modern Nordic version of "generalized reciprocity." The Americans created "moral markets" of evaluation and repudiation; whereas, as we will see, the Nordics regenerated the norms and values of kinship into a supremely modern form of reciprocity.

religion is in many respects a remarkably homogeneous phenomenon, contending claims to the contrary notwithstanding; an understanding of any part of evangelicalism can serve to illuminate the whole.[778] 2) This particular institution, in purely denominational terms, presented a reasonably representative sample of American religiosity; it draws students from a host of church communities in rough proportion to their size in the national population. 3) Speech and behavior *within* evangelical communities tend to differ markedly from presentations *without*—in the "secular" world. Teaching and scholarship within evangelical institutions, in particular, are driven by altogether different rationales—*cultural logics*, if you will—of meaning, motivation, and significance that are largely camouflaged, hidden from the outside world. Hence an investigator chances upon phenomena within such a community that he will encounter nowhere else—certainly not in the more general media-oriented and saturated national arena.[779] Elsewhere the guard is up, vigilantly projected and maintained.

Now since this work largely represents a definition of evangelicalism in and of itself and I have depended upon the unfolding of its contents for a full account of the phenomenon in question, this particular preliminary exercise has been foregone. Those readers requiring a routine introductory

---

[778] Of course there are all sorts of variations within evangelicalism. Daniel Radosh's point that ". . . . American evangelicalism is a tremendously heterodox society that is not well represented by its shrillest component, the religious right" is well-taken (*Rapture Ready! . .* , 2008, 304). Note, however, that he wrote those words prior to the ascension of Donald Trump to power. See my "For What It's Worth: The Cultural Origins of 'Alternative Facts' " for the role evangelicals have assumed in his administration. But when academicians like T.M. Luhrmann dip into such a small, potentially unrepresentative sample as she did with the church sect, The Vineyard, in *When God Talks Back: Understanding the American Evangelical Relationship with God* (Knopf 2012), the same rule of thumb applies. There are many currents within evangelicalism that are largely insignificant socially and politically. As Radosh notes in a 2006 Gallup survey, "44 percent of American adults, or about 86 million people, identified themselves as either evangelical or born-again." (op. cit., 6) *Significance* (a central theme of this book) comes *and goes* and must be assessed in terms of *degrees* of social and political impact.

[779] It is instructive that the only valuable admission or contribution one evangelical apologist in particular makes in his entire study concerns precisely this point, contained in a two-page section titled "Signals": "Evangelicals in the mainstream often use 'signaling' to communicate with other believers without alerting a secular audience. . . . depends upon implicit, subtle, and often disguised messages." (D. Michael Lindsay, *Faith in The Halls of Power: How Evangelicals Joined the American Elite*, Oxford University Press, 2007, 152-3.)
—"The early presidential speeches [of George Bush] were written by evangelical Michael Gerson. Gerson's writings were laden with Biblical language that served as coded messages to those who are part of the club. . . ." (Monique El-Faizy, *God and Country: How Evangelicals Have Become America's New Mainstream*, Bloomsbury, 2006, 204.) The reader may be put in mind of Michael Cohen's testimony before Congress, wherein he spoke repeatedly of the "code" Donald Trump used to implicitly direct and sanction illegal conduct.

description, say, of "fundamentalism" and "evangelicalism," or an extended account of the distinguishing features of various denominations or sects, are easily referred to other more traditional tracts.[780]

Above and beyond my story of this small academic community there have loomed some rather larger themes and issues that concrete details have served to evoke and illuminate. At the risk of redundancy, I have argued that evangelical religion represents the ideological heart of American culture, in that the inherent logic of its religious ideas has underpinned (and/or buttressed) a good many aggressive promotions and defenses of American society, domestic and international, throughout our history.[781] We have encountered an evangelical worldview *and* ethos that is grounded in two basic idioms: a dualistic vision cleaving the elements of society into neat, separate Christian and secular categories, and the "moral market"[782] imperatives of

---

[780] In the bibliography, see Catherine L. Albanese, Matthew Avery Sutton, Nancy Tatum Ammerman, Alan Peshkin, George M. Marsden, Garry Wills, Martin Marty, and Christian Smith, among others.

—For a review of the matter of survey definitions among sociologists and pollsters, see Conrad Hackett and D. Michael Lindsay, "Measuring Evangelicalism: Consequences of Different Operationalization Strategies," *Journal for the Scientific Study of Religion*, Vol. 47, No. 3, Sept., 2008. A fairly reliable estimate of evangelicals in the United States would run anywhere from thirty to forty percent of the total population. Hence the support for Donald Trump in polling never dipped below 35%, his rock-solid evangelical base.

—Yet I must confess having taken to Thomas A. Tweed's well-grounded definition of the larger category from which evangelicalism sprang, however contested the category has become: "Religions are confluences of organic-cultural flows that intensify joy and confront suffering by drawing on human and suprahuman forces to make homes and cross boundaries." (*Crossing and Dwelling: A Theory of Religion*, Harvard University Press 2006, 54.) Yes, that will do nicely, for now.

—I would also recommend Ross Douthat's deftly written *Bad Religion*. . . . (2014) for an adequate description of the current condition of Christianity in America, one that unfortunately relies almost exclusively on secondary published sources. But, by all means, read his book, and then luxuriate in the full knowledge that, having completed *Paradise Joe's*, the reader will already own a deep understanding of the phenomenon, the acquisition of which so clearly eluded Mr. Douthat's poor readers.

[781] Garry Wills formulates this a little more generally: "Neither Jefferson nor Madison thought that separation would loosen the impact of religion on our nation. Quite the opposite. . . . [separation brought a] greater moral force. . . . The first nation to disestablish religion has been a marvel of religiosity, for good or ill. *Religion has been at the center of our major political crises, which are always moral crises*—the supporting and opposing of wars, of slavery, of corporate power, of civil rights, of sexual codes, of the 'West,' of American separatism and claims to empire." (*Under God. . .* , 25.) {emphasis added}

[782] The phrase "moral market thinking" comes from Garry Wills's *Nixon Agonistes: The Crisis of the Self-Made Man* (New York: Houghton-Mifflin, 1968), the most compelling analysis of American political culture ever penned.

a formal individualistic system of ethics, the two merging to form a matrix of symbols and expectations—a cultural calculus or logic, if you will—which is then applied in the apprehension and evaluation of persons, objects, relationships, and even societies. The first shares much with "natural" religion and was present in the early Christian church as well as in other Western religions; the second emerged from uniquely American political and cultural developments. Both occupy the centerpiece of a peculiarly American personality, that which most clearly distinguishes the American from European societies; both also prove the source of many of our most enduring internal "cultural contradictions." [783]

Now I should explain what I have in mind by the phrase "ideological heart." The term, ideology, has been used so loosely and carelessly at times to render it almost meaningless. When I write of an ideological dynamic I am referring to an *acceleration* of meaning and motivation. For my purposes ideology represents an *extraordinary source of meaning and motivation employed in the aggressive promotion and/or defense of a particular group, community, society, or "worldview."* To my way of thinking a worldview is not in and of itself ideological.[784] Religions are not in and of themselves ideologies. They can be-

---

—Kevin Kruse traces other contributing threads, arguing, for example, that the push to retroactively invent a Christian nation "had its roots not in the foreign policy panic of the 1950s but rather in the domestic politics of the 1930s, and early 1940s. . . . corporate titans enlisted conservative clergymen in an effort to promote new political arguments embodied in the phrase 'freedom under God' . . . . this new ideology was designed to defeat the state power its architects feared most—not the Soviet regime in Moscow, but Franklin D. Roosevelt's New Deal administration. . . . With ample funding from major corporations, prominent industrialists, and business lobbies such as the national Association of Manufacturers and the US Chamber of Commerce in the 1930s and 1940s, these new evangelists for free enterprise promoted a vision best characterized as 'Christian libertarianism.' " So ideologized, church membership soared from 16% in 1850, 36% in 1900, to 49% in 1940 and eventually 69% in 1960. (*One Nation Under God* . . . , XIV-XV.)

—Or, more generally and recently, the collateral implications: "This book is about the Greens [the owners], but it is also about how a set of American values, in which success in business is viewed as a qualification for success in any area of life; in which the United States is first and foremost a Christian country and religious freedom is the magnanimous gesture of that powerful majority; and in which individualism and property rights trump free access to and public ownership of knowledge and learning." (Candida R. Moss & Joel S. Baden, *Bible Nation: The United States of Hobby Lobby*, Princeton University Press, 2017, viii.)

[783] The phrase was first introduced, I believe, by Daniel Bell (1976).

[784] Hence my reading strays somewhat from an influential standard, Clifford Geertz's "Ideology as a Cultural System," in *The Interpretation of Cultures* (New York: Basic Books, 1973). Similarly, with respect to a slightly different juxtaposition I agree with "Seeman (2010) [who] argues that if you 'read [Geertz's] essay while systematically replacing the word "religion" everywhere it appears with the word "culture" [you can see] how little the meaning of that essay changes when religion actually drops out.' " (Michael Lambek, "What Is 'Religion' for

come ideological in thrust and focus, but they are not necessarily so. Individuals, groups, communities, and societies can be *more or less* ideological in an identifiable, systematic, and measurable fashion. To lump all worldviews together as ideologies of a sort is to render judgments as to degrees of intensity in outlook exceedingly difficult to make.[785]

Anthropology? And What Has Anthropology Brought to 'Religion'?" in Janice Boddy and Michael Lambek eds., *A Companion to the Anthropology of Religion*, John Wiley & Sons 2013, 20, 30, ff#30.) For indeed although religion can at times seem to inform the entire culture, marked distinctions remain, just as a culture can become largely ideologized without growing completely indistinguishable from, or incapable of returning to, a prior condition of cultural normalcy.

—Harvey Cox's definition is somewhat similar to mine. See *Religion in the Secular City. . .* , 61.

—Nor are ideologies "rational-actor" reward systems: "Thus, ideologies are ideological as they shape, control, and deliver religious rewards or what might be called 'spiritual capital.' " (James K. Wellman, Jr., *Evangelical vs. Liberal: The Clash of Christian Cultures in the Pacific Northwest*, Oxford University Press 2008.)

—One of the few things I find reasonably accessible in Étienne Balibar's largely abstruse "critical" neo-Marxist take on secularism and religion concerns ideology: "I shall make no secret of the fact that this also represents an effort on my part to rehabilitate a category that has become rather unfashionable today: ideology. . . . The aim is emphatically not to reduce any and all discourse to an 'ideological function,'. . . . The equation that we must keep in mind cannot take the form culture + religion = ideology, but must rather be written culture + religion ± X = ideology. Ideology, as a combination of culture and religion in variable 'proportions,' always exhibits a structural deficit." Well, sort of heading in my direction. (*Secularism and Cosmopolitanism: Critical Hypotheses on Religion and Politics*, Columbia University Press 2018, 34, 37.)

—Mary Douglas refers to an essay by Louis Dupré that raises some interesting issues about Marx's conception of ideology, as well as his much later "critical theory" descendants: "Marx's Critique of Culture and Its Interpretations," *The Review of Metaphysics*, Vol. 34, No. 1, Sept., 1980. See especially the final paragraph.

—Jonathan Haidt comes very close via an afterthought: "Here's [Erikson and Tedin's 2003] . . . simple definition of ideology: 'A set of beliefs about the proper order of society and how it can be achieved.'8 And here's the most basic of all ideological questions: Preserve the present order, or change it?" Perhaps we do well to add: Or foist it upon others, as well—the evangelical mandate. (*The Righteous Mind: Why Good People Are Divided by Religion and Politics*, Penguin Books 2013, 323.)

[785] Ideology and *identity* are intimately linked, as James Morone writes of American Puritanism:

> The Puritans groped back to the tried and true—they found terrible new enemies to define them. The saints constructed their "us" against a vivid series of immoral "them"[s]: heretics, Indians, witches. Each enemy clarified the Puritan identity. (*Hellfire Nation. . .* , 33.)

—It is in this sense that Claude S. Fischer misses the point of the resilience of the Puritan mentalité in American culture, a contemporary relevance extending beyond mere Victorian sexuality: ". . . . most scholars probably agree with historian John L. Brooke that 'historians have long since abandoned any interpretation grounding the American nation in Puritanism.' " (*Made in America. . .* , 107.)

The Amish, for example, to cite a reasonably well-known American sect or group, do not strike me as an ideological community or the bearers of a religious ideology. For this reason I do not think of them as evangelical or ideological. Their beliefs are not *accelerated* or mobilized into a defensive or offensive posture; for the most part they are not deploying forces on an imaginary field of battle against some clear and present danger. They are not crazy about the "modern world" surely (in fact they quite unabashedly sell their own image and wares in the marketplace of culture[786]), but they do not hover in a condition of constant alert.[787]

The parallels between evangelicalism and radical Islam prove striking, as when Hamid Dabashi labels the Shiite variant of Islam a "religion of protest," wherein "Shiism is not so much a sect or a minority tradition of Islam, but a comprehensive and variegated version of the entire faith. It is 'the dream/nightmare of Islam itself as it goes about the world . . . a promise made yet undelivered to itself and the world.' It is 'the hidden soul of Islam, its sigh of relief from its own grievances against a world ill at ease with what it is.' The paradox comes when such a religion assumes power, as in Sfavid Persia (and Iran today), becoming a 'state majority religion with an enduring minority complex.' " As we have seen all too tragically with the evangelical administration of Donald Trump, one cannot govern on spite and resentment—on bread and circus rallies—alone. Indeed, how does one assume the reins of power and effectively govern the very same Leviathan against which one has perennially protested and heaped derision upon? No wonder the incessant internecine attacks upon the very institutions he has been assigned to oversee and guide. For like Shi'ism, evangelicalism above all remains a heat-and-heresy-seeking guided missile of a "moral force or conscience"—an ideology of protest, not of governance. Similarly, a historically developed complex of "having been wronged by the existing powers, which lies at the heart of Shi'ism, contributes to the notion [nay, even *ensures*] that 'the veracity of the faith remains legitimate only so far as it is combative and speaks

---

[786] Laurence R. Moore, *Selling God: American Religion in the Marketplace of Culture*, New York: Oxford University Press, 1994, 11.

[787] As David Nirenberg (reviewing the work of Shahab Ahmed) argues that when a religion, like Islam, loses the rich and diverse historical *contexts* of its development, where it is seen as "the sum of everything that has ever been lived or experienced as Islamic," then it begins to focus on the *literalness* of "text[s] of revelation" and overlooks the "context of revelation." This "characteristic of Islamic *modernity*" arose largely in my estimation when the West began to loom as a perceived danger to Islam, and like 20th-century extremist Zionism and evangelical Christianity jettisoned considerations of context for the clear and present dangers identified and targeted by ideology. (David Nirenberg, "What is Islam? [What is Christianity? What is Judaism?]," *Raritan*, Vol. 36 #2, Fall 2016.)

truth to power, and (conversely) almost instantly loses that legitimacy when it actually comes to power.' "[788]

All along, the modern American evangelical "Religious Right" has been equally ideologized and mobilized, standing in bold relief to both the Amish and many of their own 19th and 20th century antecedents, as we discovered in the chapter on deep and shallow history. Although there are still some unresolved questions as to the precipitating events[789] that led to the rise of this political movement, or the precise source of their apprehensions of clear and present danger, it is now indisputable that abortion—and the larger *bete noire* of *secularism*, in general—remain among the most enduring incendiary issues (*apparitions* even) sustaining the movement's ongoing sense of urgency.[790] The Roe v. Wade Supreme Court decision of 1973 legalizing

---

[788] As quoted in Malise Ruthven's review of Dabashi's *Shi'ism: A Religion of Protest*, in *The New York Review of Books*, 12/22/2011, 90-1.

[789] Randall Balmer relies upon Paul Weyrich, one of the gurus of the Religious Right, who insists that the more incendiary event was not "pornography, school prayer, the proposed Equal Rights Amendment . . . and abortion. . . . What changed their [his phrase, the "moral majority's"] mind was Jimmy Carter's intervention against the Christian schools, trying to deny them tax-exempt status on the basis of so-called de facto segregation." (Randall Balmer 2016, 112.)
—The broader racial impetus and reaction is well documented in *Reversing Roe*, a documentary film by Ricki Stern and Annie Sundberg.
—The most complete account of these and other perceived federal intrusions into family and religious life, encouraging a siege mentality to descend upon the evangelical community, can be found in William Martin's *With God on Our Side: The Rise of the Religious Right in America* (1996). See especially Chapter 4, "The Battle of Anaheim," and Chapter 8, "The Moral Majority."
—And even earlier were "The key decisions—*Engl v. Vitale* in 1962, which forbade state-sponsored prayer in schools, and *Abington v. Schempp* in 1963, which banned mandatory Bible reading. . . ." (Robert D. Putnam & David E. Campbell, *American Grace: How Religion Divides and Unites Us*, New York: Simon & Schuster, 2010, 115.)
—Francis Schaeffer's role in all of this is briefly covered in Molly Worthen's otherwise disappointing *Apostles of Reason: The Crisis of Authority in American Evangelicalism*, Oxford 2014, 213.
—Easily the best book I've encountered on this whole matter of the Religious Right and the so-called culture wars is Dan Gilgoff's *The Jesus Machine: How James Dobson, Focus on the Family, and Evangelical America Are Winning the Culture War*, New York: St. Martin's Press, 2007.

[790] One seriously misguided young academician contends otherwise. There was no perception of threat from the outside but the contentious issue of ecumenism (finally resolved) that lay behind the formation of the Religious Right, argues Neil J. Young. What is more, Catholics and Mormons had joined the fray, setting aside their separatist tendencies: ". . . . these three faiths had been thinking deeply about each other and the very question of Christian unity. . . . it was the latest iteration of a religious debate that had gone on for decades, sparked by the ecumenical contentions of mainline Protestantism *rather than by secular liberal political victories*." (*We Gather Together: The Religious Right and the Problem of Interfaith Politics*, Oxford University Press, 2016, 5.) {emphasis added} One scarcely knows how to respond. How embarrassing?

abortion, at the time a more galvanizing event among conservative Catholics,[791] nonetheless has grown over the years into the cynosure of evangelical politics.[792] *Paradise Joe's* can help us understand the deep cultural origins and nature of that ideological impetus and animus, serving to place it in an appropriate historical lineage and contemporary context.[793]

---

[791] Andrew Hartman, *A War for the Soul of America: A History of the Cultural Wars*, University of Chicago Press, 2015, 93.

[792] James Morone agrees: "The high tide for liberalism and privacy came with *Roe v. Wade* in 1973 . . . . With *Roe* the court had almost fully dismantled the Victorian sexual regime—and roused a completely new era of hellfire politics. The long socially progressive swing ended, and the political pendulum headed back towards the politics of personal morality." (*Hellfire Nation* . . , 444.) Unfortunately, he misses the mark by arguing that the evangelical backlash of the '70s focused upon the individualism of sin, not the social bugbear of *secularism*: "These new Victorians scorn the Social Gospel reflex that blames the system. Individuals, they insist, are responsible for their own behavior—and for our common problems." (450; but he almost gets it right on 453.) Nothing could be further from the truth, as we have seen.
—See Kristin Luker's *Abortion and the Politics of Motherhood* (University of California Press 1985, 126-38) on *Roe v. Wade* and "The Emergence of the Right-to-Life Movement."
—If one overlooks an excruciatingly painful introductory chapter (see a subsequent note), a useful general reference is Dallas A. Blanchard's *The Anti-abortion Movement and the Rise of the Religious Right: From Pulpit to Fiery Protest* (New York: Twayne Publishers 1994). See also: R. Marie Griffith, *Moral Combat: How Sex Divided American Christians and Fractured American Politics* (Basic Books 2017).
—Yet another piece of the larger puzzle: "At the first GOP convention after the 1973 *Roe v. Wade* decision, with Nixon's downfall and the ascension of the hapless Gerald Ford, the party was nervous about its waning base. Senator Jesse Helms of North Carolina, always alert to a divisive issue, suggested taking a stance on abortion. . . . An anti-abortion plank was readily added. Evangelicals had been permissive on the procedure into the early 1970s. . . . But that changed once *Roe* was applied nationwide, and Republicans saw a chance to pick up more of the evangelical vote." From Andrew Hacker's review of *The Great Alignment: Race, Party, Transformation, and the Rise of Donald Trump* by Alan I. Abramowitz (Yale University Press 2018), *The New York Review of Books*, 9/27/18, 73.
—In Hanna Rosin's account of the evangelical political training college, Patrick Henry University, one student named Derek produced a skit for the campus talent show, wherein he conducted an imaginary interview with four upperclassmen thirty years later: "All of them had turned out to be utter failures except one, who was a Supreme Court Justice about to provide the critical vote in overturning *Roe v. Wade*." (Hanna Rosin, *God's Harvard: A Christian College on a Mission to Save America*, Harcourt Books, 2007, 19-20.)

[793] Examples abound: "Evangelicals thus argued that the growing power of the state reflected the power of secular humanism in American culture. Senator Jesse Helms, an evangelical from North Carolina, declared on the floor of the Senate, 'When you have men who no longer believe that God is in charge of human affairs, you have *men attempting to take the place of God by means of the Superstate*,' . . . . [And Tim LaHaye followed with:] as secular humanism made its way into government, 'humanist social planners' had begun to establish 'a one world socialist state, where Plato's dream of three classes of people would be fulfilled.' " (Bowman, *Christian: The Politics*. . . , 211-12.)

By concentrating primarily on a small community, by conducting a "case study," a good deal of what I have presented cuts against the grain of current academic research into these matters, particularly that in sociology. I find this only mildly troubling since, with a few notable exceptions,[794] social scientific accounts of evangelicalism have provided only marginal assistance in the conception and preparation of this volume. Sociologists, in particular, tend to carry into their investigations an overbearing load of theoretical and methodological baggage, at times dispensing an almost impenetrable fog of jargon with somewhat predictable abandon, producing analyses that have a distant, telegraphic feel to them. From these guiding theoretical templates are usually generated testable propositions (the "science" part), coupled with the tabulation and evaluation of so-called "hard data" from questionnaires and other sources.[795] Most of our social scientific understanding of religion

---

[794] Although they share some of the problems discussed, I did find the two aforementioned case studies by Nancy Ammerman and Alan Peshkin insightful and generally amenable to the argument advanced in this book. Among journalistic accounts, I admired much of the piece by Frances Fitzgerald: "Reflections: Jim And Tammy," *The New Yorker*, 23 April 1990.

[795] In this respect, Andrew Greeley and Michael Hout's *The Truth About Conservative Christians: What They Think and What They Believe* (University of Chicago Press 2006) warrants a monograph-length appraisal that unfortunately cannot be undertaken here. Aside from the hubris of their claim to have discovered "The Truth," which proves alarming enough, there are a host of methodological, analytical, and interpretive problems. Briefly, I question the following assertions: 1) that there has occurred a "demonization of Conservative Christians in the higher media and the scholarly academy. . . . [and] bigotry against them." (4) Yet no references or examples are cited; moreover, "demonization" is an inappropriate, biased, loaded *religious* term. The "scholarly academy," *au contaire*, has bent over backward to analyze the phenomenon objectively—too much so in my estimation (or simply tends to discount the relevance of evangelical religion for serious study). I challenge the authors to provide even one example of such academic "demonization." 2) That conservative Protestants are ". . . . far too varied in their political views to be President Bush's political base, as everyone seemed to think. . . . [journalists, public intellectuals] are **monumentally ignorant** of the faith and behavior of the citizens who fit under the rubric of 'conservative Christians'. . . . Clearly, claims that Conservative Protestants have hijacked the nation's politics are greatly exaggerated. They are *only modestly different* from Americans of other large religious groups. . . . Reporters who ask us to comment on 'trends' seem to have mistaken a trend in how they cover elections [*fake news?*] for a trend in how Americans actually vote . . . . [our data] challenges the images of religiously inspired culture wars and partisan polarization. . . . [we, and others] continue to point out *the glaring gap between religious and political conservatism*. . . . On balance the conservative leanings give Republicans an advantage, but it is *clearly an error to equate religious and political conservatism*." (2, 42-48) Unfortunately, the rise of Donald Trump and his veto-proof 80% super majority among evangelical voters requires no further comment. Indeed, the reader of this book could have easily foreseen the political triumph of Trump and evangelicalism. 3) That, perhaps most glaring—no, egregious and embarrassing—of all, the pattern of responses to their survey questions reveals ". . . . the overwhelming similarity between the Conservative and Afro-American Protestants. . . . [indeed] When they differ it is almost always the Afro-Americans who take the more doctrinally conservative position." (37) And this similarity, they argue, disproves the claim that religious conservatism is strongly related to or determines political

rests upon these kinds of theoretical and methodological instruments.[796] Yet this seemingly automatic taking of general conceptions into the study of particular social and cultural phenomena often proves a debilitating habit. I am unaware of any golden rule of sociology which grounds the discipline *exclusively* in general patterns of conduct.[797] Indeed what could prove more all-

---

conservatism. For you see it has nothing to do with the political views of blacks, which are overwhelming leftist. It therefore proves that evangelicals defy any easy religious-right political stereotype or classification. Unfortunately (again), the authors, in their doctrinal, methodological, data biases, cannot get beyond the numbers. There is, in fact, a vast *cultural, historical,* and *political* difference between the religiosity of American blacks that the author's conventional model/survey questions can neither detect nor explain. (Just how one might go about this was explored and demonstrated in my Appendix A, Evangelical Apartheid: The Statistical Tests.) {emphases added above}

—Now as for the claim that mere statistical prowess ensures impartiality and "The Truth," Pippa Norris and Ronald Inglehart find much to be desired in Greeley's work elsewhere, citing reams of contradictory data: "To conclude, as Greeley [2003] does, that religion is still 'relatively unchanged' in the traditional Catholic nations of Europe seems a triumph of hope over experience, and *sharply at odds with the evidence. . . .* [and contrary to Greeley and Hout's claims above] in the 2000 presidential election, *religion was by far the strongest predictor of who voted for George W. Bush and who voted for Al Gore.*" ("Sellers or Buyers in Religious Markets? The Supply and Demand of Religion," *The Hedgehog Review,* Spring & Summer 2006, 75, 81.) {emphases added}

—Re "truth," #2: "Religious participation is associated with morally conservative attitudes on abortion, marriage, and homosexuality in all regions of the United States, Canada, and Britain; however, *these attitudes are only associated with distinct voting patterns in the United States.*" (Lydea Bean, *The Politics of . . .* , 7.) {emphasis added}

[796] For novice academicians there could be no better primer on this kind of stilted pseudo-scientific mumbo-jumbo than Dallas A. Blanchard's otherwise well-meaning (but nearly insufferable "Chapter 1 Framing the Discussion," 4-7) *The Anti-Abortion Movement and the Rise of the Religious Right: From Polite to Fiery Protest* (New York: Twayne Publishers 1994).

—A good example of how an academician allows his research approach—a "leap-frog method" of obtaining and conducting interviews—to almost ensure the confirmation of a major thesis about "networking" can be found in D. Michael Lindsay's *Faith in The Halls of Power: How Evangelicals Joined the Elite* (Oxford University Press 2007). Here an obvious evangelical apologist masquerades as an impartial social scientist.

—Jessica Johnson spoils an otherwise worthwhile dissertation-to-book outing by constantly filtering some quite valuable material through the sieves of other academician's abstruse concepts and jargon; she would have done better to trust her own instincts. See *Biblical Porn: Affect, Labor, and Pastor Mark Driscoll's Evangelical Empire* (Duke University Press, 2018).

—Then there's one of my favorite *stop-the-presses!* moments: "Generally speaking, evangelicals as a whole tend to be highly religious people." (Corwin E. Smidt, *American Evangelicals Today*, Rowman & Littlefield, 2013.)

[797] Indeed even Emile Durkheim, widely considered to be the founder of sociology, thought more broadly of the emerging discipline: "Durkheim argued, in contrast [with Freud], that *Homo sapiens* was really *Homo duplex*, a creature who exists at two levels: as an individual and as part of a larger society. From his studies of religion he concluded that people have two distinct sets of 'social sentiments,' one for each level." (Jonathan Haidt, *The Righteous Mind. . . , 261.)

inclusive—bristling with both innumerable details and sweeping vistas, long narrow corridors and broad avenues leading to who-knows-where-and-what—than a society?

In this regard, American sociologists of religion have not done themselves proud.[798] One doyen of American academicians and promulgator of

---

—And as for Max Weber: "The purpose of sociology was not to discover general laws but to understand human action in all its complexity. This emphasis on the unique rather than the universal made his work difficult to categorize. Not a few of his colleagues were tripped up by his arguments—errors he attacked in print with lacerating criticism." (Peter Gordon, "Max the Fatalist," *The New York Review of Books*, 6/11/2020, 33.)

—Then again observe the nearly opposite tendency, indulged in by evangelical college academicians (as we have seen) and some social scientists and historians who are Christian, that of eschewing any approach which seeks to link religious phenomena with social, economic, or cultural—with underlying "material"—factors or causes. As complains Joseph Bottum: "The trouble with all [all??] such sociological explanations is that they require their subjects to be nearly idiots, congenitally incapable of self-awareness or self-examination. . . . Modern sociology. . . seems not to possess much clear understanding that people *actually believe* what they believe. . . . it cannot admit genuinely supernatural events." (*An Anxious Age...*, 49.) Of course, nothing could be further from the truth: the lion's share of secular university academician's who study religion are in fact Christians and readily confess as much. But by and large, of course, they tend not to openly "admit genuinely supernatural events."

[798] One of our most distinguished living sociologists, Peter Berger, perhaps reflecting his strong Weberian sensibilities (shared by this author), attributes the "monumental" failure of the social sciences to anticipate let alone explain four "highly significant developments of the post-World War II period" to 1) the " 'fetishing of method'," or that " 'that which cannot be quantified cannot be studied,' and that has meant a tremendous trivialization" and 2) the "neo-Marxist ideological wave overcoming the field" in the '60s and '70s, where "science became propaganda. . . . I would say sociology has become a pretty depressing field with individuals and some centers doing good work." (Charles T. Mathewes, "An Interview with Peter Berger," *The Hedgehog Review*, Spring & Summer 2006, 160.)

—Another sociologist of religion with Weberian instincts similar to Berger, Martin Riesebrodt of the University of Chicago, struggles in *The Problem of Salvation: A Theory of Religion* (2011, published originally in German) to re-orient the field back in Weber's direction. Unfortunately he also demonstrates too little appreciation or understanding of the cultural grounding of religion in society, let alone the particular role it plays in the U.S. Here is the best he can do with the "secularization theory" problem: "One of the interesting and important implications of Riesebrodt's practice-based theory is that it 'reenchants' our understanding of religion. Religion has not disappeared in the modern world but rather developed autonomously just as other social sectors have done. Riesebrodt argues, 'for that reason, it is quite conceivable that religious institutions will gain more independence and importance as a result of secularization'—a term Riesebrodt reserves for process of institutional differentiation." (Mary Ellen Konieczny, Kelly H. Chong and Loren D. Lybarger, "Theory as a Tool in the Social Scientific Study of Religion and Martin Riesebrodt's *The Promise of Salvation*," *Journal for the Scientific Study of Religion*, Vol. 51, No. 3, September 2012, 405.) Space forbids an adequate critique, other than to briefly observe that his concept of "liturgy" is a thoroughly western, Judeo-Christian, sociological idiom. Would Riesebrodt call the yearly celebrations of Hawaiians for their fertility god, Lono, liturgies? Or mythologies? Religious "practices" or a tribal "rituals"? What is more, are the modern societies of Ireland, Italy, and the United States—perennially hovering around the very top of global religiosity survey scales—growing increasingly religiously fragmented? their "religions" developing, *trending* into "autonomous

a very well-worn conception, "civil religion," Robert Bellah, perhaps would have us overlook his regrettable (albeit quite understandable) 1960s prediction of the disappearance of traditional forms of American religion in *Beyond Belief: Essays on Religion in a Post-Traditional World.*[799] Bellah, and nearly every sociologist who followed in his wake,[800] indulged a seemingly irresistible

---

institutions?" Typically, sociologists rarely can distinguish cultural trees from social forests. Cultural idioms drive societies, not the reverse. Patterns of social action reflect underlying patterns of cultural meanings.

[799] New York: Harper & Row, 1970.

—And all its variations, e.g.: Richard K. Fenn, "Toward A New Sociology Of Religion," *Journal for the Scientific Study of Religion*, Vol. 11, No. 1, Mar., 1972.

—Harold Bloom, writing from an altogether different academic tradition (but having failed to learn from the mistakes of others), assures us: "I am pretty well convinced . . . that Mormonism will become the dominant religion of the entire American West, a process that is already well underway." (*The American Religion: The Emergence of the Post-Christian Nation*, New York: Simon & Schuster, 1992, 195.) "Post-Christian," unlike "Post-Modern," is a snappy academic buzz-word that connotes an ineluctable developmental trend.

—The anthropologists also: ". . . . the evolutionary future of religion is extinction. . . will erode and become only an interesting historical memory." (Anthony Wallace, *Religion, An Anthropological View*, Random House, 1966, cited in Harvey Cox, *Religion in the Secular City.* . . , 39.)

[800] One notable exception—in an entirely different context and take upon the relationship between ethnic groups and larger national "cores"—is Michael Hechter's *Internal Colonialism: The Celtic Fringe in British National Development* (University of California Press 1973). The argument perfectly summarized in a nutshell on the jacket cover:

> These phenomena call into question widely accepted social theories which assume that ethnic attachments in a society will wane as industrialization proceeds. This book presents the social basis of ethnic identity [not the reverse?], and examines changes in the strength of ethnic solidarity in the United Kingdom in the nineteenth and twentieth centuries. In addition to its value as a case study, the work also has important comparative implications, for it suggests that internal colonialism of the kind experienced in the British Isles *has its analogues in the histories of other industrial societies.* Hechter examines the unexpected persistence of ethnicity in the politics of industrial societies by focusing on the British Isles. Why do many of the inhabitants of Wales, Scotland, and Ireland continue to maintain an ethnic identity opposed to England? Hechter explains the salience of ethnic identity by analyzing the relationships between England, the national core, and its periphery, the Celtic fringe, in the light of two alternative models of core-periphery relations in the industrial setting. These are a diffusion model, which predicts that intergroup contact leads to ethnic homogenization, and *an internal colonial model, in which such contact heightens distinctive ethnic identification.* His findings lend support to the internal colonial model, and show that, although industrialization did contribute to a decline in interregional linguistic differences, it resulted neither in the cultural assimilation of Celtic lands, nor in the development of regional economic equality. The study concludes *that ethnic solidarity will inevitably emerge among groups which are relegated to inferior positions in a cultural division of labor.* {emphases added}

disciplinary urge to inject or project what might be called "secular trend" dynamics into virtually every analysis and scenario.[801] The most general of these is the quite persistent, pervasive notion of "secularization." Taken whole cloth from European sociological traditions,[802] this and other conceptions have proven exceedingly rigid, seemingly incorrigible at times, encouraging academicians to force assorted American religious and cultural phenomena into more general theoretical molds.[803] So that while Peter Berger, for example, gave us an engaging overview of the social forms and dynamics of religion in *The Sacred Canopy: Elements of a Sociological Theory of Religion*,[804]

The historical analogy here will become more obvious in time. Substitute "evangelical solidarity" for "ethnic solidarity." (Fair disclosure note: Hechter was a student of Immanuel Wallerstein, who wrote extensively about core and periphery dynamics of "world systems"; I was, briefly, a student of Hechter's at the University of Washington.)

[801] A shout out here to a trio of sociologists of religion who deftly employ data analysis to examine a crucial assumption that had heretofore gone unexamined, namely that growth in the size of conservative Protestant affiliation over the last few decades was due to movement from mainstream Protestant denominations to evangelical denominations. In fact, they claim that demographic (higher birth rates) and other factors were responsible. (Michael Hout, Andrew Greeley, and Melissa J. Wilde, "The Demographic Imperative in Religious Change in the United States," *American Journal of Sociology*, Vol. 107, No. 2, September 2001.)

[802] Rodney Stark captures the entire historical sweep of the idea in a few succinct introductory pages of "Chapter 14, Atheism: The Godless Revolution That Never Happened," in *What Americans Really Believe: New Findings From The Baylor Surveys of Religion*, Baylor University Press, 2008.

[803] And more broadly, as R. Laurence Moore writes of his profession: "In my opinion no centrally important cultural component of American life is more regularly neglected in synthetic accounts of American history than religion. That is because most American historians since World War II have not only become secularists, as I classify myself, but have accepted Weberian assumptions that a secularization finally destructive of religion is an inevitable tendency of modernization. . . . they have proved to be so dead wrong." (*Selling God* . . . , 10-11.) [But not completely wrong, as we will see, but *generally* so, as is the usual sociological contretemps.]

—"In effect, American urban history has accepted an implicit secularization thesis without really examining its assumptions or implications. In so doing, the field not only reflects the secularism of our own era and guild but also its inheritance of sociological and neo-Marxian interpretive traditions that assume the long-term incompatibility of urbanization, modernization, rationalism, and religion." (Kathleen Neils Conzen, "Forum: The Place of Religion in Urban and Community Studies," *Religion and American Culture: A Journal of Interpretation* 6, no. 2 {Summer 1996}, 110.) [Again, fair disclosure note: I was also, briefly, a student of Ms. Conzen's at Chicago.]

—As for the attention of sociology to religion in general: "Writing on the place of religion in the social sciences, Craig Calhoun (1999) remarked that there is probably no topic that matters so much to the average American yet receives such short shrift from American sociologists." (Philip S. Gorski, "The Return of the Repressed: Religion and the Political Unconscious of Historical Sociology," in Julia Adams et al. eds., *Remaking Modernity: Politics, History, and Sociology*, Duke University Press, 2005, 188.)

[804] New York: Anchor Books, 1969. See p. 129 for the origin of the "proximity" thesis.

many academicians who immediately followed in his wake simply embraced his and other general accounts of "secularization" as undeniable givens, irrespective of problematical cultural contexts and consequences.[805] And, as we have seen, American society is one hell of a problematical context.[806]

—"The best-known exponent was Peter Berger, who told *The New York Times* in 1968 that 'religious believers are likely to be found only in small sects, huddled together to resist a worldwide secular culture.' " (Ian Johnson, "China Gets Religion!" *The New York Review of Books*, December 22, 2011, 56.) A position he later recanted, based upon "the weight of the evidence. . . . by the late '70s or early '80s—most, but not all, sociologists of religion came to agree that the original secularization thesis was untenable in its basic form, which simply said modernization and secularization are necessarily correlated developments. I followed most people in the field; I went through the same process of rethinking." (as quoted in Charles T. Mathewes . . . , 152.)

—A good reference: Kevin M. Schultz, "Secularization: A Bibliographic Essay," *The Hedgehog Review*, Spring & Summer, 2006.

[805] Considerations of space forbade the inclusion of a host of direct examples and derivations drawn from the most prominent sociologists in the field—Robert Wuthnow, James Davison Hunter, Marsha Witten, Susan Rose, and Michael S. Horton, among others. My apologies.

—The not-for-a-moment imagined unintended tragic consequences of promoting this train of thought ought now haunt any conscientious academician:

> While most commentators on this sordid history [the slaughter of half-a-million Ethiopians by the 1974 regime of Megistu Haile Mariam] have, like Mezlekia, emphasized the material roots of Ethiopia's troubles, Ethiopian philosopher Messay Kebede has steadily offered an interpretation that focuses instead on the indoctrination of Ethiopia's intellectual elites in *Western social theories that paired secularization with modernization* and taught the way of progress was to be achieved only at the cost of absolute retreat from backyard native traditions. . . . while socialist states in Africa and Latin America fell like dominoes through the 1990s, *the toxic cultural impact of the militant socialist appropriation of secularization theory remains thick in the atmosphere*. (Wilson N. Brissett, "Report: Secularization in the Global South," *The Hedgehog Review: After Secularization (special double issue)*, Spring & Summer, 2006, 149, 146) {emphases added}

—And elsewhere: "When Party pragmatists took control of China after the Cultural Revolution, they assumed that re-opening temples was a minor gesture of reconciliation to elderly believers who would soon die out—in the orthodox Communist view of the world, religion belongs to an obsolescent period of history that will fade away as material prosperity and rationality gradually take hold." (Ian Johnson, op. cit.)

[806] *Some* historians, by contrast, have led a more substantial rebellion: "Still, the United States keeps refuting the standard expectation that modernity erodes faith." (Morone, *Hellfire Nation.* . . , 411.)

—Unfortunately, Mr. Berger, although he acknowledges the errors of the original modernity and secularization thesis, nonetheless entered the new century still amenable to what I call sociological "trend" dynamics, still thinking and writing more broadly and *generally* in terms of ". . . . alternative globalizations, opening up the intriguing possibility of alternative modernities." Still seemingly oblivious to the central role evangelicalism plays in American life, he insists that "All of this is very pertinent as one turn's one's attention to religion. For historical reasons that are not difficult to specify. The United States is in the vanguard of the

It might seem inevitable that sociological secular trends analysis and the malingering secularization thesis[807] eventually must deal with the apparent reality of an American religious exceptionalism of sorts. Much ink has been spilt addressing the issue.[808] And indeed, for example, yet another school of sociologists of religion has emerged advancing yet another line of attack, this time employing so-called rational actor, market behavior models to explain what makes America special. In this instance exceptionalism gets accounted for in terms of supply-and-demand and government regulation indices. (Hmmm, micro-economic market models creeping into sociology?[809]) And

---

contemporary 'Hellenistic' pluralism. Diana Eck has called the United States the most religiously diverse society in history—a slight exaggeration, perhaps, but plausible all the same."

Of course, American academicians like Berger who live in large urban university settings (his unself-reflective term is "faculty-club culture"), tend to regard urban villages like Jackson Heights (or, as in his anecdote, a ride up 16th street in Washington D.C.) as typifying American religious diversity. The ironic consequence of constitutional "disestablishmentarianism" is that it eventually produced just what Jefferson and Madison *both hoped and feared most*: thriving religious ferment (and diversity) *and* the Religious-Right takeover of a major political party and eventually the White House itself. (Peter Berger, "Globalization and Religion," *The Hedgehog Review*, Vol. 4, No. 2 {Summer 2002}, 8-9).

—J. D. Clark wonderfully demonstrates the vacuity of historically-impoverished sociological abstractions like the secularization thesis in his rich, complex "Secularization and Modernization: The Failure of a 'Grand Narrative'," *The Historical Journal* 55, 1 (2012), 161-94.

—And yet Jeremy N. Thomas advances a rather compelling claim that secularization has proceeded in the United States at an "internal" micro level among the Pro-Life movement (as documented within the pages of *Christianity Today*) via the adoption, for example, of "two secular anti-pornography narratives" to bolster and even "replace. . . traditional values" narratives. Hence, as we will see later, a kind of sacralization of formerly secular idioms occurs, but of an entirely different form from that envisaged by traditional secularization theory. ("Outsourcing Moral Authority: The Internal Secularization of Evangelicals' Anti-Pornography Narratives," *Journal for the Scientific Study of Religion*, Vol. 52, No. 3, September 2013.)

[807] We shouldn't let anthropology entirely off the hook here, for as Marshall Sahlins recalls of their own twist on secular trends: "They were firm believers in what might be called despondency theory. The logical antecedent of dependency theory, despondency theory envisioned the inevitable collapse of indigenous cultures under the shattering impact of global capitalism. Demoralized and paralyzed, the people would be left historically motionless, trapped in the aimless anomie of a cultural void." To the surprise of anthropologists, the natives largely thrived via the fomentation of cultural oppositions to the "White Men," whom they certainly more befuddled than emulated—like Captain Cook, for example. ("Two or Three Things I Know. . . ," 401-2.)

[808] Sheer declining numbers of church-goers is but one of three embattled elements or "meanings" of what Peter Beinhart designates as traditional American exceptionalism. He is right not to read too much into those trends (as the reader will see) and to single out conservative champions of these three receding mythical elements—religiosity, patriotism, equality—as their own worst enemies, undermining them far more than their liberal nemeses. ("The End of American Exceptionalism," *The Atlantic*, February 2014.)

[809] It is almost an act of kindness on my part to squirrel the following items away in a footnote. Perhaps no other piece of evidence demonstrates and confirms the *bankruptcy* of the sociology of religion (let alone modern academic sociology in general) than R. Stephen Warner's

so a significantly different American religiosity gets explained away by dises-tablishmentarianism alone. Hands-off government and a free religious mar-ketplace generates "energetic competition between churches. . . . [which] expands the supply of religious 'products,' thereby mobilizing religious ac-tivism among the public."[810] Simple and familiar enough, as we've been through this drill before.[811] Unfortunately for its advocates, as Norris and

---

widely cited "Work in Progress toward a New Paradigm for the Sociological Study of Religion in the United States," *American Journal of Sociology*, Volume 98, No. 5. March 1993. From the abstract: "This article reviews recent literature on U.S. religious institutions and argues that a new paradigm is emerging in that field, the crux of which is that organized religion thrives in the United States in an open market system, an observation anomalous to the older para-digm's monopoly concept." And who'd have thunk it could have gotten any worse?

—Perhaps we shouldn't be surprised that it actually did. Some twenty years or so later quite a few American academicians, mostly sociologists I believe, *congregated* to reevaluate the sub-discipline of the sociology of religion. I encourage the reader to compare their efforts with mine. Not satisfied with the damage already done over the last half-century, some of that embarrassment (and futility) continues and even gets compounded. Again, sadly, they seem to acknowledge a landscape strewn with train wrecks, but how to avoid future disasters escapes them. See: Christian Smith, Brandon Vaidyanathan, Nancy Tatom Ammerman, José Casa-nova, Hilary Davidson, Elaine Howard Ecklund, John H. Evans, Philip S. Gorski, Mary Ellen Konieczny, Jason A. Springs, Jenny Trinitapoli, and Meredith Whitnah, "Roundtable on the Sociology of Religion: Twenty-Three Theses on the Status of Religion in American Sociol-ogy—A Mellon Working-Group Reflection," *Journal of the American Academy of Religion*, Decem-ber 2013, Vol. 81, No. 4, 903–938.

—Just before he died, Robert Bellah had a more generous reaction to the above in the same journal issue: "Twenty-Three Theses: A Response." He suggested, all too gently and politely: time to walk the talk.

[810] Pippa Norris and Ronald Inglehart, *Sacred and Secular: Religion and . . .*, 95.

[811] I suspect too, as mentioned earlier, that there are some unacknowledged underlying as-sumptions here that many academicians who are Christians and study religion carry with them that draw them to these models, as coincidentally explained by Norris and Inglehart: "These [Supply-side] accounts posit that the need for religion is unwavering and universal. . . . This approach assumes, without providing any theoretical justification [let alone empirical evidence], that the mass desire for religion is constant and invariable." (ibid., 245.) Hence the reluctance to consider other more demand-side factors and contexts that may impact levels of religiosity.

What is more, Norris and Inglehart's "existential security" thesis [coming] may violate the assumptions of many "faith-based" academicians as to the inherent positive nature and role of religion in societies. No doubt this idea of a purely instrumental association between deprivation (or inequality) and religiosity—invoking potential aspersions—grates mightily on the raw, bias-polished nerves of some.

—As it obviously rubbed Christian pollster, George Gallup, who in 2008 sought to indirectly test a derivative proposition during the "great recession," as reported by Frank Newport: "No Evidence Bad Times Are Boosting Church Attendance: An average of 42% have attended regularly all year" (*GALLUP®*, December 17, 2008).

—And then there's Christian academician R. Scott Appleby's unfiltered account of the Serbo-Croatian war's impact upon all faiths: "In the early phase of the conflict, the everyday expe-rience of fighting and atrocities made most members of the various ethnic groups emphasize their national and religious differences. For others, however, faith provided solace to help

Inglehart aptly and amply demonstrate, the claim proves eminently *testable*, or as Karl Popper would put it, *falsifiable*. Once again statistical model worshipping and marshalling sociologists get hoisted on their own petards.[812] Scatter plot graphs of the data reveal that no such relationship actually exists:

> Moreover, in Catholic post-industrial societies the relationship is actually *reversed*, with the highest participation evident in Ireland and Italy where the Church enjoys a virtual religious monopoly, compared with the more pluralist Netherlands and France, where churchgoing habits are far weaker. [Just the opposite also, in fact, of what Jefferson and Madison imagined for America] Nor is this merely due to the comparison of post-industrial societies: the global comparison in all nations confirms that there is no significant relationship between participation and pluralism across the broader distribution of societies .... *Contrary to the supply-side theory* ... no significant relationship exists between any of these indicators of religious freedom and levels of religious behavior.[813]

---

people cope with the personal tragedies war dispensed on such a massive scale. Churches and mosques in 1994 and 1995 were filled with far more worshippers than before the war." (*The Ambivalence of the Sacred: Religion, Violence, and Reconciliation*, Rowman & Littlefield, 2000, 74.)

[812] None of which is to suggest that the collection and appraisal of data *on and in appropriate occasions and contexts* does not yield valuable insights, as we have seen. For one marvelous example of the astute recognition of the interaction of social and cultural dynamics in national development, see Ian Morris, *The Measure of Civilization: How Social Development Decides the Fate of Nations* (Princeton University Press, 2013), especially the brief section, "Society," on the framing of respective sociological and anthropological "unit[s] of analysis." (22-3.)

[813] Pippa Norris and Ronald Inglehart, "Sellers or Buyers. . . ," 85, 87. {emphasis added} *I urge the reader to gain online access to this article; it is the most important companion piece to this volume.* See also the larger study from which it originated: op. cit., 2004/2nd ed. 2011.
—Undeterred by such findings, other supply-side academicians continue on with rational-actor model explanations of modern American televangelism: "With this study we join *a growing cohort of religious scholars, sociologists, and historians who make the case for a supply-side analysis of religious vitality. . . .* religious suppliers thrive in a competitive spiritual marketplace because they are quick, decisive, and flexible in reacting to changing conditions, savvy at packaging and marketing their ministries, and resourceful at offering spiritual rewards that resonate with the existential needs and cultural tastes of the public. . . . what Finke and Stark suggest with religious economy: *religion thrives precisely when it appeals to the tastes and preferences of its 'consumers.'*" (Shayne Lee & Phillip Luke Sinitiere, *Holy Mavericks. . .* , 3, 171.) {emphases added} But why do consumers *flock* to the *products* offered by these particular "religious suppliers"? Just because they mimic or resemble appealing secular goods? And why such a huge spiritual *marketplace* here in America and virtually nowhere else in the Anglo-Saxon world? From what source and to what ultimate effect?
—Perhaps reflecting the unfortunate influence of Rodney Stark at Washington, UW sociology professor Steven Pfaff reiterates an embarrassing erroneous claim: "Hence much of the difference in religiosity across societies can be explained by the relative competitiveness of the firms that comprise a religious 'marketplace' and by the extent to which governments regulate that marketplace." ("The Religious Divide: Why Religion Seems to Be Thriving in the United States and Waning in Europe," in Jeffrey Kopstein and Sven Stinmo eds., *Growing Apart? America and Europe in the Twenty-First Century*, New York: Cambridge University Press, 2008, 26.) / See also Jörg Stolz's well-meaning but tortured effort to integrate all this within a "Weber perspective." ("Salvation Goods. . . ," 2006.)

So what do Italy, Ireland, and the United States have in common that explains such high rates of religiosity? It certainly has nothing to do with free market induced pluralism and rudimentary kinds of church participation. Then again, perhaps more importantly, why no *evangelical* movements to speak of in either Italy and Ireland and not much religion at all, let alone evangelicalism, in most of Europe?

Norris and Inglehart arrive at a rather startlingly original conclusion, even more so given that it is largely social or sociological in nature—that is, it rests upon the assignment and appraisal of *variables* that are tangible,

---

—Jeff Sharlet claims that the market model explanation began with Rodney Stark, now at that evangelical academic hotbed, Baylor University. Unfortunately Sharlet accepts the value of the model far too easily. (*The Family. . .* , 312.)

—These sociologists appear to have ignored or overlooked one of the definitive earlier studies that indirectly addressed these matters. With respect to the widely-held untested assumption that the rise of evangelicalism and the Religious Right in the United States drew Christians away from more moderate "mainstream" Protestantism, the actual (demographic) data showed otherwise, contradicting an additional supporting "supply-side" view of the dynamics at work. "Likewise the arguments about the 'strength' of conservative denominations [wherein it is claimed that] . . . they are gaining share in the religious marketplace (Finke and Stark 1992; Iannaccone 1994)." (Michael Hout, Andrew Greeley and Melissa J. Wilde, "The Demographic Imperative in Religious Change in the United States," *American Journal of Sociology* , Vol. 107, No. 2, September 2001, 490.)

—Then again, perhaps most embarrassing—and literally blinding—of all is Larry Witham's *Marketplace of The Gods: How Economics Explains Religion*, published by Oxford University Press in 2010, who in a comprehensive survey of the historical players addressing the issue nonetheless, *inexplicably*, makes no mention whatsoever of the landmark work of Norris and Inglehart. Go figure. In politics, we would call this a "cover-up."

—A reviewer of a more recent book of David Martin (who refers to Martin as one of the "doyens" of the field) perpetuates the marketplace myth: "His sociological critique of an ethnocentric, linear understanding of modernity and of Enlightenment partisanship is constant. . . . In Europe, the most secularized area of the world, secularity functions, implicitly or explicitly, in dialectic with the master narrative and values of the Christian civilization. *The United States, of course, has been and remains religious because of its particular history of church-state relations and the ensuing voluntary character of religious affiliation. Most important for the present state and the future development of Christianity, Martin finds the great expansion of Pentecostalism and charismatic Christianity in the 'inspirited' two thirds world. Pentecostalism, as a voluntary association operating below the state, from Indonesia and China to Brazil and Nigeria, has taken on the form of a transnational cultural revolution."* (Nikos Kokosalakis review of *The Future Of Christianity: Reflections On Violence and Democracy, Religion and Secularization* by David Martin, *Journal for the Scientific Study of Religion*, Vol. 51, No. 1, March 2012, 198.) {emphasis added} Note: ". . . of course. . . ."

—Scot Peterson argues that even the grandmaster of laissez-faire capitalism, Adam Smith, would find the current use of market models to explain religiosity problematical. ("Rational Choice, Religion, and the Marketplace: Where Does Adam Smith Fit in?" *Journal for the Scientific Study of Religion*, Vol. 48, No. 1, Mar. 2009.)

—See " 'Practical Divine Influence': Socioeconomic Status and Belief in the Prosperity Gospel," Scott Schieman and Jong Hyun Jung in the *Journal for the Scientific Study of Religion*, Vol. 51, No. 4, December 2012, for an interesting analysis of a 2006 PEW survey of Americans. They find socio-economic status negatively related to heightened religiosity but with some complicating twists.

measurable, although very basic, conventional, and "self-reported," as exemplified by two survey questions about faith: "How often do you pray?" and "How important is religion to you?" These are followed in turn by an additional query, one having to do with household income, which might give some readers pause. Household income? Questions about faith—"indicators" of religiosity—paired with a question about money or income? How odd. We can only hope that in another set of readers the juxtaposition conjures more than confusion, better yet even the ghost of Weber and *The Protestant Ethic and the Spirit of Capitalism*. And so what on earth might income have to do with religiosity? Well, quite a bit, as it turns out, as some may have already surmised.

> Our answer rests on patterns of human security and, in particular, conditions of socio-economic inequality. What matters for the societal vulnerability, insecurity, and risk that we believe drives religiosity are not simply levels of national economic resources but their distribution as well. . . . *the level of economic inequality proves strongly and significantly related to both forms of religious behavior, but especially to engage in individual religiosity through prayer.*[814]

Sure enough, economic inequality is significantly related to religious participation (R=.496) and prayer (R=.614)[815] and the United States exhibits the greatest concentrations and the strongest relationships of all. Although Italy, Ireland, and the States show somewhat greater income inequality than other countries in the sample scatter plot, and the latter is certainly the wealthier of the three—indeed of all the others by far—Norris and Inglehart quite correctly single out the inherent *insecurity* of American society as a particularly decisive factor. This insecurity represents what some methodologists might call an "intervening variable," for in marked contrast with the social democracies of Europe "Americans face greater anxieties than citizens in other advanced industrialized countries about whether or not they will be covered by medical insurance, be fired arbitrarily, or be forced to choose between losing

---

[814] Ibid., 87. {emphasis added} The economic insecurity thesis goes far towards explaining the extraordinary expansion of Pentecostal evangelicalism in largely third world societies around the globe, as even Pentecostal apologists acknowledge. See Allan Heaton Anderson, *To The Ends of the Earth. . .* , op. cit.

[815] Ibid. In this instance, as I understand it, a simple R, or a correlation coefficient of .496 (Table 3: "Pearson simple correlations without prior controls"), means that, for example, changes in religious participation rates are significantly (not due to random variation or sampling error) correlated to changes in household income. Although their Table 3 shows almost no relationship between "religious pluralism" and the two religious indicators, there is a very mild relationship between the two indicators and "state regulation of religion" (.427/.423) which, again, is contrary to the supply-side mantra. Hence to my mind the evidence in this one regard is quite suggestive, just not definitive.

their jobs and devoting themselves to their newborn children." *Indeed, once again, if that were only the half of it.*[816] In other words, the greater wealth of the United States gets neutralized as a factor directly impacting rates of religiosity (for we might expect lower participation and prayer—lower religiosity indicators—due to higher income) by an inherent unequal distribution of wealth whose comparative influence is compounded by the intervening factor of *a systemic insecurity that largely mirrors the insecurity felt by residents of more impoverished nations across the globe.*[817] In other words, we observe here the same kind of destabilizing, unsettling impact caused by economic deprivation— but one originating from an entirely different source, a politically-generated *social uncertainty* that most European social democracies eliminated decades ago.[818] One major task of this book has been to explore the origin and nature

---

[816] See Frederick Solt, et al (2011) and Gregory Paul (2009) in the Selected Bibliography for corroborating papers/work that I came across just a week before *PJ's* went to press.
—For some reason, some American sociologists read another narrative into all of this:

> For all the continuities, American character did change in some ways. The vast expansion of physical and economic security, greater stability and predictability, and the abundance of food, goods, and services endowed more individuals with more freedom and confidence to plan their own futures, to demand autonomy, and to expand equality. Abundance, as historian David Potter emphasized, made liberty and equality—and democracy—possible for the masses. (Fischer, *Made in America. . .* , 243.)

—Cracks in the façade of American exceptionalism (again, the irony) make an appearance in all sorts of oddly related ways: "After listening to the priests and poring over news articles, I started to wonder whether the two trends—belief in the occult and the rising demand for Catholic exorcisms—might have the same underlying cause. So many modern social ills feel dark and menacing and beyond human control: the opioid epidemic, the permanent loss of blue-collar jobs, blighted communities that breed alienation and dread." Again in a typically odd pronouncement, Pope Francis "has declared. . . . [that Satan is] a *personal being* who assails us", an ironic invocation and acknowledgement (applicable mainly to an American context) of missing personal relationships to be zero-sum filled either by Jesus *or* his nemesis. "Polls conducted in recent decades by Gallup and the data firm YouGov suggest that roughly half of Americans believe demonic possession is real. The percentage who believe in the devil is even higher, and in fact has been growing: Gallup polls show that the number rose from 55 percent in 1990 to 70 percent in 2007." (Mike Mariani, "Why Are Exorcisms on the Rise?" *The Atlantic*, December 2018.) The reader will find my earlier discussion of what I have called the "fear of complete reversal" instructive in this regard.

[817] "Here is the real core of the religious problem. Help! Help! No prophet can claim to bring a final message unless he says things that will have a sound of reality in the ears of *victims* such as these." (William James, *The Varieties of Religious Experience*, 1902, quoted in Lydea Bean, *The Politics of . . .* , 221.) {emphasis added}

[818] For just one telling example:, no better boots-on-the-ground account of the yawning difference between the United States and Scandinavian Europe exists than Anu Partanen's *The Nordic Theory of Everything: In Search of a Better Life* (New York: HarperCollins, 2016). The "Finnish journalist who is now a U.S. citizen" documents the culture shock, the "crippling anxiety"

that overwhelmed her upon her move to America to join her lover and eventual husband. The experience led her to reflections upon "... whatever 'culture' means...," the identification and comparisons of which seemed to lie at the heart of that which sets the two societies apart. As we will see in a subsequent extended note, the difference here is not a matter of traditional Norwegian village charm and close-knit family relationships set in opposition to modernist suburban American individualism and anomie, or cultural vacuums. In unraveling cause and effect, things get a little more complicated here. For as Partanen readily admits, among the "wonderful things" she discovered in America was "what it means to be part of an American extended family; what's it's like to actually get to know your neighbors on an American block; how good it feels the be welcomed and called a friend by some of the warmest, most generous, and outgoing people on earth." By contrast she finds her own Finns colder, less socially gifted, occasionally more uncommunicative, and just as selfish and even more individualistic than Americans. Whatever the author's own personal gifts may have to do with her reception in (and reading of) America to the contrary notwithstanding, she raises a host of intriguing comparative issues and metrics. But note, right off, that where she lives, New York City, is by no means a representative slice of America. In fact I've always thought of NYC as the only European city in the United States. Crown (and the other) Heights may in fact be more *international* in scope and character than all of Europe combined. What is more, the American nation is riven by regional and racial differences that make the identification and evaluation of "existential security" a very complex undertaking.

—Michael Booth, an American journalist (married to a Dane and a resident himself) who readily acknowledges a temperamental antipathy to "cozy time... *hygge*" and exorbitant tax rates, and hell-bent upon unmasking and debunking the Scandinavian hype, reluctantly concludes after a sustained examination of the dirty underbelly reality of the Nordic miracle that, as far as the so-called American Dream is concerned

> In Scandinavia it is a reality. These are the real lands of opportunity. . . . [according to the London School of Economics] The four main Nordic countries occupied the top four places on the list ["social mobility"]. . . . for all the collectivism and state interference in the lives of the people who live here, there is a far greater freedom to be the person you want to be, and do the things you want to do. . . . Really, as far as I am concerned there is only one place to look for the economic and societal role model of the future. . . . The Nordic countries have the answer. . . . [and] though they may look alike at first glance, the Nordic peoples are wildly, fascinatingly different from one another. . . . [where immigration is, to the surprise of many] turning these sometimes monotonous monocultures into kaleidoscopic multiethnic models of diversity." (*The Almost Nearly Perfect People: Behind the Myth of the Scandinavian Utopia*, New York: Picador, 2015, 368-70.)

of this peculiarly American insecurity as well as other social and cultural dynamics[819] closely associated with it.[820] And yet here although Norris and Inglehart appear to have hit the nail on the head with regard to a general global relationship between economic insecurity and religiosity, there is something *understandably* missing from their analysis.[821] For surely the

---

[819] The work of Dan Kahan and colleagues, summarized in "Cultural Cognition as a Conception of the Cultural Theory of Risk," proves useful here. Although I take mild issue with his formulation of cultural "ways of life," he identifies and addresses some crucial personal and social cognitive dynamics that help us understand differences in the perception of all sorts of physical, environmental, social, and cultural danger, what he—and others in a large community of researchers—deems the assessment of "risk." Individuals perceive risk through the lens of the particular cultural reference group they inhabit. Some of these more general dynamics (although his survey samples are exclusively American) can help explain what we might call the European-American cultural cognition gap. Take the seemingly inexplicable phenomenon of Donald Trump and his rock-solid evangelical base. Perhaps beyond the particular cultural idioms and dynamics I will explore throughout the remainder of this book are some more general "psychometrics" that come into play, such that "Individuals bear cultural predisposition toward risk—a tendency (founded on identity-protective cognition) to view some risk claims more congenial than others on the basis of latent characteristics indicated by values they share with others. This predisposition not only endows culturally diverse individuals with opposing 'prior' beliefs about risk. It also decisively regulates their experience with information about the truth or falsity of those beliefs. . . . individuals end up in a state of cultural conflict—not over values but over *facts*—that the mere accumulation of empirical data cannot be expected readily to dispel." (Originally located online—see p. 29—but now found also in Sabine Roesner et al. eds., *Handbook of Risk Theory: Epistemology, Decision Theory, Ethics, and Social Implications of Risk* (Springer Publishing 2012).

[820] Such as, for example, some intriguing attachment theory research conducted by Lee A. Kirkpatrick and Phillip A. Shaver, who discovered in an admittedly small sample of "mail survey" respondents that individuals who grew up having experienced "insecure" or "avoidant" relationships with their mothers became significantly more religious ("having a personal relationship with God") and reported significantly higher rates of conversion experiences as adolescents and later as adults than those who classified their experiences as "secure or anxious/ambivalent. . . . These results suggest that God and religion may function in a compensatory role for people with a history of avoidant attachment; that is, God may serve as a substitute attachment figure." ("Attachment Theory and Religion: Childhood Attachments, Religious Beliefs, and Conversion," *Journal for the Scientific Study of Religion*, Vol. 29, No. 3, September 1990, 315.)
—An even more recent and innovative experimental examination of some of these issues can be found in Andreas Birgegard and Pehr Granqvist's "The Correspondence Between Attachment to Parents and God: Three Experiments Using Subliminal Separation Cues," *Personality and Social Psychology Bulletin*, Vol. 30 No. 9, September 2004.

[821] For, after all, the main point of their article is to refute—once and for all, let's hope—rational actor market model accounts of the "exceptionalism" of American religiosity.
—A few years later, Inglehart returned to the topic, still not quite capturing the American difference with a further generalization: "Unhappy people tend to turn to religion. Conversely, in most countries with a long religious tradition and high levels of subjective well-being, religiosity is linked with happiness. . . . [But, then again] those at the atheist end of the scale are the happiest of all." (Ronald F. Inglehart, "Faith and Freedom: Traditional and Modern Ways of Happiness," in Ed Diener, John F. Helliwell. . . . eds., 377, 380.)

religious contexts of Italy and Ireland, however similarly and highly related to inequality, are quite distinguishable from the American religious milieu, and their political contexts accordingly so also. In a moment, a suggestion as to what might lie at the heart of this difference.

Although Norris and Inglehart make no mention of it, because of their work Marx and Engels might with some justification begin stirring once again in their graves. Perhaps I wasn't the only one for whom these more recent findings conjured up that ancient declaration: "religion is the opium of the people."[822] Surely their analysis of the data today begs the proposition that no matter the society, the *more* impoverished the individuals and families the *more* attractive, embraced, and practiced will be the religions. The relationship holds among, or between, as well as within, nations.[823] Perhaps the coincidence never occurred to them. Another useful Marxian maxim (which exhausts my list) concerns the internal dynamics of history: over the long haul of social transformations, at some seemingly indeterminate point in time, *quantitative* changes tend to produce or morph into *qualitative* changes.[824] As a cultural sociologist, I might maintain that the reverse tends to occur with as great a frequency, with equally meaningful and significant

---

—Then again, is a turn to religiosity completely, totally, a function or consequence of economic (and other insecurities)? Consider the possibility that:

> Equally, however, religion can contribute to anxiety; [Let's not forget that] in Weber's famous analysis in *The Protestant Ethic and the Spirit of Capitalism. . .* it is activity in worldly matters (adhering to a capitalist work ethic and saving money) that serves to offset the anxiety produced by religion (the uncertainty of salvation) rather than the reverse. (Michael Lambek, "What Is 'Religion'. . . , 10.)

[822] From *A Contribution to the Critique of Hegel's Philosophy of Right* (1844).

[823] Robert Orsi wrote about the letters sent to the Chicago shrine of modern Saint Jude, ". . . . processed by a large office staff in downtown Chicago, and in tiny advertisements dotting the classified section of virtually every American newspaper from the 1930s to the present. St. Jude's overwhelmingly women petitioners typically asked the 'patron saint of lost causes' to solve specifically modern dilemmas: increasingly complex marriages, the human consequences of the Great Depression, the horror of World War II, the persistence of sickness and death when twentieth-century medicine promised and often delivered cures." (in Butler, "Jack-in-the-Box Faith. . . ," 1365.)
—Even the snippets of dialogue reported from her "team's" very few interviews with Latino and Asian immigrants who acknowledged evangelical beliefs largely dwelled upon the socioeconomic and personal crises to which their new faith brought aid and comfort. For whatever the reasons behind their emigration to America, evangelicalism supplied new forms of the missing cultural infrastructures they had left behind. (Janelle S. Wong, op cit., 65-66 esp.)

[824] Friedrich Engels made more of this concept than Marx, as in *The Dialectics of Nature* and *Anti-Dühring*.

effects, and sometimes more so, as we have seen. Which might also give us pause to wonder: which actually comes first here, the horse or the cart? The quantitative or the qualitative change? In the particular case of Norris and Inglehart's account, variation or change in individual and/or national economic inequality (a measurable quantity) is significantly related to variation in rates of personal prayer or congregational participation (other measurable quantities). But again, in a slight modification, which comes or came first, quantity #1 or quantity #2? Forget for the moment any kind of sequence or its reversal. Which is the more determinative quantity? Those who quickly conclude that inequality is the obvious driver of the relationship ought be careful here. For however useful these kinds of generalizations, they only explain—or better yet, *correlate*—so much. Obviously, the authors' perspectives were limited to social or sociological data, wherein *quantitative* differences (two specific religiosity variables) were correlated with one *quantitative* difference (income variable).[825] But what accounts for the vast *qualitative* differences

---

[825] In the second revised 2011 edition of their study the authors respond to one reviewer's "perceptive criticism. . . . [that they] '. . . . do not offer any evidence that the *subjective experience* of anxiety actually motivates religious values, relying instead on objective criteria of health and wealth.' " The well-taken Weberian-like point here being that the personal/social psychological mechanisms that connect feelings of insecurity (motives) to resulting religious beliefs and behaviors need to be identified, not just assumed. Give us the direct links, not just vague correlations. As even they acknowledged, referencing the first edition: ". . . . psychological perceptions of risk and insecurity needed further analysis." And so in one of two new concluding chapters in the 2011 edition they report that ". . . . a comprehensive review of the scientific literature investigating to what extent religion provided an effective coping mechanism for life stresses, based on evidence from survey or experimental methods, found that three-quarters of all such studies confirmed a relationship." (254) Also, I am unaware of any published responses from "supply-side" advocates, for whom sheer free market competition—not inequality or "existential insecurity"—explains high levels of American religiosity.
—Now as for the question as to whether or not the United States represents an exception to this relationship between socio-economic vulnerability and religiosity, the authors waver somewhat, with good reason. Here the self-reported indicators of religiosity ("importance" and "practice") trace different mid-level relationships to poverty than to more extreme levels of poverty (Figure 12.4, 263). But the data provides only very general indicators of religiosity, allowing no way to isolate population sub-categories, such as evangelicals or African-Americans. I suspect that what we would see among evangelicals is a more modest relationship respecting inequality and religiosity, but one compounded, as suggested earlier, by insecurities of an altogether different nature, whose characteristics and impact the data would prove useless to discern let alone measure. What is more: "It therefore appears that the typical socio-economic profile of churchgoing is indeed somewhat distinctive in the United States when compared with other wealthy countries."(268) But, all told, even though "the United States does display higher than average levels of religious values and practices. . . this pattern should not be exaggerated. . . . The security thesis presented here, suggests that neither the United States nor Western Europe is an anomaly that requires special explanation."(269) Indeed, but just in terms of "the security thesis"; the other anomalies have enormous significance for us.
—Prior to publishing their revised 2011 edition, Norris and Inglehart consulted extensively with Robert Putnam and David Campbell (2010), as the latter two "emphasize a very different

between the United States, Ireland, and Italy? By now the reader might have anticipated the direction in which we are headed: *viz.*, that the historical *and* contemporary American cultural context differs *significantly* from those of Ireland and Italy. Few can or would argue otherwise. Yet the *origin*, *nature*, and continually spewing *source* of that unique cultural context, that difference, is not so obvious.[826] As we have seen, Charles Taylor has thrown up his hands in despair over the matter; market-dynamics-spouting sociologists have come up empty, embarrassingly so; and earlier American sociologists have already issued mea culpas concerning their now largely discredited secularization theses. Indeed the latter are still peeling egg from their faces, and well they should.

Perhaps it is time for wiping the slate clean? Starting over? And in this regard, *may I have the reader's attention please?*[827] Allow me to introduce another

---

set of factors. . . ." generating high levels of American religiosity, among them that an ". . . . ethnic distinctiveness swamps any socioeconomic differences, and these ethnic differences can be traced deep into history. . . . that the United States is an immigrant nation, and the process of immigration reinforces religious identification, as people cling to familiar institutions in a strange land." (271) Unfortunately, the intensity and significance of this "clinging" varies according to the particular sects, religions, conditions, and contexts involved. There is no general sociological immigration effect at work here. For, otherwise, what then explains the enduring originality of religious tradition-busting evangelicalism, and especially its episodic waxing and waning? At some point, they were all immigrants (as were Mormons also, or so they tell us). Low religiosity Canada and Australia are stuffed to the gills with similar waves of immigrants. Both pairs of academicians strain to make the data and their seemingly contradictory claims compatible with the other's. Space forbids a discussion of how in my estimation they are both right and wrong in certain respects, but neither mix really matters. The American difference transcends race, ethnicity, socioeconomics, and conventional religiosity indicators; it emerges from a cultural difference, created and driven by a host of complex, particular, academic-discipline-defying dynamics, as we have seen.

[826] As we have seen also with Norris and Inglehart, teasing out the nuances of cultural or religious contexts by data crunching proves intimidating. If, for example, as Peter Baldwin suggests in *The Narcissism of Minor Differences: How America and Europe Are Alike*, that crime in New York City compares favorably with that of Madrid, Spain, well then whatever explains the presence of unescorted young ladies—of all manner of groupings and sort—strolling unmolested through the streets of Madrid late at night and into the morning without the slightest concern for their own safety, something one rarely sees in NYC, even in Manhattan. However comparable the social data, the cultures are oceans apart. Perhaps there's simply no *accounting* for the positive effects of cultural *charm*.

[827] BTW, my own regression analysis (a far more rigorous tool than the Pearson correlations of Norris and Inglehart) of the survey data collected to test the central thesis of this book yielded an R^2 regression coefficient of .64. The data set from which these two authors coax moderately significant correlations fall quite a bit short of the natural science-like verification numbers of my own guiding proposition. And so the reader should go away assured that the so-called qualitative nature of my *cultural* interpretations have been put to the fire of an empirical test, as documented in appendix A. Also it should be noted that the argument or thesis of this book—the case study results and their implication for American evangelicalism in general—were largely completed before any critical test of the hypothesis was conducted. The

kind of dynamic here, as the very basic, very *general* social or sociological variables and data—"indicators"—that Norris and Inglehart *crunch* and interpret can only take us so far. We just might surmise from their correlations alone that Ireland, Italy, and the United States are pretty much alike when it comes to conventional benchmarks of income inequality and religiosity. But what about the latter, the religiosities themselves? Rates of participation and prayer don't tell us much. They do mention additional compounding American social insecurities but do not follow up; they appear satisfied for now to allow the sleeping dog of the proverbial *correlation is not necessarily causation* incongruity to slumber on undisturbed. But we cannot. And so at the risk of beating fauna metaphors to death, there still lumbers a large elephant in the room of their marvelous study that warrants some accounting for, and that beast of a *cultural* indicator is American evangelicalism. As has been claimed, nothing remotely like *it* exists anywhere else in the world—neither in cultural *deep play* and *structural* contexts nor historical contexts. But why not? What else can we add to our preceding formulation of that ironic exceptionalism?

In this instance, Norris and Inglehart's recognition of "human security" indicators—income level, in particular—have sent us off in the right direction (unlike virtually all of the sociology of religion of the last half century or more). But let's extend the matter, for what distinguishes American evangelicalism from more conventional Protestant and Catholic forms of Christianity is another kind of insecurity indicator just as powerful, perhaps even more so, than economic inequality. For whereas the Norris and Inglehart correlations emerge out of an insecurity or *fear* driven by the perception of and

---

author was indeed risking all on one throw of the dice. Although I stand ready to be corrected, I suspect that never before have the observations and conclusions from an anthropological case study been formulated into an all-encompassing cultural proposition that was then subjected to a sociological statistical test. Imagine Clifford Geertz returning from Bali and being asked to formulate a critical test of the "deep play" of the Balinese cockfight. In "Thick Description: Toward an Interpretive Theory of Culture" he quite deftly skirts the verification issues that plague the soft social sciences, impressionistic ethnographies in particular, falling back upon Weber's notion of "webs of significance . . . . I take culture to be those webs, and the analysis of it to be therefore not an experimental science in search of law but an interpretive one in search of meaning." (*The Interpretation of* . . . , 5.) What I have offered instead is a *cultural sociology* employing all manner of empirical tools in the pursuit of both the *meaning and significance* of evangelicalism in American life. And I *prove* it.
—I rather like Daniel Bell's guiding concept and formula for culture: "For structuralism, culture is the hidden code of significant form. For me, culture is the set of answers, coherent or discordant, the anguished responses to the significant questions of human existence." As will become all too apparent, this author fully embraces, and works within, both conceptions. ("The Return of the Sacred?". . . , 333.)

reaction to *socio-economic danger*,[828] modern American evangelicalism generates an additional, compounding set of indicators, an alarm system grounded in the perception of an altogether different (but nonetheless closely associated and compounded) kind of *cultural danger*,[829] that of *secularism* unleashed and rampaging over the socio-cultural landscape, a threat as imminent and family-imperiling as any drought or famine.[830] Hence we can add the additional

---

[828] Many years ago Paul Goodman expanded upon our notions of economic security: ". . . . research directly on the subject, by Frederick Herzberg on Motivation to Work, shows that it is defects in the intrinsic aspects of the job that make workmen 'unhappy.' A survey of the literature (in Herzberg's *Job Attitudes*) shows that Interest is second in importance only to Security, whereas Wages, Conditions, Socializing, Hours, Ease, and Benefits are far less important. . . . [But] The investigators do not seem to inquire about the usefulness of the job. . . . My guess is that a large factor in 'Security' is the resigned reaction to not being able to take into account whether the work of one's hands is useful for anything; for in a normal life situation, if what we do is useful, *we feel secure about being needed*. The other largest factor in 'Security' is, *the sense of being needed for one's unique contribution*, and this is measured in these tests by the primary importance the workers assign to being 'in' on things and to 'work done being appreciated.' " (*Growing Up Absurd*. . . , 22-3.) {emphases added} Hence the particular American context of "existential insecurity" may bring additional dimensions or cultural "indicators" into play beyond the simpler economic security issues that are addressed in more general global surveys.

[829] The intensification or ideologization of religiosity in the face of any sort of insecurity characterizes radical fundamentalisms in general, as Peter Berger observes, one of whose first casualties is toleration:

> Every fundamentalism responds to that vulnerability and says, 'look, join us and you will no longer be uncertain as to who you are, how you should live, what the world is.' That is very different from traditional religion, traditional Islam or any other. A person who lives in a taken-for-granted traditional world can afford to be quite tolerant. The one who doesn't share that world is interesting, maybe even amusing, like somebody who believes the world is flat. It doesn't threaten us. But when you are dealing with an attempt to restore a certainty that has been challenged, chances are you can't afford to be very tolerant, and the one who is outside your community of belief is a threat. You have to convert him or you have to segregate yourself from him, or in the extreme case, liquidate him. In that sense, I would say every fundamentalism is a modern phenomenon. (as quoted in Mathewes. . . , 159) {emphases added}

—Jonathan Haidt contends that "Brains evaluate everything in terms of potential threat or benefit to the self, and then adjust behavior to get more of the good stuff and less of the bad," this strategic trait obviously stemming from "selfish" genes that get selected, enhancing the survival prospects of individuals. What is more, a similar alignment characterizes human groups: they also both appraise threats and benefits as a unit and exhibit social qualities and features that have undergone an equally selfish, preemptive, "multi-level" process of natural selection. (2013, 64, 224.)

[830] As I suggested earlier, Johann Hari's *Lost Connections: Uncovering the Real Causes of Depression—and the Unexpected Solutions* (Bllomsbury 2018), despite its apparent topic, is another work,

accelerating element of ***cultural insecurity*** to this more general mix of *existential insecurity*. We can trace the apprehension of instigating indicators of clear and present dangers all the way back to the occult folk religions brought

---

along with Norris and Inglehart's, that can serve as a companion volume to *Paradise Joe's*. However, to reiterate somewhat, what Hari identifies as general sources and contexts underlying personal depression I would re-characterize as more intense particular features of American society responsible for a kind of *social and cultural* depression, many of whose symptoms are the loneliness and disenchantment that ultimately are linked to what I would call the cultural anti-depressant or opiate of evangelicalism. Yet although *Lost Connections* cites a good many of the socio-cultural dysfunctions and conditions that can, in our cultural context, send individuals hurtling towards evangelicalism, that is by no means the larger point of his book. For example, regarding just the insecurities related to inequality:

> . . . . depression is, in part, a response to the sense of humiliation the modern world inflicts on many of us. . . . Even the middle class—even the rich—are being made to feel pervasively insecure. . . . having an insecure status was the one thing even more distressing than having a low status. . . . If Robert's insights apply to humans, then Richard and Kate knew that in highly unequal societies like the United States they would find higher levels of mental distress, and in highly equal societies like Norway they'd find less. So they embarked on a massive research program to find out, sifting enormous amounts of data.
> When they were finally able to plot data on a graph, they were startled by how close the relationship was. *The more unequal your society, the more prevalent all forms of mental illness are.* (120-121). {emphasis added}

The parallels are stunning. For our purposes the point here is that these sorts of relationships generalize across the board; most importantly, grounded in Hari's telling claim that the source of our clinical depressions lies not *within* individuals themselves, as psychiatrists and pharmaceutical companies would have us believe, but *without*, in the environmental conditions that assail us. But, in particular, American insecurities are grounded in cultural mentalities and idioms that have driven the society towards a greater inequality that foments those insecurities, all the while simultaneously annihilating virtually all the succoring forms of *both* traditional European cultural life ("connections") *and* the potential for a European-like progressive egalitarian social democratic welfare state, or safety net, that could ameliorate and temper, if not eliminate, these socio-economic uncertainties. *Indeed the very same external social conditions he identifies as causes (seven in all) of individual depressions also reflect, and are responsible for, the larger cultural disenchantment of American society, whose sum total symptomatic cultural depression has sponsored the emergence and continual resurgence of evangelicalism, whose virulence is largely fueled by ideological insecurities, whose deeper sources are perceptions of the clear and present cultural dangers posed by secularism,* as we have seen. Hence the decidedly *cultural origins* of the continued dysfunctional *exceptionalism* of American evangelicalism.

—Hence also, once more, the more general observation and principle that ideologies conceived and grounded in opposition, or of protest, are inherently incapable of producing or guiding healthy governments or societies, as has been widely noted as a major difference between Shias and Sunnis in Islam. Similarly the case of Pentecostalism in Africa: ". . . . I was able to develop my account of Pentecostal political theology in Nigeria based on ethnographic material. The empirical research brought me to argue that Pentecostalism there takes the form of a negative political theology, which is to say that its conception of sovereignty did not provide grounds for theocratic authority nor could it provide a stable basis for community." (Ruth Marshall, "Christianity, Anthropology. . . , 352.)

on the boats from Europe and Africa—and, oh, the threat of red devils lurking ever present in the woods to the west of pale-faced Puritans. And then much later with the collapse of bankrupt robber-baron capitalism and the appearance of the moral market usurping New Deal of FDR,[831] tired old dogmas reemerged, energizing a hastily retreating resistance. And then more recently the apprehension of external dangers assumed a more distinctly cultural form with the reaction to the perceived advance of a secular-humanistic-driven federal government, manifesting itself in the decades-long *anxiety-ridden* opposition to Roe v. Wade, that liberal Supreme Court-generated pox on Puritanism.[832] These and other closely-related cultural phobias underlay and galvanized the *fear* and *insecurity* reaction of the Tea Party and the Religious Right, a cultural fomentation contributing to, if not culminating ultimately, in the election of Donald Trump.[833] Yes this kind of exceptionalism

---

[831] In the beginning of Roosevelt's "Second New Deal" with the passage of "the Works Progress Administration and the Social Security Act" religious organizations felt their burdens considerably lightened, or as one clergyman wrote in response to the administration's request for feedback: "For the first time in our history we have a National Administration that is seeking to realize practically all the objectives of the 'Social Creeds' of the Churches—Catholic, Protestant, Jewish." The tide turned though when moral market concerns re-emerged: "But a few clergy expressed concerns that would grow more widespread by the late 1930s, particularly among conservatives and evangelically oriented white Protestants." It wasn't, however, until decades later that "big government" complaints were vented against the institutional remnants of the New Deal. (Alison Collis Greene, "The Welfare of Faith," in Matthew Avery Sutton and Darren Dochuk eds., *Faith in the New Millennium: The Future of Religion and American Politics*, Oxford 2016, 142-3.)

—"In his programmatic 1992 book *The Tragedy of American Compassion*, [Marvin] Olasky argued that there was a process of social decline in the 20th century, when welfare state builders turned away from an early American 'understanding of compassion that was hard-headed but warm-hearted' and based on a Calvinistic understanding of a 'God of both Justice and Mercy'.... *This book has been very influential in the American Religious Right as a statement against state intervention and or individual self-help*." (Sigrun Kahl, "The Religious Roots of Modern Poverty Policy: Catholic, Lutheran, and Reformed Protestant Traditions Compared," *The European Journal of Sociology*, 2005, 46: 91-126.)

[832] Indeed wasn't it H. L. Mencken who defined Puritanism as "The haunting fear that someone, somewhere might be happy"? (From *A Mencken Chrestomathy*, 1949.)

[833] It wasn't until late in 2019, after reviewing the most significant and highly-touted books on evangelicalism of the last few decades, that I finally encountered a text that got some of this right. Kudos to Christian Smith for at least this much—on why evangelicalism was thriving during the period he studied: ".... because it is—or at least perceives itself to be—embattled with forces that seem to oppose or threaten it . . . thrives on distinction, engagement, tension, conflict, and threat. . . . the perception of crisis serves to invigorate and mobilize evangelical vitality, rather than to undermine or disintegrate it." Unfortunately, like most academic sociologists, Smith attempts to explain and buttress this by reference to a host of general discipline and other social scientific concepts that rattle like skeletons in the closet. The particular point here surely rings true to even most innocent laymen and women. He should have just let his survey data and interview materials speak for themselves. And although I thought I would never be caught saying or writing such a thing, I invite the reader to compare

has something very much to do with evangelicalism, our very uniquely American form of religiosity.[834]

As we have seen and will continue to experience, the "moral" dimensions of evangelicalism—nature, content, logic—are what render the kinds of social policies that have proven so successful in neutralizing "existential insecurities" in European social democracies virtual non-starters in American politics. In Finland, for example, we discover a society that has managed to temper the effects of industrialization and modernization by extending the *securities* of traditional village culture to the nation as a whole. The mantra that it takes a village to raise a child should be expanded to "it actually takes a whole nation to raise children successfully," a cultural maxim in either form that is largely anathema in the United States, with particular virulence among evangelicals and their Republican cohorts. To universalize the social responsibilities of the family as do the Nordic nations, documented by Anu Partanen with such clarity and depth in a book that should be required reading for all Americans, would mean an extension of the role and duties of government to the point of committing a severe violation of the moral market ethos that underlies and guides much of American society. *One great irony in all of this is that the individualism and freedom—the moral market ideology—so extolled and promoted by certain political sectors in America produces (ala Weber) the unintended*

---

his exclusive use of descriptive statistics to the more sophisticated data analysis and critical tests (correlation/regression) I cite earlier in this chapter and employ in Appendix A. E.g., how would one test (falsify) the eight propositions he advances in chapter four? As one data-driven sociologist on my dissertation committee demanded of me: "Can you prove it?" Only much later could I answer, yes. Perhaps we might ask Smith to address the same question. (Christian Smith, *American Evangelicalism: Embattled and Thriving*, University of Chicago Press, 1998, 89, 121.)

[834] At this point I simply must give a shout out to an academician who has capitalized on her dual Canadian/American background to produce one of the very few insightful (and virtually non-existent *comparative*) studies on evangelicalism in North America. With respect to perceptions of clear and present danger:

> But in both American churches, these narratives of Christian nationalism defined liberals as the villains of the story, as political and cultural out-group responsible for America's "moral decline." In both Canadian churches, I heard a rather different narrative, which blamed the loss of a "Christian Canada" squarely on the church itself. . . . In both American churches, liberal politicians and political groups were frequently mapped as salient adversaries to "our" influence in society as Christians. . . . Within both American churches, I found that a broader set of key people were "captains" for culture war politics within their congregation, who modeled a strong conservative or Republican political identity. (Lydea Bean, *The Politics of . . .* , 15.)

consequence of an extreme inequality that severely reduces the independence—and increases the dependence upon private and public charity and assistance—of a significant portion of Americans. By universalizing the social responsibilities of the state upfront, and not trailing along afterwards, the Nordic way of doing things actually generates and supports a village-like traditionalism of individualism and independence. This strategy turns back the ill effects of modernization by using national governments to recreate social conditions in a bracingly new form that mirrors the equality and security of traditional Nordic village life. What appears to many conservative American critics as a freedom-squashing socialism produces outcomes that would be celebrated stateside in any other context.

Hence evangelicalism and religiosity in general make no appearance in the Nordic region not due as much to a vestigial cultural richness of these societies but because the culture-eviscerating economic modernism, materialism, and inequality that dominates American society has been usurped and countermanded by a *Nordic theory of everything*. . . . an ethic nationalizing the *security* of a traditional village support system for the ultimate benefit of all its citizens. Much more so than other European nations that have succeeded in the *folklorization* of traditional occultic and other idioms, the Nordic nations have made an additional equally audacious leap or transition to what we might even call an *ultra-modern*, transformational, politically-generated-and-sustained, security-preserving form of society.

For whereas some Americans have embraced the notion that it takes a whole village to raise a child as a liberal Democratic mantra, the Nordic way has extended the principle in the only way that makes such villages even remotely possible. Indeed, it takes a whole national society to create and sustain the villages that raise the children. And that requires, above all, genuine culture, or at least reasonable approximations.

This is what Paul Goodman anticipated in *Growing Up Absurd*: "In such a utopian society, as was aimed at by modern radicals but has not eventuated, it would be very easy to grow up. There would be plenty of objective, worthwhile activities for a child to observe, fall in with, do, learn, improvise on his own. That is to say, *it is not the spirit of modern times that makes our society difficult for the young; it is that that spirit has not sufficiently realized itself.*"[835] Exactly, however ironic and tragic.

Unfortunately, evangelicalism and conservative moral market assumptions hang like albatrosses around the necks of a *both* too-modern *and* too-anachronistic American society and culture. As Partanen observes, we [you Americans] are "handicapped by an almost pre-modern form of depend-

---

[835] 230. {emphasis added}

ency." [836] Our in many ways dysfunctional, undemocratic Constitution, a malingering vestige of slavery, would seem to doom any movement towards a politically-generated, Nordic-like social awakening. By marked contrast, the Scandinavians, unconstrained by a puritanical, evangelical, moral market, hubris-embedded order, were free to experiment, and what has resulted over more than a half-century, as Paul Krugman never tires of reminding us, are societies that are truly the envy of the rest of the world.

Herein lies an even greater irony—to double-down, once again—of any Nordic/American comparison. American evangelical moral market individualism renders impossible the kind of government-generated social security blanket that preserves and supports the independence of citizens in Scandinavia, one that has created a genuine dependence-free individualism. Hence the tragic reversal of outcomes, as American individualism-based distrust of government generates society-wide webs of dependence, if not sheer incarceration, an unintended consequence of its own misguided celebration and application of moral individualism. The Nordic way frees citizens of burdens and responsibilities that hinder their independence and individuality, a complete reversal of the American bourgeois intention, experience, and outcomes. Decades—nay literally a few centuries—of indoctrination may have rendered a large portion of the America public incapable of understanding that

> .... the goal [of the Nordic ethos] has been to free the individual from **all** forms of dependency within the family **and** in civil society: the poor from charity, wives from husbands, adult children from parents, and elderly parents from their children.[837] {emphasis added}

Although an ostensibly horrific prospect to American ideologues, to do so is to clear the interpersonal playing field of "ulterior motives and needs" that can get in the way of genuine relationships and responsibilities, an almost anachronistic, pre-modern throwback, whereby, ironically again, ".... empowered individuals can engage in [genuine] personal relations in the modern age."[838]

Unfortunately, we Americans continue to wallow in paradoxical cultural contradictions of our own making, wherein the state is the enemy of freedom,

---

[836] Partanen, op. cit., 33.

[837] Ibid., 51-2. {bold emphasis in original}

[838] Ibid., 53. Note that Ronald Inglehart indirectly addressed this issue in a later paper, "Faith and Freedom: Traditional and Modern Ways to Happiness," in Diener, Helliwell. . . . eds., 351-388.

not the source of "existential security" and our own ultimate liberation. Indeed no foreign invasion could have more deeply enslaved us. Max Weber must have foreseen the future of America when he warned in the *Protestant Ethic and the Spirit of Capitalism* about an unhinged materialism morphing into an "iron cage" of our own making. Although he got it quite wrong that "In the field of its highest development, in the United States, the pursuit of wealth, [has been] stripped of its religious and ethical meaning. . . ," he nonetheless proved spot on in anticipation of the cultural consequences: "For in the last stage of this *cultural development*, it might well be truly said [quoting Goethe]: 'Specialists without spirit, sensualists without heart; *this nullity* imagines that it has attained a level of civilization never before achieved.' " [839]

And finally, more recently, what I call the *secular trends bias* of academicians re-emerged during the administration of Barack Obama, when it seemed as though the evangelical Religious Right might have descended to the nadir of its influence, resigned to embracing the obstructionism of the Republican Party, perhaps reduced to the role of mere malcontented apparatchiks egging on Tea Party extremism (or even simply blending into them).[840] Understandably, some observers yielded to a few all too tempting anticipations and hastily-drawn conclusions of their own making, convinced that the evangelical political uprising had run its course, about to expire in a self-destructive, internally-triggered implosion of sorts. Omens could be found in demographic trends, and the last few years of the Obama administration all too easily encouraged a spate of prognostications heralding the ultimate demise of evangelical religion and of Christianity in general. Once again, storm-cloud trends appeared ominously on the horizon. Out west the takeover of that monumental symbol of evangelical prosperity theology, Robert Schuller's Crystal Cathedral, by the Catholic diocese of Orange County in 2013, a demographic testament to the "surging population of more than 1.2 million Catholics, many of them immigrants from Latin America and Southeast Asia," seemed to confirm the shifting balance of power. Some observers allowed the encouraging ascension of a *half* black man to the White House to color their reading of the tea leaves of other trends, as did one "religion correspondent for the *Orange County Register*," who

---

[839] 181-2. {emphases added}

[840] Of the Tea Party, Jill Lepore writes that they embrace "a set of assumptions that, conflating originalism, evangelicalism, and heritage tourism, amounts to a variety of fundamentalism." Indeed they treat the founding documents as sacredly Biblical in stature, "to be read in the same spirit with which religious fundamentalists read, for instance, the Ten Commandments." (From *The Whites of Their Eyes*. . . , quoted in Gordon S. Wood, "No Thanks for the Memories," *The New York Review of Books*, 1/13/2011, 40.)

prophesized that "In a few years, perhaps a decade or two, religious America will catch up to Orange County's present. . . America will remain exceptionally religious. But traditional evangelical Christianity will no longer be a dominant presence in that religiosity. . . . [for] *the reality, largely unnoticed outside church circles, is that evangelicalism is not only in gradual decline but today stands poised at the edge of a demographic and cultural cliff.*"[841] According to John S. Dickerson, "a former investigative reporter turned evangelical pastor, evangelical Christianity is hemorrhaging members, money and influence." As he concludes in *The Great Evangelical Recession*, 'The United States has shifted into a . . . post-Christian age   . . . . No one disputes this.' "[842] *No one, indeed.*

Long before these secular trends began to assert themselves,[843] Harvey Cox wrote a swan song of his own, following up his own paean to an earlier secular trend, *The Secular City*, with *Religion in the Secular City*, wherein although recanting his earlier miscues nonetheless continues twenty years or so later on to hurdle past the evangelical political revolution as an unfortunate bump in the road, anticipating a more sustainable post Religious-Right future, one dotted by "basic Christian" Potemkin villages, a landscape fully recovered from that earlier unfortunate scorched-earth cultural episode. For him the combined trends—towards a more Latin American-flavored Catholicism—were all moving in a new positive direction.[844]

And yet the election of Barack Obama proved only a fleeting watershed event in American political and social life. Whatever obstructionism he encountered in Congress or in the "Red States" was attributed largely to the last gasp of political and religious extremism in America. Two years later in 2010, Robert Putnam and David E. Campbell published *American Grace: How*

---

[841] Jim Hinch, "Where Are The People?" *The American Scholar*, Winter 2014. {emphasis added}

—To be fair, some predictions based upon survey data are understandable. Eboo Patel presents a PRRI 2016 American Value Atlas table showing a quite dramatic "Decline of White Christians by Age Group" from 64% of Americans 65 years or older to 25% 18-29 years old. (Eboo Patel, op. cit., 117.)

[842] Ibid.

[843] And even longer before that, Alexis de Tocqueville fell prey to a similar secular trends bias when he drew upon census data to project that "If the Union continues, the basin of the Mississippi is evidently marked out, by its fertility and its extent to be the permanent center of the Federal government. . . . In a few years the states that founded the Union will lose the direction of its policy. . . ." (Phillips Bradley ed., *Democracy in America, Vol. 1*, New York: Knopf, 1972, 400.)

[844] Harvey Cox, *Religion in the Secular City*. . . . 1984, 107. Cox largely interprets the demographic trends for theological purposes: ". . . with the passing of the modern age, the epoch of 'modern theology' which tried to interpret Christianity in the face of secularization is also over. A fundamentally new theological approach is needed." (20)

Religion Divides and Unites Us,[845] a highly praised study relying primarily upon survey data, the authors reporting religious trends that appeared to parallel shifting social and political currents. For our purposes the study yields a couple of telling, if not embarrassing, observations: "Since this fact is not widely understood, it is worth reemphasizing—*the evangelical boom that began in the 1970s was over by the early 1990s, nearly two decades ago. In twenty-first century America expansive evangelicalism is a feature of the past, not the present.*"[846] Ooooops.

As was then *supposedly* well-known, that prior "boom" of an increase drew largely from declining mainline Protestantism, although the population of self-reported "evangelicals" fluctuated from 23% in 1973 to 28% (at its peak) in 1993 back down to 24% in 2008. So that all during the apparent rise of the Religious Right the number of survey-identified evangelicals either grew or declined a few percentage points at the very most. The "boom" would appear due not to a demographic shift but to heightened political mobilization.[847] The trends instead ominously portended an ultimate decline in both numbers of evangelicals (although "what the evangelical churches have lost in adherents over the last two decades has mostly been made up for by the evangelicals' zeal"[848]) and traditional Religious-Right activism.[849] With the necessary qualifications kept firmly in mind, one left the highly-praised Putnam and Campbell treatise fairly persuaded that evangelical religion in America was wavering on the last legs of its social, cultural, and political influence, about to go down for the count.[850]

---

[845] Simon & Schuster 2010. Of course, this spare selection doesn't do justice to their findings.

[846] Ibid., 105. {emphasis added}

[847] Putnam and Campbell are wise to question the "purely demographic factors" (e.g., birth rates) some sociologists of religion have advanced to explain shifts in evangelical numbers and influence. (ibid., 109-110) Then again, ten years or so earlier Michael Hout, Andrew Greeley and Melissa J. Wilde ("The Demographic Imperative. . . ," 2001) had claimed something entirely different based upon equally rigorous survey data.

[848] Ibid., 107.

[849] Not so fast: "Red states have higher birth rates than blue states, which means that over time the country should become increasingly conservative. *Wall Street Journal* columnist James Taranto points to what he calls 'the Roe effect.' He says the right to abortion has diminished the number of Democratic voters because it is, de facto, pro-choice women who have abortions and children tend to gravitate toward their parents' values. If pro-choice women are having fewer babies than pro-life women, there will be fewer pro-choice voters in the next generation, the argument goes. The effect is heightened, Taranto holds, because the racial groups that have the most abortions proportionately—blacks followed by Hispanics—also have higher rates of Democratic voting than non-Hispanic whites." (Monique El-Faizy, op. cit., 238.)

[850] Here is Alan Wolfe, a somewhat rare evangelical operating within the belly of the secular academic beast: "Along with their changing demography has come a new political sensibility. While strongly committed to their faith, *Evangelicals accept the separation of church and state and share*

A 2016 study makes an even stronger demographic case for the impending disappearance of evangelical religion from American life, Robert P. Jones of the Public Religion Research Institute's provocatively titled *The End of White Christian America*. No doubt the study was researched and completed prior to the election of that same year. Based upon the Institute's 2014 *American Values Survey* and two terms of Barack Obama, the die appeared irreversibly cast:

> Perhaps most tellingly, 2007 was the year that it became clear that the Christian Right had lost its ability to influence the nominating process for Republican Party presidential candidates. . . . [and] Mitt Romney's defeat in 2012 showed that despite its appearance of vitality, the Tea Party is better understood *as a late-stage expression of a White Christian America that is passing from the scene.*[851]

---

the culture of toleration of the rest of their society. . . . *Evangelicals have made their peace with American culture. . . .* They insist on the importance of strong moral dispositions and watchfulness against sin, but they are also part of a society that wants to emphasize the positive and uplifting over the negative and depressing. . . . *Evangelicals are now part of the mainstream. . . .*" ("Faith, Freedom, and Toleration," in E.J. Dionne Jr., Jean Bethke Elshtain, and Kayla M. Drogosz eds., *One Electorate Under God? A Dialogue on Religion & American Politics*. PEW Forum Dialogues on religion and Public Life. Wash. D.C.: Brookings Institution Press, 2004, 224.) {emphases added}. Ooooops again.

—Five years later, John Meacham reported on forecasts of the serious decline of born-again Christianity in a long article in *Newsweek* magazine: "The End of Christian America," April 3, 2009, the more dire prognostications of which he did not entirely share.

—More recently, political scientist Mark A. Smith spent six years of the Obama administration working to arrive at the conclusion that the "culture war" was overblown by a few intellectuals and academicians, that religion in general and evangelicalism in particular represent the tails that get wagged by the larger dog of secular culture and not the other way around: ". . . . the culture warriors all agree on the desirability of individual rights and representative democracy. . . . the culture war is best described as a struggle between people with overlapping worldviews who fight over their differences. The issues dividing them often do not persist . . . . Americans are now nearly unified in denouncing slavery, discrimination, child abuse, and domestic violence. . . ." Professor Smith spends most of his book belaboring the obvious point that religions are not impervious to larger encompassing social and cultural contexts and cherry-picking what he calls the "full range of actual and potential issues." That most Americans accept that the planet is not flat ("denouncing slavery") proves scant compensation for a substantial minority's continued belief in an 8,000 year-old earth, climate change denial (grounded in dispensational millenarianism), immigration xenophobia, second amendment gun-rights extremism, federal government phobia, Jim Crow bigotry and/or racism, and the fear of a spreading secular humanism. By turning a blind eye to white supremacy ideologies, sexual predation, domestic spousal abuse, and the spurning of strangers, the large evangelical minority of Americans reveals its true colors. See *Secular Faith: How Culture Has Trumped Religion in American Politics*, University of Chicago Press, 2015, 218-21 especially.

[851] Simon & Schuster, 2016, 98. Ooops, again.

—"The incomplete revolution conservatives directed in the 1970s *makes the problems they face today deep rooted and difficult to overcome. Contrary to the conventional wisdom, conservatism will not be easily remade simply with a new person in the White House* or fresh leadership on Capitol Hill." (from the Epilogue of the editors: Bruce J. Schulman & Julian E. Zelizer eds., *Rightward Bound: Making*

Observe here one painful secular trend-induced blunder of an anticipation or expectation after another.[852] But are any of these prognosticators suitably embarrassed? Are any experiencing *sociological secular trends remorse syndrome—SSTRS?*[853] Better yet, have any of them paused to ponder the consequences

---

America Conservative in the 1970s, Harvard University Press, 2008, 292.) Ooops, ooops, again. [emphasis added}

—Even earlier D. G. Hart sensed a sea-change: "This generational succession [shift leftward] suggests that the days of goodwill and harmonious relations between evangelicals and conservatives may be coming to an end. . . . reaching the threshold of irreconcilable differences. . . . [cites Frances Fitzgerald quoting Joel C. Hunter, "an evangelical pastor of a large church in Orlando. . ."]: 'What has passed for an "evangelical" up to now is a stereotype created by the people with the loudest voices.' A new constituency of born-again Protestants is emerging, 'like the force of a tsunami under water.' E. J. Dionne, a columnist for the *Washington Post,* told Fitzgerald that *the era of the Religious Right was over."* (*From Billy Graham to Sarah Palin: Evangelicals and the Betrayal of American Conservatism,* Grand Rapids: Eerdmans 2011, 2, 179; and with reference to Frances Fitzgerald, "The New Evangelicals," *New Yorker,* June 30, 2008.) {emphasis added}

[852] Quite recently, Professor Janelle S. Wong of the University of Maryland addresses some of these secular trend assumptions head on, discovering a more complex demographic situation. Instead of a white evangelical American population proportionately shrinking away, she reports an influx of "Latinx" and Asian evangelical immigrants bolstering the original white evangelical head count. In examining large sets of questionable survey data and conducting a series of unimaginative interviews with immigrant populations (by her "team"), she nonetheless is one of the few academic social scientists who has actually gleaned some insight from such data. Drawing also upon Lydia Bean's comparative study of Canadian and U.S. evangelical church communities, she demonstrates an understanding of the "in-group embattlement" mentality (although leaning too heavily, and mistakenly, upon conventional sociological reference group theory), an outlook that sets American evangelicalism far part from identically-named Canadian sects. Unfortunately she fails to directly apply the lessons learned, for it is the absence of any such perception of clear-and-present-danger from outsiders, or a persecution complex, and also any closely related well-honed distrust of government (historical contextual cultural dynamics—not the "effects of race" or contending ideas of "national community," as she frames it) that so clearly distinguishes these new evangelical immigrants from their conservative white American counterparts. Given the uncertainties attending the resulting ethnic and ideological mix, she understandably shies away from predicting the extent to which these newly arriving evangelicals will merely rush in to take up the demographic slack, fortifying the original base, or chart some new directions of their own. (*Immigrants, Evangelicals, and Politics in an Era of Demographic Change,* The Russell Sage Foundation, 2018.)

[853] Certainly not the reigning doyen of American sociologists of religion, Robert Wuthnow, who riding the wave of this forecasted decline predictably relied upon data-based sociological (institutional or "organizations theory") factors for an explanation: "In contrast, Wuthnow argues [in 2007, *After The Babyboomers.* . . .] that the decline in religious adherence among younger Americans (roughly, those under age 35) can be understood as the result of short-term, historically specific failure of institutional adaptation. . . . the life course has undergone a radical transition over the past 30 years; now, most Americans take until their midthirties to achieve all markers of adulthood, and many never do, remaining childless and spending long periods of adult life without a spouse / partner. Given this reconfigured life course, Wuthnow argues that American religious institutions have failed to provide ministries that are

that might have rained down upon the nation had Donald Trump proven even moderately focused and competent enough to fully carry out his stated Religious-Right political agenda?[854] Among the many well-meaning observers searching for answers, Malcolm Gladwell advanced an academic journal-borrowed explanation: the election reflected both gender bias and "moral license." The public felt good enough about itself for electing Barack Obama that it could turn right around and indulge in some lingering subliminal venting: I've/We've been virtuous, so a little compensating self-indulgent badness on our part might be overlooked, if not thoroughly excused. A bit far-fetched perhaps, but one arguable scenario nonetheless.

A little closer to home and to the truth, I suspect, is that evangelicalism is not going away anytime soon, for a host of reasons that can no longer be denied or explained away with conventional sociological terms and dogma, emanating as they do from a slew of metastasizing cultural dynamics of disenchantment with which the reader has now become all too familiar. For as we've intimated throughout the book, perhaps too optimistically, *were that only the half of it.*

---

relevant for the first 10-15 years of adult life." (Penny Edgell, "A Cultural Sociology of Religion: New Directions," *Annual Review of Sociology*, 2012, Vol. 38, 253.) The diligent reader might have already guessed that the direct opposite in fact obtains, for it is precisely these kinds of "insecurities" that propel young people towards non-traditional evangelical religious forms.

[854] As I write there still has been no published account of the impact of Donald Trump's conversion to evangelical Christianity upon the composition and thrust of his administration. I would be happy to share my own take on the matter upon request: "For What It's Worth: The Cultural Origins of Alternative Facts," 2017. (See my other items in the Selected Bibliography.) But, of course, the Religious Right was well aware of the evangelical connection from the very beginning, as is made readily apparent by even a cursory Amazon search for books on Donald Trump, keyword: *hagiographies.*
—Two of the earliest accounts I have located: ". . . . had breakfast with [televangelist Paula White] a few months earlier at the Trump International Hotel on the edge of Central Park. Donald Trump is a personal friend of White's, and she frequently stays at his hotel during her frequent visits to New York. The staff there know her and greet her warmly and deferentially. . . . [she also] leads a Bible study for the Yankees [baseball team]. . . ." (Monique El-Faisy, op. cit., 2006, 21); and Julie Zauzmer, "Acts of Faith: Paula White, prosperity preacher once investigated by the Senate, is a controversial pick for the inauguration," *The Washington Post*, 12/29/16.

Selected Bibliography

Albanese, Catherine L. *America: Religions and Religion*. Belmont: Wadsworth, 2nd ed., 1992.

Alexis de Tocqueville. *Democracy in America, Vol. 1&2*. Phillips Bradley ed., New York: Knopf, 1972.

Anderson, Allan Heaton. *To The Ends of the Earth: Pentecostalism and the Transformation of World Christianity*. Oxford University Press, 2013.

Anderson, Kurt. *Fantasyland: How America Went Haywire A 500-Year History*. New York: Random House, 2017.

Ammerman, Nancy Tatum. *Bible Believers: Fundamentalism in the Modern World*. New Brunswick, New Jersey: Rutgers University Press, 1987.

Appleby, R. Scott. *The Ambivalence of the Sacred: Religion, Violence, and Reconciliation*. Rowman & Littlefield, 2000.

Aslan, Reza. *Zealot: The Life and Times of Jesus of Nazareth*. Random House, 2013.

Atwood, Margaret. *The Handmaid's Tale*. Toronto: McClelland and Stewart, 1985.

Bailyn, Bernard. *The Ideological Origins of the American Revolution*. Cambridge: Harvard University Press, 1967.

Baldwin, Peter. *The Narcissism of Minor Differences: How America and Europe Are Alike, An Essay in Numbers*. Oxford University Press, 2009.

Balibar, Étienne. *Secularism and Cosmopolitanism: Critical Hypotheses on Religion and Politics*. New York: Columbia University Press, 2018.

Balmer, Randall. *Mine Eyes Have Seen The Glory: A Journey Into The Evangelical Subculture In America*. New York: Oxford University Press, 1989.

_____. *Evangelicalism in America*. Waco: Baylor University Press, 2016.

Bartkowski, John. *Remaking the Godly Marriage: Gender Negotiation in Evangelical Families*. Rutgers University Press, 2001.

Barzini, Luigi. *The Italians*, Atheneum, 1964.

Bean, Lydea. *The Politics of Evangelical Identity: Local Churches and Partisan Divides in the United States and Canada*. Princeton: Princeton University Press, 2014.

Beinart, Peter. "The End of American Exceptionalism." *The Atlantic*, February 2014.

Bell, Daniel. *The Cultural Contradictions of Capitalism*. New York: Basic Books, 1976.

_____. *The Winding Passage: Essays and Sociological Journeys, 1960-1980*. Abt Books/Basic Books, 1980.

Bellah, Robert. *Beyond Belief: Essays on Religion in a Post-Traditional World*. New York: Harper & Row, 1970.

_____. "Religion & Power in America Today." *Commonweal*, 3 December 1982.

_____ et al. *Habits of the Heart: Individualism and Commitment in American Life*. New York: Harper & Row, 1986.

_____. "Max Weber and World-Denying Love: A Look at the Historical Sociology of Religion." *Journal of the American Academy of Religion*. 67/2, 1999.

_____. *Religion in Human Evolution: From the Paleolithic to the Axial Age*. Cambridge, MA: Harvard University Press, 2011.

_____. "Twenty-three Theses: A Response." *Journal of the American Academy of*

Religion. December 2013, Vol. 81, No. 4.

Bercovitch, Sacvan. *The Puritan Origins of the American Self.* New Haven: Yale University Press, 1975.

Berger, Peter L. *The Sacred Canopy: Elements of a Sociological Theory of Religion.* New York: Anchor Books, 1969.

Birgegard, Andreas & Pehr Granqvist. "The Correspondence Between Attachment to Parents and God: Three Experiments Using Subliminal Separation Cues." *Personality and Social Psychology Bulletin,* Vol. 30 No. 9, September 2004.

Blodgett, Geoffrey. "A New Look at the Gilded Age: Politics in a Cultural Context." In D. W. Howe ed. *Victorian America.* Philadelphia: University of Pennsylvania Press, 1976.

Bloom, Harold. *The American Religion: The Emergence of the Post-Christian Nation.* New York: Simon & Schuster, 1993.

Blythe, Ronald. *Portrait of an English Village.* New York: Pantheon Books, 1980.

Booth, Michael. *The Almost Nearly Perfect People: Behind the Myth of the Scandinavian Utopia.* New York: Picador, 2015.

Boswell, John. *Christianity, Social Tolerance, and Homosexuality: Gay People in Western Europe from the Beginning of the Christian Era to the Fourteenth Century.* Chicago: University of Chicago Press, 1980.

Bowler, Kate. *Blessed: A History of the American Prosperity Gospel.* Oxford University Press, 2013.

_____. *Everything Happens For a Reason and Other Lies I've Loved.* Random House, 2018.

Bowman, Matthew. *Christian: The Politics of a Word in America.* Cambridge, Massachusetts: Harvard University Press, 2018.

Bronowski, Jacob. *A Sense Of The Future.* Cambridge, Massachusetts: The MIT Press, 1977.

Bruner, Jerome S. *Beyond the Information Given: Studies in the Psychology of Knowing.* Jeremy M. Anglin ed. W. W. Norton, 1973.

Buerge, David M. "Missions in the Wilderness: Seattle's early religious leaders imposed moral order on an unruly frontier town. . . ." *The Weekly,* 25-31 December 1985.

Buettner, Dan. "The World's Happiest Places." *National Geographic,* November, 2017.

Butler, Jon. *Awash In a Sea of Faith: Christianizing The American People.* Cambridge, Massachusetts: Harvard University Press, 1990.

_____. "Jack-in-the-Box Faith: The Religion Problem in Modern American History." *The Journal of American History,* March 2004.

_____. *God In Gotham: The Miracle of Religion in Modern Manhattan.* Cambridge, Massachusetts: Harvard University Press, 2020.

Butterfield, Herbert. "Christianity in History," in Philip P. Wiener, ed. *Dictionary of the History of Ideas, Vol. 1.* New York: Charles Scribner's Sons, 1973.

Butterworth, Michael L. "Saved at Home: Christian Branding and Faith Nights in the 'Church of Baseball'." *Quarterly Journal of Speech,* Vol. 97, No. 3, August 2011.

Bynum, Caroline Walker. *The Resurrection of the Body in Western Christianity, 200-1336.* New York: Columbia University Press, 1995.

_____. *Christian Materiality: An Essay on Religion in Late Medieval Europe.* Zone Books, 2011.

Cacioppo, John T, & William Patrick. *Loneliness: Human Nature and the Need for Social Connection.* New York: Norton, 2008.

_____ & James H. Fowler, Nicholas A. Christakis. "Alone in the Crowd: The Structure and Spread of Loneliness in a Large Social Network." *Journal of Personality and Social Psychology,* 2009, vol.97, no. 6.

Calder, Nigel. *Einstein's Universe.* New York: Penguin Books, 1980.

Cash, W. J. *The Mind of the South.* New York: Alfred A. Knopf, 1941.

Clark, J. D. "Secularization and Modernization: The Failure of a 'Grand Narrative'." *The Historical Journal* 55, no. 1, 2012.

Clark, Norman H. *Mill Town: A Social History of Everett, Washington, from Its Earliest Beginnings on the Shores of Puget Sound to the Tragic and Infamous Event Known as the Everett Massacre.* Seattle: University of Washington Press, 1972.

Cox, Harvey. *The Secular City: Secularization and Urbanization in Theological Perspective.* Macmillan Co., 1965.

_____. *Religion in The Secular City: Towards a Postmodern Theology.* Simon & Schuster, 1984.

Davis, David Brion. *Revolutions: Reflections on American Equality and Foreign Liberations.* Cambridge: Harvard University Press, 1990.

Demos, John. "Satan in Salem." *The New York Review of Books,* 12/3/2015.

Di Giovanni, Janine. "The Vanishing: The plight of Christians in an age of intolerance." *Harper's Magazine,* December 2018.

Diamond, Sara. *Spiritual Warfare.* South End Press, 1989.

Diener, Ed, John F. Helliwell, & Daniel Kahneman eds. *International Differences in Well-Being.* Oxford University Press, 2010.

Dionne Jr., E. J., Jean Bethke Elshtain, & Kayla M. Drogosz eds. *One Electorate Under God? A Dialogue on Religion & American Politics.* PEW Forum Dialogues on Religion and Public Life. Wash. D.C.: Brookings Institution Press, 2004.

Dochuk, Darren. *From Bible Belt to SunBelt: Plain-Folk Religion, Grassroots Politics, and the Rise of Evangelical Conservatism.* New York: W.W. Norton, 2011.

Douglas, Mary. "The Effects of Modernization on Religious Change." *Daedalus,* Vol. 111, No. 1, Religion (Winter, 1982).

_____ & Steven Tipton eds. *Religion and America: Spiritual Life In A Secular Age.* Boston: Beacon Press, 1983.

Douthat, Ross. *Bad Religion: How We Became A Nation of Heretics.* Free Press, 2012.

Dupont, Carolyn Renee. *Mississippi Praying: Southern White Evangelicals and the Civil Rights Movement, 1945-1975.* NYU Press, 2013.

Dupré, Louis. "Marx's Critique of Culture and Its Interpretations." *The Review of Metaphysics,* Vol. 34, No. 1, Sept., 1980.

Edgell, Penny. "A Cultural Sociology of Religion: New Directions." *Annual Review of Sociology,* 2012, Vol. 38.

Eldredge, Niles. *The Monkey Business: A Scientist Looks at Creationism.* New York: Washington Square Press, 1982.

El-Faizy, Monique. *God and Country: How Evangelicals Have Become America's New Mainstream*. New York: Bloomsbury, 2006.

Eliade, Mircea. *The Sacred and the Profane: The Nature of Religion*. New York: Harcourt Brace Jovanovich, 1959.

Engen, Abram C. Van. *City on a Hill: A History of American Exceptionalism*. New Haven: Yale University Press, 2020.

Erikson, Erik. "Wholeness and Totality—A Psychiatric Contribution." Reprinted in Carl J. Friedrich ed. *Totalitarianism* (Proceedings of a conference at the American Academy of Arts and Sciences, March 1953). Cambridge: Harvard University Press, 1954.

Eskridge, Larry & Mark A. Noll eds. *More Money, More Ministry: Money and Evangelicals in Recent North American History*. Grand Rapids: Wm. B. Eerdmans Publishing Co., 2000.

Everett, Daniel. *Don't Sleep, There Are Snakes: Life and Language in the Amazonian Jungle*. London: Profile Books, 2008.

Fischer, Claude S. *Made in America: A Social History of American Culture and Character*. Chicago: University of Chicago Press, 2010.

_____. *Still Connected: Family and Friends in America Since 1970*. Russell Sage Foundation, 2011.

_____. *Lurching Toward Happiness in America*. MIT Press, 2014.

Fischer, David Hackett. *Albion's Seed: British Folkways in America*. New York: Oxford University Press, 1989.

Fitzgerald, Frances. "Reflections: Jim and Tammy." *The New Yorker*, 23 April 1990.

_____. *The Evangelicals: The Struggle to Shape America*. Simon & Schuster, 2017.

Fitzgerald, Timothy. *The Ideology of Religious Studies*. Oxford University Press, 2000.

Flanagan, Sabina. *Hildegard of Bingen, 1098-1179: A Visionary Life*. London: Routledge & Kegan Paul, 1989.

Friedman, Howard Steven. *The Measure of a Nation: How to Regain America's Competitive Edge and Boost Our Global Standing*. Prometheus Books, 2012.

Froese, Paul & Christopher D. Bader. "God in America: Why Theology Is Not Simply the Concern of Philosophers." *Journal for the Scientific Study of Religion*, 2007, 46(4).

_____. *America's Four Gods: What We Say About God and What That Says About Us*. Oxford University Press, 2010.

Frye, Northrop. *The Great Code: The Bible And Literature*. New York: Harcourt Brace Jovanovich, 1981.

Frykholm, Amy Johnson. *Rapture Culture: Left Behind in Evangelical America*. Oxford University Press, 2004.

Gallup, George. *Religion in America, 1982*. Princeton Religion Research Center. Princeton, New Jersey.

Gardella, Peter. *Innocent Ecstasy: How Christianity Gave America an Ethic of Sexual Pleasure*. Oxford University Press, 1985.

Gaskill, Malcolm. *Between Two Worlds: How The English Became Americans*. Basic Books, 2014.

Geertz, Clifford. "Religion as a Cultural System." Originally published in M. Banton ed., *Anthropological Approaches to the Study of Religion*. London: Travistock Publications Ltd, 1966/reprinted in *The Interpretation of Cultures: Selected Essays*. Basic Books, 1973.

_____. *Islam Observed: Religious Development in Morocco and Indonesia*. New Haven: Yale University Press, 1968.

Gerson, Michael. "The Last Temptation." *The Atlantic*, April 2018.

Gilgoff, Dan. *The Jesus Machine: How James Dobson, Focus on the Family, and Evangelical America Are Winning the Culture War*. New York: St. Martin's Press, 2007

Godfrey, Laurie R., ed. *Scientists Confront Creationism*. New York: Norton, 1983.

Goodman, Paul. *Growing Up Absurd*. New York: Random House, 1956.

Goodwyn, Lawrence. *The Populist Moment: A Short History of the Agrarian Revolt in America*. New York: Oxford University Press, 1978.

Goody, Jack. "Religion and Ritual: The Definitional Problem." *The British Journal of Sociology*, Vol. 12, No. 2, June, 1961.

Gorski, Philip. "The Return of the Repressed: Religion and the Political Unconscious of Historical Sociology." In Julia Adams et al. eds., *Remaking Modernity: Politics, History, and Sociology*. Duke University Press, 2005.

_____. and David Kyuman Kim/John Torpey/Jonathan Van Antwerpen eds. *The Post-Secular in Question: Religion in Contemporary Society*. New York: NYU Press, 2012.

_____. *American Covenant: A History of Civil Religion from the Puritans to the Present*. Princeton: Princeton University Press, 2017.

Gould, Stephen J. "Cardboard Darwinism." *The New York Review of Books*, 25 September 1986.

Greeley, Andrew and Michael Hout. *The Truth About Conservative Christians: What They Think and What They Believe*. Chicago: University of Chicago Press, 2006.

Greven, Philip. *The Protestant Temperament: Patterns of Child-Rearing, Religious Experience, and the Self in Early America*. New York: A Meridian Book of The New American Library, 1979.

Griffith, R. Marie. *Moral Combat: How Sex Divided American Christians and Fractured American Politics*. Basic Books 2017.

Gutman, Herbert G. *Work, Culture, & Society in Industrializing America: Essays in American Working-Class and Social History*. New York: Vintage Books, 1977.

Hackett, Conrad and D. Michael Lindsay. "Measuring Evangelicalism: Consequences of Different Operationalization Strategies." *Journal for the Scientific Study of Religion*, Vol. 47, No. 3, Sept., 2008.

Haidt, Jonathan. *The Righteous Mind: Why Good People Are Divided by Politics and Religion*. Penguin Books, 2013.

Harding, Susan Friend. *The Book of Jerry Falwell: Fundamentalist Language and Politics*. Princeton: Princeton University Press, 2001.

Hari, Johann. *Lost Connections: Uncovering The Real Causes of Depression and the Unexpected Solutions*. London: Bloomsbury, 2017.

Harrison, Robert Pogue. *Juvenescence: A Cultural History of Our Age*. Chicago: University of Chicago Press, 2014.

Hart, D. G. *From Billy Graham to Sarah Palin: Evangelicals and the Betrayal of American Conservatism*. Grand Rapids: Eerdmans, 2011.

Hartman, Andrew. *A War for the Soul of America: A History of the Cultural Wars*. Chicago: University of Chicago Press, 2015.

Hartman, Laura M. *The Christian Consumer: Living Faithfully in a Fragile World*. New York: Oxford University Press, 2011.

Haselby, Sam. *The Origins of American Religious Nationalism*. Oxford University Press, 2105.

Hechter, Michael. *Internal Colonialism: The Celtic Fringe in British National Development*. Berkeley: University of California Press, 1975.

Hedgehog Review, The. "Religion and Globalization." Summer, 2002.

_____. "After Secularization (special double issue)." Spring & Summer, 2006.

_____. "Does Religious Pluralism Require Secularism?" Fall, 2010.

Hedges, Chris. *American Fascists: The Christian Right and the War on America*. Free Press, 2006.

Hick, John & Paul F. Kitter eds. *The Myth of Christian Uniqueness: Towards a Pluralistic Theology of Religions*. Mary Knoll, N.Y.: Orbis Books, 1987.

Hidaka, Brandon H. "Depression as a Disease of Modernity: explanations for increasing prevalence." *Journal of Affective Disorders*, 2012 Nov: 140 (3).

Hirst, Paul Q. *Durkheim, Bernhard and Epistemology*. London: Routledge & Kegan Paul, 1979.

Holland, Tom. *Dominion: How The Christian Revolution Remade The World*. Basic Books, 2019.

Holmes, Arthur F. *The Idea of a Christian College*. Grand Rapids: Eerdmans, 1975.

_____. *Contours of a Christian Worldview*. Grand Rapids: Eerdmans, 1983.

Horton, Michael S. *Beyond Culture Wars: Is America a Mission Field or Battlefield?* Chicago: Moody Press, 1994.

Hout, Michael, Andrew Greeley, and Melissa J. Wilde. "The Demographic Imperative in Religious Change in the United States." *American Journal of Sociology*, Vol. 107, No. 2, September 2001.

Howe, Daniel Walker ed. *Victorian America*. Philadelphia: University of Pennsylvania Press, 1976.

Hunter, James Davison. *American Evangelicalism: Conservative Religion and the Quandary of Modernity*. New Brunswick: Rutgers University Press, 1983.

_____. *Evangelicalism: The Coming Generation*. Chicago: University of Chicago Press, 1987.

_____. *Culture Wars: The Struggle To Define America*. New York: Basic Books, 1991.

Jaeger, Gertrude and Philip Selznick. "A Normative Theory of Culture." *American Sociological Review*, 29.

Johnson, Paul E. *A Shopkeeper's Millennium: Society and Revivals in Rochester, New York, 1815-1837*. New York: Hill&Wang, 1978.

Jones, Robert C. *The End of White Christian America*. New York: Simon & Schuster, 2016.

Jordan, Mark. D. *Recruiting Young Love: How Christians Talk About Homosexuality*. Chicago: University of Chicago Press, 2011.

Junger, Sebastien. *Tribe: On Becoming and Belonging.* Twelve, Hachette Book Group, 2016.

Lindsay, D. Michael. *Faith in The Halls of Power: How Evangelicals Joined the Elite.* Oxford University Press, 2007.

Kahan, Dan M. "Cultural Cognition as a Conception of the Cultural Theory of Risk." In Sabine Roesner et al. eds., *Handbook of Risk Theory: Epistemology, Decision Theory, Ethics, and Social Implications of Risk.* Springer Publishing, 2012.

_____. "What's Really Wrong with Shaming Sanctions." Yale Law School Research Paper #125 preliminary draft, undated.

Kahl, Sigrun. "The Religious Roots of Modern Poverty Policy: Catholic, Lutheran, and Reformed Protestant Traditions Compared." *The European Journal of Sociology,* 2005, 46.

Kammen, Michael. *People of Paradox: An Inquiry Concerning the Origins of American Civilization.* New York: Knopf, 1975.

Kagan, Jerome. *The Nature of the Child.* New York: Basic Books, 1984.

Keister, Lisa A. "Religion and Wealth: The Role of Religious Affiliation and Participation in Early Adult Asset Accumulation." *Social Forces,* September 2003, 82(1).

Kellogg, John Harvey. *Man, the Masterpiece, or Plain Truths Plainly Told, About Boyhood, Youth and Manhood.* 1886.

Kett, Joseph F. *Rites of Passage: Adolescence in America, 1790 to the Present.* New York: Basic Books, 1977.

Kirch, Patrick Vinton. "When Hawaii Was Ruled By Shark-like Gods." *The New York Review of Books.* December 3, 2015.

Kirkpatrick, Lee A. and Phillip A. Shaver. "Attachment Theory and Religion: Childhood Attachments, Religious Beliefs, and Conversion." *Journal for the Scientific Study of Religion,* Vol. 29, No. 3, September 1990.

Konieczny, Mary Ellen, Kelly H. Chong, and Loren D. Lybarger. "Theory as a Tool in the Social Scientific Study of Religion and Martin Riesebrodt's *The Promise of Salvation*." *Journal for the Scientific Study of Religion,* Vol. 51, No. 3, September 2012.

Kotesky, Ronald L. *Psychology from a Christian Perspective.* Nashville: Abingdon, 1980.

Krus, Kevin M. *One Nation Under God: How Corporate America Invented Christian America.* New York: Basic Books, 2016.

Kyle, Richard G. *Popular Evangelicalism in American Culture.* London: Routlege, 2018.

Lacorne, Denis. *Religion in America: A Political History.* New York: Columbia University Press, 2011.

Laderman, Gary. "The Disney Way of Death." *The Journal of the American Academy of Religion.* No. 1, March 2000.

Lambek, Michael. "What Is 'Religion' for Anthropology? And What Has Anthropology Brought to 'Religion'?" In Janice Boddy & Michael Lambek eds., *A Companion to the Anthropology of Religion.* John Wiley & Sons 2013.

Lears, T. J. Jackson. *No Place of Grace: Anti-Modernism and the Transformation of American Culture, 1880-1920.* New York: Pantheon Books, 1981.

Lee, Shayne & Sinitiere, Phillip Luke. *Holy Mavericks: Evangelical Innovators and the Spiritual Marketplace.* New York University Press, 2009.

Lepore, Jill. *The Whites of Their Eyes: The Tea Party's Revolution and the Battle Over American History*. Princeton: Princeton University Press, 2010.

Luhrmann, T. M. *Persuasions of the Witch's Craft: Ritual Magic in Contemporary England*. Cambridge: Harvard University Press, 1989.

_____. *When God Talks Back: Understanding the American Evangelical Relationship with God*. New York: Knopf, 2012.

Luker, Kristin. *Abortion and the Politics of Motherhood*. University of California Press, 1984.

Mahmood, Saba. *Religious Differences in the Secular Age: A Minority Approach*. Princeton: Princeton University Press, 2016.

Mansfield, Stephen. *Choosing Donald Trump: God, Anger, Hope, and Why Christian Conservatives Supported Him*. Grand Rapids: Baker Books, 2017.

Marsden, George M. *Fundamentalism and American Culture: The Shaping of Twentieth-Century Evangelicalism, 1870-1925*. New York: Oxford University Press, 1980.

_____. *Understanding Fundamentalism and Evangelicalism*. Grand Rapids: William B. Eerdmanns Publishing Company, 1991.

Marshall, Ruth. "Christianity, Anthropology, Politics." *Current Anthropology*, Vol. 55, Supplement 10, December 2014.

Martin, David. *The Religious and the Secular: Studies in Secularization*. New York: Schocken Books, 1969.

_____. *The Breaking of the Image: A Sociology of Christian Theory and Practice*. New York: St. Martins, 1979.

Martin, William. *With God on Our Side: The Rise of the Religious Right in America*. New York: Broadway Books, 1996.

Marty, Martin E. *A Nation of Behavers*. Chicago: University of Chicago Press, 1976.

_____. *Pilgrims in Their Own Land: 500 Years of Religion in America*. New York: Penguin Books, 1985.

_____. *Modern American Religion, Vol. 1: The Irony Of It All, 1893-1919*. Chicago: University of Chicago Press, 1986.

_____ & R. Scott Appleby. *The Fundamentalism Project, Vol. 1: Fundamentalisms Observed*. Chicago: University of Chicago Press, 1991.

Mathewes, Charles. "An Interview with Peter Berger." *The Hedgehog Review*, Spring & Summer 2006.

Masuzawa, Tomoko. *The Invention of World Religions: Or, How European Universalism Was Preserved in the Language of Pluralism*. Chicago: University of Chicago Press, 2005.

May, Rollo. *Love and Will*. New York: Norton, 1969.

McLoughlin, William G. *Revivals, Awakenings, and Reform: An Essay on Religion and Social Change in America, 1607-1977*. Chicago: University of Chicago Press, 1978.

Meacham, Jon. *American Gospel: God, the Founding Fathers, and the Making of the Nation*. Random House, 2006.

_____. "The End of Christian America." *Newsweek*, April 3, 2009.

Miller, William Lee. "The Seminarian Strain: Church and Statesmen in the Democratic Party." *The New Republic*, 9 July 1984.

Moore, R. Laurence. *Selling God: American Religion in the Marketplace of Culture.* New York: Oxford University Press, 1994.

Moreton, Bethany. *To Serve God and Walmart: The Making of Christian Free Enterprise.* Harvard University Press, 2009.

Morgan, Murray. *Skid Road Seattle—Her First Hundred Years.* New York: Ballantine Books, 1971.

Morison, Samuel Eliot. *The Oxford History of the American People.* New York: Oxford University Press, 1965.

Morone, James A. *Hellfire Nation: The Politics of Sin In American History.* New Haven: Yale University Press, 2003.

Morris, Ian. *The Measure of Civilization: How Social Development Decides the Fate of Nations.* Princeton: Princeton University Press, 2013.

Moss, Candida. *The Myth of Persecution: How Early Christians Invented a Story of Persecution.* New York: HarperOne, 2013.

_____ & Joel S. Baden. *Bible Nation: The United States of Hobby Lobby.* Princeton: Princeton University Press, 2017.

Mulder, Mark T. *Shades of White Flight: Evangelical Congregations and Urban Departure.* Rutgers University Press, 2015.

Mutz, Diana. "Status threat, not economic hardship, explains the 2016 presidential vote." *PNAS Proceedings of the National Academy of Sciences,* May 8, 2018, 115 (19).

(*NEB*) *New English Bible, The.* New York: Oxford University Press, 1971.

Nichols, Donald M. *Seattle Pacific University, 1891-1991: A Growing Vision.* {Archives}

Nirenberg, David. "What is Islam? (What is Christianity? What is Judaism?)" *Raritan* Vol. 36 #2, Fall 2016.

Nongbri, Brent. *Before Religion: A History of a Modern Concept.* Yale University Press, 2013.

Norris, Pippa and Ronald Inglehart. "Sellers or Buyers in Religious Markets? The Supply and Demand of Religion." *The Hedgehog Review,* Spring & Summer 2006.

_____. *Sacred and Secular: Religion and Politics Worldwide.* Cambridge University Press, 2011.

O'Gieblyn, Meghan. "Exiled: Mike Pence and the evangelical fantasy of persecution." *Harper's Magazine,* May 2018.

Pagels, Elaine. *The Gnostic Gospels.* New York: Random House, 1979.

_____. *The Origin of Satan.* New York: Random House, 1995.

Painter, Nell Irwin. *Standing at Armageddon: The United States, 1877-1919.* New York: W. W. Norton, 1987.

Palmer, R. R. & Joel Colton. *A History of the Modern World.* 3rd ed., New York: Alfred A. Knopf, 1965.

Partanen, Anu. *The Nordic Theory of Everything: In Search of a Better Life.* New York: HarperCollins, 2016.

Patel, Eboo. *Out of Many Faiths: Religious Diversity and the American Promise.* Princeton: Princeton University Press, 2018.

Paul, Gregory. "The Chronic Dependency of Popular Religiosity Upon Dysfunctional Psychosociological Conditions." *Evolutionary Psychology,* 7 (3), 2009.

Peale, Norman Vincent. *The Power of Positive Thinking.* Prentice-Hall, 1952.

Peretti, Frank. *Piercing the Darkness*. Westchester: Crossway Books, 1989.

Peshkin, Alan. *God's Choice: The Total World of a Fundamentalist Christian School*. Chicago: University of Chicago Press, 1986.

Peterson, Mattie. "Footprints in the Sands of Time." Unpublished memoir, May 7, 1960, Seattle Pacific University Weter Library Archives.

Peterson, Scott M. "Rational Choice, Religion, and the Marketplace: Where Does Adam Smith Fit in?" *Journal for the Scientific Study of Religion*, Vol. 48, No. 1, Mar., 2009.

Pfaff, Steven. "The Religious Divide: Why Religion Seems to Be Thriving in the United States and Waning in Europe." In Jeffrey Kopstein and Sven Stinmo eds., *Growing Apart? America and Europe in the Twenty-First Century*. New York: Cambridge University Press, 2008.

Polanyi, Michael. *Personal Knowledge*. Chicago: University of Chicago Press, 1962.

_____. *Science, Faith, and Society*. Chicago: University of Chicago Press, 1964.

Popper, Karl. *The Open Society and its Enemies, Vol. I: The Spell of Plato*. 5th rev. ed., Princeton: Princeton University Press, 1966.

Preston, Andrew. *Sword of the Spirit, Shield of the Faith*. Alfred A. Knopf, 2012.

Putnam, Robert D./Campbell, David E. *American Grace: How Religion Divides and Unites Us*. New York: Simon & Schuster, 2010.

Quinones, Sam. "The Penance of Doc." *The Atlantic*, May 2019.

Radosh, Daniel. *Rapture Ready! Adventures in the Parallel Universe of Christian Pop Culture*. New York: Scribner 2008.

(REB) Revised English Bible. Oxford & Cambridge University Press, 1989.

Reno, R.R. & Barbara McClay eds. *Religion and the Social Sciences: Conversations with Robert Bellah and Christian Smith*. Eugene: Cascade Books, Wipf and Stock Publishers, 2015.

Robertson, James Oliver. *American Myth, American Reality*. New York: Hill & Wang, 1980.

Robinson, Marilynne. "Fear." *The New York Review of Books*, September 24, 2015.

_____. "Which Way to the City on a Hill?" *The New York Review of Books*, July 18, 2019.

Rose, Susan D. *Keeping Them Out of the Hands of Satan: Evangelical Schooling in America*. New York: Routledge, Chapman and Hall, Inc., 1988.

Rosin, Hanna. *God's Harvard: A Christian College on a Mission to Save America*. Harcourt Books, 2007.

Rothstein, Richard. *The Color of Law: A Forgotten History of How Government Segregated America*. Liveright 2017.

Rousseau, Jean-Jacques. *The Social Contract and Discourses*. London: J. M. Dent & Sons, 1978

Sahlins, Marshall. *Stone-Age Economics*. New York: Aldine de Gruyter, 1972.

_____. *Culture and Practical Reason*. Chicago: University of Chicago Press, 1976.

_____. *Islands of History*. Chicago: University of Chicago Press, 1985.

_____. "Cosmologies of Capitalism: The Trans-Pacific Sector of 'The World System'." Radcliffe-Brown Lecture in Social Anthropology, *Proceedings of the British Academy*, LXXIV, 1988.

_____. *How "Natives" Think: About Captain Cook, For Example*. Chicago: University of Chicago Press, 1995.

_____. "Two or Three Things I Know About Culture." *The Journal of the Royal Anthropological Institute*, Vol. 5, No. 3, September 1999.

_____. *The Western Illusion of Human Nature*. Prickly Paradigm Press, 2008.

Sale, Roger. *Seattle: Past to Present*. Seattle: University of Washington Press, 1976.

Sandin, Robert. *The Search for Excellence: The Christian College in an Age of Educational Competition*. Macon: Mercer University Press, 1982.

Schieman, Scott and Jong Hyun Jung. " 'Practical Divine Influence': Socioeconomic Status and Belief in the Prosperity Gospel." *Journal for the Scientific Study of Religion*, Vol. 51, No. 4, December 2012.

Schluchter, Wolfgang. *The Rise of Western Rationalism: Max Weber's Developmental History*. Translated, with an Introduction, by Guenther Roth. Berkeley: University of California Press, 1981.

Schulman, Bruce J. & Julian E. Zelizer eds. *Rightward Bound: Making America Conservative in the 1970s*. Cambridge: Harvard University Press, 2008.

Sharlet, Jeff. *The Family: The Secret Fundamentalism at the Heart of American Power*. Harper, 2009.

_____. *C Street: The Fundamentalist Threat to American Democracy*. Back Bay Books, 2011.

Sica, Alan. *Max Weber and the New Century*. Transaction Publishers, 2004.

Slotkin, Richard. *Regeneration Through Violence: The Mythology of the American Frontier, 1600-1860*. Norman: University of Oklahoma Press, 1973.

Smilde, David. *Reason to Believe: Cultural Agency in Latin American Evangelicalism*. University of California Press, 2007.

_____ & Matthew May. "Causality, Normativity, and Diversity in 40 Years of U.S. Sociology of Religion: Contributions to Paradigmatic Reflection." *Sociology of Religion*, 2015, 76:4.

Smith, Christian. *American Evangelicalism: Embattled and Thriving*. Chicago: University of Chicago Press, 1998.

_____. *Christian America? What Evangelicals Really Want*. Berkeley: University of California Press, 2000.

_____. *What is a Person? Rethinking Humanity, Social Life, and the Moral Good from the Person Up*. Chicago: University of Chicago Press, 2010.

Smith, Christian, Brandon Vaidyanathan, Nancy Tatom Ammerman, José Casanova, Hilary Davidson, Elaine Howard Ecklund, John H. Evans, Philip S. Gorski, Mary Ellen Konieczny, Jason A. Springs, Jenny Trinitapoli, and Meredith Whitnah. "Roundtable on the Sociology of Religion: Twenty-Three Theses on the Status of Religion in American Sociology—A Mellon Working-Group Reflection." *Journal of the American Academy of Religion*, December 2013, Vol. 81, No. 4.

Smith, Huston. *The World's Religions: Our Great Wisdom Traditions*. Harper SanFrancisco, 1991.

Smith, Mark A. *Secular Faith: How Culture Has Trumped Religion in American Politics*. Chicago: University of Chicago Press, 2015.

Solt, Frederick, Philip Habel, and J. Tobin Grant. "Economic Inequality, Relative Power, and Religiosity." *Social Science Quarterly*, Vol. 92, 2, 15 April 2011.

Sparks, Michael F. "Ambiguity and Social Behavior in Max Weber: A Systemization." unpublished paper, 1993.

————. "(What Really Happened) Donald Trump, The Empty Vessels of Evangelicalism, & The End of the World (or New Wine into Old Wineskins)." unpublished article, 2017.

————. "For What It's Worth: The Cultural Origins of 'Alternative Facts'." unpublished article, 2018.

Srikantan, Geetanjali. "Towards New Conceptual Approaches in Legal History: Rethinking 'Hindu Law' through Weber's Sociology of Religion." In Thomas Duve ed., *Entanglements in Legal History: Conceptual Approaches, Vol 1*. Frankfurt: Max Planck Institute for European Legal History, 2014.

Stanley, Brian. *Christianity in the Twentieth-Century: A World History*. Princeton: Princeton University Press, 2018.

Stark, Rodney. *What Americans Really Believe: New Findings From The Baylor Surveys of Religion*. Waco: Baylor University Press, 2008.

Steensland, Brian. Review of *Moral Ambition: Mobilization And Social Outreach In Evangelical Megachurches* by Omri Elisha; *Emerging Evangelicals: Faith, Modernity, And The Desire For Authenticity* by James S. Bielo. *Journal for the Scientific Study of Religion*, Vol. 51, No. 2, June 2012.

Stern, Scott Wasserman. *The Trials of Nina McCall: Sex, Surveillance, and the Decades-long Government Plan to Imprison "Promiscuous" Women*. Beacon, 2018.

Stolz, Jörg. "Salvation Goods and Religious Markets: Integrating Rational Choice and Weberian Perspectives." *Social Compass*, 2006, 53 (1).

Subramanian, Samanth. "A Port in a Storm: A community's quest to save its harbor." *Harper's Magazine*, April 2018.

Sutton, Matthew Avery. *American Apocalypse: A History of Modern Evangelicalism*. Boston: Harvard University Press, 2014.

————— & Darren Dochuk eds. *Faith in the New Millennium: The Future of Religion and American Politics*. Oxford, 2016.

Swartz, David R. *Moral Minority: The Evangelical Left in an Age of Conservatism*. University of Pennsylvania Press, 2012.

Sweeney, Douglas A. *The Evangelical Story: A History of the Movement*. Grand Rapids: Baker Academic, 2005.

Tolentino, Jia. *Trick Mirror: Reflections On Self-Delusion*. Random House, 2019.

Toulmin, Stephen. "Rules and their Relevance for Understanding Human Behavior." In T. Mischel ed., *Understanding Other Persons*. London: Blackwell, 1971. Just one among many writings by, and conversations with, him that greatly influenced my thinking on these matters.

————. "The Mozart of Psychology." *The New York Review of Books*, 9/28/1978.

Turkle, Sherry. *Alone Together: Why We Expect More from Technology and Less from Each Other*. Basic Books, 2017.

Turnbull, Colin. *The Human Cycle*. New York: Simon & Schuster, 1984.

Turner, Frederick Jackson. *The Significance of the Frontier in American History*. (Presented first as a paper to the American Historical Association at the 1893 Chicago World's Fair.)

Tweed, Thomas A. *Crossing and Dwelling: A Theory of Religion*. Harvard University Press, 2006.

Veblen, Thorstein. *The Theory of the Leisure Class: An Economic Study in the Evolution of Institutions*. 1899.

_____. "Christian Morals and the Competitive System." (1910) Reprinted in *Essays in Our Changing Order*. New York: Augustus M. Kelley, 1964.

_____. *Absentee Ownership and Business Enterprise in Recent Times: The Case of America*. Boston: Beacon Press, 1967.

Vidich, Arthur and Joseph Bensman. *Small Town in Mass Society: Class, Power and Religion in a Rural Community*. Princeton: Princeton University Press, 1968.

Warner, Stephen R. "Work in Progress toward a New Paradigm for the Sociological Study of Religion in the United States." *American Journal of Sociology*, Volume 98, No. 5. March, 1993.

Weber, Max. *From Max Weber: Essays in Sociology*. C. Wright Mills & H. H. Gerth eds. New York: Oxford University Press, 1946.

_____. *The Protestant Ethic and the Spirit of Capitalism*. New York: Charles Scribner's Sons, 1958.

Weinstein, Michael L. & Davin Seay. *With God On our Side: One Man's War Against an Evangelical Coup in America's Military*. New York: Thomas Dunne Books/St. Martins Press, 2006.

Wellman, James K., Jr., *Evangelical vs. Liberal: The Clash of Christian Cultures in the Pacific Northwest*. New York: Oxford University Press, 2008.

Whitehead, Andrew L., Samuel L. Perry, & Joseph O. Baker. "Make America Christian Again: Christian Nationalism and Voting for Donald Trump in the 2016 Presidential Election." *Sociology of Religion: A Quarterly Review* 2018, 79:2.

Williams, Daniel K. *God's Own Party: The Making of the Christian Right*. New York: Oxford University Press, 2010.

Williams, William Appleman. *The Roots of the Modern American Empire: A Study in the Growth and Shaping of Social Consciousness in a Marketplace Society*. New York: Random House, 1969.

Wills, Garry. *Nixon Agonistes: The Crisis of the Self-Made Man*. Boston: Houghton-Mifflin, 1969.

_____. *Inventing America: Jefferson's Declaration of Independence*. Garden City, New York: Doubleday & Company, Inc., 1978.

_____. *Under God: Religion and American Politics*. New York: Simon & Schuster, 1990.

_____. *Head and Heart: American Christianities*. New York: The Penguin Press, 2007.

Winiaerski, Douglas L. *Darkness Falls on the Land of Light: Experiencing Religious Awakenings in Eighteenth-Century New England*. University of North Carolina Press, 2017.

Witham, Larry. *Marketplace of The Gods: How Economics Explains Religion*. Oxford University Press, 2010.

Witten, Marsha G. *All is Forgiven: The Secular Message in American Protestantism*. Princeton: Princeton University Press, 1993.

Wolfe, Alan. "The Opening of the Evangelical Mind." *The Atlantic*, October 2000.

Wong, Janelle S. *Immigrants, Evangelicals, and Politics in an Era of Demographic Change*. The Russell Sage Foundation, 2018.

Wright, Lawrence. *Saints and Sinners*. New York: Alfred A. Knopf, 1993.

_____. "Remembering Satan—Parts 1&2." *The New Yorker*, 17&24 May 1993.

Wright, Robert. *The Evolution of God*. Little, Brown & Co., 2009.

Wuthnow, Robert. *The Restructuring of American Religion: Society and Faith Since World War II*. Princeton: Princeton University Press, 1988.

_____. *The Struggle For America's Soul: Evangelicals, Liberals, and Secularism*. Grand Rapids: Eerdmans, 1989.

_____. *God and Mammon in America*. New York: The Free Press, 1994.

_____. *Producing The Sacred: An Essay on Public Religion*. Champaign: University of Illinois Press, 1994.

Young, Neil J. *We Gather Together: The Religious Right and the Problem of Interfaith Politics*. Oxford University Press, 2016.

Zauzmer, Julie. "Acts of Faith: Paula White, prosperity preacher once investigated by the Senate, is a controversial pick for the inauguration." *The Washington Post*, 12/29/16.

Zuckerman, Phil. *Society Without God: What The Least Religious Nations Can Tell us About Contentment*. New York University Press, 2008.

Index

(including a few entries from the appendices)
Essential concepts, themes, and sources are emphasized in **bold** type.

C

Cacioppo, John, 371, 375, 382-83

Calvinism, characterizations of, 61-62

Campolo, Anthony, 172, 177, 233, 239-242, 251, 308-09, 353-55, 367

Carter, Stephen, 15, 19, 356

casuistry, 19, 397

Cato's Letters, 390

causal reductionism, 220

CCW, [*see* Christian Commitment Week]

chapel, 176, 229, 231-38, 243-44, 271, 280, 295, 298-99, 327, 349-353, 357, 372-73, 377

recordings of, 111-112, 181, 346-47

Christian College Consortium, 70, 132-134, 136-137, 198, 313

Christian Commitment Week (CCW), 235, 238, 298, 328

prayer chain, 358

Christian Scholar-Servant Model, 158, 209, 257

Christian Student Union, 138

city on a hill (John Winthrop), 49, 123, 252

Civil War, 34, 97, 130, 389-90

Clinton, Bill, 15, 269-70, 341

Clinton, Hilary, 270, 431

Podesta email server, 218

communism, cultural antipathy towards, 85, 105, 115-17, 238, 289, 387

complexes of meaning, 51

Conference of the Free Methodist Church, 25

conspicuous invidious distinctions, 214, 243, 269

Covid-19 pandemic 2020, 228

Cox, Harvey, 106, 394, 473, 480, 502

Crazy Eddie, 8

creation science, 190, 198

critical realism, 219, 222, 224, 226, 229

Cromwell & English Puritanism, 223, 390, 437

Crouch, Paul, 64, 287

culture/cultural

apartheid, 29, 195, 248, 288, 388, 413, 426-27, 478

cause/effect, 15, 489

depth and intensity, 118-20

disenchantment, 89, 92, 94-95, 97-100, 105, 118-19, 273, 292, 387, 395-96, 398, 403, 405, 411, 429, 447, 449, 452, 461-63, 469, 496, 506

insecurities, 22, 390, 399, 406, 408, 411, 417, 419, 453, 460, 467, 469, 491-92, 494, 496, 498, 505

logics, 51–52, 55, 73, 82-83, 99, 105, 117-19, 152-53, 177, 232, 360–361, 378, 394, 399, 470

sociology, 14, 494

vacuum(s), 140-41, 389, 398, 401, 409, 417, 444, 446, 450-53, 460, 465, 469, 473-474, 477, 489

Cuomo, Mario, 227

D

daycare, 314-15

Daugherty, Paul, 4

declensions [see sacred/profane declensions]

deep (and shallow) history, 51–52, 58, 82-83, 121, 286, 476

depression (economic), 89, 91-92

emotional, 236, 241-242, 346, 372, 374, 382, 460, 466-67, 496

Dewey, John, 85, 180, 292

discipleship groups, 229

disestablishment (arianism), 75, 389, 394, 441, 483-84

Disney, Walt, 341-42, 391-92

divine intervention, 192-93, 207, 227

divorce rate, 30, 338

Dobson, James, 244, 308, 475

Douglas, Mary, 14, 411, 456, 473

dualism, 53, 152, 211, 273

opposites, 4, 70-72, 143, 159, 392,

453, 505
definition of, 69, 333, 336
Durkheim, Émile, 6, 53, 186-87, 410,
413, 421, 478

E

economic development, 93, 100, 120, 200
markets, 74
order, 87, 90, 92, 97
transformation, 33
egalitarianism, 54, 87, 96, 166, 176-77,
255, 296, 308, 389, 442
egalitarian logic, 298
Einstein's theory of relativity, 190, 200
Eldredge, Niles, 198, 202-03
electromagnetic energy, 200
Elementary Forms of The Religious Life, The
(Durkheim), 53, 186
Eliade, Mircea, 18, 53, 279, 334
empty vessel, 142, 179, 191, 409, 435
entire sanctification, 255-56, 263
epistemology, 179, 186-87, 225, 227, 232,
415, 490
equality *vs.* hierarchy, 174
Equal Rights Amendment (ERA),
475
Erickson, Joyce, 164-65, 259-62
Erikson, Erik, 327, 333, 393
ethnic diversity, 37
ethnography, 11, 13
European cultural ancestors, 79
European societies, 10, 401, 442,
466, 472
evangelical bonds, 295
American sexual malaise, 339
Authoritarianism/Egalitarian-
ism, 296
burden of sexuality, 315
Christian sexuality, 298
family, 308
under siege, 313
fear of total reversal, 331
marriage market, 306
100% mentality, 326

mystification and magnification,
319
onanism, 321
Satanic Ritual Abuse Syndrome,
314
sexual wild card, 334
students, 309
Superior Christian Family, 312
survey, 302
Swaggart spectacle, 335
evangelical Christian college
academic superiority *vs.* intellectual expediency, 144
balance *vs.* heterogeneity, 148
brokenness, 148
eternality *vs.* specialized education, 150
freedom and truth, 143
holistic education, 150
homogeneity, 148
imbalance, 148
inferiority, 144
instrumental values, 150
intellectual integrity, 144
intrinsic values, 150
logic of, 136
modern, 131
open *vs.* closed systems, 140
unity of truth *vs.* parcelization of
truth, 140
wholeness, 149
logic, guiding terms of, 313
resurgence, cresting wave of, 130
signal of distinction, 159
evangelicalism
contemporary fluorescence of, 122
cultural cauldron of, 342
definition of, 152, 427, 470-71
exceptionalism, 49, 79, 217, 342, 388,
391, 410, 429, 435, 437-38,
441, 443-44, 456, 458, 483,
488, 490, 494, 496-97
existential insecurity, 21, 410, 460,
484, 489, 492, 495-96, 498, 501
exotic, 7, 12, 16, 97, 105, 181, 197, 201,
214, 265, 401, 429, 463

Grantham, Winfred A., 33, 45

Great Awakenings, 39, 129, 439-40,
443, 446

Greeley, Andrew, 14, 269-70, 477-
78, 481, 486, 503

Griswold, Wendy, 10

H

Haidt, Jonathan, 46-47, 63, 409-11,
414, 473, 478, 495

Hansacker, J. J., 106-07

happiness issue, 262, 329, 375, 393,
399, 401, 405, 410, 450,
456-57, 460, 462, 464, 490

Harding, Susan Friend, 71, 240,
290-91, 337, 432, 439

Hari, Johann, 382, 401, 453, 466,
495-96

Harrison, Robert Pogue, 400,
402, 453

Hechter, Michael, 479-80

higher education, 13, 127-28, 130-
31, 133, 137, 144, 148,
155, 157-58, 160, 192,
207, 214, 250, 283, 394

Western notions of, 137

Hirst, Paul Q., 187-88

Hofstader, Richard, 439

holiness, 63, 93, 255-56, 394, 463

movement, 93, 263

Holmes, Arthur, 130, 137-38, 139, 142,
145, 149, 151, 254, 268, 282

holy man, 173, 374

homogeneity, 134, 148, 285, 437

homosexuality/gay, 265-66, 301, 325,
328, 330-33, 368-69, 378, 407,
478

Hunter, James Davison, 64, 227, 270,
296, 455, 459, 482

hypocrisy, 63–64, 67–68, 147, 239, 269-
70, 283, 397, 434-35

of moral neutrality, 147

I

Idea of a Christian College, The (Holmes),
137, 168, 268

ideological

acceleration, 56, 116, 119-120, 122,
315, 399, 453, 472

cultural heritage, 213

elasticity, 276

emotional baggage, 339

fortress, 174

infrastructure, 111

intensity, 118-19, 121-22, 231-
32, 399

interpretation, 97

reaction, 53, 117, 119, 162

uniformity, 134

*ideology, definition of, as cul-
tural acceleration*, 472

immigrants, 33, 37, 44, 84, 273, 447,
491, 493, 501, 505

immigration/emigration, 81, 387,
390, 442, 489, 491, 493, 504

imperialism, 17, 106-107, 109-10,
112

in but not of the world, 248, 397

individualism of sin, 265, 269, 476

indulgence, 41, 46, 48, 69, 95, 150,
183, 277, 329

industrial capitalism, 89, 92

industrial habits, 101

industrialization, 48, 93, 95, 97-98,
105, 273, 480, 498

inequality, Biblical mandate of, 309

inerrancy (of scripture), 166, 172,
418, 432

*infinite regress of qualifica-
tions*, 195-96, 205

integration, 55, 136, 139, 143, 150, 157-
62, 164, 178, 189, 195-96, 207,
213, 232, 257, 259, 262, 283,
237, 263, 290, 442

of faith and learning, 136, 139, 150,
158, 161, 213

L

labor movement, 35, 92–94, 96
  theory of value, 221, 225
laissez-faire capitalism, 75, 91, 97, 102, 486
Lemcio, Eugene, 161, 174-75, 177-78
Lewis, C. S., 191, 209, 244
Liberal Arts Week, 171
liberal theology, 232
Lincoln, Abraham, 72, 96, 223, 388, 444
Lockerbie, Bruce, 233
loneliness, 347, 370-77, 379-80
lonely mask, 370
love gifts, 66-67
Luhrmann, T. H., 20, 266, 315, 344, 401, 467, 470
Lyusi, Sidi Lahsen, 56-57

M

MacArthur, Douglas, 91, 114
Manchurian Candidate, The, 116, 430
Manichean one-upmanship, 300
Marit's confession, 362
marriage, 87, 177, 242, 252, 266, 295-98, 306-07, 309-13, 316, 321, 324-25, 334-38, 340, 346, 463, 478, 491, 408, 425
  anticipated climax in, 316
  evangelical code of, 336
  market, 306
Marty, Martin, 13, 39, 92, 129, 269, 286, 391, 471
Marx, Karl, 6, 98, 147, 200, 221-22, 225, 264, 413, 440, 457, 473, 491
  dialectical materialism, 225
  labor theory of value, 221, 225
  quantitative/qualitative change, 121, 200-01, 461, 465
mask(s), 146, 254, 343-44, 346-48, 351-52, 356-57, 360-61, 365, 368, 370, 374, 377, 379-81, 400
mass psychology, 263

masturbation, 41, 299, 321-324, 326, 335-36, 340, 360, 365
materialism, 67-69, 103-04, 233, 239, 225, 277, 397-98, 499, 501
  consecrated, 68
  sacred, 69
Mather, Cotton, 18, 355
Matthews, Mark Allison, 40
May, Rollo, 318
McKenna, David, 127-29, 131-34, 138-40, 143-44, 146-49, 152, 157-59, 161, 175-76, 182, 185-87, 191, 194, 198-201, 232, 236, 249-54, 256, 277-80, 282-84, 296, 313, 344, 348, 352, 356, 371, 397
McKeown, Bruce, 256
McMartin pre-school daycare center case, 314
McNeill, George E., 93-94
meaning and significance, 21, 51, 234, 344, 392, 430, 446, 494
methodological atheism, 226
militarism, 53, 105, 114, 121, 333
militarization of Christian spirit, 114
Moore, Roy, 270
monopolization of pos./neg. qualities, 194-96, 203, 205
  infinite regress of, 195
moral market, 20, 46-49, 58-59, 62-63, 65-68, 73-82, 116-18, 122, 387-88, 391, 396-98, 401, 469, 472, 497-500
Moses, 8, 92, 347
mutual submission, 242, 296-98, 309, 311, 316, 334
Mutz, Diana, 432